These Also Believe

A Study of

MODERN AMERICAN CULTS
&
MINORITY RELIGIOUS MOVEMENTS

CHARLES SAMUEL BRADEN, Ph.D.

Professor of the History and Literature of Religions
Northwestern University

New York THE MACMILLAN COMPANY *1949*

Acknowledgments

The author gratefully acknowledges his deep indebtedness to the following publishers and owners of copyright for permission to quote from their copyrighted publications. In such a work as this it has been of especial value to be able to quote directly from these authoritative sources. The Church of Jesus Christ of Latter-Day Saints, Salt Lake City; Columbia University Press, New York; Thomas Y. Crowell Co., New York; The Deseret Book Co., Salt Lake City; The Deseret Sunday School Union, Salt Lake City; Destiny Publishers, Haverhill, Mass.; Dodd Mead and Co., New York; Fleming H. Revell and Co., New York; Henry Holt and Co., New York; The Herald Publishing Co., Independence, Mo.; Hillman-Curl, New York; Ernest Holmes, Los Angeles, Calif.; Hodder & Stoughton, London; Little, Brown and Co., Boston; The Macmillan Co., New York; Moral Rearmament, Washington, D. C.; National Spiritualist Association, Washington, D. C.; Psychic Books, Eaton Rapids, Mich.; Psychiana Inc., Moscow, Idaho; Routledge and Kegan Paul Ltd., London; Charles Scribner's Sons, New York; Stevens and Wallis, Salt Lake City; The Theosophical Society, Adyar, India; Truth Research Publications, Los Angeles, Calif.; The Unity School of Christianity, Kansas City, Mo.; The University of Chicago Press; The Watchtower Bible and Tract Society. He is also grateful for the faithful help of his secretaries, in particular, Miss Lydia Trippe, for their painstaking and untiring service in getting the manuscript ready for the press.

To My Grandchildren

Preface

Concerning the cults and minority religious groups in America
much has been written. In general the purpose of the writers seems
to have been either to exploit the strange, bizarre elements which
many of them do undoubtedly contain, and so to interest and amuse
the reader, or to expose their weaknesses, refute their claims, laugh
at their idiosyncrasies and so to discredit them. The writer was
recently asked to speak at a city-wide religious education conference
dinner in a great mid-western city, on the significance of the
modern cults. Beside his plate as he sat down lay an envelope with
the bold inscription: "God's truth concerning the cults, please read
before speaking." Inside the envelope were a dozen or more
pamphlets, each alleging that some one or other of the cults was
the direct work of the Devil, designed to lead the unwary to a
very unpleasant eternity in Hell. This is the typical point of view of
much that has been written, especially by ultra-conservatives.

True, there have been some excellent, relatively objective, studies
of individual groups, as may be seen in the annotated bibliography in
Appendix A of this book. But by far the greater bulk of the writing
concerning the separate movements has been violently partisan,
either for or against. In some cases, this is due in part to the fact
that they are relatively new and still subjects of violent controversy.
There is great need for careful scholarly study of most of them.
Such study is made extremely difficult because some of the movements, perhaps naturally enough in view of what they have suffered
at the hands of certain writers, are too distrustful of outsiders to
be willing to allow them free access to the indispensable first-hand
materials which they alone control. Thus those who attempt to
write fairly and impartially are severely handicapped and must use
what materials they can find. Some of the movements, still definitely
on the defensive at some points, may indeed have something to fear
from a perfectly open scrutiny of all the facts concerning their
beginnings. But it is doubtful if anything of essential value is ever

lost thus. It is the history of religious movements that incidental factors—which may at one time have seemed very important—are frequently lost by the wayside, and in the perspective of time this loss has meant decided gain.

But whatever may be said concerning studies of single movements, few books if any containing brief studies of some or all of the modern cults have been written from the standpoint of objective scholarship. The writer knows of none now in print, covering any considerable proportion of the movements, which fulfill this description. There have been some recent studies of individual movements or related groups by social psychologists and sociologists as social phenomena, and the attempt has been made to analyze the types of motivation which draw people into them. More such studies are greatly to be desired.

The present study attempts very briefly to do eight things: (1) to present the essential historical facts concerning the rise and development of each group considered, with as much objectivity as may be possible under the limitations upon original source materials imposed by the refusal of some groups to allow access to their files; (2) to set forth as simply and clearly as possible the major distinctive religious ideas each holds, and, in so far as may be, out of what these ideas arose; (3) to show at what points each agrees with and differs from normative Protestant or Catholic belief; (4) to describe and, to the extent possible, to account for, the distinctive form of organization employed in each; (5) to indicate the significant religious, social, economic, or other practices exhibited by each group; (6) to point out what seems to be the basic motivations to which each dominantly appeals; (7) to note current trends in the present-day life and thought of the various movements where such appear; and finally, (8) to make some attempt at generalizations concerning the movements, on the basis of comparison of one with another and with the majority religious groups.

It will be noted that there is here stated no purpose to evaluate the movements, to show where they are right or wrong, strong or weak. Undoubtedly there will, here and there, be evidence and possibly even a direct statement of the author's evaluation. But this is not his primary purpose. Readers will of course evaluate them, and it is perfectly proper that they should do so. It is the author's conviction that a true evaluation of anything must rest squarely upon a faithful consideration of all the facts available. These it is the writer's purpose to provide to the degree possible within so brief a compass as a single book which considers so many movements.

It is the conviction of the writer that everyone who writes a book on religion ought to let his readers know his general point of view, in order that they make allowances for his possible biases in drawing their own conclusions concerning the matters on which he writes. The reader is warned, therefore, that the author has been a lifelong Methodist, is an ordained clergyman, who has been a university teacher in the field of the History of Religion for many years. He is a graduate of liberal schools and remains an "unrepentant liberal" to the present. He holds no brief for any particular cult nor is he violently opposed to any. He believes that in general the cults represent the earnest attempt of millions of people to find the fulfillment of deep and legitimate needs of the human spirit, which most of them seem not to have found in the established churches.

Besides studying the original and secondary source writings of each he has sought wherever possible close personal contact with founders or present day leaders of the groups, in order to get, in so far as possible, the "inside view" of what they are attempting. But he has also sought to get the mind of the "little people," the everyday followers of the movements, in order to know what they think the cults offer and what they report getting from them. These contacts with the leaders and people have been an enriching experience. To have known personally such men as Frank B. Robinson, Charles Fillmore, Father Divine, and other less well-known figures in these movements has been a real privilege. The almost—but not quite—universal readiness of the cult leaders to help a sincere investigator to an understanding of their movements has made the study a pleasure. The author here records his deep debt of gratitude to all those obscure and more prominent persons who gave of their time and information so generously.

It will be noted that some of the chapters—particularly upon the more recent movements—are much longer than the rest. This is no accident. In the case of Father Divine, Psychiana, and "the I Am movement" there have been no adequate studies, certainly none comparable to what is here presented. It must be frankly stated that the author feels that his main original contribution to the field lies in these chapters. Certainly he has made a more extensive firsthand investigation of these than anyone else to date who has written at all objectively. There are at least two monographs on Father Divine, but they are of the spectacular or exposé type, for the most part, and seem never to have made any serious attempt to get the "inside" point of view.

The others, except the Liberal Catholic Church, have been written about often enough from one point of view or another, and the author can claim no particular originality for his treatment of them. It does, however, seem that a treatment of the whole group by a single author with a definitely objective point of view is desirable.

What to include and what to omit has been a problem. No single volume could contain an adequate discussion of all the movements which might be classed as cults or minority religious groups in America. By the term cult I mean nothing derogatory to any group so classified. A cult, as I define it, is any religious group which differs significantly in some one or more respects as to belief or practice from those religious groups which are regarded as the normative expressions of religion in our total culture. If any reader who belongs to a group discussed here prefers to think of himself as a member of a minority religious group rather than a cult, there can be no objection. The subtitle of the book, it will be noted, is Modern Cults and Minority Religious Groups. All the so-called cults are minority groups, but there are many minority groups which would not necessarily fall under the definition of a cult as given above.

I have confined the discussion to groups that have either originated in America or have had, perhaps, their major development here. To have included groups of foreign origin would have been impossible in a single volume.

Some American groups that have been important are on the wane. Some have so far lost what was distinctive in their earlier history that they are no longer thought of as significantly different. Others are just beginning and may eventually surpass in influence and popular appeal many of those discussed here. In order that the book may serve as a useful reference work and afford at least a little information concerning most of the "non-regular" religious bodies, a brief dictionary of movements is appended with some notation, in most cases, of some sources to which the reader may go for details not provided in the brief sketch included in the dictionary.

The field is a continually expanding one. New movements continue to arise. Old ones change constantly. The writer will welcome correspondence about any of the groups which will add to his knowledge and understanding of them. And he will especially welcome information about new movements that arise from time to time.

Evanston, Illinois

CHARLES S. BRADEN

April, 1948

Contents

25

235

277

Contents

Chapter One

The Peace Mission Movement
of Father Divine

I. *I GO TO A BANQUET*

"I think we will go in now to the communion table," said Father Divine. He led me from his private office room across a corridor and through a crowded hallway where scores of people seemed to be waiting to see him as he passed. They shouted and stretched their hands toward him as we moved slowly into the large dining-room. The room, which was of substantial size, was filled with tables arranged in "U" shape, all ready set for the banquet which was to follow. The tables were covered with immaculately clean white table cloths. At each place was a setting of delicate china of attractive design, with community plate silver service and two glasses. One of the glasses, a tall stemmed goblet, held a white napkin partially unfolded in conical shape and in each of these stood a small American flag. It was a most attractive sight. Above the center table was a neon sign reading "Father Divine's Holy Communion Table." In the middle of the head table, arranged in "V" shape, were a dozen gleaming silver coffee pots and, arranged within the "V" were the forks, spoons, and other utensils with which the food was to be served. Father Divine took his place directly at this central point. As he sat down, the whole company who had assembled around the tables took their seats and the banquet began. There were perhaps two hundred people at the table. There were easily that many more present, some standing behind the chairs of those seated at the table, others sitting on chairs or on the floor within the "U" formed by the tables. At once someone struck up a song and the whole

I

crowd joined enthusiastically in singing. A pianist, who was a master of boogie-woogie, accompanied the singing, and somewhere a bass drum and cymbals were heard accentuating the rhythmic quality of the song.

It was a happy, enthusiastic crowd. Father Divine sat smiling, all eyes centered upon him as song after song was sung, many of them directly in his own praise.

The singing was led by a group of young girls who, I came to know, were the "Rosebuds." Their fresh young voices and happy laughter contributed much to the joyous character of the occasion. Most of the songs, I was to learn, had been written by the "Rosebuds" or adapted from already existing tunes. In many cases both words and music were a product of their creation. The singing was all done without benefit of songbooks. I failed to see once in seven banquets, and perhaps as many more meetings of Father Divine's groups, any use of printed helps to the memory, and yet they sang their songs, first, second, and on through the last stanza, without a hitch. Some of the songs they sang, not once, but many times. Some of them were mere choruses, repeated over and over, one forty times by actual count. Sometimes the songs would start very, very slowly and softly. Then the tempo would be stepped up, at the same time increasing in volume, until it was sung as rapidly as a football yell and almost as explosively. Then it would begin to die down again and cease as it had begun. One of the songs, repeated times without number, was this:

> "I am not alone
> I am with my Father
> He walks within me
> He talks within me
> He gives me peace, love, joy and happiness
> I am not alone
> I am not alone."

Another was repeated almost as frequently:

> "Father Divine is God
> Father Divine is God Almighty
> He is God, is God, is God."

Sometimes the singing was accompanied by appropriate gesturing. One favorite ran thus:

"Oh, can't you see he is God to you and me
He's the one who came to set us free.
I want to be rolled up, wrapped up, tied up in his love
And let the rest of the world go by."

Familiar tunes are used for some of them. "Mary Lou" was
wedded to the following words:

"Father Divine, I love you.
In my heart, I need you.
Everyday I am celebrating to you with songs and praises
Because I love you,
Sweet Father Divine."

Others were sung to the familiar tunes of "Anchors Aweigh"
and the Notre Dame football song.

While they sang, the serving women began to bring in the food.
These women, who are trained particularly to serve, and who constitute part of the staff which Father Divine carries with him from
banquet to banquet, were dressed in white satin and were extremely
neat and attractive in appearance. Some were white and some were
of dark complexion. They began first with the serving of vegetables.
Each heaping bowlful of well cooked vegetables was brought to
Father Divine so that he might bless it before it was passed. This
he did by putting in a serving spoon or fork and passing it to his
right or left to start it on the long round of all the tables. Each guest
served himself as much of each dish as he desired and then passed it
on to his neighbor.

Eleven different cooked vegetables passed in quick succession:
steamed rice, green beans, green peas, boiled cabbage, sweet corn,
squash, succotash, stewed tomatoes, lima beans, greens and carrots.
I, not knowing what to expect, had begun by taking a little bit of
everything but soon saw that this was not wise and became more
selective. Then came platters of meat. It will be recalled that this
experience was still in war time and rationing had not yet been lifted.
First came three or four cold cuts, including baked ham. Then
appeared the hot, freshly cooked meats: roast beef, beef curry, meat
loaf, fried chicken, roast duck, roast turkey, beef steak, each heaped
high on the platters which were passed around the festive board.
Then came salads: fruit salad containing Persian melon, cantaloup,
alligator pears, and lettuce, and sliced tomato salad. Next came

breads: hot corn bread, hot rolls, white bread, brown bread, rye bread, raisin bread, and for good measure, crackers, accompanied by a good serving of butter. There was cranberry sauce for the roast turkey, apple sauce for the duck, and jams and jellies in profusion. The drinks consisted of iced tea, iced coffee, and iced water. I was assured that I could have hot coffee if I wanted it. Dessert consisted of two kinds of cake, one of them with fruit and whipped cream. On another like occasion, great heaping bowls of ice cream of two or three flavors were circulated around the table. Along with all of this went sweet pickles, mixed pickles, ripe olives, green olives, and all the condiments that would ordinarily be served on such an occasion. The average number of different dishes served at these banquets is around fifty-five.

As the food was being passed and eaten, person after person rose to his feet and gave testimony as to what Father Divine had done for him. Some of them became exceedingly emotional as they told of the joy that had been given them. Some of them shouted, some fell to the floor, some swayed about with hands raised high over their heads in an ecstasy of religious feeling. Meanwhile the songs were continued: songs of praise and thanksgiving, and songs, not only of religious character, but of real social significance, dealing with such matters as enacting the Bill of Rights in every community, of putting down racism, of getting an anti-lynching bill through Congress, of stopping the World War and of the retribution which was sure to follow individual sin and social unrighteousness.

Finally our appetites were sated. A general sense of well-being was upon us. All were waiting in great expectation for the moment when Father Divine would push back his chair from the table and rise to speak. When he finally did so, a wild burst of enthusiasm greeted him. They shouted, "God! God!" They stretched loving hands toward him. One heard such exclamations as, "Oh, that beautiful body!", "Peace, Father!", and other like expletives.

He always begins his after-dinner discourse with some such formula as this: "Peace everyone. Good health, good appetite, good fortune." Then he begins to speak. He is not an impressive figure. He is short, somewhat stocky, with a round pleasant face and a genial winning smile. He begins invariably in a low tone. All his halls are equipped with public address systems so that those least favorably seated in the room and in other rooms in the building can hear without effort. No one knows what he is going to say. One wonders if he knows himself. When once asked by a curious investigator about the preparation of his speeches he declared that he did not make preparation for them, but spoke under the inspiration of the moment. Not a little ridicule has been poked at Father Divine for his frequent use of big words and high-sounding phrases. It has been said that his speech is not always coherent, that he is frequently vague and indefinite, and that he uses terms which a great many of his hearers would not understand. There is a measure of truth in all of this. It is not easy to follow him. Yet as one reads the verbatim reports of his speeches which are carried week after week in the official publication of the movement, the *New Day*, one cannot help being impressed with the fact that there is a good deal of meaning in many of his utterances. There is much of common sense and of genuine wisdom in what he says. He makes abundant use of the Bible. To this I shall refer in detail later. There is not a little repetition of familiar phrases and stereotypes, if one takes the trouble of following through his published statements, but, on the whole, when one considers that he speaks from one to four or five times a day, almost every day of the week, and to congregations containing many of the same people but nevertheless, in the main, different groups, and when it is considered that he apparently does not make studied preparation, the range of his discussions is fairly wide.

He speaks for fifteen or twenty minutes, sometimes a little longer, and then sits down. After the applause he usually rises again to invite anyone present to say anything that he may wish to say. No pressure is put on anyone to speak, but any guest or any member is privileged to rise and speak what is on his mind. Since there are usually some visitors present, there is nearly always some speaking by outsiders. This is particularly true of followers of Father Divine from other sections of the country—from Chicago or Minneapolis, from Ohio or California or England, or from any one of the distant groups. These persons seem almost overwhelmed by the occasion, and some of them are quite unable to finish their speeches because of the emotion that overwhelms them. I cannot forget the case of a young Negro from California who had looked forward for years to seeing Father Divine's face. When the invitation was given for guests to speak, he arose. "Peace, Father," he said. "I want to thank you for the opportunity to be here and look upon your glorious body. I want to thank you, Father." His voice broke. "I want to thank you, Father," he began again. Then in a shaking voice, with tears streaming down his face, he cried, "Oh, God!" and sat down, burying his face in his hands. The joy of it was too much for him.

When all present have spoken who feel moved to do so, Father usually arises and says, "We will now take our leave, and as we go, let those who have waited so patiently take our places and be filled even as we have been filled. Good health, good appetite, good fortune to you all." Then he files out of the room accompanied by eager followers, and one can hear the shrieks of delight as he passes through the crowd in the hall waiting to get into the banquet room. He was to go on this particular occasion to another banquet at Pine Brook Hotel in the lovely hill country of New Jersey. We had been at the banquet table from about 7 o'clock until about 9:30 o'clock. We then drove some fifteen miles into the country to a hotel recently purchased by his followers, where, after a lively meeting in an auditorium, we sat down again about midnight to an even more abundant feast than we had enjoyed in the early evening. The banquet finished about 2:30 o'clock in the morning and possibly five hundred people, all told, were fed. By that time this investigator was thoroughly wearied, but for an hour and a half he sat in a private apartment talking with Father Divine, who seemed quite tireless. Altogether it was the best of the four interviews which I was permitted to have with him. As I left him to return to New York, at about 3:30 in the morning, he was planning to drive back to Philadelphia, where he would serve another banquet before the break of day. I didn't feel that I could take it.

II. *FATHER DIVINE*

Father Divine's Peace Mission Movement, the official name of his group, is one of the most unique religious movements that has appeared. Many prophets have arisen and not a few Messiahs, but seldom has God himself in human form assumed leadership of a movement. Yet that is precisely the belief of Father Divine's followers concerning him. Father Divine is God, to them.

How did such a belief arise? Whence came this strange figure, who if he does not often proclaim his own divinity in so many words, nevertheless accepts the homage and adoration of his followers who declare that he is none other than God.

The difficulty in tracing its origin prior to the Sayville, Long Island, period which began in 1919, is great. Attempting to discover it, even while a great many of the people who saw it arise are still living, is likely to inspire respect for researchers who seek to unearth the beginnings of obscure movements in the long ago.

How old is Father Divine? Where was he born? Once asked the date of his birth, Father Divine replied with a scripture verse which reads, "Before Abraham was, I am." That wasn't much help. Two books[1] written about him identify him with one, George Baker, who is then traced back to Savannah, Georgia. Two courts have accepted the identification, although Father Divine himself has denied under oath that he was ever known as George Baker.

For the purposes of this chapter it does not greatly matter, since the interest here is in a movement which is actually functioning and appeals to large numbers of people through its teaching and ministry, regardless of where or when its founder was born, or what he may have been in his past. We are concerned about where he got certain of his ideas and practices, as will appear in a later section, but his followers are attracted to him not by what he may have been in his childhood or youth, but by what he is saying and doing now.

His biographers associate him with various earlier movements. Under the influence of one Father Jehovia, a colored Baptist preacher, whose real name was Samuel Morris, he is said to have taken the name, "The Messenger," and to have set out to convince the world that he was himself God incarnate.

Mr. J. R. Moseley, a widely known religious figure, in a recent book, *Manifest Victory*,[2] writes that in 1914 at Valdosta, Georgia, he visited a "little bright-faced colored man who was in the Valdosta jail, because he was calling himself 'God.'" Inquiring if there was anything he could do for him the prisoner replied that he did not accept money, but that he would be glad to have bread which he might share with his fellow prisoners. Mr. Moseley succeeded in arranging for his release. Later word came from a state institution about a strange case there, of a man who knew Moseley. Again his release was arranged and he later came to Macon, Mr. Moseley's home, and they had a long conversation on religion. Years afterward, on reading of the work of Father Divine, it occurred to Mr. Moseley that he might be the man he had befriended. And so it proved, when on a visit to New York he made contact with the now famous

[1] R. W. Parker, *Incredible Messiah,* Little, Brown and Co., Boston, 1937 and John Hoshor, *God in a Rolls-Royce,* Hillman-Curl Inc., New York, 1936.
[2] Harper and Brothers, New York, 1941, pp. 106-109.

Father Divine. They had several interviews and found genuine spiritual kinship. In correspondence with Mr. Moseley, I inquired carefully if he was sure that the prisoner was actually calling himself "God" at that time. He replied positively that he was. This pushes his claim of divinity back further than any other dependable source I have discovered.

Hoshor asserts that he came to Brooklyn in 1915 and with twelve followers established himself in Prince St., Brooklyn, where, he says, the communal system, which is so central now in the movement, was first put into effect.

It was as Major Morgan J. Devine that in 1919 he purchased a home in Sayville, Long Island. From that time the movement began to attract wide attention and its subsequent history is easy to follow. It began very quietly. Major and "mother" Devine opened their home generously to all who cared to come. Some became members of the household, going out to work in the surrounding territory, but living in the Devine home. Many came to meals, which at first were served without charge. They were happy occasions with much singing and shouting. Devine seemed to have an inexhaustible supply of food. He preached to his guests at the tables, and insisted upon high moral standards. Gradually the crowds increased. Harlem had heard about the grand banquets and came in ever larger numbers. The feasts lasted late into the night.

Sayville residents became alarmed. Their objection was partly to the noise which they found disturbing. But also the race question was involved, for most of those who enjoyed Major Devine's hospitality were colored. All sorts of attempts were made to get him to move. There was talk of evil things which went on in the night. It is claimed that private detectives were put in the house ostensibly as inmates to discover the truth. Was Devine carrying on intrigues with his female followers? They found not the slightest irregularity. It is even charged that women were hired to try to seduce him, but were wholly unsuccessful. Feeling ran high and Father Divine was arrested and brought into court on charges of taking funds from his followers and refusing to return them when they desired to leave—an out and out "frame up," Divine claims, and there is not a little evidence to justify his assertion.

At last, partly because so many were coming from Harlem, and the Sayville house was no longer adequate, and partly because of the continual hostility of Sayville residents who sought by every means to embarrass him, he moved to Harlem, and the movement began to grow and spread as it never could have done elsewhere. Mission after mission was opened. Restaurants, stores, garages, homes for men, homes for women, and schools, sprang up all over Harlem. The sect soon spread to other cities in New Jersey, Pennsylvania and Connecticut. In time it swept northward along the Hudson river to a pleasant rural section of New York near Kingston, which came to be called the Promised Land. His followers came to be numbered not by the hundreds but the thousands, and finally Father Divine began to talk in terms of millions. How many there actually were no one knows, because no statistics are kept, or at least none are made public. (See section: "Is the Movement Growing?" pp. 11 ff.). Branches sprang up in distant places—in the midwest, on the Pacific coast, and in foreign countries. It was on the way to becoming a world movement.

The organization is fairly simple. Local churches exist as in other movements. Father Divine is pastor of most those in and around New York and Philadelphia, but there are assistant pastors in most of the larger groups who look after the churches very much as pastors of the established churches do. In connection with many of the churches there are Kingdoms, or Heavens, as popularly called, separate hostels for men and for women which provide comfortable living quarters at a very low cost. (See section on Economic Aspects, pp. 27 ff.). Members do not have to live in these hostels, though many do. They may live outside, though those of the inner circle must live within. In these centers a highly moral atmosphere is maintained. Non-members may live in them also, but no immorality, profanity, smoking or other evil habits are permitted. Those who become members of the inner group may not marry, or if married must live separately, as brothers and sisters. Children are cared for usually in some of the women's hostels.

The principal meetings of the groups are the banquets which are really communion services, though there are also meetings at which food is not served. The latter are known as Righteous Government meetings. Where Father Divine cannot be present, as in distant cities, his messages are read from the official weekly paper, the *New Day*, and his picture may be placed at the head of the table where he would ordinarily sit. The local churches are self-supporting, and probably bear whatever deficit there may be because of the banquets. It is a strange rule that only members of a given local church may contribute to that church. However, guests at a banquet may contribute more than the modest sum which is charged everyone, except Father Divine, his staff, and any special guests who may be present. The churches are organized with a board of trustees who hold the property, and other officers who bear special responsibilities. The more detailed functioning of the movement will appear in the course of the discussion of its social and economic aspects.

Various publications have been issued by the movement since it appeared in New York. The first was *The Spoken Word*. It gave way in 1936 to the *New Day*, a weekly paper usually of forty-eight pages which publishes a verbatim report of everything Father Divine says in public or in private. He is always accompanied by at least one of his numerous secretaries (there were sixteen when I visited him in 1945) who records in shorthand every word he utters. This is avidly read by his followers wherever they are. *The World Herald* was published for a time beginning in 1936, but was discontinued. They have published some tracts, but as yet no books.

All has not been peace and harmony within the movement. Some of his most devoted and influential followers have left him. Some have led dissident movements. None has maintained itself for any length of time. Some have come back humbly penitent as, for example, "Faithful Mary," and been accepted once more into the fellowship.

"Mother" Divine shared his work during the Sayville period and until about 1942 or 1943. Then she dropped out of the picture. Evidently she died. Death, as we shall see later, has no place in his system, so notice is never given of the passing of a member.

The world was startled in the summer of 1946 by the announcement of the marriage of Father Divine to an attractive young white woman who becomes now "Mother Divine." In view of Father's attitude toward marriage, this caused consternation among the followers despite his assertion that this was but a "spiritual marriage." Correspondence with various followers indicated that some were quite disappointed and even a little bitter about it. But after considering it carefully, some of them, who were at first much troubled, found great significance in it. One man wrote, "The purpose of this marriage as stated and exemplified by Father and his bride needs to be understood and given out universally. Surely it will awaken 'a new birth of freedom under God,' if we can rise above . . . the sin and bondage of human propagation. There must be something much finer than all this sordidness and suffering brought about by selfish passion and lust." A young white woman wrote, "Even before the first explanatory *New Day* came, one of the ideas I had formed was that Father was now married to us all, that he had spiritually united us all into one family. And those who are willing to accept this virtuous amalgamation will find joy and happiness in being married to Father, just as I found. It made Father even more real to me." It is quite probable that not a few failed to find in it this high significance and have been permanently alienated by it.

III. *IS THE MOVEMENT GROWING?*

It is impossible to assess the numerical strength of Father Divine's following. He is completely non-statistical in his interest. He is wont to speak of the millions of his followers, yet there seems to be no sure way of checking on his claims. In the first place, they do not have a membership list as other movements do, or better, as other churches do. The minority groups do not, as a rule, run to statistics. When in personal conversation I would ask him some question designed to get a fairly exact estimate as to the number of societies or the number of inmates of a given kingdom, Father Divine's usual reply was, "I don't bear record of that." Thus it is quite impossible to assert with certainty whether or not the movement is growing. Father Divine himself declares that it is. I find rather generally the impression among outsiders that it has passed its peak of popularity and is receding.

The only basis I have been able to discover upon which any judgment can be rested is the published report of the number and location of the various centers of the movement which appears from time to time in the official publication, now the *New Day*. By tabulating the data thus given in an October number of the journal of the years 1934–44,[3] it is possible to see whether the movement seems to be expanding, at least in so far as organized centers are concerned. It tells nothing about the size of the groups listed. Thus, while there may be more groups noted, the number of followers may actually have diminished in a given year, and vice versa. Furthermore, it it specifically stated in each listing that the list is not complete. There

[3] Less regular publication of the list of groups after 1944 makes it more difficult to get comparative data for later years. However, on pp. 16–17 data for February 1946 are given.

is no way of knowing how nearly complete it is. However, it is safe to assume that if there were a great many more, the list would be longer than it actually is. Some few may be omitted in a given month's issue, but why would they continue to be omitted month after month if they were active centers?

The groups are usually classified into two divisions, those "Kingdoms, Extensions, and Connections under Father's Personal Jurisdiction," and "Other Peace Missions, Extensions, and Connections." Within these they are further subdivided according to location. The city and street address of each mission is indicated, and they are further grouped by states or countries in which they are found. It is thus possible to see into what parts of the country and the world the movement is spreading, and whether within any given region it is increasing, holding its own, or diminishing. Again it should be noted, we are dealing here only with groups or centers, and know nothing about their size or activities.

A summary of the tabulation follows:

TABLE I *Summary*

Number of Kingdoms, Extensions and Connections

	1934	'35	'36	'37	'38	'39	'40	'41	'42	'43	'44
Under direct Jurisdiction of Father Divine in New York State	14	15	20	20	19	25	27	44	50	56	48
In Other States	12	2	2	2	2	2	2	1	1	3	3
Extensions and Connections	46	117	129	114	141	125	128	123	125	108	103
Total	72	134	151	136	166	152	157	178	176	167	154

According to the totals there were more than twice as many groups in 1944 as in 1934. But the peak year seems to have been 1941 with 178. From that there was a gradual decline to 154 in 1944. The number under Father Divine's personal jurisdiction which are all located within a radius of 150 miles of New York City and in the four states, New York, New Jersey, Connecticut, and Pennsylvania, increased steadily until 1943 when they reached the total of 59. The maximum number of "extensions and connections" was reached in 1938 with 141. But this had fallen to 103 in 1944. The marked increase in the number of Kingdoms in New York State is probably to be accounted for by the development of the so-called "Promised Land" near Kingston, New York, where numerous farms were purchased by Father's followers, and where cooperative farming, which took many out of the crowded city, was undertaken. Strong opposition developed in the counties involved. This, coupled with problems of man-power shortages in war time, has greatly affected the back-to-the-country phase of the movement, though it has been by no means abandoned. It had been expected that these upstate farms would find an outlet for their produce through the cooperatives in the city, and to a certain degree this actually did occur; but city inspection, whether fairly or unfairly exercised (the writer does not know), made it impossible to bring in their dairy products, and, by so much, interfered with the success of the farming venture. The farms are operated at present by only a skeleton crew. On the other hand, agricultural work is carried on more actively in New Jersey, not far from Atlantic City.

In general, the obstacles put in the way of the development of the movement in New York State has resulted in the gradual withdrawal from New York and the beginning of concentration in Pennsylvania and New Jersey. The official residence of Father Divine himself has been moved from Harlem to Broad Street, Philadelphia, and the activities in the "city of brotherly love" have been expanded rapidly in the last few months. One of the chief difficulties in carrying on his own work personally from New York City is the fact that a judgment has been rendered against Father Divine for the repayment of a sum of some thousands of dollars to one, Verinda Brown and her husband, which they allege they turned over to Father Divine when they joined the movement back in the Sayville days. According to Father Divine, the claim is utterly false. They at no time gave him any money, he says, and even if they had done so they had long since been reimbursed for it by having lived with him without any charge. Furthermore, he alleges that both Verinda Brown and her husband confessed in a written statement in the judge's chambers that their claim was false. Later, however, they repudiated the statement and the judgment was handed down against him.

In all the interviews I had personally with Father Divine, it was over this that he became most excited. "My followers have often begged me to let them pay it off and so remove the embarrassment to our work, but I will not permit it. The claim is unjust; it is false. I will go to jail before a penny is paid on such a dishonest claim." And one knew from the tone of determination in his voice that he would do just that. Elsewhere, pp. 27 ff., we discuss the general financial operations of the movement. If what we there state, on the basis of numerous personal testimonies, is true, then there is every reason to credit Father Divine's sincerity in his branding this an outrageously unjust "frame up," designed to hurt his movement.

Nevertheless the judgment still stands. Since he has moved his residence to a neighboring state, the legal process cannot be served upon him unless he appears in New York. Happily, according to New York law, it cannot be served on Sunday, so Father Divine can spend Sunday in Harlem and usually does so at one of his several Missions in that area. But since Father Divine has left Harlem, many of his followers have likewise left and gone to be near him in Philadelphia. Hence many of the restaurants, stores, work cooperatives, and other activities carried on "in the Spirit of the Father," have forsaken Harlem. The personal loyalty to Father Divine and the desire to be near him are among the most notable features of the entire movement.

How far has the movement spread? Where outside of the orbit of his personal supervision are his followers to be found?

A glance at the table, p. 17, shows that it has been found at some time from 1934–44 in twenty-six states of the Union and in Washington, D. C. Of these, nine are southern states: Alabama, Florida, Georgia, Maryland, North Carolina, South Carolina, Oklahoma, Texas, and Virginia, and if Missouri be considered southern, as it probably should be on questions involving the Negro, there were ten. In no one of these were there ever more than three centers; in most of them not more than two. Georgia has had none since 1941; Alabama has never had more than one. Oklahoma and Texas had each one in 1935 only. Evidently the movement has not made much headway south of the Mason and Dixon line, a fact readily to be understood in view of the teaching of Father Divine concerning the relationship of the races.

Outside of the New York, New Jersey, Pennsylvania region, the largest concentration of the movement has been in California. There were nine groups listed in 1934. In 1935, the number had jumped to

20. The subsequent years reported were respectively, 23, 16, 22, 18, 18, 17, 16, 16. The greater number of these were to be found in the San Francisco area. The number of societies was substantially less in 1945 than in the peak year 1936. Whether this means fewer individual followers, there is no sure way of knowing.

The next largest concentration has been the state of Washington, where the number of societies listed from 1934–44 was respectively, 2, 10, 11, 11, 9, 8, 10, 8, 8, 8. Neighboring Oregon reported one mission in 1936 and 1937, but none since.

Next in importance numerically is Ohio where the record runs respectively from 1934, 4, 6, 4, 8, 6, 6, 6, 6, 6, 7. No other state has registered more than three centers in any one year; several of them have never had more than one group. Kansas had one in 1934 and 1935, two in 1936, one in 1937, and then disappeared from the list. The movement appears in 1944 in twenty-one states. Including those under Father Divine's personal supervision, it is found in twenty-five states in all.

But the movement has spread beyond the continental United States. Centers are listed in Canada, British West Indies, Panama, Switzerland, England, and Hawaii. As early as 1934, there were two extensions in Canada. The listing in subsequent years of the decade were, 7, 9, 5, 8, 6, 4, 8, 6, 5, 7. Australia enters the list in 1935 with two groups. There were none listed in 1936, but beginning in 1937 and continuing through 1944, the numbers were 2, 4, 5, 8, 6, 5, 6, 5. The British West Indies was reported first in 1935 with one group and so through 1936 and 1937. Since 1938, each year, four groups have been listed. Panama had two each through 1938–41, and three since. Switzerland has shown considerable variation, possibly due in some way to the war. It appears first in the listing in 1935 with four groups. In 1937 it jumped to twelve, and has registered subsequently beginning with '38, 14, 1, 8, 8, 9, 9, 9. One must suppose that the drop to one in 1939 must have been due to some clerical error or failure to report. It seems hardly likely that the societies simply disappeared in such large proportion, only to appear in substantial strength in 1940.

Publication of the list of Peace Missions and Extensions was omitted in 1945. The list reappears in 1946 but seems to be much reduced. For example, in the February 23rd issue the number of Missions under Father's personal jurisdiction was 56 as over against 51 in 1944. Thirteen of these were in Philadelphia. But the number of other Missions, Extensions and Connections had fallen to 39 from 103. A number of states are not represented in the list. Whether this is an actual shrinkage is not certain, for, as observed, the lists do not claim to be complete. But why so many should have dropped out in so short a time is not clear. The writer definitely knows of a group in Illinois, yet none is reported. In how many other cases is this true?

It has not been my privilege to make contact with the groups outside of the Atlantic states (except in Chicago and Minneapolis where they are not large and the white members outnumber the colored,) but it has been reported frequently that on the West coast the percentage of white followers is much greater than in the East. I have heard estimates that run as high as 70% white in the West. In England and Switzerland it is predominantly white, and presumably also in Australia. From my several visits to banquets in New York, New Jersey, and Pennsylvania, I estimated that about 10% of those present were white persons.

One cannot get any information on this matter from either Father Divine or his followers. They refuse to make any distinction of color. Indeed, as already stated, they refuse to use such terms as black or white. One can therefore only guess at the racial composition of the movement as a whole.

TABLE II

A detailed tabulation of the available statistics of the Movement follows; based upon data published in *New Day*, Vol. 2, October 20, 1938, page 100, and an October number of each year to 1944, and a February issue, 1946.

Listed as Kingdoms, Extensions, and Connections under Father's Personal Jurisdiction

	1938	1939	1940	1941	1942	1943	1944	Feb. 1946
New York City	16	22	24	24	30	30	29	14
New York	3	3	3	20	20	26	19	24
Connecticut	2	2	2	1	1	1	1	1
New Jersey						2	2	4
Penn. (Phila.)								13

Other Peace Missions, Extensions, and Connections

	1938	1939	1940	1941	1942	1943	1944	Feb. 1946
Alabama	1	1	1	1	1	1	1	1
Arizona	1	1	1	1	2	1	1	—
Australia	4	5	8	6	5	6	5	4
Brit. West Indies	4	4	4	4	4	4	4	3
California	22	18	18	18	17	15	16	7
Canada	8	6	4	8	6	5	7	2
Colorado	1	2	2	2	2	1	1	—
D. C.	2	2	2	2	2	2	2	2
England	—	1	1	1	1	1	1	1
Florida	2	2	2	2	1	1	2	1
Georgia	2	1	2	2	—	—	—	—
Hawaii	—	—	—	—	3	3	1	1
Illinois	2	3	2	2	2	2	2	—
Kansas	1	—	—	—	—	2	—	—
Maryland	2	2	1	1	3	2	2	1
Massachusetts	2	3	2	—	2	1	1	—
Michigan	—	—	—	—	2	2	2	1
Minnesota	3	3	3	2	2	2	2	1
Missouri	3	1	1	1	2	2	1	—
Nebraska	1	2	2	2	—	2	2	—
New Jersey	17	20	22	16	7	4	4	—
New York	16	16	10	12	12	10	8	2
N. Carolina	1	2	3	3	2	2	2	—
Ohio	8	6	6	6	6	6	7	—
Panama	2	2	2	2	3	3	3	2
Pennsylvania	7	8	8	7	7	8	5	—
S. Carolina	1	1	1	1	1	1	1	1
Switzerland	14	1	8	8	9	9	9	6
Virginia	2	2	3	2	2	2	2	—
Washington	11	9	8	10	8	8	8	3
Wisconsin	1	1	1	1	1	1	1	—

IV. SOCIAL IDEALS OF THE MOVEMENT

If it may be said of some of the minority religious groups that they are largely egocentric and have little concern for the social order, no such statement can be made concerning Father Divine's Peace Mission. Father Divine does, to be sure, strongly emphasize the necessity of individual salvation, and is insistent on personal integrity. But that is not the end of the matter. He has a veritable social passion and never ceases to preach the remaking of the social order. The individual is never left to stand alone. And the ultimate end which he envisages is no less than a perfected society *here on earth*—a true Kingdom of God.

Father Divine's is no other-worldly faith. He promises no heaven hereafter. One hears reiterated over and over in the testimonies given in the public meetings, the joy of believers in the fact that they do not have to wait until after death to secure the benefits of salvation. They are already participants in the joys of the Kingdom. They enjoy the personal presence of God. They are sustained daily here and now by his bounty. They expect confidently that this will never end. To be sure, there is the larger world about them which has not yet acknowledged the rule of Father Divine, and in which they experience opposition and sometimes serious injustice. But God's will must ultimately prevail, and the world will recognize him or be destroyed. Meanwhile within the little microcosm they have built for themselves they find the security and joy and satisfaction which they so deeply crave.

To perceive that this is a profoundly social movement one needs only to attend a service, read the mottoes on the walls and listen to the songs, or give attention to the speeches of Father Divine. Manifestly the people are religious, but one finds certain words appearing over and over again which indicate the social interest at the heart of it. These words particularly struck the writer: "Americanism," "brotherhood," "equality," "the Bill of Rights," "Democracy."

"Americanism is our religion," proclaims one placard in a meeting room. Another, "Let there be an International Bill of Rights."

Father Divine himself said to me, "Americanism, Democracy, and Christianity are synonymous." But how does he define Americanism? Another placard found in the various centers says: "What does Americanism consist of? Amalgamation of all Races, Colors, Creeds." Here one is plunged into the very center of the movement. No note is more insistently struck than that of the equality of the races—and no movement in America is more definitely itself an inter-racial movement. In it there is no distinction of color. White and black mingle freely, and white and black sing with apparently equal enthusiasm the crusading songs in which racial discrimination is condemned and the ideal of racial brotherhood proclaimed. Note, in the hymn which follows, the reaction against the segregation commonly practiced on the street in public carriers, places of recreation, in schools, in restaurants, and in church.[4]

---

[4] The *New Day*, Vol. 9, September 8, 1945, p. 44.

We shall have the *Same Rights*
Not only *Equal* but the *Same*
Side by side, we shall ride
The *Same* car, bus and train.
We shall play in the *Same* parks,
Study our lessons in the *Same* schools.
There shall be the *Same Equal Rights*
For you, and you, and you!

Forever more we shall have the *Same Rights*.
We shall dine face to face.
Eternally there shall never be
Known a creed, color or race.
We shall live together
And worship God in the *Same* pew.
There shall be the *Same Equal Rights*
For you, and you, and you!

Or this:

America, America,
Blot out that line of demarcation
Unify with your fellow man;
That's the only way to save this nation.
Wipe out that Mason and Dixon line
It only breeds vice and crime
Wake up! Step up! You're way behind!
Copy after the fashion of Father Divine.
America!

Perhaps their most hopeful statement of the anti-racism ideal is
to be heard in the following song which sees a day in which even
in Texas and the farthest parts of the South, segregation will be
wiped out.

Away down in Texas
And in the farthest parts of the South
We shall eat and drink together,
Racism shall be wiped out.
There will be no more race riots and lynchings,
There will be no more division or strife
When they recognize *God's Body*
They will value each other's life.
Father will make them love each other so much

With or without an anti-lynching bill
They will know that they are brothers
And will not desire to kill
Away down in Texas
And in the farthest parts of the South.
They will enact the Bill of Rights in every community,
Racialism shall be wiped out!

The late Senator Bilbo became for them the symbol of racial big-otry. An issue of the *New Day* carried in bold, black-faced headline type the following which filled the entire front page: "DOWN, DOWN, DOWN WITH BILBOISM!"

There was also an anti-Bilboism song, sung frequently, and with more fervor than almost any other. It was accompanied with vigor-ous stamping of the feet.

D-O-W-N, down with Bilboism! Down! Down! Down!
Up with Democracy! Let it flood city, village and town;
Let it sweep through the country
And give its subjects the very Same Rights!
Let every woman, man, boy, and girl,
Help Democracy's banner to be unfurled,
And clean out the Senate
Of all lynch-mob violent leaders;
And when they start to filibuster, don't allow them to talk;
Just snatch them off the floor and send them for a walk!
For Democracy shall flourish in the land of the free,
And its subjects shall have Life, Happiness and Liberty!

One could veritably feel the building tremble as they shouted "Down, down, down."

It is this inter-racial program which probably occasions more difficulty than any other and it is certainly this which keeps the movement from expanding into the south. But there is one feature about it which robs it of the major objection alleged by representa-tives of the white race. There is no such thing as inter-marriage, therefore no intermingling of the two blood streams. All sexual rela-tions are strictly forbidden. Men and women are rigidly segregated. There are hotels or "heavens" for men and for women. Even married couples are forbidden to live together.

Father Divine's Movement has a definite social program. They have worked out and published a detailed statement of just what it is that they seek to accomplish in the area of human relations. At a convention held in 1936 under the name, International Righteous Government, a platform was adopted which sets forth not only the social aims which they hold, but also by what means these goals are to be realized. The main features of the platform are as follows:

(1) "The immediate repeal of all laws local and national that are contrary to the spirit and meaning of the Constitution of the United States and its amendments.

(2) "Immediate legislation in every state in the United States and all other countries making it a crime to discriminate in any public place against any individual on account of race, creed or color; abolishing all segregated neighborhoods, all cities and towns and making it a crime for landlords and hotels to refuse tenants on such grounds; abolition of all segregated schools and colleges and all segregated areas in churches, theatres, public conveyances and other public places.

(3) "Immediate destruction by nations and individuals of all fire-arms and instruments of war within their borders, saving those that are used for law enforcement. The true followers of Father Divine will refuse to fight their fellow men for any cause whatsoever."

It is apparent, however, that despite this utterance, Father Divine and his followers have supported the recently ended World War II. Father Divine was very active in selling war bonds, and often in public has made a point of emphasizing the support his group has given to the government in this emergency. Furthermore, a number of their songs sung in recent months have been definitely militant, calling for the support of their fighting brothers at home and abroad. Only a very few of Father Divine's followers appeared in Conscientious Objector's camps or have gone to prison for conscience's sake in their opposition to war. It will be recalled that this platform was first adopted in 1936.

(4) In the fourth plank in the platform he returns once again to the race issue and calls for legislation, "making it a crime for any newspaper, magazine or other publication to use segregated or slang words referring to race, creed or color of any individual or group, or write abusively concerning any."

(5) Plank five is against legislation providing for compulsory insurance, public liability, or any other form of insurance.

(6) The sixth plank calls for the abolition of capital punishment in all states.

(7) Plank seven has to do with healing. It will be recalled that healing is often practiced by Father Divine and notable claims for healing are constantly published in their literature. This plank opposes compulsory vaccinations, operations and treatment by physicians. When the authorities or physicians take charge of the patient, "they must guarantee a complete cure and guarantee the life of the individual or be liable for damages in the event of his death."

(8) The eighth plank is against lynching which, it asserts, must be outlawed in all states and countries.

(9) The ninth plank reverts once again to the race issue calling for legislation making it unlawful to withhold work from any Civil Service employee on account of race, creed or color provided he or she is qualified to do the work.

(10) The tenth plank refers to the return of all stolen goods or their equivalent not only by individuals but by nations, "this to include all territories taken by force from other nations."

All four of the remaining planks of the platform concern themselves with racial issues. According to the eleventh plank legislation should make it a crime for an employer to discharge an employee when it can be proven "that it was on account of race, creed or color." Plank twelve calls for legislation prohibiting labor organizations from discriminating against members on account of race, creed or color. A rather novel addition is that any labor union which limits the hours and days of work per week "must guarantee at least that much work per week to its members, and if it calls a strike, pay its members, while they are out of work, the full amount they are demanding from their employers. Otherwise all obligations for dues must cease." Plank thirteen calls for the repeal of all laws, government rules and regulations requiring individuals to designate themselves as being of a certain race, creed or color in signing any kind of papers, especially immigration, citizenship, passport, or legal papers. The final plank calls for legislation forbidding payment of different wages or salaries to workers, skilled or unskilled, technical or professional, on the basis of race, creed or color. Likewise they would forbid discrimination in any way in the hiring of help, on the grounds of race, creed or color.

Thus it can be seen that in seven of the fourteen planks of the platform the race issue is raised.[5]

---

[5] The entire platform as adopted by the International Righteous Government convention, New York City, January 10–12, 1936, A.D.F.D., is published in the *New Day* in July 28, 1945, Volume 9, No. 30, pages 40 and following.

The Righteous Government platform is based upon the belief that the principles of righteousness, truth, and justice, in order to become a reality, need to be established universally, not alone in the minds and hearts of people, but through the legislative process.

Equal opportunity, which is at the heart of the social program, can only be secured in our present society through legislation. The Constitution of the United States enunciates the principles but there is need for specific legislation to make its principles effective, and Father Divine seeks to influence legislation to this end. That he is not wholly doctrinaire in the position that he takes is evident when it is recalled that he has more than once, through the influence he exercises over his followers, sent them to the polls or kept them away in such numbers as to effect vitally the results of elections. More than once, also, his followers have definitely raised the issue of the legality of requiring the declaration of race origins, through the refusal to sign applications on which this information was sought, and in some cases the authorities have been obliged to accept the information without declaration of race.

The Righteous Government program has a very definite economic outlook, also, and offers specific planks concerning the reshaping of our economy in line with the general principle of equality of opportunity. The details of this section cannot be given here, but it includes such principles as government control of all idle plants, machinery, tools, and equipment, which, when owners refuse to operate them, will be made available to workers on the cooperative, non-profit basis; provision for government projects of social utility to give unemployed workers opportunity to work; abolition of tariff schedules and the adoption of free trade; and finally, limitation upon the amount of profit that one may take. One interesting plank which is very much insisted upon in his own group is a demand for legislation making it a criminal offense for anyone, while he owes a just debt to anyone else, to spend money except for the necessities of life.

There is an educational department, and definite planks are adopted regulating educational procedure. Naturally enough it must be completely open and free of any race or color restrictions. No text books shall be used which refer to racial conflicts or differences. The desirability of a universal language is asserted in one plank, and, elsewhere than in the platform, he has advocated that this one language be English. The Righteous Government Platform is the ideal that has been set up. It has been slightly modified from time to time since its first promulgation. Theoretically there are supposed to be periodical meetings, called Righteous Government meetings, in which the membership discusses questions dealing with the Righteous Government Program and from time to time a report is made of the progress being made toward the realization of the ideals expressed in the platform. The writer recalls one report which was given at a meeting he attended in which certain legislation that had been passed in certain states and by the national Congress, was declared to be in fulfillment of the Righteous Government Platform. It seemed a little far-fetched to the writer, because they seemed to feel that it was a direct victory for the Righteous Government and that said legislation was at least to some extent the result of the efforts being made by Father Divine. He has declared publicly: "I am in Congress doing so and so," or "I am in Florida bringing certain reforms to pass," and his followers seem to accept this as a statement of fact.

One of the ways in which Father Divine operates is not simply to preach in his own meetings what he believes to be right; he frequently writes letters to those in authority both here and in other parts of the world suggesting what ought to be done in a given case. Such letters are to be found printed in the *New Day* from time to time. One recalls a message to Hitler, another to Hirohito, and at times to different places within our own country.

Internationally, Father Divine has a definite platform. It appears on letters that he writes. Colored stickers, for putting on letters, contain messages of this sort. One of these is done in red, white, and blue, and represents the two hemispheres, east and west, flanked by two doves of peace with olive branches in their mouths. The headline is, "For a Just and Lasting Peace." Then follows, "Why not propose at the international conference of nations, the unification of all the mutual and allied sovereignties of the universe, and let the united countries of the world be one big universal allied sovereignty? By the unity of spirit, mind, aim, and of purpose, let all of the allied sovereignties unite consolidatedly and the Four Freedoms will be made a reality." Another which appeared earlier but is still frequently found on letters of his followers gives the substance of a cablegram sent to Hitler, Chamberlain, Daladier, President Benes, and President Roosevelt, on September 20, 1938, A.D.F.D. "Why not propose purchase of coveted Czechoslovakian territory, with Sudetans helping to pay for annexation, substituting

cooperation and Peace for terrible unhuman warfare consequences?"
—signed, Father Divine. There is added a statement made by
President Roosevelt: "It is my conviction that all people under the
threat of war today pray that Peace may be made before, rather
than AFTER war."

Father Divine's plan for inter-American solidarity will not make
South Americans very happy, for his plan would definitely make
the United States the controlling factor in the Western world from
the extreme north to the straits of Magellan.

However one may evaluate his proposals for achieving the ends
he seeks, it must be admitted that here is a religion with a concrete
social, political and economic program, designed to make its
ultimate ends possible of realization. If they seem to some grandiose
and unattainable, it must at the same time be observed that some of
them are exceedingly sensible and have much to commend them.
He has an educational program. Many thousands of followers have
become literate, intelligent citizens because of the stimulus they
have received from him. He does have an economic program. Many
people have been lifted out of misery and unhappiness and poverty
through the operation of his system. He has a political ideal. His
people are told to revere the Constitution of the United States. Many
of them know it by heart and can repeat the Declaration of Independence without a mistake. They do operate, on occasion, as a
political unit when moral issues are at stake, and they are effective.
However mistaken he may be about some things or even many
things, there is not a little in his program to command the respect
and even the admiration of those who cherish the Christian ideal
and seek its realization in the lives of men.

One of the taboos of the movement is any use of the customary
race terms that are employed to distinguish people. They never
speak of "Negroes." If it is necessary to use any term of racial differ-
entiation the most they will do is to speak of the N's or the B's
(blacks) or the W's (whites). The circumlocutions required to
distinguish race or color are interesting. In talking with me personally about such things, Father and various of his followers would
speak of "those of my complexion" or "those of your complexion,"
or in general speech "those of another complexion." They will not
countenance the customary distinctions to the extent of dignifying
them with names. Father Divine insists that it is *vulgar* to use such
terms as Negro, White, etc. "My followers," he frequently asserts

in his sermons, "will not be so vulgar as to speak of N's or D's (darkeys)", etc.

It is something of a shock to the average white observer to see the freedom with which colored and white live in the same hotels, share the same rooms, eat at the same tables, with a complete apparent lack of the consciousness of differences. This is particularly notable among the Rosebuds, the young girls' group which usually forms the choir and keeps the music going during the banquets and in the public meetings. Here fresh-faced, young, dark and white girls sing side by side without the slightest trace of any difference between them. There is no grouping of whites together. Nor does this seem to be at all by design, rather a result of personal choice. They seem to sit together because they like each other. Nor is there any grouping of whites together at the communion tables. Some of them get to sit at the first table, some do not, and often have to stand, as do the colored folk, awaiting the second table. Cantril professed to find that there was a special deference shown to the whites.[6] I personally did not notice this among the members of the group. It is true that white visitors are given a place up near the head of the table where Father sits. But that may well be because they are guests. A colored guest also, particularly if he be a person of distinction, will be shown the same courtesy. There is no doubt that Father Divine likes to have guests at the communion meals. He undoubtedly is glad for whatever advantage may accrue to his movement from such visits. Since his movement runs counter to the general mores of the dominant group, in respect to race, especially, but also in respect to the economic principles he teaches, it would be strange if he did not welcome the friendly visits of persons of influence who, by their very presence, even though motivated chiefly by curiosity, tend by so much to give a certain "respectability" to his movement. "If so and so visits such a place and eats with them, and even speaks a word of appreciation for their work, it can't be wholly bad," is likely to be the attitude of many who learn of such visits. Since it is chiefly white opposition that must be broken down, it is not unnatural that white visitors of influence are shown every courtesy. Personally I cannot recall any particular deference shown to anyone because of color. I saw some very humble colored persons treated as guests also and seated in the preferred location.

[6] Hadley Cantril, *Psychology of Social Movements*, pp. 127 ff.

It is undoubtedly true that among many of the rank and file of colored followers the almost unconscious attitude of deference to white persons persists. It has been so long a necessity of their very existence as a part of the community, that they do not quickly lose it when they become members of this inter-racial group.

Among those closest to Father Divine are his secretaries, of whom seven out of sixteen are white girls. One of these acts as chauffeur as well as secretary. Of course, a mere three days' observation is all too short a time on which to base a sure judgment, but certainly there was no apparent distinction among them on racial grounds. It would be too much to suppose that, being human, there exist no feelings of rivalry, possibly some envy or jealously among them, but to the outer world these are not apparent. White and colored among them vie with each other in their loving service to Father Divine. Some it may be, are older, more experienced, better trained, and more capable than others, but so far as could be observed the factor of race or color did not enter in the slightest degree to affect their relations with each other or with Father Divine.

Some white men have been prominent in the movement and stood close to Father Divine. John Lamb, his chief secretary for a number of years, was "of the other complexion," as Father Divine would say. But he is no longer intimately associated with the movement. White women seemed much more numerous than white men. Most of these were middle aged or beyond. Aside from the Rosebuds who are the younger group, I did not see many white women of younger years. A number of the older white women were retired school teachers. The beautiful home for retired school teachers at Riverton, New Jersey, about fifteen miles out of Philadelphia undoubtedly accounts in part for this. There, in the former home of a rich industrialist, are beautifully furnished quarters where retired members of the teaching profession may live at nominal expense amid delightful surroundings.

V. ECONOMIC ASPECTS

Father Divine's Peace Mission is not simply a religious movement. It is at the same time a definite social and economic movement as well. Indeed, it is the economic aspect of the movement which has probably excited more curiosity and interest than any other phase of it. The questions most frequently heard concerning Father Divine are, "How does he do it? Where does the money come from?

Who pays for all this?" And it must be said that no one has satis-factorily answered these questions as yet. Those 10- and 15-cent meals, for example! You can go into any of the Peace restaurants and for 15 cents get a substantial meal, consisting of an abundant serving of meat, potatoes, a vegetable, bread, butter, and a drink—either coffee, tea, or milk. Formerly a salad and dessert were pro-vided also. As late as 1941 they were advertising, "We specialize in fried chicken." Now a salad may cost from three to five cents, and dessert five cents. That is a complete meal costing not over 25 cents! How can that be done in a day like this? Or the banquets, better named the Communion meals. These meals have often enough been described, yet until I had actually sat at the table, I had not really quite understood how elaborate they were. One's first experience of such a meal is overwhelming in more ways than one, and he is constrained to ask whence comes all this? Who pays for it? How can they afford it?

Or one goes down to Atlantic City to the once elegant Brigantine, a million dollar resort hotel, and discovers that he can get lodging there for $2 per week—yes, per week, not per day. (This hotel was given up to the Government as a hostel for refugees during the war at a rental of a dollar a year.) Or go, as I did, to lovely Pine Brook Hotel, twenty miles out of Newark among the pleasant New Jersey hills, and lodging can be had for as low as $1.50 per week, with meals at fifteen cents, or with dessert and salad at twenty-five cents. Thus one could have a week in the country with complete meals for as little as $6.75. But how can they do it?

When I asked that question, one of Father's secretaries spoke up. "Do you not recall the feeding of the four and five thousand by Jesus? He had, to begin with, only five loaves and two fishes. Yet they gathered up twelve baskets of the fragments that remained over." That seems to be the answer accepted by many of Father's followers. A German farmer in New Jersey who wrote me a thirty-two-page letter explaining Father Divine, said, "If they prepare ten pounds of meat, they then can serve ten thousand people, so is God's blessing. When they take a piece of meat out of the pot there is another piece in the place." A white woman told me of seeing Father pour thirteen cups of coffee out of an eight-cup pot. When his attention was called to it, she said he went right on pouring cup after cup from the same pot without replenishing it. One is reminded of the widow's cruse of oil. These people, many of them, verily believe that the day of miracles is not past and, of course, logically, if Father Divine is God, there would be no difficulty in believing that he could do these things.

But this is a skeptical age, and such an answer will not satisfy hard-headed investigators. There must be some answer that fits better into the twentieth century. Father Divine obviously must have money, lots of it. Where does he get it?

Well, I asked him that very directly. His answer was equally direct. "I haven't any money. I do not own a thing personally. Yet my needs are always taken care of."

"But all these properties, these Kingdoms, are they not yours?" I asked.

"Not one," he replied. "They all belong to my followers."

And despite the fact that investigators have sought long and diligently by fair means—and not so fair, sometimes—no one has been able to discover that he does have any money or any property. He pays no income tax, because he has no income, though his followers do pay substantial amounts in taxes.

An explanation that has been widely published and accepted and which I myself accepted and published at one time is that on coming into the movement the entrant surrenders all his property and assets into Father's hands in return for the assurance that he will be securely provided for in Father Divine's Kingdom.

If, it is argued, that were done, and if members of the movement should, as it is asserted by some writers, turn over to Father for disbursement the income they receive when they go outside to work, there would be plenty of money to provide these banquets and all the other benefits which the movement affords its members.

This sounds plausible, and would be, for myself, a sufficient explanation—if it were true—but I am personally no longer convinced that it is true.

It is true that such charges have been made by some who were one time members of the group, but who became disgruntled and left it. The best known of the cases is that of Verinda Brown and her husband who sued Father Divine for the return of a substantial sum, some $3,000, which they allege they turned over to him on joining the movement and from their continued earnings afterward. This has already been referred to (p. 13, Is the Movement Growing?). I expressed there my own belief that the claim was false. This conviction is based on extensive reading in the reports of the case, especially, in the *Spoken Word*, the official publication at that time. There appear declarations and even affidavits of other persons who were in the movement at the time which discredit completely the claim of the Browns. If the sworn statement of this couple, who obviously have something personal to gain from the payment of this sum of money, is to be considered, why ought not the sworn statements of others in the movement, who have nothing personally to gain by their declarations, be given consideration also? I refer to such persons as John Lamb who for a long time, as his secretary, stood quite close to Father Divine, although he has since withdrawn.

He asserts that he "saw many offer Father Divine money and property in return for blessings received, but he always refused it." He himself offered $2,000 to Father Divine to be used in his work, desiring to become a member of his household. He swears that Father Divine said he could not accept it, that he "never accepted contributions, donations or love offerings from anyone."

Charles Callow, another follower, made affidavit that, becoming interested in Father Divine at Sayville, he "offered a sum of money to turn over to anyone he might suggest." It was refused, since he never solicited or accepted gifts. He owned certain apartments on 135th Street. He invited Father Divine to come and live in his home as his guest since Father was often speaking in meetings in Harlem and elsewhere. Divine consented in March, 1932, and for eight months Mr. Callow's home was regarded as headquarters. In 1933 one Lena Brinson leased a building at 20 W. 115th Street, larger and better suited for his work. She invited Father Divine to move there, and made available an apartment on the top floor. Mr. Callow then closed his own home and moved into the 115th Street apartment and helped to maintain it. Father Divine had nothing to do with financing it.

If Verinda Brown and later Faithful Mary's charges were printed in the public press, why not some of the testimony of others whose character has never been questioned? For example, there is the affidavit of Priscilla Paul, who asserts that as a fellow worker of Verinda Brown she had heard her testify often to the effect that "Father Divine had done so much for her she could not thank him adequately, and that he would not allow her to do anything for him but give him her heart." [7] Or, again, consider the affidavits of

---

[7] *Spoken Word*, June 22, 1937, p. 52. See other affidavits in this issue.

Blessed Real and that of Satisfied Justice,[8] who was a secretary to Faithful Mary and who swore that Faithful Mary had not turned over profits to Father Divine.

Convinced as I was when I first made contact with Father Divine and his followers that it was his method to take over their assets, I was greatly surprised when he declared that he accepted no money from any of them. I sought at every opportunity to find out from the followers whom I met whether this was a fact. Repeatedly I asked individuals, "What did you turn over to Father Divine when you joined the movement?"

Generally their reply was, "What do you mean—turn over property to Father? Why you can't give him anything. He's always giving things to us." Riding back to New York in the early morning hours after a banquet in New Jersey, I put the question to my five companions in the car. One of them replied, "Why, the only thing I brought to Father was my sins." All asserted categorically that no one is ever asked to give anything to Father, but that on the contrary, he will not accept anything from any one of them. I pressed the questions upon two highly intelligent white members of the group, one of whom holds a doctorate of philosophy from a high ranking American University. The couple has been closely associated with the movement for several years. They asserted positively that Father Divine refuses to accept even a small gift from anybody. It can be readily seen that it would be easy, if he would do so, for people to seek some personal privilege from him by such gifts. Mrs. X. also said that if one wished quite anonymously to make some little gift to one of his secretaries or members of his staff, who, incidentally, are paid no salaries, it could be done, but if the name of the donor were known, the gift would be returned to him immediately. Again and again Father Divine returns money gifts made to him by mail, thanking the donor but refusing the gift. This particular couple has never known anyone, in the years they have been associated with him, to be asked to give up any property or money. Certainly these people would not be easily fooled. And certainly they have no personal ends to serve through misrepresentation of Father Divine. As a matter of fact the husband of the couple is critical of some aspects of the movement and is not himself a full-fledged member. He has made a painstaking study of it which, it is to be hoped, will some day be published. He finds a

[8] *Id.*, pp. 56–57.

very different explanation of the so-called mystery, and in what follows I am to a considerable degree indebted to him. He courteously accorded me the privilege of reading part of his unpublished manuscript. I had already begun to suspect where the true answer lay. His help and my subsequent observation served to confirm my belief that the answer lay in the clever economic foundation of the movement-on cooperation. This is the principle that underlies the whole structure. So far as I have been able to discover this has not been set forth by anyone who has written on the subject of Father Divine.

First, it should be said that the Peace Mission Movement is not one single cooperative, economically. Rather it is a congeries of small cooperatives operating upon principles taught by Father Divine and brought into a spiritual unity by the common loyalty and devotion which all the members feel toward him. This spiritual unity will be seen, however, to have very practical consequences; indeed, it seems to be the *sine qua non* of the effectiveness of his whole economic program. Without this common loyalty it is doubtful if the individual cooperatives could succeed as well as they do.

Second, it should be said that Father Divine himself claims to have no holding in any of the cooperatives, and to profit in no financial way from their operation, although of course his movement prospers financially as these business ventures succeed, and people are attracted to it, in many cases, by the factor of economic security which it offers. Father Divine personally declares that his part in the cooperatives is chiefly that of adviser. In some cases apparently the original suggestion is made by him that a cooperative be formed. Thus it becomes known that Father Divine is interested in the purchase of a hotel building, or a farm, or a garage. An offer comes to him personally. If the offer seems advantageous he may suggest that a group of his followers organize and buy it. But frequently the followers conceive an enterprise on their own initiative. They then come to him for advice. The transactions of Father Divine and his followers are always on a cash basis. They may even bring him the cash with which to make the payment as their agent, thus giving rise to stories of the large sums of money which he carries about in a black satchel. Of course, the possibility exists that Father Divine is profiting financially and very cleverly concealing the fact. But his followers do not believe it. They often seek to thrust money or gifts upon him, despite his refusal to accept them.

The insistent belief that there must be something not quite above board about the whole financial arrangement arises chiefly from the difficulty the average American has in conceiving a type of belief or organization in which money plays only a minor role—where it is only a kind of necessary evil, because of the surrounding environment which depends upon money or exchange for its very existence.

But suppose that money comes to be considered not as an end, but only as a means to securing certain values, and suppose further that those values could be secured without money, or at best with only a very limited amount of it. Then obviously the amassing of money would hold no appeal for people. This seems literally to be a fact among many of Father Divine's followers as it is a fact among some other groups such as some, though not all, monastic orders.

Father Divine himself literally has, personally, everything he needs without having to spend money at all. In every one of the centers a suite of rooms is always furnished for him. They are comfortably and, in some cases, luxuriously furnished. He presides at one or more banquets almost every day of the week and there is a private dining room for him and his staff in many of the centers where he can be served at any time he desires. He is embarrassed constantly by the desire of individuals and groups to give him personal gifts, clothing, hats, etc. He lacks nothing of the necessities and even comforts of life. He owns not even a car; it is furnished by devoted followers, and, at least at present, it is in no sense a luxury car. He does not even buy the gas or oil, or pay for the up-keep of the car. Yet a car is always at his disposal. He can command a superabundance of personal service. Secretaries are always at his disposal for his office work. Money is for him almost completely unnecessary.

Of course, many will think this may not last and that he must be salting something away for the time when the bubble bursts. But does he regard the whole movement as a bubble? One of the most marked characteristics of Father Divine, as I observed him, was his complete confidence in the future of his movement.

Clearly not all his followers enjoy all the advantages which surround him personally, but there is a faith among them in the ability of Father Divine to secure for them all that is needful—*in this present life*. They feel this so strongly that they are quite willing to forego the ordinary monetary rewards men seek and to devote their time and energy to making possible the successful operation of the various enterprises of the Peace Mission. It is this fact which makes it possible to operate them at the low prices they are able to charge.

Several factors enter into the cost of doing business in, let us say, a restaurant. There is capital investment which seeks a return. It has to pay, and the desired return ordinarily is a fairly high percentage—what the traffic will bear in many cases. Then there is the cost of equipment and materials—the food, the rent of the building or its upkeep, heat, light, etc., if owned, and finally the cost of management and labor.

If the investors demand a high rate of return, if rent is high, if equipment is lavish, if food is bought in the open market, geared to a profit system, if labor and management demand the highest possible rewards, then obviously meals cannot be served at fifteen to twenty-five cents.

But what if the investors are interested, not in the accumulation of wealth, but only in a modestly comfortable living, and desire only that their capital serve the cause in which they believe, without any return to them personally? One charge is at once eliminated. Suppose, again, that the restaurant is operated in a cooperatively owned building which does not have to make a profit, but is meant primarily to serve the cause. Clearly the rent item will be much less than what a straight commercial rent charge would be. This is actually the case of probably most of the Peace Mission restaurants.

Then the cost of equipment; if expensive, luxurious equipment and fixtures are provided the cost is inevitably increased. But suppose it is only modestly but comfortably furnished without any conspicuous luxury element, solidly built and durable as well as simple —as is actually the case. The charge upon the selling price need not be heavy.

But food costs. Everybody knows that. Nevertheless, even here economy may be practiced. If food is purchased in the open market, which is geared to the profit system, only buying in quantity or buying second-grade materials will cut the cost to an extent. But once more, suppose that much of the produce, at least, comes from cooperative farms, not operated for profit, or that meats and vegetables be bought from cooperative stores and markets, where profit is not the motive. In such a case substantial savings can be effected, which may serve to reduce the cost of the meals.

Finally, let us look at the cost of service, the cooking and serving of the meals, and the cost of management. If everyone must be paid substantial wages, and if the service is elaborate, the cost of meals will inevitably be raised. But once again, suppose the people who manage the restaurant, and those who prepare, cook, and serve the meals are interested not in income, but in service, and consider that in contributing their labor on a subsistence return they are serving God—Father Divine. Then a major cost factor is affected.

Actually, it is a fact that these restaurants are run as service institutions, not profit-makng ventures. Most of them are located in cooperatively owned buildings, so that rent is low; they buy either from cooperatively run farms, or stores and markets where the profit element is reduced to a minimum. And too, some of the employees of the restaurant perform their various tasks as a service for which they receive not wages, but maintenance—maintenance, let it be remembered, in hotels or kingdoms which are run on the same principles. They get their food in the restaurants themselves where the cost is low—for the reasons just given.

When all these facts are taken into consideration it does not seem so remarkable that meals are served at fifteen and twenty-five cents. The Bureau of Labor Statistics reports that the cost of food per week in American cities, in February 1946, for a family of five, with an income of $1,500–2,000 per year after taxes, was $14.91, or just over 14 cents per meal.[9] But note that here, (1) buying is done in small quantities, (2) in a system definitely run for profit, and (3) in a system in which relatively high wages are paid for labor and management. Of course this represents the cost of meals in the home, not in a public place, hence the rent and labor costs do not enter. It is thus roughly comparable to the Peace Mission restaurant meals.

But even if meals could be served for fifteen to twenty-five cents, how about the elaborate banquets where food appears in such variety and abundance? Who pays for them? In an earlier period apparently they were served without charge to any who might come. Now, however, the regular fifteen- twenty-five-cent charge is made to all those who are not of Father's helpers or guests—fifteen cents, unless salad and dessert are eaten, otherwise twenty-five. It is left up to each individual to say whether he took the extras or not. But one can pay more if he wishes and many do contribute

[9] *Monthly Labor Review*, Vol. 62, #2, February 1946, p. 299.

much more than the minimum, just out of gratitude for the privilege of being near Father Divine and enjoying his bounty. It is not unusual to give as much as five dollars or more. But there is no compulsion and I have heard Father Divine say publicly, "If any one tries to collect more from you than the minimum charge, please report it to me."

As one thinks carefully of the matter, he is bound to reflect that, after all, regardless of the number of varieties of food offered, each person can consume only so much, and after he has attended one or two banquets, he, knowing what to expect, passes most of the dishes on without taking any. Conceivably, therefore, the cost of the meal might be met by the amount taken in by the collectors. If the expense is not so covered, it is made up by the local church or group in which the banquet is given, or from any profits that accrue from the hotel or kingdom where it is served. This would not be in any case a heavy charge, and since the banquet or communion table is the central feature of the group life—an occasion for the sharing of experience, the joys of fellowship, and for seeing and hearing the beloved Father, it would not be a serious burden upon the group. Consider the fact that they pay no ministerial salaries, maintain few churches that are separate from income-producing properties, do not pay for music, and in such educational or eleemosynary work as they do, pay only maintenance or subsistence to those who carry on the work. Nor do they support an expensive home or foreign missionary program.

The original cost of the rather elegant china and silver service must not have been inconsiderable, but well-to-do people have come into the movement and have undoubtedly made substantial contributions toward their purchase. After all, the very attractive dishes, I noted, were of Japanese manufacture, and such ware is not prohibitive in price. Father Divine does not say that his followers must not make gifts to the local groups, even though he will not accept such gifts personally.

How do they provide lodging in a great city for $1.50 to $2 per week? There seems to me nothing mysterious about this after having been personally conducted by Father Divine through a number of his Kingdoms, both in New York and in Philadelphia. Let me describe a typical hotel for sisters which I visited.

On the ground floor there were the lobby and office, parlors and lounge rooms, and the dining room and kitchen, all nicely and comfortably furnished. On the upper floors were rooms, smaller and larger, with adequate bathroom facilities, usually shower baths, and a few tubs. They were scrupulously clean, comfortably and attractively furnished. In the smallest of the rooms was at least one double bed and a dresser. Every bed I saw had an attractive spread of the candlewick or damask variety. In the larger rooms would be three, four or as many as twelve double beds and dressers. I began to see the answer to the economic question. No room would bring less than $4 a week and that would be a small room. On the other hand the one with twelve beds would bring up to $24 per week or almost $100 per month.

A little calculation will help to see the total picture. Suppose that the capacity of one of the hotels was 100 young women. That would mean $150 to $200 per week income, which would amount to some $8,000–$10,000 per year. The girls do most of the work of caring for their beds and rooms. But allow five persons full time to care for the building. If paid regular wages that would be a fairly large item, but recall that their service is a labor of love, for maintenance only. Since they live at the same cheap rate of $2 per week and a maximum of $.75 for three meals a day, they could be kept at $10 per week, $520 per year each and be given a little cash. That would mean an expense of $2,600 for service. Add an equal amount for repairs and upkeep—recalling here that this is all done on a maintenance basis also and that therefore a great deal could be done for the amount indicated. That would bring the total up to $5,200. Add for extras enough to make the total cost $6,000 and there would still remain a profit of from $2,000–$4,000. This would represent a return of 3% on an investment of $66,000–$132,000. While I did not secure an exact statement of the cost of any of the properties visited, I seriously doubt if any of them would have cost as much.

Because the price is low, occupancy of the hotels runs close to 100% the year round. The one thing that is sacrificed by the roomers is privacy. They live in dormitories. This will appear to many as a hardship in contrast to the background of a roomy private house where everyone has his own room. But if put alongside the crowded, often unsanitary kind of living, in congested city areas—and that is the lot of a great percentage of colored members—this undoubtedly represents something approaching luxury. There is no infraction of the city ordinance in any case. Here the sexes are segregated and at least there is cleanliness and physical comfort. It is a genuine service that Father Divine is rendering in furnishing such hostels to his flock.

Thus there does not seem to be so much mystery about the system as popularly imagined. It looks like very wise planning. What actually happens is that Father Divine and his followers never build new buildings. They watch the market for real estate bargains which will serve their purposes, and buy properties at very advantageous prices. Often the buildings are in bad condition and need repair. The cost of this would perhaps be prohibitive if one had to pay current prices for everything and make a fair return on the investment. But for Father Divine it is not so difficult.

To explain what I mean, let me introduce "Generous Henry." (That is, of course, not his cult name, but he is a real person well known to the writer and the statements about him are facts.)

Henry told me, on inquiry, that he could live in New York in one of the men's kingdoms and keep a good Buick car—all for $10 per week. That seems amazing, but remember the cost of the room and meals. Also there are cooperative garages and he can buy his gasoline at a one cent profit per gallon from the dealer instead of the usual three or four cent profit.

"How much do you earn per day when you work?" I asked him.

"Twelve dollars is a minimum if I work for wages, though I usually take contracts upon which I net a much better return," he replied. He is an artisan.

Now consider the significance of this. He can earn in one day enough to live on the rest of the week. Where else can this be done?

"What do you do the rest of the time?" I inquired.

"Well," he answered, "I am one of the maintenance force for keeping up the properties of the various Peace Missions."

"How much do you get when you work thus?"

"Only maintenance," said he. "Sometimes I may spend three months continuously working at the renovation of some building in the movement, and get no money at all. But of course, I eat well and have lodging and the upkeep of my car during that time."

Consider the implications of this. By working one day a week he is able to earn enough so that he can *give* his service freely to Father Divine whom he loves. That is one day for himself, six days for God.

Here is the secret of Father Divine's amazing achievements—the free service of devoted followers without any desire for financial return, but only the privilege of being near or working for him whom they love.

Actually, of course, not all the followers work most of their time. Henry was in the midst of completing a $1,000 contract for outsiders when I talked with him. He is a hard-working, successful artisan, and when he and others work for any outsider they charge about what anyone else would charge for the same kind of work. However, he will give an honest day's work where many an outsider will not. If he earns and accumulates money, what does he do with it?

Well, he doesn't drink. This is strictly taboo. Likewise he doesn't smoke or use tobacco in any form—another taboo. He doesn't gamble. He doesn't spend money on vice since he has been reformed. He doesn't often, or perhaps ever, go to the movies. He doesn't carry insurance, so he pays no premiums. That is the result of a definite belief they hold. To take out insurance, whether accident, health, or life, is to exhibit distrust of God's power to keep one. He is single, so has no family to support. It is easy to see that if he or any other follower has a fairly well paying job, he will either not work all the time, and so have free time to serve Father in some capacity—whether as footman, cook, secretary, assistant minister, or maintenance man—or he will accumulate money, which he will either contribute to the movement, by supporting some local church group, or he will buy war bonds. (Large amounts were bought by Father's followers.) Or again, he may invest in some of the cooperatives which are constantly springing up.

When the million-dollar Brigantine Hotel at Atlantic City was to be sold for $50,000 it was not difficult to find a number of followers with money to put into it. Other examples are the Pine Brook Hotel in New Jersey, or Krum Elbow across the Hudson from the late President's Hyde Park home, or the lovely estate of the former president of the Campbell Soup Company at Riverton, New Jersey. It was these accumulations of capital which bought the farms in the Promised Land in Ulster County, New York. There is or need be little mystery about it.

There are scores of small cooperatives, garages, meat markets, building contractors, painters, and artisans scattered about New York, Newark, Philadelphia, and other cities in that area. Each is independent of the other, though some of the same individuals may have investments in several. All are loyal to Father Divine's principles and all are mutually friendly. Wherever possible they help each other out, making a better price to each other than to the general public, but at no actual loss to themselves.

Again consider Generous Henry. He is a carpenter, and contracts for small building and repair operations. He is associated with a group of artisans who practice bricklaying, plumbing, painting, etc. They work together wherever advantageous. He owns not a few tools, which he must move about from job to job. He does not own a truck. But there is a trucking cooperative operating in his area. A member of this cooperative will willingly transport his equipment to a new location at a slack hour of the day when he might otherwise be idle, charging only enough to pay the cost of his gas and his time, but much less than he would charge an outsider. In his turn, Henry will work for the truckers at a convenient time for himself and at a very reasonable charge. Through this kind of mutual aid the individuals and the cooperatives greatly strengthen each other and the movement as a whole.

I once asked Father Divine whether his cooperatives were run on Rochdale principles. He seemed not even to know the name, Rochdale. He does, however, have definite principles which govern all Peace Mission enterprises. These he explains in a letter written to an inquirer in 1937.

"Any business enterprise should be purchased completely by those who are the buyers and paid for in cash without mortgages, notes, or any trust or loan whatsoever [sic]; and it should be distinctly understood that such business is to be owned and operated by those in charge as joint tenants, not as tenants in common but as joint tenants, with right of survivorship, each business being an individual independent enterprise or being an individual independent unit."

In 1937 the question of employees' compensation arose. The state insisted that the Peace Cooperatives observe the usual requirements upon employers in this respect. Father Divine held that this would involve the violation of certain of his principles. To clarify the situation a resolution was passed and published officially defining the relationship of persons engaged in their operation. Incidental light is thrown upon the organization of the so-called cooperatives. The resolution reads:

"Each place of business, Peace Mission Extension, and Connections, is an individual unit under the control of the various representatives of the Peace Mission engaged in activity therein.

"Those serving as co-workers do so gratis, it being understood that such co-workers are not employees but joint tenants with the individual or individuals who lease such places.

"This manner of cooperative activity is now and has always been carried on by followers of Father Divine and is not intended as an evasion of any law.

"It is understood, the believers of Father Divine voluntarily give their services to the Cause gratis, without compensation.

"It is further understood that the co-workers and Representatives of the Peace Missions are willing to TRUST GOD wholeheartedly according to our conscious conviction.

"Therefore—in summary, we will not remain on public welfare, neither seek further aid. We will not take out insurance and will resign what we now have for the purpose of giving our whole hearts, souls and minds to that to which we are converted—nor will we take out compensation or liability or other insurance. We will also refuse to receive old age pensions, insurances, veterans' pensions and other compensations. All this is done through their conscious conviction of such being a violation to their religious belief and not according to their religious discipline.

"Therefore, we the undersigned, do hereby respectively request the exemption from such obligations as above-mentioned, according to our constitutional rights, for the advancement of Moral Betterment, Honest and Human Liberty and Justice under the Constitution of our Great Country." [10]

Such principles cut across the social security plan at present observed by the United States government. These people are so completely convinced that their security lies in their relation to Father Divine—God—that they refuse all other attempted guarantees of future security. Obviously when they employ outsiders who do not share their ideals, they must pay current wages. Also they have to make the proper Social Security return to the United States government. But to avoid this complication groups of workers are formed, such as one described by Generous Henry. Let us call it the "Peace Sun Workers." In this group are associated ten artisans, carpenters, plumbers, plasterers, painters, etc. Each man is free to contract for

---

[10] *The Spoken Word*, Vol. 3, July 3, 1937, p. 21.

jobs as opportunity affords, but when his contract calls for the service of other than his own specialty he calls in the proper members of the group rather than hiring outsiders. They are then regarded as partners and not employees, and hence are not subject to the social security requirements. The exact financial arrangement within the group may vary according to the job. Compensation may be in terms of wages or in the form of a proportionate share in the total income from the job.

VI. *RELIGIOUS IDEAS*

If we have emphasized, and rightly, the social and economic features of Father Divine's Peace Mission, it must not be forgotten that it is first, last, and always a distinctly religious movement. It is out of certain basic religious convictions that the practical social and economic beliefs and practices naturally flow. What are these religious ideas? How do they differ from the ideas held by the Christian groups out of which Father Divine himself came and from which come most of his followers. Has his movement a recognizable system of theology?

From a superficial reading of Father Divine's sermons as they are published in the *New Day* one is likely to emerge with the impression that, except at perhaps two points, he is just an evangelical Christian holding about the same general ideas one would find in almost any Evangelical Church. Man is a sinner who must repent and turn to God in order to obtain a salvation, which he is not, himself, able to attain. Jesus Christ came to earth as the revelation of God's love for man and laid down in the gospels the conditions under which man might be redeemed. Unless man repents and turns to God he is lost.

The major point at which difference appears is in his identification of himself with God. Here is something unique among religious cults. Now and again men have arisen to claim that they were prophets of God, some that they were Messiahs, some that they were incarnations of deity. But here appears one who proclaims boldly— or at least it is proclaimed for him by his followers—that he himself is God—and none other. Does Father Divine himself assert that he is God?

Well, concerning what his followers think there cannot be the slightest doubt. One only needs to listen a little while to their

songs and testimonies to be convinced that they have no slightest
hesitation in affirming that he is God in the flesh.

Listen to the yell of the Rosebuds (the young girl group) given
with all the enthusiasm of a football crowd:

> 2, 4, 6, 8
> Who do we appreciate
> Father Divine, Father Divine
> God! (explosively)

Or this:

> 1, 2, 3, 4
> 3, 2, 1, 4
> Who for
> What for
> Who'd you think
> We're yelling for?
> F-A-T-H-E-R, Father, D-I-V-I-NE, Divine
> That's the way we spell it
> Here's the way we yell it,
> Father Divine, Father Divine,
> God! God! God!

Their songs are replete with assertions of his divinity, thus the
chorus sung over and over again at the banquets:

> Father Divine is God,
> Father Divine is God Almighty,
> Is God, is God, is God!

Without the slightest hesitation they ascribe to him every attribute
that Christians ascribe to their God. He is the very creator of the
universe.

> Listen, World, we want you to know
> That Father Divine is the God we adore,
> He is the One that created the heaven and earth,
> He is the One that brought this spiritual birth,
> So why stand by and criticize
> The One who can open your blinded eyes?
> Listen! Stop and realize
> That your God is here and not in the skies!
> Now, Mr. Preacher, we know it hurts

But you know, God's tired of you playing church,
He is here to show you in the actuated words
And that is why your jealousy is stirred
But Father is merciful, if you'll confess
How you've robbed the poor, barring their success
For hunger will cause a man to steal
But your time is out, for God is revealed! [11]

In the excitement of the public meetings and communion meals one hears the most extravagant claims of divinity for him.

"Father, I know you're God," is a most frequent testimony. But also in their publications, in cold type, one gets no less extravagant assertions as to his divine nature. Each of his printed sermons is introduced by a longer or shorter statement by the secretary who transcribed the material. Looking through only three issues of the weekly paper the *New Day*, the following epithets were found applied to him:

Dean of the Universe
Master of Omnipotency
Beloved Savior
Master and king
Beloved Lord and Savior
Our Lord and Savior, King Sweet
Beloved King
Supreme Poet of the Universe
Author and Finisher of all past, present and future dispensations
Great interpreter of all Creation
Omnipotent interpreter.

I personally asked many of his followers the direct question, "Do you believe Father Divine is God?"

Their answer was invariably in the affirmative. Once I asked it of "Generous Henry."

"Absolutely," he replied. "He couldn't be anything else and do the things he does," and he cited what Father Divine does, not alone in a material way.

"Those banquets," he said. "Did you ever see anything like that?"

I admitted that I had not, but I said that through the practice of cooperation such a thing might be possible.

[11] The *New Day*, Volume 8, October 14, 1944, p. 6.

He couldn't see it, nor could he explain whence these things come. "Father hasn't any money," he said. "We don't furnish it. How does it come?"

He cited also the effects wrought in the lives of men, in his own, first of all, for he had been a derelict, a drunk, so given to drink that if he could not get liquor he would drink anti-freeze compound. Now he had absolutely no desire for drink. Others had been redeemed from every sort of crime, and were now upright citizens, loyal servants of God, Father Divine. "Nobody but God could do that," he declared.

This I found to be the prevailing view. They believe he is God because nobody but God could do what he does; he heals the sick, and raises the dead. (Yes, that has been claimed for him, though I have never heard that he himself has ever made such a claim). I had pointed out to me a white woman, a Canadian, who, they told me, had been four days out of the body, but had been restored. A devout follower composed a song celebrating the event, which I heard given for the first time. Soon the crowd had taken up the song and was singing it. The burden of it was:

"When Father said 'Peace,' she arose!"

Father Divine gives them economic security. He makes them over into new men and women, morally and spiritually. "Nobody but God could do all this."

I sought to discover how persons of more education and culture looked upon him.

An intelligent white woman testified to her firm conviction that he was God. She claimed she was not psychic, yet she had seen him in various forms. Once as he was arriving at one of the Kingdoms, she ran out to the car to ask him for a blessing on a toothache from which she was suffering. (This is a very common custom among the followers.) Describing her experience, she said, "Suddenly I saw an aura of all colors above his head. His face was young and beautiful. Another person seeing me said I was as white as a ghost."

"Sometimes," she said, "Father speaks through me. I never prepare what I am to say, but his Spirit gives me words and thoughts that I could never utter of myself." This was corroborated by her husband, a university trained man who avers that he also has seen the aura about Father's head. He says that some have seen him with three faces.

I sought to get at just the way this man, who is not completely committed to the following of Father Divine, but is greatly attached to him, thinks of him.

"How do you think of Father Divine in relation to divinity?" I asked.

"As an incarnation of God," was the substance of his reply.

"Probably I too," he wrote me later, "would have been repelled at the thought of people calling Father Divine, God, if I had not studied Oriental religions. The Christian religion got off on the wrong foot in the early days when the idea was built up of Jesus as a personal potentate, or King, with all the attendant hierarchy of popes, cardinals, bishops, etc. This is a sort of God-Emperor notion, like Hirohito. This put God off as something apart from the masses . . . we have tried to break away from this type of thinking, but again and again I have found that the notion still lingers that Jesus was a personal God-King. To me, the power of God was made visible and manifest in Jesus so that men could see that God really did deal in the affairs of men. The same is true of other sublime beings like Krishna and Buddha. They escape mortal measurements. They embody the highest we know, and we have no alternative but to call them God. And, far from limiting God, Jesus made his power manifest." He then quoted the famous formula concerning incarnation enunciated by Krishna in the Bhagavad Gita:

"When virture is decadent, when righteousness is trodden under foot, ever and again I re-incarnate myself to re-establish my kingdom. I come into being in every age for the protection of the good, for the destruction of the wicked and for the establishment of religion." [12]

"It is true," he continues, "that God may also be incarnated in abstract principles or ideals which uplift the world, but when these saving ideals are embodied in an individual, we have 'the word made flesh.' "

This would seem to be the view held by many who have come to follow him from some other of the minority religious groups, such as New Thought or Theosophy.

Walter Clow Lanyon, an Englishman and a lecturer in the metaphysical field who has published several books in which many of Father Divine's sayings appear, says in the dedication to one of

[12] Book IV.

them, "In my search for truth I had met many wonderfully enlightened souls, noble and fine; some official stone casters; and a Judas; from all these I received help, but it was never until I contacted Father Divine that I fully realized the Presence of the Power here and now. Not as something to be used to produce results, but as the very actuality of Being itself." [13]

But of still greater interest is the question as to what Father Divine thinks about himself. Does he consider himself as God, and has he always done so?

There is no doubt that he accepts without the slightest protest the assertions of his followers. He sits calmly at the banquet table and listens to the most extravagant utterances concerning himself. In the *New Day* appear published statements attributing divinity to him which he could certainly prevent if he so desired. In one of the trials in which he has figured he was asked directly concerning his divine status. Without making a direct statement of his own view, he said:

"I teach that God has the right to manifest Himself through any person or thing He may choose. If my followers, however, believe that I am God and in so doing they are led to reform their lives, and experience joy and happiness, why should I prevent them from doing so?" [14]

Many have sought to get a direct statement from him, the writer among them. In an extended interview I pressed the question of his deity.

"Do you have any personal record where I say I am God, or where I say I am not God?" he asked.

I was obliged to admit that I did not have such a record. [15]

"What would be the difference what my version would be concerning myself? . . . That should not be the question in anyone's consideration."

"What then should be the question?" I countered.

His reply was: "Jesus said, and I say unto you, 'Then who do you say I am?'"

"Yes," I admitted. "Jesus said that to Peter."

---

[13] *It Is Wonderful.* E. K. Reader, London.

[14] Quoted by R. A. Parker, *The Incredible Messiah*, p. 74. Little, Brown and Co., Boston, 1937.

[15] Some months later a statement appeared in the *New Day*, in which he says: "I, God, said it volitionally." Volume 9, December 9, 1945, p. 25.

"But it would be a little unfair for me to ask you that immediately," Father said, "for it is better revealed than told. I withdraw that question until later."

"It would not give you justice to say one way or another without your rightful contact with me. . . . If I be God or the 'other fellow' (he will not use the term 'devil') it would not justify you to speak too radically or quickly or even to think too radically or quickly until you have had a chance to investigate. The investigation should come through the Spirit and not through the theory of man, for it is corrupt. . . . So if, to justify the situation and to answer your question more explicitly—if you contact me harmoniously —mentally and spiritually, I will tell you explicitly."

He urged me to study his movement, to visit his various centers in New York and Philadelphia and see what he was doing before I made up my mind concerning him. It all sounded a little like the reply of Jesus to some who came to question him concerning himself. "Go tell John the things ye have seen and heard: the blind receive their sight, the lame walk, the lepers are cleansed, the deaf hear, the dead are raised up, the poor have good tidings preached to them." Lk. 7:21. Father did not ask me later what I had decided.

But if he will not declare it unequivocally, and I can recall no statement that I have heard or seen from him that does so, it can readily be inferred from the hearing or reading of almost any of his numerous sermons. Typical is the declaration made in a sermon, October 6, 1945.

It is good to dwell together in Unity—to dwell in the Oneness of GOD! By the Unity of the Spirit, of Mind, of Aim and of Purpose you are here, enjoying the Blessings of the Supernatural Presence of ALMIGHTY GOD, not only so, but being Supernatural, Invisible and Intangible, but made Natural, Tangible, Real and Practical for your comfort and for your convenience.[16]

In a letter to one who had apparently criticized him he wrote:

I received your letter a few weeks ago, but have just got to it today and write to say in response, the mortal versions of your human mind, being corrupt, have sought to dethrone ME from MY *Godship degree;* hence, you have taken the mortal, human theories of men and their finite versions of things and tried to

---

[16] The *New Day,* Volume 9, No. 40, October 6, 1945, p. 7.

weigh ME and MY supreme plan of life upon the abominable scale of your mind, but truly is it given, "Judge not the Lord with feeble sense." [17]

This seems clearly enough an assertion of divinity. "My Godship degree," "judge not the Lord," "MY supreme plan of life," in contrast with "finite versions."

Often in quoting from the scriptures he refers to them as having been spoken by himself, thus:

"Did I not say scripturally in the Book of the Law, 'I will make you the head and not the tail?' Did I not say, 'Lift up a standard for MY people?' Did I not say, 'Tell Israel her transgressions and the House of Jacob her sins?'" [18]

Again, "I AM the Lord your GOD! I said in the Book of the Law, I am visiting the iniquities of the fathers upon the children from the third to the fourth generation." [19]

He frequently speaks as though he has at his command the natural forces of the universe. To an interviewer he once said, "I have known even the floods and storms and tornadoes to work harmoniously with ME and with MY Work and Mission. It is a marvelous thought to ME although it may sound somewhat superstitious; but to ME it is a reality, it works." [20]

The last statement seems to put him a little on the defensive as I observed him to be on more than one occasion in personal conversation. Indeed, he seems in his utterances to oscillate between the character of ordinary preacher about God, and God himself, the former character predominating. But now and again in moments of exalted discourse, or sometimes in judgment, he puts on the vestments of divinity.

Shortly after the disastrous accident in which a great airplane crashed into the Empire State Building, Father Divine spoke at one of his banquets on the necessity of repentance for the city of New York. He said in effect that the people of New York thought that the disaster was terrible, "but unless the inhabitants that escaped that terrible accident repent, they shall also likewise perish. God has declared it. Aren't you glad? MY hand is outstretched still. Repent

[17] The *New Day*, Volume 9, September 29, 1945, p. 34.
[18] The *New Day*, Volume 9, September 29, 1945, p. 6.
[19] The *New Day*, Volume 9, September 29, 1945, p. 12.
[20] The *New Day*, Volume 9, September 1, 1945.

or the city will weep and mourn and her representatives . . . must weep." [21]

Apparently he was feeling the severity of criticism against him and his work. For his critics he prophesied retribution. "Those who criticize MY work and MY message and ME as a person I say retribution is assured and is sure to you and to your city until your representatives and your city as a population repent in dust and ashes and confess their sins and forsake them by confessing them to ME and MINE, the ones they have abhorred and despised. MY hand is outstretched still." In a later sermon he said, "You will hear from me over and over again until that wicked city New York and its inhabitants repent." [22]

Among the most revealing records are the printed Office Talks which appear from time to time in the *New Day*. He has a numerous office staff which he carries about with him from one center to another, so that wherever he may be he can carry on his arduous task of letter-writing and general administrative work. Sometimes a statement in a letter he has just read, or a question from a staff member, will call forth extended comment by Father Divine. These are taken down verbatim and published. Recently one appeared on the subject, "How to Answer Critics Concerning Father Divine's Deity." Apparently some criticism of their belief in Father Divine as a Deity had been reported to him. To this Father Divine made a reply: "If one should question you concerning where did your God come from, you could answer them or call them into question and ask them 'How did their God, the one whom they are representing become to be God?' It is none of their business. They did not question how their God came into being . . . some will ask 'How did you come to be God and how did you first start out? Was it revealed to you?' Some will ask in all sincerity apparently, but yet without the right concept of the truth. They are asking mortal-mindedly and scientifically, but not infinitely and not recognizing the infinite mind and that is why they cannot fathom it out. It is a wonderful thought. Wonderful! Wonderful! Wonderful!"

He went on to say, "When Jesus was asked of himself, he did not say, 'I am Mary's son that was born thirty years ago,' for then he would have been limited to the thirty years and much more or longer. But he knew that 'Before Abraham was, I AM.' Abraham as a man had a beginning. But as I have none, you have no record from whence I came, but yet I declared, 'Before Abraham was, I AM.' It is wonderful, etc." [23] He went on to suggest that they should compare the results that the God of their questioners was about to produce and compare with what he, Father Divine, was producing. He ended, "There is nothing to fear because you have everything to hope for and to show that Your GOD is as real as theirs from every angle expressible. It is wonderful, wonderful, wonderful!" [24]

To an interviewer who asked about when he was born he said: "In my opinion I see life without the beginning of days and without the end of life—eternal—therefore, I could not justifiably give, I might say, a legible answer to that question because I do not see MYSELF as one that had begun at some certain time. I see the impersonal and yet personified, and I believe, as life goes on, it will evolve and take on and shape and form itself in many different expressions of its creation. It is Wonderful!

"Therefore, it is not justifiable, in MY opinion, to limit MYSELF to that which may be deemed flesh or person or personality, not the individual, nor the individuality even of MYSELF nor the individuality of Jesus." [25]

Much stress is laid by his followers upon the Body of God. They frequently speak of him as "God's body" or as just, "the Body." As to why he appears in the body as he does, he gives an interesting explanation. He was speaking of enacting the Bill of Rights which seems to signify to him chiefly the erasure of all racial distinctions among men. "I enacted the Bill when I formed this BODY out of all of the likenesses of all of you. I have some of the likeness of the English, some of the likeness of the French, of the German, of the Irish and some of the likeness of the Africans. I have some of the likeness of all of them. That is why all are the same. That is, I have formed MY BODY out of the blood that I created all nations and therefore the blood that runs in these veins is the blood that out of which I formed all nations." [26]

In almost every address he makes at the banquets he stresses the fact that his physical presence is not necessary in order that his

---

[23] The *New Day*, Volume 9, September 15, 1945, p. 13.
[24] The *New Day*, Volume 9, September 15, 1945, p. 13.
[25] The *New Day*, Volume 9, September 1, 1945, p. 33.
[26] The *New Day*, Volume 9, October 27, 1945, p. 21.

people may enjoy the benefits which they seek. They may contact him spiritually any time and in any place. And, indeed, thousands of his followers have never seen him in the flesh, yet testify, in their letters, to the help that he has afforded them in many ways. A typical statement, of the sort I personally heard him make more than once is: "You need not contact ME Personally, especially, but make your mental and spiritual contact. If you are sick or afflicted or ill in any way whatsoever, MY Spirit can reach you and can adjust matters satisfactorily, for you need not see ME Personally. And again I say, I do not use material methods, neither do I make a physical effort, neither do I use material remedies to reach one's condition in the case of sickness or afflictions, but I reach them when they contact ME mentally and spiritually." [27]

From the evidence cited thus far there can be no doubt that he does consider himself to be divine. Has he always thought so? Or, if not, when did he begin to assume the role of God?

It is impossible to answer this with certainty, for there is a lack of published data on his earlier career. However, his disciples were certainly referring to him as God early in his Sayville period. Hoshor thinks that this was at first only a complimentary title given him by grateful individuals who had experienced his bounty. This seems to me quite likely. Used at first only in this way, it was repeated again and again until they actually came to believe it. After all, who but God could do all he was doing for them?

Hoshor tells of a man who had been a paralytic but was healed. He leaped from his wheel chair and ran out into the street shouting, "God and Father Divine healed me. I can walk! I can walk!" Evidently at that time God and Father Divine were two distinct entities in the minds of his followers. But they were soon to be merged into one.[28]

Some writers fix the moment of his own direct recognition of his deity as the time when he heard of the death of Justice Smith, who had presided at the trial of the Sayville case brought against Father Divine by Sayville residents, who were seeking to force him to leave their city. The defendant, Father Divine, was found guilty, but leniency was recommended by the jury. However, Justice Smith refused to hear the plea for leniency and sentenced him to

---

[27] The *New Day*, Volume 9, September 6, 1945, p. 12.
[28] John Hoshor, *God in a Rolls-Royce*, Hillman-Curl, New York, 1936, p. 54.

the maximum penalty. Frequent warnings were uttered during the trial that judgment would fall upon the court if it found Father Divine—God—guilty. When the verdict and judgment were announced, a Divine follower is said to have remarked, "Do not pity Father Divine, rather pity the Judge who sentenced him." Three days later Justice Smith, who had apparently been in good health, suddenly died. When news of his death was brought to Father Divine in his cell, he is reported to have said, "I hated to do it."

Whether this report is literally true, the writer has no way of knowing. Parker does not report it. There is no doubt, however, that this event confirmed in the minds of his followers the conviction that he was indeed God. Some thirteen years later a follower who knew of this author's intention of writing concerning Father Divine, wrote: "The privilege granted you to study this movement carries with it the responsibility and reward of presenting facts, or the retribution of misrepresentation." (Personal correspondence.)

However, evidence has already been introduced (pp. 7–8) from a source which I consider quite reliable that Divine was calling himself God as much as thirty years ago, when he was imprisoned in the Valdosta, Georgia, jail. Mr. Moseley, who reported his encounter with him at that time, has reiterated in personal correspondence his assertion to that effect.

Whenever it began one gets the impression that the conviction has strengthened with the passing years.

But apart from the very distinctive claim that he is God, what content does he give to the idea of God? How does it compare with other current concepts held in the various recognized religious traditions?

The answer is that in most respects it does not differ much from what is generally accepted among fairly conservative Christian groups. Certainly he uses all the adjectives descriptive of His nature employed in orthodox theology. He is omnipotent, omniscient, omnipresent, and also "omnilucent."

He frequently speaks of God as impersonal, in the manner of Christian Science and the New Thought groups. He seems to have been influenced not a little by the latter.

If one were to attribute to him a philosophical position, which he probably does not, consciously at least, recognize, it would be something like this: God is the suprapersonal, if not the impersonal, ultimate reality—the ground of all existence. He affirms occasionally the unreality of matter: "So that is the thought, to know the Allness of God and the nothingness of matter." [29]

But God is also intensely personal, and usually is referred to in highly personal terms. He becomes real by being "tangibilated" in history, in Jesus, and in himself, and is deeply concerned about humanity's needs. Thus he says: "God is no longer an imagination; God is no longer to be discerned as something to scare the children of men, to frighten them into submissiveness and into obedience to Him, but to be discerned as a LOVING FATHER, a HUMBLE SERVANT and as the REDEEMER and SAVIOR of men! That is the purpose for which I came.

"That is why you have beautiful homes wheresoever I AM! That is why you have plenty to eat and to drink! That is why you have clothes to wear, I say! That is why you have plenty of nice, comfortable automobiles to ride in! For GOD is no longer a supposition to be discerned as destructive and wrathful, but as LOVING and KIND and COMPASSIONABLE. Aren't you glad?" [30]

He is constantly spoken of as Father. He is Perfection. He is Love. He is, of course, Creator, and is represented as active in nature and in history. He works through natural forces to effect his will. He is Good, and of course he is One. The unity of God is frequently stressed. While I have neither seen in the reports of his speeches nor heard any reference to the Trinity by name, he often speaks of the Holy Spirit, and in general he seems definitely to belong in the Trinitarian group. He regards Jesus as Divine, and the way-shower to God. "No man cometh unto the Father but by Me." "None knoweth the Father save the Son and those to whom the Son revealeth Him."

God, in order to be made real to humanity had to take personal form. Says Father Divine, "Jesus came in a Personal Body, to make the PRACTICALITY of your DEVOTION to the ALMIGHTY a LIVING REALITY—no longer something imaginary. Without a Body Form GOD would remain a Mystery.

"If GOD had not changed the versions of men by coming in a BODILY FORM to bring into their recognition and realization HIS ACTUAL PRESENCE, the KINGDOM of GOD and GOD HIMSELF would have been a mystery as a supposition, an imagination and not a realization; as something impractical and unprofitable as far as your bodies and present life's existence are concerned; would have been unprofitable and impractical even as the earth was in the beginning of the creation! Can you not see the mystery?" [31]

He distinguishes, however, between Jesus and Christ. For example, he does not use the abbreviation B.C. for the pre-Christian era, but rather B.J.—before Jesus.

"I say B.J., not B.C.," declares Father Divine, "because it was before Jesus, yet, in my opinion it was not before Christ." [32] Jesus, he seems at times to regard as merely the temporal and physical embodiment of the Christ. His use of the term, "the Christ," at times seems closely akin to the usage of the Unity group. At other times there is no noticeable distinction in his use of the terms.

But whatever the name he uses, he asserts that it is upon Jesus' teachings and work that his own message and work are based. Indeed, it appears, on occasion at least, that he himself stands in the same relation to God that Jesus does. "When I went into the Temple," he declares, "I overthrew the table of money-changers, and any temple I get in I will overthrow graft and greed in them and the love of money I will cast out of them, for it is the root of all evil." [33] Frequently he quotes sayings of Jesus, as having been uttered by himself. Thus to quote: "When I, in the Sonship Degree, said, 'Lay down the world, take up your cross and come and follow me!' I said it not in vain. I was showing you the way to go home. Showing you the way to go home!—a place of Rest where you would be free from barriers and limitations by following the Footsteps of your SAVIOR, for truly said He in the Name of ME, 'I AM the Way, the Truth and the Life. No man cometh to the Father but by Me!' You could not get to the FATHER save by the Way of JESUS as the Wayshower! As the Sample and as the Example I portrayed the Life of CHRIST and exemplified it among you and have shown you the way to go, which is the way to come.

" 'No man cometh to the FATHER but by Me,' said He. But by you coming through the Way and the Teaching of Jesus you have found ME, and in finding ME you can say in reality, 'I have found that which I sought so diligently and mourned because I

[31] The *New Day*, December 4, 1941, p. 71.
[32] The *New Day*, Volume 9, September 1, 1945, p. 33.
[33] The *New Day*, Volume 9, November 17, 1945, p. 25.

found it not!' The Way of CHRIST is the Way of Life, is the Way of Health and it is the Way to Eternal Glory; it is the Way to Eternal Pleasure, it is the Way to all Success and all Prosperity, it is the Way to Victory over all undesirable conditions, it is the Way to an Eternal Emancipation and Peace on earth and Good Will toward men! This is what you have found in ME!" [34]

Herein are revealed some of his basic ideas regarding the work of Jesus, or Christ. He is Savior, way-shower, example, life-giver, health-giver; he is the giver of eternal pleasure, success, prosperity, and victory over all undesirable conditions; he is eternal emancipation, and the bringer of peace on earth and good will to men.

Asked directly by an interviewer whether he accepts the teachings of Jesus and the Bible, he replied: "Positively! The Life and the Teaching of CHRIST as exemplified and as brought to fruition in the Person of Jesus, we endeavor to reproduce it—not only reproduce it but reincarnate it and bring it to fruition in the hearts and lives of ourselves as individuals and transmit it to others by harmonization." [35]

Father Divine makes constant use of the Bible. The assertion of Hoshor that, "he uses quotations from scripture as a very minor adjunct," [36] is quite mistaken. It is true that he usually claims that what he is saying is his own word, for was it not he, God, who revealed himself in the scriptures? Illustrations of this were given above. The fact is that he has an amazing acquaintance with the Bible and seldom preaches without allusions to one or many sayings taken from it. It is true that he does not often read a lesson from the Bible in public, nor does he give the reference to the quotations he uses beyond saying, "as the scriptures declare," or some such introductory remark. His quotations are sometimes free, rather than exact, but the great majority of them are verbatim. Sometimes he quotes but a phrase, sometimes an entire paragraph—but always from memory. Nor are his quotations only the old familiar ones that everybody knows. He quotes from every part of the Book. A casual examination of but one number of the *New Day* disclosed the use of more than thirty different Bible verses in the first three sermons reported, which would be a good average for most preachers. Some of them he repeated over and over again. They were taken from

---

[34] The *New Day*, Volume 9, No. 40, p. 7.
[35] The *New Day*, December 4, 1941, p. 56.
[36] Hoshor, *God in a Rolls-Royce*, p. 136.

Exodus, Psalms, Proverbs, Isaiah, Jeremiah, Matthew, Mark, Luke, John, Acts, Romans, First Corinthians, First Peter, and Revelation—fourteen different books in all. John appears most frequently as the source, then Revelation, Matthew, and the Psalms. Whether this would be the case usually is not certain, but the writer gathers the impression that John's gospel is perhaps his favorite reliance.

His use of the Biblical material is sometimes highly original, and would not be recognized as legitimate interpretation by scholars. But in this he is not peculiar. One's judgment of the correctness or incorrectness of the use of scripture by a given individual tells perhaps as much about the judge as the one judged. Sometimes his interpretation seems fantastic to the writer, but on the whole there seems to be far less distortion of the probable original meaning the writers intended to convey than will be found among many who stand in the so-called orthodox tradition. Particularly, if one leaves out the application of scripture to his own person, which is of course a rock of stumbling to all the orthodox, and most of the liberals as well, there is much of common sense in his use of the Bible. On his use of it as a moral guide few would find fault.

He plainly regards the Bible as the revelation of God or as the word of God. I have seen nothing to indicate that he holds any theory of verbal inspiration. The fact that he often quotes loosely rather than exactly would seem to prove that the exact wording is not of primary importance. Of course, if, as he definitely declares, it was he, God, who inspired the ancient writers, he might justifiably be allowed to modify their wording on occasion. Undeniably he speaks as his own authority, and does not require the support of any other.

Asked on one occasion if he speaks by inspiration or if he prepares his messages he replied, "Well, I would not deem it necessary to prepare a message." [37] He gives an interesting description of the origin of a saying which is basic in all his teaching and which is repeated with great frequency in his addresses. "The Spirit of the Consciousness of the Presence of GOD is the Source of all supply, and it will satisfy every good desire. I said it by composition. I brought it forth volitionally when men questioned ME at one time 'Where do YOU get so much money from and how can YOU do it?' Volitionally as a thunderbolt out of a black cloud, it came

[37] The *New Day*, Volume 9, September 1, 1945, p. 32.

forth as a dynamic explosion as you have never heard before, 'The Spirit of the Consciousness of the Presence of GOD is the Source of all supply!' " [38]

He encourages his followers to read the Bible, though there does not seem to be any adequate provision for systematic instruction in it. Most of his adult followers have come out of a conservative, evangelistic background and have already a certain familiarity with the Bible.

To the followers who are near and are privileged to see him and who regard him as God, the living word which he speaks is bound to be of greater import than the reported ancient sayings of prophets, or even of Jesus. But what of the others who live at a distance from him? Naturally they use the Bible, but their main reliance also is upon the reported sayings and acts of Father Divine.

Probably no founder of a new religious group ever had his every saying so completely and accurately reported as Father Divine. As stated above, he has a large staff of secretaries who accompany him wherever he goes and take down whatever he says. There were several secretaries at the time I visited him, and at no time save when he was conducting me through the various Kingdoms did they fail to get a substantially accurate report of all that either of us said. At one interview there were eleven secretaries present, all taking down our conversation in shorthand. At the banquet tables they always sit near him at the table and record whatever he says. He dictates all his correspondence and publishes a good deal of it. Whenever a member comes for an interview—and he has many such interviews every day—whatever he says is written down. Often when no one is present but the staff, he will give what they call an "office talk," and it is carefully recorded. Even the most commonplace announcement that visitors are invited to speak if they wish is carefully preserved, and most of whatever is recorded sees the light in the official publication which is currently the *New Day*.

That this body of material is regarded in the light of scriptures seems clear from the use that is made of it, for when he is not physically present at a meeting or a banquet, selections are read from the *New Day*. Indeed, they are sometimes read while Father Divine is sitting at the table. Here is undoubtedly a new Bible in

[38] The *New Day*, Volume 9, September 29, 1945, p. 3.

the making, and if the movement goes on after the founder's death (he says he is not going to die), it will certainly look upon these preserved utterances as the very word of God. It seems somewhat strange that some collection of his utterances has not yet been made. One English follower has included many of them in several volumes which he has written,[39] but they are merely selected passages upon which the author comments, and not a systematic or topical arrangement; nor is there any continuity manifest. This will one day be done. It is conceivable that Father Divine may himself make such a selection. As it is, the sayings are scattered through large unwieldy bound volumes of the successive publications that have carried them.

There may be a definite purpose in the fact that a Bible is seldom, or never, seen in his meetings or banquets, and never a song book. A rather cryptic statement appears in one of his recent addresses. Does he mean that the use of the Bible and hymn books might interfere with their apprehension of himself as deity? At all events he declared, "I have closed the Bible and the Hymn books that you might know your Lord." [40]

Man, in Father Divine's teaching, is a sinner standing in need of salvation. Just what sin is thought to be, it is not easy to discover in his reported utterances. He is very specific as to what are the chief sins which man commits, but does not attempt to define sin in the abstract. Certain it is that sin stands between man and God. Perhaps disobedience to the will of God comes as near as anything else to being what he means. I have found no reference to such a thing as original sin as held in the orthodox tradition, though there is constant recognition of the influence of heredity upon a man's actions. "Curb your hereditive tendencies," he admonishes. But apparently man has freedom to choose the way he will go, and he is judged for his failure to make the right choice. He must repent and seek forgiveness if he would attain to salvation. "He must be born again," he declares, for "except a man be born again he cannot see the Kingdom of Heaven." [41]

[39] Walter C. Lanyon, *Behold the Man*, London, L. N. Fowler & Co., 1933.
Id., *The Eyes of the Blind*, London, L. N. Fowler & Co., 1932.
Id., *It Is Wonderful*, London, E. K. Reader.
Id., *Out of the Clouds*, London, E. K. Reader, 1934.
[40] The *New Day*, Volume 9, October 20, 1945, p. 2.
[41] John 3:3.

In all that I have read of his sayings, or personally heard, there seems to be nothing of the forensic element of satisfaction in the salvation scheme. He makes little of the death of Christ. Man is a sinner, called by Jesus to repentance and given direction as to what he must do if he would attain to salvation. This is continually being pointed out by Father Divine. First of all man must repent. Repentance that is genuine means restitution to the degree that that is possible. This is a point of special emphasis with Father Divine. Words are not enough. Intention is not enough. One must literally undo the evil he has done, in so far as that is possible, before he can claim that he is saved. He certainly cannot join the movement, or get a new name until this has been done. Hence it is that every issue of the *New Day* carries many pages filled with accounts of the repayment of old debts, the restitution of stolen money or goods. One follower, a white man, told me he had been working for four years to pay back ill-gotten funds and that he was just about to finish it off and be received. Another, a magnificent-looking young man, told me it had cost him more than ten thousand dollars to even up his score and get into the movement. But sometimes it is not just the repayment of money. Talking between two and three o'clock in the morning about this very matter, Father Divine said to me: "Would you like to hear the personal story of one of our men?" I replied that I would like nothing better. He sent out at once and invited one we may call Mr. Condor, to come in. He entered diffidently, yet joyously, for to be summoned by Father and allowed to be in his very presence is a boon to be sought after.

"Peace, Father," he said.

"Peace, Brother," replied Father Divine. "Will you not tell this brother your story?"

"Of course, Father. I thank you," he said.

Then followed one of the most fascinating experiences I can recall. The man, a coal black brother, told with flashing eyes, and with vivid pantomime this remarkable story.

"I lived in the deep south in the country. With an older brother I worked on a farm and we used to drink hard liquor. One day a white young man of about our age was drinking with us and he took away a quart of whiskey. We tried to get it back. He refused. Some days after I took my shotgun and said, 'I'm a goin' after my whiskey.' I went over to his place and demanded my liquor. He refused to return it, so I shot him dead. Then I had to git out, and

I got. After some fifteen years in the North one day I met Father Divine and I was converted. But I had killed a man. How could I make that right? I went to Father and told him and said, 'Father, what can I do?' He said, 'Go back and give yourself up to the sheriff.' "

To anyone who knows what happens to Negroes who kill a white man in the deep South this will seem the ultimate test of good faith.

"So I went back," he said, "and I hunted up the sheriff of the county and I said, 'Sheriff, I killed so and so seventeen years ago and I've come to give myself up.'

"The sheriff, he looked at me hard as though he couldn't believe what he'd heard.

" 'You killed a white man?'

" 'Yes, sah!'

" 'And you are giving yourself up?'

" 'Yes, sah.'

" 'Well, what makes you do that?'

"And I said: 'I met Father Divine and I was converted and he told me I must come back and give myself up.'

"The sheriff remained quiet for a while and then he said, 'If Father Divine can make a man do what you've just done, then you go along back up North and stay with him. You're free—go.'

"And I came back. But I've tried several times since to give myself up to a judge and they all say the same, 'Thank Father.' "

"Thank you," said Father. "And now, brother, tell me, do you drink whiskey any more?"

"Law, no," he replied. "Why, I wouldn't even chew gum now!"

The sins that Father Divine frequently dwells on are the ones the evangelist in the orthodox tradition preached against: drinking, gambling, sex irregularity, and stealing. To this he adds the use of tobacco. Over and over again he declares, "No follower of mine would drink liquor. My followers do not smoke cigarettes." The ban on sex extends even into the family, and husband and wife are required to "live evangelically," separate quarters being furnished for men and women. The record of the movement in reference to sex aberrations is remarkably clear. He constantly stresses "the virginity of Mary and the Holiness of Jesus" as the ideal to be sought after. Speaking of the desire of some to join the

"Rosebuds," the young girls' organization, and the "Crusaders," the boys' group, he said, "True Rosebuds must be Pure, must be Virtuous, must be True! Must be free from self-indulgences, must be free from vice and crime and sin and debauchery of every kind! They must be free from human fancies, pleasures and tendencies, and refuse to indulge in them from any angle whatsoever." [42]

His insistence upon truth and honesty is constant and extremely rigorous. I have personally never had contact with any group which seems so absolute in the definition of honesty. One who finds a penny on the street will not keep it, but advertise it in the *New Day*. Here are a few entries in the lost and found column of a recent issue. "A penny found on J. car, a pocket comb, a yellow pencil, a red ration point, 2 small hat pins, 2 coat buttons, 1 ear bob, etc., etc." [43]

To fail to work steadily while on a job is to steal. To take a tip is wrong, and even to accept bonuses or gifts from employers, or compensation for days when one does not work, are also considered wrong. In a recent number of the *New Day*, Father Divine gives explicit instruction concerning such matters. He cites as scriptural basis for this teaching Ex. 23:8, Dt. 16:19; Prov. 15:27; Eccles. 7:7; Is. 1:23; Chron. 19:7, and Prov. 17:23.

But these personal sins of the flesh are by no means all. As indicated elsewhere, he has a strong sense of social evil, and even greater than the individual sins are the failures to enact the Bill of Rights, to live democratically, to be brothers to all men. It is here that he stands in sharp contrast to the purely individual emphasis of the older evangelistic tradition. For a more extended comment on this aspect of his teaching see the sections on the Social Ideals and the Economic Aspects of the movement.

Salvation is found through the acceptance of the Gospel. Repentance and restitution are a first demand, but that is only the beginning. A poem, printed apparently with approval in the *New Day*, sums up rather well what is required for salvation.

"So the Keynote to Salvation,
  To solve every, every problem,
  Is to accept of the Gospel of your SAVIOR
  And adhere to HIS message!

[42] The *New Day*, Volume 9, December 15, 1945, p. 5.
[43] The *New Day*, Volume 9, December 15, 1945, p. 36.

And then you will find Peace, Joy, Life and Happiness,
And Love and Unity,
That not anything can scatter.
It is wonderful! Wonderful! WONDERFUL! WONDERFUL!

So the first thing to do is to accept of the Golden Rule
And live the Life of CHRIST, for nothing else will do.
If you think it is too great and too wholesome to live,
Accept of the Golden Rule and Democracy as it is given
And live it and express it until you can get more!

For when you live it continually,
The Spirit of Love will eventually flow,
And all the Blessings from your SAVIOR will come directly
    to you
And you need not to call it the Golden Rule!

The Life of CHRIST is fully exemplified,
And that Love that Jesus Spoke of is materialized.
It is wonderful. Wonderful. WONDERFUL! WONDERFUL!" [44]

It will have been noted that here there is no reference to the death of Christ, but rather to his life and message—and no reference to any life hereafter. This is quite true to Father Divine's thought. His salvation idea is this-worldly, not other-worldly. He never tires of reiterating his teaching that heaven, as commonly taught, is wrong, and that it must really be experienced here and now.

"They who are teaching a heaven above the sky are teaching something mystical and imaginary and not a reality. They have not a leg to stand on!" [45] he declares. Or again, "I am taking you out of the imaginary heaven, for—the first heaven and first earth are passed away. I am cancelling that imaginary heaven and earth out of your consciousness— How can the Kingdom come when you have the imaginary heaven in the way. Get it out of the way and the new Heaven and Earth can come in." [46]

Heaven is really but the realization of the Kingdom of God and that is not something only for a future life and another world. It has already come. In one of his sermons he says, "We are privileged to understand that the Kingdom has truly come. The Kingdom is not a place geographically to go, but a place in consciousness

---

[44] The *New Day*, Volume 9, October 6, 1945, p. 17.
[45] John Hoshor, *God in a Rolls-Royce*, p. 233.
[46] W. C. Lanyon, *It Is Wonderful*, pp. 221–222.

where all can go to—that they might be partakers of the Nature and Characteristics and mind of Christ that was in Jesus the Great Love Master. When this Life shall have developed in mankind, there will be no more occasion for worrying, for then and there the Kingdom has truly come. The Law of the Spirit of Life that was in Christ Jesus has truly made You free from the law of sin and death.—" [47]

Again a decade later he said: "The Kingdom has truly come and the Will is now being done right here on earth, as it was in the fondest imagination of all Christianity, yea, of all humanity, for I have brought it from the fondest and most glorious imaginations of the children of men. I have drawn the ESSENCE and the SUBSTANCE of the Kingdom from their fondest imaginations and I have brought them through the process of Tangibilization and Materialization. I have TANGIBILATED AND MATERIALIZED the ESSENCE and the SUBSTANCE of your fondest imagination of heaven as imagined by the most conscientious and sincere religions! I AM bringing both it and them through MATERIALIZATION, for it has truly come on EARTH as it was in that imaginary heaven! ("So true, Lord!" verified the multitude spontaneously.) Enjoy thou this and be thou ONE in ME, and from every barrier and all undesirable conditions you are FREE! Aches and pains are dispelled. Ailments and complaints will all go when you recognize GOD'S ACTUAL PRESENCE and weep and sigh no more!

"When you recognize GOD'S ACTUAL PRESENCE and bring your bodies into subjection you will be able to see and know definitely GOD is actually with you here and now! And such a Conviction will cause you to act differently and think differently. By acting differently and thinking differently and by taking on NEW CHARACTERISTICS and a NEW DISPOSITION you will be a NEW CREATURE automatically, and you will not even have the old character you once had. You will put off the old man with all of his deeds and you will put on the New Man, CHRIST JESUS, in Whom you should live!

"You will not even feel like you once felt; you will have New Characteristics and a New Disposition; you will be a New Person! You will not even so much as smell like you once smelled, because

[47] *World Herald*, November 19, 1936, p. 4.

a new nature and a new disposition, new characteristics and new ideas and new opinions will make you different completely, WITH-OUT as well as WITHIN you—and WITHIN as well as WITH-OUT! That is the mystery!" [48]

But if the Kingdom of God is earthly, what of those who die? That question I asked Father Divine personally. His reply was very definite. "My true followers do not die."

"But, surely," I said, "people who have been in your movement have died. I am certain I have read of such cases."

But he only repeated his statement, "My true followers do not die."

"Do you mean to say," I inquired, "that the fact of the death of a follower is prima facie evidence that he was not a true follower?"

He nodded his head in assent.

Here is one of the places at which Father Divine has been most harshly criticized. He will apparently have nothing to do with the burial or the disposal of the remains of one of his deceased disciples.

Does he then not believe in immortality? His teaching at this point is vague. There are some indications that he holds to a belief in reincarnation, but he is never explicit on the matter. For example:

"When you cease to function as a person the impersonal One or the inner man functions, and that inner man functions through you and you have been the visible expression of the inner man; you are the visible expression of the mental and spiritual conception. The outer expression is but the outward appearance of your mental and spiritual conception. The visible is to reveal the inner, and when the visible ceases to exist the inner is just as operative and as expressive, can and will be more—whatsoever to you—than it could dare be with the outer." [49]

I asked a very intelligent white woman follower how she thought of the matter. She declared that she did not expect to die.

"But," I said, "suppose that you should die. What, then, would become of you?"

"Then," she replied, "reincarnation would take place." But she admitted that this idea might have come to her from Unity which she had once followed. She then tried to give the distinction which she says Father Divine makes between Spirit and Soul. The Soul as

[48] The *New Day*, Volume 9, October 6, 1945, p. 8.
[49] The *New Day*, Volume 9, September 1, 1945, p. 26.

the "mortal I am" dissolves at death. Concerning the destiny of Spirit she was not clear, but it was evident that she thought that it went on in some form. I have not found the distinction made by Father Divine in anything I have read from him.

In an "office talk" concerning bereavement he revealed, though not too clearly, some of his thought concerning the life hereafter.

"God is the life and the length of your days; therefore you should live and never die. Therefore, that life that was in the person that has passed on, it is just as operative; it has just gone into the invisible; but when you get the right concept of it, it can be visibilated—that same life, that same spirit, that same mind—and GOD will give it a body as it pleases Him. That Scripture 'GOD giveth it a body as it pleases Him,' the spirit is it that will be re-embodied if necessary and the Christ shall take on the body of the one that was called your father. It is just the same; he functioned through the body and lived in the body and you called him father or daddy or something of that sort. Hence, when the outer man passes on, the inner man, the real One, but in the likeness of you, and you may physically be shaped and fashioned and have the features somewhat like Christ in that body, also shaped and fashioned like unto you and you like unto it, and you called him father or called him daddy, but Christ, GOD, has always been your Father and you never had another. . . . GOD has always been your Mother and you never had another. If this be your mother, Christ is that Mother in that body, your FATHER MOTHER GOD! Christ is as though it is she, or as though it is she or her who is in that likeness, but every sense of an expression of good and love to or for you is the Christ in the person, and when the body ceases to function, that individual that was that man cannot die, it is infinite and with the right concept you cannot be bereaved, but GOD is present with or without a person and will your every hunger feed and will supply your every need and can and will be with thee more than the personal father could dare be. . . . So, with these thoughts you will not have an occasion to fret nor worry, neither be bereaved, because the very spirit and the life and the mind of that person that is incorruptible, it is undefiled, it fadeth not away and it is just as much with you today as it was before it left the person, and the spirit is just as happy and more happy because it is impersonal now, you see. It is GOD embodied until it is re-embodied; you see the mystery? Until it is reincarnated or reimpregnated in some other person to be to you and to itself and to others, just what it was in the first one." [50]

Clearly Father Divine does not himself expect to die, nor do his followers expect it. It is at this point that one sees grave danger to the movement. While he has insisted frequently that it is not necessary to see him personally to contact his spirit, his followers are likely to receive a terrible jolt when the announcement of his death comes, as, of course, non-followers confidently expect that it will. This was certainly true of many followers of the *I Am* group when Mr. Ballard, the founder, who was supposed "to make his ascension," simply died.

I once asked one of the followers, "What will happen to the movement when Father Divine dies?"

"But he isn't going to die," he countered. "Yes," said I, "I understand your belief to that effect, but just *suppose* that he should die?"

"I can't imagine it," he said.

"You know he travels about in a motor car a great deal. Just suppose that one day there is a crash and he, Father Divine, is killed," I said, feeling something like a heel to be pursuing the matter so far.

He was silent a moment as if trying to take in such a possibility. Then he said gravely, "I don't know. I suppose I might just as well go back to my old life, or follow anybody else if Father Divine should die."

He was probably typical of the Divine following.

Salvation, then, is here and now. The Kingdom of God is already come. It will go on extending itself—out beyond Harlem and Jersey and Philadelphia until it takes in all mankind. This leaves a lot of questions unanswered, but so does Father Divine.

Although healing is not a major element in the work of Father Divine, and is seldom emphasized in his public utterances, it does undoubtedly constitute one of the strong appeals to his followers. Listening to the testimonies given in the meetings and at the banquets one hears remarkable stories of healing experienced by the witnesses. Many of them seem wholly incredible to skeptical auditors, but the cures are related circumstantially, exact details of time and place being given—the nature of the ill, the diagnosis of orthodox physicians, the failure of all scientific attempts to alleviate the suffering, resulting hopelessness, then the discovery of Father Divine,

[50] The *New Day*, Volume 9, September 1, 1945, p. 26.

and the cure. The writer has not had the opportunity to check up on any of the testimonies given, to prove whether or not the stories were correctly told, whether the illness was what the sufferer thought it was, whether the physician who made the diagnosis was competent, or whether his treatment was the best-known scientific treatment available. Such a check would be most interesting, and would be clearly indicated if the writer's purpose were that of accrediting or of discrediting the movement. But from the standpoint of merely trying to understand and describe the movement, it is unnecessary. The fact is that the people testifying believe themselves to be reporting the facts honestly, and other people hearing their testimonies are moved to seek relief from their ills at the same source—and often enough find such relief. They, themselves, then become witnesses to the healing powers of Father Divine, and so the movement grows.

If one listens long enough he will hear claims of the healing of almost every kind of disease, both functional and organic. At one of the banquets a sister said: "I love you, Father, because you healed me of a leaky heart." A white woman said, "You healed me of acute indigestion. No medicine helped until I looked on your body."

A heavy set, elderly colored woman said, "I remember how in 1935 I had suffered from cancer. Someone asked me if I knew Father Divine. I said no, I didn't. They gave me a copy of the *Spoken Word*. I read Father's message in it. The spirit within said he was God. Father's picture was in the paper. I never saw anything so light up as that picture. I had then some glasses. I couldn't read without them. I said, Father, thank you to take off these glasses. That was in 1935. I've never had on glasses since that day. I know Father Divine is God. He healed that cancer completely. Though I'd never seen him, I got to trust him."

Many of such declarations are made in the midst of highly emotional testimonies given at a meeting charged with feeling, and to the accompaniment of cries of approval—"Amen," "Yes, Father," "So true." One might under such circumstances be impelled to embellish the facts somewhat. Overstatement on an occasion of that nature might be understandable and easily forgiven. But what of the testimonies given in the quiet of one's own home, over the dinner table?

I recall one such, given to me by a white woman of intelligence and charm. In the beginning she had never seen Father Divine. She had lived in a distant city. But she was a sufferer. Her case had been diagnosed by physicians as cancer. She could get no relief. She was desperate. Then someone told her of Father Divine—how he had effected some remarkable cures. This friend suggested that they go to the local headquarters of Father Divine in her home city and see what they could find out. Accordingly, one day they knocked at the door of a humble apartment and were graciously received by a young colored woman who asked them to sit down. Mrs. Blank was given a seat on a low bench along one wall of the room. They had hardly opened the conversation when Mrs. Blank suddenly began to feel ill. She experienced a violent internal agitation in the region of her cancer. She felt she must get out into the open air lest she faint. "Perhaps Father Divine has done something to you," said the worker. As Mrs. Blank arose from the seat she noticed that just behind where she had been sitting there hung a picture of Father Divine. She went out into the street, and returned home. "From that time, more than ten years ago," she declared, "I have not suffered." The cancer disappeared and she regained her former vigorous health. Naturally she became a devoted follower of Father Divine, though doing so brought about the disruption of her home. She was forced by her husband to leave the house and was left with the problem of making a living for herself and her two children. Later she moved to New York so that she might be near Father Divine.

In talking with her, I said: "But are you sure that you had cancer?"

"That is what the doctors said I had," she replied, "and it was that for which they were treating me, without results."

"Well, have you ever undergone any medical examinations since," I asked, "so that you can be quite sure that you are completely cured?"

"Why should I?" she countered. "I was sick, desperately in pain. The doctors could do nothing for me. This thing happened. I am no longer suffering. I feel well and strong. Why should I bother about getting their corroboration of what I know has happened?"

It sounded not a little like the testimony of one in the gospels when someone sought to inquire concerning the healer and the healing. "This one thing I know, that whereas I was once blind, now I can see."

I once got much the same reply when I asked one of the directors of Unity why they did not get corroboration by competent doctors of the testimonies to healing which they publish in their magazine. People feel themselves to be ill. They seek the proffered ministry of Unity and they are restored to health. "Does it matter," he said, "what the doctor says if they really feel well?"

One can think of a suitable reply, but from the standpoint of a believer it is easily to be seen that such corroboration is not important.

How does Father Divine purport to heal the sick? There seems to be no such definite philosophy of healing here as in Christian Science or in Unity. Indeed, it seems very simple, as stated more or less casually in a recent issue of the *New Day*.

"Some have come to Me from time to time and said, 'Father, wouldn't you lay hands on me to heal me?' I say, I do not make a physical effort, neither do I use material methods, and I will not use material remedies to reach your condition, but as you contact me mentally and spiritually, I will heal you from all your ailments and complaints. That is, if you will live exactly according to my teaching, the Spirit of my presence within you, through concentration will heal you by harmonizing with it and bringing your body into subjection to it." [51]

Father Divine does not condemn people for resorting to physicians when they are ill, but he feels it is unnecessary. In his addresses, he often says, "If you are sick all you need to do is to call upon my name and you do not have to see anybody or anything."

In an interview with Dr. M. Bach, Father Divine sets forth his ideas on healing. "If one gets sick and for any cause the Spirit does not reach his condition, I say get a physician, but if they have implicit faith and unshaking confidence and live exactly according to my teaching, I do not believe they will be sick, to that end, they will not need to have a physician." [52]

A follower is slightly more specific. She says, that while he asks that in case of illness his people seek to make contact with his Spirit in order to be healed, he evidently recognizes that for some reason, possibly through ignorance or because of some subjective hindrance, they may not be able to do so. In such a case, according to her, he says, "If after three days you cannot make contact with

[51] The *New Day*, Volume 9, November 17, 1945, p. 8.
[52] The *New Day*, Volume 9, September 1, 1945, p. 34.

me, then call a doctor. I work through doctors." (Related in personal conversation.)

Numerous interviews with people seeking healing appear in the *New Day*. There is nothing striking about his procedure. One may well imagine that as in the case of Naaman, the leper, who sought healing at the hands of Elisha, they feel disappointed that he does not do something—lay hands on them, or prescribe something definite for them to do. He only sits and talks quietly with them and inquires as to the nature of the malady. Then he bids them contact him spiritually, always declaring that his physical presence is not necessary at all, and most importantly, bidding them "live exactly according to my teaching." They must have implicit faith. This is encouraged sometimes by the recital of what has occurred in like cases. If they do "this" they will not be sick. His very manner, the complete confidence with which he announces this, begets confidence, which is the secret, psychologically, of faith healing the world over. And people are healed, many of them. If they are not healed it seems, implicitly at least, to be proof that they have not made the contact with his spirit or have not lived "exactly according to his teachings," though I have not heard or read of such a statement from him.

VII. *THE SOURCES OF THE MOVEMENT*

Seldom, or never, does a religious movement arise that is wholly original. Usually it grows out of some previously existing movement or movements from which it differs at significant points. Generally it is possible to discover what the main sources were from which a new movement draws. Is this possible in the case of Father Divine's Peace Mission? To a certain degree, yes, it is.

Where the life story of a founder of religion is well known, it is fairly easy to see what influences have played upon him. But in the case of Father Divine, very little is surely known of his past. Therefore, most of the answer must come from a study of what he says and does, and how that compares with other known religious teachings with which he may have had some contacts. If it then appears that he actually did at one time have some contact with such groups, it is fairly certain that he has drawn upon them for some of his teachings and practices.

No one, acquainted with old-fashioned evangelistic Christianity, can doubt for a minute that this forms a backdrop for everything else in the movement. Father Divine was reared in it, steeped in it, and, while the content of his thought is very different, he manages to create the authentic atmosphere of old-fashioned revivalism in his public meetings. He knows his Bible, as shown elsewhere. He quotes it extensively, quite contrary to the assertion of some writers. His addresses are liberally salted with appropriate Bible verses, just as is the case with the evangelist, though Father Divine's interpretations of the verses might shock the latter. He encourages vocal and often physical response on the part of his listeners. Often in the course of his remarks he exclaims suddenly, "Aren't you glad?" And the cries of "Yes, God Almighty," "So true, Father dear," and the like, spur him on to further utterances, sometimes at a heightened emotional level.

Again, he encourages public confession and testimony. This is a constant element in the banquet meetings. Anyone is privileged to rise and confess, or testify or express himself in poetry and often in song. If he is emotional in this, the crowd emotion is stirred, and frequently the vocal response of the group drowns out the one who testifies, or requires that he shout even louder and louder. There seems no limit to the time one may take in this way. Both Father and the crowd have endless patience. Extreme religious ecstasy is not infrequently witnessed—expressing itself in all sorts of ways. I saw people fall to the floor in a trance. I saw others with arms stretched above the head, with hands and fingers all aquiver, reel about on the stage or among the communion tables most wildly, colliding with people or chairs or tables. I saw one fall against Father Divine himself, another fell over a food-laden serving table. But Father Divine sat completely unmoved and oblivious to the disorder. This sort of thing unquestionably roots in old-fashioned evangelistic religious practice.

Then the music! Here, while the verbal content of the songs is very different, as shown elsewhere, the type of music and the enthusiastic manner in which the crowd joins in, is of the evangelistic order. The music is highly rhythmic, usually, the beat accentuated by the accompaniment of a bass drum and/or cymbals, plus a skillful boogie-woogie type of piano accompaniment stressing in the lower bass register the rhythmic beat of the songs. Add the repeated singing of choruses, a familiar technique of the evangelist singer, and one can easily see that a major source of the movement, on the side of religious behavior and experience, is old-fashioned evangelistic Christianity.

There is certainly also the ring of the evangelistic preacher in his denunciation of the sins of the flesh—gambling, dishonesty, stealing, drinking, smoking, and the like. Fortunately, this is not the end of his catalogue of sins, for he is also a preacher of social righteousness, as few evangelists ever are. But his heritage seems fairly clear at the point of condemnation of the familiar personal vices.

But there are phases of his teaching that are entirely foreign to the evangelistic tradition, namely—his emphasis upon economic security and healing.[53] In these two emphases can be seen, I think, a reflection of influences emanating from the New Thought group. I do not now refer to his remarkable economic arrangement described above, (pp. 27 ff.,) through which his followers have been enabled to enjoy a financial security they have never before known. Here he has broken new ground and gone far beyond any New Thought group known to the writer.

The reference is rather to the constant teaching of the availability of unlimited abundance, sufficient to meet every human need, if only the conditions for its utilization are properly met. He has a formula which he repeats times without number, and which he evidently regards as basic in all that he teaches concerning the enjoyment of economic security.

"The Spirit of the Consciousness of the Presence of God is the Source of all supply and will satisfy every good desire. . . . The abundance of the fullness of the Consciousness of good—no place is vacant from the fullness thereof."

To anyone who is acquainted with New Thought teachings, and particularly with Unity, this has a very familiar ring. Nowhere stated in exactly these words, the idea expressed is found in the writings of the exponents of New Thought. Here are a few typical statements:

"There is an all sufficiency of all things, just as there is an all sufficiency of air. The only lack there is is our own lack of appropriation." [54]

"There is a kingdom of abundance of all things, and it may be

---

[53] Healing, it is true, was frequently practiced by the evangelist, but Father Divine uses a very different technique, as we have seen.
[54] Charles Fillmore, *Prosperity*, p. 15.

found by those who seek it and are willing to comply with its laws." [55]

"It is impossible that in this universal mind that fills everything there can be any such thing as absence. There is no lack of anything anywhere in reality. The only lack is the fear of lack in the mind of man." [56]

There is abundance for all. No one need experience any lack. Establish right relations with the Source of all supply, employ the proper techniques (see pp. 170 ff.) and everything one needs is available. If one suffers lack, it is his own fault. He has not made the right effort.

Thus the basic idea is a New Thought concept. But so also is the method whereby one is enabled to attain the fulfillment of his need. Here is a typical statement.

"The thing you vividly visualize, you tend to materialize! You can visualize the negative and produce it and realize it if it was nothing but a supposition. You can bring it into your recognition and realize something that you did not want or do not want by visualization. When it goes through the process of materialization by your visioning it vividly, you materialize it. You reproduce it and bring it into outer expression and you become to be the personification of the negative instead of the positive! Can you not see the Mystery?" [57]

We have said that the healing emphasis is found occasionally in Evangelistic Christianity. But with Father Divine it is a constant, if not a principal point of emphasis, as it is in the New Thought movement, and the method used approximates much more closely to the New Thought method, though it is not identical. There is no laying on of hands or anointing the sick person, or praying over him as the evangelistic healers do. The patient is told simply that he must make contact with the Spirit of Father Divine, i.e., with God.[58] He is encouraged to think positive thoughts of health, not negative thoughts of "lacks or illnesses," for one tends to become what he thinks. This is the New Thought way.

And finally, the addition of the element of happiness, upon which great stress is laid, looks also in the direction of New Thought, for

[55] *Id.,* p. 16.
[56] *Id.,* p. 52.
[57] The *New Day,* Volume 9, September 29, 1945, p. 3.
[58] See section on healing, pp. 67 ff.

health, wealth or prosperity, and happiness are the trinity of values which New Thought offers its followers. The further stress upon happiness here and now, and not in another world, is closer to New Thought than the other-worldly ideal of the older Evangelists.

Other evidence of New Thought influence may be found in Father Divine's frequent use of such phrases as, "the Christ in you."

But if he displays evident signs of New Thought influence, through what channels have such influences come? There is no certain way of knowing. If Parker is right in associating him with Father Jehovia in Baltimore and later with Bishop St. John Divine, both of whom seem to have held some views bearing likeness to New Thought, it could have come through them. The former is said to have taught his own identity with the Supreme Spirit, which in turn might be regarded as only an extension of the divinity in man which many New Thought teachers hold and preach.

Whether he was ever influenced by the reading of Unity literature—for he reads very little—it is impossible to say, but he told the writer, personally, that at one time in his career as Father Divine he had made it his business to circulate widely some of Unity's publications. As I recall it, he invested something like $5,000 a year in disseminating religious books. Prominent among those circulated were some of the Unity books. At any rate, it appears that he must have felt that they were in line with what he was himself teaching. He expressed great personal admiration for Charles Fillmore, the founder of Unity.

But if Father Divine appears to have drawn heavily from the older evangelistic Christianity and New Thought, whence came the intense social passion which marks his ministry? Whence his strong insistence upon the equating of Christianity, Democracy, and Americanism, and his powerful promotion of racial equality? Certainly he did not get these from either the older revivalistic Christianity of New Thought, which are both strongly individualistic in their outlook.

His sensitiveness to racial discrimination is, of course, a product of his own experience and that of his race. He has been so often, himself, the victim of racial bigotry, and he has seen so often the bitter sufferings of his people, that his ardent desire to get away from inter-racial hatred, distrust, discrimination, and exploitation is most natural. It would be strange if he had not sought by some means to counteract these evils. That he should have thought of defining religion in terms of democracy and social justice is not explained in terms of his older evangelistic Christian or New Thought backgrounds. Here seems rather to be some reflection of the Social gospel emphasis in more recent decades, though I have not found any evident avenue through which this influence might have come to him. Of course, it is always possible that he went back to his gospels and found for himself what the "social gospellers" found when they sought to get behind the doctrinal accretions of the centuries and discover the real teaching of Jesus. Concern for his own people he might have gotten from Marcus Garvey, one-time Messiah of the colored race. But his was a narrow racialism, while Father Divine's drive is for a universal brotherhood that ignores race, creed or color.

One fairly certain influence upon Father Divine is that of Roman Catholic monasticism, for his organization seems in many ways to be patterned upon it. This may be seen in the essentially monastic organization of the inner circle of his followers. Note, first of all, that it is celibate, a rather remarkable fact if one considers the age in which it appears and the fact that it is accepted wholeheartedly by so many people. He expressed to me in personal conversation his admiration for Catholic nuns, and in public discourse he frequently dwells upon the "virginity of Mary" and the "Holiness of Jesus" as ideals to be realized in the community.

Furthermore the essentially communal living is very much like that of monks and nuns, except that the vows seem not to be permanent. Nor are the members of the group withheld from contact with the outside world, as some monastic groups are. Those who are in the inner circle get no fixed salary, as far as I can discover, but are abundantly taken care of. When they need clothes, clothes are provided, or shoes, or books, or pocket money, or vacation expenses, or anything else really needed. They have only to ask for these things, just as monks and nuns do. One might characterize this inner circle as a kind of *lay monasticism*. Undoubtedly it is Roman Catholic influences that have produced this feature of his movement.

How many of these various elements that blend in Father Divine's movement were consciously chosen and incorporated into it, and how much has been the result of quite unconscious syncretism, no one can say with certainty. Probably most of the process has been quite unconscious as it is in most movements, but it is also probable that some of it is the result of deliberate choice, made with the view to meeting the needs of his people and to attracting a following to himself. After all, he is a keen student of human nature and of human need in the present age. With rare skill he has set himself to minister to it in the most effective way possible.

VIII. *WHAT OF THE FUTURE?*

Will the movement prove to be a permanent one, and go on after the death of its founder—supposing that he is mistaken in his claim that he is God, and that he will prove to be only mortal like the rest of us? It is difficult to believe that it will. That which seems to hold it together is the intense personal loyalty of the membership to Father Divine in the flesh. To be sure, he frequently asserts that his personal, bodily presence with them is not necessary. Yet the fact remains that the movement is most vigorous and active where he appears in person. And even those who belong to the branches in other cities at a distance cherish the desire and hope of going to New York or Philadelphia to see and be near him. Hundreds, possibly thousands, do so every year.

If he should die, having led his followers to believe that he would not do so, would they not suffer a profound disillusionment and many of them fall away? He has not prepared them by any theory of reincarnation or otherwise to achieve a rationalization of his disappearance from their midst. Doubtless some would be able to do so. Probably the more intellectual among them could do so and would, for example, the Doctor of Philosophy from whom I have already quoted. (P. 46.) And there would be others. But the poor people, the fearful, the needy, the dependent, who are attracted to him by reason of their very insecurity and helplessness. Would they continue to follow? This may well be doubted, even when one goes on to say that these folk have found much beside economic security in following him. The very strength of the appeal is the immediacy of its ministry. Not in some indefinite future, but now, here, at once, there is help of the most concrete sort. Without Father Divine in person, the movement may indeed go on in some form, but there is little ground for belief that it will go on as it now is, or that it will continue to attract large numbers of people. It will be interesting to follow it through the years and see to what extent this prediction may be fulfilled.

Chapter Two

Psychiana

I

In the year 1929 a tall, breezy westerner walked in to an advertising agency in Spokane, Washington, and expressed a desire to have an advertisement placed by them in certain periodicals. The man was a complete stranger to the agency. They took the ad, read it through and handed it back to him saying, "The ad is not well written. It will never bring any results; besides the subject matter is such that it will make no appeal to periodical readers." They, therefore, suggested that he save his money and not attempt to buy space. He persisted in his desire to go ahead with it. They asked him how much money he had for an advertising campaign. He told them five hundred dollars. That sum, they said, was sufficient to buy but a single ad in one paper, and that, if he had no more to spend, he would be better advised to forget the whole matter. They ended by saying that they, at least, did not care to accept his commission.

The man was troubled but undiscouraged and turned away saying, "Well, either you people are crazy or I am," and went elsewhere to dispose of his ad. Subsequent events seem to have proven rather conclusively that it was not Frank B. Robinson who was crazy, for that ad has appeared continuously in hundreds of magazines in every part of the world and has brought a percentage of replies quite beyond that of most commercial ads. For eighteen years it has been a continuous producer. Literally millions of people have read it and been moved at least to inquire further about what it offered.

The ad was somewhat as follows: In the upper left-hand corner there was a picture of Frank B. Robinson. In black capital letters across the top it read, "I TALKED WITH GOD." Then followed in solid type a fairly long paragraph stating what issued from this talk with God. The ad closed with the statement, "You, too, can talk with God. Write to etc., etc." Since then the ads have been varied in their makeup and detailed content, but the general import has been the same; and into little Moscow, Idaho, there flows a continuous stream of inquiry as to how men and women of every class, and race, and circumstance can find the solution to their problems which "Psychiana," the name of the movement, purports to offer.

"Psychiana" is primarily a mail-order religion. It has few local organizations, but seven ordained ministers, owns comparatively little property, save the headquarters, and recognizes but one source for its teaching, namely the founder himself, who is the center around which gathers whatever unity the movement boasts. He did, at one time, start to organize local "Psychiana" groups, but gave it up and for years deliberately refused to sanction the formation of such bodies. He would not ordinarily disclose to any individual in a given city or region the names of any others in the same community who follow his teaching. It was not unusual to see advertisements in local papers expressing a desire to get in touch with other persons who were interested in "Psychiana." [1] Dr. Robinson, the founder, does from time to time make public appearances in certain centers, and wherever he is advertised to speak he is usually thronged with listeners. He has, however, made the deliberate choice of exercising the greater part of his influence through the medium of advertising in newspapers, periodicals and by radio.

There is a formally recognized legal corporation know as "Psychiana," which enjoys all the rights and immunities that are granted to religious groups under the law of the state of Idaho. It enjoys complete autonomy and is obliged only to conform to the constitution under which its corporation was approved by the state authorities. Thus "Psychiana" enjoys exactly the same status as the Roman Catholic Church. The head of the corporation Sole known as Psychiana is its founder, Dr. Frank B. Robinson who holds the office of Archbishop of Psychiana. He, and four other ordained clergymen, is the ruling body of this religion, with power to ordain ministers for the purpose of spreading the truths as taught by

---

[1] Quite recently this policy has been changed. A recent letter from Dr. Robinson says that they are forming local groups as rapidly as possible now.

Psychiana. They are empowered to ordain other bishops or ministers of the corporation.[2] The management of the corporation is vested in the archbishop and his successor, but should it be terminated at any time by Dr. Robinson or his successor, all properties and funds vested in the corporation legally must go, not to himself, or his family, but to some institution of a religious or benevolent character similar in kind to "Psychiana" itself.

As a religious corporation "Psychiana," like the Roman Catholic church and other institutions so incorporated, is not required to make an accounting of its funds or property to the state or any other authority. By reason of its being a religious organization, it enjoys all tax exemptions generally extended by the state and nation to such institutions.

The headquarters of the movement are at Moscow, Idaho, where Dr. Robinson and a staff of some one hundred employees keep in touch with the thousands who yearly write in for information and subscribe for the successive sets of lessons and other publications. For years Dr. Robinson undertook to answer correspondence inspired by the reading of his lessons, or his many books, but in more recent times, the burden of this correspondence has grown too heavy for him personally to reply to every letter. Even so, he does actually reply to a good many of them personally.

Before the outbreak of the war, he had begun to establish branch offices in foreign cities and was circulating a considerable number of his lesson sheets in dozens of countries all over the world. Naturally the war put a stop to this international spread of the movement. Even Canadian people had difficulty getting his lessons, since it was extremely difficult to make remittances of cash out of the country. Thus, during the war years, his efforts were confined almost exclusively to the United States. Even so, the mails were flooded constantly with inquiries, perhaps more numerous because of the troubles that piled up on people during the critical war period. The writer was in Dr. Robinson's office in Moscow one morning when the mail came in, and the actual count for a day and one-half was over nineteen hundred requests for further information. The average was at that time about thirteen hundred per day.

These inquiries come from all kinds of people in every part of the country, since his ads appear in all sorts of periodicals, save the more

[2] Information direct from Dr. Robinson.

exclusive type of magazine read by limited groups of people. But in the popular press, the "slicks" as well as "pulps," in weekly and daily newspapers, from the Atlantic to the Pacific, his ads appear with regularity. Detective magazines, adventure magazines, occult magazines, the *Police Gazette, Pathfinder, Popular Science*, fashion magazines, business magazines, magazines of almost every sort carry the good news which "Psychiana" purports to have for the world. In the office at Moscow, an elaborate set of records is kept of every ad, where it appears, how many times it appears, and an ingenious plan has been worked out by Dr. Robinson to show whether a given ad in a particular paper is producing sufficient results to justify its continuance. It was the writer's privilege to study this record in the various magazines and to try to discover if there was any close correlation between the type of magazine, the percentage of inquiries made, and the number of people who ultimately subscribed for the lessons.

A sampling of twenty-five magazines of all kinds, including the widest extremes, revealed a range of returns varying from 3% to 21%. That is, from 3% to 21% of those who read the ads and wrote in for further information, finally subscribed for the lessons. The highest yield, of 21%, was from readers of a magazine dealing with the future. Two astrology periodicals accounted for 18% and 14% returns. Two detective story publications gave returns of 16 and 15% respectively, while a third returned 11%. One movie and radio publication resulted in 14%, but another movie sheet gave but 8% returns. A favorite of the old-time, barber shop, male clientele showed a 14% return. What claims to be the most widely circulated Sunday newspaper magazine section, accounted for a 13% return. A nationally circulated newspaper almanac returned 14%.

Here, to be sure, are relatively high returns but by no means all of them can be held to interest special classes or groups of people. Who, for example, are the people who read detective fiction? Many of the great and near great are said to find escape from their heavy responsibilities in following some famous sleuth. At least they read the detective books. Whether they also read the detective magazines, there is no sure way of knowing.

The lowest return, 3%, was from a nationally circulated weekly paper. It may be that it circulates chiefly among small-town and rural folk, for the next lowest, 4%, was from readers of a paper definitely known to have that class of readers. But at the same time a specifically designated mid-west farm paper yielded a 9% return. A nationally read popular priced "slick paper" weekly made about the average return which according to Dr. Robinson was at the time about 7%. A well-known national veterans' magazine yielded 5%.

If any generalizations can be drawn from such figures they might be the following: Readers of magazines dealing with the future, reflecting thereby some insecurity in the present, show a relatively high response to Psychiana, though one wondered why one such should register more than twice the return shown by another of similar nature. Readers of detective magazines respond well. Also the readers of rural and small-town circulation magazines seem to respond to a less degree than any others. This may be significant. They may be on the whole less insecure, better adjusted than their urban brothers, and hence feel less need for what Psychiana has to offer.

The founder keeps close watch upon this record, and as soon as any given ad proves unproductive, it is withdrawn, or when any magazine fails to make an adequate return, when one of the tried and successful ads is employed, it is no longer used as a medium. The same careful check is made of the results of radio advertising. At one time he was heard over eighty stations, mainly on the west coast. Here, too, he could tell whether a station was paying its way, and was quick to exclude those that were unprofitable.

The third approach to the public made by Dr. Robinson was the direct mail appeal. This means simply that he procures extensive lists of names and addresses from name brokers, and sends to each a circular which varies from time to time, but which generally carries, in one form or another, the material or appeal found in the ad described earlier, "I Talked With God." A sample of the initial appeal of these follows:

One, recently circulated, has a red mass across the top of the page with lightning points suggesting electric power. Upon it in extra large white caps is the legend I TALKED WITH GOD

and

SO CAN YOU—IT'S EASY

Four paragraphs of explanation and exhortation follow. On the other side of the sheet at the top in large white caps on an electric red background appears

THIS POWER IS FOR YOU

Four additional paragraphs carry in detail the appeal of the movement. Scattered sentences are: ". . . if your life lacks anything good, be it financial, domestic, or spiritual, or otherwise, if it is good, the Power of which we speak can supply that lack and supply it NOW. You can draw on this staggering Power at will. At any hour of the day or night. In any emergency. In sickness or health. If the desire is right YOU CAN HAVE IT NOW. . . . You may find the Power of God and actually use it to bring to you and yours, WHILE YOU ARE ALIVE, a super-abundance of happiness, peace, comfort, financial security, domestic happiness—in fact everything for your own good. NOW. . . . You may learn to use this fathomless, pulsing, throbbing ocean of spiritual power just as you learn to use chemistry, physics or mathematics. Moreover you need make no outward show of religion. This is not necessary. . . . We are giving accurate, scientific instructions which if followed by you for about 15 minutes each day, seldom fail to reveal the fullness of THE POWER OF GOD."

The lists come from many sources. One positive requisite of every list is that it contain names of persons who have responded to some kind of an advertisement by mail. Simple telephone directory lists are not sufficient. Theoretically anyone who has bought any article by mail is a good prospect for some other offer made through the same medium. So, annually, Dr. Robinson buys millions of names of people who have bought books, or hardware, agricultural implements, or typewriters, or patent medicines, in short, anything that can be bought by mail. Here again the same careful businesslike record is kept in the headquarters office. The record tells the number of names on a given list, from what source the list came, the amount paid for it per thousand and then the net results in the number of inquiries and the final number of those who subscribed for the lessons of the movement; so that at a single glance at a card in the file, it is possible to determine how productive a given list is.

Again the writer made an attempt to discover whether there was any correlation between the percentage of lessons sold and the kind of list reported by a given mailing. As in the case of advertising through magazines there was a wide range of percentages, but again it was difficult to draw any certain conclusion. The highest percentage of all was from a list of persons who had responded to some sort of a lonely hearts appeal. A return of 20% came from a group dealing with the power of thought. The next highest, 16%, came from a list of people who had bought fish. It seems that in an unguarded moment, Dr. Robinson had bought a large list of names from a fish dealer. Not seeing any particular relationship between buying fish and a religious appeal, it occurred to him to make a sample mailing of only 2,000 names. To his great surprise the net return was as indicated, very high—16%. Still distrustful of any correlation, he made another mailing of several thousand which gave a return somewhat under average. A Theosophical group list brought 15%; the followers of Yogi 14%; customers of a New Thought writer, 13%; two astrological lists 12% and 11%; a list of a famous strong man, 6%; a parent's organization, 6%. Lowest of all, 0%, was recorded by a list from an aristrocratic fashion sales organization. If any conclusion may safely be drawn, it is both here and in the case of the magazine list that persons who have been interested in the occult, or the mysterious, or the future seem to respond more readily than readers of other types.[3]

Once an inquiry has been made by an individual, there is a routine follow-up which is regular and persistent. At stated intervals over a period of weeks and months successive appeals go out to the one who has made the inquiry. If, after several letters which are mailed weekly, there is no result, no further appeal is made until months later when another letter goes out and so on for an indefinite period. Sometimes people who have not succumbed to the first dozen appeals will succumb to an appeal made a year later, though the law of diminishing returns operates here, as might be expected.

Once the individual has subscribed for the lessons which may be a series of twelve, or twenty or seventy-five, and even a larger series is in preparation, each two weeks he receives a small pamphlet of instruction which he is supposed to read and master and follow carefully until his next installment comes. Thus there is maintained between the office and the individual an intimate contact over a period of months. In the early days, correspondence was invited. Later it was positively discouraged, but the present policy is to welcome it.

Payment for the lessons is made either in one lump sum, with a substantial discount for such payment, or in small installments at bi-weekly or monthly intervals during the period covered by the study of the lessons. The cost of the lessons has varied from one

[3] See above, pp. 81–82.

time to another during the years of the movement's existence, and at one time the experiment was made of making no stated charge but allowing the individual to make such a contribution as he might be moved to make. This scheme resulted in a substantial loss for the corporation during the year that it was tried, and the plan was abandoned. Every year large numbers of lessons are sent without cost to people who are unable to bear the expense, and a substantial discount from the regular price is often made to persons who are poor. Any prisoner in the United States can have a set of the lessons free of charge if he will write in for it, and many hundreds of them have availed themselves of the opportunity.

Naturally, not all who begin the series on the installment plan see it through to the end. A careful follow-up is maintained by the office which attempts to keep people up to date, but, even so, some, for one reason or another, drop out and leave unpaid a part of the sum they originally promised to pay. The actual average return is about three-fourths of the gross lesson price, exclusive of discounts for cash. The advertisements carry a standing offer of a refund of the entire sum paid if the individual is dissatisfied. Now and then a subscriber asks for his money back, and invariably receives it without question, but the number is very small in proportion to the many who complete their payments.

The number of individuals reached by the movement, and the enormous labor involved in maintaining touch with all its members, may be indicated by the fact that annually the movement uses some twenty-five million ordinary envelopes. A considerable amount of the printing is done by a well-equipped printing shop which the movement itself maintains, but often enough their own facilities are inadequate, and they have to go to outside printers to furnish the millions of sheets which are annually called for by people who are appealed to by the offerings of Psychiana.

Dr. Robinson estimates, although there is no absolute count, that in the twenty years the movement has been in existence, he has enrolled at least a million individuals as students for his lessons or for his books, many of which contain the core of his teachings. This million people is made up of individuals from every class of society, the rich and poor, educated and uneducated, the white and the black, from small towns and cities, from all of the United States and the whole world. A glance at the address files maintained by the headquarters indicates that they are perhaps more largely located in the far west than elsewhere, but are liberally distributed over every other section of the country. There is no way of telling what percentage come from the various strata of society. The writer has seen testimonial letters from hundreds of people, taken at random from the files, and certainly there was every class represented among them. If the larger percentage came from the more needy groups it would be not an unnatural state of affairs, since it is they who most need the things which "Psychiana" has to offer. How many continue to practice the teachings of the founder after the regular period of study, there is no way of knowing. Some knowledge of human nature and some slight check upon a few score of subscribers to the lessons led the writer to believe that a great many of them do not continue actively to profess or practice the teaching, though they will admit to some permanent influence of the movement upon their lives. A considerable number do continue to subscribe for successive sets of lessons and to buy the numerous books which the founder continues to produce, but what percentage do this, there is no way of telling for certain. Dr. Robinson recently estimated it at 75%. The lack of a corporate body of followers which might bring mutual stimulus and help and encouragement to its members will seem a genuine weakness to those who are convinced of the importance of the reinforcement, that comes through social confirmation, in the maintenance of a vigorous religious philosophy of life.

When the founder was asked what would become of the movement after his own death, since there was no organized body to carry on his teachings, his reply was that he had sown the seed and he must leave to the future the harvest; that he was content to have performed this function, a most necessary one; and that he believed it never would die, but rather grow. Students of the history of religious ideas and institutions will be inclined to question his judgment at this point. His recent change of policy in the direction of organizing groups may change the picture very greatly.

II

Dr. Frank B. Robinson is Psychiana. Any story of the growth and development of the movement must include the story of his life. What, if anything, is there in the experience of Frank B. Robinson to account for the movement that he founded?

He has told his story in *The Strange Autobiography of Frank B. Robinson,*[4] and in it one finds an adequate explanation of the direction that he has taken in his later years. Many of his most characteristic outlooks and attitudes seem definitely to grow out of the experiences of his childhood and early manhood. Take, for instance, the strong anti-church bias which he displays in almost every chapter of anything he writes. Its roots lie in certain harsh experiences with organized religion which have left an indelible mark upon him. The salient facts, as given by him, may be stated briefly.

He was born in 1886. As to where he was born, there has been controversy. He states that he was born in New York, on the occasion of a visit to that city by his parents. In 1940 some of his enemies, knowing that his parents were English, brought a charge against him in the courts for having falsified, on a passport upon which he traveled in Europe in 1934, the place of his birth. He was acquitted of the charge which apparently should have established the fact of his having been born in America. Yet, only a little later, deportation proceedings were brought against him by the Bureau of Immigration and he was permitted to leave the country and enter again on a proper visa in order to clear up his status with the immigration authorities. Evidence was introduced in the trial against him, purporting to come from his father, to the effect that he and Mrs. Robinson had never visited New York. That Frank B. Robinson had consistently, from an early time, represented himself as having been born in America, was apparently the basis of his acquittal, since it seemed evident that no fraud had been intended even though a mistake on his part might have been made. At any rate, that seems to be the only likely explanation of the contradictory situation as revealed in the acquittal and the subsequent attempt at deportation.

Regardless of the place of his birth, Dr. Robinson, in his autobiography, states that his early childhood was spent in England where his father was a Baptist minister. His mother, whom he idealizes in his life story, died when he was quite young and his father remarried. For his mother he had the greatest respect and affection, but not so for his father. He, according to Frank Robinson, was an unworthy minister who frequently engaged in drunken brawls, and carried on intrigues with female members of his congregation. This, he alleges,

[4] Psychiana, Moscow, Idaho, 1941.

was his first contact with the church and it has left him embittered against it.

Life was not happy for himself and a younger brother after his father's second marriage. He alleges repeated cruel treatment by both parents, treatment which he felt ill became a representative of the Gospel of Christ. He was put into a naval school by his father, much against his will, but succeeded by clever strategy in getting out. At the age of fourteen, he declares, he and his younger brother were put on a steamship for Montreal, Canada, with passage paid and $2.50 cash between them. No provision was made for them in Canada other than a letter to a Canadian Baptist minister whom the father did not even know personally, commending the two boys to his care. The Baptist minister lived a distance of several hundred miles from the port of entry and when finally, thanks to the help of strangers, the two boys reached the town where this minister dwelt, and went to his house, they were rudely rebuffed because it was not a propitious time. They were only grudgingly aided when later they came back to the minister's home. This second contact with the Christian church and its ministry likewise left a deep and lasting impression upon the mind of Frank Robinson.

His youth and early young manhood was spent in or near Toronto, in a variety of jobs. Despite the unfortunate contacts he had had with the church, he was accustomed to attending services, though writing thirty years later he reports most of those contacts in such a way as to reflect little credit upon the church. As a young man in Toronto he sang in choirs and engaged in young people's religious meetings, displaying some skill as leader, and was finally given a scholarship in the Baptist training school of Toronto where he began to prepare for the Christian ministry. In this school, according to his own story, he made a good record and was warmly commended by his benefactor who had furnished him the scholarship. On this occasion, he reports, he was ordained to the Baptist ministry. But he writes that he was never quite at ease in the training school. He could not believe or accept the theology that was taught there. He found himself asking questions of his teachers and getting unsatisfactory answers. At last he felt he could no longer continue his studies and thus broke with the school and went out to work again.

The writer visited Toronto in the summer of 1945 and while there met and talked with some of the people who had known him in his youth. Among them was one of the professors who knew him in the Bible Training School, the one alone for whom Robinson expressed great respect in his account of his school days. While the professor did not, of course, know intimately all that was going on in the mind of young Robinson, and while, from the professional angle some of the events reported by Dr. Robinson looked quite different, he did recall clearly the youth who nearly forty years before had studied under him.

About this time Robinson began to drink. Though he claims never to have drunk hard liquors, he did use beer heavily and was often under its influence. He wandered about from job to job, unhappy and discontented. He drifted to the west coast. From time to time he went back into religious circles. On one occasion he joined the Salvation Army and played the bass drum in the Army's band. Apparently here, too, he found hollowness and insincerity. He asserts that one of the Salvation Army lasses attempted to seduce him, so he became disgusted and left the Army. Years passed. He became a pharmacist and worked for short periods in a dozen cities in western Canada and the United States, intermittently reforming and returning to his drinking.

All this time, he alleges, and indeed from early childhood, he had had a great hunger for God, partly, it may be, because of his mother who was herself a deeply religious person and whose influence upon him was very great. He speaks often of this hunger to know God and relates frequent attempts to discover God in and through the churches, or through the ministers of the churches. Again and again he was disappointed and asserts that they had no answer to give him when he asked them to show him the reality of God. How much of this sort of thing actually happened and how much he may have read back into his earlier experiences, it is impossible to say with certainty. Dr. Robinson is of a mystical turn of mind and no doubt must have been so from childhood up. There is no reason to suppose that he may not have had some deep unsatisfied longing for a deeper experience of God. But his quest was never successful. There was always an unappeased hunger which drove him on to the discovery of God.

Meanwhile he had married, but still drifted from one pharmacist's job to another with no sense of permanence in any community.

Then came a great change in his life. As he tells it, his final, clean break from all forms of religion, as he had known them, came one Sunday morning in a beautiful church in Hollywood, where, he says, he made up his mind that the world needed something very different from "the religious hodgepodge that minister handed out that beautiful Sunday morning." Finally, he says, he had the courage to throw away and disbelieve everything the church had told him about God. He was alone in his home on Sunday when he made his decision which, he said, "will mean so much to this world and to future generations." He decided he would see if he could not find God by some other means. As he stood there in his room, he writes, he lifted his eyes to God and said, "Oh, God, if I have to go to hell, I will go with the consciousness that I went there earnestly trying to find you." Then a remarkable thing happened. Instead of feeling condemned for denying that the church knows anything about God, there came to him a wonderful peace and rest. At last he knew he was on the right track. He knew that God, as that great spirit must exist, was not to be found in anything the church teaches. From that time on, he says, he knew that his childhood dreams were to come true. He was sure "that the revelation of God he was to bring to the world would be the most amazing revelation this religious world has ever known." [5] The experience deepened and a strange power, he says, came into his life. All fear left him and he came to know a deep abiding peace. He came to know that God was a living reality here and now, and began to feel a strong impulse to share this experience with others.

What influences had brought him to this experience, it is impossible to say with complete certainty, but there is one indication in his autobiography that he was influenced by the reading of Robert Collier's *The Secret of the Ages*. He says, "I shall never forget the day the spirit of God spoke definitely to me. . . . I had been lying under a tree in Grant High Park, studying some works along the religious New Thought line. The particular set of books, as I recall it, was a volume called *The Secret of the Ages* by Robert Collier. . . . These small books helped open the way I was trying to tread, and my gratitude is to Bob Collier for having written them." His experience sounds very much like the conversion experience other religious leaders have reported. The following description of it in his own works may help to understand its nature.

"I lay perfectly still, not a move, just completely resting in the

---

[5] *Autobiography*, p. 187.

Great Spirit, God. Then God opened the veil which is supposed to separate us mortals from God, and though God and I are very close now, I shall never forget that day. The future opened up like a rose. I cannot describe it—such moments are not described by any words in any language; they are spiritual moments and are spiritually discerned. A great, infinite peace stole over me. I was overwhelmingly happy. There, in those few seconds, for that is all they were, I suppose, I saw victory ahead. I saw the road I was to travel. I saw the home we now live in. I saw the answer to the criminal trials which were to come later. I saw everything in one flash, exactly as it happened, and for this reason I am so absolutely sure of the future. It was undescribable. Let me just try to describe it by saying that the Spirit of the Infinite God spoke to me. All I could do was to lie and shout, 'Glory to God—Glory to God in the highest,' and I did shout. The tears rolled down my cheeks, for God had at last revealed Himself to me, and had done it through methods entirely removed from any theological organization on the face of the earth." [6]

Immediately after describing the experience which became the turning point of his life, he makes an observation which seems strange, but it is of a sort that is found again and again throughout his subsequent career, statements which put a considerable strain upon the credulity of his readers. He said, "One strange thing about that experience was that I saw the home in which I now live and the grounds and the very identical pipe organ I have." [7] The next day, he relates, he met a famous English lady who was visiting in Portland. He had never seen her before. He had as yet related this religious experience to no one, yet the woman said on meeting him, "I should like to talk with you, sir." When they had walked into a nearby park and sat down on the bench, she said, "What is this religious experience you recently had?" Having told no one about it, he was naturally amazed that she should know about it. Then the woman exclaimed, "It is beautiful to realize that I have personally met the man whom God is to use to bring in the Great Day of God." [8]

That conversion experience he says "changed me and made me.

[6] *The Strange Autobiography of Frank B. Robinson,* p. 191.
[7] *Id.*
[8] *Id.,* p. 192.

It equipped me with the strength to do the work which is mine to do. It put the seal of the most high God on my life exactly as I knew it would be put on me sooner or later." [9]

Frank. B. Robinson considers himself a prophet of God. He says so explicitly again and again and again throughout his writings. To quote some of his statements, speaking of himself, "You have met the prophet of God." "I was born for the express purpose of revealing the power of the spirit of God." "I say to you as a prophet of God." "My message comes direct from the God of the universe." "I happen to be one of the very few prophets, etc." "Through this humble prophet of God." "Very seldom does God raise up a prophet. I know I was raised up." [10] "I am a true prophet of God." "I am the prophet God has sent." [11] He writes by direct divine inspiration according to repeated assertions. For example, "What I have written has been written by the direct inspiration of God." "The spirit of God dictates what I write." "The spirit of God is upon the writer of this book." [12] One of his published volumes bears the title "*A Prophet Speaks*." Thus there can be no doubt about it. He claims to be a prophet of God, I have heard him repeatedly say the same thing in personal conversation.

He makes claims of very unusual powers. Some of these claims seem utterly incredible, yet they are solemnly made in print and repeated in private, personal conversation. Here the reference is not to miracles of healing of which he claims to have performed great numbers, but miracles that are quite incapable of any explanation such as those of healing which may be plausibly explained. For example, he tells that on one occasion he was driving to Portland, Oregon. At a certain point along the highway, a front tire blew out. He had no way of fixing it, but, he says he never gave the tire a thought. Instead, he turned his thoughts inward "to where God is." The rest of the story is in his own words.

> I sat on the running-board of the car and for about fifteen minutes communed with God. The flat tire was completely forgotten. When my moments of communion with God were over, I climbed into the car, started the motor and drove to Arlington. Suddenly I remembered the flat tire. Stopping the

[9] *Id.*
[10] *Your God Power*, pp. 58, 41, 161, 163, 171, 179, 211.
[11] F. B. Robinson, *Your God Power*, pp. 318, 343.
[12] *Id.*, pp. 344, 336, 347.

car, I looked, and the tire was up to its regular pressure and not a soul had touched it.[13]

Other stories equally or even more remarkable are told in his book under the title *Blood on the Tail of a Pig*.[14] In this, Dr. Robinson tells of an experience he had while driving on one of his many trips. He found himself following a truck which, for some inexplicable reason, he did not want to pass, as was his usual custom when on a highway. When he drove a little closer, he saw in the truck a pig whose tail was bleeding profusely. He pulled ahead and motioned the truck-driver to stop. When asked the cause of the pig's injury, the hard-looking driver replied that he had struck the animal with a piece of board with nails in it when the pig would not enter the truck. After the truck had gone on, Dr. Robinson relates that he was so overwhelmed not only by this man's cruelty, but also by the human sufferings in Europe, that he sat for some minutes wondering what he could do to change the cruel hearts of men. The tears streamed down from his eyes. Looking up he said, "Spirit of the Living God, help me to do something for that poor pig." He continued his drive, and in a short time had caught up to the truck. When he looked at the pig again he was amazed to see absolutely no traces of blood or an injury on its tail. Once again he stopped the truck to verify his observation. The frightened driver declared that he had done nothing whatever to remove the blood. Then the thought came to him, "Your sympathy and your uttered word have healed the tail of that pig."

Another experience took place in Dr. Robinson's home one Christmas Eve after his family had retired. He was seated in his study when he felt a "Power, so strange, so beautiful—it cannot come from this earth—this Power—truly, I have never known anything like this before." While in this condition, he heard a slight noise in the adjoining room. He thought, "It is one of our gold-fish which has flipped out the bowl on to the floor." He went to see, and sure enough there it was. Instead of reaching for the fish to put it back in the bowl, he felt impelled by something outside himself to order the fish back into the aquarium. He stopped and clapped his hands, "Get back into that bowl," he commanded, and instantly the fish was back again in the bowl. "The fish could do nothing else than

---

[13] *Ibid.*, p. 174.
[14] Psychiana, Moscow, Idaho, 1941.

obey me, for God is in this house tonight. God is in me." He returned to the desk in his study. It occurred to him to send out a desire that the gold-fish come to him. He held out his hand and on the instant three gold-fish lay flat in his right hand, their little gills heaving. He tossed them into the air with a command to get back to the aquarium. Then he walked into the dining room and looked, and there they were swimming around as usual and his hand, he says, was still wet. "This experience," he says, "told me one thing. It told me never to doubt the existence of God again."

His dog "Ching" was heard sniffing along the bottom of the closed door leading into the hall. The door was fast shut. "I wanted to see 'Ching,' " he writes, "so with no thought that it could happen, I called 'Here, Ching.' Instantly, bounding through both closed doors, came 'Ching.' " To make sure he was not dreaming, he opened a drawer in the desk, took out a scissors and clipped a tuft of hair from the dog's back. The tuft of hair was laying on his desk the next morning. After a few moments he said to the dog, "Go back to bed now, 'Ching.' " Without a moment's hesitation, he leaped through both doors and was gone. "From this experience," says Robinson, "I knew that God had chosen me to be the medium through which the whole world could be made conscious of the presence of God, even though that presence is invisible to the mortal eye."

Such experiences, I reapeat, put a heavy strain on one's credulity, but it is interesting to discover that many people accept implicitly the truth of Dr. Robinson's statements and believe that these things happened exactly as he told them. Later will be related some of the remarkable healings that he claims to have performed which are also accepted unhesitatingly as true by his followers.

In his later writing may be detected what appears to be some Theosophic influence upon him that the writer had not observed earlier. It appears in a 1943 book, *Your God Power*, where he quite definitely describes himself as an Adept. Now the term Adept comes from Theosophy and, of course, originally from India. Among Theosophists it is held that there are Mahatmas, "great souls" or, sometimes, Adepts, who by reason of an unusual achievement of spiritual quality, come to have wisdom and powers not vouchsafed to ordinary individuals. It was from such that Madam Blavatsky and Annie Besant claim to have received communications, giving them knowledge of hidden wisdom. Frank Robinson, in his own writings, refers to himself as one of the Adepts. He defines them thus: "There are those of us who, after many years of living with the consciousness of God, may rightfully be called Adepts or Masters. They are those who usually, after many years of tribulation, search, and close communion with God have found the place where the whole Realm of the spirit of God opens to them. These Adepts know God. They are able instantly to project themselves in the Realm of the Spirit of God and they know what the future will bring forth." [15]

Not many achieve the distinction of becoming Adepts or Masters. He asserts that there are not more than one-half dozen alive today, and he knows most of them. He places three of them in India, one in England and perhaps two in the United States, all of whom he has met and knows. Furthermore they know him. Indeed, they knew him "forty years ago, long before he ever became an international religious figure." [16] One of the Adepts who lives in Egypt, he declares, is over one thousand years old. He claims to have seen him on a visit to Egypt some years ago. He asserts that he had given no intimation to this Egyptian Adept that he was coming to Egypt, yet the day before he arrived in Alexandria, said Adept had sent word to the British authorities that Robinson be allowed to see him at once. Not only that, said Dr. Robinson, "in his communication he called me by name. He definitely knew through spiritual communications alone that I was in Egypt."

The Adepts have strange powers. Dr. Robinson asserts that he saw one of them look at a china platter "and immediately demolish it by the power of the unseen God in him. I saw a dozen sparrows instantly killed and all brought back to life again, all through the power of God in the Adept. This sounds very much like the experiences related by Yeats-Brown in *Lives of a Bengal Lancer* and Paul Brunton in *A Search in Secret India*.

When the writer asked him if he had had any contact with Theosophy he declared that he had not, except to speak to a group once in Los Angeles. Furthermore, he professed not to have read their literature. When it was suggested that the term "Adept" was once used by Theosophists he said, "No, it is Indian-Yogi." He said he had read books on Hinduism though he did not say what he had read.

---

[15] F. B. Robinson, *Your God Power*, p. 292.
[16] *Id.*, p. 295.

He did have the fourteen-volume *Sacred Books and Literature of the East* on his library shelves. He said he had spent a short time in India once when on a trip around the world.[17]

III

Although Dr. Robinson seriously objected to me when I classified Psychiana as essentially a branch of the New Thought movement, it is just that. To be sure, it differs at some points from other "New Thought" groups, but that is the very genius of the New Thought. It permits wide individual differences while holding to certain other well-defined common aims. As a matter of fact, Dr. Robinson mentions that just before the crucial experience which was the turning point of his life, he had been "studying some work along the religious new thought line"[18] and he mentions particularly *The Secret of the Ages* by Robert W. Collier. Whether Robert W. Collier is a constituent member of the International New Thought Alliance, the author does not know for certain, but the general outlook and emphasis in his teaching as well as his techniques are very similar to those held and practiced by leaders of the various branches of the New Thought. Furthermore, Frank B. Robinson has at times been in close contact with Dr. Ernest Holmes of the Institute of Religious Science at Los Angeles who is a major figure in the New Thought movement, a former president of the International New Thought Alliance. At one time a merger of the efforts of Dr. Robinson and Dr. Holmes was seriously considered, and indeed they did collaborate in certain public meetings held in Los Angeles. Serious consideration was given to making the Institute of Religious Science the school for the preparation of ministers of Psychiana. This, it should be said, was at a time when Dr. Robinson actively contemplated the formation of local groups of followers, a plan later abandoned but now once again a part of his system. The two men agreed on one occasion to collaborate in the publication of a book but certain disagreements arose and the work was not finally published. All this may serve, however, to indicate the affinity between Psychiana and the New Thought. The fact that Psychiana has its own name would create no barrier on the part of the New Thought Alliance

---

[17] F. B. Robinson, *Your God Power*, p. 295.
[18] *Strange Autobiography of Frank B. Robinson*, pp. 188–189.

to his being a constituent member of that movement, for the various regional "New Thought" groups have quite different names.

In one of his lessons [19] he mentions specifically being helped by Emily Cady who was a noted New Thought leader, author of the basic textbook of Unity, which has, during part of its history, been a member of the International New Thought Alliance. He says her writings "gave me a lot of help in my early metaphysical studies, and while I do not agree with Mrs. Cady in many things she teaches, I can and do agree with her on many other points." He further says, "I should like to have every student of mine, when he has finished these lessons, send for that book."

Also, in a personal conversation he told of attending a Truth Center, which is a New Thought branch, years before he had thought of starting a movement. Later on when this was mentioned as a possible evidence of New Thought influence he declared that he had gone in merely to get out of the rain. The incident is cited only for what it may be worth.

Robinson pays his respects to the New Thought movement in one statement in *Your God Power* where he says, "There are over sixteen millions of Americans who belong to New Thought organizations. (Where he gets his statistics in this as in other statements in his book it is impossible to say). They find some truth there but they can never find the fullness of the power of God there so long as these dear New Thought people insist on basing their teachings on Jesus instead of on God." [20]

It is interesting to note in this connection that in the earlier editions of the lessons put out by Dr. Robinson, a great deal more importance was given to the place of Jesus than in subsequent editions. It was the author's privilege to read the first set of lessons issued in 1929 of which Dr. Robinson has only a single copy, carefully kept in the safe in his office, but loaned to the author for his examination. At that time, the series of lessons was shorter, indeed but ten all told, and, of these ten, at least one half were given up to an exposition of the teachings of Jesus concerning the availability of power. Evidently there has been a change of emphasis in Dr. Robinson's teaching.

The characteristic emphasis, found in most New Thought organi-

[19] *Psychiana*, Moscow, 1932, Lesson 4, p. 11.
[20] F. B. Robinson, *Your God Power*, pp. 338–339.

zations on the availability of health, happiness, prosperity, as well as inner peace, is found throughout the Psychiana lessons, indeed they seem to be at the center of interest. Quoting directly from Dr. Robinson a sequence of statements will illustrate this fact. "The power of God exists. God wants you to know the fullness of that power and He has made provision for you." [21] . . . "All the power of God is instantly available *always* for you". . . . "You can intelligently and scientifically apply and use the invisible power of God in your life against any and all circumstances which exist which are not as they should be." . . . "There can be no lack in your life which the Spirit of God cannot fill. There can be no illness not even death itself which the power of God cannot banish." [22] . . . "You have now, right here on this earth, and under your complete control, all the power there is in the Realm of the Spirit of God." [23] . . . "There can be no problem in your life that you cannot solve. There can be no lack that you cannot fill. There can be no problem that the Spirit of God cannot answer because that spirit lives in you and you are the only one who controls the flow of the spiritual power of God." . . . "It is utterly impossible for you to draw upon the Spirit of God in you for anything and have that spirit fail you." [24] . . . "There are no limitations to the Spirit of God. There is nothing, absolutely nothing, you can need for your own good which the Spirit of God cannot bring to you. I don't care if it's a million dollars or ten million dollars. With the Spirit of God *in you*, why there is nothing to it. All you do is stay in earnest enough to direct the Spirit of God into the proper channel. Impress upon it what you want and the immutable Spirit of God will supply it." [25] . . . You can materially and physically bring from the creative Realm of the Spirit of God *anything you need for your complete physical and material happiness.*" [26] . . . "There is no room for illness or disease where the Spirit of God is. The two cannot live in the same house together. One has to go. If God stays and continues to give life, illness must go." [27]

The central teaching of Psychiana centers about God. It is doubtful if any religious group places greater emphasis upon God than does Frank B. Robinson. The writer was impressed in his personal contacts with the founder at the almost continuous reference in their

---

[21] F. B. Robinson, *Your God Power*, p. 32.
[22] *Id.*, p. 33.   [23] *Id.*, p. 39.   [24] *Id.*, p. 43.   [25] *Id.*, p. 90.
[26] *Id.*, p. 97.   [27] *Id.*, p. 116.

conversation to God. As we talked in his office, as we lunched or dined together, as we walked about the street, he was constantly insisting upon the power of God in its relation to human problems and the necessity of making this power known to man. He seemed utterly obsessed with the idea.

A number of his books exhibit in their title this same God-centered emphasis. They are his *Pathway to God, God and Mr. Bannister, Your God Power, The God Nobody Knows,* etc., etc. His whole teaching revolves around the fact that there is in God a sufficient answer to every human need. It is a matter of interest then to ask how he thinks about God. What is his conception of God?

In the first place, it should be said that he is in no sense a systematic thinker. Nor is his thought at every point self-consistent. One looks in vain for a carefully thought-out and reasoned statement concerning God's nature, but in this respect he is no different from many another religious leader. Indeed, few founders of new forms of religion have been careful or systematic in their definition of terms. As a matter of fact, in reading his books and talking with Frank Robinson, one finds him at one time thinking of God in purely impersonal terms, as naked power, while at another time he seems to refer to God as a warmly personal humanlike being. For example, he says, "While the Realm of God is charged and supercharged with power, that power is silent, motionless, emotionless and completely devoid of feeling." [28]

Or again in one of his lessons series he says that the common idea is that God is a personality, but "the statement is erroneous. God is invisible life. In 'It' we live and move and have our being." [29] Further on in the same lesson, he declares, "This power is no personality, it never was a personality and it never will be a personality. It has, however, a personal existence for you and me by its Law." [30] Again, he says: "There is no personality of any kind connected with this creative Life Principle or Spirit—It is a *Law*." [31]

The fact of God's existence is basic. It is the one thing that one must believe in, he says, as he begins a series of his lessons. Granted the existence of God, he goes on to show God's nature and how

[28] F. B. Robinson, *Your God Power,* p. 119.
[29] *Psychiana* Lesson 4, p. 12, Moscow, Idaho, Copyright 1932. All subsequent references to Lessons are to this series.
[30] *Id.,* Lesson 4, p. 14.
[31] *Id.,* Lesson 3, p. 11.

God fulfills human needs. The existence, however, must be accepted to begin with. God is the creator, though the process through which God works in creation is definitely the evolutionary process. Indeed, one of his books, *A Prophet Speaks*, is, in part, a rewriting of the story of creation in terms consonant with the evolutionary theory that God creates through the evolutionary process. God is "a mighty operating spiritual law of Power." [32] He frequently uses the neuter pronoun "It" rather than the masculine pronoun "He" when describing or speaking of God. Sometimes God seems just to be Law or just Power. Yet God lives, "God cannot be anything but a Living, Vital, Powerful, Operating Spirit. God was never a human being." [33] "God is invisible life, capable of manifesting without physical form." [34] God seems to be immanent in the universe when, indeed, he is not to be thought of, pantheistically as the universe itself, as sometimes appears. He declares "this thing in us *which lives, which sees, which breathes, which thinks,* that invisible motivating power in each of us is the Spirit of the living God;" [35] and again, "within you is the only place you can find God." [36]

But God is sometimes very definitely personal as appears for example in the following from his book, *The God Nobody Knows*.

> I know beyond any shadow of a doubt that there exists in this universe a God who is so potent, so powerful, so sweet and so satisfying that for me to deny His presence would be the very worst kind of blasphemy . . . and He exists as the most dynamic, pulsating, throbbing power there is in this world today. . . . Because He cannot be seen, He has not been believed. [37]

Again, "To me God, as he exists today is far sweeter than any earthly thing I know. He is far more precious and what is more, He is far more powerful, and for me to say that I love Him is speaking the truth." [38]

Dr. Robinson is wholly Unitarian in his concept of God, and will have none to share His power and glory. One of his pet aversions is what he persists in calling "the crucified God idea," upon which he pours unlimited scorn. Indeed, one of his books bears the title *Crucified Gods Galore*. There is hardly a chapter in any one of his

[32] F. B. Robinson, *Your God Power*, p. 35.
[33] *Id.*, p. 38.   [34] *Id.*, p. 38.   [35] *Id.*, p. 38.   [36] *Id.*, p. 42.
[37] F. B. Robinson, *The God Nobody Knows*, p. 112.
[38] *Id.*, pp. 115–116.

writings, and he has written much, which does not refer slightingly to the Christian idea of the crucified God, as though God could be crucified. This leads to a general statement of his attitude toward Jesus.

Apparently in his earlier career, Jesus played a more central role in his thinking. There seems to be a growing impatience in his utterances concerning Jesus when thought of as God. In one of his books, *The God Nobody Knows*, he takes pains, in one chapter, to list fifty-eight reasons why Jesus cannot possibly be regarded as God. In the course of his argument one gets something as to his own definition of God. He says in the beginning of his argument, "The essential attributes of an existing God and creator and 'upholder of all things' are infinitude, omnipotence, omniscience, omnipresence, and any being not possessing all these attributes to repletion [sic] or possessing any quality or characteristic in the slightest degree incompatible with any one of these attributes cannot be a God in a divine sense, but must of necessity be a frail, fallible, finite being." [39] Then follow declarations, based mainly upon the scriptures that Jesus in no sense can claim these particular attributes, that indeed he disclaims them on many occasions, and hence cannot be God.

But to say that he rejects the dogmatic assertion of orthodox Christianity with reference to Jesus, does not mean that he makes no use of Jesus in his teaching. On the other hand, he does, over and over again, use Jesus as an example of one who knew the power of God and was able to apply it in practical ways to the meeting of human needs. Jesus, he asserts, has been completely misunderstood by the Christian church and the real value of His ministry, which was that of showing the illimitable possibilities that lie in the knowledge and use of the power of the Almighty, has been obscured. Jesus was able to heal because he knew the power of Almighty God and dared to use it. Likewise, he was able to perform miracles which, by the way, do not in the least trouble Frank B. Robinson, because he tells stories of his own ability to do unusual things which run quite beyond the power of ordinary mortals to perform, save through the power of Almighty God. It is the contention of Psychiana that all the power that was available to Jesus is equally

[39] *Id.*, pp. 172–173.

available to men here and now who know and understand the nature and the power of Almighty God. The church, he asserts, over and over again, in its religion built about Jesus, has obscured the real truth which Jesus illustrates in His own Life, and in so doing has obscured man's vision of God rather than clarified it. It is his further contention that the church can only be redeemed and made to serve the purposes of God when it is willing to relinquish the mass of what he calls superstition and magic, with which it has surrounded God and Jesus, and learns the simple truth of the availability and power of Almighty God for present purposes. Jesus, then, is only a man, or put it, a great and good man, and is not central to man's chief quest which is to know the power of Almighty God. The author has discovered nowhere in Dr. Robinson's writings evidence that the nature and character of God are to be defined in terms of Jesus, as is the universal belief of Christian people. Possibly it has been overlooked, but if it is in his writings, it is of very minor importance.

Of his own personal regard for Jesus as a man, he often writes. "I have learned to love this Galilean character". . . "this much misunderstood carpenter man and myself have become pals, as it were, sometimes in the stress of a busy life, I weaken just a little . . . in such moments, however, I remember his superb strength in the face of all obstacles and, revived with the power this man of Galilee knew so well, the weakness is always turned into overwhelming strength. . . ." [40]

Concerning the church's teaching as to salvation, he has, of course, violently opposed it. He oversimplifies the conservative statement of the doctrine of Christian salvation and makes it appear ludicrous. He apparently wholly ignores the fact that wide reaches of the Christian world hold a very different concept of salvation. Nowhere does he recognize what moderately intelligent, liberal Christians would define as salvation. Taking the doctrine in the oversimplified form in which he represents it, he proceeds to laugh it out of court. He does not himself define salvation in so many words. But it appears from his writings that salvation, for him, means the achievement of a relationship to or an understanding of the nature of God, which renders the power of God freely available to the individual man for his own uses. Salvation certainly does

[40] *Psychiana*, Lesson 13, p. 5.

not mean for Robinson salvation in another world. Indeed, in repeated instances, he states definitely his own agnosticism with reference to any life beyond the present, though he does not deny that such may be a fact. His insistence is constant that man's great concern must be with the here and now. His persistent quarrel with the churches is their promise of something to come hereafter, in another life, but not available now. His contention is that all the power of Almighty God is available to everyone here and now and that means the achievement of the consciousness of this available power and its use for whatever the individual himself may need.

In the advertisements which attract followers to Psychiana this is the point of major emphasis. "You do not have to believe in a 'Crucified God.' You do not have to wait until after you have died. You can have what you need now through the power of Almighty God." Nor does he limit need to the realm of the moral and spiritual. If you need health, health can be had *now*. If you need a job, it can be had now. If you need money, money can be had. Anything you need, whatever it may be, is possible through the power of Almighty God.

There is apparently no limit to what one may secure through this power. Dr. Robinson even speaks at times as though death itself could be overcome through the power of Almighty God. Certainly the most deadly of diseases are amenable to cure through this means. He tells of numerous cases of malignant cancer, and of deep infections that have been almost instantly healed through the power of Almighty God. It is undoubtedly this practical aspect which makes a major appeal to the followers of Psychiana. Men feel themselves helpless and impotent in adversity, and in the face of illness insufficient to carry on under the various stresses which life brings them. They see his advertisement in the papers, "I Talked With God," and then the description of what followed thereafter. Here appears to be a way out of their difficulties, and they write for further information concerning this supposedly powerful new faith. Concerning the techniques of achieving these ends we shall speak later. There remains yet one aspect of his teaching which calls for some detailed discussion, namely, what of its moral value?

It is probably at this point that the greatest objection is likely to be raised to the teaching of Psychiana. If just any need can be met, does not that open the way to selfishness which is the antithesis of the Christian ideal? May not one seek to attain through the power of God things that will be dangerous or harmful? Then what moral content is there in Dr. Robinson's teaching? Does it hold up a moral ideal? Does it tend to make people seek after the good?

In the many writings of Dr. Robinson which the writer has examined in an attempt to understand his system, he has followed the custom of marking the passages bearing on what appeared to be the crucial questions raised by his teaching. One that he has kept constantly in mind in reading was the matter of moral teaching. It must be said by way of summary that there is strikingly little in what he has written that bears directly on the moral question. Certain questions do seem to emerge, for instance, in Dr. Robinson's *Autobiography*, as to the moral discrimination shown in his writing. One recalls his report of little shady practices carried out while employed in business that one of genuinely sensitive conscience would have been likely to omit or offer some apology for. To be sure, he holds his employers, who were sometimes Christian men, up to censure or ridicule because of the moral failings which they exhibited, while at the same time serving as officials in the local church. But while some slight suggestions of this sort appear, apparently the heart of his moral philosophy is to be found in such a statement as the following: "This world is so sodden with materialism, whiskey, sex satisfaction, that very few seem to want to find God in them or anywhere else." [41] Or again, "All I ask you to do is to keep on with these studies, do faithfully what I ask you to do and then, behold, the glory and the Power of the spirit of God will baptize you with moral and spiritual power." [42] And then this strange statement, quoted, apparently, approvingly, by Dr. Robinson from the words of another person to whom had come the consciousness of what God really is. "I used to be afraid to do something that was wrong, but now I am never afraid because I know that if I want to do a thing, it is right." [43] Something of this same philosophy is implied in the following: "Well, Dr. Robinson, is there not a chance of your falling away and getting back into the world again?" "I have never left the world and I have nothing to fall away from. I can go out and get drunk tonight if I want to and there is nothing that can stop me. I don't want to, but if I did, that is exactly what I would do, for when a man knows the God consciousness in him,

[41] F. B. Robinson, *Your God Power*, p. 80.
[42] *Id.*, p. 91.   [43] *Id.*, p. 138.

he still is the same free will agency he was before. But I have yet to see the man or the woman who ever really knew God, who ever left God." [44]

Perhaps the most explicit statement involving moral teaching is as follows: "But when America awakens to the fact that the power of the spirit of God is available with all its mighty power to all, here and now, believe me, this world will change completely. Wars will cease, illness and death will be no more, for the life-giving power of the spirit of God is more powerful than the phenomenon we call death. There will be no more tears, no more sorrow, no more suspicion of the other fellow, no more crime, no more immorality, no more whiskey and brothels, no more sex-mad young men and women, no more cigarette smoking, bridge playing, whiskey drinking, dog-loving, church members, for the sham of present day religion will be cast off, and in its place will come the power of Almighty God." [45]

In lesson three of the already quoted Psychiana series there appears a certain amount of moral exhortation. "Be absolutely on the level with yourself and with your fellow men and women. Downright crookedness will invariably defeat the law and there is no need for it in the first place. So as a matter of business alone, if for no other reason, be on the level with everyone for your own good. Every wrong deed brings its own reward and may hinder the workings of the God Law. When you know this mighty Law better, automatically you will never bother your head with anything that does not comply with the God Law. I am not preaching now, for I quit preaching a long time ago. I am merely telling you that you will get along faster playing the game on the square with everybody." [46]

"Live a clean life. Be absolutely on the level with everyone and if there is anything that needs cleaning up in your life, get it cleaned up. You will find the God Law works more effectively when the thoughts are undiluted and free than it can be if these thoughts are not that way." [47] "Unbelief or doubt of God is the only sin there is in the universe." [48] "While this unseen God-power can and will bring you the necessary material joys of life, it also can bring the

[44] *Id.*, p. 212.
[45] Robinson, *Your God Power*, p. 332.
[46] Robinson, Lesson 3, p. 16.
[47] Robinson, Lesson 5, p. 14.
[48] Robinson, Lesson 9, p. 7.

many spiritual joys. It can and does bring to the one knowing it the finest and highest and noblest impulses possible. It lifts one out of all moral wrong. It cleans up a dirty life. It makes the one intent and desire of life for a fuller and more complete knowledge of the great God-Law itself. It has no time for rottenness. In fact, the one knowing the God-Law to the full will not commit very much rottenness—Man motivated by the spirit of the living God never will do them. He is too big a man in the first place and he knows it is a violation of the Spiritual Law in the second place." [49]

By way of summary then, it appears that there is not much that can be called specifically moral teaching in the writings of Dr. Robinson. His assumption is that when one possesses the God Law or consciousness, mortality takes care of itself. One does not want to do evil, though perfectly free to do so. In personal conversation with Frank B. Robinson, the author brought up the matter of his moral teaching, and to his assertion that the knowledge of God was all that was required, asked," But what of the nature of God? Does it not make a tremendous difference in the moral outcome of such knowledge itself whether the character of God is moral or not?" The impression he got from the conversation was that Dr. Robinson was assuming, without being conscious of it, the Christian ethical content in the character of God. But that, it was pointed out to him, might need to be made explicit for persons who had not been taught the ethical character of God as seen in Jesus. As a matter of fact, in the ethic which does appear as assumed, yet not explicit, and in the few specific ethical references in his teaching, it is evident that Dr. Robinson himself works under the limitation of a rather narrowly conservative Christian ethic and apparently associates these ideas with God. Save, as it appears indirectly, in his horror of war, and he has a great deal to say about that subject, he does not display much consciousness of the great social evils of our day. So far as can be observed, he revolts against the death and destruction involved in war, but discloses little disposition to analyze the causes of war, or to condemn the narrow selfishness of our economic set-up, which is one of the major causes of modern war. He is, for example, an ardent opponent of the rather mild New Deal ideas with reference to the economic and social order, and during the 1944 campaign, circulated, at his own personal expense, vigorous letters supporting

[49] Robinson, Lesson 15, p. 10.

the rather reactionary Republican candidate. Indeed, the major criticism that the socially minded religious liberal would bring to bear upon his movement would be on the score of its rather narrowly individualistic concept of what is good and right and the failure to recognize one of the primary teachings of Jesus, namely that of humility and the giving of self for the good of others.

Dr. Robinson is exceedingly generous as an individual. He can always be counted upon for a substantial contribution to any good cause, and he does much in a personal way for the relief of human distress. He is civic minded. He has made a gift of an attractive park to the public, known as Robinson Park. But until quite recently his movement has undertaken no social expression. Its first such expression, so far as is known to the writer, was the founding of a Youth Center in Moscow at a cost of $16,000. In a personal letter of January, 1946, Dr. Robinson stated that in its first three months it had paid a membership of five hundred young people.

Concerning Dr. Robinson's attitude toward, and use of the Bible, little need be said. He does not believe it in any sense to be the inspired word of God, as held by orthodox Christians. It is full of myths and legends, utterly unscientific and not trustworthy even as a guide to a knowledge of God. Indeed, as used by the church, it has continually led men astray or obscured the truth about God. He quotes from it now and again, showing some familiarity with the text of scripture, but not nearly so frequently as Unity or the New Thought groups in general. For years he circulated through his organization two volumes purporting to prove conclusively the falsity of the Christian and Jewish claims for the Bible.[50]

As to the claim that the church is a divinely instituted organization, he is completely unconvinced. As already stated, he can find nothing good in the church, and looks upon it and its ministry as one of the chief obstacles to the discovery by men of the true nature of God. Rather than help men to God, they obscure Him and mislead earnest seekers after knowledge. It is the supreme business of the church and the ministry to make God real. They have failed and are failing according to Robinson. "If the churches would only make God real to men," he said to the writer, "I, (meaning Psychiana) wouldn't last over night." We have already found the basis

---

[50] Joseph Wheless, *Is It God's Word*, Psychiana, n.d. Moscow, Idaho, *Id.*, *Forgery In Christianity*, n.d. Moscow, Idaho.

for this attitude in his childhood and subsequent unhappy experiences with the church and the ministry.

This attitude to the church, so constantly reiterated finds a ready hearing among many who write to him, for they, too, have often enough had some unfortunate experience with the church. But it also repels not a few, as the writer has discovered in a check up on some of those who have purchased his lessons, but have been alienated almost at the beginning by his bitter attacks upon the church, and have failed to go further in their study of his system.

It is basic to the philosophy of Dr. Robinson that the "Unseen or the Spiritual Realm is the Real and Permanent Realm from which all material things must come." Man and woman were first of all spiritual beings, having no such thing as a physical body at all—either that or they possessed a physical body and were not conscious of it, which means the same thing. He proves this by citing the Genesis story that man and woman were naked and knew it not. That is, they were utterly unconscious of their physical bodies. "The fact of the matter is," he says, "that the first created couple, as this mighty Life Spirit made them, had no sense of the physical at all." In the story of the fall—it should be stated that he, of course, regards the story as purely mythical—God told them of one thing which they must not do, "that if they did so Inevitable Death must follow." Then came the snake—"it might just as well have been a porcupine," he says. It said: "Did God say that you would die? Well, that is not so, don't worry about that, you will not die." Rather their eyes would be opened. "But instead of bringing life to them, it brought death. Now note carefully: this death is what we call life today."

"Had the man and woman said to the snake, 'Oh, yes, we will die—God said so,' I would not be here writing this to you, neither would you be in your room reading it. Neither would there be a single solitary thing in the universe contrary to the great immutable God, not excepting the earth itself. Had there been no disobedience on the part of the first couple, there would be nothing physical in the entire creation. Right here is the actual deed that brought upon this earth all the misery, poverty and death that it has ever seen, that the man and woman believed the snake in preference to believing God." Hence his statement, elsewhere quoted, that "Sin is unbelief." "Prior to their disobedience there was no such thing as physical consciousness. That came when their eyes were opened.

When the same eyes are closed that were opened in the garden, then and then only, can man be what he was before the fall. This Jesus came to do, as we will see later." [51]

IV

When the needy individual in search of health, wealth or happiness has seen the advertisement from Moscow and has subscribed for the series of lessons, what does he have to do to achieve the desired results? What are the techniques through which Psychiana works? I have already said that in general Psychiana fits into the general New Thought pattern. This, not alone in what it offers to do, but also to a certain extent in its techniques. The underlying theory is that Power, or the Power that one needs, to effect the desired ends, is available if only one knows how to release it. Power is God, or the God-Law, or the Creative Spirit. The individual does not know this power. It is the prophet's function to acquaint him with it. This is done first of all by a rather carefully worked out set of lessons, starting simply and advancing step by step more deeply into the matter. There is an intellectual content of teaching which is contained in the lessons, and which the student is supposed to master week by week, studying each one thoroughly before the receipt of the next one, for they come to him at two-week intervals.

A notable feature of the lessons, and not of the lessons alone but of all of the books which the founder has published, is that of awakening, through the power of suggestion, a lively sense of expectancy in the student. For example, inserted in each one of the lesson pamphlets is a yellow sheet with a short message upon it. The one which accompanies Lesson I begins, "You are about to begin a journey, a wonderful adventurous journey." Early in the first lesson occurs the phrase, "This course of instruction is entirely different from anything ever put in print before." [52] Again, in the second lesson, "In this second lesson you will find the first faint glimpse of the Power of the God-Law. You will, at this point, begin to see something of the immense possibilities lying in your own hands. You will see that the Power involved in your life success

---

[51] Lesson 8, p. 1, and 8-9 *passim.*
[52] Lesson I, p. 4.

and happiness comes from the unseen or Spiritual Realm. You will also instantly recognize the logic of what I am showing you." [53] And a little later in the same lesson, "There is coming to you, as you read this, renewed hope as you begin to faintly grasp the staggering possibilities which are yours, as you realize that it is possible for you to instantly contact this mighty God-Law as it is. There is also coming to you now the impression that I know how to lead you right and you have mentally said to yourself, 'This fellow knows what he is talking about.' " [54] Once more, in lesson three, "You will find this one of the most interesting and enlightening lessons of the whole course. It is also one of the most important of them all." This statement appears in several of the lessons.

But in addition to the content of the teaching there is a very definite but rather simple method to be used by the student, and it is carefully stated in each lesson just what one is supposed to do. The first thing one must do is to relax. There should be a special time for the appropriate exercises. This might be in the morning, during the day or at night, but should be regularly kept. In the very beginning of the period one must seek complete relaxation. The relaxation is helped by deep breathing which he explains does not have any effect upon the Spiritual Realm, but does have a "mighty good effect on your physical body and as you are going to enjoy increased life with its blessings from now on, it will do no harm for you to keep your physical body in good shape. If you want to make it a habit to breathe slowly and deeply, filling your lungs to their utmost capacity without straining, and then slowly exhaling, it will be a mighty fine thing." [55]

No particular posture is called for. One may "rest in an easy chair, or lie on the bed or on the davenport." "There need be no unnatural straining of any kind, but give your body a chance to rest." Then, breathing deeply, "close the eyes and repeat as many times as you care to, slowly and very quietly the following sentence: 'I believe in the power of the living God.' This should be repeated slowly as many as thirty or a hundred times, then, 'get on your feet and, standing erect if feasible, say the same sentences three or four times aloud if there is no one around.' " In other unoccupied moments of the day it is to be repeated mentally as many times as

[53] *Psychiana*, Lesson II, p. 2.
[54] *Id.*, Lesson II, p. 9.
[55] *Id.*, Lesson I, p. 11.

possible. "The more times you repeat it the more definite the results I am after will be." [56]

Subsequent lessons go more into detail. An unusually favorable time to relax is in bed. "Lie as limp as a rag, close your eyes. There always is in every man's closed eyes a certain area which, when you learn how to find it, is the very thin veil between you and the God-Law of the Universe." This he speaks of as the "bright spot," or "white spot." "There is nothing mysterious about this at all, nothing mystic, nothing supernatural, it is perfectly natural. In fact one of the most natural things I know of is for a man to begin to realize that the Living God-Law is an actual thing which can be contacted here and now by every normal man and woman." [57] When the white spot appears, the student should direct into the very "depths of his mentality and right into the white spot," a new affirmation which goes beyond the earlier one, "I am finding the Power of the Living God." You need not know it, but there is a scientific reason for all this, and throughout the course, Dr. Robinson tries to explain just what the scientific reasons are. He does not appeal through the mysterious or the supernatural. Everything is natural. In this he differs from many of the religionists of the day. One may not be satisfied with his explanation, but at least his intent seems clear. "A thought," he says, "is part of the creative God-Law, and you yourself are now using this mighty God-Law for the first time in your life." [58] Meanwhile you must "keep all negative thoughts out of your head by keeping it filled with this thought. Do you see what I am doing now? I don't want you ever to let one single thought of failure, ill health, or poverty enter your head. Never mind how poor you are, how unhappy, how big a failure you are, keep this one thought in your mind to the exclusion of all other thoughts for the next two weeks." [59]

Here if nowhere else may be seen the typical New Thought influence, the power of thought, the necessity of affirmation, the necessity of excluding the negative thoughts, since thought tends to express itself concretely.

From the fifth lesson on no specific affirmations are required, rather, one is to use whatever affirmation best fits his case. Typical affirmations are suggested by way of illustration. If it is success

[56] Lesson I, p. 11.   [57] Lesson II, p. 8.   [58] Lesson II, p. 9.
[59] Lesson II, p. 9.

that is desired one might affirm, "I am more and more successful";
if it is health that is desired, he might affirm, "The living God is
making me whole"; if happiness is sought, he might repeat, "I
am happier-happier-happier." But he is exhorted to keep on affirming.
And affirmations must be made with confidence. "Remember," he
writes, "a wishy-washy system of affirming will get you nothing,
just that. But the grim jaw, the clenched fist, the stiff spine, the solid
back-bone, the determined will, in other words, The Faith, will
bring the answer every time, and it will bring it in the moment
when you least expect it." [60] One should be always expectant. "Look
for the things you are needing to happen. Keep those thoughts
uppermost in your thought realm and realize that your desire and the
actual thing itself are but different ends of the same thing, that your
desire and the actual manifestation of the thing desired, are in the
spiritual realm, both the same thing." [61]

While all abundance resides in the Spiritual Realm it is available
only to those who fulfill certain requirements. "Money does not
drop from the sky into your lap. Health will not immediately manifest itself if you are not in a state of mind to receive it. The conditions necessary for the blessings and gifts from the Spiritual Realm
to manifest are: First, an absolute faith in the existence of the all-
creative intelligence which created you in the first place. Second,
the desire for what you want, impressed into the spiritual realm
with never wavering precision. Third, the ability to follow the
leadings of the Spiritual Realm, from whence these things must
come. If you are a weakling, become strong. The God-Law likes
nothing better than to have you put yourself to the test." [62]

In the twelfth lesson a new note is struck. A new affirmation is
suggested, "a new affirmation of truth for you, and also a very
powerful one." It is, "I thank thee Father that thou hast heard me."
"There is no better way to obtain things from the Spiritual God-Law
than to acknowledge the fact that your needs have been made known
and will be answered and provided." This affirmation, he declares,
is very dynamic. "I have seen more results achieved from this one
affirmation than from any other." [63] This will, of course, be recognized as the affirmation of Jesus on the occasion of the raising of

---

[60] Lesson XI, p. 13.   [61] Lesson IX, p. 10.   [62] Lesson XII, p. 7.
[63] *Id.*, p. 8.

Lazarus. The introduction of the concept of Father in connection with the impersonal God-Law is interesting.

In the fourteenth lesson he advances a step farther. Here the emphasis is not on affirmation but on listening. If relaxation was sought before, let it be still more complete, for nothing less than actual spiritual contact with the power of the mighty Life Spirit is at stake. "Not one single move. Keep absolutely still. Not a strained stillness at all, but an absolute and utter relaxation of every nerve and every muscle. Then forget everything in you, cast it out, and listen. Forget who you are if you can. Forget everything, just lose yourself in the great cosmic consciousness of the universe. Keep wide awake, intently listening. At sometime or other, and before you have been doing this 'waiting on God' exercise very long, there will come a moment in your life, while you are doing this exercise, probably, when it will seem that the whole realm of heaven has been opened up to you. You may want to shout, and if you do, shout. You may want to sing, and if you do, sing. It will fill you with a spiritual peace that you never knew before. It will transform you. It will make you extremely happy." [64]

Then follows a very interesting statement reminding one somewhat of the old "once in grace, always in grace." He says, "Once this flash is recognized you need never fear further about your relationship with the Master-Intelligence behind the universe. Of course, it is possible even after that for you to do things which might break this connection, but the law is that after this consciousness is established you never will do many things you are not supposed to do. You will not commit many of what Christians like to call 'sins.'" "But," he adds, "a good many things which the church would have you believe are sins, are nothing of the kind." [65] What ones he refers to he does not state.

This seems to be the climax of the lesson series. There is no advance beyond it, though repeatedly the student is exhorted to the practice of quietness. One suggestion is that they turn their thoughts toward him as at a stated hour each day, he plays hymns on the pipe organ in the music room of his home in Moscow.

He does not attempt to make it easy. He does not promise quick returns. He says specifically that they may delay long in coming.

[64] Lesson XIV, pp. 8–9.   [65] *Id.*

But if the conditions are met, the results are assured sooner or later. If man is poor, sick, unhappy, a failure, it is because he has not opened, as yet, the channels through which the God-Power can manifest in him plenty, health, happiness or success. The method has, however, been made clear. "The only way the Spirit of God can manifest in your life and bring Life's good things to you is by you actually and literally speaking this Supreme Power into existence. It responds to the Spoken Word. . . . The secret of achievement is in your own hands." [66]

If in the course of the lesson series, the emphasis was largely upon material blessings, he does come at the end to a different emphasis. "The attainment of these things is by no means the assurance of real happiness, real satisfaction or real success in life; for real success in life lies not so much in getting as in giving. Real satisfaction in life lies not so much in material accumulation as it lies in the accumulation of the finer spiritual things of life; and real happiness lies not so much in the amassing of a fortune as it lies in the fact of the conscious realization of one's inseparableness from this vast spiritual God-Realm." [67]

It will have been noted, no doubt, that so far there has been no reference to prayer. What does the founder of Psychiana have to say about prayer, one of the central practices of most of the religions? He will have none of it, at least as he seems to think Christians generally conceive it, namely, as petition. He writes, "No prayer of any kind ever enters into my life, there is no need of it. My knees are never bent at the bedside. That would be idolatry and pagan superstition. I know that the God-Law knows better than I the thing for which I am best suited. I also know that there is absolutely no need for me to beg and implore God to do this for me or that for me. I know a far better way. I know that it is the law of the Spiritual Realm that God has already prepared for me and you whatever we can take. Knowing this either praying or petitioning are quite futile and absolutely unnecessary. I simply depend on the God-Law and the results are sure." [68]

Yet in another paragraph in a later lesson he defines prayer in quite a different manner and, as such, apparently uses it. He says, "Prayer is not asking for anything. Prayer is simply expressing the desire of your heart into the great spiritual realm of the God-Law; and then having faith enough to start the spiritual realm to work,

[66] Lesson XII, p. 9.   [67] Lesson XVIII, p. 3.
[68] Lesson XII, p. 5.

actually bringing to you the things you need. That is prayer. That is the kind of prayer that wins and there is no other kind of prayer." [69] Were he more familiar with the literature on prayer, he might recognize in his "listening exercise" the elements of the prayer of communion, and in his affirmation, "I thank thee, Father, that thou hast heard me," the prayer of thanksgiving.

One other statement, this time bearing on the moral aspect of man's approach to God. He declares, "Nor is prayer necessary to contact this marvelously potent power, nor is repentance, nor is salvation. It is as free as the air we breathe." [70] It is precisely this lack of moral sensitiveness of the individual in the presence of God that will seem to many Christians the chief weakness of Robinson's teachings. For to the Christian, God is not alone power. He is also goodness, and in the presence of moral perfection there is always a sense of moral unworthiness, or at least humility. We have seen in another place that the moral note is not altogether lacking in his teachings though it is more implicit than explicit, but here, by his specific utterance, he seems to make the moral character of the student in his approach to the Spiritual God-Realm a matter of indifference.

V

Who are attracted by the movement? According to statements by Dr. Robinson about equal numbers of men and women subscribe to the lessons. "Their average age is from forty to sixty years. Seventy-nine percent of them are 'white collar' people in the $3,000 a year class. Not lunatics as one monthly publication called them." [71] For years, he told the writer, he kept account of the church affiliation of subscribers, though he no longer does so. He found that 73% of them came from some church or other, and that of these, 50% were Roman Catholics. Do they continue their relationship to the church? he was asked. He was of the opinion that most of them dropped out. "Generally after being with me," he said, "they just don't go to church." This seemed to be particularly true of the Roman Catholics, he thought. [72] He declared that the largest percentage of his followers were of more than average mentality.

All of the above statements are from the founder himself. It is

---

[69] Lesson XVI, p. 8.   [70] Lesson XI, p. 13.
[71] *The Strange Autobiography of Frank B. Robinson*, p. 208.
[72] On another occasion and in public he declared in answer to a question that about 90% of the people retained their church membership. Of course they might do this, but not go to church.

difficult to get a fair objective picture of the movement as a whole. He seemed quite willing to have any check made upon them that would get at the facts. For example, he gave the writer the names and addresses of all his subscribers in a given city, with full permission to follow up by interview or correspondence, and find out anything possible concerning them. Of the list given just about half and half were men and women, thus confirming his estimate of the relative proportions of each. All of those with whom contact was established were or had been members of some church or other. Only one was of Roman Catholic background, but then the city was predominantly Protestant, and not even half of the list responded to letters from the writer. Almost all of those interviewed would fall within the age group he indicated as average.

Reactions were both positive and negative. Since the number involved is too small to be significant, no fair basis for an evaluation of the movement as a whole is afforded by the check, but some interesting light is thrown on the question as to why people seek Dr. Robinson's help. A few brief excerpts from specific case studies will be of interest to the reader.

Miss A, a woman well past middle age, reports that after many years as a home missionary of one of the great denominations, she became greatly troubled by her health and other circumstances, and seemed to find her customary religious resources insufficient to meet her need. Just at that time she saw Dr. Robinson's advertisement, "I Talked With God," and it occurred to her that here might be found the help she so greatly needed. So she subscribed for the lessons. Her first reaction was favorable, but as she got further into the lessons and came upon his bitter denunciation of the church, she began to change her mind. Her whole experience with the church and with the ministry had been so different from that of Frank B. Robinson that she found herself very seriously disagreeing with him and, indeed, soon found such a barrier raised in her own mind against his teaching that she discontinued the lessons. Asked if she found any benefits from the techniques of relaxation and affirmation, she said she had not. She does not understand how he could be of any help to anyone who cherishes regard for church. She herself has never deviated from her loyalty to the church.

Mrs. B, a well-to-do woman, member of the Episcopal church, had lost her son in the war. She was terribly grief stricken, for the son had been very close to her. She wanted comfort. She felt she couldn't confide in anyone. Just at this time she saw one of Robinson's ads, and thought that here she might find help. She worked through the full twenty lessons, and did find help. She sent for another of his books, but in it she said he expressed no belief in the after life, and she was disappointed in him. She continued in active fellowship with the Episcopal church. When the writer thanked her for the interview and said that he would not quote her by name in anything she had said, she replied, "Use my name if you wish. I am perfectly willing to let anyone know that the lessons helped me."

Mr. C, a lawyer, wrote: I have received your letter concerning Psychiana. As my reaction to it was thoroughly unfavorable, I do not wish to discuss it. I hope you will consider this reply to your request final.

Miss D, a colored woman of about fifty years of age, a practising chiropodist, said that about a year before she had been "feeling rather low" when she received a nice letter from Dr. Robinson, evidently a direct mail approach, so she sent for his lessons. "Did they help you?"

"Yes, indeed," she replied. "I found them very helpful."

"Were you ill?" she was asked.

"No, I wasn't sick but they made me feel much better." She didn't say in what way.

"What was your church background?"

"Episcopalian."

"Are you still one?"

"I sure am. Nothing is going to take me out of the church."

"But Dr. Robinson is quite anti-church in his attitude."

"Yes, I know, but I don't pay any attention to that. He helps me just the same. I just take what helps me. I don't bother about the rest." It appeared that she felt the same way about his hostility to the "crucified God" idea. She doesn't let it bother her. She disclosed that she also sometimes goes to the Christian Science church. "I go around to all of them but I'm Episcopalian and that's what I am always going to remain." She is a great admirer of Dr. Robinson. She has his picture and several of his other books. She sometimes sits quietly at the evening hour when he is playing the organ in his home. When told that Dr. Robinson had recently been in the city she was quite excited. "Why didn't he come to see me?" she cried. "But then I suppose he has so many he couldn't do that." She has already been instrumental in getting some of her patients to send in for the lessons and she talks about it with them. She practices the habit of relaxation before going to sleep every night.

Mrs. E wrote: "I beg to be excused from any discussion of the so-called Psychiana, as I am in no way interested, and my only thought is that it is nothing but a money-making scheme, pure and simple. I could find nothing in the lessons except a repetition of words, not even very grammatically strung together, and cancelled the subscription, as I was convinced it was just a fake, and money was too scarce with me to afford such waste. It certainly bore little resemblance to what could be called religion, and as I am first, last, and always an Episcopalian, I shun such fakes. It had sounded as if there might be something worth while about it, but when I got the so-called lessons, I found out that it was just another cult. I do not wish to discuss the matter at *any* time."

Mrs. F, a women of possibly fifty years of age, evidently in very comfortable circumstances, had studied Psychiana in one of the first years of its appearance. She had been born a Roman Catholic, and as a girl had been very religious. She used to be greatly worried about whether in confession she had forgotten anything and would suffer for it. She used to take as much as forty minutes in confession and then waken in the night, fearful that she had omitted something.

Finally, she suddenly made up her mind that if she were going to hell for some minor oversight, she might as well go to hell for the whole thing, so she gave up her Catholic faith. After about a year she suddenly wondered how she could ever have believed the things she did, but she was still hungry for God. This quest led into many paths, one of them Psychiana. "I was seeking God," she said, "when one day I saw his ad, 'I Talked With God,' in a periodical and I thought he might help me, so I secured the lessons."

"Did they help you?"

"Yes, they showed me some things for which I am grateful, but I have found so much greater satisfaction from other systems that I never followed Psychiana beyond the first set of lessons."

"Did you follow his techniques?"

"Yes," she replied, "I found them much like Mr. Coué. I am French, you know."

She did not get to the point where she saw the 'white spot,' but she did get to hear voices. She regards Dr. Robinson as not very deep —helpful to some people, but lacking in the ability to lead into the deeper experience of God. She has at various times tried not only

Psychiana, but the I Am, Ontology, a branch of New Thought, Theosophy, and has had some contact with Christian Science and Spiritualism. She believes in the Masters or Adepts of Theosophy. When told that Dr. Robinson had claimed to be an Adept or Master, she shook her head. "If he were, he wouldn't proclaim it." A real Master never does, she thinks. She does not find satisfaction in the church. She does not get there a sense of the reality of God. This she gets most satisfactorily from meditation. She uses affirmations and says that she has had some truly wonderful experiences. Once during the interview she made a remark that was probably a genuine bit of self-revelation, "I guess I'm an escapist."

Mrs. F wrote: "I studied this form of religion for about three months only and never practiced it, finding Dr. Robinson's tenets unconvincing. The only thing I remember about the course at all is that with each lesson a number of leaflets were enclosed in pink, yellow and blue, announcing a new book written by the doctor, promising the fulfillment of all one's desires, material and spiritual, if purchased and studied diligently. These books all seem to emit from the pen of Dr. Robinson on a mass production basis."

Mr. G wrote: "I did not finish the course. Statements were made in the lessons that did not harmonize with the Bible so I gave it up."

Miss H was an attractive woman of some thirty-five years of age, holding an important position in the business world. She had grown up in a "hard-shelled Baptist" family. She was teaching in the Sunday School when she came to the conclusion that she couldn't go on teaching the faith of her parents. It was a serious break. Later she attended a Methodist church, but didn't find it very different. The minister couldn't answer her questions. She would find out the answers in heaven, she was told, if she were good, and managed to get there.

She was hungry for God. She tried various things. Spiritualism attracted her. She was told that she was psychic. She sometimes hears her name called clearly. She says she hasn't quite the nerve to follow it up and experiment with it. She has some remarkable premonitions, but seems definitely not to want to follow Spiritualism. Then one day she saw the Dingle system advertised. She bought the lessons and went through most of the set. She got real help, especially from the breathing exercises. She found peace and contentment. But evidently she was not completely satisfied, for seeing the "I Talked With God" ad, she sent for the lessons and worked through them.

At first she said she thought it was silly to read the lessons over and over again, as advised by Dr. Robinson. But when she did it, she found there was a reason, for presently the things she was told she would experience, she did begin to experience. So she completed the twenty lessons and found them exceedingly helpful. Once she was healed. She had had a bad fall. Going home at night her back was very sore. She bathed it in hot water and massaged it. It was still painful. As she retired, she made use of an affirmation of health. She said that it seemed almost as though under the cover there were electric light bulbs. Next day she had not the slightest trace of soreness. She found that the practice of the system brought her peace. She was able to control her temper, she said, and that was not easy. She had no difficulty in getting the 'white spot.' Indeed she had had that before ever studying with either Dingle or Dr. Robinson.

Now she is studying Unity and Rosicrucian literature and finds them interesting. She does not attend church anywhere. She apparently does not miss what many find in corporate worship.

Thus the reactions to Psychiana are both positive and negative. The balancing of favorable and unfavorable reactions here observed is no index to the general reactions of the multiplied thousands that subscribe to the lessons. There is no way of getting at the facts. The writer was given the privilege of reading, and copying, such as he might wish to, a sheaf of over a hundred letters that had come in about the time he visited Moscow. To what extent they were a selected lot he cannot say. The fact that they were all favorable, to at least some degree, is probable evidence that they were. But it is also probable that those who were dissatisfied with the lessons would simply cease to send in their bi-weekly installment, without necessarily writing out what they thought of the lessons. Dr. Robinson specifically states on all the application blanks that the money for the course will be refunded if the purchaser is not satisfied. Now and then someone requests a refund, but the number who do so is negligible, he reports. On the other hand he stated that the collections on the lessons and book orders runs to only about 75%. This, however, he says, is higher than the average on installment mail order collections.

If this reported loss seems high, it is only fair to ask what percent of those who join the churches remain faithful, particularly to the financial obligation which they assume in their membership vows. (At least in some churches, if not all, there is included the promise to support the church and, if not explicit, it is the commonly expected thing.)

That many people get help of many kinds through Psychiana is beyond doubt. The gratitude expressed in many of the letters is nothing short of pathetic. They come from all sorts of people. Only a few can here be quoted, and without name or address, but the writer guarantees that he has seen the original letters, a great many of them written by hand, with date, address and personal signature. He has not checked them for accuracy, but they bear on their very face the mark of genuineness. The writers may not have known what was the matter with them. They may have been mistaken, in health cases, in the diagnosis of their ills, but that they believe they have been helped, there can be no doubt. And when people believe they have been helped, they have been helped, at least temporarily.

Mrs. H writes: "Thank you a million times for making life worth living."

A letter from Mrs. S says, in part: "When I joined you I was surely discouraged. Seemed there was nothing left for me but despair. After I got my first lesson, I began to take a new lease on life. Now I have a swell job and am planning the much desired home very soon. I would not exchange my Psychiana lessons and work for the world's wealth, and do without them."

Mr. E declares: "After taking only three lessons and following your simple exercises, I am beginning to see things happen. I was able to purchase my wife a new washing machine. Something they said would be impossible. (This was in 1944.) Anyone thinking Psychiana won't work, tell them to write me a line."

Mrs. M writes: "Enclosed please find P.O. order for $100 for which please send me four copies of *Your God Power*. I have been so blessed that I feel I must help others find their God-Power that they too may be blessed."

Mr. P is grateful for material benefits: "I've wanted a little business of my own for a long time, but I never thought I would be able to see my dream come true and *in such a short time*. I am now in partnership with another fellow and we have a nice little business, and besides, I am receiving almost everything I have asked the God-Law for. It's so simple and easy. I am still amazed at the way it works, and from now on I am depending on the law for everything."

Many write of health benefits. One of the constant emphases of Psychiana is on the power of the God-Law to heal. "Do you want health?" appears frequently in his advertising.

Mrs. J writes: "I feel a considerable change in life, both in health and happiness, and also a slight change in material success. Before starting these lessons, I felt tired and worn out. No energy to go any place but work and back home, always worrying and afraid something would happen to my children, and life just seemed hopeless. But now all that has left me. I don't fear anything now, and I feel perfectly well, spiritually and physically. I feel nice and fresh when I wake up in the morning. My work goes so much easier and I am not as tired as I used to be at the end of the day."

Miss H had had a very bad throat ailment and could get no relief. Alone and a stranger, she finally wired Dr. Robinson for help. He evidently responded. In a letter a few days later, after apologizing for bothering him, she states: "Within twelve hours the swelling was all gone and in twenty-four hours the soreness was gone." Naturally she was grateful.

Many times a day there come long-distance telephone calls or telegrams or letters asking for specific help in cases of illness. One woman wrote: "My daughter is sick and has been for four years. I want you to help me and ask God to guide the doctor to the trouble so they can cure her, etc." Dr. Robinson's reply is characteristic of his method:

"If your daughter is not well at this time you must keep in mind that there exists in you more of the healing power of the Spirit of God than you will ever be able to use. Your job is to throw this power against the illness or disease, for no disease or illness can withstand this great God-Power. We shall remember your daughter spiritually at this time. Remember that you must have faith in this God-Power. Faith is not something mysterious or something hard to use. Indeed you must have faith in many ways in order to live one day of life. Faith in the God-Power operates in exactly the same way. Your faith in the God-Law should be as natural and easy as eating and drinking, and you may use it NOW."

The writer was one day in Dr. Robinson's office when there came a long-distance call from more than halfway across the continent, asking for help in the case of a serious illness of a member of the family. Dr. Robinson took the receiver. He listened to the story of the illness. "Are you one of my students?" he asked. Apparently the speaker was enrolled. "Then go to your studies and get lesson thirteen on healing and use the techniques described there."

What the voice at the other end of the line said at that point could not be heard, but Dr. Robinson replied: "You can throw out all physical conditions that are unfavorable, for the power that created life is there. All that you need to do is to carry it into action."

Evidently the person speaking had made the attempt to do this, for Robinson said: "In that case you are not getting through to the Realm of God."

"But I have tried," the voice must have said, for Dr. Robinson countered: "I want you to quit trying and just realize the Power of God." After listening to some further remarks from the one calling, he ended the conversation, saying: "At nine o'clock, be thinking about me here in Moscow. I'll send some thought waves your way and see what happens," and hung up the reciever. All in the day's work! He permitted the writer to see dozens of telegraphic requests for help, as well as his replies.

Sometimes, he says, he has requests that he come long distances personally, in order to heal the sick. He says he has been offered as much as $10,000 if he would come. In the earlier days of the movement he did sometimes make such trips but seldom does so now. He never makes any charge for healing, he asserts.

The last case to be cited has a bearing upon the moral effects of the teaching. Just what effect, it is left to the reader to judge.

"My biggest problem for the past fifteen years has been drinking and getting drunk. I tried many times to quit by will power. I was just about at the end of my rope and my wife had almost reached the limit of her endurance when I received your announcement." Another direct mail approach, evidently.

Saturday noon after getting the lessons, "I went home instead of to a honky tonk and lay down for half an hour allowing my mind to dwell on the subject and literally to 'talk to God.' When I got up I felt different than at any time in my life. I went out into the back yard and helped my wife all afternoon cleaning the back yard. I just didn't WANT to drink. I had no desire to drink, but the feeling was different from the times when I didn't drink by using my will power. I seemed calm and was not trying to squelch an almost overpowering upsurge of the desire to drink. My wife does not understand what has 'happened' to me, nor do my former drinking cronies—they probably think I have 'got religion'—I don't know.

I do know that I am happier than I have been and feel as though some heavy weight has been lifted from my mind and heart.

"My lost desire for drinking and getting drunk is not the only benefit I have received from the course. There are literally hundreds of little things that have changed. I am no longer self-conscious, nor do I suffer from an inferiority complex I once had, which may have been the reason for drinking so much. I have no temper tantrums any more and it is hard to get me 'riled up' about anything. I never worry any more if the going gets tough. I get out under the stars and talk it over with God and the problem always works itself out with amazing simplicity. I am still in debt, but I still do the best I can and am doing better than a year ago. Each month I wonder a little just how I am going to get by (I am one of the forgotten 'white collar' workers) but I make it some way, and along this line there have been some unusual things happened to help me for which I have no explanation other than my practice of talking it over with God as you taught me to do." If the story stopped here the moral would be clear, but he continues:

"Let me cite one instance in the latter case. Shortly after starting the course I decided to see if it would help my luck any on a game they have here known as 'policy.' I lay down one evening when all was still and contacted the bright spot of which you spoke. Keeping my mind clear of all thought, I lay inanimate for some time and saw clearly printed on the white spot the numbers 14, 47, 76. The next day I played them and caught $18 for a dime. I played them two or three times since that date, but if I didn't need the money absolutely, they did not come out. I have almost quit playing the game entirely as, for some reason, I have almost the same feeling as not drinking beer, just an intangible feeling telling me it is not worth while. Two or three weeks ago, I was down to my last three or four dollars and still a week to go until pay day. As I always do now when things get tight, I let my thoughts soar 'out of this world' seemingly, and although I was sitting at my desk at the office, the flash came to me to play these same numbers, although it had been months since I had played them. I did. Eighty-four dollars, the maximum, is what I got. With this proof and the changes in my mental, moral and matrimonial life, do you wonder that I am convinced of the truth of your teachings? I would no more consider making an important decision without contacting the God-Power than I would walking down Main Street without my pants. Thanks a million for showing me the way to a better, cleaner, more hopeful way of life than I have ever known."

While healings are frequent, "This has never been a 'healing' movement, and never will so long as I head it," writes Dr. Robinson. "Cancer and other incurable diseases have melted away before the Power of the Great Spirit, God, yet these things, unusual as they are, are but sidelights on the greater work we are doing," [73] which is that of making God real to men. No such theory of illness as found in Christian Science is held. Illness and pain are real, terribly so, but health is the natural state and the Power of the God-Law is sufficient to overcome disease if one will but make the proper contact. There is no hocus-pocus about the manner of healing. He tells of having had a telegram from a student saying that her sister was dying of cancer. Would he come and heal her? He replied that it would be impossible for him to come, and that it was not necessary. She nevertheless wired him. "I will wire you $5,000 if you will come." He replied by wire: "Madam, if you wired me $50,000 I could not come. It will not be necessary for the Spirit of God is not to be bought with money." Two days later, he says, he received a message saying that her sister, dying of cancer two days before, was well.[74]

He asserts that he never publishes a testimonial of a remarkable healing—and he frequently does this in his promotional literature—without first getting a recognized physician in the community to investigate the case, what the illness was, and to what extent the person was really healed. This statement he has in his safe, he declares, before he publishes the testimonial of healing. He frequently makes an offer of $5,000 to anyone who can bring evidence that any of the published testimonials are false.

Thus it appears that many people are helped in many ways. That they might have gotten help from many other sources, including the very churches in which they did not seem to get it, is equally certain. It was in most cases the receipt of a direct mail communication from Dr. Robinson, or the reading of one of his ads, just at the time of their great need, that induced them to make the contact with him which brought them the help they so much needed. The fact that he uses such a variety of periodicals and name lists and match covers and the radio, results in his reaching multitudes of

[73] *The Strange Autobiography of Frank B. Robinson*, p. 207.
[74] *Id.*, p. 69.

people whom the churches would never reach. It is in a sense a new way of "going into the highways and hedges" of the world with his gospel.

Dr. Robinson, as stated before, is in a sense, Psychiana. The years are passing. He is getting older. He has had one very serious attack of coronary thrombosis. He is an indefatigable worker. He works much beyond what any man of his age ought to work. In a recent personal letter, written while on a vacation trip—the first in many years—he asserted that he was in the best of health, able to do as much work in a day as ever. He is a vigorous person, has a splendid physique, but the human frame of the best men wears out.

What will happen when he is no longer able to carry on the movement? Will there be any one capable of taking his place as leader? Recently his son Alfred has become business manager of Psychiana and seems disposed to push it with vigor.

Owing to Dr. Robinson's hitherto definite policy of forming no society, there is no close-knit organization self-conscious of its mission and committed to its continuance and promotion. Thus there seems little likelihood that it will continue permanently unless some change should be introduced into it. This could be done, indeed there appears some tendency to encourage students to get together now, where in an earlier period this was discouraged.

Dr. Robinson has written much. With vigorous promotion an organization could be built upon his teachings after his demise. Even without any organization, it would undoubtedly go on for a time under its own momentum, for at any given moment there are many thousands of subscribers to the lessons who have just begun. And there will continue to be a market for his books for some time to come. But that will run out eventually, unless continuously cultivated. Much depends upon the son, who will undoubtedly succeed his father. He has been too recently brought into a place of importance in the movement to be able to predict with assurance as to what the future may hold for it.

Dr. Robinson has himself been a veritable dynamo of energy, and there is a real vitality in his message. Certainly his unique method of using the mails has brought help to multitudes whom the churches do not touch, and for whom they perform no ministry. Some thoughtful churchmen, while feeling that his treatment of the church is more violent than the facts warrant, have nevertheless been constrained to see, both in his method of propaganda and the techniques he recommends to his students, something which the church and the ministry might well take into account.

But whether it lives or dies it will stand out prominently as a remarkable movement, born just at the end of a period of great prosperity, and drawing to itself, during the great depression and the Second World War, multitudes of those who felt deeply the need for a ministry which for some reason or other they failed to find within the established churches. It stands as symptomatic of that period of confusion, uncertainty, insecurity and fear.

Chapter Three

New Thought

New Thought is a very general term. There is no single organization that can claim the title as its exclusive name. Rather, it represents a general point of view held by a multitude of people, organized into numerous smaller or larger groups which share it, but which differ very widely in many other respects. They are found under many different names. Some names represent but a single local organization, others represent a regional or it may be a nationwide network of local groups who follow some one particular branch of New Thought. Many of these affiliate in what is known as the International New Thought Alliance. A recent book, published in 1944 by the Alliance, *Mind Remakes Your World*,[1] contains articles by thirty-six leaders of New Thought, designed to represent a "true cross-section of the spiritual philosophy and methods for practice which are today being taught by leading teachers, authors and lecturers in the New Thought field." Contributors are indicated as belonging to eighteen different groups as follows:

Church of Truth	Unity Truth Center
Institute of Religious Science	Home of Truth
Unity Church of Truth	Christian Assembly
Divine Science	Church of Advanced Thought
Unity Center	New Thought Temple
Chapel of Truth	Church of the Healing Christ
Center of Religious Education	Metaphysical School of Health
Unity Metaphysical Center	Radiant Life Fellowship
Absolute Science Center	Institute of Man

[1] Dodd, Mead and Co., New York, 1944.

Some of these names may represent only a local church but several of them, such as Divine Science, Home of Truth, Church of the Truth, Institute of Religious Science, and Unity, which no longer belongs to the Alliance, are organizations of considerable size and influence. In the brief dictionary of movements in the Appendix, some of the larger of these are discussed briefly. Others, which really represent the New Thought point of view, do not belong to the International Alliance, for it is a purely voluntary association. We have seen that Psychiana definitely is New Thought in outlook, and I Am has in it not a little that is typical of that viewpoint.[2] Robert Collier, author of *Secret of the Ages*, who seems to have no organization but operates largely through books and lessons, definitely fits the New Thought pattern, as do others who are teaching and writing.

What is the New Thought outlook? In the introduction to the above-mentioned book it is stated: "While there is a wide range of opinions among New Thought leaders, teachers, practitioners and laymen, this one underlying purpose runs through the entire Movement: the immediate availability of God; conscious and practical application of spiritual thought force to the solution of human problems; the inevitability that good shall come to every soul; the belief in immortality and the continuity of the individual stream of consciousness and the external expansion of the individual life; the awakening not to an absorption of man's identity in Deity but to his complete unity with the Whole. Thus every man becomes an individualized center of God Consciousness, eternally expanding."

While this is doubtless true of that body of New Thought followers who join together in the International Alliance, it would not be true of all those who are spiritual descendants of the original New Thought impulse, but who have developed along more secular lines and would probably dissent from some of the more theological phrases in the statement. They would not, many of them, necessarily believe in "the inevitability that good shall come to every human soul," or in immortality, or that a man is "an individualized center of God Consciousness, eternally expanding."

But our interest in this book is the religious, not the secularized "success" group, and we may well accept the statement as representative of that phase of it. Certainly, there could be no more

2 See pp. 97–98.

authoritative statement made than that coming from a committee representative of the International Alliance.

This New Thought movement which, it is estimated by the compilers of the book, influences fifteen to twenty million people in America (p. xii) and of which it is reported that William James once said, "together with Christian Science, it constitutes a spiritual movement as significant for our day as the Reformation was for its time",[3] had its beginning in New England about the middle of the nineteenth century. While it may be traced to a particular individual as its founder, it was, as a matter of fact, the logical outcome of a movement of thought or perhaps better an intellectual climate which partly produced, and was partly produced, by a galaxy of influential thinkers which included William Ellery Channing, Theodore Parker, Ralph Waldo Emerson, Thoreau, Bronson Alcott, and others of lesser stature but like mind. By many Emerson is regarded as the real spiritual father of New Thought.

Not that these men all believed alike. They did not, but they had some things in common. They all, in one way or another, refused to be bound by tradition. The older orthodoxy could not hold them. They were all in rebellion against the current Calvinism which had so long ruled New England religious thought. They were not afraid of innovation. They were hospitable to new ideas. Due to their preaching and writing and teaching a new spirit of freedom was in the air, making it easy for a new movement to attract thoughtful minds.

They were alike, too, in their confidence in the powers of man himself, that went beyond that of the older theology, which believed in his depravity and his incapacity, unaided, to do much for himself or his own salvation. They had great respect for the human mind, a profound conviction that a man's mind was meant to be used, and they claimed the freedom to use it. This was a potent factor in the breakdown of the authority of religion which was characteristic of the New England of that period. It was this recognition of mind and its central place in the world that became the core of New Thought teaching.

This growing freedom and liberality of thought opened men's minds to appreciation of the values in other cultures than their own. The west was becoming conscious of the thought of the Orient.

[3] J. R. Mosely, *Manifest Victory*, Harper and Brothers, New York, 1941, p. 38.

Translations of oriental sacred literature and philosophy were being made and circulated in the west. Emerson particularly fell under its influence. His whole outlook was affected by it, and through him the thought of the period was colored; but so also were Thoreau, Bronson Alcott, and other teachers, preachers and writers of the day. The high immanentism, or near pantheism of Emerson and of the whole Transcendentalist school, owed not a little to oriental thought. This tended to obscure the sharp distinction between God and man, and man came to be regarded as divine himself or, if not wholly divine, possessed of a degree or spark of divinity. In this lies one of the major roots of the New Thought movement.

If any one person may be said to have been the founder of the movement it was Phineas P. Quimby of Portland, Maine. As a mental healer whose reputation spread far beyond the city in which he practiced, he was sought out by a Mrs. Patterson, later to be known as Mary Baker Eddy, then suffering from a chronic spinal affliction, and she was healed by him. Out of this experience eventually came Christian Science. The degree to which she was indebted to Quimby was a violently debated question (see pp. 184 ff.) and in the course of it much was said to the discredit of Quimby, his method of healing and the philosophy which underlay it. The very existence of the Quimby Manuscripts, written by him over a period of years, was called in question. But whatever Christian Scientists may say about him and his writings the New Thought people recognize in him and his early reflections, embodied in the now published Quimby Manuscripts, the basis of the beginning of their movement.

Quimby was born in 1802, the son of a blacksmith. He became a clockmaker and worked for many years at his trade. His formal education was meager, but he is said to have been a thoughtful person and to have read in the fields of philosophy and science what was available to him at the time. He became greatly interested in hypnotism, through one Charles Poyen, a French hypnotist who gave a series of lectures in Belfast, Maine, where he was then living, in 1838. Under the tutelage of Poyen, he began himself to practice hypnotism on anyone who would submit himself to the experience. Finding an unusually suggestible subject, one Lucius Burkmar, he traveled about the country giving hypnotism exhibitions. After a time, Quimby returned to his trade and Burkmar associated himself with another hypnotist who used him, under the hypnotic spell, to diagnose the ills of patients who came to him and to prescribe the remedy, which is said, usually, to have been one which his employer manufactured and sold, doubtless at a nice profit.

This detail, while seemingly unimportant, is however, of real significance. When again Quimby employed Burkmar, he himself experimented in the diagnosis of disease through his hypnotic subject. And here, too, the subject prescribed remedies. Sometimes, however, the remedy suggested would be expensive or difficult to secure. In such cases, Quimby, who had no part in the selling of the remedies, would suggest that he make a simpler, less expensive prescription. The subject did so and the result seemed to be just the same. The patient was cured by one just as readily as by the other. This caused Quimby to reflect that the healing, therefore, lay not in the medicine but in the mind. Here was his first step on the way to mental healing. But he did not end here. The fact that he did at one time employ hypnosis in healing gives some color to the charge, leveled against him by the defenders of Mrs. Eddy's originality in the field, that he healed by "animal magnetism," a charge against which Mrs. Eddy herself, then Mrs. Patterson, vigorously defended him in a newspaper article immediately after her remarkable healing. (*Portland Courier*, November 7, 1862.)

Convinced that the healing process was a mental one, he dispensed with the help of Burkmar and began to experiment with healing through suggestion without resort to hypnotism. He did continue to use some manipulation of the heads of his patients, first dipping his hands in water, but he always said that this was no necessary part of the healing but one designed to establish confidence in the patient. Dakin asserts that Mrs. Eddy continued for some time in her early instruction to teach "this method of establishing a working relationship with ailing patients." [4] (What his source for this statement is he does not say.)

Quimby made no specific charge for his services, rendered no bills, kept no accounts, and ministered mostly to those who were poor or were unable to get help from orthodox physicians. He did not believe, apparently, that any special virtue in himself accomplished the healing, for he is said to have laid it as a requirement upon some of his patients that they teach the secret of their healing to at least two other persons during their lifetime.

[4] Edwin F. Dakin, *Mrs. Eddy*, Charles Scribner's Sons, New York, 1930, p. 50. See also, Bates and Dittemore, *Mary Baker Eddy*, Geo. Routledge and Sons, London, pp. 141–142.

He was a thoughtful individual and given to making notes of his thought from time to time. These notes, eventually assembled and published as the Quimby Manuscripts, form the basis of much in New Thought.

Long before their publication he was in the habit of allowing his patients to read them and even make copies of them. This, it is alleged by some, rightly or wrongly, Mrs. Patterson did, and on the basis of them built her own system. Defenders of Mrs. Eddy's originality, on the other hand, assert that she took some of his fragmentary notes, rewrote or revised them, including in them the results of her own reflection and returned them to him. It is thus that they account for the almost verbal identity that is to be found between some of Quimby's published thought and her own, for example, the section, "recapitulation" which now appears in *Science and Health*, but was at one time circulated in pamphlet form under the title "Science of Man." The other side asserts that she carried away in 1864 a copy of his writings called "Questions and Answers," which for years she made the basis of her instruction, and finally published as the *Science of Man* in 1870.

Certain it is that Mrs. Eddy was the first to publish. The Quimby Manuscripts did not appear until many years later. When they did, however, the various writings were dated and, if the dates are correct, priority in certain of the ideas undoubtedly goes to Quimby. The opposing side casts doubt upon the authenticity of the Manuscripts which were so long locked up in the possession of George Quimby, son of the mental healer.

Quimby was not religious by orthodox standards, but in his writings, if accepted as authentic, there appears a deep religious and philosophic interest. He seems to have thought that he had discovered the method that Jesus and his disciples had used in their healing ministry. He believed that these marvelous cures were wrought not miraculously but by the employment of natural forces and could, therefore, be duplicated in the present. His method, according to his son, George, was "to change the mind of a patient and disabuse it of its error and establish truth in its place, which, if done, was the cure." [5]

In one of his notes he wrote, "Can a theory be found capable of practice which can separate Truth from Error? I undertake to say

[5] Quoted in *Mind Remakes Your World*, p. xii.

there is a method of reasoning which, being understood, can separate
one from the other. Man is made up of truth and belief and if he
is deceived into a belief that he has or is liable to have a disease, the
belief is catching and the effect follows it." Disease being in its root
a wrong belief, change the belief and it will cure the disease. By
faith we are thus made whole.[6]

But he was, says *Mind Remakes Your World*, "completely convinced that the Creative Spirit within us is God and that we have
immediate relationship to the Divine. This relationship is creative." [7]
Some of his notes dealt with such topics as Spiritualism, Religion,
Truth, Error, and one bore the title, "Scientific Interpretation of
Various Parts of the Scriptures." When one of his admirers, who
had been healed by him, declared that Quimby was reproducing "the
wonders of Gospel history, he wrote an essay entitled "A Defense
Against Making Myself Equal with Christ." Sometimes he called his
discovery the Science of Christ, though usually he referred to it as
the "Science of Health." Once, at least, he called it "Christian
Science." [8]

But when in 1866 death claimed Phineas P. Quimby, there was no
movement of any kind to carry on his work. Mrs. Eddy wrote Julius
A. Dresser, suggesting that he was best fitted to do so. But he, at the
time, felt no disposition to assume the responsibility.

It was Warren Felt Evans, a Swedenborgian clergyman who was
healed by Mr. Quimby, who was the first to begin to teach the system and write about it. He wrote two books before Mrs. Eddy
published *Science and Health* in which he stated Quimby's point of
view. This, incidentally, ought to be taken into account in any
complete consideration of the Quimby controversy. In 1869 he
wrote in *The Mental Cure* concerning Quimby's ideas: "Disease being in its root a *wrong belief*, change that belief and we cure the
disease. By faith we were thus made whole. . . . The late Dr.
Quimby of Portland, one of the most successful healers of this or
any age embraced this view of disease and by a long succession of
most remarkable cures proved the truth of the theory and the
efficiency of this method of treatment." [9] Other books by him
were *Mental Medicine*, 1872, *Soul and Body*, 1875, the year *Science*

[6] *Id.*, pp. xii & xiii.
[7] *Id.*, p. xii.
[8] *The Quimby Manuscripts*, p. 249, 2nd ed., p. 131 and p. 388.
[9] Quoted by Dakin, *op. cit.*, p. 108.

and Health appeared, *The Divine Law of Cure,* 1881, *The Primitive Mind Cure,* 1885, and *Esoteric Christianity,* 1886.

Julius Dresser, also healed by Quimby, was an enthusiastic believer in his system but, refusing Mrs. Eddy's suggestion that he take up Quimby's work, went west to California. Returning in 1882 to New England he became an active leader and promoter of Quimby's thought. It was he who engaged in the rather bitter controversey with the Christian Scientists over Quimby's possible influence upon Mrs. Eddy. It was through the Dresser family—the son Horatio became the historian of the New Thought Movement—that the Quimby Manuscripts were finally published.

Evans and Dresser may, therefore, be said to have been the most influential figures in the actual organization of the movement which came to be known as New Thought. But others, several who had belonged to the New Church (Swedenborgian), were also teaching and practicing the Quimby method of healing. Some adhered more strictly to it than others. Each developed it in his own way and gave it the name he desired. Thus there was much New Thought activity and teaching but no general organization.

Dresser points out that in the earlier phase of the movement its emphasis was chiefly on mental healing where indeed it was in Quimby's own practice. But he says: "Interest in mental healing gave the disciples of the New Thought a point of view, a way of approaching all questions, a way of looking at life as a whole; it gave an impetus toward individualism, toward freedom; it implied religious liberalism; it implied idealism as a working or practical philosophy. Hence, the special interest is related with all other interests and we find disciples of New Thought advocating it as an all-inclusive program. If they sometimes made their work too broad and so lacked definiteness, if they sometimes claimed too much for their special interest, it was because their first desire was to gain recognition for their point of view with a sufficient emphasis to achieve results. The devotees were eager to show that New Thought not only stood for a method of healing, but a philosophy, a positive or affirmative idealism; hence, for religion, applied Christianity, the rediscovery of the doctrine of healing." [10]

But the differing groups holding so much in common naturally

[10] Horatio W. Dresser, *History of the New Thought Movement,* Thomas Y. Crowell, New York, 1919, p. 190.

drew together. The first national convention was held in San Francisco in 1894 and others followed, in Chicago, 1895, Kansas City, 1896, and St. Louis, 1897. The first convention held under the name New Thought met in Boston in 1899. A convention under the name International Metaphysical League was held in New York in 1900. In 1903 at Chicago, 1904 in St. Louis and 1905 International New Thought Conventions were held. In 1908 the name was changed to The National New Thought Alliance and in 1914 the present International New Thought Alliance was formed.

The movement had by this time become international in scope with societies in England, on the continent, in South Africa, Australia, South America and elsewhere. In England the usual name for it was The Higher Thought.

In 1916 they adopted a declaration of purpose which has not since been significantly altered. It read: "To teach the infinitude of the Supreme one, the Divinity of Man and his infinite possibilities through the creative power of constructive thinking and obedience to the voice of the Indwelling Presence which is our Source of Inspiration, Power, Health and Prosperity."

In 1917 they adopted at their St. Louis Convention a Declaration of Principles to which the movement still adheres. Since no summary statement could do full justice to it the entire declaration is here included. It bears out the earlier statement offered in the introduction to *Mind Remakes Your World.*

"We affirm the freedom of each soul as to choice and as to belief, and would not, by the adoption of any declaration of principles, limit such freedom. The essence of the New Thought is Truth, and each individual must be loyal to the Truth he sees. The windows of his soul must be kept open at each moment for the higher light, and his mind must be always hospitable to each new inspiration.

"We affirm the Good. This is supreme, universal and everlasting. Man is made in the image of the Good, and evil and pain are but the tests and correctives that appear when his thought does not reflect the full glory of this image.

"We affirm health, which is man's divine inheritance. Man's body is his holy temple. Every function of it, every cell of it, is intelligent, and is shaped, ruled, repaired, and controlled by mind. He whose body is full of light is full of health. Spiritual healing has existed among all races in all times. It has now become a part of the higher science and art of living the life more abundant.

"We affirm the divine supply. He who serves God and man in the full understanding of the law of compensation shall not lack. Within us are unused resources of energy and power. He who lives with his whole being, and thus expresses fullness, shall reap fullness in return. He who gives himself, he who knows and acts in his highest knowledge, he who trusts in the divine return, has learned the law of success.

"We affirm the teaching of Christ that the Kingdom of Heaven is within us, that we are one with the Father, that we should not judge, that we should love one another, that we should heal the sick, that we should return good for evil, that we should minister to others, and that we should be perfect even as our Father in Heaven is perfect. These are not only ideals, but practical, everyday working principles.

"We affirm the new thought of God as Universal Love, Life, Truth and Joy, in whom we live, move, and have our being, and by whom we are held together; that His mind is our mind now, that realizing our oneness with Him means love, truth, peace, health and plenty, not only in our own lives but in the giving out of these fruits of the Spirit to others.

"We affirm these things, not as a profession, but practice, not on one day of the week, but in every hour and minute of every day, sleeping and waking, not in the ministry of a few, but in a service that includes the democracy of all, not in words alone, but in the innermost thoughts of the heart expressed in living the life. "By their fruits ye shall know them."

"We affirm Heaven here and now, the life everlasting that becomes conscious immortality, the communion of mind with mind throughout the universe of thoughts, the nothingness of all error and negation, including death, the variety in unity that produces the individual expressions of the One-Life, and the quickened realization of the indwelling God in each soul that is making a new heaven and a new earth.

"We affirm that the universe is spiritual and we are spiritual beings. This is the Christ message to the twentieth century, and it is a message not so much of words as of works. To attain this, however, we must be clean, honest and trustworthy and uphold the Jesus Christ standards as taught in the Four Gospels. We now have the golden opportunity to form a real Christ movement. Let us build our house upon this rock, and nothing can prevail against it. This is the vision and mission of the Alliance."

New Thought is, according to the description of its own leaders, metaphysical, though not, they say, in the strict philosophical sense. Metaphysics in New Thought, they explain, "means a practical idealism, which emphasizes spiritual sensation and the accessibility of spiritual mind power, acting in accord with law and available to all people. From this standpoint 'Christian Metaphysics' means the philosophy of the New Testament, practical as a science." [11]

These leaders freely recognize the influence of many systems of thought. "It has borrowed much from the idealistic philosophies of the ages, particularly Plato, Socrates and the Neoplatonists—has been profoundly influenced by the Old Testament, the precepts of Buddha and the Sacred Writings of the East—the Spiritual philosophies of the Middle Ages; and in our own country is particularly indebted to Emerson and many others." [12] In this frank acknowledgement it differs sharply from Christian Science.

In distinction from orthodox Christianity its belief is not Trinitarian, though some, like Unity, do have a triune concept of a kind. It is philosophically monistic. "Our Life is immanent in the universe and is both Center and Circumference of all things visible and invisible." It is quite generally held by the orthodox that their thought is pantheistic, though it must be admitted that the line between an extreme concept of immanence and that of pantheism is but a thin one. As a matter of fact, many Hindu thinkers deny that the typical Vedanta idea of God is pantheistic. It is, of course, certain that the sharp, clearly drawn distinction between God and man and the world, characteristic of most Christian thought, is never found in New Thought. This is one of the major appeals of New Thought to many who have been repelled by the rigidity in the thought of God in much of the teaching in the established churches. Particularly in a day of evolution and the new physics this idea seems to many to be more easily acceptable.

Yet while talking of God as Life, Principle, Light, Love, Truth, etc., they, at the same time, stress the Fatherhood—the Motherhood also—of God, and his goodness, for God is the good. Unlike Christian Science they do not deny the reality of the material world. "The physical world is Mind in form," declares Ernest Holmes in

[11] Quoted in *Mind Remakes Your World*, p. xi.
[12] *Id.*, p. xi.

his *New Thought Terms and Their Meanings.*[13] If they speak, as sometimes they do, of the unreality of matter, he continues: "This does not deny the physical body or other physical objects, it merely affirms that all form is the manifestation of the energy of Mind. Mind is Substance and projects form." [14]

God is good. Evil is but "a term used to imply the opposite of good." It is "not a thing in itself but an absence of what is felt to be good or pleasing, as darkness is an absence of light, or death an absence of life. What might seem evil to one man might be seen as good by another." [15] "Evil and pain are but the tests and correctives that appear when man's thought does not reflect the full glory of the good, in the image of which he was made," to paraphrase one of the declarations of principles. Sin is defined as man's mistakes. "Sinful" and "mistaken" seem to be synonymous terms. Little is said about such a thing as forgiveness of sins. "Repentance" is a word evangelical Christians miss in their teachings.

It is interesting that in *New Thought Terms and Their Meanings,* quoted from above, there is no definition of sickness, illness, or pain, though the "treatment for pain" is stated as "a realization of its opposite which is peace, calmness, joy and perfect circulation." [16] Nor does the term health appear.

Man is a spiritual being, created in the image of the Good or God. He is, however, endowed with freedom to choose his own way. The divinity of Man and "his infinite possibilities through the power of constructive thinking and obedience to the voice of the Indwelling Presence" is a cardinal doctrine. (Statement of Purpose, 1916.)

Salvation is a present experience and is not to be thought of as otherworldly, though most New Thought believes in some type of immortality. Heaven is here and now, they affirm. Some groups such as Unity believe in reincarnation, others and probably the greater majority do not. Heaven is defined by Holmes as "Harmony, Wholeness, Health, Physical well-being, Happiness, Mental peace, poise and well-being." [17] Hell is "the torment of experiencing that which contradicts truth." [18] Just what the thought is of life beyond

[13] Ernest Holmes, *New Thought Terms and Their Meanings,* Dodd, Mead and Co., New York, 1942, p. 86.
[14] *Id.,* p. 86.   [15] *Id.,* p. 41.   [16] *Id.,* p. 105.   [17] *Id.,* p. 58.
[18] *Id.,* p. 58.

the crisis of death is not wholly clear. In a previously quoted statement of common belief held by New Thought groups occurs a phrase in which they attempt to state it as "the awakening not to an absorption of man's identity in Deity, but to his complete unity with the whole." But since Deity elsewhere is identified with the Whole and since "absorption" would seem to mean complete "unity with," there does not seem to be a real difference. What they seem to be trying to protect is the persistence of "the individual stream of consciousness." Perhaps they have done so in the words employed. It does not seem so certain to this writer.

What is perfectly clear is that the older stress upon an otherworldly heaven and hell of eternal reward or punishment is rejected and this is a pleasing thought to many who grew up under the older orthodoxy, but no longer find it possible to believe it, for many reasons.

Jesus is thought of as illustrating through his life and teachings "the nature of Reality as Love, Wisdom and Law." [19] In one place it is affirmed that the purpose of the whole New Thought Movement is to "prove the teachings of Jesus relative to the Spiritual Universe and Man's relationship to it." [20] Its early exponents, just as Mrs. Eddy in Christian Science, thought that they had discovered the real teachings of Jesus. "With Jesus," its leaders say, "it has insisted that faith shall be made manifest in works." [21] When, however, the term "Christ" is used, it is sharply distinguished from the historic Jesus. Christ is defined as "Divine Sonship. The Spiritual Principle in Man. The Presence of God in man as man. The True man, the Real man, the eternal man. The consciousness of God with us and in us." [22] When Christ is spoken of as the incarnation of God it is meant that "Every man is an incarnation of God; anyone who recognizes this and lives in conscious and harmonious union with Spirit, automatically becomes Christ." [23] It is obvious that here is a sharp difference from orthodox or even liberal Christian thought, and in reading their literature without this understanding one might easily be misled. Jesus Christ as Savior, "does not refer to Jesus Christ as a person, but to the Christ principle in all people which

[19] *Id.*, p. 71.
[20] *Mind Remakes Your World*, p. xi.
[21] *Id.*, p. ix.
[22] Holmes, *New Thought Terms and Their Meanings*, p. 20.
[23] *Id.*, p. 21.

Jesus revealed. It refers to accepting his method and using it in our own personal lives." [24] The Kingdom of God is within as Jesus taught, they say. It refers "to the invisible essence of Reality governing everything in accord with Divine and harmonious laws of Love, etc., from the human viewpoint the Kingdom of Heaven means a consciousness of harmony." [25]

If as sometimes happens, they speak of the Holy Trinity, it means "Spirit as Absolute Intelligence, Mind as Law, Form as Manifestation." [26]

The New Thought use of the Bible, particularly the New Testament, is constant, though probably less on the whole than that of Unity; and the more secularized forms make comparatively little use of it. The fact that Holmes defines Bible as, "The Sacred book or books of any race of people; a book containing the sacred writings of any religion which is used as an authority," [27] may serve to indicate that the Christian Bible is held in a very different regard than among the orthodox. Certainly there is no rigid idea of the inspiration of the Bible, and its authority has the authority of truth only, wherever that may be found. Where they do use it they are likely to use it allegorically or symbolically, though in general not to the same degree exhibited in Unity.[28]

Concerning the church little is said. In general New Thought does not demand exclusive membership in its groups. Members may, if they so desire, continue in the membership of their traditional churches, and many do. Each individual must be loyal to the truth he sees. This generous tolerance is an appealing feature of it to many people.

The moral teachings of the movement are not significantly different from those of the churches. They stress chiefly the individual rather than the social. As a movement, as stated in connection with Unity, they have little or no social outreach, relying rather on remade individuals to remake society. They support few institutions of charity, have little or no part as groups in pressing for a better economic or social order, though as individuals they may participate in such efforts. They theoretically stress the Brotherhood of Man, believe not alone in the profession but in the practice of their principles "not on one day of the week, but in every hour and

---

[24] *Id.*, pp. 71–72.   [25] *Id.*, p. 73.   [26] *Id.*, p. 60.   [27] *Id.*, p. 14.
[28] See pp. 172–173 ff.

minute of everyday sleeping and waking, not in the ministry of a few, but in a service that includes the democracy of all." (Declaration of Principles.)

As a matter of fact, probably the major impact of New Thought on American life has been, not so much through their organizations as through the public lectures and writings, not necessarily labelled as New Thought, of their greater leaders. Who can measure the influence of a single book such as that of Ralph Waldo Trine's *In Tune with the Infinite* which has sold over a million copies and is circulated just as any other book without a special New Thought label? Many of their books are published not by a denominational publishing house but by commercial publishers as a sheer matter of profit. Or who can estimate the influence of Orison Swett Marden and his books, or his magazine, *Success* which was on all the news-stands for many years. And many of New Thought's characteristic ideas are to be found in Emerson's writings.

Emmet Fox is said to have the largest congregation in New York—some say in the world. Every Sunday he fills Carnegie Hall and his noon lectures on Wednesday are thronged. In Los Angeles Ernest Holmes attracts an enormous following. Less outstanding figures in other cities draw large numbers to their ministry, a great many of whom never become members of New Thought groups as such.

Healing continues to be a major consideration. With so many sick people there are always those to whom this appeal comes. They affirm health as the natural state of man. They do not deny pain, it is very real, but it can be overcome, and their technique, like that of Unity, is largely that of affirmation and denial. Denial, says Holmes, has its use in mental treatment "where argument is used in dissolving the condition, but is not needed as the student reaches the higher plane of thought. Here there can be only affirmation as the Eternal Perfection, that is All in all, is perceived." [29] In another place he says, "Affirmation is the greatest and fundamentally the only creative agency in the universe." [30] "Whatever you mentally affirm and, at the same time, become inwardly aware of, Life will create for you." [31]

So not only in the matter of health, but also of economic affairs,

[29] *New Thought Terms and Their Meanings*, pp. 31–32.
[30] Ernest Holmes, *This Thing Called Life*, p. 37.
[31] *Id.*, p. 39.

and in life generally, affirmation plays an important part, if one is to enjoy good health, prosperity and happiness. New Thought makes much of the discipline of quiet, the cultivation of the art of meditation and of affirmation. Prayer takes generally the form of affirmation and of gratitude, not alone for what is received but in anticipation of receiving that which is confidently affirmed. There is no doubt that many troubled spirits are greatly helped to calm and inner adjustment through the practice of their religious techniques.

On the whole the appeal of New Thought is to intelligent people. It could hardly be expected to have a mass appeal. Yet many humble and little educated folk have also found help through its ministry, particularly the ministry of healing; and not a few who have sought it for economic reasons have through it won a larger success and plenty.

New Thought, we conclude as we began, is not so much an organization as it is a point of view. As such its influence is enormous and there is nothing to indicate that it is in any way decreasing. On the contrary, it seems to be extending its influence, directly or indirectly, upon the life of the American people.

Chapter Four

Unity School of Christianity

The Unity School of Christianity is located at Kansas City, Missouri. Its work, like Psychiana, is done largely by mail, although it does have group organizations, or Unity Centers, scattered all over the United States. At the great center in Kansas City, Unity has an extensive correspondence with individuals throughout the United States and the entire world. One department alone—Silent Unity— weekly receives on the average at least 10,000 letters, telegrams, or telephone calls from out of the city, all of which must be answered. It has a large publishing plant in which all of its magazines—*Unity, Weekly Unity, Daily Word, Progress, Good Business,* and *Wee Wisdom*—are published. In addition, it publishes numerous books, and issues tracts and lesser printed materials in almost incredible numbers.

It is a most interesting institution to visit. The spirit of the place is utterly unique. Most of the employees are students of Unity, or if they are not when they first come into the organization, they usually become such, according to Mr. Lowell Fillmore, manager of the plant. One cannot be long in the building without being conscious that it is a deeply religious institution. Thus at ten o'clock, in the case of the writer's visit, all work in the great office stopped and there was a period of complete silence for a little while. Then one of the department chiefs led in a quiet affirmation of religious faith. Again at eleven o'clock, work stopped, and over the public address system in every part of the building could be heard, as workers reverently paused, the Lord's Prayer. Once again, precisely at twelve o'clock, there was complete silence in Unity Inn, the vegetarian restaurant run by Unity, partly for its own employees, but widely patronized by non-Unity students. Then someone led in an affirmation of protection for the men in the Armed Forces throughout the entire world.[1]

The employees seemed contented, and several to whom the writer spoke said that it was a grand place to work. An attempt was once made by the A.F. of L. to unionize the workers in the plant, but when a vote was taken under the supervision of the War Labor Board, the decision of the employees was against unionization. They are paid union wages and are accorded certain privileges such as vacation on pay, club membership at Unity Farm, with facilities for swimming, games, fishing, picnics, and various other outdoor sports, all at a very nominal sum per year. The plant has had no serious labor trouble throughout its entire history as an employer.

The chief departments of Unity are the Editorial Department, the Manufacturing Department, the Field Department, which relates the Unity School to the various Unity centers throughout the world, and perhaps most important of all, the Silent Unity. In addition, there is an educational program for the training of future leaders in Unity centers. This latter school is conducted during the summers at Unity Farm, Lee's Summit, Missouri.

It is the intention of the movement ultimately to move out of the city entirely, to Unity Farm—a magnificent 1,300 acre farm some seventeen miles from the center of Kansas City, Missouri. Here it is planned to erect ultimately a magnificent set of buildings to house every department of the work. It will call for a settlement of some 2,000 people when it is completed. Already several of the buildings have been put up and are in use. A striking 170-foot tower dominates the landscape, and around it is a beautifully land-scaped area where the other buildings will be located. On the Farm, in addition to provisions for the school, the printing plant, mailing rooms, offices, etc., there are already in use a club house for em-ployees, a swimming pool, golf links, tennis courts, picnic grounds, and other recreational facilities. Even fishing is available in the thirteen-acre lake which provides water for use throughout the entire Farm. The Farm itself, well situated in a fertile area of Mis-souri, will find an outlet for its products in a modern market at the nearby crossing of two important highways. Here on the Farm the entire work of the institution will be carried on. The school will

[1] Since the close of the war the prayer has been changed to one for peace: "Let there be peace on earth, dear Father, and let it begin with me."

be held throughout the year, with shorter school terms during the summer, and numerous conferences. An excellent hotel is already on the grounds, later to be very greatly enlarged, and Unity Tea Room—vegetarian, like Unity Inn in Kansas City—provides eating facilities for all who are guests at the Farm. At present Unity offers its facilities freely to other religious organizations, when not employing them for its own purposes.

There is no disposition, as in some other religious communities, to live communally. Every family will have its own living unit. There will be dormitories for the single men and women workers. Salaries will be paid at current rates and each will be free to go and come as he pleases. Plans for the development of the Farm, including all the buildings and equipment, are in charge of Rickert Fillmore, son of the founder. A man of considerable artistic talent, with a background of study in architecture and art, he is also a practical, large-scale farmer, proud of the yield of fields, herds, and various produce under his management. When the Farm is completed it will, indeed, be one of the unique religious institutions in the whole of America.

Unity began with no intention of founding a new sect or denomination. It still claims categorically that it is not a church or a sect, but a school. As already stated, probably most of its work is done through its literature which circulates widely among the membership of many of the Protestant and Catholic churches and Jewish synagogues, but it has actually developed into a sect which does have its own local membership, its own meeting places, its own worship services, and its own ministers. Indeed, it is indistinguishable in most respects from any other religious denomination. This, it is explained by Unity leaders, came about quite naturally. People received great benefits from Unity teaching. They desired to share those benefits with others. They formed classes for the study of Unity principles—classes made up, in part, of persons who were active members of local churches, but were attracted to the particular teachings of Unity. At first no meetings were held at the accustomed hour of church services, but Unity began to draw into its membership persons who either were not, at the time, related to any church, or never had been. Yet they desired to have a worship service, and preferably, at the convenient hour used by the majority of churches. Thus at last Unity came to have its own worship services at the regular hours of church service.

Even so, they still insist that they do not wish to take anyone out of his own church, and Unity leaders have repeatedly told the writer that they discourage people from leaving other churches to come into their own. How widely this is true one has no way of knowing. When people actually withdraw from other churches they are welcome to membership in Unity.

That these Unity groups are real churches may be easily seen if one studies their little book of rituals, for they do have a book which is widely followed. It is published by the Unity School at Kansas City. In this book one finds an order of service for baptism, though water is not used in the service, but rather, flower petals.[2] There is also a communion service, though it differs in detail from the practice of the majority of churches. However, a part of the ritual is definitely taken from the Episcopal book of common worship. Also, there is provided a form for marriages and for funerals, as well as for the installation of officers. In a typical Unity service, hymns are sung, prayers are offered, and a sermon is delivered. Thus there can be no doubt that Unity does function as a church, whether it be meant to do so or not.

The Unity groups, usually called Centers, are not an integral part of the Unity School of Christianity, they declare. Organized into an annual conference with appropriate officers, they are held to be entirely independent of the Unity School of Christianity, and free to go their own way. Lowell Fillmore, son of Charles Fillmore, the founder, and himself manager of the Kansas City school, is secretary of the National Conference, but he asserts that this is by no means a necessary relationship. The connection between the Unity School and the Centers is maintained through what is called the Field Department. Also, ministers in the Unity churches are supposed to have completed courses of training in the Unity School and are ordained by the Unity School. Thus there does seem to be a rather close connection between the two.

The chief Unity Center in Kansas City has as its present meeting place a part of the total Unity building at 917 Tracy Avenue. There is, however, in prospect a new Unity Center, to be built at the cost of half a million dollars as a memorial to Myrtle Fillmore, co-founder of the movement. It will be located in the country club

---

[2] A letter from Mr. Lowell Fillmore states that flower petals are used only in the case of children. The practice is not advocated by Unity School, but is one adopted by some Unity ministers of their own volition.

section of Kansas City, at some distance from the present site. Money for this memorial Center will, of course, come from many people outside of Kansas City who loved and admired Myrtle Fillmore. Many of these gifts will be made through the Unity School, as well as direct.

Thus it becomes increasingly difficult for an outsider to justify the assertion of the Unity School that it is not a denomination or a sect. Probably no one would object to their being a denomination or sect. Everyone would be inclined to say that it is their privilege to be a church, to hold church services if they wish to. But why should they assert that they are not effectively a church when in reality they seem so clearly to be one?

Quite the most remarkable department of Unity is the one known as Silent Unity. In the upper floor of the main Kansas City building, something over one hundred workers are employed every day and sometimes through the night in answering the thousands of letters, telegrams, and telephone calls that come from all over the United States and even from foreign lands, requesting help through prayer. For Silent Unity is primarily a service performed through prayer. For more than fifty years, now, this department has been carrying on its quiet work. Requests for help of every kind pass through its workers' hands. Many want to be healed. Many are in financial difficulty, and many are facing grave decisions that must be made. Normally, according to Mrs. Rowland, the director of Silent Unity, the requests for healing are most numerous. However, in periods of depression, the financial problem becomes more prominent. At the time the writer visited it (1945) the greater number of requests had to do with the solution of difficult family problems, most of which were occasioned directly or indirectly by the war.

When a request for help comes in, whether by mail, telegram or telephone, the case is assigned to some one of the Silent Unity workers. He or she, for there are both men and women in this department, takes it up and makes the affirmations appropriate to the case. Thus he or she will affirm health or prosperity or the right solution of the difficult problem. At stated periods during the day, all the Silent Unity force gathers in a meeting room for meditation and prayer, and if a case presents some special difficulty, a worker may bring it to the attention of the whole group and ask their combined prayers that the help needed be given. Normally, the name of each person is carried on the worker's list for thirty days, unless word has been received indicating that the need has been met.

Thus far it is prayer alone, or affirmation, which has been employed, but the service of Silent Unity does not end with prayer, though they will be quick to affirm that this is their most powerful means of securing help. Each person's letter, telegram, or telephone call must be personally answered. If it is a very commonly repeated request of rather general character, and lacking in specific detail, an appropriately worded form letter may be used. If the case has special angles, if specific individuals are mentioned, and if counsel is sought in a very definite direction, then the worker, drawing upon his wide experience and training, writes letters of counsel and advice, which, quite apart from any religious help, would in many cases afford the petitioner very real assistance. It was the writer's privilege to read various letters which had just come into the office, especially ones dealing with marital difficulties, and to see the entire correspondence that ensued. Sometimes, many letters are exchanged before the case is closed.

In effect, Silent Unity offers not simply a religious solution, but affords much excellent personal counsel given by persons who are well trained to help through such counsel. The results of this ministry are undoubtedly not always completely satisfactory. Many do not get their problems solved, but on the other hand, many claim that they have found in Silent Unity just the thing that they most needed. *Unity*, the best known publication of the movement, regularly publishes articles from this department, containing letters from persons who have been helped through Silent Unity. One reads of some remarkable cures of diseases of the most terrible nature, such as cancer, tuberculosis, heart affections, blindness, deafness—indeed, almost every kind. Precisely the same kind of testimony appears in the *Christian Science Journal*, and may be heard in the midweek Christian Science meetings.

Are the healings genuine? Are people made well from grave diseases? Obviously, in many cases the diagnosis of the disease is the patient's own, rather than that of the doctor. And too, the patient may have thought he had something much more serious than he had. Also, the purported cure is not certified by any outside source. The writer once asked one of the Unity leaders why some certification was not insisted upon. Would not a healing, attested to by medical authority, and so reported, inspire confidence in people and strengthen their faith in the method of Unity? He did not seem impressed with the necessity or even the desirability of such certification. Enough for him that people said they were ill and later said that they had been cured, that they were in pain, and that they now no longer felt the pain. The whole operation is based, he said, on faith— not upon proof, and the intromission of an intent to prove might even be counter-productive and lessen men's faith rather than increase it.

There can be no reasonable doubt that many people are greatly helped by this ministry of Silent Unity. Its reputed success through half a century has aroused in the minds of many people a strong sense of expectancy or faith, and it is, as the Unity people properly recognize it to be, the faith, which ultimately effects the cure. One may not believe entirely, or even at all, their theory concerning the working of Silent Unity. For example, Mr. Charles Fillmore, himself, the founder, declared that through right prayer or affirmation there is a certain effective lodging in the ether, itself, of a power which grows ever greater as it is added to by the continued projection into it of the affirmations of truth used by the Silent Unity workers. He claimed that this becomes enormously effective as it is brought to bear upon the ills of humanity. In speaking of this, Mr. Fillmore used, as an illustration, what he asserted to be a fact— that Thomas A. Edison, just before his death, was working on an invention to recapture the actual words of Jesus which by some means had impressed themselves on the ether and are still capable of being apprehended, if only man had the proper technique for doing so.

The initial impulse to the foundation of Unity [3] came undoubtedly through Christian Science, which had been established, first, in Kansas City in 1887, by J. S. Thatcher, who opened there the Kansas City School of Christian Science. Charles and Myrtle Fillmore were members of the first class, organized and taught by Eugene B. Weeks of Chicago. Myrtle Fillmore, suffering from tuberculosis and about to give birth to her third child, Royal, was miraculously healed. She became an ardent exponent of Christian Science, and by 1890 her husband was won to the cause.

[3] I am indebted for much of what follows, even when not specifically noted, to Prof. James W. Teener, then of Park College, Missouri, who wrote a doctoral dissertation at the University of Chicago on Unity. It is the most thoroughgoing research study of Unity that has thus far been made. Unfortunately it was never published.

It is true that they never became members of the mother church, nor was their understanding and exposition of Christian Science ever quite that of its founder, Mrs. Eddy. They apparently never met Mrs. Eddy in person, but received their instruction under some of Mrs. Eddy's followers or former students. In a personal letter Mr. Lowell Fillmore particularly mentions that both his father and mother studied with Emma Curtis Hopkins, wife of an Andover college professor, and, for a year, assistant editor of *The Christian Science Journal*. Mrs. Hopkins, after disagreement with Mrs. Eddy, came to the midwest metropolis and founded the Christian Science Theological Seminary. Charles Fillmore was ordained by the school in December, 1890.

Mrs. Gestefeld, one-time follower of Mrs. Eddy and a gifted writer, published *A Statement of Christian Science*, an explanation of *Science and Health*, but in it she disagreed with Mrs. Eddy at a number of points. Among other things, she entirely ignored "malicious animal magnetism," and asserted that Mrs. Eddy's declaration that "there is no matter, no body, no world, no anything, but God and man, who is spiritual and not material," was only a misleading half truth. This brought a sharp rejoinder from Mrs. Eddy and expulsion from the First Church of Christ, Scientist. Mrs. Gestefeld's reply in a pamphlet—*Jesuitism in Christian Science*—was warmly approved by Mr. Fillmore in his magazine, *Modern Thought*, (I, 12, December, 1889), and he published many contributions from her pen in the ensuing decade. Unable to come to lecture in Kansas City, her lectures were used in class.

So strongly were the Fillmores influenced by Christian Science that their magazine, which began under the name *Modern Thought*, was changed to *Thought* in 1890, and in smaller letters across the word "Thought" was written "Christian Science."

But, meanwhile, a controversy had broken out concerning the right to use the name "Christian Science" by those who differed in their definition of the term from Mrs. Eddy. The Fillmores had quoted from, and copied freely, articles from Mrs. Eddy. But Mrs. Eddy was already trying to bring the entire movement under her personal control, and it did not suit her purposes that others should use the name under which she was building her movement. *Christian Science Thought* thus was informed that her articles were not to be reproduced by other publications.

This attempt at authoritarian control alienated Charles Fillmore. From the first he had stood for the recognition of Truth where-ever it might be found. He believed that no single individual or movement possessed all truth. He had declared in an article, "Truth Bows at No Human Shrine," that, "no man nor woman, nor angel or archangel has a copyright on truth; that all claims of exclusive inspiration of whatsoever nature are fraudulent, and that such claims are never made by those who have an apprehension of the real Christ principle." (*Modern Thought*, I, June, 1889). Accordingly, the *Christian Science* was dropped from the name of the magazine, which continued to appear simply as *Thought*, Mr. Teener asserts that, "Mrs. Eddy is the only individual severely criticized in the fifty years of their magazine's history." (Thesis, *Unity School*, Page 26.)

The principal points of difference with Christian Science, as defined in Boston, and shared by a number of rebel followers, including the Fillmores, were their repudiation of "malicious animal magnetism" and their interpretation of the world and man. They agreed with the definition of God as "Mind, Intelligence, Life, Love, Spirit," but they drew very different conclusions with respect to man and the material world. Boston said, "Man is God's changeless image and likeness forever. God and man are all in all, therefore there is no sin, sickness, or death." As a corollary of this, neither the world nor matter is real. The "outlaw" group on the other hand, "affirmed a living soul which forever images God, and a 'substantial environment' known as the material world. Man is composed of an existent soul and a material body." (Teener, Thesis, Page 27.)

Mrs. Eddy, they charged, ignored the real world, and the material body—and while denying that such things as sin, sickness, or death, existed, her loyal followers were treating these very things and getting results.

Unity does not deny the reality of the material world or of human experience. Sin, sickness, death are real, but they can be overcome, and Unity possesses precisely the techniques by which they may be overcome, as we shall see later.

While Unity got its first impulse from Christian Science, its real affinity is with the New Thought group rather than with Christian Science as it exists today. Not that Unity now recognizes itself as a member of the International New Thought Alliance, for it does not, and for reasons which will later appear. But its genius is essentially that of the New Thought movement in general, and its philosophy runs much closer to the New Thought than to Christian Science. Indeed, the New Thought movement and Christian Science stem from the same source, for it was the work and teaching of Phineas P. Quimby to whom both must ultimately be referred. This is not to say that Christian Science is wholly derived from Quimby, for obviously it is not. It is a moot question discussed elsewhere [4] in the volume as to exactly the degree of influence Phineas P. Quimby had upon Mary Baker Eddy, but that she did get her start through Quimby no one can deny, and that not a little of her method of healing grew out of her own healing under the teaching of Quimby, seems quite clear to unprejudiced students of the genesis of both movements.

It has already been indicated that certain disciples of Mrs. Eddy in the Chicago area, who thought they were teaching Christian Science, departed significantly from her teaching and the direction they took was precisely the direction in which the New Thought Movement as a whole has been moving. Indeed, these same Chicago outlaw Christian Scientists were among those who were influential in the formation of the first nation-wide movement which later came to be called the New Thought movement. Among these dissenters from the Eddy version of Christian Science were numbered the Fillmores, co-founders of Unity. The early history of New Thought was that of individual healers who, adding to the teachings of Quimby ideas of their own, formed local groups known by a great variety of names such as Divine Science, Home of Truth, Practical Christianity, Livable Christianity, etc. The central interest of the entire group was, in that early day, healing of the body. Later was to be added emphasis upon prosperity and happiness. Scattered as they were throughout the country, they recognized certain common interests, so naturally they developed a nationwide movement to which the schools of various names became affiliated.

As early as 1892, the International Divine Science Association was organized. During the World's Fair at Chicago there was held the Columbian Congress of Christian Scientists. They were not the orthodox Christian Scientists. In 1894, a national convention was held in San Francisco and in 1896 the meeting was in Kansas City, the home of the Fillmores. On the program that year Mr. and Mrs. Fillmore both appeared. Successive congresses were held in St. Louis in 1897, and in Boston in 1899 was held the first convention under the name of New Thought.

In 1897, the Fillmores made a statement, somewhere in their

[4] See pp. 187 ff.

official publication, which was somewhat at variance with the majority of the members of the New Thought body. They said, "We find by experience that concentration is necessary to success, and we wish to confine these pages to that specific doctrine and Holy Ghost power taught and demonstrated by Jesus Christ." This was much more definitely oriented toward Christian doctrine than most New Thought groups were willing to accept, and eventually it led to the separation of Unity from the general movement. In 1903 the group reorganized under the name—The New Thought Federation, and Unity continued a member of the Federation until 1906. In that year, Mr. Fillmore felt that much of the material and program was far from his own understanding of New Thought, and so withdrew Unity from membership.

From that period on, for a number of years, little reference is made to New Thought in their publications. Mr. Fillmore asserted in 1915 that Unity was not to be thought of as a branch of New Thought or Christian Science, but rather as primitive Christian. "We understand and teach the truth given by Jesus Christ in its holiness. This means that we include in our doctrine the great plan of salvation for the race which Jesus inaugurated. New Thought ignores this and Christian Science attenuates its fundamental facts until they lose the force and power necessary to complete the salvation of the body." [5]

By this time, however, Unity had grown to such a point that it seemed highy desirable to the New Thought Alliance that they be drawn once again into the movement. Therefore, in 1919, at the meeting of the International New Thought Congress at Cincinnati, the leaders inquired by wire of Unity concerning the conditions under which they would be willing to unite with them. In reply, the Fillmores said that they would enter the Alliance only if what they called the Jesus Christ Standards which they stated as follows were adopted: "The Universe is spiritual and we are spiritual beings. This is the Christ message to the twentieth century and it is a message not so much of words as of works. To attain this, however, we must be clean, honest, and trustworthy and uphold the Christ standard in all things. Let us build our house upon this rock and nothing can prevail against it. This is the vision and the aim of the Alliance." [6]

[5] Quoted by Teener, *op. cit.*, p. 32.
[6] *Unity*, Vol. 51 (Nov. 1919), p. 471.

The Alliance voted to accept the statement without amendment, so Unity became once more a member of the New Thought group. Indeed, they acted as hosts to the Congress the following year at Kansas City. For three years they continued in this relation, but in 1922 the directors of Unity voted unanimously to retire from the Alliance. The reason given was that "the other New Thought had insisted upon putting their own interpretation on the Jesus Christ Standard rather than accepting the ideals as they had been working them out." [7]

The particular points of differences seem to have been the teaching concerning eternal life, which according to Unity, "Is to be one here and now by the process of body refinement, and body refinement can be achieved by mental realization of oneness with the Absolute, plus the renunciation of such sinful habits as the lust for meat, tobacco, sex, dancing, and all the pleasures that exalt sense above the soul. Thus man can overcome death." Most New Thought groups, however, thought that death was the entrance into a higher life.[8]

There were practical difficulties, also, the chief of which were the maintenance of an open platform and the circulation of field lecturers from other groups through Unity Centers, which introduced a difference in teaching and caused the leaders of the Group Centers much difficulty. Also, Mr. Fillmore felt that the International New Thought Alliance, instead of maintaining a connection or a loose federation of groups, was trying to "make the Alliance another school of New Thought people." Since 1922, Unity has had no relation to the New Thought movement.

When I spoke to Mr. Fillmore and his sons about this personally, they did not seem to recall the details as given by Mr. Teener in his carefully documented study, but they do feel that they represent something essentially different from New Thought generally. When I said, however, "But Unity does emphasize the same general ends which are characteristic of all New Thought organizations," they readily admitted it, and when I further stated that many of their techniques of attaining the ends were likewise similar they could not deny it. When I still further suggested that it seemed to me that the main difference between Unity, as I understood it, and the New Thought movement, in general, was the relatively closer ap-

[7] Teener, *op. cit.*, p. 34.   [8] Teener, *op. cit.*, p. 35.

proximation of Unity to orthodox Christian thought, they also manifested agreement. I recall saying to them, jokingly, "Why, most of the people of our churches who read your literature don't even see that there is anything wrong with it," and they were good enough to laugh heartily. Whether or not Unity and New Thought will ever again unite in any organization, cannot be predicted, but as, probably, the largest and strongest, numerically and institutionally, of any of the New Thought groups, Unity does not feel so keenly the need of association that lesser groups may be inclined to feel.

II. *WHAT IT TEACHES*

Many of the practical emphases and some of the ideas of Unity have already appeared in what has thus far been said about the organization and its founders. But what precisely are its major beliefs and whence do they come? Basic to everything else is the fundamental concept of the nature of God. In speaking of God, almost the identical terms are used that are found in Christian Science: Life, Mind, Principle, and Spirit. Charles Fillmore says in his book, *Christian Healing:* "The truth is that God is Principle, Law, Being, Mind, Spirit, All Good, omnipotent, omniscient, unchangeable, Creator, Father, Cause and Source of all that is." [9] Yet this does not necessarily tell the whole truth about God, for in another place he declares: "Language is the limitation of mind; therefore, do not expect the unlimited to leap forth into full expression through the limited. Words can never express that which God is." [10] Both personal and impersonal terms are used in addressing God, but the thought of God as personal is regarded as a limiting concept. "From the teaching that the Deity is a person we have come to believe that God is changeable; that He gets angry with His people and condemns them; that some are chosen and favored above others; that in His sight good and evil are verities, and that He defends the one and deplores the other. We must relieve our mind of these ideas of a personal God ruling over us in an arbitrary manner." [11] "We

[9] Charles Fillmore, *Christian Healing*, Unity School of Christianity, Kansas City, Missouri, 1909, p. 15.
[10] *Jesus Christ Heals*, Unity School of Christianty, Kansas City, Missouri, 1944, p. 23.
[11] *Jesus Christ Heals*, p. 34.

must drop from our minds the idea that God is circumscribed in any way or has any of the limitations usually ascribed to persons, things, or anything having form or shape." [12]

But do not such attributes as love, power, and mind, betoken personality in God? Mr. Fillmore seems to anticipate such a question, and his answer is definitely no. God, for example, is love, but, he says, "God is not loving. . . . God does not love anybody or anything. God is the love *in* everybody and everything. God is love. Man becomes loving by permitting that which God is to find expression in word and act. . . . God exercises none of His attributes except through the inner consciousness of the universe and man." [13] Likewise, God is Power, but not powerful; he is Wisdom, but not intelligent, and so on through the list of attributes.

"Drop from your minds," he writes, "the belief that God is in any way separated from you, that He occupies form or space outside of you, or that He can be manifested to your consciousness in any way except through your own soul." [14] In the attribute of Mind is found the "meeting ground of God and man." . . . "We cannot describe God with human language, so we cannot describe mind. . . . We can only say: I am mind; I know God is mind; He knows. Thus knowing is the language I use in my intercourse with God." [15] The "knowing," as he further develops it, seems to reduce to the "immediate" knowledge that comes through communion as known to the mystic. He declares that he can offer no way to its understanding beyond that of "showing you in the simplest way how to come into conscious relations with the source of omnipresent wisdom, life and love, by taking with you in the silent inner realms, the first steps in the language of the soul." [16] "God lives in you, and you depend upon Him for every breath you draw. . . . You could not think a thought or speak a word or make a movement, were He not in it." [17]

God is always accessible. "He must be just as accessible as a principle of mathematics and as free from formalism. . . . Jehovah God is always within reach of every man, woman and child." Indeed, "God is your highest self and is in constant waiting upon you. He loves to serve, and will attend faithfully to the most minute details of your daily life." . . . "Never be formal with God. He cares

[12] *Id.*, p. 29. [13] *Id.*, p. 27. [14] *Id.*, pp. 27–28.
[15] *Jesus Christ Heals*, pp. 31–32, *passim.*
[16] *Id.*, p. 33. [17] *Id.*, p. 36.

no more for forms and ceremonies than do the principles of mathematics for fine figures or elaborate blackboards. . . . You cannot use God too often. He loves to be used, and the more you use Him, the more easily you use Him and the more pleasant His help becomes. . . . He will do you a favor just as quickly if you ask in a jolly, laughing way as He would if you made your request in a long, melancholy prayer. God is natural, and He loves the freedom of the little child." [18] Also, God is good, All-good. [19]

Unity thinks of God as Trinity, which fact brings it much nearer in language to the orthodox churches than any of the other New Thought and similar groups. In the *Metaphysical Dictionary*, a principal source book of the movement, it is stated: "The Father is Principle, the Son is that Principle revealed in a creative plan. The Holy Spirit is the executive power of both Father and Son carrying out the creative plan." [20] Again, Mr. Fillmore says: "We might also say that the Father is Being in the Absolute, the unlimited, the unrelated. Son is the I Am identity of Being. Holy Spirit is the personality of Being . . . the personality of God . . . neither the all of Being, nor the fullness of Christ, but is an emanation, or breath, sent forth to do a definite work. Thus circumscribed, He may be said to take on, in a sense, the characteristics of personality, a personality transcending in its capacity the concept of the intellectual man." [21] The fact that in scripture the Holy Spirit speaks, searches, reveals, reproves, etc., implies, he thinks, "distinct personal subsistence." Or again, the Holy Spirit is the "law of God in action." He says that "what writers ascribe to Jehovah in the Old Testament the writers of the New Testament ascribe to the Holy Spirit." [22] The Holy Spirit is "the interpreter of Christ." He "comes to men in this day as in the past, and reveals to them how to overcome the erroneous states of consciousness that have been evolved, or in which they are cast through association. A higher, a more far-seeing guide than the mere intellect is necessary, and that guide has been provided for in the Holy Spirit." [23] There is much in this that runs parallel to the teaching of orthodox Christianity. It is perhaps because of the

[18] *Talks on Truth*, Unity School of Christianity, Kansas City, Missouri, 4th ed., 1943, pp. 11–13, *passim*.
[19] *Jesus Christ Heals*, p. 15.
[20] *Metaphysical Bible Dictionary*, Unity School of Christianity, Kansas City, Missouri, p. 629; also *Talks on Truth*, p. 134.
[21] *Talks on Truth*, pp. 134–135.
[22] *Id.*, p. 135.   [23] *Id.*, p. 138.

familiar orthodox language, though the meaning is not always the same as in orthodoxy, that many members of the churches read the Unity literature, and find help in it, but never think of leaving their traditional faith to join the movement.

That there is substantial difference in the understanding of terms is evident when the matter is pursued in greater detail. Thus the explanation of the creation is said to involve the Trinity, but in a way never found, to the reader's knowledge, in orthodox thinking. Says Mr. Fillmore in his *Mysteries of Genesis:* "The first chapter of Genesis shows two parts of the Trinity, mind and idea in mind. In the second chapter we have the third part, manifestation. In this illustration all theological mystery about the Trinity is cleared away, for we see that it is simply mind, idea in mind, and manifestation of idea." [24]

The familiar change of divine name from the first chapter, in which Elohim is used, to the second chapter, where Jehovah or Yahweh appears, is declared by Mr. Fillmore to represent a distinction within the God-head.

The place of Jesus Christ in Unity is very important. We have already seen that he is accepted as the second person of the Trinity, as interpreted. Mr. Fillmore says: "The man that God created in his own image . . . is Spiritual man. This man is the direct offspring of Divine Mind, God's idea of perfect man. This is the only-begotten Son, the Christ, the Lord God, the Jehovah, the I Am. In the second chapter this Jehovah, or divine idea of perfect man, forms the manifest man and calls his name Adam." [25] Here Christ is equated with Jehovah. In another place he speaks of Jesus as "a perfected soul who attained creative power in a cosmic evolution previous to human history." "This world and everything in it was brought forth by Him in many earthly incarnations." [26] He appeared variously as Moses, Elisha, David, and others. "These," says Mr. Fillmore, "were his days at school, and he arrived at a state of consciousness, while manifesting as Jesus of Nazareth, where he remembered his past lives." [27]

He was more than just Jesus of Nazareth, "more than any other

---

[24] Fillmore, *Mysteries of Genesis*, Unity School of Christianity, Kansas City, Missouri, revised edition, 1944, p. 12.
[25] *Id.*, p. 12.
[26] *Unity*, December 12, 1936, p. 6.
[27] *Unity*, Volume 14, p. 149 (1901).

man who ever lived on earth. He was more than man . . . because there came into His manhood a factor to which most men are strangers . . . the Christ consciousness. The unfoldment of this consciousness by Jesus made Him God incarnate, because Christ is the mind of God individualized, and whoever so loses his personality as to be swallowed up in God becomes Christ Jesus, or God man." [28]

Jesus Christ cannot be separated from God, nor can it be told where "man leaves off and God begins in Him. To say that Jesus Christ was a man as we are men is not true, because He had dropped that personal consciousness by which we separate ourselves into men and women. He was consciously one with the absolute principle of Being. He had no consciousness separate from that Being. He *was* that Being, to all intents and purposes." [29]

Here is a Christology high enough surely to satisfy the most exacting orthodox standards. But when the nature of the work of Christ is considered, a tremendous difference appears, though liberal Christian thought would find less in it with which to quarrel.

It is through the Christ, or Christ consciousness that man achieves salvation, according to Unity, as in orthodox belief, but both the meaning of salvation itself and its method of attainment are radically different. Logically, therefore, the consideration of what salvation means may well be introduced at this point, and then the work of Christ in its accomplishment set forth.

What does salvation mean in Unity? Well, first of all it does not concern itself with an otherworldly state to be achieved in a life beyond this. It is not an escape from everlasting punishment in hell. Two distinctive notes are found in the Unity thought that are foreign to orthodox, or even liberal Christian belief. They are: (1) the belief in reincarnation, and (2) the doctrine of the "regeneration of the body."

The idea of reincarnation is common in the Orient, especially in India, but there has also been a strain of it in the West. Particularly has this been true within the last century with the opening up of the East to travel from the West, and the increasing acquaintance with oriental thought, made possible by the translation and circulation of oriental scriptures and other writings in English. Also the many Orientals who have come into the West to lecture, to write and to teach, have played an important part in its introduction. Mr. Fillmore

[28] *Talks on Truth*, p. 169.   [29] *Talks on Truth*, p. 169.

may have gotten the idea from any one of various sources. Theosophy has been the most potent factor in its introduction to the American people. The whole Transcendentalist movement in New England, out of the midst of which New Thought came, played with the idea, even though it did not wholly embrace it.

Death, according to Mr. Fillmore, is but a temporary laying down of the physical body. He likens it to sleep. "We fall asleep," he says, "without any sense of apprehension and for a little while the soul leaves the body. If we have a good conscience we rest peacefully and acquire strength for a new day's work. If worried, anxious, or guilty, we are troubled by dreams that distress us." So, he says, is death. When death occurs, "the soul leaves the body to mortal dissolution, yet it does not fail to return in due time to take up a body—as long as it believes in the limitations of sense. . . . If his life has been according to the Golden Rule, he 'wraps the drapery of his couch about him and lies down to pleasant dreams'; his soul basks in the sunshine of a world Elysian and his hope of heaven is for a season fulfilled." [30] Nowhere, that writer has discovered, does he enlarge extensively on the idea of heaven, and it will be noted that here only by silent inference is there any reference to any opposite state, corresponding to the distressing dreams of the anxious, troubled sleeper. However, a little later on he is more explicit. The rich man who, in the parable, left Lazarus to lie neglected in poverty and disease at his door, affords an illustration of what happens to the wicked after death. "In Hades he lifted up his eyes, being in torment." Says Mr. Fillmore: "Material selfishness starves the soul and devitalizes the physical body . . . when death overtakes such a one, the inner, as well as the outer life, changes environment. The material avenues are lost to the outer, and the soul finds itself in a hell of desires without the flesh sensations with which to express itself . . . the body consciousness, the peace of union for all the attributes of man, has been removed, producing in the life consciousness a great gulf or chasm that cannot be crossed, except by incarnation in another body." [31]

In answer to the oft-repeated question: "Where is my loved one who is dead?" he replies that man is a complex being. He is spirit, soul, intellect, and sense consciousness "out of which the body is formed." At death "the spiritual ego reverts to its original essence

[30] *Talks on Truth*, pp. 47–48.   [31] *Id.*, pp. 156–157.

in the bosom of the Father; soul falls asleep until the next incarnation. Body and sense consciousness are earthbound and in due season they disintegrate." [32] That ordinarily man does not recall his former births is obvious from the failure of humans to do so. Yet now and then there is a flash of memory in the case of some individuals. Mr. Fillmore, in personal conversation with the writer, affirmed that he had definite knowledge of certain of his own personal reincarnations.

Salvation here, as in most of the faiths that hold the doctrine of rebirth, is attained when the cycle of birth is broken and man "comes to birth no more again." To Mr. Fillmore, that is, Unity, the final goal is eternal life which is attained when the true spiritual body replaces the physical body and man becomes like Jesus Christ. And "this is to be accomplished here in this earth." [33] Here appears the second distinctive teaching of Unity. Further it is affirmed that all men will one day attain it. Thus Unity is "Universalist" in its salvation ideal. Here is no election, no conditional salvation. Ultimately no human being is lost. Meanwhile rebirth goes on. "In each incarnation that goal is brought nearer if Spirit is given opportunity to express itself."

"Eternal life means conscious existence in the body," declares Charles Fillmore.[34] It is not necessary to die. "Christianity shows how to come right back into life, and that is the only salvation for men. *If you believe faithfully in the Christ life you will never die.*" (Italics are the author's).[35] Here is a daring doctrine. It is paralleled in Father Divine's teaching; indeed, Father Divine may well have gotten it from Mr. Fillmore whose teaching, as we have seen, he greatly admired. Mr. Fillmore has the courage of his convictions and asserts, as the writer personally heard him do, that he believes he will not die. This startling statement came in response to the author's question as to what he, Mr. Fillmore, thought would happen to the movement when he, the leader, passed off the scene. He was, at the time of the interview, ninety-two years of age. He is a small man, very slightly built, and has, since his youth, been a cripple. A tubercular condition of the hip, healed by faith, left him with one limb shorter than the other, so that he had to wear a heavily built up shoe to compensate, and in his earlier and more recent years has

---

[32] *Talks on Truth*, p. 159.   [33] *Id.*, p. 159.
[34] *Talks on Truth*, pp. 150–151.   [35] *Id.*, p. 150.

walked with a cane. He walks with a decided limp, but asserts that he is constantly improving, that the limb is gradually becoming longer, and he believes it will ultimately be completely restored. He is remarkably vigorous considering his years, and still does an amazing amount of work. He is regularly at his desk, writing for the various Unity publications and revising his numerous books, for successively new editions, and preparing still other volumes. He is young in mind and spirit and utterly sincere in his belief that he has found the secret of eternal life in the body.

He believes that Jesus promised such eternal life and that "our understanding of the laws of mind substantiates His assurance in this respect. The mind can be so filled with thoughts of life that there will be no room for a thought of death. Death can never take possession of the body of one whose mind is thoroughly charged with ideas of life." [36]

This, then, is salvation. What part in it does Jesus play? To see this it will be necessary to go back to the beginning and see what happened. Man was created a spiritual being, and would "never have known matter or material condition" if he had followed the leading of his higher consciousness. But he did not do so, and "we exist today in a state of lapse so far as our relation to God and the orderly movement of His idea in creation are concerned." The "fall of man" is in a measure true. "It is the recognition of this higher consciousness and the reorganization of our place in Being that we are seeking . . . we want to know the shortest way to it. That way is the Jesus Christ way." [37]

But mental states, once they are formed, tend to persist. "Thought emanations" tend to crystallize about a form they have made, despite strenuous efforts of man to break through them. A whole race, says Mr. Fillmore, "might be caught in the meshes of its own thought emanations and, through this drowsy ignorance of the man ego, remain there throughout eternity, unless a break were made in the structure and the light of a higher way let in." Indeed, "this is just what has happened to our race. In our journey back to the Father's house we became lost in our own thought emanations, and Jesus Christ broke through the crystallized thought strata and opened the way for all those who will follow Him." [38] . . . "He became the

[36] *Talks on Truth*, p. 150.   [37] *Talks on Truth*, p. 164.
[38] *Id.*, pp. 165–166.

way by which all who accept Him may 'pass over' to the new consciousness." He made a "connection between our state of consciousness and the more intense one of the Father—He united them —made them a unit—*one*—hence, the at-one-ment, or atonement through Him." [39]

That which died on the cross, continues Mr. Fillmore, "was the consciousness of all mortal beliefs that hold us in bondage—such as sin, evil, sickness, fleshly lusts, and death—which He overcame. His 'overcoming' made a great rent in the sense consciousness and opened a way by which all who desire may demonstrate easily and quickly." [40] But it was not so much his death on the cross as his overcoming death, the resurrection, that opened "the way for every one of us into the Father's kingdom." [41]

But how shall the work of Christ be made effective? It is not through "belief" in him. "The whole secret of the demonstration of Christ is that we shall come to realize our original sinlessness"— not realize in the sense of "be conscious of," but rather "to attain to." "Sin and the consciousness of sin are the cause of all darkness and death." [42] "We must be perfect even as Jesus Christ was perfect. There is no other way." . . . "If I am in any degree a sinner, I have in that degree a corruptible dead body. I must, then, be guilty of the carnal mind. And what is the remedy? I must get rid of carnality; that is all. The quicker I do that, the quicker I shall become alive." [43] And do not forget that it is eternal life in the body which is the desired goal.

Of course, there is a technique worked out to enable man to attain to the Christ consciousness, and along with the ultimate salvation goal there are many proximate goods that are attained, including health, prosperity, and happiness—the well-known and generally recognized New Thought values. Of all the means, it is the affirmation that is most strongly stressed and constantly employed, both by individual and the group.

Since eternal life in the body is the goal, illness which threatens the body must be overcome. Health becomes a desideratum, not merely because it is more comfortable for the individual, but because, unless it can be maintained, death may result, bringing the necessity of further rebirths, and a postponement of salvation.

[39] *Id.*, p. 166.   [40] *Talks on Truth*, p. 166.   [41] *Id.*, p. 164.
[42] *Id.*, pp. 154–155.   [43] *Id.*, p. 155.

The basic Unity theory of healing is that health is natural, sickness unnatural. "Our ills are a result of our sins," writes Mr. Fillmore, "or our failure to adjust our mind to Divine Mind." . . . "When the sinning state of mind is forgiven and the right state of mind established, man is restored to his primal natural wholeness." [44] More picturesquely, and in greater detail, he has discussed health and illness in another place. Here he says that according to physiology, the body has two sets of cells, the living and the dead. At the center of the live cells is a little electric light, while the dead cells are dark. When man is healthy the light cells predominate—in sickness, the dark. "Meta-physicians," he declares, "have discovered that they can light up the body cells by affirming life and intelligence for them." Such an affirmation might be—"I am alive with the life of Christ. I am intelligent with the intelligence of Christ." Making this affirmation throughout the day and at night, until it becomes a part of your consciousness, is "an important step in demonstrating eternal life." [45]

He goes on to say that, "the body is shocked to death by the violent thought voltage of the unwise mind." Selfishness leads to strife, anger, and hate, and these emotions "generate currents of thought whose volts burn up the body cells in the same way that a live wire sears the flesh. Hate burns out the connections in the glands exactly as the excessively high current burns out a fuse in your house lighting system. Then the lights go out and death of the body sets in." [46]

Obviously, if this is the case, then the remedy lies in love, peace, and harmony. God is love, and "to live in God-Mind, man must cultivate love until it becomes the keynote of his life. We must love everybody and everything, ourselves included. . . . Affirm the infinite love as your love and you will find that there will be generated in your mind and body an entirely new element. . . . Center your love thought upon God, and you will find love for your fellow men growing marvelously." [47]

A most interesting theory of disease is set forth in a chapter on Micro-organisms. It is a commonplace of medical knowledge that many diseases are caused by germs, but physicians only seek to put them out of action, never inquiring into their origin. This, he says,

[44] *Jesus Christ Heals*, p. 5. [45] *Talks on Truth*, p. 152.
[46] *Id.*, p. 152. [47] *Talks on Truth*, pp. 152–153.

is a superficial way of dealing with them. But the "students of mind" know whence they come. "Every mental process is generative. . . . Thinking is formative—every thought clothes itself in a life form according to the character given it by the thinker. This being true, it must follow that thought of health will produce microbes to build up healthy organisms, that thoughts of disease will produce microbes of disorder and destruction." [48] "Every thought that flits through the mind of every man, woman and child in the universe produces a living organism, a microbe of a character like its producing thought." Thus there are microbes produced by anger, fear, hate, and envy, after their kind, and once let loose in the world they "have no respect for anyone." "So," he says, "the fears, the doubts, the poverty, the sin, the sickness, the thousand erroneous states of consciousness have their microbes." [49] There is even a special death microbe, and he cites, as authority in the medical world, the story of a certain Dr. Parker of New York who claims that "death is caused by a specific microbe that can be recognized and bred just as the microbes of various diseases." He does not identify the paper in which the story was published.

If all this be true, then obviously the important thing is not simply to kill the microbes, but to get at their source and prevent their appearance. "To apply the remedy to the poor little microbe is like trying to stop the manufacture of counterfeit money by destroying all that is found in circulation." [50]

Cease then "making disease microbes and turn your attention to higher things. Make love alive by thinking love. Make wisdom the light of the world by affirming God's omnipresent intelligence. See in mind the pure substance of God and it will surely appear. This is the way to destroy microbes—this is the antidote for disease germs. The real, the enduring things of God are to be brought into visibility in just this simple way." So simple is it that the least educated man can do it. "One does not have to know about anything whatsoever except God." [51]

From what has been said concerning healing it is clear that a different theory underlies it from that held in Christian Science. Unity does not deny the reality of pain and sickness. When the writer asked Mr. Fillmore if he believed that pain was real, he re-

[48] *Id.*, p. 18.   [49] *Talks on Truth*, p. 21.   [50] *Id.*, p. 21.
[51] *Id.*, p. 26.

plied, "Yes, real, but not permanent." Microbes actually exist, even though they are caused by thoughts. But evil microbes can be destroyed by good microbes which also actually exist, and which are produced by good thoughts.

This brief statement is doubtless an oversimplification of the teaching concerning healing. The fundamental theory is here stated accurately, but there are many other incidental factors involved. For instance, diet is important. Most Unity followers are vegetarians. Unity Inn on the farm, and Unity Tea Room in Kansas City are both vegetarian restaurants, with the exception that they now serve fish. The change of policy in introducing fish was the result of a change in Mr. Fillmore's own practice. For many years he was a strict vegetarian, though he said personally to the writer, "Unity does not make a fetish of food . . . if you think spiritually you automatically select the more refined types of food . . . but do not be a food fanatic. Unity has never excluded from its membership those who are not vegetarian."

For many years Mr. Fillmore would not eat even eggs, milk, or cheese, and, of course, never meat. In more recent years he has modified the rigor of his practice and now includes eggs and dairy products. His inclusion of fish in his diet was the result, as he told the writer, of what might be called a special revelation. He had felt for some time a "lack of mental expression." He was not thinking with his usual clarity. In a flash one day, he said, the words came to him, apparently out of thin air, "Your brain lacks phosphorus; eat fish." And since that day he has done so. Mr. Fillmore can laugh and joke about the matter. The author recalls the good-natured badinage concerning the merits of vegetarianism that passed between father and son, Rickert, while dining in the latter's home on Unity farm. The son does not hold to the vegetarian regime.

Then there is the matter of sex. The teachings of Unity on this subject are not so rigorous as those of the I Am. However, there is no question but that the indulgence in sex expression for other than purposes of procreation is regarded as an evil. In *The Twelve Powers of Man*,[52] Mr. Fillmore writes, "Through the sins of the sex life (casting away of the precious substance) the body is robbed of its essential fluids and disintegrates. The result is called death, which is the last great enemy to be overcome by man. Immortality

[52] Unity School of Christianity, Kansas City, 7th ed., 1943.

in the body is possible to man only when he has overcome the weaknesses of sensation and conserves his life substance." [53] Or again: "Sex sensation has made a broken cistern of man's consciousness; for generations the life stream has been turned into this receptacle and lust has robbed the bodies of the whole race making them mere shells, void of life. The failing eye, the deaf ear, the festering or withering flesh, all bear testimony to this perversion of God's life." [54] Teener, after an exhaustive study of the entire Unity literature says that Unity does not completely condemn those who practice generation—the only permitted use of sex in its external manifestations. "They are providing bodies for souls that have lost out in a previous incarnation and are waiting to try again. . . . They may for the time be doing a good thing, but they must realize that they cannot escape the heartache, disease, and death which are concomitant to that plane of living." [55]

"So long as your eyes see sex and the indulgence thereof on any of its planes, you are not pure. You must become mentally so translucent that you see men and women as sexless beings—which they are in the spiritual consciousness." [56]

These are but two of the areas in which controls are a necessary part in the achievement of the ultimate goal, which is eternal life in the body. As a matter of fact, there are Twelve specific Powers which man possesses—the proper development of which contributes to the final ends. An entire book is required in their description and discussion of the laws under which they operate. Each of these powers is located in a particular part of the body, as indicated in a drawing in the book, and each of these twelve powers is thought of as represented by one of the twelve disciples. Here we can only name the powers and their apostolic representatives, and locate them. "Jesus, the I Am, or central entity, has His throne in the top of the head, where phrenology locates spirituality." The others are as follows:

Faith—Peter—center of brain.
Strength—Andrew—loins.
Discrimination, or Judgment—James, son of Zebedee—pit of
     stomach.

---

[53] *Id.*, p. 23. [54] *Id.*, p. 165. [55] *Thesis*, p. 170.
[56] *Twelve Powers of Man*, p. 167.

Love—John—back of heart.
Power—Philip—root of tongue.
Imagination—Bartholomew—between the eyes.
Understanding—Thomas—front brain.
Will—Matthew—center front brain.
Order—James, son of Alphaeus—navel.
Zeal—Simon, the Cananaean—back head, medulla.
Renunciation, or Elimination—Thaddeus—abdominal region.
Life Conserver—Judas—generative functions.[57]

For a full exposition of this scheme the reader must go to the book itself. It should be said that Mr. Fillmore does not regard the physiological designations of these faculties as arbitrary. The detailed study of the scheme and its application is one of the practical techniques for the maintenance of health and the attainment of salvation.

Unity's concept of man has already been suggested, in part, in the discussion of the idea of salvation and the Twelve Powers of Man. Basically, man, like God, is triune in his nature, as befits one made in the image of the triune God. He is Spirit, Soul, and body. He is, says Mr. Fillmore, "omnipotent Spirit. He expresses himself through soul which makes a dwelling place called body." [58] He is endowed with free will. He made the wrong choice. Instead of opening his mind to the divine intelligence and knowing the creative law, he took the way of blind experimentation and ended in disaster, from which he had to be saved through Christ. Man is a creature of infinite possibilities. He is a son of God having "in embryo all the faculties and powers of that from which he came forth." [59] He is capable of attaining all that Jesus attained, of whom Mr. Fillmore says, "He was consciously one with the absolute principle of Being. . . . He was that Being to all intents and purposes." [60] For did not Jesus pray, "That they may all be one, even as thou Father art in me and I in Thee." (John 17:21). In another connection, he declares: "in man a wonderful being is in process of creation. This being is spiritual man, who will be equal with God, when he overcomes or handles with wisdom and power the faculties of the body.[61] This and other references to God and man and the world lead Dr. Teener

[57] *The Twelve Powers of Man*, p. 16.
[58] *Unity*, Volume 8, p. 421, 1897.
[59] *Talks on Truth*, p. 163.
[60] *Talks on Truth*, p. 169.
[61] *The Twelve Powers of Man*, p. 163.

to observe that, "while Unity leaders attach both personal and impersonal symbols to their concept of God, their pattern of thinking is always pantheistic . . . the casual adornment of the pantheistic structure with personal symbols sometimes gives Unity's God idea the appearance of a hybrid, but it is only in appearance. God is still the inexorable Principle at the source of all existence." [62]

A part of the teaching of Unity is the availability of abundance of supply, such that no one need suffer lack. One of Charles Fillmore's books bears the title *Prosperity.* "It is perfectly logical," he declares, in the foreword, "to assume that a wise and competent Creator would provide for the needs of His creatures," and that—"the supply would be given as required, and as the necessary effort for its appropriation was made by the creature." "What we need to realize above all else," he says, "is that God has provided for the most minute needs of our daily life and that if we lack anything it is because we have not used our mind in making the right contact with the supermind and the cosmic ray that flows from it." [63] "There is a kingdom of abundance of all things, and it may be found by those who seek it and are willing to comply with its laws." [64]

But what are the laws? Well, first, "Every idea of personal possession must be dropped out of mind before men can come into the realization of the invisible supply. They cannot possess money, houses, or land selfishly, because they cannot possess the universal ideas for which these symbols stand. Nobody can possess any idea as his own permanently." [65] "Make a definite and detailed covenant with the Father, lay your desires, appetites and passions at His feet and agree to use all your substance in the most exalted way. Then you are seeking the kingdom and all things else shall be added unto you." [66] This is, of course, an appeal to the direct word of Jesus. It is open to everyone. "Every one of us can strengthen his hold upon the thought of divine substance until it becomes a powerful idea, filling the whole consciousness and manifesting itself as plenty in all our affairs." [67]

If one squares his desires with these conditions his wants will be

[62] Teener, *Thesis,* p. 121.

[63] Fillmore, *Prosperity,* Unity School of Christianity, Kansas City, Missouri, 4th ed., 1940, p. 6.

[64] *Id.,* p. 16.   [65] *Id.,* p. 17.   [66] *Id.,* p. 20.

[67] Fillmore, *Prosperity,* p. 22.

met. He has still to make use of specific affirmations such as: "The all-providing Mind is my resource, and I am secure in my prosperity," [68] or, "I trust Thy universal law of prosperity in all my affairs," or, "Divine love bountifully supplies and increases substance to meet my every need."

Both affirmation and denial are to be used. If, for example, you are "fearful that you will not be provided with the necessities of life for tomorrow . . . or for your old age, or that your children will be left in want, deny the thought. Do not allow yourself for a moment to think of something that must be outside the realm of all-careful, all-providing good." [69] "Do not say that money is scarce; the very statement will scare money away from you. Do not say that times are hard with you; the very words will tighten your purse strings until Omnipotence itself cannot slip a dime into it. Begin now to talk plenty, think plenty, and give thanks for plenty." [70] . . . "If your purse seems empty, deny the lack and say: "You are filled even now with the bounty of God my Father, who supplies all my wants.'" [71]

Unity, more specifically than any of the other groups which stress the power of God to supply man's economic needs, stresses the necessity not only of receiving, but of giving. They emphasize tithing as the road to prosperity—not, however, in a legal sense as is sometimes done. Right giving, says Mr. Fillmore, is the key to abundant giving. One of the publications of the movement bears the title *As You Tithe You Prosper.*[72]

If this fact is held in mind, a revised version of the twenty-third psalm which is offered at the end of one of the chapters of *Prosperity* as a "prosperity treatment," will not seem so almost sacrilegious as it does to many who see or hear it. It reads:

The Lord is my banker; my credit is good
He maketh me to lie down in the consciousness of omnipresent
    abundance;
He giveth me the key to His strong-box
He restoreth my faith in His riches
He guideth me in the paths of prosperity for His name's sake.
Yea though I walk through the very shadow of debt
I shall fear no evil, for Thou art with me;

[68] *Id.,* p. 63.   [69] *Id.,* pp. 92–93.   [70] *Id.,* pp. 103–104.   [71] *Id.,* p. 114.
[72] Meyer, L. E., 3rd ed., *Unity,* Kansas City, 1944.

Thy silver and gold, they secure me,
Thou preparest a way for me in the presence of the collector;
Thou fillest my wallet with plenty; my measure runneth over.
Surely goodness and plenty will follow me all the days of my life;
And I shall do business in the name of the Lord forever.[73]

As will already have been evident in what has been said, Unity makes a constant use of the Bible. It encourages its reading and distributes it through its sales division. In this respect it is much closer to Orthodoxy than any other branch of New Thought. To be sure, the Bible is not regarded as the only or final authority. Mr. Fillmore is quoted by Teener as saying: "Scripture may be a satisfactory authority for those who are not themselves in direct communion with God." Nor is it the only sacred book for which respect is felt. Other sacred books are not to be despised, but taken as "records of men as to what their experiences have been in communing with the Omnipresent God." [74]

The best clue to Unity's attitude toward the Bible is to be found in Mr. Fillmore's *Mysteries of Genesis*, in which he interprets the entire book as he understands it. "It is," he says, "interesting, if not accurate" from the standpoint of the student of history. "The faithful good man finds in it that which strengthens his righteousness, and the overcomer with Christ finds it the greatest of all books as a guide to his spiritual unfoldment." [75] Biblical words have an "inner and and outer significance," and it is, of course, the inner that is of real consequence. It is this which his study purports to give. A few examples will suffice to indicate its nature. It is clearly the symbolical or allegorical method he uses. Thus in the creation story, "waters" represents unexpressed capacities. "Day" is the "state of mind in which intelligence dominates." "Firmament" is "faith," etc. "Yahweh," the Hebrew word for God, signifies the union of "wisdom and love as a procreating nucleus," for "Yah" is masculine, "weh" is feminine, and these correspond to wisdom and love.[76] Thus the female, as well as the male element, is found in God.

In Unity, while Mr. and Mrs. Fillmore's writings are highly es-

[73] Fillmore, *Prosperity*, p. 69.
[74] *Twelve Powers of Man*, p. 115.
[75] Fillmore, *Mysteries of Genesis*, p. 10.
[76] Fillmore, *Mysteries of Genesis*, p. 32.

teemed and much used, there has not appeared, in so far as the writer has observed, a tendency to regard them as sacred or inspired writings, as in the case of some other movements. It is still the Bible, interpreted and made meaningful by the commentaries and teachings of the Fillmores that is at the basis of Unity. It is this that makes Unity more palatable to the orthodox taste than that of some of the other movements.

Unity, in so far as it is true to its founder, is not, and cannot be a church, although as above indicated it has now taken on almost all the distinctive aspects of a church. Mr. Fillmore distrusts organization. There is something self-defeating in attempting to organize a religious faith into a church. The minute a man organizes his religion, he writes, "he ceases to be guided wholly by the free Spirit of truth and to that extent he falls away from the true church." [77] Jesus never organized a church, he argues, "nor did he authorize anyone else to do so. . . . Whoever attempts to organize it on earth, with creeds, tenets, or text books of any kind or description as authority, is in direct opposition to His word and His example. He gave but one guide and source from which His followers should receive their inspiration—the Holy Spirit." [78] Anyone who pretends through creed or book to be an infallible guide, or who through organization of a church seeks to save men by rules and tenets, obstructs the soul's progress. He defines the true church as "a state of consciousness in man. . . . The very body of each man and woman is a temple in which the Christ holds religious services at all times." [79]

He says, "The church of Jesus Christ still waits for a minister that will represent it as it is—an organization in heaven without a head on earth, without a creed, without a written line of authority. This church exists and must be set up in its rightful place—the minds and hearts of men. It can never be confined to an external organization. Whoever attempts such a movement, by that act ceases to represent the true church of Christ." [80]

Holding such an idea, it must be a matter of some concern to its founder that Unity is developing into a rather inflexible organization. An official Statement of Faith was adopted in 1921.[81] A Unity Annual Conference was organized in 1933 and it is difficult to see

[77] *Talks on Truth*, p. 109.   [78] *Id.*, p. 102.   [79] *Id.*, p. 103.
[80] *Id.*, p. 109.
[81] *Unity's Statement of Faith*, Kansas City Unity School, 1938.

in what respect it differs significantly in function from the denominational bodies in Protestantism. It prescribes that before ordination, candidates must take certain courses determined by the Unity School at Kansas City. Membership in the conference is subject to yearly renewal. Only Unity literature is allowed to be used, and regular reports must be made to the Field Department of Unity School. None but those approved by Unity School may preach from their pulpits. Surely here the crystallizing process is going on rather rapidly. Mr. Fillmore organized "Unity Church Universal" in 1924, but soon abandoned the idea of a church. He is, of course, faced by precisely the same problem that faces all those who promulgate new ideas. If the new idea does not get institutional formulation, it is not likely to have widespread influence, nor to perpetuate itself. If it does form an institution, it faces all the hazards that go with institutions. There is nothing new in the dilemma.

Unity has built up an impressive institution in Kansas City. The Fillmores had nothing to start with. The total investment in plant, farm, and Unity Centers now runs into millions of dollars. How has it been done? It has been a rule, says Mr. Fillmore, to make no charge for the services rendered, for example—healings through Silent Unity. Gifts are accepted, if grateful beneficiaries wish to send them in, and many do in quite generous amounts. The literature is sold at very reasonable prices. Their books, which are of about two hundred pages, are on very good book paper and in good cloth bindings, and sell for only one dollar. Their pamphlet material is printed in good form on good paper at very modest prices. There can be little profit there, one would think. Their periodicals are very well gotten up—some of them illustrated in color. Not a little of their material is bought in an open market at current rates, though, of course, it must be in keeping with Unity's general purposes. Yet they are priced at a figure which would certainly not seem designed to return much profit.

They do circulate in large numbers. One small monthly publication has well over a quarter of a million circulation (1945). Their children's magazine runs well up toward two hundred thousand subscribers. In all, the total number of monthly subscriptions goes far beyond a half million,[82] and—counting four and a third issues

---

[82] Mr. Lowell Fillmore stated in a letter in March, 1948 that their "combined circulation or paid subscriptions" is more than a million. One periodical in Spanish circulates 20,000 copies free of charge.

monthly of their weekly paper—they mail out close to a million and a half periodicals each month. How many read them nobody knows for certain. Counting the books and magazines it would not seem at all improbable that as many as five million people are to some degree readers of their literature. One often finds it in homes of Methodists, Baptists, all sorts of Protestants, and even Catholics. One of the Unity leaders told this story as having happened not so long ago. A Catholic woman was not happy in her religious life. She found a copy of *Unity* and it greatly helped her. She felt uncomfortable, however, at going outside the church and so confessed to her priest that she had read *Unity*. To her surprise she discovered that he, too, was reading it. He told her that if she used it rightly there was no reason why she could not read it and still remain a good Catholic.

Within the week during which this was being written, a woman Methodist minister told the writer that she reads two of the periodicals. Indeed, she said that quite recently she had been in ill health, had written Silent Unity for help, and had been healed. How many there are throughout the country who are not Unity followers but who have had like experiences, can never be known. That such persons give financial support to the movement is altogether probable.

But if Unity does not ask for money and does not tell people how much, or to what exent they ought to give it, it does suggest that giving is a part of life and that as one gives and shares so he prospers. Naturally Unity benefits by much of their giving. Unity calls these gifts "love gifts," as does the I Am, who probably borrowed it from Unity.

At the time the writer was visiting Unity they had just announced a half-million-dollar Unity Center for Kansas City which was to be a memorial to Myrtle Fillmore. There would be no campaign or drive, they said, though there would be plenty of publicity. Already substantial gifts have come in. Many contributions have come from quite unexpected sources from outside the membership. A wholly unknown woman once handed Mrs. Lowell Fillmore $25 for it in a public place. Mr. Lowell Fillmore's clothes cleaner, not in any way connected with the movement, handed him $50 for the memorial.

At one time no charge was made for food or service in Unity Tea Room, the guest giving whatever he felt moved to give. But this became an embarrassment to outsiders who thought they might not be giving enough and so stopped coming. Now a regular charge, modest enough, yet not too low, is made and the place is thronged.

Charges have been made from time to time to the effect that the Fillmores were getting rich out of the movement. In a bit of litigation a court statement was made showing that each of the Fillmores received a salary—comfortable—but not out of line with the responsibilities they carried, and certainly not comparable to salaries received by men in the business world who carry equal responsibility. The movement is incorporated as a non-profit organization. But that it does prosper financially there can be no doubt.

One of the devices which has been in use for over thirty-five years and which has brought substantial sums to Unity is the Prosperity bank. Anyone may have one for the asking. It is a small triangular pasteboard container. On the front where the coin slot is located, is printed a picture of the façade of the Unity School at Kansas City, with the text, "Thou, O God, art my mighty resource." On the back is the statement "The Spirit of the Lord Goes Before Me, and My Prosperity, Success and Happiness Are Assured," and other scriptural verses. A border of stars encloses the texts, one of which is to be checked off each time a deposit is made. A sheet of instructions accompanies the bank explaining its purpose and providing for a drill to be carried out each day, "including prayers, affirmations and self-examination." When the coin is deposited one is to declare "God is in charge of all my affairs, and abundant good is manifested for me daily." "As you faithfully follow the drill you will be led to take the right steps to bring your good into manifestation," says a letter which accompanies the bank. At the end of the seven-week period for which the bank serves, remittance is to be made to Unity for whatever purpose the donor may direct, for literature, for himself, or for others, or as a gift to Unity's work. Over 13,000 requests are received monthly, declared Mr. Lowell Fillmore in 1946. Many use the banks regularly year after year. The reports on these banks are very gratifying, says Mr. Fillmore, though how much is realized from this source is not disclosed.

Among the many printed items circulated by the movement are cards about the size of a post-card, suitable for enclosure in letters. These are sold in truly large numbers. A few titles will indicate their nature: "This is Friendship"; "On Spiritual Inheritance"; "Beatitudes for a Housewife"; "Calmness"; "The 23rd Psalm"; "Think on These Things"; etc. Most of them carry no special mention of Unity except the very inconspicuous Unity imprint in very small type somewhere on the card. One, "Metaphysical Gadgets," suggests thirteen affirmations indicated for various situations, e.g.—"I go to meet my good"—(To be used when answering the doorbell or on the way to an appointment); "There is nothing lost in Spirit"—(To be used when something seems to be mislaid); "Peace"—(To be used when there is a disturbing noise, or when you are afraid); or "I am Spirit, and Spirit cannot be sick"—(To be used when somebody remarks that you are not looking well).

The emphasis, in these and other Unity publications and in their practice in the great plant at Kansas City, is upon religion as a constant factor in all of life, rather than merely occasional. One other of the cards entitled, "God Bless this Automobile"—for the use of automobile owners and drivers—is an apt illustration. It reads in part: "This is God's car. God's hand is at the wheel. . . . The driver of this car is an emissary of Spirit. God's wisdom inspires in him alertness, good judgment, and quick decisions," etc. Someone was mean enough to point out that the affirmation had not kept some of Unity's own cars from being involved in accidents. But a driver, conscious of the declarations on the card, would undoubtedly be a safer driver for carrying it.

What of the moral emphases of this movement? We have already made some reference to their moral theory. A word of summary will, however, be in point. As to the nature of evil, it is a little difficult to get a wholly clear picture. At times it seems to be unreal and non-existent,—at other times a terrible and positive force. Mr. Fillmore writes in *Christian Healing:* "Good is all; evil is that which might be if man forsook his guiding light. In the serene mind of God there is no duality, no good-and-bad, no understanding-and-ignorance. The brilliancy of all-knowing Mind dissolves all shadows, all negations." [83] Here evil is evidently negative. Man is free and may will to go his own way, apparently thus producing evil. Satan, says Mr. Fillmore, "is the personal mind that tempts man to try experience without knowledge." [84] In his exposition of the "Fall of Man," in Genesis, he writes: "Man fell because he did not keep his mind on the source of life. He departed from spiritual consciousness and saw both good and evil." And again, as noted above, he envisages two possible choices for man: Satan's way, in which "through

[83] Fillmore, *Christian Healing*, p. 451.
[84] *Id.*, p. 51.

experience of evil man gains by contrast a concept of good"; and God's way, in which, "through consciousness of good, man sees that evil is unreal and unnecessary." [85]

A little farther on he says that if man follows God's way his mind will be "so charged with good that evil will be to him totally unreal." But there is surely a difference between "being unreal" and "being unreal to him." Nowhere does the problem seem clearly resolved, but if Mr. Fillmore has not solved it satisfactorily, he is not alone among founders of religious systems of thought. There is not a little similarity here, it seems to the writer, to the Qualified Monistic philosophy of India. But whatever the ultimate philosophy of good and evil, man finds himself in a moral struggle and good must win out in that struggle if he is to achieve salvation.

Generally speaking, the moral teaching of Unity is of the familiar individual type prevalent in the churches. It undoubtedly emphasizes the Christian virtues of purity, honesty, kindness, generosity, etc. They are not as rigorous in their prohibitions as some of the movements. The attitude toward sex has been pointed out. They do not drink and generally do not use tobacco. Mr. Fillmore, in a half facetious passage in his *Talks on Truth*, is advocating the free access of the individual to God. There is nothing "too wicked or unholy to ask God about," he writes. . . . "If you want a drink of whiskey, a dress, a car, a house, or if you are thinking of driving a sharp bargain with your neighbor . . . ask God for guidance in a moment of silent soul desire." [86]

But the emphasis is almost wholly on the individual—the theory apparently being that good individuals naturally make a good society. There is no evident social drive in Unity. They have no social program, organize no campaigns, carry on no organized social expressions of religion. They have no hospitals, orphanages, clinics, or relief agencies, though individual Unity followers doubtless participate in such movements as individuals. That they firmly believe that social results will flow from the practice of their teachings, is evident. Mr. Fillmore in his *Prosperity*, sees, as a result of the fulfillment of the required conditions of the elimination of the motive of personal selfish possession, the dawn of a new era, when the "principle of universal substance will be known and acted upon, and there will be no lack. Supply will be more equalized. There will not

[85] Fillmore, *Mysteries of Genesis*, p. 48.
[86] Fillmore, *Talks on Truth*, p. 12.

be millions of bushels of wheat stored in musty warehouses while people go hungry. There will be no overproduction or underconsumption or other inequalities of supply, for God's substance will be recognized and used by all peoples. Men will not pile up fortunes one day and lose them the next, for they will no longer fear the integrity of their neighbors nor try to keep their neighbor's share from him." [87] But again it may be noted that Unity differs in no significant way from the average churches in this respect.

Unity is a strong, going concern. Mr. Fillmore is now a very old man. He does not think he will die. But suppose he should. What effect would it have on the movement? Very little—it seems to the writer. Myrtle Fillmore, the co-founder of the movement, had held the same belief. Yet she died. It did not seriously affect the movement. It was quickly observed that she had a great mission to perform and had renounced her already attained eternal life in the body in order to perform it. It would undoubtedly be the same with Mr. Fillmore, for it must not be forgotten that they hold the doctrine of reincarnation. When the writer pressed the question and said, "Yes, Mr. Fillmore, but suppose you should possibly be mistaken and should one day succumb, like the rest of humanity to death. What then? Would you be reincarnated?" His answer was yes. Already he has ceased participation in the active management of the movement, save in the capacity of counsellor, giving himself largely to writing. His sons manage the enterprise now and they are capable men. They, too, are now getting on in years. Will there be successors to carry on, when they are forced by age to retire and then pass off the scene?

There seems to be little doubt that there will be, though it will not come from the Fillmore family. The Unity movement as a church is growing. Already it has a stability far surpassing that of most of the New Thought and similar movements. That they will always go on in the same way, and keep the Unity School in its flourishing state, and always maintain complete loyalty to the Fillmore teachings, may not be certain. But it has now become, to all intents and purposes, a church—an organization—despite Mr. Fillmore's fear and distrust of organization, and it is through this, chiefly, that the teaching of the Fillmores will live on in American life.

[87] Fillmore, *Prosperity*, p. 23.
Word came after the book was in press that Mr. Charles Fillmore died on July 5, 1948.

Chapter Five

Christian Science

Christian Science is a stable, well-recognized religious body with more members than many of the smaller denominations in America which are not dealt with in the present book. Why include it among the modern cults and minority religious movements? For this there are several reasons. First, because, despite the fact that it is national in scope, indeed international, there are literally millions of people who have never seen a Christian Science church or met a Christian Scientist personally, to whom Christian Science is only a name. Christian Science is largely an urban movement. Only a comparatively limited number of smaller communities, aside from those that are suburban, have Christian Science churches, and there are practically none in the country. Second, Christian Science is significantly different at a number of points of belief and practice from what are generally regarded as normative religious beliefs and practices in America. It requires explanation if it is to be understood. Third, there exists almost nothing in written form concerning Christian Science which is not rather highly partisan. It is usually written about by those who would attack it or those who would defend it. Neither may be fully trusted to give a wholly objective picture of the movement. Not necessarily that either side is consciously dishonest in its statements, but personal bias of writers leads inevitably to a selection of material that favors their point of view.

Christian Science went through a stormy period of controversy. Against no modern religious movement has so bitter an attack been made, unless it be Mormonism. It has been condemned, argued against, belittled, ridiculed, in periodicals, pamphlets and books, until Christian Scientists have become hypersensitive and feel on the defensive whenever even well-founded observations of disinterested scholars are made concerning it. No other organization known to the author is so zealous in attempting to correct any supposed misstatement concerning itself. There is, as is well known to those who have written concerning Christian Science, a Committee on Publications in each state, whose business it is to watch the press for anything that might, from their point of view, reflect unfavorably upon the faith, and immediately attempt to have it rectified. The author has more than once had his attention called to his own supposed misstatements, with a request for correction in a future edition of the book. Indeed, material has been offered and received on the basis of which to make the correction. As a matter of fact materials have been gratuitously furnished the writer as a basis for the preparation of this chapter by said committee. It is hereby gratefully acknowledged, and it has been taken into account. Will the Committee be satisfied if the writer does not accept this material as over against other source materials, and will he believe that the writer's conclusion is a wholly honest attempt at objectively presenting the movement?

Perhaps it will be of help both to the general reader and to possible Christian Science readers if the writer presents his own viewpoint concerning not only Christian Science but religions in general. In the foreword this has already been done in a general way. Toward Christian Science he holds the same attitude that he holds toward all the others. In it he sees much that is of value. He recognizes the helpfulness of its ministry to thousands of persons, many of whom did not find that same helpfulness in other churches to which they belonged. He sees great strength in some of its positions—but also great weakness in others. He sees points of great vulnerability in it just as he sees them in other faiths including his own. Obviously he does not accept their beliefs, else he would be a Christian Scientist, but he sees no serious reason to attack them, or to impugn their sincerity in holding the beliefs they cherish, even when he is wholly unconvinced by them personally. He has a profound conviction that truth is its own best defense, and looks upon the insistent desire to establish it and defend it at every point as unnecessary, and, possibly, a reflection of a not too great confidence in it on the part of its defenders. Old Gamaliel uttered a profound saying when in his defense of the early apostles before a group who were for killing them he said, "if this undertaking is of men it will fail, but if it is of God you will not be able to overthrow them." [1]

Particularly open to criticism is the attempt to keep out of circulation books and articles which seem to reflect upon the movement. To resort to the boycott of booksellers who distribute a book which has been condemned by the movement is, it would seem to the author, definitely out of keeping with the well-known democratic American concept of freedom of the press. Furthermore it just is not effective. A biography of Mrs. Eddy which displeased the official leadership of Christian Science was made almost a best-seller by the attempt on the part of the movement to suppress it. A five-dollar book which by reason of the price naturally has a very limited circulation, quickly became a dollar book, thanks to the advertising it got through the attempt to secure its suppression. If anyone doubts that this was done let him read a pamphlet, *The Blight That Failed*, published by Blue Ribbon Books, New York, or an article "The Christian Science Censorship," by Craig Thompson, in the *New Republic*, December 11, 1929.

Has the time not arrived when a dispassionate study of the movement including the life of the founder ought to appear, not alone from the standpoint of the general reader, but for the good of the Christian Science Movement itself? It was of course inevitable in the early days that much of the discussion should center about Mrs. Eddy. She was the movement for many years. Unfortunately she did not begin her great work until she was a middle-aged woman. Her early years were years of illness and maladjustment which gave the very impulse to seek health and stability which resulted in her discovery of Christian Science. But they were years which contained much that made her vulnerable to attack by enemies. The fortunes of Christian Science have been so closely tied up with its founder that any attack upon her has seemed to be an attack upon the faith. She must be defended at any cost. And that defense has been a difficult one. There has come to be an official Life of Mrs. Eddy, that of Sibyl Wilbur written in 1907 and any life story that is not in agreement with it is wrong. To be sure, in more recent years Lyman Powell, an Episcopalian clergyman, who in his earlier ministry had written a sharply critical book about Christian Science, published a life of Mrs. Eddy, in which he supposedly had complete access to the

[1] Acts 5:38-39.

files of the movement in Boston. It proved so favorable that it is now recommended almost equally with that of Miss Wilbur. But if Powell had free access to Christian Science files he seems quite to have disregarded the abundant non-official sources to which other writers have had access. Thus it does not, as it seems to the writer, represent an adequate historical treatment of the subject, for historical writing calls for the careful consideration and weighing of conflicting or differing source materials, and in a case as controversial as that of Christian Science, should call for some occasional statement by the writer as to why he reaches the conclusion he does.

So long as Christian Science chooses to rest the case for its general teaching on the person of Mrs. Eddy it is sure to run into trouble. So long as it insists upon the complete originality of Mrs. Eddy in all that she taught, so long will they have difficulty, for the patient research of scholars, who have no axe to grind, seems to indicate very clearly the influences that played upon her. Certainly she gave them final form. Certainly there is much that is original, in the best sense, in the combination of various elements. Certainly she was a remarkable person to have achieved, late in life, the success that she did, and against formidable opposition.

But is not the teaching the important thing, rather than the origin of it? Is it not this, however it came, that must continue to validate itself in the experience of man if the movement is to continue to live and influence men and women?

Some Christian Scientists are coming to see this. Grateful as they are to Mrs. Eddy, they are saying that it is what she taught that is important, and not her person. Of course if she were divine that might not seem to be the case—but this, leading Christian Scientists deny, and there is certainly no official teaching that she was more than human. That she was "inspired" in her writings is of course common belief, but so was Isaiah according to orthodox Christian and Jewish belief, yet no one would suggest that he was more than human.

It is no part of the writer's purpose here to give the story of Mary Baker Eddy's life. She was born July 16, 1821, at Bow, New Hampshire, the youngest of six children of Mark and Abigail Baker. She received the ordinary education of a district school, though her brother is said to have taught her more advanced subjects during the summer vacations. She was an impressionable child. In later years she told of having frequently heard her name called when a young child and would run to ask her mother what she wanted. But the mother had not called. Finally she answered as the child Samuel had done, but never again, she says, "to the material senses was that mysterious call repeated." [2] She was not a strong child, indeed she was a partial invalid for several years. She was much interested in writing, was given to poetry. Not a few of her poems were published in newspapers and magazines of that day.

It was when she was already past forty, and had been twice married that there occurred certain events which were to have a very important influence on her life. During one of her frequent physical attacks, from a spinal affection, she heard of a man in Portland, Maine, one Phineas P. Quimby, who was accomplishing marvels of healing, and that not by medicine. She resolved at once to go to him and seek her own healing. Accordingly in the year 1862 she appeared in Portland, made contact with Quimby and was healed.

It was from this man, most non-Christian Science writers believe, that she got the beginnings of her ideas of healing, though none claim that she did not add to Quimby's thought and even modify it very significantly. But the Christian Science official view is that Quimby was at best a mesmerist healer and that far from getting anything from him, it was she who gave to him some of the ideas that later he promulgated, and which became the basis of the rise of the New Thought Movement. Here the issue is squarely joined. One side says that Quimby allowed Mrs. Eddy, then Mrs. Patterson, to read and copy some manuscripts which he had, over a number of years, been writing, setting forth the ideas that lay back of his healing.

Sibyl Wilbur, the official biographer, discusses Quimby as a hypnotist, a Mesmerist, making use of animal magnetism, and something of a charlatan. She asserts that there never were any Quimby manuscripts and quotes an unidentified writer in *Human Life*, April, 1907, as her authority, he claiming to have been told by Quimby's son, George, that the supposed manuscripts were copies of copies of things his father had written down on odd pieces of paper from time to time, made by his mother or a Miss Ware.[3] These originals he had locked in his safe and would permit no one to see, and said that he would not publish them until after Mrs. Eddy's death. She

[2] *Retrospection and Introspection*, pp. 8–9.
[3] Sibyl Wilbur, *The Life of Mary Baker Eddy*, Christian Science Publishing Society, Boston, 1938, p. 98.

says, "the conclusion seems warranted that there is nothing worthy of the name of manuscripts in the Quimby safe." [4]

On the other hand, according to Mr. Julius A. Dresser there were over 800 closely written pages covering more than 120 subjects. Here is a clear conflict of supposed facts. It is difficult at this distance in time to discover precisely what the facts were. Other factors have to be taken into account. Chief of these are the extended correspondence which Mrs. Patterson carried on with Quimby, of which a number of the letters have been published in facsimile, and certain articles which she wrote concerning him which appeared in various New England papers.

There can be no doubt that she was deeply and favorably impressed by Quimby and his ideas. Her praise of him in an article in the *Portland Courier*, November 7, 1862, is superlative. She insists in so many words that his method could not have been "animal magnetism" or "electro-magnetism." She had tried healers of this kind. "But," she says, "in no instance did I get rid of a return of all my ailments because I had not been helped out of the error in which my opinions involved us. My operator (the magnetic healer) believed in disease, independent of mind; hence I could not be wiser than my master. But now I can see, dimly at first, and only as trees walking the great principle which underlines Dr. Quimby's faith and works, and just in proportion to my right perception of truth is my recovery. The truth which he opposes to the error of giving intelligence to matter and placing pain where it never placed itself, if received understandingly, changes the currents of the system to their normal action; and the mechanism of the body goes on undisturbed . . . this is a science capable of demonstration. . . . The truth which he establishes in the patient cures him . . . and the body . . . is no longer in disease." [5]

[4] *Id.*, p. 91.
[5] Quoted by Edward F. Dakin, *Mrs. Eddy*, Charles Scribner's Sons, New York, 1930, p. 46, used by permission of the publishers. It was this book to which reference was made on page 182. Dakin has been universally condemned by Christian Scientists. Judge Clifford P. Smith said of it, "The biography by Dakin . . . is distinctly biased and hostile. It presents a false picture by what it contains and what it omits. Its tone is callous and flippant. Mostly, its material is from the Milmine book and from other hostile sources, etc. . . ." The writer holds no brief for the conclusions reached by Mr. Dakin, or by Bates and Dittemore whose book, *Mary Baker Eddy, Truth and Tradition*, was also excoriated by Christian Scientists. Certainly Dakin does descend to ridicule of Mrs. Eddy, and so vitiates to some extent

This quotation from Mrs. Eddy, herself, quite apart from any manuscripts, seems clearly to establish one fact, namely that she had gotten from him one of the basic doctrines which she later taught, that of opposing "truth to error" as a means of healing. It was not wholly unnatural that she, at a later time—many years later —as the head of a growing religious body, under heavy opposition, should have seen fit to deny any influence of Quimby and to excuse this and other utterances as the result of having "my head so turned by animal magnetism and will power, under his treatment, that I might have written something so hopelessly incorrect as the articles now published in the Dresser pamphlet." [6] But the objective student who does not recognize "animal magnetism" can hardly be expected to accept it as a sufficient explanation of such a statement.

Then, too, certain other statements of Mrs. Eddy lead the careful student to question her later repudiation of Quimby's influence.

The date generally recognized as the time of the real discovery of Christian Science was 1866, after the death of Quimby, which had occurred in January 16, 1866. The occasion was a fall upon the ice resulting in what she describes as a near fatal injury, as a result of which the doctor, she says, told her she would never walk again. But in two days she did walk, and this marvelous experience of healing "was the falling apple that led me to the discovery how to be well myself and how to make others so." [7] The doctor forty years later made affidavits in which he transcribed from his records, made of the case at the time of its occurrence, and in this there appears no indication that he regarded her condition as hopeless. He says, indeed, "I did not at any time declare or believe that there was no hope for Mrs. Patterson's recovery." This latter statement was of course not in the transcript, and might possibly have resulted from a lapse of memory after forty years. More convincing, however, is

---

the value of his book, since it lays him open to the charge of bias, and makes the reader, who seeks to approach the matter objectively, distrustful of his other conclusions which may be perfectly sound. However, both books do quote liberally from original sources not easily available to everyone, and it is chiefly this material which I have taken from these authors in the present treatment. The original sources can of course be checked. The fact that Mr. Dittemore wrote to the Board of Directors in Boston regretting his attitude toward the Mother church government can in no sense be taken as denying the authenticity of the original materials his book contains.

[6] Boston *Post*, March 7, 1883. Quoted by Dakin, *op. cit.*, p. 44.
[7] *Retrospection and Introspection*, p. 24.

the casual statement, "I visited her twice on February first (the day of the fall), twice on the second, once on the third, and once on the fifth, and on the thirteenth of same month my bill was paid." He adds a little later, that on the 10th of the August, following, he again attended the patient, visited her three times and prescribed the usual remedies for the bad summer cold and cough from which she was suffering.[8]

However, on February 14, Mrs. Patterson wrote a letter to Mr. Julius A. Dresser, fellow patient of Dr. Quimby, which is published in full by Horatio W. Dresser in the *Quimby Manuscripts*,[9] also in Georgia Milmine's *Life of Mary Baker Eddy*.[10]

In this she recounted the fall on February 1 but declared, "in two days I got out of bed alone and will walk; but I confess I am frightened, and out of that nervous heat my friends are forming, in spite of me, the terrible spinal affliction from which I have suffered so long and so hopelessly. . . . Now can't you help me? I believe you can. I think I could help another in my condition."

The official biographer explains the letter as a "backward glance to Quimby and Quimbyism."

The letter she said was written to a former patient of Quimby, for Quimby was now dead and "could not obtrude his unformulated theories between her mind and its own spiritual apprehensions." [11] Mrs. Patterson in her letter had said to Mr. Dresser, "I am constantly wishing that you would step forward into the place he has vacated. I believe you would do a vast amount of good, and are more capable of occupying his place than any other I know of."

The official biographer comments that the former patient, whom she, for some reason, never names, "replied that he did not know how Quimby had performed his cures and doubted if anyone did," and declined the task of "reviving Quimbyism or attempting to stand in the shoes of the mesmerist." So she says, "There was a closed door against that refuge from her own responsibility, a refuge which had presented itself to her mind as at least a temptation. Quimby was dead. Quimbyism had perished with him. No one remained of those who had gathered around him in life to perpetuate his peculiar influence. Her fall had destroyed the very work she had so long

[8] Quoted by Dakin, *op. cit.*, pp. 61–62.
[9] Thomas Y. Crowell Company, New York, 1921, p. 163.
[10] Doubleday Page & Co., New York, 1909, p. 69.
[11] Wilbur, *op. cit.*, p. 129.

credited him with. Everything must begin anew for her; life must be made completely over. She was forced to turn to God." [12]

One other consideration may be added. In 1883 Mr. Julius A. Dresser published a letter concerning pioneer work done by Quimby in mental science before 1866. Mrs. Eddy in a letter in the *Boston Post* wrote that "We made our first experiments in mental healing about 1853." [13] But again when Mr. Dresser in 1887 lectured in Boston on Quimby's discoveries and aroused considerable public discussion, Mrs. Eddy asserted in the *Christian Science Journal*, "As long ago as 1844 I was convinced that mortal mind produced all disease." [14]

What can one do in such a case but leave judgment to the readers? But the objective writer can hardly refrain from an expression of his own conclusion on the basis of the evidence, of which admittedly he has by no means presented the whole—the limitation of available space forbids that—though he has read most of what has been alleged on both sides of the controversy.

His own belief is that Mr. Quimby did make some very important discoveries in the realm of mental healing. For a brief discussion of this see the chapter on New Thought. He is recognizedly the basic figure in the beginning of the New Thought Movement. Mrs. Eddy learned much from him both as to theory and practice. It is probable that her conversations with him planted ideas in her mind upon which she reflected deeply, for she was a thoughtful person. Quimby was not primarily a religious person in the usual meaning of that term, although basically he was. Mrs. Eddy was profoundly religious. It was natural, therefore, that she should invest the whole matter with deep religious meaning. It is not without significance that Mr. Horatio Dresser, the historian of the New Thought Movement, should stress the fact that the earlier phases of the New Thought Movement emphasized primarily the *mental* phase of healing, in distinction from the *divine* element. And there has always been a dominantly secularist wing of the movement.

Mrs. Eddy was a constant reader of the Bible. She thought she found in the Bible the truth which was dawning upon her, and her formulation of that thought was in religious and Biblical terms. She made a religion of it.

Moreover that she was not a merely slavish borrower from

[12] *Id.*, p. 130.   [13] March 1883.   [14] June 1887.

Quimby is evidenced by the fact that their philosophies differ radically at certain points, though the basic practice in healing differs but little if at all.

Moreover both Quimby and Mrs. Eddy were living in an intellectual climate that had in it the germs of both New Thought and Christian Science, and conceivably either might have arrived at the place he ultimately attained without ever having met the other. But historically, of course, they did meet. That climate was Transcendentalism, which was a combination of the Kantian philosophy of idealism with elements of Hindu philosophy which had crept in through the widespread circulation among intellectual readers of newly translated Hindu religious and philosophic classics. Emerson is full of it, so is Thoreau, and Bronson Alcott was deeply touched by it.

Mrs. Eddy may never have read the *Upanishads*, the basic philosophic texts of Hinduism, but she may well have been acquainted with them at second if not at first hand. She makes no definite reference in her writings to them, but some of the fundamental ideas there set forth could have been taken directly from Hindu sources, for example, the whole idea of the unreality of matter. Whence did it come? To be sure there was Berkeleian idealism which held that things had real existence only in ideas, or for that matter the Platonic concept of things as the shadows of ideas, which were the reality. And of course there is the new physics which demolishes the older concept of "hard" matter and resolves it into a phase of energy, but Mrs. Eddy knew nothing of that. However, her followers are finding great comfort in such a novel concept of matter and regard it as a substantiation of the truth of Mrs. Eddy's thought.

The closest approximation to the thought of Mrs. Eddy is to be found in the Hindu concept of the one Real, and the illusory character of all else. So, also, her fundamental denial of the reality of evil and suffering is an almost exact restatement of one phase of Hindu thought.

Now it is conceivable, of course, that she was wholly original in this discovery. This must be admitted. But when she was steeped in an intellectual atmosphere of which this formed a part, it must also be admitted that she may have been either consciously or unconsciously influenced in her thought by it.

Such an assertion is unwelcome to Christian Scientists. The author has already been admonished of his error by the Committee on Publications for suggesting elsewhere such a possibility.

The reason for this concern is not hard to discover. Such an explanation is doubtless felt to reflect on the *Christian* character of Christian Science, and there is an obvious desire to maintain this character in a dominantly Christian, or so-called Christian culture. But to say that she has borrowed from Hinduism is not to say that the movement is not Christian, although many have denied, wrongly as the author thinks, that it is. Christianity is multiform. Who can say exactly what is and what is not Christian? Christianity itself in its historic development has incorporated ideas from many sources, Hebrew, Greek, Roman, North European and even American. Why should it not incorporate ideas from the East? As a matter of fact Christianity in India is being definitely colored by Hindu thought in some respects. Mrs. Eddy may or may not have made a plausible synthesis of Hindu and Christian ideas. That is a matter of personal judgment, depending very much on the point of view of the person exercising judgment. But that she has taken ideas from, or similar to some Hindu thought and given them a Christian and a Biblical setting there can be no reasonable doubt. And that, it must be conceded, she has every right to do if she so wishes, and whosoever will has a perfect right to follow her in her thinking. But of course it must ultimately validate itself before the bar of public opinion on the bases of the intrinsic truth that it contains. Calling it Christian or non-Christian does not establish its truth or falsehood. Saying that Mrs. Eddy, the channel through which it was brought to the world, was original in her discovery of it, or humanly dependent upon Mr. Quimby or other sources, does not establish its truth or falsity. Neither will the allegation that Mrs. Eddy was a petulant, irritable, disagreeable person of little personal ability who purloined her system from a greater mind, Quimby or some other, as some represent her, nor that she was the perfect paragon that she appears to be in the official literature of the movement, wholly inspired from above in her discovery and development of Science.

It is no part of the author's intent to praise or condemn it, to prove it true or false, but to convey, in so far as he may, an understanding of it to those who may desire to know. If by its teaching, it more or less successfully makes sick people well, unhappy people happy, evil men good, selfish men generous, nervous people calm, in the name of Christ or the Christ within, he will not feel like denying its right to call itself Christian any more than he would that of the many other imperfect human institutions calling themselves Christian which achieve, however imperfectly, the same general results.

The nine years between her discovery of Christian Science which she asserts was 1866, and the publication of the first edition of *Science and Health* in 1875 were difficult years. Her second marriage, to a dentist, Dr. Patterson, had not proved to be a happy one. She had no settled home for any length of time, but moved from place to place, living in rented quarters, or in the homes of friends who were attracted, at least at first, by her teachings. The story of those years differs so greatly in the official life and in those by her critics that it is difficult to suppose they are writing about the same person. In the one she is a gentle, loving, but much misunderstood figure persecuted by others for the truth which she was unfolding; in the other she is a determined woman who exploits her friends, abuses their hospitality, giving little or nothing in return, only to turn upon them bitterly when they are no longer willing to endure her presence. Where lies the truth? Probably in neither extreme statement. On the one hand, there is a too facile explanation of some of the alleged facts produced by the critics, which are likely to convince only those who are already convinced. On the other hand, there seems at times to be a disposition on the part of the extreme critics to put the worst possible construction upon a given episode. From it all there emerges a figure who, however notable her later achievement as founder of a new faith, definitely has "feet of clay." All of which is exactly what those expect who do not raise her to a plane of divinity.

They were undoubtedly years of struggle. Much of her time was employed in writing out her thought, bringing into form what ultimately appeared as *Science and Health*, in 1875. During these years she began to train students as, what later came to be called, practitioners. Hiram Crafts was the first, a shoe-maker of East Stoughton, Mass., who after five months of instruction advertised in May, 1867, in Taunton, Mass., "Would say unhesitatingly I can cure you, and have never failed to cure Consumption, Catarrh, Scrofula, Dyspepsia and Rheumatism. . . . If you give me a fair trail and are not helped I will refund your money." [15]

Mrs. Eddy herself—then using the name Mrs. Mary B. Glover

---

[15] Quoted by Bates and Dittemore, *Mary Baker Eddy, The Truth and the Tradition*, George Routledge and Sons (Routledge and Kegan Paul, Ltd.,) London, 1933, p. 120. See footnote on sources, pp. 185–186.

—advertised in *The Bower of Light*, June 20, 1868; "Any person desiring to learn how to heal the sick can receive from the undersigned instruction that will enable them to commence healing on a principle of science with a success far beyond any of the present modes. No medicine, electricity, physiology or hygiene required for unparalleled success in the most difficult cases. No pay is required unless this skill is obtained. . . ." [16]

In 1870 she taught Richard Kennedy her system and entered into partnership with him. They took rooms in Lynn, and Kennedy hung out his sign. He was to pay Mrs. Eddy one-half of his earnings. Also he was to refer to her anyone who might be interested in training in the healing art. This arrangement brought her a number of students who signed an agreement to pay her $100 for her course of twelve lectures and 10% of their income from practice, or one thousand dollars in case of failure to practice.[17] Later the fee was raised to $300. The movement was now definitely under way.

But the way was not easy. Her teaching provoked opposition. Not all her students succeeded. Some refused to pay the 10% of their income. She sued. The matter came into court and she lost. In the report of the court incidental information, based upon Mrs. Glover's own testimony, indicates that she was still using manipulation as part of her method, as it had been of Dr. Quimby's.[18] But she came to the conclusion that it was not necessary and sought to eliminate it. Much later she was to regard it as a fundamental denial of the spiritual nature of healing, saying, "when you manipulate patients you trust in electricity and magnetism more than in Truth. . . . You weaken or destroy your power when you resort to any except spiritual means." [19]

When she began to teach her students to discontinue it, Kennedy objected and eventually their disagreement led to a parting of the ways. He destroyed the contract between them and sought another office. She was to regard him ever afterward as an enemy who sought by Malicious Animal Magnetism, M.A.M., to injure her.[20]

In 1875 she established herself in a new home which she had purchased and here, tradition has it, the writing of *Science and*

---

16 Bates and Dittemore, *op. cit.*, p. 124.
17 *Id.*, p. 138.
18 Bates and Dittemore, *op. cit.*, pp. 141–142.
19 *Science and Health*, 181:9-13, *passim*.
20 See pp. 213 ff.

Health was completed. Here she started once more with five students. And it was in this same year that the first organization of a society was effected. A small group of people formally agreed to contribute regularly toward a fund for the rental of a public hall and the employment of Mary Baker Glover "to preach to us or direct our meetings on the Sabbath of each week." The first public meeting of the society was held June 6 in Templar's Hall, Lynn, Mass. For six years the young movement continued in Lynn, growing slowly, though violently opposed by pulpit and press. The publication of *Science and Health* made for her both friends and enemies. Its early distribution was very discouraging, but Mrs. Glover at once set about the work of revising it for a second edition. Meanwhile, in 1877, she married her third husband, Asa Gilbert Eddy, taking the name now so familiar to all the world.

In 1879 the movement was granted a charter under the name "The Church of Christ (Scientist)," with headquarters in Boston, though Mrs. Eddy continued for a time to reside in Lynn. In 1881 she founded the Massachusetts Metaphysical College in the Lynn home. That year saw the withdrawal of a substantial number of the group, but the remainder formally ordained her as their pastor. There were probably fewer loyal followers at the end of her years at Lynn than in the first year, but a start had been made in Boston. She resolved to leave Lynn and go thither. The Metaphysical College was moved to the larger city and continued its work of instruction beginning with seven students.

Gilbert Eddy's health began to fail. Despite all her healing efforts he passed away on June 3, 1882. Here was a severe blow to a healing movement. She attributed it to "arsenical poisoning," according to the Boston *Daily Globe*,[21] "the result of a malicious mesmeric influence exerted over his mind by certain parties here in Boston, who had sworn to injure him." Mrs. Eddy was for the third time a widow. She was sixty years old. She was faced by the most formidable odds. She might have given up. But she did not. The account of the phenomenal success she achieved in the remaining twenty-seven years of her life is one of the most remarkable success stories in American life.

In the same year, 1882, Calvin Frye joined her. He was to be one of her most devoted followers, her personal secretary, her most

[21] June 2, 1882.

trusted counsellor, for the remainder of her life. He kept a diary which has been invaluable to an understanding of Mrs. Eddy during her years of success. In 1883 she founded the *Christian Science Journal*, announced as an "Independent Family Paper to Promote Health and Morals." Here were later to appear the names of all accredited practitioners and all local Christian Science Societies throughout the world, a most valuable source therefore in a study of the extension of the movement.

While the little group in Boston was slowly forging ahead, Mrs. Eddy's students had gone, some of them, to distant places to practice healing and to teach others the art. Disciples in Chicago invited their leader to give a course of lectures there as early as 1884, and she did so, leaving an enthusiastic group to carry on and develop into a strong church. Though her early followers had been drawn largely from among the workers in industrial Lynn, in Boston men and women from the more privileged groups began to be attracted. Some of them were persons of notable gifts who were to occupy places of distinct leadership in Christian Science. Augusta Stetson, who was later to develop her great church in New York, and to be the center of one of the greatest storms in a stormy period of growth, first became interested in Science in 1884. In 1886 was organized the National Christian Scientists' Association, proof that the movement had grown far beyond a local setting. Also land was purchased for the erection of a church building in that year. In 1888 Mrs. Eddy went again to Chicago and spoke to over eight hundred enthusiastic delegates to a Christian Science convention in Central Musical Hall. She was given a remarkable ovation.

During her years in Boston she had been pastor of the local group as well as leader of the expanding movement. She felt that the time had come in 1889 to retire from the local leadership and devote her whole strength and energy to the larger movement. She therefore left Boston to take up residence in Concord, N. H. She closed forever the Massachusetts Metaphysical College where so many of her followers had been trained, and even caused the disorganization of the Boston Society. She offered to deed a property suitable for a church edifice on condition that the church legally disband.

In place of the local Boston church which, though legally disbanded, had continued informally, Mrs. Eddy organized the "Mother Church" in 1892. In the terms of the deed conveying the property the government of the church was vested in a self-perpetuating

Board of Directors whom she first appointed. They were to elect the pastor and other leaders, maintain services of worship, and make necessary rules for carrying out the purposes of the church. The property was to revert to the donor in case of neglect to carry out the conditions of the trust deed. They were to erect a church to cost not less than $50,000 within a period of five years.[22]

Twelve "charter members" of the new church organization were appointed to pass upon all "candidates for admission," including all former members of the Boston group. These twelve chose twenty others and these thirty-two were to be called First Members of the First Church of Christ Scientist [23] provided they accepted the tenets which Mrs. Eddy had prepared, and which still remain only slightly changed as published in the *Church Manual*.[24] To these First Members at a public meeting fifty-nine other members were added, and thereafter the membership increased rapidly. At the second annual business meeting report was made of 2,897 members, only about one-twentieth of whom were Boston residents. Christian Scientists from all over America were invited through the *Journal* to join the Mother Church. It had now become a national, not a local body, the head of all Christian Scientists everywhere. It was governed by rules adopted by the Board of Directors and by a number of by-laws sent down by Mrs. Eddy herself and added to as occasion arose, during her lifetime. These constitute the *Church Manual* by which the church is governed today. The first section of Article XXXV concerning the *Church Manual* asserts that nothing can be adopted or amended or annulled without the written consent of the Leader. Thus her control as long as she lived was complete, and since she cannot now give written consent, it is impossible ever to change them in any way. Most living institutions have left themselves some possible legal way to change with the passing years. Mrs. Eddy left Christian Science no such possibility. It thus becomes a relatively inflexible movement. One may venture to guess that ways will be found to reinterpret some of the language used in the by-laws in the course of time.

When Mrs. Eddy ceased to act as pastor, another was appointed in her place. It was the custom to have pastors in all the churches. In April, 1895, however, Mrs. Eddy handed down a by-law which

[22] *Church Manual*, 89th Edition, pp. 128–138.
[23] *Id.*, p. 18.   [24] Pp. 15–16.

"ordained the Bible and *Science and Health with Key to Scriptures,* as pastor on this planet of all the Churches of the Christian Science denomination." Christian Science pastors acquiesced without opposition to the by-law and it has ever since been the law of the church. As afterward modified in the *Manual,*[25] it ostensibly applies only to the Mother Church, but it is the universal practice among Christian Science churches. Local churches are regarded as branches of the Mother Church and all Christian Science readers, lecturers, and teachers must be members of the Mother Church. Local churches generally have adopted as their own the *Church Manual,* and are guided by it in every particular. A Board of Lectureship was set up and each church is expected to call for a lecturer at least once a year. Lecturers must send written copies of their lectures to the Clerk of the Mother Church before their delivery. No debate or public discussion on Christian Science is permitted without consent of the Board of Directors.[26] A Committee on Publications is ordained for the Mother Church and in each state and in Canada for the purpose of correcting false or misleading statements in the public press concerning Christian Science or its founder. Members are forbidden to buy, sell, or circulate incorrect statements of Christian Science, or to buy from publishers or book stores who have on sale "obnoxious books." [27] It is on the basis of this rule that Christian Scientists are today sometimes urged to bring pressure to bear upon booksellers not to handle books regarded as unfavorable to Christian Science. "Obnoxious" is of course capable of various interpretations. It could mean immoral, obscene, pornographic, but in the context in which it appears, following directly a section dealing with "incorrect statements of Christian Science," its reference seems clear.

The *Manual* prescribes conditions for joining the church. One who is not a member of any church, excepting one of the branches of the Mother Church, who knows Christian Science and reads understandingly the textbook and other books by the founder; who is "Christianly qualified" and accepts the formal tenets of the Mother Church may become a member. On the application blank he must state specifically that he has severed his relationship with any church of which he was once a member. No dual membership is possible in Christian Science as in so many other groups.

[25] Art. XIV, Sec. 1   [26] Art. X.   [27] Art. VIII, Sec. 12.

A definite and invariable order of service is prescribed for every public occasion and rigidly followed. A Board of Publication is required to publish requisite lesson material to be followed strictly in all the churches. The reading of portions of scripture by the Second Reader followed by the reading of correlative passages from *Science and Health with Key to Scriptures* by the First Reader is the heart of the worship services, taking the place of the sermon. The same lesson is used in every Christian Church on the same day the world around.

Each branch church is allowed to have its own form of government, and is not under the control of the Mother Church.[28] No branch church may have other branches.[29] Nor may branch churches hold conferences except within a state, for certain definite purposes.[30]

The Mother Church was dedicated in January, 1895. In it a room was set apart as "Mother's Room," for the personal use of Mrs. Eddy who was seventy-four years of age. It is beautifully furnished. Though apparently occupied but once by Mrs. Eddy it has become one of the most sacred spots for Christian Scientists who visit it in large numbers every year. It is no longer open to non-members of the churches.

The building seems small, quite dwarfed by the magnificent extension which was built and dedicated eleven years later. Towering above all the surrounding buildings its great dome is a Boston landmark now, to which thousands and thousands of Christian Scientists from all over the world are drawn every year to attend public services. But the original Mother Church still holds the affection of Christian Scientists, probably because of its closer association with their revered Leader. Across the street is the great luxuriously appointed Publishing House which was dedicated at the height of the depression without a cent of indebtedness, but rather a surplus in the building fund. It thus stands at once as a symbol of the rapid growth of the movement and of the appeal of a gospel of healing in a world where sickness is so widely prevalent.

Success had come to Mrs. Eddy beyond anything that could have been predicted. She continued, in her retirement at Concord and later at Chestnut Hill, a suburb of Boston, to revise *Science and Health* periodically, and write extensively. In 1908 she caused to

[28] Art. XXIII, Sec. 1, *Church Manual.*
[29] Sec. 3.   [30] Sec. 1.

be founded *The Christian Science Monitor*, one of the really great newspapers of America, which we have already characterized. The years brought troubles not a few. Some of her students, dissatisfied with some aspects of Christian Science, or irked by the highly centralized control exercised by Mrs. Eddy and the Mother Church, broke away and founded movements of similar nature, but differing in some respects. Mrs. Augusta Stetson in New York, Mrs. Bill in London, Mrs. Gestefeld and Mrs. Hopkinson in the Middle West and others became leaders of dissident movements. Some of these later became affiliated with the New Thought Movement. It was not easy to hold them all. Nevertheless the movement spread widely not only throughout America but the world.

Mrs. Eddy lived until 1909. She had become a legend long before she passed from the scene. Her control had been so absolute, and was so thoroughly exercised through a small group in the Mother Church, that her death made little or no change. There have been inner struggles for power since, but the outside world has known little about them. The church has gone on growing and continues to grow. The successive decennial religious census shows the following: 1906, 85,717; 1916—; 1926, 202,098; 1936, 268,915.[81]

While the church has been more largely urban than otherwise there has been a steady growth in the number of societies in smaller towns.

Sunday Schools are maintained for the instruction of children and youth, and reading rooms are provided by most churches and societies where Mrs. Eddy's writings may be read or borrowed, and the periodical literature is available for use or purchase. Mid-week testimony meetings are held, usually on Wednesday nights, where opportunity is given for those who have been healed or otherwise helped by Christian Science to voice their gratitude and share their experiences with others. This is probably the growing point of the movement. Many who hear these testimonies are led to inquire further and often to accept the teaching, particularly if they are themselves in need of healing.

The churches are in general prosperous. Unlike so many of the minority groups, far from losing social prestige by joining them, many feel that they raise their social standing. The churches are well located, not on the side streets. They are usually attractive and in

[81] No statistics are reported in the 1916 Census.

the cities imposing. Lacking in the symbolism used in other churches they feature in their interiors the sayings of their Leader as well as of Jesus. Although to persons who come from the liturgical churches the worship service may seem rather barren, it nevertheless is dignified. The music is often that of the Protestant churches in general, though the words of the hymns carry the teachings of the church, and seem strange to those familiar with the traditional words.

Christian Science gets its people to read. Many of them dedicate regular periods of the day for reading and study of Science, and this pays rich dividends. They likewise encourage meditation. On the whole their method does seem to produce calm, quiet, poise, in the individual which so many harried people in our modern world who do not have a time to read and meditate and pray, seldom achieve.

WHAT IT TEACHES

What are the teachings of Christian Science concerning the great central concepts of religion. What does it teach concerning God?

It is well to begin here, for in this particular faith everything else derives from that idea. Out of it flows logically everything else Mrs. Eddy taught, for "God is All." [32] Whatever is not God is unreal, insubstantial, non-existent, the result of mortal error. "God is the only real substance." [33] Matter, things, are not substantial. "The objects cognized by the physical senses," she says, "have not the reality of substance." [34] Matter is "nothing beyond an image in mortal mind." [35] It is "mortal error. Spirit is the real and eternal; matter is the unreal and temporal." [36] Again, "matter has no life, hence it has no real existence." [37] That which seems to be real, but in truth is unreal, is of course an illusion. Mrs. Eddy does not often use the identical word, illusion, to express the idea of the illusory character of the physical world of apparent reality as is commonly the case in Indian thought, but now and again she does so explicitly; thus, "Matter and death are mortal illusions." [38] And in the glossary of terms contained in *Science and Health*, which she felt it neces-

[32] *Science and Health*, 339–7, 366–29, 532–24. Page references are to the 1910 and subsequent editions of *Science and Health* as finally revised by Mrs. Eddy. The second number in the citations refers to the line or lines on the page indicated by the first number.

[33] *Id.*, 468:22.   [34] *Id.*, 311:26–27.

[35] *Science and Health*, 116:18.

[36] *Id.*, 468:11–13.   [37] *Id.*, 584:11.   [38] *Id.*, 289:29.

sary to define, doubtless because many of them are there used to signify something else than their usually accepted meanings, Mrs. Eddy specifically defines matter as "mythology; mortality; another name for mortal mind; *illusion* . . . that which the mortal mind sees, feels, hears, tastes and smells only in belief." [39] When one further inquires as to what she means by "mortal mind" the definition given is: "nothing claiming to be something . . . mythology; error creating other errors," etc.[40]

God, it appears therefore, is the only reality, the one real. Any other apparent existence is the result of ignorance, error, mortal mind. Thus far the resemblance to Hindu thought is remarkably close, whether derived from it or not. Mrs. Eddy does not, however, refuse to predicate anything with reference to the nature of God. It is undoubtedly her Christian heritage which leads her to attribute to God the many qualities with which she endows him. Thus her formal definition of God in the glossary is: The great I Am; the all-knowing, all-seeing, all-acting, all-wise, all-loving, and eternal; Principle; Mind; Soul; Spirit; Life; Truth; Love; all substance; intelligence." [41] Elsewhere she equates God and good.[42] In what she calls "a platform," set forth in the chapter on The Science of Being, in *Science and Health*, she elaborates her concept of God. God is infinite, the only Life substance, Spirit or Soul, the only intelligence of the universe, including man.[43] "God is what the scriptures declare him to be—Life, Truth, Love . . . Mind . . . in reality one Mind only, because there is one God." [44] "God is All in All . . . nothing possesses reality nor existence except the divine Mind and His ideas." [45] "God is individual incorporeal . . . all inclusive . . . reflected by all that is real and eternal and by nothing else . . . He fills all space." [46]

God is also triune, but here Mrs. Eddy departs sharply from Christian orthodoxy, for "Life, Truth, and Love constitute the triune Person called God—that is the triply divine Principle, Love. They represent a trinity in unity, three in one—the same in essence, though multiform in office." [47] This seems quite different from the traditional Trinity. She goes on, however, to approach that somewhat more closely when she says further: "God the Father-Mother; Christ the spiritual idea of sonship; divine science the Holy Com-

[39] *Id.*, 591:8–15, *passim.*   [40] *Id.*, 591:25–27.   [41] *Id.*, 587:5–8.
[42] *Id.*, 587:19.   [43] *Id.*, 330:11–12.   [44] *Id.*, 330:19–24, *passim.*
[45] *Id.*, 331:11–13.   [46] *Id.*, 331:18–25, *passim.*   [47] *Id.*, 331:26–30.

forter. These three express in divine Science the threefold, essential nature of the infinite." [48]

Mrs. Eddy makes much use of the Father-Mother concept. It has been suggested that this may have come to her from the Shakers who stressed it in their teaching. There was a Shaker colony not far from where she spent part of her early life, and she almost certainly would have heard the term used. It expressed for her more adequately the character of God than the sole term Father. The real embraces all, therefore it embraces all the qualities supposedly inherent in both the sexes. The element of tenderness and love and compassion are better represented in the mother aspect of deity. She says: "Father-Mother is the name for Deity, which indicates His tender relationship to his spiritual creation." [49] Is she here doing something of what Roman Catholics do in elevating the Virgin to the office of the "Mother of God"?

The third "person" of the trinity "the Holy Comforter" she equates with divine Science. This has been taken to mean that she regarded her own teaching as the Holy Ghost or Holy Spirit or Holy Comforter. Color is lent to this understanding by her statement, "The terms Divine Science, Spiritual Science or Christian Science, or Science alone, she employs interchangeably, according to the requirements of the context. These synonymous terms stand for everything relating to God, the infinite, supreme, eternal Mind." She goes on to say, however, that "the term Christian Science relates especially to Science as applied to humanity." [50] Christian Science was the name she gave historically to a divine Science that had existed from the beginning of the world. Once at least she equates it with the "Word of God." [51] "Christ in divine Science shows us the way," [52] He demonstrated divine Science to his disciples "by healing the sick and the sinning." [53] He said: " 'But the Comforter . . . shall teach you all things!' When the Science of Christianity appears, it will lead you into all truth. The Sermon on the Mount is the essence of this Science." [54]

Most of the terms which Mrs. Eddy uses to describe God seem to be abstract, especially when capitalized. Is God for her impersonal? Let her reply in her own words.

[48] *Id.*, 331:30 ff.   [49] *Id.*, 332:4–5.   [50] *Id.*, 127:15–16.
[51] *Id.*, 503:12.   [52] *Id.*, 242:10.   [53] *Id.*, 271:14–15.
[54] *Id.*, 271:19–24.

"Do I believe in a personal God? I believe in God as the Supreme Being. I know not what the person of omnipotence and omnipresence is or what the infinite includes, therefore I worship that of which I can conceive, first as loving Father and Mother, then as thought ascends the scale of being to diviner consciousness, God becomes to me as to the apostle who declared it, 'God is love-divine Principle, which I worship, and after the manner of my fathers so worship I God.' " [55]

As a matter of fact she oscillates continually between the personal and impersonal thought of God, though she never uses the neuter pronoun to designate God as the more logical Hindu thinker does. God is always *He*, capitalized. She seems to have reacted strongly against the extreme anthropomorphic concept of God widely current in her time, as now, and to have associated the idea of personality of God with form. This she cannot allow.

"We must learn," she writes, "that God is infinitely more than a person or finite form can contain; that God is a divine *whole*, and *All*, an all-pervading intelligence and Love, a divine infinite Principle." [56] In so saying she seems almost to anticipate a fairly commonly held idea among modern theologians, that God is not so much *impersonal* as suprapersonal. But she freely uses the language of psychic anthropomorphism. God sees, hears, knows, loves, reveals purposes, inspires, thinks, is good, tender, kind, compassionate. In this she is true to her Christian heritage.

Her idea is generally held to be pantheistic. Certainly the statement "God is all" tallies with the generally accepted meaning of the term pantheism. She does not, however, like the term and definitely denies that it is true of her thought.[57]

She distinguishes clearly between Jesus and Christ. In this Christian Science and the whole New Thought group are at one.[58] She writes in *Science and Health:* "Christ is the ideal truth that comes to heal sickness and sin through Christian Science and attributes all power to God. Jesus is the name of the man who more than all other men, has presented Christ, the true idea of God, healing the sick and the sinning and destroying the power of death. Jesus is the human man, and Christ is the divine idea; hence the duality of Jesus the Christ." [59]

55 *Id., Miscellaneous Writings*, p. 96, 107th ed., 1912.
56 *Miscellaneous Writings*, p. 16, 107th ed.
57 See her *Christian Science Versus Pantheism*.
58 Cf. pp. 140 ff.
59 *Science and Health*, 473:10-17.

Jesus only demonstrated Christ, thus proving "that Christ is the divine idea of God—the Holy Ghost, or Comforter, revealing the divine Principle Love, and leading into all truth." [60] Note the identification of Christ with the Comforter. Jesus was born of the Virgin Mary. In his birth without the intervention of a human father, that is, conception by the overshadowing of Spirit, or idea Mrs. Eddy saw the possibility of the ultimate elimination of the necessity of marriage. In the resurrection there will of course be no marrying nor giving in marriage.[61] But, "until it is learned that God is Father of all, marriage will continue." [62] Would this ever occur in this life? Whether Mrs. Eddy ever thought so or taught so, is a matter of difference of opinion, but that some of her followers thought that she did is a matter of historic record. Great embarrassment to the cause resulted from the announcement of a one-time follower that she had conceived a child spiritually. Among the followers of Mrs. Stetson, well-known Christian Science leader in New York, the idea was definitely held and taught.

Mrs. Eddy asserts that she never knew of more than one case of belief in "agamogenesis," and this was held by an unmarried woman who was suffering from incipient insanity, and specifically declares "I discredit the belief that agamogenesis applies to the human species." [63]

In saying, "I and the Father are one," Jesus was not referring to the corporeal Jesus, but to "the divine idea or Christ" who is eternal.[64] The Christ was "invisible and imperceptible to the so-called personal senses" until he was manifested by the corporeal Jesus. After the ascension "the human material concept, or Jesus, disappeared while the spiritual self, or Christ, continues to exist in the external order of divine Science, taking away the sins of the world, as the Christ has always done, even before the human Jesus was incarnate to mortal eyes." [65]

In her conception of the work of Christ, Mrs. Eddy reacted vigorously against the traditional ideas of the atonement as somehow designed to satisfy something in the mind of God before salvation could be granted to humanity. The work of Christ is directed

[60] *Science and Health*, 332:19–22.
[61] Matthew, 22:30.
[62] *Science and Health*, 64:26–27.
[63] *Id.*, 68:16–26, *passim*.
[64] *Id.*, 334:1–3.
[65] *Science and Health*, 334:10–20.

manward, not toward God. "The atonement of Christ reconciles man to God; not God to man," she writes, "for the divine Principle of Christ is God, and how can God propitiate himself?" [66] This, Jesus aids in doing "by giving man a truer sense of Love, the divine Principle of Jesus' teachings, and this truer sense of Love redeems man from the law of matter, sin and death by the law of the Spirit —the law of divine Love." [67] Jesus' work was exemplary. He "did life's work aright . . . to show them (mortals) how to do theirs," but he did not do their work for them "nor relieve them of a single responsibility." [68] "His consummate example was for the salvation of us all, but only through doing the works which he did and taught others to do." [69] "Pinning one's faith without works, to another's vicarious effort" will not avail.[70] "Whosoever believeth that . . . divinity is appeased by human suffering does not understand God." [71] "One sacrifice, however great, is insufficient to pay the debt of sin. The atonement requires constant self-immolation on the sinners' part. That God's wrath should be vented upon His beloved Son is divinely unnatural. Such a theory is man made." She admits that the atonement is a hard problem in theology but offers as its "scientific explanation" this: "that suffering is an error of sinful sense which Truth destroys, and eventually both sin and suffering will fall at the feet of everlasting Love." [72]

Man is to work out his own salvation along the path opened for him by Jesus as the way-shower. Both faith and works are necessary and a man's faith is attested by his works.

But what is the meaning of the salvation which is thus achieved?

Is salvation a present experience, is it this-worldly, or does it take place in a future world and on another plane? She defines it formally in the Glossary as: "Life, Truth, and Love, understood and demonstrated as supreme over all; sin, sickness and death destroyed." [73] A recent and eminent Christian Science leader speaks of it as entrance into a "haven of perfect being." [74] Since the ideal includes the destruction of sickness, it obviously has to do with the present world in which sickness afflicts human kind. One who is

---

[66] *Id.*, 18:13–15.   [67] *Id.*, 19:6–10.   [68] *Id.*, 18:6–9.
[69] *Id.*, 51:19–21.   [70] *Id.*, 22:23–27.   [71] *Id.*, 22:27–29.
[72] *Science and Health*, 23:1–10, *passim*.
[73] *Id.*, 593:20–22.
[74] *Id.*, Albert F. Gilmore, *Christ at the Peace Table*, Prentice-Hall, New York, 1943, p. 51.

sick, or believes he is, has certainly not attained to salvation. We shall return later to deal with this, for it is central in Christian Science teaching. Here only let it be noted that it is a phase of the total salvation ideal. "The atonement . . . includes man's redemption from sickness as well as sin . . . a whole salvation." [75] And sin! However unreal it may be it is something with which man is profoundly concerned here and now. The destruction of sin is held to be a present possibility, so again, salvation has to do with the present life. What is sin? Mrs. Eddy does not specifically define it, but usually brackets it with sickness and death as above. It is worse than sickness, she says once.[76] Sin alone she says elsewhere, "brings death, for sin is the only element of destruction." [77] As a matter of fact she asserts that along with sickness and death it is a delusion,[78] an illusion,[79] whose "only reality is the awful fact that unrealities seem real to human erring belief until God strips off their disguise." [80] If one equates sin with evil as he may in most cases, then it is said to be "nothing," [81] unreal,[82] an illusion,[83] temporal not eternal,[84] lacking in power and intelligence.[85] Yet because mortal mind conceives of it as real, it is a problem to be dealt with and belief in it must be overcome. In the last analysis the only way to escape the misery of sin is, says Mrs. Eddy, "to cease sinning. There is no other way." [86] It will not do to "pray and repent, sin and be sorry," if one lacks the "practical repentance which reforms the heart and enables man to do the will of wisdom." [87] Sin can be overcome in this life. Indeed, the attainment of moral or Christian perfection is held up as an ideal, to be achieved by extracting error from mortal mind, and this is accomplished by pouring in "truth through flood-tides of love." [88] "Sin can and must be forgiven. God is forgiving. But it cannot be forgiven when it is not forsaken." [89]

But salvation is not limited to this life. Life is eternal and goes on after the bodily existence is ended. Man is immortal, because he is spiritual. He has always existed and "is always beyond and above mortal illusion of any life, substance and intelligence as existent in

[75] *Miscellaneous Writings*, 107th ed., p. 96.
[76] *Science and Health*, 408:3.
[77] *Id.*, 196:9–10.   [78] *Id.*, 204:10.   [79] *Id.*, 494:23.
[80] *Id.*, 472:27–29.   [81] *Id.*, 287:18.   [82] *Id.*, 71:2; 339:9; 186:16.
[83] *Id.*, 480:23.   [84] *Id.*, 569:25.   [85] *Id.*, 399:1.   [86] *Id.*, 327:12–13.
[87] *Id.*, 19:21–24, *passim*.
[88] *Science and Health*, 201:16–18.
[89] *Id.*, 202:1.

matter." [90] Death is but a "belief." [91] It is a "dream from which mortals must waken." [92] It is "an illusion, the lie of life in matter, the unreal and untrue, the opposite of Life." [93] "Any material evidence of death," Mrs. Eddy says, "is false, for it contradicts spiritual facts of existence." [94] There is to be sure, "a change called death," [95] but in reality "man in Science is neither young nor old. He has neither birth nor death." [96] "Sin brought death, and will disappear with the disappearance of sin." [97]

It is because of this kind of teaching that death, or "the change called death" occurring within the ranks of Christian Scientists has always been an embarrassment, though Mrs. Eddy herself recognized its inevitability. Man has not yet attained to the state in which he can demonstrate eternal life and overcome death; but that death may finally be overcome is firmly held by Christian Scientists today. No official ritual was ever provided for funerals by Mrs. Eddy, though she provided an exact and unvarying order of service for other occasions. Many of her followers quite expected that Mrs. Eddy herself would not die, and when the "change called death" came, thought that she would be resurrected, though the official leadership of the movement disavowed any such a belief.

What lies beyond the "change called death"? Certainly not the heaven or hell of traditional Christian orthodox thought. There is no such thing as an everlasting hell. Hell she defines as "mortal belief; error; lust; remorse; hatred; revenge; sin, sickness, death, suffering and self-destruction, self-imposed agony, effects of sin, that which worketh abomination or maketh a lie." [98]

Nor is heaven a locality, "but a divine state of Mind in which all manifestations of Mind are harmonious and immortal, because sin is not there, and man is found having no righteousness of his own, but in possession of the 'Mind of the Lord.' " [99]

She does, however, speak of life as going on upon another plane or state of existence, [100] and communication is possible between those on the same plane, though never between those on different planes. [101]

[90] *Id.*, 302:15–18.   [91] *Id.*, 380:2–3.   [92] *Id.*, 429:17.

[93] *Id.*, 584:9–10.   [94] *Id.*, 584:15–16.

[95] *Id.*, 254:17; 290:16; 487:6; 572:24; 172:9; 82:20.

[96] *Id.*, 244:23–24.   [97] *Id.*, 426:28–29.

[98] *Science and Health*, 588:1–4.

[99] *Id.*, 291:13–18.

[100] *Miscellaneous Writings*, 34:17; also p. 42.

[101] See Chapter IV, *Science and Health*.

But little detail is supplied, however, concerning that life. Once she wrote:

"Man is not annihilated, nor does he lose his identity by passing through the belief called death. After the momentary belief of dying passes from mortal mind, this mind is still in a conscious state of existence; and the individual has but passed through a moment of extreme mortal fear, to awaken with thoughts and being as material as before. . . . Spiritualization of thought is not attained by the death of the body, but by a conscious union with God. When we shall have passed the ordeal called death, or destroyed this last enemy, and shall have come upon the same plane of conscious existence with those gone before, then we shall be able to communicate with and to recognize them." [102]

Apparently new bodies appropriate to that existence are acquired. Mrs. Eddy says: "Mortals waken from the dream of death with bodies unseen by those who think that they bury the body." [103] Indeed there may be a succession of bodies. "Mortal belief dies to live again in renewed forms, only to go out at last forever." [104] Here appears a comparatively adequate basis for a belief in reincarnation, and some one-time Christian Scientists have taught reincarnation as a fact, [105] though Christian Science does not hold any such view. What seems quite definite is that life goes on and that some kind of progression takes place toward the ultimate goal, never very clearly defined. Mrs. Eddy writes:

"Mortal mind creates its own physical conditions. Death will occur on the next plane of existence as on this, until the spiritual understanding of Life is reached. Then . . . will it be demonstrated that 'the second death hath no power.' " The period required for this dream of material life . . . to vanish from consciousness 'knoweth no man . . . neither the Son, but the Father.' This period will be of longer or shorter duration according to the tenacity of error." [106]

"Reaching the spiritual understanding of Life." What does that mean? Recall the phrase of Albert F. Gilmore, "haven of pure

[102] *Miscellaneous Writings*, 107th ed., p. 42.
[103] *Science and Health*, 429:17–18.
[104] *Id.*, 556:10–12.
[105] See Swihart, *After Mrs. Eddy*, Henry Holt and Co., New York, 1931, pp. 237 ff.
[106] *Science and Health*, 77:8–18, *passim*.

being." Is it final mergence of the soul in "the All?" I have found no such statement in any Christian Science writings. Heaven she calls "the harmony of being." Harmony does not connote unity of being, but separateness, with all the elements of opposition removed. "Christ in divine Science shows the way to it. It is to know no other reality—to have no other consciousness of life—than good, God, and his reflection, and to rise superior to the so-called pain and pleasure of the senses." [107]

For whom is salvation possible? Is it universal? Apparently so. "Universal salvation rests on progression and probation, and is unattainable without them," she writes.[108] But at least the possibility that some might not attain to it is found in one passage: "If a man should not progress after death, but should remain in error, he would be inevitably self-annihilated. Those upon whom the 'second death' hath no power are those who progress here and hereafter out of evil, their mortal element, and into good that is immortal, thus laying off the material beliefs that war against Spirit and putting on the spiritual elements in divine science." [109]

Mrs. Eddy declared concerning the Bible, it "has been my only authority. I have had no other guide in 'the straight and narrow way' of Truth." [110] The use of the Bible in Christian Science is constant. In Christian Science churches there is no sermon. Its place is taken by the reading aloud of the Bible and the correlative passages in *Science and Health*. It is used, that is, as understood and interpreted by Mrs. Eddy. One example of her method of interpretation must suffice. Let the reader examine the entire *Key to Scriptures* which is always bound up with *Science and Health*. This covers only a part of Genesis and Revelation, but her method could be applied to any part of scripture. It was the method of allegory and symbolism. Thus: "Spiritually followed, the book of Genesis is the history of the untrue image of God, named a sinful mortal. This deflection of being, rightly viewed, serves to suggest the proper reflection of God and the spiritual actuality of man as given in the first chapter of Genesis. Even thus the crude forms of human thought take on higher symbols and significations, when scientifically Chris-

---

[107] *Id.*, 242:9-12.
[108] *Id.*, 291:12-13.
[109] *Miscellaneous Writings*, 2:24 ff.
[110] *Science and Health*, 126:29-31.

tian views of the universe appear, illuminating time with the glory of eternity." [111]

Here is the interpretation of Gen. 1:3. "And God said let there be light; and there was light." "Immortal and divine Mind presents the idea of God: first in light; second in reflection; third in spiritual and immortal forms of beauty and goodness. But this Mind creates no element nor symbol of discord and decay. God creates neither erring thought, mortal life, mutable truth, nor variable love." [112]

Science and Health with Key to the Scriptures is a second scripture to the Christian Scientists. This is seen in the constant use made of it, and the authority that is accorded it, equal to or greater than the Bible itself, since the true meaning of the latter is known only through the interpretation given it in *Science and Health*. That Mrs. Eddy considered herself inspired in its writing is scarcely open to question. Christian Science rests upon it. Indeed, it is the exposition of Christian Science, and concerning Christian Science she writes in *Science and Health*: "Christian Science is unerring and divine." [113] She refers to the "divine origin and operation of Christian Science," [114] the "divine basis of Christian Science; [115] the Divine Principle of Christian Science; [116] the divine rules of Christian Science"; [117] and declares specifically that *Science and Health* "is the voice of Truth to this age and contains the full statement of Christian Science." And in another connection she writes "since the divine light of Christian Science first dawned upon the author, etc." Surely there can be no doubt that both she and her followers regard it as of divine inspiration.

Mrs. Eddy defines the church as "the structure of Truth and Love; whatever rests upon and proceeds from divine Principle . . . that institution which affords proof of its utility and is found elevating the race, rousing the dormant understanding from material beliefs to the apprehension of spiritual ideas and the demonstration of divine Science, thereby casting out devils or error, and healing the sick." [118] She is here obviously defining Christian Science as church, and not the orthodox Christian church, which she was sure had lost

[111] *Science and Health*, 502:9–17.
[112] *Id.*, 503:18–25.
[113] *Science and Health*, 99:15.
[114] *Id.*, 272:24.　[115] *Id.*, 388:7–8.　[116] *Id.*, 495:29.
[117] *Id.*, 462:4.　[118] *Id.*, 583:12–18.

the pristine purity of the primitive Christian Church. She was not content to have her followers continue on within the churches. They must be brought into the true church—that which she had founded and formed into a closely knit, highly centralized body of believers.[119] We have already described the organization which has grown out of her teachings.[120] Christian Science was bitterly attacked by and in the churches in the years of its earlier development—indeed is even yet the frequent object of attack by conservative ministers. It was natural enough, therefore, that Mrs. Eddy should have reacted vigorously against such attacks. But if she saw the weaknesses and mistakes of the Christian churches, she also came early to recognize the value and necessity of organization in the extension and transmission of truth. In the end she created her own church and so saw to it that her understanding of the truth should have a channel through which it might flow out into the life of the world.

The moral teachings of Christian Science are the ones commonly accepted in the orthodox churches. There is nothing different here. It undoubtedly makes for individual honesty, truthfulness, purity, kindliness, generosity. "The use of tobacco or intoxicating drinks is not in harmony with Christian Science," writes Mrs. Eddy. Any sex indulgence or sensuous pleasure is frowned upon. Even the necessity of sex in procreation is regarded as something less than ideal and will ultimately disappear as man progresses. Celibate existence is therefore a distant goal, an ideal finally to be realized, though not for the present possible of attainment. No marriage ceremony is provided in the *Church Manual*, though it is required that if a Christian Scientist marries,[121] the ceremony should be performed by a legally authorized clergyman.

But here as in the teachings of so many of the churches, there is little stress upon the social implications of the teachings of Jesus. Perhaps the most notable social outreach of Christian Science is the

---

[119] *Church Manual*, Art. IV, Sect. 2.
[120] Pp. 195 ff.
[121] Art. IX, Sect. 1, *Church Manual*.

Rev. Irving C. Tomlinson writes in *Twelve Years with Mrs. Eddy*, Christian Science Publishing Co., Boston, 1945, p. 112: "Originally Mrs. Eddy had no plans for establishing a new denomination, for, as I heard her state many times, she confidently expected that the Christian Church would welcome her discovery and adopt the healing ministry as an integral part of its activity." But when they refused, "it was only natural then that Mrs. Eddy and her followers should seek to have a church of their own."

Christian Science Monitor which is in no sense a house organ or propaganda sheet, but a newspaper of high order, probably the cleanest, most wholesome published in America. It refuses to report the scandalous, the sinister, the more debasing type of news, but rather the important, the constructive, the wholesome happenings of the day. Christian Science has developed few social institutions even of the merely ameliorative type such as are common among the churches, hospitals, orphanages, homes for the aged, good will industries, schools or colleges, save for the specific teaching of their own particular doctrines.

Nor have they been known as crusaders for social righteousness. Little social passion has been generated by Christian Science, even though it is to be credited with the development of a fine type of individual piety. This is of course most natural. If evil and sin are regarded as but illusions, unreal, the opposite of good, perhaps it is illogical to be found to be deeply concerned about them. To build hospitals for the care of sickness would perhaps be to dignify mortal error beyond its just merit and would be confusing to outsiders, who might reasonably question, on the basis of popular understanding or misunderstanding of Christian Science, why there should be needed hospitals to treat that which is unreal and has no existence. Of course even Christian Science leaders recognize that people need to be helped, that they are desperately unhappy and seem to feel pain, even if the pain is not real. Why therefore might there not be set aside places to which people might go, when suffering from error, where conditions favorable to the correction of error might be provided. As a matter of fact three such institutions are maintained, one in Boston, one in Concord, and one in San Francisco, California.

Christian Science, as we have seen, has a definite set of beliefs—a philosophy, and appeals to many persons precisely as philosophy. But the thing which draws people into Christian Science is its healing ministry. Christian Science preaches a gospel of present healing as an important phase of man's whole salvation. It began with healing, Mrs. Eddy's recovery from illness led to her acceptance or elaboration of a philosophy to support it. The healing came first, and it is chiefly so among the adult membership of the movement, or rather among those who have come into the church as adults. They do, of course, rear children in the faith, and for them the teaching may come first, though always reinforced by the fact of healing.

Does Christian Science really heal people? Of course it does. To argue the contrary is to run counter to an array of facts that simply cannot be ignored. Christian Science heals. Not always, of course, not every case, possibly not every disease, although there is testimony to the healing of almost every kind of disease known to man in Christian Science literature or, if not recorded in the literature, it has been heard in the testimony meetings which play a most important role in the life of the church. Often the testimony is to healing of diseases named without benefit of expert diagnosis, and unconfirmed by any competent objective observer. But discounting all this, there can be no doubt that myriads of people have been healed, and have stayed well, thanks to the help of Christian Science.

How are they healed? Christian Science healing is not mental they believe. It is set off sharply against the so-called mental healings practiced by other healers. It is not, says Mrs. Eddy, as so often imagined, "only a phase of the action of the human mind, which action in some unexpected way results in the cure of disease. . . . On the contrary . . . the physical healing of Christian Science results now, as in Jesus' time, from the operation of divine Principle, before which sin and disease lose their reality in human consciousness and disappear as naturally and as necessarily as darkness gives place to light and sin to reformation." [122] If, as Mrs. Eddy, says, "the cause of all so-called disease is mental, a mortal fear, a mistaken belief or conviction of the necessity and power of ill-health," [123] then the remedy is indicated—get rid of the mistaken belief. This one may do with no outside help. Reading of *Science and Health* is itself one of the best ways to achieve this, and many testify to having found health in precisely this way.[124] But resort to a practitioner is usual, for the practitioner is one who has been prepared by a special course of training to know the truth about so-called disease and to know how to show the supposed sufferer the error in which he is involved, and hence point the way to a cure. The chapter of *Science and Health*, entitled Christian Science Practice, seems to be addressed chiefly to those who would help in the healing of others. Here, for example, are directions for treatment of a fever:

"If the body is material, it cannot, for that very reason, suffer with a fever. Because the so-called material body is a mental concept

[122] *Science and Health*, p. xi:1-13, *passim*.
[123] *Id.*, 377:26-27.   [124] *Id.*, 422:5 ff.

and governed by mortal mind, it manifests only what that so-called mind expresses. Therefore the efficient remedy is to destroy the patient's false belief by both silently and audibly arguing the true facts in regard to harmonious being—representing man as healthy instead of diseased, and showing that it is impossible for matter to suffer, to feel pain or heat, to be thirsty or sick. Destroy fear and you end fever." [125]

Or take one of the most frequent maladies, the common cold. "If your patient believes in taking cold," writes Mrs. Eddy, "mentally convince him that matter cannot take cold and that thought governs this liability." [126]

The first thing in any treatment is to allay the patient's fears. If fear be removed the patient is healed. The leader is advised to call the disease by name silently, not audibly, and mentally to deny it. He is to argue, again mentally, not audibly, "that the patient has no disease," to insist mentally "that harmony is the fact and that sickness is a temporal dream. . . . Realize the presence of health and the fact of harmonious being, until the body corresponds with the normal conditions of health and harmony." [127] If such effects can be wrought silently and without audible argument, why might not healing be done at a distance or in absence? Are Mind and its effects subject to space considerations? Not at all, declares Mrs. Eddy. "Science can heal the sick who are absent from their healers, as well as those present, since space is no obstacle to Mind." [128] So absent healing is frequently practiced.

But if constructive effects can be wrought in another "mentally" or in absence, may not evil effects also be produced? If one may do another good thus, may he not also do him evil?

This very logical inquiry opens up naturally one of the darker chapters of Christian Science history, one that many who are devout followers of the movement would prefer to forget. But unfortunately it is too much a part of it to be neglected. It may well be that unfriendly critics of Mrs. Eddy have overemphasized the importance of Malicious Animal Magnetism, or M.A.M. in Mrs. Eddy's life, but it certainly cannot be wholly erased from the record. Mrs. Eddy was accustomed to attribute her ills and difficulties to the M.A.M., or the mental malpractice of some of her enemies. Richard

[125] *Science and Health*, 376:17–26.   [126] *Id.*, 377:1–3.
[127] *Id.*, 412:10–27, *passim.*   [128] *Id.*, 179:5–7.

Kennedy, an early student, was charged with exercising such mental malpractice against her, also Daniel H. Spofford and others. A case was brought in the courts at Salem, Massachusetts, by a Lucrecia L. S. Brown, complaining "that Daniel H. Spofford is a mesmerist and practices the art of mesmerism, and that by his power and influence he is capable of injuring the persons and property and social relations of others and does by said means so injure them." [129] Mrs. Eddy attended the trial which resulted in the dismissal of the case. She later asserted that the suit had been brought contrary to her advice and judgment. But say Bates and Dittemore "In both the second and third editions (of *Science and Health*), written before and after the Brown case, she repeatedly demanded that the courts take cognizance of the crime of mesmeric influence." [130] In current editions she says that "all mental malpractice arises from ignorance or malice aforethought. It is the injurious action of one mortal mind controlling another from wrong motives, and it is practiced either with a mistaken or a wicked purpose." [131] This is a clear statement of the possibility of such control. When her loyal followers seemed to waver in their loyalty she would warn them of the subtle influence of M.A.M. For example when Julia Field-King was recalled from London it was because M.A.M. had affected her. "Mother never has and cannot be mistaken in her diagnosis of M.A.M.," she wrote. [132] One of the charges made against Mrs. Stetson, most influential of Mrs. Eddy's followers, who had an enormous following in New York, was that "Mrs. Stetson attempts to control and injure persons by mental means; this being utterly contrary to the teachings of Christian Science." [133] Mrs. Stetson was forced to withdraw A by-law, Art. VII, Sect. 8, forbids intentional malpractice by any member, since the Golden Rule must be followed in the practice of Christian Science. Particularly forbidden is mental malpractice upon the Leader or her staff under pain of exclusion from the church.

To ward off the attacks of M.A.M. upon herself and her move-

[129] Quoted from the court record in Newburyport *Herald*, May 16, 1878.

[130] *Mary Baker Eddy*, pp. 193–194.

[131] *Science and Health*, 451:28–30.

[132] Bates and Dittemore, *op. cit.*, p. 350, quoted from a letter to Mrs. T. K. from M.B.E.

[133] Quoted by Bates and Dittemore, *op. cit.*, p. 439.

ment Mrs. Eddy is said to have named certain persons close to her who would "take up" the supposed malpractitioner and so counteract their destructive power. Both Dakin and Bates and Dittemore give instances of this, particularly in the closing years of Mrs. Eddy's life. Sibyl Wilbur and Lyman Powell make no reference to it. The former base some of their statements upon the Journal of Calvin Frye, who was closer to Mrs. Eddy than any other person. For example an entry for November 15, 1883, says in part: "Mrs. Eddy has had a belief of difficulty of breathing for the last two days and got only temporary relief from it; this morning at about four o'clock she called me to help her. . . . This morning she discovered that the mesmerists were arguing to her inflammation and paralysis of muscles of lungs and heart so as to prevent breathing and heart disease with soreness between the shoulder blades [sic]. She experienced the greatest relief when she and I took up Kennedy and Arens to break their attempts to make her suffer from aforementioned beliefs, and she said, 'I have not breathed so easy for two days.' " [134]

For a number of years in the 80's M.A.M. was much referred to in the *Journal*. In 1887 a special department was devoted to it. Apparently some of the followers thought she gave too much attention to it, for in the October, 1885, issue she wrote:

"Those who deny my right or wisdom to expose its crimes are either participants in this evil, afraid of its supposed power, or ignorant of it." Modern-day Christian Scientists are disposed to say little about M.A.M. I discover that sometimes Christian Science college students seem to know nothing at all about it. Asked concerning the place it plays in contemporary Christian belief and practice, a prominent Christian Scientist said that it is no longer stressed as in the past, although the possibility of its existence and influence is not denied.

Is Christian Science growing? Since the movement does not publish statistical reports, there is no way of knowing certainly the facts. The successive religious census reports give the following figures, 1906, 85,717; 1916, —[135]; 1926, 202,098; 1936, 268,915; but how nearly complete they are is uncertain. There is one way, how-

[134] Quoted by Bates and Dittemore, *op. cit.*, p. 228.
[135] Statistics for 1916 are not given in the census report of that year.

ever, of discovering whether the movement is going ahead, at least in the number of its societies and whether it is spreading. The *Christian Science Journal* has for at least four decades published monthly a list of the churches and societies, their location, time of meeting, etc. Comparing these lists by decades, it is possible to ascertain whether more centers have been opened in a given state or country. This does not tell how many members any individual church or society may have. A society is an incipient group not organized formally as a church. There must be at least three members to form a society, and a church may be organized with seventeen members. Some societies are of substantial size, some churches quite small, some very large. The *Christian Science Journal* lists 2103 organized groups in the United States in November, 1946. If the average church had as many as 150 members the total membership would be 315,450. But the U. S. Religious Census 1936 gives 87 as the average size of the local groups, not counting the Mother Church in Boston, of which the majority are also members. The average including the Mother Church was 105 in 1926, and 127 in 1936. Unless the average has increased there would actually be fewer members now than reported in the religious census for 1936 when there were 2113 organizations, ten more than in 1946. The number of societies listed outside of the United States in November, 1946, was 594, not including Germany or Rumania concerning which information is totally lacking. This would make the world total, 2697. It is doubtful if the foreign groups have as large an average membership as those in the United States since in many places they are very small. If they were to average 150 per group the foreign membership would reach 89,100. If, as seems much more likely, the average were 100, the number would fall to just a little less than 60,000. On this basis the total world membership would be certainly not more than 375,000.

A few statistics concerning some typical areas will be enlightening as to growth and expansion. First, Massachusetts, the state of its origin.

In 1916 there were 60 organizations in 56 cities or towns, 44 of them churches, 16 societies.

TABLE IV *Christian Science in Massachusetts*

	Cities Occupied	Total Organizations	No. Churches	No. Societies
1916	56	60	44	16
1926	65	69	53	16
1936	76	79	63	16
1946	77	82	70	12

This represents a gain of 15% in the number of organized groups 1916–26, 14% 1926–36, and 4% 1936–46. Whether the groups are large or small there is no way of knowing.

Indiana may be taken as a fairly representative middle western state. Here the growth is as follows:

TABLE V *Indiana*

	Cities	Total Organizations	No. Churches	No. Societies
1916	61	61	33	28
1926	76	80	47	33
1936	75	79	47	32
1946	73	78	54	24

Here there was a very substantial increase in the number of organizations 1916–26, but a slight decrease in each subsequent decade. A detailed comparison of the listing for 1916–26 revealed that five groups disappeared during the decade while twenty-one new ones appeared. Eight of those in the 1926 list dropped out but six new ones were added by 1936. Six of the 1936 list do not appear in 1946, but five were added. The net gain in organized groups 1916–46 was 27 groups or 26%.

A number of the societies became churches, but some of the churches also became societies. Thus Angola was listed as a society in 1916, and 1926, as church in 1936, but as a society again in 1946. Peru reported a society in 1916, a church in 1926, but a society in 1936 and 1946.

Illinois reports the total member of organizations for the four decades as 101, 122, 133, 128, a 20% growth 1916–26; 10% 1926–36; and a loss of 9% 1936–46. The total increase in organizations 16–46 was 26%. Chicago, Illinois, accounted for 17, 19, 22, and 23 organizations respectively in the same period.

New York City listed 14, 37, 33, and 33 by decades, an increase of 164% during 1916–26 and a decrease of almost 9% during 1926–36 and to 1946. The net increase 1916–46 was 123%. Again it must be indicated that this tells nothing as to the size of the churches. The number of members may actually have increased.

California has shown substantial growth. Here the count was as follows:

TABLE VI *California*

	Cities	Total Organizations	No. Churches	No. Societies
1916	128	152	83	69
1926	192	233	88	145
1936	211	275	209	66
1946	221	276	214	62

Here again the expansion was notable during 1916–26. They were in 50% more cities and had 53% more groups at the end of the decade. The increase in the number of organizations in the next decade was, however, but 15%; and that during 1936–46, almost negligible, only one group in the ten years, though they had entered 10 new cities or towns. There was, however, probably a numerical gain in the membership, for while in 1926 there were but 88 churches and 145 societies, there were in 1936, 209 churches and but 66 societies. The division in 1946 was 214 churches, and 62 societies. The increase in the total number of organizations over the thirty-year period was 81%; in the number of cities occupied, 73%.

Los Angeles listed 10, 25, 35, and 38 organizations in the same years; Oakland had no group in 1916, but 8, 9, 9 in the succeeding decades while San Francisco, also without a church in 1916, listed 9, 11, and 12 in 1916, 1926, and 1936.

Turning to the South, a few typical states revealed the following:

TABLE VII

	1916		1926		1936		1946	
	Cities	Org.	Cities	Org.	Cities	Org.	Cities	Org.
Mississippi	11	11	6	6	12	12	12	12
Virginia	9	9	12	12	14	14	12	12
Tennessee	7	8	6	9	7	10	9	11
S. Carolina	1	1	5	5	5	5	5	6
N. Carolina	10	10	15	15	19	19	21	21

A net gain of but one organization in thirty years in Mississippi, three in Virginia and four in Tennessee indicates but slow growth there, though in North and South Carolina the increase was more notable.

From all this it is impossible to draw any very definite conclusions except that there seems to have been a rather rapid growth up to 1926 and but moderate growth since that time, always, of course, it must be remembered in the number of organizations.

The expansion abroad is seen in the following table:

TABLE VIII

Christian Science Groups in Certain Countries Outside of the United States

	1916	1926	1936	1946
Africa	6	12	30	31
Asia	5	12	26	25 *
Australasia	9	19	54	63
Netherlands Indies and Philippines		2	4	5
Europe				
France	2	2		
Germany	9	28		
Sweden	1	2	4	5
Switzerland	4	10	22	36
England	76	137	257	292
Scotland	4	6	10	16
Canada	44	51	76	72

* Not including Japan.

There are scattered groups in other European countries as well as in Latin America which are not included here. No generalization as to rate of expansion is possible here, for it has proceeded at quite different rates in different areas, but it has in most countries forged steadily ahead. England has accepted Christian Science more widely than any other country. It experienced an 80% increase in the 1916–26 decade; 88% in the next; and 36% in the last ten years. Canada had fewer groups in 1946 than 1936. It appears to have been the only one to experience a loss. And even here there may actually have been an increase in membership.

What of the future of Christian Science? Will it continue to grow and expand throughout the world? There is every reason to believe that it will. So long as there are people who suffer physical ills, there will always be an appeal in it. For people want to be well. They want it desperately. Any movement with the record of successful healings that Christian Science has need not fear the future. And to those who find in it healing, must be added a significant number who finds in its total philosophy some definite appeal.

Christian Science is well established. It owns well located, impressive buildings in most large centers, which inspire respect. There is even prestige value in belonging to it, a statement which can be made of very few of the movements described in this book.

That its early rate of growth will be maintained may hardly be expected. Already it seems to have reached the "plateau" which appears in the growth curve of most new movements. But that it will continue to grow, and to expand into new territory, may be expected, and that it will find increasing social acceptance seems quite probable. That it may have to undergo some internal changes, some relaxation of the rigorousness of its central control, seems altogether likely. There may be serious cleavages within before this is accomplished. But it will go on, and it will continue to draw from the established churches substantial numbers of those who do not find in those churches the satisfaction of what they regard as their legitimate needs.

Chapter Six

Theosophy

In the newer religious movements in America women have played a much more important role than in the older groups. Modern Spiritualism began with the Fox sisters; Mrs. Eddy founded Christian Science; Edna Ballard had probably more to do with founding "I Am" than the now Ascended Master, Guy Ballard, her husband; Myrtle Fillmore is recognized as co-founder of Unity; Amy Semple McPherson founded The Four Square Gospel Church; and most of the history of Theosophy can be written around two women, Helena P. Blavatsky and Annie Besant.

Helena P. Blavatsky, or H.P.B., as she is usually called in Theosophic writings,[1] was of Russian birth. Her family was of the nobility with a long line of aristocratic ancestry behind it. She was reared, after her eleventh year, when her mother died, in the home of her grandparents. She is said to have been a strong-willed, spoiled child, whom only her grandmother knew how to control. She had an unusual mind and could easily grasp what she was interested in making the effort to master. She learned at least eight languages and many dialects. She herself declared that as a child she was never alone, but always had invisible companions. She was definitely what is now known as psychic and developed the power of mediumship. It was during the period of her youth that Spiritualism became a widespread interest not alone in America but in Europe as well, and she early acquired an interest in it. Indeed, it was through this interest that she was ultimately led to the founding of Theosophy as a distinct movement. She is said to have practiced medium-

---

[1] We shall follow this practice generally in the remainder of the chapter.

ship professionably at one period in Egypt, where she spent some time.

At only seventeen years of age she was married to General N. V. Blavatsky, apparently against her will, for she soon left him and returned to her family, who sent her back to her father. Fearful that he would oblige her to go back to her husband, she escaped and for some years led a wandering life. Just where she went or how she spent those years is not known for certain. All sorts of charges have been leveled against her character, among them that she led a wild life. On the other hand, Theosophists generally believe that it was during these years that she was led in her search for truth to the retreat of the Great White Brotherhood in the Himalaya mountains, "where she garnered the priceless knowledge with which she afterwards enriched the world's literature." [2] This authority declares that H.P.B. met her Master and Guardian, on the physical plane, in London in 1851, only three years after her marriage. It was under his guidance and direction that she "passed from strength to strength in her power to control many unusual forces, by means of which she produced the phenomena which caused so much skepticism, opposition, and shock to a materialistic and conventional world." [3] The reference to phenomena is to such things as are quite casually and frequently related as simple facts by the same writer; for example, at teatime one afternoon in India, there was no water with which to make the tea, and the servants could obtain none. "Helena P. Blavatsky came to the rescue by putting an empty bottle in the loose sleeve of her gown and then bringing it out filled with the clearest filtered water." [4]

Long after the founding of the movement, when she was resident in India, charges of fraud were made against her which many believe to have been thoroughly substantiated, and the enemies of the movement made much of them.[5] Finally, she felt it wise to leave India, the headquarters of the movement, and established herself in London. But Theosophists today do not seem to be troubled about Helena P. Blavatsky's character. Some frankly admit that she was certainly no saint. The truth of what she brought from the Masters they say, has been so often validated through other sources and by other

[2] Josephine Ransom, *A Short History of the Theosophical Society*, Theosophical Publishing House, Adyar, India 1938, p. 32.
[3] *Id.*, p. 32.   [4] *Id.*, p. 146.
[5] See below, pp. 232 ff.

means that modern Theosophy need spend little time in attempting to defend the character of their founder. This is not yet true of most of the other movements, especially Christian Science, which will brook no criticism of Mrs. Eddy or any challenge of her originality in the discovery of Christian Science, but leap at once to her defense.

Whatever the truth about her character, there is no doubt that Theosophy owes more to Helena P. Blavatsky than to any other person in its founding and as the channel through which most of its teaching has come.

In 1872 she came to New York where she interested herself in Spiritualism, as the historian of the movement says, "to explain its phenomena, expose its frauds, to enlarge its spiritual scope, and to give it the dignity in the world of science which was its due." [6] She observed the work of various mediums of note and wrote freely about them. It was on a visit to observe a notable medium, William Eddy, that she met for the first time Henry S. Olcott, called usually Col. Olcott, with whom she was to join in organizing the Theosophical Society, in 1875, in New York City, and with whom she was to labor for many years in elaborating both the teaching and the organization of the movement. In her scrapbook which she kept for many years, telling the story of the movement, she pasted as a first entry an article by Col. Olcott concerning her arrival in Chittenden, the home of William Eddy, with the legend "The curtain is raised— Henry S. Olcott's acquaintance on October 14, 1874, with Helena P. Blavatsky at Chittenden." [7]

Henry Steel Olcott was but a year younger than Helena P. Blavatsky, born of Puritan ancestry in Orange, New Jersey, August 2, 1832. His parents were members of the Methodist Church. He early became interested in scientific agriculture, and through the founding of an agricultural school exercised not a little influence on agricultural education in the United States. He wrote several books on agriculture, and became one of the agricultural editors of the New York *Tribune*. He was a soldier in the Civil War, and rose to the rank of Colonel. He also studied law and was admitted to the bar, specializing in the field of Customs, Revenue and Insurance. He was active in the writing of the legal regulations under which insurance companies operate in the United States. He was recom-

[6] *Id.*, p. 33.   [7] *Id.*, p. 57.

mended at one time as Secretary of the United States Treasury but, through a political shift in the administration, the appointment was never made. It is evident, however, that he was a man of ability and of considerable reputation.

The Colonel had been interested in Spiritualism from its first appearance with the Rochester knockings, but it had played no important role in his life. Then one day he read of the Eddy séances, went to Chittenden to observe them, and wrote his impressions to the New York *Sun*. His article aroused widespread interest and the New York *Daily Graphic* sent him back to study the phenomena further and write his observations. It was these articles that drew H.P.B. to Chittenden, more to meet Olcott than to witness the Eddy phenomena. But the meeting linked their lives and eventually produced the Theosophical movement.

There is much that is common to Spiritualism and to Theosophy. They are both firm believers in the separateness of the essential ego and the body it inhabits temporarily. Both believe that death is but an incident in the total life cycle of an individual, though the spiritualists do not generally believe in rebirth at the physical level. Both believe that the living may have communication with the dead, though in different ways, and that the dead may greatly influence the lives of the living, though again in a different manner.

Madame Blavatsky's explanation of the ordinarily observed spiritualistic phenomena, at least as recalled at a later period, was quite different from that currently held, and, indeed, from that held by Col. Olcott. Mrs. Ransom says, "As regards the phenomena she witnessed, and often controlled, she said how her own recollections and brain images were drawn from her memory and disfigured in the confused amalgamation that took place between their reflection in the medium's brain which instantly sent them out, and the shells which sucked them in like a sponge and objectivised them—a hideous shape with a mask on. She could watch the process." [8] The "shells," she explains, were understood by H.P.B. as "cast-off astral remnants of those who had passed onward." These had nothing to do with the real ego which went on to a higher plane and lost all touch with earth, and could be reached by the living only in thought and love, especially during sleep. "The law prevents them descending to us." "According to the sensuous affinities of these shells, con-

[8] *Id.*, p. 58.

tracted of course while still on earth, would be their attraction to mediums. Whatever cravings they had they would blindly satisfy through the medium, or urge him to develop it." [9]

"At times," writes H.P.B., "I used to see one of such phantoms quitting the medium's astral body, pouncing upon one of the sitters, expanding so as to envelop him entirely, and then slowly disappearing within the living body as though sucked in by its every pore." [10]

She and Col. Olcott were not in agreement and argued long over the matter. In the early relationship there is little or no reference to any bearing of Eastern philosophy on the subject. One writer asserts that there was no mention of Hinduism or Buddhism or of the Masters in the earlier phase of the movement. [11] Mrs. Ransom apparently recognizes this and explains H.P.B.'s silence concerning it as due to Olcott's lack of knowledge of oriental thought. [12]

The degree to which H.P.B. was interested in Spiritualism as late as 1874, may be seen in a passionate letter she wrote to the London *Spiritualist*. For fifteen years, she wrote, she had fought her "battle for the blessed truth." She had become a "wanderer upon the face of the earth" in its behalf. Knowing America to be the cradle of modern Spiritualism she had come thither "with feelings not unlike those of a Mohammedan approaching the birthplace of the Prophet." Spiritualists had allowed themselves to be ridiculed and slighted by anyone who wished. She was unwilling not to take up the challenge and defend it. [13] This she did vigorously through articles, pamphlets and letters to the press. One man asserted that he could, with a few yards of the proper fabric, reproduce any of the materializations reported of the mediums. She countered that at the Eddy séances she had herself summoned seven spirits she had met in her travels, dressed in various types of costumes, and that one of them had brought her a medal of honor granted to her father and buried with him in Russia. She offered $500 if he could produce anything like that. He did not accept the challenge, but through the incident H.P.B. got national and even international publicity that proved valuable to her. [14]

[9] *Id.*, p. 58, f.n. 2.
[10] *Incidents*, pp. 177–179. Quoted by Ransom, *op. cit.*, p. 60.
[11] Farquhar, *Modern Religious Movements in India*, p. 220.
[12] Ransom, p. 60.
[13] Ransom, *op. cit.*, p. 62.
[14] *Id.*, pp. 60–61.

Whatever of truth there was in Spiritualism there was in it, undoubtedly, a great deal of fraud and imposture. Both H.P.B. and Olcott were active in exposing fraud wherever they found it. The most notable such case was that of the famous mediums, Mr. and Mrs. Holmes, who had been widely credited with producing true materializations. This activity involved them in extensive controversy, both in America and Europe, and attracted to them a great many people who later became part of the Theosophical Society, among them William Q. Judge, who was afterward to play a conspicuous role in the fortunes of the Society.

Both H. P. B. and Col. Olcott while defending Spiritualism, despite their exposure of such frauds as they discovered, felt that there was need for developing the philosophy underlying it, a task that had been conspicuously neglected, they thought. They discovered in Gerry Brown, editor of *The Spiritual Scientist*, one who sympathized with this aim, and directed their efforts to building up the periodical, which was having financial difficulties at the moment. A "Miracle Club" was announced as forming for spiritualistic investigation and open only to a limited few men of scientific attainment and reputation who would offer a guarantee to the public of the validity of any conclusions they might reach. A brother of the editor, Charles A. Dana, was to be the medium, and the results were to be published in *The Spiritual Scientist*. But the medium failed them and the Club came to nothing.

At this point it becomes impossible to write of the history of the movement without reference to the "Masters," for certainly all Theosophic sources explain the actual founding of the movement as the fulfillment of a plan and a result of definite orders from the Masters. It is difficult to get back of these Masters, for the dates of the exact appearance of the letters upon which much of the history is based is uncertain. Were they written later and dated earlier?

H.P.B.'s apartment in New York had become the gathering place of a number of people attracted to her by her spiritualistic interest and her apparent ability to produce phenomena. She must have been, from all accounts, an intriguing personality. On the evening of September 7, 1875, an engineer, Mr. George H. Felt, gave a lecture to some seventeen persons on "The Lost Canon of Proportion of the Egyptians." This prompted active discussion, in the course of which, Col. Olcott suggested in a note to H.P.B. "that it would be a good thing to form a Society to pursue and promote such occult research." H.P.B. agreed.[15] This sounds to the outsider like a natural and logical explanation of the beginning of the Society. Later there appears a note, in H.P.B.'s scrapbook, apparently in her own handwriting, which reads: "M ∴ brings orders to form a Society—a secret Society like the Rosicrucian Lodge. He promises to help." There is no date given. The whole "Important Note" reads as though it might have been written at some time after the period to which it refers. It is an explanation of the course she had taken in the exposure of the fraudulent character of the Holmes' materialization of "Katie King." "I had to save the situation," she declares, "for I was sent from Paris on purpose to America to *prove* the phenomena and their reality and show the fallacy of the Spiritualistic theory of Spirits." Sent by whom? By the Masters! She recounts that M ∴ had helped her in the exposure.[16]

Mrs. Annie Besant later wrote (in *Lucifer*, April, 1895, p. 105): "She, Helena P. Blavatsky, has told me herself how her Master bade her found it, and how at his bidding she wrote the suggestion of starting it on a slip of paper and gave it to W. Q. Judge to pass to Col. Olcott, and then the Society had its first beginning." [17]

Regardless of who made the first suggestion of a society, the result of it was that at an adjourned session held the next evening, September 8, 1875, definite steps were taken which eventually resulted in formal organization of the Theosophical Society. Col. Olcott was made president, H.P.B. secretary. Col. Olcott is reported as having proposed that the society be formed to investigate science and religion . . . "to be the true friend of religion and the enemy of scientific materialism . . . to be a nucleus around which might gather those willing to work together to organize a society of occultists, begin to collect a library, and to diffuse information concerning those secret laws of nature which were so familiar to the Chaldeans and Egyptians, but were unknown to the modern world of science."

But when the constitution and by-laws were finally completed and the Society formally launched, in a public meeting on November 17, 1875, with an inaugural address by the president, Col. Olcott,

---

[15] Ransom, *op. cit.*, p. 77.

[16] "The Important Note" is reproduced in facsimile in C. Jinarajadasa, *The Golden Book of the Theosophical Society*, The Theosophical Publishing House, Adyar, India, 1925, p. 7.

[17] Ransom, *op. cit.*, p. 77, f.n.

the object of the Society was simply stated as: "to collect and diffuse a knowledge of the laws which govern the universe."[18] Membership was open to all applicants in sympathy with the aims of the Society, on nomination by two fellows or members and approval of the Council. There were to be active, honorary and corresponding fellows. In 1876, however, a change was effected making it a secret society with the usual passwords and signs of recognition common to such fraternities. There were now to be three sections of membership and in each section three degrees. The first section was regarded as probationary and the time required for passage from one degree to another was indefinite, all was to depend upon merit. The second section was to be somewhat on the order of Masonry with secret rituals, but it apparently was never fully developed. The third section was almost the equivalent of a monastic order. It is described thus in an early circular "printed for the information of correspondents." "To be admitted to the highest degree of the first section, the Theosophist must have become free of every leaning toward any one form of religion in preference to another. He must be free from all exacting obligations to society politics and family. He must be ready to lay down his life, if necessary, for the good of Humanity and of a brother fellow of whatever race, color, or ostensible creed. He must renounce wine, and every other description of intoxicating beverages and adopt a life of strict chastity. Those who have disenthralled themselves from religious prejudice, and other forms of selfishness, but have made a certain progress towards self-mastery and enlightenment belong in the second section." Members of the third section might withdraw at will, but were still bound to strict secrecy regarding anything received by them under restrictions.[19]

Likewise the object of the Society had undergone restatement. In part it was stated as follows: "to influence its members to acquire an intimate knowledge of natural law and its occult manifestations". . . to study to develop their latent powers, and inform themselves respecting the laws of magnetism, electricity and all other forms of force—"to oppose the materialism of science and every form of dogmatic Theology, especially the Christian, which the Chiefs of the Society regard as particularly pernicious; to make known among the western nations the long suppressed *facts* about

[18] *Golden Book*, p. 23.   [19] *Golden Book*, p. 26.

Oriental religious philosophies, their ethics, chronology, esoterism, symbolisms; to counteract . . . the efforts of missionaries to delude the so-called 'Heathen' and 'Pagans' as to the real origin and dogmas of Christianity and the practical effects of the latter upon public and private character in so-called civilized countries; to disseminate a knowledge of the sublime teachings of that pure esoteric system of the archaic period which are mirrored in the oldest Vedas, and in the philosophy of Gautama Buddha, Zoroaster, and Confucius; finally, and chiefly, to aid in the institution of a Brotherhood of Humanity, wherein all good and pure men of every race shall recognize each other as the equal effects (upon this planet) of one Uncreate, Universal, Infinite, and Everlasting Cause." [20] At least three things in this statement are a notable addition to the original declaration of purpose, the increased occult emphasis, the hostility to dogmatic Christianity with consequent opposition to Christian missionary activity, and, perhaps most notable, the turning to the oriental religious philosophies as the source of true understanding of the nature of things.

Jinarajadasa, an Indian, now president of the Society, and the editor of the *Golden Book* is quick to point out that the apparent anti-Christian emphasis was in no sense opposition to Christianity, *"as the body of teachings given by its Founder,"* rather dogmatic Christianity, which the founders remembered "had often martyred those who tried to reach out into the larger spheres of truth not under its dominion" and which, in the "materialistic" form preached in the orthodox churches, "resulted in a social condition which held the masses in economic subjection, and . . . upheld a social system which was profoundly unethical and anti-Christian." Furthermore, "the spread of these narrow forms of Christianity, which were inseparable from missionary effort," they felt, "did great harm to many oriental peoples." [21]

What was it that turned the Society eastward in its search for truth? According to the Theosophist it was, of course, the Masters, whose home was in the East. But who were the Masters, and how did they function in relation to the nascent Society?

The idea of the Masters is undoubtedly of oriental origin. Jinarajadasa specifically says "no doctrine in Theosophy . . . is new, not

---

[20] The entire circular is reproduced in *The Golden Book of the Theosophical Society*, p. 26.

[21] *The Golden Book*, pp. 27–28, *passim*.

even that of the existence of the Masters . . . but the fact of the existence of Adept Teachers has not only appeared logical, but to many it has become the center of all their Theosophical Idealism. For if evolution is a fact, and if also the soul of man is immortal then the necessary result of evolution must be the slow transformation of all souls into the grade of Masters of the Wisdom. Furthermore, as evolution has been a principle in the universe since the beginning of time, it is obvious that somewhere in past ages Masters of the Wisdom must have existed. So, then, also, what the Masters are today, each one of us, whatever his failings now, will be some day." [22]

Whatever the original source of the concept of Masters, it is through Theosophy, and chiefly through H.P.B. that the Masters have become known in the West. Some movements, originating since her time, have carried the idea even farther and created a whole host of new Masters, particularly the I Am Movement, but also in some phases of New Thought they have appeared, e.g., Psychiana. Also Rosicrucians use the concept.

In *Isis Unveiled* written during the years 1876–77, published in 1877, and in the *Secret Doctrine* which appeared in 1888, H.P.B. disclosed the nature and functions, as well as the hierarchy of organization of these Masters, all of which is accepted as literal fact by Theosophists generally.

There is a mighty hierarchy, she declares in *Secret Doctrine*, in descending scale from the first Mighty One, the Lord of the World, the Pratyeka Buddhas and Buddhas, the Manu, Bodhisattva, Mahachohan, the Chohans, and then the Adepts or Masters. Below the Masters on the scale are the Arhats, and the initiates of three degrees and finally the *chelas*, or accepted probationary pupils. Plato, St. Paul and Moses are recognized as initiates, and there are a number of them now living in many countries. Only a few who have attained Masterhood remain on earth "to promote its evolution in accord with God's plan." Some fifty or sixty are said to be thus engaged. They prepare for themselves physical bodies which last sometimes, it is said, hundreds of years, though of course they are not limited to their physical bodies. They reside temporarily or permanently in many different places—including Tibet, the one most commonly associated with them in popular thought, but also in China, India, Egypt, Syria, Hungary, possibly Greece, in England and in Yucatan

---

[22] *The Golden Book,* pp. 1–2.

in the Americas.[23] They have been seen by many people on numerous occasions, it is asserted.

There is room here only to name and describe a few of the better known ones. Master Morya, or M, as generally designated, was one of two Masters who were instrumental in the founding of the Society, and it was he who furnished H.P.B. the plan of her important book, *The Secret Doctrine*. It is his function "to guide men and form nations." His residence is near Shigatze, Tibet, but he travels extensively. His body is that of the Rajput Indian type, "expressing power, strength, and imperious dignity." [24]

The other Master who had to do with the beginnings of the movement was Serapis, who is "a fair Greek by birth," but has done most of his work in Egypt. He is "distinguished and ascetic, blue-eyed, with sunny red-gold hair." His special interest is "in Harmony and Beauty." [25]

Master K.H. was first met by H.P.B. in 1868. In a former incarnation he was Pythagoras. His present body form is that of a Kashmiri Brahman, and "his keynote is Wisdom." He is concerned with religion, education and art. He engages much in meditation, "sending out streams of thought and benediction." His residence is near that of Master M in Tibet, but he, too, travels, and has been seen, it is reported, by various Theosophists. [26]

The Venetian Master is "the most handsome of all the members of the Brotherhood." Adaptability and tact are his keynote. His body is "Venetian with Gothic blood." In a former incarnation he was Plotinus, originator of Neo-Platonism. He is concerned with astrology, "to know the exact time to do or not to do things." [27]

Master Jesus has as his keynote "intense Purity and a fiery devotion that brooks no obstacles." He has charge of "the saints and mystics of *every* religion." The Christ occupied his body and founded the Christian Church, of which he is now the Shepherd and guardian, "inspiring, disciplining, purifying it century after century and now pouring forth the stream of Mystic Christianity." He lives among the Druses on Mt. Lebanon, as a Syrian in body. Among his other incarnations are Apollonius of Tyana, and Ramanuja, in India.[28]

Other Masters are Hilarion, The Prince Rakoczi, who, interestingly enough, was incarnated as Christian Rosenkreuz, 1378–1484.

---

[23] Ransom, *op. cit.*, p. 54.   [24] *Id.*, p. 50.   [25] *Id.*, p. 51.
[26] *Id.*, pp. 50–51.   [27] *Id.*, p. 51.   [28] *Id.*, pp. 52–53.

With this Rosicrucians, belonging to AMORC, will hardly agree, since there never was a Christian Rosenkreuz. Also, the I Am group should be interested in knowing that he was once, also, Francis Bacon. In addition, among many others, there are Master Jupiter, Master Djual Khool, and, living in England, two Masters who, in their last lives, were known as Sir Thomas More and Thomas Vaughn.[29] There seems to be none resident in America, except in Yucatan, for they do not apparently recognize the legitimacy of Frank B. Robinson's assertion that he is an Adept, nor that of the I Am Accredited Messengers who report a branch of the Brotherhood at Mt. Shasta, California.

When asked what holds the Brotherhood together, Master K.H. is reported to have replied: "Duty," which "for us is stronger than any friendship or even love, as without this abiding principle which is the indestructible cement that has held together for so many millenniums, the scattered custodians of nature's grand secrets—our Brotherhood, nay, our doctrine itself—would have crumbled long ago into unrecognisable elements."[30]

Aside from their varied *cosmic* activities the Masters fulfill many other functions. They "send out thought forms of high intellectual power, to be caught and assimilated and used by men of genius"; help "the so-called dead"—"watch tendencies of events"; . . . "correct and neutralize as far as the law permits, evil currents, balancing forces that work for and against evolution, strengthening good, weakening evil"; . . . "break the bonds of orthodoxy, dogma and hardness of thought which clog human growth"; and "above all" form the Guardian Wall around humanity within which it can progress, "uncrushed by the tremendous forces that play around our planetary house."[31]

How do the Masters make themselves known, and who are able to communicate with them? It is believed by Theosophists that H.P.B. made contact with some of them during the years of wandering immediately following her marriage. How this meeting was effected, and how she communicated with them is not certainly known. She notes in her scrapbook, as above indicated, that she was "ordered" to aid in the Holmes fraud case; that M brought *orders* to form a Society. To some of her associates, letters written

[29] *Id.*, pp. 52–54, *passim.*
[30] Ransom, *op. cit.*, p. 54; quoted from *The Mahatma Letters*, p. 351.
[31] *Id.*, pp. 55–56.

on material paper in the English language came from the Mahatmas or Masters. Whence did they come? It is generally believed by Theosophists that they were "materialized," just as in the case of other reported phenomena connected with H.P.B. Col. Olcott in 1875 received his first letter from "the Brotherhood of Luxor." It is reproduced in facsimile in *The Golden Book*, page 13, and numerous other letters followed through the years. A. P. Sinnett received many such, published under the title *Mahatma Letters*. They continued to come after the death of H.P.B. through Annie Besant. for many years head of the Society.

Naturally such phenomena were regarded by the unbelieving world as of doubtful authenticity and there is an immense literature attempting to prove them fraudulent, the work of clever people, designed to deceive the public. Years later the Society for Psychic Research attempted to get at the truth. They examined both H.P.B. and Col. Olcott in England, and sent a representative to India to investigate, on the ground, reported claims of fraud practiced by the principals. As a result the Society for Psychic Research gave an adverse judgment, branding H.P.B. as "one of the most accomplished, ingenious and interesting impostors in history," a judgment which was carried in an Encyclopedia Britannica article for many years, but has more recently been withdrawn, though the Society for Psychic Research has never officially reversed its judgment. Of course the Theosophical Society bitterly rejected the decision, and claims that it was completely mistaken and grossly unjust. They blame very largely the Christian missionaries of India who were, it is true, hostile to the leaders of Theosophy. This hostility is perhaps not unnatural in view of the attitude assumed by them toward the missionary enterprise. Col. Olcott wrote to Dyananda Sarasvati, founder of the Arya-Samaj, a reform movement in Hinduism, violently opposed to Christianity, saying that the group of westerners including himself and H.P.B. "place themselves at your feet and pray you to enlighten them . . . finding nothing in Christianity to satisfy reason or intuition, and repelled by its imperfections they turned to the East for light and openly proclaimed themselves the foes of Christianity." [32] And H.P.B. once wrote in the New York *Echo*, "The Theosophical Society means, if it cannot rescue Christians from modern Christianity, at least to aid in saving the

[32] *Id.*, pp. 115-116.

'heathen' from its influence." [33] In an article in *The Religio-Philo-sophical Journal* she wrote: "It is universally known that this most important object is to antagonize Christianity and especially Jesu-itism." [34]

On the other hand, there was direct testimony on the part of people who lived for an extended period in the headquarters at Adyar to the effect that definite mechanisms were provided there to produce phenomena. To be sure, the Theosophic group asserted that this testimony was false and given as a result of resentment felt at being put out of the residence into which they had been taken, when penniless and in need of shelter, because H.P.B. had known Madame Coulomb during her residence in Egypt. It was very much a question as to which to believe, the Coulombs or H.P.B. and her coterie of followers. It was easier for most people to believe that H.P.B. was employing devious methods in the production of her phenomena than to credit the phenomena themselves, even if no ulterior motives were involved.

This is not the place to reopen the controversy, though the reporting of it is a necessary part of the story. To those with occult tendencies the appearance of such phenomena offers no obstacle to belief in Theosophy, for, to such persons, that is the expected thing, the nature of the world being what they believe it to be. The effort to understand the movement requires that their best leaders be al-lowed to explain how all these things come about.

The most lucid explanation the writer has seen is that of Charles W. Leadbeater, for many years one of their most distinguished leaders and writers. His explanation is undoubtedly over-simplified, for in this particular case he is writing a very elementary outline of Theosophy.

It is all a matter of vibration, he says—we do not quote him ex-actly but paraphrase what he writes. Man gets all his information of the outer world by means of some kind of vibration. Now, if he can succeed in making himself more sensitive to additional vibra-tions, he will get greatly extended information. He will become *clairvoyant* which means simply an extension of normal vision. But if he greatly increases his sensitivity to higher and more subtle vibra-tions he finds entire new worlds opening up to him. He discovers

[33] *Id.*, p. 118.
[34] *Id.*, p. 118.

that there lies about him a vast unseen universe which, though he is unconscious of it, affects him in many ways. But with his heightened sensitivity he becomes able "to observe them scientifically, to repeat his observations many times, to compare them with those of others, to tabulate them and draw deductions from them." This he says has been done thousands of times. The Adepts or Masters are those who have done it to the fullest extent, but Theosophical students, including himself—though he does not here say so—have been able themselves to verify what the Masters have told them. Things that were formerly mysteries are thus cleared up. The difference between ordinary science and this higher science is that science dedicates its energies to the improvement of its instruments of investigation, while the science of the soul aims rather at the development of the observer. And as in the case of science so in this science of the soul, "full details are known only to those who devote their lives to its pursuit." [35]

Returning to the fortunes of the Society, its auspicious beginnings were not followed immediately by any great activity. H.P.B. was chiefly engaged in the writing of *Isis Unveiled* which is a basic textbook of the movement, aided by Col. Olcott. There was little development of the section on degrees, indeed not much beyond continuation of the meetings in H.P.B.'s apartment.

But in the same year the Society was formed, another Society was formed in India which Jinarajadasa says was under the central impulse from the unseen which had led to the founding of the Theosophical Society. This was the Arya Samaj, founded by Dyananda Sarasvati as a reformed movement in Hinduism. The two societies had much in common, and for the first two or three years worked closely together. Indeed, on May 22, 1878, the Society voted to accept the proposal of the Arya Samaj to unite with itself, and changed its name to the Theosophical Society of the Arya Samaj of India, and resolved that it, together with "its branches in America, Europe, and elsewhere, recognize Dyananda Sarasvati, Pandit, founder of the Arya Samaj, as its Director and Chief." [36]

However, only a few months later the full rules of the Arya Samaj were received and a new decision was taken to return to separate organizations, but to form a link-society to be known as The

[35] *An Outline of Theosophy*, 3rd ed., Theosophical Book Concern, Los Angeles, 1916, pp. 8–12, *passim*.
[36] Ransom, *op. cit.*, p. 116.

Theosophical Society of the Arya Samaj of Arya-Wart, members of which would belong to the other two, but this never developed any strength, and by 1880 died out. [37]

Extensive correspondence took place between the respective leaders, and it was this probably, as it seems to an outsider, that led H.P.B. and Col. Olcott to decide to go to India, although it was purportedly on orders from the Brotherhood, according to Theosophical writers. This they did in 1878, setting up headquarters first in Bombay, but in 1882 at Adyar, where it has ever since remained.

The intimate relationship with the Arya Samaj lasted only a short time, however. Although Dyananda was regarded by them as an "Adept of the Himalayan Brotherhood," it soon became evident that they were not moving in the same direction. The Samaj, it seemed to H.P.B. and Olcott, was too sectarian for their broad universal faith and Dyananda distrusted the recurring "phenomena" or miraculous element of the Theosophical Society. Thus they drew apart and after a violent attack by Dyananda and his complete repudiation of membership in the Theosophical Society, they severed all relations. But the Society was in India to stay.

Here was started the magazine, *The Theosophist,* and a publishing society. Olcott traveled widely in India, lecturing on the common aims of Theosophy and Hinduism. He and H.P.B. went to Ceylon, made contact with Buddhism and were warmly received. The Society grew and prospered. The appreciative attitude of these westerners toward Hinduism and its thought naturally produced a most favorable impression on Hindus. The fact that they have generally been on the side of India, rather than of their Western overlords, has not been unrecognized by the Indians. This in later years was in rather sharp contrast to the attitude of many of the missionaries, although there have always been those among the missionary group who have stood squarely with the Indians in their aspirations toward a free India. Later Mrs. Besant, then president of the Society, was president of the Indian National Congress.

Meanwhile the organization was growing in America, England and on the continent, and was to spread throughout the entire world. Col. Olcott continued as head of it and became a world traveler in its behalf. H.P.B. left India in 1885; worked in various European countries, beginning her *Secret Doctrine* in 1886. Differ-

[37] *Id.,* pp. 119–120.

ences arose between herself and Col. Olcott on organizational matters, she threatening to secede from the Adyar group and establish an autonomous movement in Europe. Olcott, who had been something of a dictator in his rule of the organizations, was obliged to make some concession and as a result the Esoteric section of the Society was formed, of which H.P.B. became the head, with the declared purpose of promoting the esoteric interests of the Theosophical Society by the deeper study of esoteric philosophy. It was to have no connection with the Exoteric Society, "save in the person of the President Founder." [38] Private Lodges of the Esoteric group were granted charters.

Madame Blavatsky settled in London in 1890, continuing her literary work, directing the new Esoteric group, and serving as Secretary of the Society. She died in 1891, at the age of sixty, having the satisfaction of seeing the Society solidly organized and exercising a worldwide influence on the religion and philosophy of the West. Enigmatic, unpredictable, willful, brilliant, yet capable of great charm, and of undoubted intellectual gifts, she left a deep mark upon the world of religious thought. Whether, without the stabilizing influence, the organizing ability, and the capacity of Henry Steel Olcott to win men to his views, she could have left so deep a mark is altogether doubtful. But this she did have. It is a tribute to her powers that she was able to take this influential man out of his chosen career and make him the instrument of her purpose.

Two years before Helena P. Blavatsky passed on an English woman, Mrs. Annie Besant, wife of an Anglican clergyman, who had herself, however, lost her religious faith, became an atheist, and separated from her husband, became a convert to Theosophy and joined the Society. She was later to become its President and to direct its fortunes for more than a quarter of a century. Next to Madame Blavatsky herself, she has probably done more to shape the developing Society than any other figure.

In 1888 the principle of autonomous sections had been accepted by the Society and there were now vigorous branch sections in various parts of the world. Of the American branch, William Q. Judge, one of the original group who surrounded H.P.B., was president. In the year 1894 charges were made that Judge was "issuing

[38] *Id.*, pp. 251-252.

letters purporting to be in the handwriting of a Master with His signature," some of them bearing the impress of the "Delhi Seal," bought many years earlier by Olcott because he thought it resembled the cryptogram of the Master M.[39] Judge denied the charges. The upshot of the affair was the secession in 1895 of the American section, almost entire, for it had complete confidence in the integrity of Mr. Judge. There was formed the Theosophical Society in America which has continued until the present to maintain its own activities. Its general objectives were essentially the same as those of the parent society, but there was less of a disposition to exalt the wisdom of the East. Mr. Judge in a statement made in his defense had said that it was not the desire of the Masters "to turn the Theosophical Society into a solely Eastern Movement, nor have us run after the present East, and its exoteric teachers . . . the cycle required work in the West for the benefit of the world. The new Race was being prepared in the West, and to divert thought back to the teachers of today in the East would be dangerous." [40]

Mr. Judge was made life president of the new Society into which apparently all but fourteen local branches had entered. But he lived only a year, dying in 1896. The new Society was influenced greatly by Mrs. Katherine A. Tingley, who was a professional spiritualistic medium. Indeed, it is sometimes referred to as the Tingley branch of Theosophy.

The few branches that refused to secede were drawn together and recognized as the "still existing American Section." Col. Olcott, although at times suffering great physical disability, continued in active direction of the Society, traveling among its scattered sections throughout the world, and aside from his purely Theosophical activity, endeavoring to bring the Buddhist world into some sense of unity, and to promote an understanding and appreciation of the various religions. He admitted in public address some regret for the intolerance of the movement in its earlier days toward Christianity. Had this attitude not been adopted they would have had the sympathy of many Christians who were otherwise appealed to by Theosophy.[41]

Col. Olcott died on February 17, 1907, and the direction of the movement's destinies fell to Mrs. Annie Besant, who was the choice of Olcott as his successor. The pioneering work had been done.

[39] *Id.,* p. 289.   [40] *Id.,* p. 305.   [41] *Id.,* p. 284.

The major battles had been fought—and not always won. It was her task to direct the peaceful unfolding of the movement's activities, to give it an intellectual statement suited to the advancing world of thought, and to work out in practical directions the implications of Theosophical teaching. This she ably performed. Under her guidance the Adyar center was greatly enlarged and its educational efforts, to which Col. Olcott had given much attention, extended, not only in India but throughout the world. Associated with her were a group of able leaders, writers, and speakers who assisted her greatly. Among them, perhaps the most notable was Charles W. Leadbeater, who has written more lucidly and on the whole more convincingly than any other, as the present writer sees it. He became the chief figure in the founding of another movement, discussed elsewhere in this book, The Liberal Catholic Church (see Chapter VIII). Also, George S. Arundale who was to succeed her as president in 1934, and Mr. C. Jinarajadasa, one of the most prolific, if not the most lucid of Theosophical writers, the present president of the world organization.

Mrs. Besant's annual lectures at the successive anniversaries of the Movement have become classics of Theosophical writing. She began the publication of *New India* in 1914 and was consistently a supporter of the Indian aspirations for Home Rule. She was interned for a time during World War I, but was freed, and in the year 1917 became president of the Indian National Congress, a signal honor for a non-Indian to be accorded. She was first president of The Women's Indian Association, founded in 1917 with the object of furthering the progress of Indian women. At first concerned chiefly with the education of women, it later pressed the demand for equal suffrage. It publishes its own magazine and has branches all over India.

She organized the "Order of Service" which was designed to give practical effect to Theosophic teachings. It has espoused at different times many causes, national education, child welfare, antivivisection, healing, famine relief, animal protection, and particularly work for the blind. They founded and published a magazine, *The Light Bearer*, in Braille. They have also furthered music, drama and the arts.

She was especially interested in education in India, and not only carried on the schools for the outcasts begun by Col. Olcott, but sought to provide a suitable education in religion and philosophy for

Hindu youth. It was she who founded the Central Hindu College and was influential in the creating of the Hindu University of which the College became a part.

In 1908 according to *The Golden Book*, Mrs. Besant made the first public announcement of the coming of a World Teacher. An Indian boy, J. Krishnamurti and a younger brother were taken by Mrs. Besant to rear, in the belief that the former was to be the vehicle of the Teacher, and it was her task to prepare him for that service. Accordingly she and Charles W. Leadbeater assumed direction of their training, the father willingly consenting. Later, under pressure of his caste, he sought to compel the boy's return to himself by appeal to the courts. After extended litigation the final decision was adverse to the father, but it occasioned not a little difficulty and expense for Mrs. Besant and the Society, for the father made charges of immorality, reviving the sex charges against Mr. Leadbeater which had earlier led to his expulsion from the Society. Though later restored, a great deal of bad publicity for the Society resulted.

Even within the Society there was not a little opposition to the World Teacher idea, and particularly to the specific training of an individual for the role. Long afterward when the press in England and America represented her as having proclaimed Krishnamurti as the Messiah she vigorously denied the allegation and made the following explanation: "My reason for accepting guardianship of the boys was that I was told that the older had been selected to give his body as a vehicle for the World Teacher on his approaching coming, if the lad proved worthy of the privilege when he reached manhood." She had, she said, announced that Krishnamurti "was the chosen vehicle" at a closed conference in Holland the previous summer, but she never had any idea of proclaiming him as Messiah.[42]

Nevertheless, there was a distinct sense of expectancy among Theosophists in the middle twenties when Mrs. Besant brought Krishnamurti to America. The young man, a singularly charming young Indian, was enthusiastically received, and the press gave a great deal of space to his activities and sayings. To some he gave the impression of a man who was playing a role not wholly of his own choosing. He did not welcome the spotlight, and seemed to want to get away from it all. Subsequently he withdrew from any active

[42] Ransom, *op. cit.*, p. 475. Quoted from *The Theosophist*, 1926, pp. 638-639.

association with the Society, repudiated any pretensions of being a World Teacher, and eventually settled in California, where he leads a life of retirement, coming out of it only now and again to give public lectures. He has published some things that have received the attention of serious students.

In 1926 the American Headquarters was established at Wheaton, Illinois, in spacious buildings, erected for the purpose. These are to be found just a few miles from Chicago, an imposing center with offices, facilities for distribution of literature, an excellent, nearly complete Theosophical library, and accommodations for a large number of students who come for courses of study offered there. In the same year Mrs. Besant, who had laid the cornerstone of the new buildings, spent some months at Ojai, California, developing what she hoped would be the center of a great community in the distant future.

At the Golden Anniversary of the Society in 1925, the movement was found nationally organized in 43 different countries, with scattered lodges in 16 others. There were in existence 1,576 lodges or local groups, and 41,779 members. The largest number in single nations was in the United States, with 7,333 in 268 lodges. India, however, had more lodges, a total of 403, with 6,395 members, England, France and Holland following with 4,938, 2,923 and 2,673, respectively. This does not take into account other Theosophical groups such as the Theosophical Society in America, and other dissident movements, of which there were not a few.

Now more than 70 anniversaries have been celebrated, but present statistics are difficult to obtain, due to incomplete reports. Whole sections of the Society disappeared under the totalitarian regimes in Europe and the Orient. Books were burned, lodges scattered, and the members themselves, in a number of cases, were incarcerated in concentration camps. Present available information reveals that there are 45 national sections and a grand total of 1,245 lodges scattered in various parts of the world. The active membership is approximately 32,000. In India the number remains above 6,000, but in America and England, France and Holland it fell off by half during the depression years. Since the beginning of the war the Society in America has steadily increased in membership.[43]

---

[43] Information direct from the president of the American Section of The Theosophical Society.

Mrs. Besant died September 20, 1933, and was succeeded by George S. Arundale, who had been one of the earlier followers of the movement. He passed off the scene in 1945, and Mr. C. Jinarajadasa came to the presidency.

As at present organized the World Society has its center at Adyar, India. National societies are practically autonomous, and in Europe there is an International Federation that brings together the European sectional groups for conference from time to time. In the main the organization is made up of adults, but there are organizations for children. For the younger there are the Golden Chain, and Lotus Circles, and for the older ones the Round Table. In this "great attention is paid to ceremonial and a ritual based on the old tradition of chivalry, aiming at satisfying the need for self-expression and devotional feeling among young people." [44]

In addition there is a youth group, the Young Theosophists, formed in 1923 by the uniting of several youth organizations under various names with the expressed object: "To organize young members to cooperate more intensively in giving practical expression to Theosophic ideals." [45] It spread rapidly throughout the world. One modern tendency indicated as observable in the Movement at the present time is in the direction of an appeal to youth. Related to this is the serious effort being made by a group of members to integrate at the college level modern thought with the wisdom of the ancient East. A new publication, *Main Currents in Modern Thought* is being published and circulated to this end.[46] Its avowed purpose is "to promote the free association of those working toward the integration of all knowledge through the study of the whole of things, Nature, Man, Society, assuming the universe to be one, dependable, intelligible, harmonious."

In addition, there are in various countries subsidiary organizations such as the "Order of the Rising Sun" of India, which later became the "Order of the Star in the East." Of this Krishnamurti was head.

The objectives of the Theosophical Society have been stated in slightly different form from time to time, though their general purpose has remained relatively constant. Its present statement is: (1) "To form a nucleus of the Universal Brotherhood of Humanity,

---

[44] *The Golden Book of the Theosophical Society*, p. 291.
[45] *Id.*, p. 307.
[46] Published monthly at Port Chester, New York.

without distinction of race, creed, sex, caste or color. (2) To encourage the study of Comparative Religion, Philosophy and Science. (3) To investigate unexplained laws of Nature and the powers latent in man." [47]

Mrs. Besant in her lectures on the "Ideals of Theosophy" mentions four basic principles, dedicating a lecture to each. They are the brotherhood of humanity, tolerance, science or right knowledge, and the spiritual nature and therefore the perfectibility of man, but none save the first did she regard as binding on all members. The general direction of the evolution of the objectives has been toward a wider more universal outlook. Thus at one time it was the study of Eastern religions that was stressed, now it is comparative religion. Most of the intolerance toward Christianity has been eliminated, at least in the western sections, and members of Christian churches work freely within both the society and the church. A recognized leader of the Theosophists in the Chicago area at one time was superintendent of the primary department of a Methodist Sunday school.

II. *WHAT IT TEACHES*

Theosophy is clearly a syncretic system, a blending of Eastern and Western religious and philosophic thought and practice. It brings together elements from Hinduism, Buddhism, Christianity, Spiritualism, Egyptian Hermeticism, perhaps something from Jewish Kabbalism, and occultism generally. More largely Hindu and Buddhist in doctrinal teaching, it is Christian in its moral outlook. What are its major teachings, and what is its attitude toward the great Christian doctrines held generally in Christendom?

It claims, as do some of the other so-called cults, that it is not a religion. Leadbeater says "It is not itself a religion, but it bears to the religions the same relation as did the ancient philosophies. It does not contradict them but explains them." [48] Nevertheless, it deals with God, man, salvation, death, the hereafter, and moral ideals, as do all the religions.

The idea of God is essentially that of Hindu pantheism, "the one Uncreate, Universal, Infinite and Everlasting Cause," [49] as is stated

[47] *The Golden Book of the Theosophical Society*, pp. 249–250.
[48] *Outline of Theosophy*, p. 4.
[49] *The Golden Book*, p. 26.

in a declaration issued about 1878. It is an impersonal concept. H.P.B. said specifically, "We reject the idea of a personal, extra-cosmic and anthropomorphic God." [50] God is The Absolute or Absolute Principle. Typical statements are: "The Absolute does not think or exist, but is rather thought and existence." "It is beyond the range and reach of thought." In the *Secret Doctrine* she says that in the Absolute is realized "the idea of eternal non-being which is the 'one Being.' It cannot be conceived to have any relation to the finite and conditioned." [51] Yet, "All that which is emanates from The Absolute."

Mrs. Besant says categorically, "The wisdom religion teaches a profound pantheism," and again, "in theology, Theosophy is pantheistic." [52] Once more, she declares in her *Ideals of Theosophy:* "There is no grain of dust in which God's life is not immanent. There is no loftiest Deva in whom that life is not manifest. There is no other life than His; there is no other consciousness than His; there is no other Will than His; nor is there any Actor save He. There is only one life, one consciousness, and one power, and that is the life, consciousness, and power of Ishvara (God), that are in all that He has emanated." [53]

Leadbeater makes a distinction between "God as infinite existence and the manifestation of this Supreme Existence, as a revealed God, evolving and guiding a universe. Only to this limited manifestation should the term 'a personal God' be applied. God in himself is beyond the bounds of personality, is 'in all and through all,' and indeed *is* all: and of the Infinite, the Absolute, the All we can only say, 'He is.' " [54] He would have been more consistent had he said, as does Hinduism, "*It* is."

For all practical purposes, he goes on to say, man need not go further "than that marvelous and glorious manifestation of Him (a little less entirely beyond our comprehension) the great Guiding Force or Deity of our own solar system, whom philosophers have called the Logos. Of Him is true all that we have ever heard predicated of God—all that is good—that is." [55] And in his work the Logos "is undoubtedly triple-three and yet one," that is Trinity—"a

[50] *Key to Theosophy*, p. 61.
[51] *Id.*, pp. 14–15.
[52] *Exposition of Theosophy*, pp. 5 and 28.
[53] Besant, Annie, *Ideals of Theosophy*, p. 16.
[54] *Outline of Theosophy*, pp. 23–24.
[55] *Id.*, p. 24.

dogma common to all religions." [56] This threefold nature is described by Mrs. Besant in *The Inner Government of the World*, in definitely Hindu terms, as Brahma or creator, Vishnu (preserver of form), and Shiva, destroyer or liberator from form. "These three Supreme Beings, who sustain the solar system, are its Godhead, and are the fount of authority of the Occult Hierarchy which in its sublime Lords and Chiefs wields that divine authority on our small earth and inflexibly pursues God's plan of Evolution." [57]

Other lesser cosmic beings are agents of the Logos. At the head of them all stands The Lord of the World, whose keynote is Will, "for he wields the divine will on Earth." [58] Under him are the Pratyeka Buddhas who have reached the 8th stage of initiation; the Buddha, first of humanity to have reached his exalted position, as one with the Second Logos; and The Mahachohan, one with the Third Logos. These three "have reached grades of consciousness . . . beyond the fields of humanity" and are "actual manifestations of the three aspects of the Logos." [59] Representatives and agents of these higher beings are The Manu, and the Bodhisattva Maitreya, who was incarnated variously as Krishna in India, Jesus in Palestine, Mitra in Persia, Lao-tze and Confucius in China. The Masters, whom we have already discussed, form a lower group in the hierarchy, and aid in carrying out the purposes of the Lord of the World.

All this is of course quite obviously built on the Hindu model with the neuter World Soul, Brahman at the center; the Trimurti, Brahma, Vishnu, Shiva; and the lesser polytheistic beings directing and ministering to the world and man.

Jesus appears as one of the incarnations of Maitreya, borrowed from Buddhism, the Buddha yet to come; and as the Master Jesus who lent his body to the Christ. It will be recalled that in the criticism of Christianity there was none of Jesus and his teachings. But he wears no cloak of orthodoxy in Theosophy. His moral teachings are, however, basic in the movement, though Theosophists will be quick to deny the statement and declare that they are not distinctively his but are found in all religions. Certainly the theological Christ, with the doctrine of atonement as a requisite for salvation, is entirely repudiated. In an interview with the present president of the American Section of the Society, he specifically mentioned the trouble which the atonement idea gave him when he was a

[56] *Id.*, p. 25.   [57] Ransom, *op. cit.*, p. 47.
[58] *Id.*, p. 47.   [59] *Id.*, pp. 48–49, *passim.*

young man, a member of the Methodist Church, and the sense of relief and release he found in Theosophy. He was obviously reacting to the orthodox, rather than the liberal, view, as it was rather generally held and preached in the South of his youth.

The perfectibility of man is a cardinal principle in the movement. Man is a phase of the general evolutionary process which is going on in the universe—an idea taken bodily from Indian philosophy.[60]

First there is the evolution of the inorganic world, then of the organic, through the animal stages, and at last man emerges, but on a very low plane. Once having emerged, however, he never reverts to the sub-human level. At this point Theosophy departs from the Indian idea. Writes Mr. Jinarajadasa, now president of the Society: "A soul once 'individualized' and human cannot reincarnate in animal or vegetable form . . . for, were such a thing possible, a soul would gain nothing for his evolution by such a retrograde step." [61]

Evolution takes place through rebirth, but it is a long process, and the stages very uneven. Mr. Jinarajadasa distinguishes five broad classes, the undeveloped and the simple minded, who reincarnate many times in one sub-race before going on to another; the cultured, some of whom reincarnate twice in each sub-race, some even more; those on the Path who reincarnate at once under the supervision of their Masters; and finally Adepts or Masters who may reincarnate but are not obliged to do so. But they continue in their development, none the less, passing through successive stages of initiation until they become cosmic beings themselves.

To explain fully the idea of man it is necessary at this stage to state that there are seven distinct worlds or planes upon which life exists. In the earlier literature the names of the higher planes were taken from oriental sources, but Mrs. Besant wisely gave them names more easily intelligible to western folk. They are in descending order:

1. Divine World	or Adi Plane
2. Monadic World	or Anupadaka Plane
3. Spiritual World	or Atmic or Nirvanic Plane
4. Intuitional World	or Buddhic Plane
5. Mental World	or Mental Plane
6. Emotional or Astral World	or Astral Plane
7. Physical World	or Physical Plane.

[60] See an exposition of it by Mr. Warrington, late president of the American Section in my *Varieties of American Religion*, pp. 220 ff.
[61] *First Principles of Theosophy*, pp. 42-43.

Man is defined by Leadbeater as "in essence a Spark of the Divine
Fire, belonging to the monadic world." [62] He is an individual man,
a "fragment of the group soul," which manifests its ego in three
aspects, in the spiritual world as Spirit which always remains in that
world, in the intuitional world as intuition, and in the mental world
as intelligence. Man therefore, like God, is triune. This ego dwelling
on the higher planes resides in what is called the causal body. As
individual ego, "he lives unchanged (except for his growth) from
the moment of his individualization until humanity is transcended and
merged in divinity." [63] In no wise affected by what is humanly called
birth and death, the visible bodies he assumes in the process of
evolution are only temporary vestments worn and put away when
they have served their purpose.

Man has not one body but many. Besides the causal body, there
are bodies appropriate to the lower planes. Let Mr. Leadbeater explain. For some reason the evolutionary process requires the assumption of a physical body, the kind we readily recognize. But
before this can be done he must "make a connection with it through
the lower mental and astral worlds. When he wishes to descend he
draws around himself a veil of the matter of the lower mental world
which we call his mental body. This is the instrument by means of
which he thinks all his concrete thoughts—abstract thoughts being
a power of the ego himself in the higher mental world." "Next
he draws around himself a veil of astral matter, his astral body . . .
the instrument of his passions and emotions, . . . only then can he
come into touch with a baby physical body and be born into the
world which we know." [64] Thus man has at one and the same time
not only a physical, but also an astral, a mental and a causal body.
Each body is limited in its capacity to apprehend what is going on
in the spheres above it because of the higher vibration rates of
matter at those levels, just as our eyes cannot see ultra-violet rays.

Having acquired certain qualities as a result of the experiences in
the physical body, at death he "reverses the process of descent,"
laying aside successively the physical, astral, and mental bodies. The
time the astral body endures depends upon "the amount of passion
and emotion which he has developed within himself in the physical
body." When done with the astral body he lives on in the mental
body for a period depending upon "the nature of the thoughts to

[62] *Textbook of Theosophy*, 3rd ed., Theosophical Publishing House, Los
Angeles, 1918, p. 41.
[63] *Id.*, p. 42.   [64] *Id.*, pp. 42–43.

which he has habituated himself," then casts it aside and "is once more the ego in his own world." But because of a lack of full development he is not wholly conscious in that world. He is not able as yet to catch its higher vibratory rate. So after a time a desire is felt to return to a level where the vibrations are perceptible, so that he may feel himself fully alive. Therefore he repeats the process of descent into matters of denser nature, and takes on new bodies, mental, astral and physical. The only means of the full development of the ego is through these succeeding descents into the lower worlds. It is thus only "that a full cognizance of the higher worlds is developed in him." [65]

If it be asked how all this is known, the explanation is that through clairvoyance, the heightening of the perceptive capacity, it is possible actually to observe these things. The ordinary man is not really aware of much that is going on around him, even at his own level, but through many rebirths and therefore many experiences this perceptive power is increased until some perceive readily what is hidden to others. Thus there is the brutish man, evidently low in the scale of the evolutionary process, and there is the highly sensitized man of culture or even of genius to whom a whole world of experience is open, of which the brutish man can know nothing.

The Masters are those in whom the latent powers have been developed to the fullest extent, but there are others who have so developed their perceptive powers that they see what is denied to the ordinary senses. Such persons were Helena P. Blavatsky and Mrs. Besant, and Charles W. Leadbeater, who writes, "it is by means of such highly developed consciousness that we observe all these facts I am now describing," [66] referring to what has just been quoted from his pen.

Mrs. Besant and Leadbeater, as well as H.P.B., spent many hours studying, by clairvoyant means, not only the problems of human existence, but the world of physics and chemistry and of nature generally. Mr. Leadbeater in a letter to Mrs. Besant once described something of the process by which this was done. "The person who undertook the work would not give words and commas. He would offer the Ego of the pupil a concept which, when passed *by that Ego* into his lower mind would burst out into a mass of ideas which

[65] *Id.,* pp. 44-45.   [66] *Id.,* p. 45.

would clothe themselves in language. But the ideas would not be the original concept, but the ego's conception of that concept; the words would not even be directly the ego's own choice, for he does not concern himself with words. He does not use such things; they are not his language. They would be the mind's expression of what he wanted to say, but they could never be a perfect expression. . . . There has never been any such thing as verbal inspiration as it is ordinarily understood—and this in spite of the fact that it often seems to the recipient as though someone stood by and dictated every word." [67]

As a result of the experiences on the lower planes the causal body is developed. As seen by clairvoyant sight the causal body of undeveloped persons has the appearance as "ovoid" and surrounds the physical body, "extending to a distance of about 18 inches from the normal surface of that body." [68] In the case of a primitive man it "resembles a bubble, and gives the impression of being empty," though in reality it is "filled with higher mental matter, . . . colorless and transparent," because it has not yet been brought into activity. As the ego develops, this higher matter of the causal body is "stirred into alertness by vibrations which reach it from the lower bodies" and "gradually becomes a sphere filled with matter of the most lovely and delicate hues . . . beautiful beyond all conception." And the colors are significant. Unselfish affection shows itself as a pale rose color; yellow indicates high intellectual power, sympathy is green, blue expresses devotional feeling, while high spirituality reflects itself in a luminous lilac blue. [69]

Only desirable qualities affect the causal body. Evil qualities must be thrown aside as man advances "because he has no longer within him matter which can express them." The causal body increases in size as man progresses in spiritual power "because it has so much more to express . . . and in the case of one who has attained Adeptship this body is of enormous proportions." From it begins to pour out "in all directions rays of living light."

Even in the lower bodies the color scheme is evident though of a less delicate character. Pride shows itself as orange, irritability as brilliant scarlet, avarice as bright brown, deceit as gray-green, in the

[67] Ransom, *op. cit.*, pp. 91–92.
[68] *Textbook of Theosophy*, p. 46.
[69] *Id.*, p. 46.

mental body. At the astral level "a lurid brownish red indicates the presence of sensuality, while black clouds show malice and hatred, and brownish green betokens jealousy." [70]

Every thought a person has "builds a form; if the thought be directed to another person it travels to him; if it is distinctly selfish it remains in the immediate neighborhood of the thinker; if it belongs to neither category it floats for a while in space and then disintegrates." [71] It results that as a man goes along thinking he leaves a trail of floating thought forms which may float into the mind of another whose attention he attracts. A man is not responsible necessarily for a thought which floats into his mind but is responsible if he gives it lodgement, and sends it out strengthened. If all this is true, then it follows that one can greatly assist others by the intelligent direction of thought upon another person.

This being the nature and organization of man, salvation which is conceived of as for everyone, or universal, is the attainment, through the process of reincarnation, of ultimate mergence in or oneness with God; as Leadbeater says, "until humanity is transcended and merged in divinity." [72]

The principle of Karma or the "law of sowing and reaping" operates inexorably. Man is free apparently to choose his course. The conditions in any given life span are the result of one's own actions in the past, but actions in this life are determining what the conditions in the next life are to be. One "may not always be able to make himself or his conditions all that he would wish in this life; but he can certainly secure for the next one whatever he chooses." [73] The law of evolution "if left to itself would do the very best possible for every man," but "is restrained by the man's own previous actions." [74]

But what of death and of the period between births? It is spent in one or more of the other planes of existence, and the length of each depends upon many factors. Those low in the evolutionary scale scarcely go higher than the astral plane, because they do not yet think much, then return to physical plane. More highly developed individuals may spend extended periods at each of the higher levels. The astral life, says Leadbeater, in general "corresponds to what Christians (Catholic) call purgatory; the lower mental life, which is always entirely happy, is what is called heaven." [75] Hell is non-

[70] *Id.*, pp. 54–57. [71] *Id.*, p. 52. [72] *Id.*, p. 42.
[73] *Id.*, p. 103. [74] *Id.*, p. 106.
[75] *Textbook of Theosophy*, p. 64.

existent, "only a figment of the theological imagination." Man makes his own purgatory and heaven—and neither is eternal, "for a finite cause cannot produce an infinite result."

Mr. Leadbeater estimates that an average man of the so-called lower middle class, might spend perhaps forty years on the astral plane, and about two hundred on the mental. A more highly developed man, "of spirituality and culture," might have twenty years of astral life and a thousand years of mental. Specially developed persons might spend only a matter of days or hours at the astral level, but fifteen hundred years at the mental, or in heaven.[76]

The dead do not "go" to heaven. They remain about where they lived in the physical body, though they are able to float about in any direction as they desire. The astral world extends to about the distance of the moon's orbit from the earth,[77] but ordinarily the astral bodies remain close to earth, and may be all about us as we go about our ordinary day's activities. They cannot communicate with physical bodies, but may, and do, with the astral bodies of living people in sleep, when the astral body may temporarily separate itself from the physical. Thus are dreams of traveling about and of communicating with the dead and absent persons explained.

In the mental world there are, as in the astral, seven subdivisions, but one does not pass through them successively but is "drawn to the level which corresponds best to the degree of his development, and on that level he spends the whole of his life in the mental body."[78] Here he is surrounded by all the friends and "they are for him always at their best," and the state is one of immense happiness. But eventually this ends and the mental body is left. The individual is then in his causal body in which he remains, at least most do, in a more or less dreamy unobservant state since "they have very little consciousness at such a height as this."[79] But as he returns again in the cycle the period of causal life is lengthened and at the same time as he grows his capacity not only of receiving but also of giving increases, and in this lies the supreme delight of all. This happy state is, according to the gospel of Theosophy, certain for all.[80]

Evil is man-made. Most of what appears to human sight to be evil is in reality but a part of an ordered progress when we "escape from the dust-cloud raised by the struggle in this outer world and look upon it all from the vantage ground of the fuller knowledge

[76] *Id.,* pp. 64–65.   [77] *Id.,* p. 71.   [78] *Id.,* p. 94.
[79] *Id.,* p. 95.   [80] *Id.,* p. 96.

and the inner peace." [81] Then it is seen that what appeared to be countercurrents of evil prevailing against the stream of progress "are merely trifling eddies into which for the moment a little water may turn aside, or tiny whirlpools on the surface . . . but all the time the mighty river is sweeping steadily on its appointed course, bearing the superficial whirlpools along with it." [82]

The tendency to evil which man finds in himself and against which he must struggle for the mastery is explained not as the work of the devil, as the orthodox have thought. Not that there are not evil entities, for there are, but they "are man-made, every one of them, and impermanent . . . called into existence by the thought of other evil men." [83] The explanation of such evil promptings is usually from quite a different source, the matter which man draws around him at different levels in order that he many be born again on the physical plane. This matter is not dead matter, indeed "there is no such thing anywhere" rather it is instinct with life, though at "a stage of evolution much earlier than our own—so much earlier that it is still moving on a downward course into lower matter, instead of rising again out of lower matter into higher. Consequently, its tendency is always to press downward toward the grosser material and the coarser vibrations which mean progress for it, but retrogression for us." Thus the interest of the true man "sometimes comes into collision with that of the living matter in some of its own vehicles." [84]

The Bible is for Theosophy only one of the many sacred books. It is quoted freely in their literature, but since the emphasis has been so strongly upon the oriental religions, it has not played so important a role in Theosophy as in some of the other movements. H.P.B. once wrote in a letter that "there are 64,000 mistakes in the Bible." [85]

Toward the church the early leaders had only hostility. They considered it an obstacle to true religion and anyone sufficiently prejudiced to prefer one form of religion above another could not be a member of the society. As indicated above, this attitude has been modified in more recent years, so that many Theosophists now retain their church membership, and some are quite active churchmen. The failure of Theosophy to provide anything in the nature of corporate worship leaves unsatisfied many persons who find in it a

[81] *Outline of Theosophy*, p. 27.
[82] *Id.*, p. 28.   [83] *Id.*, pp. 55–56.
[84] *Id.*, pp. 56–57.   [85] Ransom, *op. cit.*, p. 127.

satisfying intellectual answer to their questions. The church supplies that need. We shall see in another chapter the rise of a new church to meet this need on a basis different from orthodoxy, the Liberal Catholic Church. (See Chapter VIII).

There is nothing distinctive in the moral teaching and practice of Theosophy. In general it is Christian, for it is merely the carry-over of the generally accepted moral teachings in which the outstanding leaders grew up, a morality found, it is true, also, in the other religions at their best. There was a strong emphasis on temperance in the earlier years of the movement. Many Theosophists are vegetarians, drawing this undoubtedly from India, but this is not a requirement. There is a broad ideal of brotherhood, a repudiation of caste, race and color as well as creed. How successful they have been in the practice of these ideals it is difficult to say. In the group in America where color is a very real problem, they have not had conspicuous success in attracting colored people, if indeed they have tried. In India, unquestionably the record has been good.

C. Jinarajadasa represents H.P.B. and Col. Olcott as being apparently anti-Christian, because Christianity as they saw it, "resulted in a social condition which held the masses in economic subjection, and which upheld a social system which was profoundly unethical and unchristian." [86]

This was written in 1925 many years after the rise of the emphasis on the social gospel, and may well reflect the projection of ideas of a later period into the past, for he is writing of what the founders were thinking fifty years before, in 1875, more than two decades before the rediscovery in Protestant Christianity of the social message of Jesus. If they did, indeed, hold such ideas it is rather remarkable. There is nothing in the history of the Society save its espousal of Indian Home Rule which identifies it conspicuously with the struggle of the underprivileged for a better share of this world's goods. It has done some work of social amelioration, but has not been noted for its philanthropic effort. Its members have been drawn from the fairly comfortable middle class, the bourgeoisie, in general from those of some education and serious intellectual interests. Its emphasis has been mainly on the individual virtues. Indeed, in its doctrine of Karma, which makes the condition in which a man finds himself the result of his own past choosing, the social

[86] *Golden Book of the Theosophical Society*, p. 28,

responsibility for much that the individual suffers does not seem to be adequately explained. For example, in times of depression millions of men are thrown out of employment and suffer real hardships and their families with them. Was it something in the past of an innocent child, victim of parental unemployment, through no fault of his own, which caused its suffering? Perhaps there is an adequate explanation of such things, but the writer has not come upon it.

The broad non-dogmatic character of Theosophy made a great appeal to many in the earlier day when the inroads of the newer scientific age were working such havoc among thoughtful religious people. Here was a faith that was not at odds with the fascinating and convincing idea of evolution, indeed it seemed to be the very application of evolution in the sphere of religion. Advancing scientific knowledge made many people highly critical of the cruder forms of thought about the after-life. Reincarnation must have seemed to not a few a far more rational and acceptable view than that of literal orthodoxy. At all events it made possible a continued belief in the ongoing life of the individual. The universalism of Theosophy as opposed to the limited Calvinistic and other orthodox conceptions of salvation likewise made a real appeal, while its optimism with reference to the inevitable progress of the world and humanity was in keeping with the growing spirit of the age. It was natural that it should attract a considerable, though never a mass following.

But is it growing today? The writer asked this question of the president of the American Section of the Society. Personal observation in a local setting had given the writer the impression that it was much less strong both in numbers and influence than it had been two decades earlier. The answer was definitely that the movement continues to grow. Local leadership in some centers has proven inadequate, and there has been definite recession here and there. Indeed, the movement as a whole has had its periods of advance and of recession. It was his opinion that it is growing rather vigorously at the present time. There is that in the modern situation which is less favorable to it than in an earlier period. The battle between science and religion is pretty well decided. Religion has come to terms with the newer scientific climate, or at least, if the mass religious expression lags, there are conspicuous liberal religious groups which offer all the scope for intellectual inquiry and investigation that the most critical minds could desire, and these do not have what has become increasingly a handicap to Theosophy as time has passed, the belief in the occult. This it becomes more difficult to accept with the increasing scientific understanding of the world.

Can Theosophy survive and grow in such a time? Well obviously, yes, because at no given time is the entire world at the same stage of development. Furthermore, Theosophy is fluid and adaptable and seems capable of interpreting the world in terms compatible with a rigorous scientific outlook. Indeed, it has made not a little capital of the new physics as a support of its contentions from the beginning. It can certainly be counted upon to attract thoughtful, if not completely critical minds, despite its occult emphasis.

It is solidly organized, owns and controls very considerable properties, all over the world; has a large literature which is read far beyond the limits of its membership. There is every reason to suppose that it will continue as it has in the past to pour a stream of influence into the thought of the West.

No movement in America has been more influential in introducing oriental thought. This is seen in new movements which have drawn a great deal from Theosophy, but have developed on a mass basis never achieved by Theosophy itself. The I Am movement is one. Its basis is definitely Theosophy, but dramatized and given a popular appeal Theosophy never could have. Unity is carrying to literally millions of readers the idea of reincarnation, though modified, to be sure, in some respects. Sections of New Thought, Rosicrucianism and even Psychiana, as has been indicated, all bear some of the marks of Theosophy upon them. All these lie rather beyond the pale of orthodoxy, though Unity less distantly than the rest. But there have arisen others which seem to operate within orthodoxy, or at least to maintain much that is orthodox in belief and practice, notably the Liberal Catholic Church, and a rather recent movement largely drawn from the Anglican church, the Order of the Cross (see pages 470–471).

But perhaps even more subtly the influence of Theosophy may be registered to some degree in the increasingly universalist view of salvation; and the disposition of Liberal Christians to think, if not in definite terms of reincarnation, at least of growth and development of the individual beyond the bounds of this mortal life.

Undoubtedly the continuous effort of Theosophist leaders to secure a greater degree of freedom for India through lectures and articles, as well as intimate participation in the struggle in India, has helped to create a world public opinion favorable to their aspirations and has helped immeasurably to hasten what has so recently been realized, the emergence of a free independent India.

Chapter Seven

The I Am Movement

In the year 1930, Mr. Guy Ballard, a mining engineer, was in the neighborhood of Mount Shasta in northern California, where, he says, he had been sent on government business. He had long known of the existence of the Brotherhood of Masters or Great Souls, made known in the West through Theosophy. In his travels in the Far East he had heard much of them. There was a rumor, indeed, that a branch of the Great White Lodge existed in this very mountain, called the Brotherhood of Mount Shasta. Deeply impressed by Mount Shasta's grandeur, each morning he would almost involuntarily salute the "Spirit of the Mountain and the Members of the Order."

He had become accustomed to taking long hikes during the days he spent at the foot of Mount Shasta, and it was on one of these long walks that the experience occurred which revealed to him the basis of the I Am teaching. That morning at daybreak he had set out without any specific destination in mind and climbed high up on the side of the mountain, enjoying the view to the south as it spread out before him. At lunch time he stopped near a mountain spring with a cup in hand. He knelt to dip up some water, when suddenly he felt as if there were an electrical current passing through his body from head to foot. Looking about quickly he saw beside him a young man who seemed, like himself, simply to be bent on a mountain walk. As he looked, the young man spoke to him, saying, "My Brother, if you will hand me your cup I will give you a much more refreshing drink than spring water." He handed him the cup which was instantly filled with a creamy liquid. Then the stranger handed it back, saying, "Drink it." He did so and was greatly astonished. The taste was delicious. There seemed to be some electrical

257

and vivifying effect on both mind and body that made him wonder what was happening.

The young man assured him that what he had drunk was directly from the Universal Supply—Omnipotent Life itself—which exists all about and is subject to our conscious control when we love enough, since the universe is obedient to the behest of love.[1] Whatever is desired can be manifested when commanded in love. It had been this that happened when he held out the cup. To give further evidence he held out his hand and immediately there appeared in it a golden disc. Then followed a longer discourse on the theme of the abundance of supply in the universe, available to those who are fitted to command it. Men do not know of the divine authority with which they are endowed. Because of this they are limited to time and space activities. There is an eternal law of life—that what one thinks and feels he brings into form. Hate, condemnation, lust, envy, jealousy, suspicion, generate, as a natural result, failure and disaster in mind and body and world. As a result of discordant feeling comes disintegration of the memory and body structure. Only the control of thoughts and feelings can enable one to transcend the evils in his surroundings. This requires discipline of a high order. The nature of that discipline he then continued to unfold.

The steps were, first of all, the quitting of outer activity of mind and body. Then follows a description of techniques which have been commonly used within the I Am movement from that time until now. This will be described in its proper place later on. Finishing the discourse, the young man declared that he had known Mr. Ballard for æons of time in a former incarnation. He had been present, he said, at Ballard's birth, at his mother's death, and it was he who had brought Ballard and Lotus, his wife, together. Then, as Ballard watched, the young man's countenance changed before him, and after a minute he saw in the young man who accosted him the master, St. Germain, a majestic figure, godlike in appearance, clad in a jewelled white robe, his eyes sparkling with light and love. The time had come, the Master asserted, when humanity must be awakened to the understanding of the fact that they have again and again been reembodied, each time in a new physical body, not by chance or accident but by a proven law. For there are no accidents, but everything has a former cause and every cause is invariably followed by an appropriate result.

[1] *Unveiled Mysteries*, St. Germain Press, Chicago, 1934, pp. 3-4.

"Come with me," he said, "and see what you were in some of your former lives." Then in an instant, Ballard reports, he was outside his physical body, seeing it clearly as it lay upon the ground. Encircled by a white flame, perhaps fifty feet in diameter, and with St. Germain's arm about him, they rose swiftly above the earth and presently looked down upon a town in southern France, where he had lived in a former incarnation, in which he became a great musician. After that he was taken to Egypt, passed rapidly over the desert, appearing finally at Luxor where he saw himself in a temple of great beauty as a ministering priest, serving alongside a high priest who was later to become his own son, Donald. A vestal virgin stood guarding the sacred fire, whom he recognized as Lotus, later to become Mrs. Ballard. As he watched, there appeared a visiting prince from afar who had designs on this same vestal virgin. The high priest, shown in vision what was to happen, was standing guard when the slaves of the visiting prince approached to seize her. Ordered to stop, the slaves still moved forward. Reaching a certain point the priest raised his right hand, pointing it directly at the slaves. As he did so a bright flash like a lightning stroke was seen and the hapless slaves fell dead upon the floor. The outraged prince strode forward, but was ordered to halt. Refusing to do so, again the fire leaped forth as the priest raised his hand, and the prince was no more.

This called for explanation from St. Germain, who pointed out that the priest had merely turned against the men their own hard selfishness and depravity. It was after this episode that St. Germain remarked that there was but one way by which the cosmic law of cause and effect, the round of reincarnation, could be avoided— namely, through the "conscious effort to comprehend the law of life." [2] To do this the God within must be earnestly sought and conscious contact made permanently with the "inner self," despite any condition in life. With this, Mr. Ballard was returned once again to his body and transported, without feeling any sense of motion, to his room in the lodge. Marveling that he thus should have been able to reach his room without being seen, St. Germain explained that it was possible to throw about the physical body a cloak of invisibility when moving among men. A moment later he was gone.

Not long afterward, Mr. Ballard found a card of thin gold on which was written with beautiful lettering an invitation to return once more to the mountain the next day. Responding to the summons

---

[2] *Unveiled Mysteries*, p. 27.

he returned up the mountain trail and had almost reached the meeting place when there suddenly appeared a panther, slowly approaching him. Frightened and tempted to run at first, there suddenly came to him the thought that he had within him the "Mighty presence of God," that this animal was a part of God's life also, and that consequently one part could not hurt another. With this realization his fear left him. He moved slowly toward the animal. As he did so its threatening eyes softened. The animal came slowly toward him until it rubbed its shoulder against him like a house cat. As he continued stroking the animal, St. Germain appeared and assured him that since he had conquered fear he would now be able to do for him what he could not have done otherwise. Holding out his hand there suddenly materialized in his palm delicious-appearing small cakes, which, when he ate them, brought a remarkable sense of clarity of mind and vision. Then St. Germain spoke to him saying that instead of using the method of the previous day, of visiting distant places, they would use "The projected consciousness." As he said this he touched the thumb of his hand between the eyes and the fingertips on top of Mr. Ballard's head. At once he felt as if a powerful electric current had passed through his body. Through projected consciousness one is able to become observer and actor in scenes of whatever time or place. After a few moments of silence he saw the Sahara Desert at a time some 70,000 years ago, with the civilization then existing. They found themselves in a magnificent building in the presence of the king who proved to be St. Germain and his daughter, again Lotus, and beside her was a young man, none other than Donald. The splendor of the court was beyond all description and the king notable in his wisdom. His teaching, of course, was the teaching of the I Am.

When this visit was over and he was returned to his former state he felt so exalted that he wanted to remain all night on the mountain and return home the next day. No sooner had he expressed the desire than he noticed a marvelous sleeping bag lying at his feet. St. Germain once again handed him a crystal cup filled with a golden fluid. When he finished drinking it the cup disappeared from his hand. Then he lay down in the sleeping bag, the panther serving as his guard through the night. Coming back to the hotel for the evening meal, he ordered a glass of milk which, to his amazement, when he touched it, became the same liquid that St. Germain had first given him. Just before retiring, while preparing for his bath, he held out his hand and a crystal-like substance precipitated and settled in his palm. Putting it in the bath the water seemed to come alive, and as he plunged into it he felt a thrill in every part of his body as though charged with an electric current of great power. After this he fell into a dreamless sleep. Experience after experience followed in quick succession.

Four days later a dove appeared upon his window sill. In its bill it carried a tiny card on which was written an invitation once again to meet his mentor, St. Germain. This time the journey was taken in still a different manner. His body was left behind with the panther to guard it while he and St. Germain flew over the mountains to the Royal Teton, where he was to see even greater wonders than anything thus far revealed. At a point where great boulders lay scattered on the mountain side, St. Germain put his hand on one of them. It opened up, leaving a passage, through great bronze doors weighing tons, into the mountain side. Within were marvelous rooms decorated with an unbelievable wealth of gold and precious jewels—rubies, diamonds, sapphires. In the center of one of the great rooms there was seen an enormous golden disc a dozen feet across, which was set with myriads of yellow diamonds in the shape of the seven-point star. Around this were seven discs of lesser size, some two feet across representing the planets and the seven colors of the spectrum. He was to learn later that Great Cosmic Beings pour through these discs their powerful currents of force. It is received by the Great Illumined and the unselfish ones known as the Ascended Masters of Light, who send it to humans on earth. The "radiation affects the seven ganglionic centers within every human body on our planet, as well as all animal and plant life." [3]

At another point there was an enormous eye representing the eye of the creator. In still another room there were records rolled on spindles which had hieroglyphics written on gold. To his amazement he found that he could read there a record of everything that had occurred since the beginning. This, anyone may train himself to read and understand, provided he is willing to give his attention and time to the self-discipline necessary to still the confusion in the outer activity of his everyday existence. In another room were containers of gold and jewels that were to be used for a special purpose. This gold was Spanish gold lost at sea or gotten from lost continents of

[3] *Unveiled Mysteries*, p. 82.

ancient civilizations. He was told about a school founded in 1887 for the Ascended Host of Masters established on the Inner planes, for the purpose of instructing those who had misused wealth and showing how it should properly be used.

Later they entered a council hall where seventy Masters gathered. Before them appeared something in the nature of a cosmic screen and upon it were portrayed, successively, the life of the lost continent of Mu, long since sunk beneath the broad Pacific, and Atlantis, submerged twelve-thousand years ago beneath the Atlantic Ocean. Here had been developed in remote ages a system of air transportation by the side of which our own modern air transportation was but primitive and crude. Then the ancient civilizations of the Gobi and Sahara Deserts came before them. They saw Egypt rise and fall, as well as the Roman Empire's growth from infancy to its fall; also the appearance of Jesus, bringing light and love and an overwhelming knowledge of the perfection of God. His coming was the revelation to the world of the power of divine love, a complete dominion over all finite things, the divine blueprint for the ages.

The pictures revealed not only what had passed, but what was to come in the far future, and the future of North America was a notable one, for it was she who was to serve as guide for the rest of the world, and to be the center of the golden age yet to come. He was assured that America would stand for a very, very long time. The pictures continued for hours. He was introduced to the great Masters, one of whom invited him to return again on New Year's Eve. After further instruction from St. Germain and having heard music such as he had never heard before, they left the retreat through a small door and passed swiftly back to Mt. Shasta to reenter the body which the faithful panther had watched over for nearly twenty-four hours.

Subsequent excursions with St. Germain took him to the Yellowstone, to Mitla, Mexico, which, it seems, was then a colony of the Incas; to Peru, where he, Lotus, and Donald had all been of the royal family; to the buried cities of the Amazon; to a secret valley somewhere in Arizona; and finally, his narrative comes to a climax in another visit to the Royal Teton when no less than seven personages from Venus also pay it a visit.[4]

---

[4] The entire narrative as given is based upon *Unveiled Mysteries*, though no specific page references are given. Very little is quoted verbatim, only that in quotation marks, and that, usually, *passim*.

This story was published under the title *Unveiled Mysteries* and became a principal text of the I Am movement. In a scientific age, it achieved a remarkable circulation and was accepted by literally hundreds of thousands of American citizens of all classes as true. The movement, although it had hard enough times in the beginning, had within ten years swept the entire country, captured enormous numbers of people in all the great cities, and was claiming more than a million followers. The writer has heard estimates by members of the movement running as high as three million. As a matter of fact no one knows just how many did accept it, for they never kept formal statistics. They do know how many groups there are. They do have record of the "one hundred percenters," which will be later described, but beyond that all is guesswork. It is a fact, however, that in the late thirties they gathered huge crowds, filling the great auditoriums of the larger cities of America, night after night, for a week or more each. Obviously not all who attended the meetings were converts to the movement, though many became so. Many were there out of curiosity, or to investigate, as was the case with the writer, but in the Chicago crowd he could tell by the way the great majority entered into the spirit of the proceedings that most of them were followers.

The meeting in Chicago was held in the great Civic Opera House. A considerable proportion of the women present wore evening dresses, many men were dressed formally. To one watching in the foyer during an intermission and as the crowd entered, there was little to distinguish it from an opera night. The Ballards were there, all of them. The crowd was enthusiastic. The dramatic entrance of the leaders, exceedingly well prepared for in advance, sent the people into a delirium of enthusiasm. They received an ovation which reminded one, at least in the length of its continuance, of a national political convention. When the leaders spoke they were interrupted again and again by prolonged applause for which an outsider could see little or no reason. They gave their decrees, which will be explained later, with an intensity seldom seen in a religious service. Deep emotion pervaded the whole meeting. It was an impressive occasion, and many must have been attracted to the movement by it.

Out of what did such a movement come? Who were its founders? What were its main teachings, and from whence were they drawn? What gave it its appeal? How were its benefits to be won? What has been its growth and subsequent fortune? To these questions we now turn.

The founders were Guy Ballard and his wife, Edna Ballard, and they have constantly associated their son Donald with them in it. In the *Unveiled Mysteries*, in every one of the various incarnations which Ballard was permitted to see, there were always Lotus, or Mrs. Ballard, and son Donald, in some relation or other. Unfortunately not too much is known about their past, and that little not certainly known. They were very obscure people before the movement assumed nation-wide proportions. None of the followers whom the writer has interviewed seemed to know, or indeed, to care about what they were in the past. They were the channels through which certain great truths had come. What else mattered? The fact that there has been something of a shadow over the reputation of Guy Ballard, whether rightly or wrongly so, may account for some of the reticence which followers exhibit in talking about Mr. Ballard's past. That record we shall have to deal with, as objective students of the movement, with no purpose of either discrediting or promoting it. But that must come later.

Guy W. Ballard was born on a farm not far from Newton, Kansas, July 28, 1878. Nothing is certainly known of his childhood. A devoted follower declares that once as a child he touched a sick boy and the boy was healed. There may be other legends in circulation concerning the period. At about fourteen years of age he went to live with an uncle at Mt. Vernon, Iowa. Although details of his early life are lacking, two things are asserted of him by those who knew him. He early became interested in mining, and as a young man engaged in selling stock in various western gold-mining ventures. He later came to be regarded as a mining engineer. What training he had for his calling must have come from practice in the field. The writer has found no record of any formal training for such a career. He seems early to have become much interested in fortune-telling and in mediums. Indeed, he became a medium himself, according to the testimony of friends, over thirty years before he launched the I Am movement. Apparently he practiced spiritualism in Chicago for a number of years.

In 1916 he married Edna Wheeler. Born in 1886 at Burlington, Iowa, she had been trained in music. She studied the harp in Chicago and finally became a professional, travelling for some time as a concert harpist. She was teaching the harp in Chicago when she met

Guy Ballard and married him. She, too, was interested in the occult. At various times they are said to have interested themselves in Christian Science, Unity, the Rosicrucian teaching, Theosophy, the teaching of the Swamis and other occult movements. They had close contact with William Pelley, organizer of the Silver Shirts, and at a later time absorbed a considerable part of his following. They became intimately acquainted with Baird T. Spalding, author of *Life and Teachings of the Masters of the Far East.*[5] At one time Spalding lived with them for a while.[6]

Their only child, Donald, was born in 1918. Apparently they did not prosper. A woman wrote Dr. Byran in 1938 that she had been invited to visit them in 1919, that she had lived with them seven months, "sharing their poverty, their sorrows, their woes, for they were as poor as the proverbial church mouse." She states that Ballard had an obsession, that of finding a gold mine. "He had dabbled a bit in mining prospecting." She financed a trip to California. They

[5] *California Press*, San Francisco, California, copyright, 1924.

[6] Authority for some of the above statements is found in the only extensive study thus far made of the I Am movement. It was made by Dr. Gerald B. Bryan of Los Angeles, who published a series of five brochures under the titles: *The I Am Experiences of Mr. G. W. Ballard; The I Am Teachings of Mr. G. W. Ballard; The I Am Doctrines of Mr. G. W. Ballard; The Source of the Ballard Writings;* and *The Ballard St. Germain;* and a full-length book, *Psychic Dictatorship in America.* These writings of Dr. Bryan are in no sense objective historical writing. They are all of the exposé type, written with the definite purpose of discrediting the movement. Dr. Bryan, a sincere student of occultism, was early attracted to the Ballards and attended their lectures with genuine interest. However, he finally became convinced that the teachings as represented were doing immense damage to thousands of people. Once he had reached this conclusion, he set about combating it with a crusader's zeal. Can such a study be used properly as a source by an objective student of the movement? The answer is, yes, at certain points. Certainly not where the author is obviously expressing his own opinion, though even this may be cited as one typical attitude toward the movement, and the recording of the various types of response to the movement is a part of its history. But where statements of fact occur, based upon letters which he has received from personal acquaintances of the Ballards, or where the author specifically states that he saw or heard certain things, these may very properly be cited. The writer knows Dr. Bryan. He is a professional man. He earns his living by the practice of his profession. He profits in no way by the publication of the material he has gotten together. Indeed, he has paid for it out of his own earnings, not at all certain whether he would ever get it back. Convinced that Dr. Bryan is a deeply sincere individual and that he serves no personal end, other than getting at what he regards as the truth, the present writer will use material from him at certain points where such material seems definitely to be in line with the testimony of other people, and in keeping with what seems to be consonant with the general picture of the movement.

went up into the mountains. He had the idea, she says, that she might lead him to a gold mine, since she was a medium and had a spirit guide. They lived in a cottage in the Sierras, near a gold mine, and every day he and she, or Mr. and Mrs. Ballard would walk out in the mountains, in search of the gold mine. "There was no money in the house," she says, "and we lived upon practically nothing." Finally she left them and saw nothing further of them until after the movement had gotten under way.[7]

Out of the next ten years come occasional stories of Guy Ballard's being involved in the sale and promotion of oil wells and gold mines which did not yield. His followers allege that these are stories told by enemies to discredit his movement. It is a fact that in 1929, March 25, the Cook County Grand Jury indicted him on the charge of "obtaining money and goods by means of the confidence game." Warrants for his arrest were drawn, but he was not apprehended. He was apparently from 1928 on, away from Chicago, in the far West. He states definitely in *Unveiled Mysteries*, in recounting certain of his experiences on Mt. Shasta and elsewhere, that he had not been with his family for two years.[8] Bryan asserts categorically that he was living during this time in Los Angeles under the name Dick Gilbert. He says that there were a number of people in Los Angeles who knew him at that time.[9]

A former member of the movement, who has, however, withdrawn from it, told the writer that Mr. Ballard "spent long hours in the occult library in Los Angeles, many times going without meals, for he was not well provided for in those days, and all the time he was probably working on this story." Somewhere in the decade 1919–1929 must be found room for his "travels in the Far East" which he mentions on the first page of *Unveiled Mysteries*. Bryan challenges his statement that he ever travelled in that part of the world and brings not a little circumstantial evidence to support his contention. The writer has made no independent attempt to ascertain the facts, or indeed, to judge of the merits of the claims made against Ballard. While such an investigation would be necessary if it were sought to evaluate the movement, it has not seemed to him necessary in recounting its history. Here the movement is. These are the claims it makes. Such and such are the responses it evokes in

[7] *Psychic Dictatorship in America*, pp. 129–131, *passim.*
[8] *Unveiled Mysteries*, p. 244.
[9] *Psychic Dictatorship in America*, p. 138.

people. Whether Guy Ballard was genuine or a charlatan, he and Edna Ballard succeeded in the short space of a decade in convincing multitudes of people that he had the truth, and built a nation-wide movement which continues to flourish, to some degree.

It ought, perhaps, to be said that of all the movements the author has studied, this seemed least willing to cooperate with him. In every case he made an attempt to get the inside story of each movement and its meaning from the founders or leaders themselves. Repeated attempts to secure an interview with Mrs. Ballard were unsuccessful. Charles Sindelar, once a very important figure in the movement, promised an interview, but failed to keep the appointment which had been duly made, having been called out of the city on business affairs. Mr. Paul Potter of Chicago did consent to an interview, which was very helpful. On the whole, however, through no choice of his own, the writer has been forced to go to the people who have been in the movement but have, for one reason or another, dropped out. Even here it was not possible to get any statement, usually, without promising not to reveal, even indirectly, the source of the information. One wrote, "I trust you will keep your word and not disclose the source of the information, as we do not wish to be subjected to the avalanche of letters and personal calls which would be our unfortunate lot." Another spoke of the fear of economic difficulties that might ensue, if it were known that he had given certain information about the cult. Such an attitude has appeared nowhere else among the cults.

After Mr. Ballard left Chicago, Edna Ballard worked in a book store known as the "Philosophers Nook," which was managed by her sister. It was chiefly occult books that were handled, and Mrs. Ballard is said to have read many of them. She published a periodical, *American Occultist*, and another, *The Diamond*. One who was very close to the Ballards at one time told the writer that in later years when they travelled about the country, they always carried a trunk full of occult books which they frequently read.

Thus the whole background of both Mr. and Mrs. Ballard is one of deep interest in the occult, a fitting background for a movement such as the I Am. Some light is thrown on the possible impulse that led Ballard to the creation of his brain child by the same correspondent who told of living with them and of bringing them to California. She says that one evening they attended a certain church. "The Priest and Priestess sat in two golden chairs with the twelve vestal virgins as the choir. Behind them was a great illuminated cross with flashing lights. During the service the very lightly clad virgins threw flowers among the audience. . . . Afterwards came the Love Feast. A virgin held a basket of strips of bread and the audience was asked to join this holy order which was non-sectarian. Another virgin held a loving cup of wine. . . . Over one hundred and fifty people went forward and partook of that sacrilegious feast. . . .

"During this scene Guy's face was a study. He was enchanted with the show but didn't join the church. As soon as he reached the sidewalk, he could not stop talking about it . . . and from what I now hear he has fashioned his own church upon the same lines, with his illumined background." [10]

Dr. Robinson, founder of Psychiana, told the writer in a personal conversation in Moscow, Idaho, that Ballard had come to see him in Moscow and told him he intended starting a movement. "Go ahead," said Robinson, "just so you don't infringe on my material." "I am going to make it dramatic," said Ballard; and certainly he did just that.

II. DEVELOPMENT OF THE MOVEMENT

The first beginnings of the I Am movement are not easy to trace. Edna Ballard had started certain secret classes in 1930, in Chicago. It will be recalled that at that time Guy Ballard was in California, where, in August, September, and October, the startling experiences narrated in the *Unveiled Mysteries* occurred, as he specifically states in his foreword to the volume. It is charged that in Mrs. Ballard's teachings she used some material from William Pelley of Silver Shirt fame. Byran quotes an unsolicited letter written him by the Pelley Publishers in 1938 as saying: "Mrs. Ballard was a student of Mr. Pelley's spiritual philosophy before she launched upon her purported mission to 'save' Christian America. All her writings and teachings are full of material which she appropriated from Mr. Pelley's writings." [11] The fact that the two movements were at that time rivals, and that the Pelley movement had apparently lost heavily to the

---

[10] Quoted by Gerald B. Bryan, *op. cit.*, p. 130.

[11] Bryan, G. B., *Psychic Dictatorship in America*, p. 33 quoting from "an unsolicited letter from Pelley Publishers, Asheville, North Carolina, January 10, 1938."

Ballards, might lead one to question the validity of such testimony. Bryan goes on, however, to draw so large a number of parallels between the two movements, that it does not seem unlikely that Pelley's materials were known and either consciously or unconsciously used by them.

Pelley had written an article in the *American Magazine* [12] in 1929 under the title *Seven Minutes in Eternity*, which told of an experience he had while living in a lonely cabin in the Sierra Madre mountains. Here one night he suddenly left his body and was carried away into eternity, from which he returned to tell of what had happened to him. Later he received messages from the Masters which he duly published in his magazine *The New Liberator*. Bryan points out that Ballard's experiences of being taken out of his body also occurred in the mountains, at Mt. Shasta, and that he, too, talked with the Masters—St. Germain chiefly, but also many others, and that he received messages from them, which he communicated to the world as their "accredited messenger." Possibly the parallelism is only accidental, but it is a fact that the Ballards succeeded in winning to their own movement a substantial number of Pelley's followers in 1934, while Pelley was in difficulty with the law in North Carolina. The treasurer of the Silver Shirts organization became the "Associate Director of the St. Germain Activities," and he was active in the promotion of the I Am movement until a serious accident a few months later incapacitated him for further service.[13]

It is true, also, that in a message from St. Germain dated August 3, 1934, reference is definitely made to "Christian Democracy," which was the name given by Pelley to his ideal political order, as upholding "splendid ideals, possible of achievement." [14] Also there was reference to Pelley's "Plan of No More Hunger" which, however, it was revealed, "is not entirely correct." So it is completely certain that by 1934 at least, the Ballards were well acquainted with Pelley and his movement. Thus it becomes easier to believe that Mrs. Ballard might well have known and used his material at an earlier date.

Just when Guy Ballard returned to Chicago is not certain. One writer mentions a secret trip in 1931, at which time he told his wife of the revelation on Mt. Shasta through St. Germain. However, it

[12] Vol. 107, March, 1929, pp. 7–9, 139–144.
[13] *Psychic Dictatorship in America*, p. 40.
[14] *Id.*, p. 31.

seems to be certain that Edna Ballard was busy laying the founda-
tions for the later movement. With the knowledge of Ballard's Mt.
Shasta experiences, communications began to come to her through
St. Germain. Her husband and herself and the boy Donald became
the Accredited Messengers through whom not only St. Germain,
but Jesus and an increasing number of Masters, speak to the world.

The first regular ten-day class was held in the Ballard home in
Chicago in 1934, with some ten persons in attendance, all pledged to
secrecy.[15] At this time messages from St. Germain were read. These
were subsequently published. Usually the date and place of each
message is given. Messages might come through either Mr. or Mrs.
Ballard, for both were Accredited Messengers. Donald was also
Accredited but no messages given through him have come under
the writer's observation.

The year 1934, then, seems to be the year of the launching of the
movement in the form in which it is now known. In that year
Unveiled Mysteries was published under the copyright and imprint
of the St. Germain Press, located then and always in Chicago. It
was incorporated in the State of Illinois for the purpose of publishing
and distributing literature. Of its three directors, two have always
been of the Ballard family, the remaining one, some more important
leader of the movement, changing from time to time.

In October, 1934, the Ballards, under the name of Mr. and Mrs.
Godfré Ray King, the *nom de plume* under which Ballard published
Unbelieved Mysteries and *The Magic Presence*, opened their first
out-of-Chicago ten-day class in Philadelphia. That they had not yet
begun to prosper financially is evidenced by the fact, often stated by
them, that they used the rent money on their home to pay their
railway fare to Philadelphia.[16] It will be recalled that the treasurer of
the Pelley movement had been won over to become their promoter.
Undoubtedly, therefore, among the first to attend the classes were
some of the followers of Pelley. There were thirty persons present
on the opening night. By the end of the series a hundred and fifty
were attending. The idea had begun to "take." It drew particularly
two kinds of people, those who were already believers in the occult,
and "patriotic" people, for, as will be seen a little later, a strong
emphasis was constantly placed on the welfare and prosperity of
the nation.

---

[15] *Psychic Dictatorship*, p. 21.
[16] Bryan, *Psychic Dictatorship*, p. 37.

A ten-day class was next scheduled in New York, with some success. Meanwhile the Philadelphia group desired another class, to which still larger numbers responded. Back again to New York— thence to the nation's capital for a class—they were finding a ready response wherever they went. The near fatal accident to their agent in Washington, already mentioned, was a serious blow, for he had connections that made it easy to get invitations from various cities. They did not have the same success in the South where they went in the winter of 1935. Indeed, they met not a little opposition. Of that period Mr. Ballard once wrote: "You will never know the forces we have been pitted against since we left Washington." [17] In an automobile accident he suffered the fracture of some of his ribs. By now they had been able to purchase a Ford car for their travel from city to city. Prosperity was beginning to crown their efforts.

From Florida they headed west to California, and Los Angeles, which was to provide them their greatest successes, and to become their home for several years, but also to witness the most formi- dable attacks made upon the movement. Of this, more later. Los Angeles has long been known as the "city of cults." Probably more such organizations flourish there than in any other city in America. The preparations for their coming had been well made. The "meta- physical" devotees had heard of some of the marvels the Accredited Messengers were relating. They eagerly turned out for the classes and poured out "love gifts" upon the founders in unheard-of amounts. Real prosperity was at last achieved.

Persons who attended the earlier classes and later became promi- nent in the movement told the writer of the relative simplicity of the Ballards in those days. Mrs. Ballard dressed modestly and with- out ostentation. They were humble, friendly, kindly, and drew peo- ple to them. One informant had the impression that the Ballards could not quite believe what was happening to them. It seemed un- real. Crowds were attending their meetings which had not yet been dramatized, as they were later. Successive classes necessitated moving to larger auditoriums, until finally they took the great Shrine audi- torium, seating six thousand people, for their classes in August 1935.

The Ford car gave way to extravagant luxury cars, and they began to live in the most expensive hotels in the various cities they visited. At the peak of their success in 1938 their entourage included four- teen persons. Between 1935 and 1938 they visited most of the great

[17] Bryan, *Psychic Dictatorship*, p. 41.

cities, holding classes in the largest auditoriums, and attracting vast numbers of people. Gradually the comparatively simple lectures with which they began gave way to highly colorful meetings, elaborately staged to center attention upon the Accredited Messengers. A complicated ritual of decrees and affirmations gave large place for audience participation.

A description of a typical meeting at that period will not be out of place, for it was characteristic of the movement as a whole as it had developed.

The enormous stage of the Chicago Civic Opera House was ablaze with light. Back center was a colossal painting of the symbol which they had adopted, and which frequently appears in their publications. It is called The Magic Presence. Against a deep blue background of sky, rising above mountains which are meant to represent Mt. Shasta and the Royal Tetons, is a human figure surrounded by a cylinder of violet or lavender, shading off into light yellow. About the head is a varicolored halo, and coming down directly into the top of the head is a ray of light from another figure in the sky which is surrounded by concentric haloes of white, yellow, orange, lavender, violet, purple, green, and blue. Radiating in every direction are powerful rays of light, one of which touches the top of the head of the lower figure. It is an exceedingly colorful symbol. At either side of the stage were two large portraits in color, one of St. Germain and one of Jesus, both works of Charles Sindelar, an artist who was drawn in the movement. He alleges that both Jesus and St. Germain sat for their respective portraits. He became very prominent in the movement. Both figures were strongly Nordic in features and quite alike in appearance, kindly, bearded figures, somewhat reminiscent of Thorvaldsen's Christ. Under the powerful spotlights which played upon these paintings they were decidedly impressive.

On the stage, besides the speaking desk with microphone, and a grand piano, there were chairs for the Ballards and others of their leaders, a pianist, a singer, and a Master of Ceremonies. The first part of the meeting was conducted by the Master of Ceremonies, at that time a Mr. Harry Rogers, who had been a successful business man in Los Angeles before he was drawn into the movement. The singer was Mrs. Rogers, who not only sang, but wrote many of the songs that the movement used. It was a lively, happy gathering. The Master of Ceremonies was clever and knew how to keep things moving. He spoke much of the success in other cities; read telegrams and other letters of greeting; made frequent reference to the Accredited Messengers, referring to them always in the most affectionate terms, and building up carefully to the moment when they would appear. The crowd was all expectancy when finally they made their triumphal entrance. As they swept on to the stage the audience arose and applauded long and enthusiastically. Mr. Ballard was a rather tall slender man with gray hair, combed straight back from his forehead, a rather thin, somewhat aquiline nose, and deep-set eyes. He moved easily, with erect carriage, across the stage, bowing to the applauding audience. He was dressed in a white woolen full-dress suit, a diamond sparkling in his shirt front. Donald Ballard, garbed very much like his father, was then a very young man, with dark hair, and a small black mustache—a rather sophisticated-looking individual. He was accompanied by his wife Margery—richly clad in an evening dress of latest fashion. She was later to divorce him.

But the climax came when Edna Ballard appeared. She was at that time in her early fifties, an extremely well preserved woman, dressed elegantly in a white silk formal gown, her hair dressed in the very latest fashion. She wore jewelled rings on her fingers and a necklace which glittered in the strong spotlight which played upon her. She smiled graciously, and inclined her head in recognition of the storm of applause that swept the great audience. She was clearly the dominant figure of the four principals, not only in her appearance, but in her manner as she took over and thereafter largely directed the proceedings. Her voice was not pleasing. It approached the strident at times, but that may have been the effect of the public address system. At all events there appeared none of the sweetness and gentleness which it is said she had shown in the earlier days of the movement. Hers was now a voice of command.

She both spoke and led in the giving of the decrees which occupied a considerable portion of the time. There were no messages from the Ascended Masters that night, though they often occurred. Mr. Ballard finally took the floor and spoke for perhaps fifteen minutes. His voice was pleasing. He spoke easily, smoothly, and with little emotion until he began talking of what he called the vicious attack upon the Accredited Messengers by certain local papers. They had been giving large publicity to the revival of charges against himself of having practiced fraud in his sale of mining stocks to some women of the community. These charges he labelled as false, and the whole but an expression of the hatred of evil entities who feared the mightly I Am and the Messengers because of their work, and sought to destroy it. Thus far, he declared, he had exercised great patience. He had not unleashed all the limitless power of the Ascended Masters. But this could not go on. If persisted in he might be compelled to loose powers of destruction that would blast forever all such evil agencies and those who allowed themselves to be deceived by them. At this point he spoke with great feeling.

The great audience, deeply stirred, applauded enthusiastically. He stood long before raising his hand to signal the applause to cease, in order that he might continue. No one among all the applauding multitude seemed for a moment to doubt that he could or would do what he had said. When he finally ended his discourse and sat down the applause continued for a long time. Obviously the Ballards had captured the great audience. The meeting had lasted for some two hours and a half, all told. No collection was taken, but those present had all been given envelopes in which they might place their "love gifts" and deposit them in the boxes, conspicuously placed at all exits. How much was given at such a meeting the public never knew, but it must have been a substantial sum. Expenses had become high at that time. Yet the income was far in excess of outlay. The Los Angeles *Times* reports that in the trial it was disclosed, through the introduction of reports by government prosecutors, that "receipts from the sale of books and love gifts during the classes conducted by the Ballards in the major cities throughout the country averaged well over $1,000 a day." As an example they cited a seventeen-day class in Los Angeles in 1938, during which "nearly $15,000 was realized from the sale of books and more than $12,000 from love gift offerings." [18] The movement was at that time nearing the peak of its popularity.

In the foyer was a display of their literature and other cult materials which were for sale. These included the books by Godfré Ray King—or Guy Ballard, the *I Am Discourses*, the song book—the magazine, *The I Am Voice*, pictures of St. Germain and Jesus, etc.

The author approached the man in charge of sales and suggested that his university library would be glad to have the books of the movement. "By all means," said he. "Take this set right along with you." The writer hesitated. "But, you may need these. There is no hurry. Why not just mail them to the library at your convenience?"

[18] Los Angeles *Times*, December 20, 1940, Pt. I, p. 2, col. 2.

"If I need anything, I have only to decree it, and it is supplied," he replied, as he bundled up the books and delivered them into the writer's hands.

Something like this went on in all the greater American cities. The Ballards were tireless workers. They were constantly speaking, attending meetings, keeping up an extensive correspondence, writing for their magazine, making radio addresses, and granting interviews. Staff meetings were frequently held, and often directions to one or another of its members, or to the whole staff, were given as though coming from St. Germain. These were accepted for a long time without question as bona fide messages from the Ascended Masters, although they always came through Mr. or Mrs. Ballard. "It did not occur to me to question their ultimate source," one of the members of the staff told the writer. Usually, therefore, they were heeded.

In the earlier period, a staff member reported to the writer, there was a spirit of the utmost harmony within the group. Both Mr. and Mrs. Ballard seemed to be humble, sincere people. No one must criticize anyone else. Only good should be spoken of anyone. It was a wonderful experience to share the group life. The Ballards, as stated above, seemed surprised at their success. But as money came in in ever larger sums, and as their power grew, a change was wrought, particularly in Mrs. Ballard. Perhaps it was only human that they should have been so affected. Power is a dangerous acquisition. Its corrupting influence upon the best of people has often enough been observed. Gradually Mrs. Ballard became hard and domineering, imperious in her demands and in her control of the group. For it was she, according to various informants close to the heart of the movement, who was the effective and aggressive figure of the Ballard family of Accredited Messengers. Orders and suggestions usually came from St. Germain, but they came through Guy, or more often, Edna Ballard. Donald Ballard is quoted by a witness in the trial as saying, "Whatever my mother wants, that's what St. Germain says." [19]

Meanwhile a permanent institutional form was developing. When the Ballards moved on there had to be some follow-up, and this necessitated some form of local organization.

At Los Angeles the Ascended Master, St. Germain, named a Seven-fold Committee, always speaking, of course, as he must,

[19] Reported in Los Angeles *Times,* December 29, 1940, Pt. I, p. 3, col. 1.

through one of the Accredited Messengers. He appointed one particular person as its chairman to carry on the work in the absence of the Ballards. Dissension developed, however, and the Accredited Messengers were obliged to cancel certain of their Eastern engagements and return to straighten out the difficulties in Los Angeles. The chairman of the Seven-fold Committee was summarily dismissed in a typewritten letter sent from Washington, D. C., signed only on the typewriter by St. Germain. It read in part:

"You are now dismissed from any further privilege or authority to serve the Messengers, Myself, or any of the Ascended Masters in this embodiment. To willingly try to deceive earnest students seeking their freedom in the Light is unpardonable. . . . Too late you will cry out in agony for the mistake you have made.

"Your earth span is very short. Make peace with your God and call on the Law of Forgiveness while there is yet time lest you deprive yourself of the opportunity in the next embodiment. Do not try to bluff such deception through any longer, less you do this thing again in the next two embodiments. When you put yourself under the Red Light, you cut off the White Light. . . . I am making this one last attempt to help you. *Choose.* The All-seeing Eye of God is upon you."

St. Germain.[20]

In some of the larger cities, notably Los Angeles, there were a number of local organizations, corresponding to local churches, each under the direction of a recognized leader. Such a group was that of Ratana Hendrickson, who had had her own organization not only in Los Angeles, but in various other centers. Recognizing, or thinking to recognize, in the Ballards' teaching much that she herself was teaching, she took her group bodily into the I Am movement and became one of the most influential leaders in Los Angeles, with an enormous following. She later left it, convinced that the Accredited Messengers were not true voices of the Ascended Masters, but the mouthpieces of evil beings, representing themselves as St. Germain and Jesus. She was one of the group included in the indictment brought in the courts, but was exonerated. Such local groups carried on regular classes, financed themselves, distributed the literature and paid in a certain portion of their income to the Ballards. The leaders evidently held their positions subject

[20] Quoted by Bryan, *Psychic Dictatorship*, pp. 49–50.

to the will of St. Germain, expressed through the Ballards. Evidence of this fact is to be found in an exchange of letters between Guy Ballard and one of the most loyal of his followers—a member of the staff on the road, and leader of a local group. The occasion of the dismissal was the conduct of the man's wife who had become convinced that the Ballards were not Accredited Messengers of the Ascended Masters, but clever exploiters of the credulity and the genuine needs of the people. The letter forms part of the court record in the trial of the Ballards:

My dear ————:

How tragic that you should be so deceived, or knowing, try to deceive me. We have a copy of ————'s terrible vicious letter written to Mr. ———— in New York trying by her vicious lies to prevent our getting the Woman's Club there—lieing that she had resigned instead of being dismissed. . . .

You have been hoping and decreeing that ———— come back into this Light and Groups. She will never come back in a thousand years. St. Germain gave her the opportunity to be silent, which she refused to do, gathering students about her at the cafeteria to try to injure us by her vicious lies. You told me she was not doing this when she sat at the table with others at various times and heard her doing it. You cannot be loyal to the Light and do this. Don't ask me to ever again believe one word of good about either ———— or ————. It is not in them. . . .

It is absolutely impossible for you to go on with your Groups with that treacherous creature in your midst. I am sure it will be much better for you to close your Groups, until such time as *you cut yourself free* from such influence if you should ever wish to do so. . . . Saint Germain has brought into our midst a fine man to take your place. . . .

You had the power in your own hands to stop all this viciousness in the beginning. What a pity you did not do it! Remember, ————, how St. Germain pled for two years to prevent this humiliation coming to you and there is no one to blame but ———— and ————.

May the Light within you reveal the full Truth of this to you. . . .

Sincerely in the Light,
G. W. Ballard.[21]

[21] Court record, District Court, Los Angeles, No. 14496-B.H., p. 30.

The reply, beautiful in spirit, reveals the degree to which its writer had accepted and, indeed, still at the time held the I Am teaching of the Ballards—and the affection he held for them:

Dear One:
    This is just a brief note to let you know that when the *telegram of St. Germain* dated November 12, 1939, arrived it seemed as though the end of the world had come for me. Certainly it was the most unexpected thing that ever could have happened. It seemed incredible to me. I do know I have given my all into this activity—my very life and soul as well. I do know that the Good which the Great Presence was able to do through me will live forever. It seems to me now as I reflect, that the continuous statements of the Ascended Masters in the Dictations saying how much was needed in getting out our decrees "as never before"—for the protection of America and all mankind—I became so imbued with the ideal of trying to render a service, that that became an all-consuming desire and possibly blinded me to other things. . . .

The letter continues describing the closing out of the Group—encloses $300 surplus funds and ends:

    Thank you, dear Ones, for your willingness to carry this wonderful message of the mighty I Am Presence to the world. Thank you for the opportunity you gave me to try to serve. . . . The only thing to live for is to render service to the Light. . . . May the Infinite blessings of the Eternal Light drench you, Lotus and Donald, etc., etc. . . .
    With all the love of my heart—

—————————— 22

Another case of similar nature shows that this must have been a not uncommon occurrence:

January 9, 1939

Mrs. M———:
    I have watched, waited and tried to bless you for many months; but since you are more and more determined to condemn the Messengers and join others to destroy This Work, it compels me to dismiss you as a Messenger of This Light.

22 Court record, District Court, Los Angeles, No. 14858-O.C., p. 31.

This means that you will no longer have the radiation of myself or any of the Ascended Beings, until such time as you correct this condition within you.

What a pity you cannot see that you are destroying yourself and all of the splendid work you have done and could do in the future. Since this is your choice I withdraw my Assistance and Association.

May the Great Light within you enable you to see your mistakes and correct them. Kindly return the letters of your Messengership to the Messengers, Mr. and Mrs. Ballard.

In the Service of Light,
SAINT GERMAIN.[23]

The great public classes continued through the greater part of the year 1939. Then, following a ten-day class in Cleveland, there came a sudden change of policy. All open sessions were banned and a new system of closed classes inaugurated—and so it continued until now. "In the future," declared St. Germain through Guy Ballard, "all classes and groups will be closed to the outside world. . . . Then the howling pack of wolves on the outside can howl to their heart's content." [24]

The occasion for this change of policy seems to have been the mounting public criticism of the movement in the press; the revival of the claims of fraud against Guy Ballard; and certain local difficulties experienced in Detroit and elsewhere. A woman attending one of the meetings refused to remove her hat. She was, she claims, forcibly ejected by white-clad ushers, or Minute Men, as they were called. Flung to the sidewalk, she asserted that she suffered spinal injuries. As a result she brought suit against the Ballards for $5,000.

Westbrook Pegler attended the Cleveland meetings and wrote a vitriolic series of articles about them that were circulated very widely and brought them much unfavorable publicity. A camera man, seeking to photograph the Accredited Messengers, was set upon by Minute Men and sustained physical injuries. He brought suit for $5,000 also and got court attachments on the Ballard's cars, and various stage properties.

In the first closed class at Washington the Goddess of Light, speaking through the Accredited Messenger, is reported as declaring that

[23] Letter included in Count 7 of grand jury indictment of Ballards, taken from photostat in court record, Los Angeles, September 14, 1944.
[24] Quoted by Bryan, *Psychic Dictatorship*, p. 232.

the Messengers (the Ballards), despite the fact that they had never so much as injured a fly, had been attacked by depraved persons in the press. But such individuals would yet come to know that they were dealing with forces too great for them.[25] Members were cautioned not to talk outside about what went on in the classes for there were spies about. No further information as to time or place of meeting was to be given.[26]

This policy undoubtedly had the effect of limiting their members, for no longer could the curious come to observe or to criticize. Even so, large numbers continued to attend the classes, for admittance to which they must now have admission cards. The very fact that it was now secret gave it an added attraction to some.

Already there had appeared a distinction within the group—in the Hundred Percenters—who were committed one hundred percent to following the I Am teachings. To be enrolled as one, it was necessary "for the I Am students to follow no other teachings, to abstain from meat, onion, garlic, tobacco, liquor, narcotics, playing cards, and to avoid all sex activities. The average student might indulge in sex activity in the procreation of the race, but the 'one hundred percenters' were required to avoid even this experience. They were taught that it was unnecessary to carry insurance because eventually every human whose body was completely purified would ascend. . . . Only One Hundred Percenters reach the stage where an ascension could be expected." [27]

Whether this is a complete description may be doubted, but it affords some indication of the general spirit of the group.

Bryan asserts that henceforth only those who "would sign a pledge of allegiance to the Ballards and their Ascended Masters could get in to the classes." [28]

But how could new recruits be attracted? Here the device is a preparatory class which the prospective member must faithfully attend for a period of six weeks, in which he is taught some of the basic beliefs and practices of the movement. If at the end of that time he has demonstrated his sincerity of interest to the satisfaction of the leader, then he is permitted to attend the regular classes,

[25] *Voice of the I Am*, February, 1940, p. 10.
[26] *Id.*, pp. 17–18.
[27] From court proceedings as reported in Los Angeles *Times*, December 11, 1940, pt. 1, p. 2.
[28] Bryan, *Psychic Dictatorship*, p. 233.

though there seem to be both elementary and more advanced classes beyond this stage.

Two young men known to the writer once entered the preparatory class. They reported that questions during the class session were discouraged, though the leader would sometimes answer them personally after class. Most of the time was spent in learning how to make the decrees. No student seemed free or willing to discuss what he had learned with the rest. It has been exceedingly difficult to get anyone still in the movement to talk freely about what goes on in the classes, or to discuss their beliefs and what results flow from them—a genuine handicap in any attempt really to understand a movement.

In the March 1936 number of the *Voice of the I Am* there is a section devoted to I Am Study Groups, by which is meant local groups, in distinction from the large classes conducted by the Messengers themselves. They are to be "closed," open only to "those who have decided to serve the Light and America, and, by perfecting themselves, be able to give still greater service."

Before each meeting the leader and students "should use the Violet Consuming Flame with great intensity, to purify the place in which it is held." Smoking should never be allowed and anyone smelling of alcohol should be excluded.

The principal purpose of the study groups is to help people understand the Teaching of the Ascended Masters, and through that to give the assistance which is requisite if America is to have protection from the discord across the Atlantic and from "cataclysmic disturbance."

It is "absolutely imperative" that there be no discussion of any kind; the entire time and attention, rather, is to be given to the reading of the texts of the movement, in the St. Germain series. This, it is asserted, is "Jesus' own request" because of the urgency of the hour. It is Jesus' and also St. Germain's request that no disclosure be made of what takes place during a group meeting. If one tells others of his experiences "he releases their energy into the surrounding atmosphere" and does not therefore receive the help intended for himself.

No charge must ever be made for this, for it is "a glad free gift of love from the Ascended Masters." All commercial and selfish motives must be eliminated. No discord or imperfection must enter the class, else the Energy of the Masters cannot come through.

An order is prescribed, including an invocation, the reading of a discourse, the visualizing by the students of the various activities of the Light Rays, for the protection of America and for healing, adoration of the "Mighty I Am Presence," as well as thanks and praise to It for Its great gifts to the world and the individual.

Questions during the reading must never be allowed, for they "break the Stream of Energy" which is powerful to bless.

The directions close with the declaration that Jesus has asked all students under this radiation "to put aside everything else they have ever learned," and enter into such communion with the Mighty I Am Presence that the Ascended Masters may be enabled to give the greatest possible assistance. . . . Any who do not wish to abide by such conditions should remain outside the groups.[29]

The year 1939 was to bring the movement a still more serious crisis—the greatest of all. On December 29, Guy W. Ballard, Accredited Messenger of the Ascended Masters, died. In most movements the death of the founder, sooner or later, is expected. Not so in the I Am. He would leave them, yes, but he would not die. He would make his Ascension. We shall later return to a more detailed discussion of this cardinal belief. Enough here to say that to make the Ascension means to arrive finally at the goal of all striving. It is to be liberated forever from the physical body, and to be free to move at will throughout the universe. Mr. Ballard had spoken much about Ascension. He had announced from time to time that certain persons had made their Ascension. No one had ever seen an Ascension, though hope was held out that some day this might even occur. Some day the Accredited Messengers would make their Ascension and become Ascended Masters. It was believed that they would do so in the physical body. In a message from Jesus, through Guy Ballard, on November 30, 1938, it was asserted that, although some had entertained the idea that the Ascension might be made after the experience of death, such was not the case.[30]

But Guy Ballard fell ill. He grew steadily worse and was in great pain. Finally, two days before his death, a surgeon was called and performed an abdominal operation, but in vain. In the early morning of the 29th of December, 1939, he died. The death certificate, of

[29] *Voice of the I Am*, March, 1936, pp. 26–29, *passim*.
[30] *I Am Voice*, January 1940, p. 6.

which the writer has a photostatic copy, indicated as the cause of his death, "arteriosclerotic heart disease," with "cardiac cirrhosis of the liver" as a probable contributing cause.

Seven days before his death a seventeen-day class had begun at the Shrine Temple, and every day Edna Ballard carried on the regular work. She told the students, according to Bryan,[31] that because of a serious crisis in world affairs "Blessed Daddy was out with St. Germain." The very day of his passing she conducted the class as usual, giving no hint of his demise. Arrangements were made for his funeral and cremation, and she herself pronounced the funeral oration on the morning of January 1, 1940. That afternoon at the class, at about the time the story broke in the public press, Edna Ballard made the startling announcement: "Our Blessed Daddy Ballard made his Ascension last night at twelve o'clock from the Royal Teton Retreat, and is now an Ascended Master." [32] There was a moment of stunned silence. Then thunderous applause broke out. But, "Our Blessed Daddy will come back," she declared, "and there will be a big temple in Los Angeles where he will some day appear in all his Ascended Master Radiance, wielding infinitely more Power of the Light Rays than before his ascension." [33] A little later the class dispersed to read in the afternoon Los Angeles papers that their Beloved Messenger had died. Many would not believe it. They were sure he had Ascended, but the first serious doubts were awakened in the minds of many others. With all the healings that he had claimed through the power of St. Germain, why should he himself have fallen victim to disease? Mrs. Ballard, at the trial, said he healed "thousands and thousands." If he had Ascended why was the body cremated? It was definitely the moment of awakened questionings for a number of leaders, according to the testimony personally given the writer by some closely tied into it. Mrs. Ballard's explanation that "The Beloved Messenger" was given his Ascension under the New Dispensation [34] did not satisfy them. The disintegration of the movement began, and it has suffered enormous losses since.

Edna Ballard carried on as before. Hers had always been the chief control, in the opinion of people who were deeply involved in it. As an Ascended Master, Guy Ballard could continue speaking

[31] Bryan, *Psychic Dictatorship*, p. 245.
[32] *Id.*, p. 251. [33] *Id.*, p. 252.
[34] *I Am Voice*, January 1940, p. 6.

to them, dictating the Message through his widow, and he has frequently done so. Soon his picture hung in the I Am meeting rooms, and "calls" were made to him as to the other Masters. His photographs were added to the list of articles advertised for sale by the movement, and the March number of the *I AM Voice* assured prospective purchasers that the pictures had been so charged by Him that those using them in contemplation and making calls to the Ascended Master might look for immediate answers.[35]

But a still further crisis was soon to be met. Even while Guy Ballard was dying, investigations were being made that led to an indictment by a Federal Grand Jury. On July 24, 1940, the Ballards and a score of their more prominent leaders were indicted on eighteen counts. In part, the indictment was as follows:

"The jury charges that the defendants 'did unlawfully, knowingly, and willfully devise and intend to devise a scheme and artifice to defraud, and for obtaining money and property by means of false and fraudulent representations, pretenses and promises from a large number of persons . . . and that class of persons who could or might be induced by means of any of the fraudulent or false devices, etc., to purchase books, magazines, etc., and each of them to become followers or who might be induced to accept the teachings of the . . . I Am movement and who might be induced to give, send and pay their money and give other things of value to said defendants.' "[36]

The trial was long drawn out and had nation-wide publicity. The hostile press made a field day of it, and the movement was badly discredited. The case was finally dismissed on September 8, 1941. The charges were renewed and a second trial, beginning December 2, 1941, continued for thirty-two days, and again national publicity was given it, particularly the more spectacular bits of testimony. A great deal of what appeared in the press was adverse, but many faithful followers testified to the value they had received and the utter confidence they had in its leaders. A Mrs. Holmes said: "Before I knew of the I Am, I was nervous, suffered from indigestion and had a slight curvature of the spine. I am now in better health as a result of the greater contact with my God. The Mighty I Am Presence to me is God in action, the power that beats my heart." [37]

[35] *I Am Voice*, March 1940, pp. 41–42.
[36] Court record 14496, Los Angeles.
[37] Los Angeles *Times*, January 8, 1941, Pt. II, p. 20.

Another declared: "I now find that the severe sick headaches I used to have are a thing of the past, that I have more energy and am calm and poised." [38]

Mrs. Schall, wife of Senator Schall of North Dakota, testified that she had spent "large amounts of money" in classes conducted by the Ballards in an unsuccessful attempt to cure her husband's blindness. "Mrs. Ballard told me to visualize a ray of light coming straight down to my husband's head and then leaving it at right angles through his eyes. I went to many, many classes, and kept putting in money, but he remained blind."

She further testified: "Mr. and Mrs. Ballard said that it was fortunate, indeed, that they had come to San Francisco when they did, because they had prevented a tidal wave and a cataclysm." Also, "All that you had to do to get precipitations from the Ascended Masters, including clothing, money, automobiles, or anything—was to visualize certain sparkles in the atmosphere—but I never succeeded in locating any sparkles." [39]

Since the charges had to do largely with obtaining money by deceptive means, the defense attorney made every attempt to show the disinterestedness of the leaders and their concern to extend the work. He cited the fact that the St. Germain Press discounted its books as high as seventy percent to the I Am corporation, which is strictly a non-profit organization, in order that it might have funds to carry on its work. He declared that Mrs. Ballard turned over 80 to 90% of the love gifts received to the non-profit corporation. She herself, in direct testimony, declared that she kept only those love gifts specifically ear-marked for her. "I've never asked a human being for a dime," she asserted. "I want the whole world to know that." [40] The defense counsel declared, at the last, that government had not proved that Mrs. Ballard had accumulated large sums of money. He declared in his opening of the defense: "We will produce evidence that Mrs. Ballard, in her will executed prior to these charges, has left everything to the non-profit company for furtherance of the work. If that is a scheme to defraud, then I'm a Chinaman." [41]

Government also introduced as evidence the will of Mrs. Ballard which provides for her son Donald a life interest not to exceed $500

[38] *Id.*, Pt. II, p. 20.
[39] Los Angeles *Examiner*, December 11, 1941, Sec. 1, p. 14, col. 1.
[40] Los Angeles *Times*, January 15, 1941, Pt. II, p. 2, col. 4.
[41] Los Angeles *Times*, January 7, 1941, Pt. II, p. 12, col. 12.

per month. This, in contrast to the relative poverty of the Ballards before the movement got under way less than ten years before, obviously seemed to them evidence of the personal accumulation of funds, even if the will did provide that the remainder of her estate was to go to the non-profit corporation for the perpetuation of the I Am activity.[42]

Much incidental information concerning the movement and the principals was included in the testimony, some of which has already been used in this chapter.

In an impassioned plea, the defense attorney dramatically asked: "Is it criminal to defraud people of frowns, disharmony, bad habits, fear of the future, and lack of a faith in a Supreme Being? If it is . . . then the jury should find them guilty of using the mails to defraud. And you will convict a new type of criminal, highwaymen who teach people to be good." [43]

The final result of the trial was the conviction of only Mrs. Ballard and son Donald, the former on seven counts, the latter on three. Mrs. Ballard was sentenced to one year of prison on each count, to run concurrently, the execution of the sentence to be suspended, and fined $8,000. Donald was sentenced to thirty days' imprisonment on each count, to run concurrently, sentence suspended and fined $400. The Ballards appealed, the judgment was reversed; government again appealed and the original conviction was sustained. Use of the United States mails was denied to the Ballards and to the St. Germain Press, so that since that date all books and articles distributed by the press have had to be sent by express. Orders are received by telegrams and in indirect ways, evidently, for the press still functions.

Meanwhile the case was appealed to the Supreme Court of the United States. This court handed down a decision in late 1946, voiding the indictment against the defendants because of the illegal drawing of the grand jury panel. Whether this will lead to a new trial, or just what its effect will be, it is too early, as this is written, to determine. A letter from a United States Mail Inspector to Mr. Gerald B. Bryan, written December 26, 1947, declared that the ban on their use of the mails was still effective.[43]

Mrs. Ballard was under probation for a year, subject to very rigid

[42] Los Angeles *Times*, January 15, 1941, Pt. II, p. 2, col. 4.
[43] Los Angeles *Times*, January 17, 1941, Pt. II, p. 1, col. 2.

restrictions that she cease operating, directly or indirectly, the I Am Movement or any enterprise connected with it, either press or foundation; that she not conduct meetings nor make use of radio programs; that she not represent self as channel of healing, or publish literature alleging that the Ascended Masters appeared to the Ballards, nor that any person could obtain help from the Ascended Masters or other deities; that she refrain from representing, orally or in writing, that the alleged powers of the Ascended Masters had the power to save the United States from destruction; in short, that she refrain from making representations as set forth in the entire indictment, and from solicitation of gifts, either directly or indirectly, during this period.[44]

The trial with its attendant publicity had wrought havoc among the members of the cult. The death of Guy Ballard—and now the indictment of Edna Ballard, was too much for great numbers of followers. The movement was rapidly falling apart.

Mrs. Ballard naturally enough desired to get away from Los Angeles. She sought permission from the court, and it was granted, to leave California. Accordingly, the Los Angeles headquarters were closed and she and son Donald left the city.

The subsequent fortunes of the movement are exceedingly difficult to follow, for almost no one seems willing to talk about it. It has become more and more secret in its operations.

Mr. Paul Potter, to whom the writer was referred by Mrs. Ballard, who herself declined a personal interview, was able to give only some very general ideas of the whole movement outside of Chicago, where he and Mrs. Potter are the leaders at the present moment. Some phases of the headquarters' activities have been moved to Santa Fe, New Mexico, and some of the publishing and literature distribution is done from there, but the real headquarters are now in Chicago. A recent issue of *The Voice of the I Am* still carries the notation: "Published monthly by St. Germain Press, Inc., Chicago, Ill.," but with the additional note: "Send all subscriptions and orders to St. Germain Press, Inc., Santa Fe, New Mexico."

Another publication called *I Am Ascended Master Youth in Action*, which was begun in 1944, is published bi-monthly by "Miracles, Inc.," Denver, Colorado, Box 2561. Here the United States mail facilities are evidently in use. The new corporation is,

[44] District Court Record, Case No. 14588, Los Angeles.

of course, not enjoined against their use. The magazine is evidently edited by Mrs. Ballard, for in a conversation reported in the November–December issue, page 30, when a question was asked about the publication of personal letters to men in the Armed Services, she replied, that any letters considered to be of interest to students should be sent in, and that she would take out anything that might not be suitable. Further discussion of the magazine will appear later. All current issues of the publications carry advertisements of the various items for sale by the St. Germain Press. Phonograph records of invocations, benedictions, and dictations from the Masters, as well as musical records of duets on harp and organ (the harp played by Edna Ballard), are sold direct from "the Santa Fe Branch of the St. Germain Press, Inc." No postal address is given for either Chicago or Santa Fé. Nor is any direction given as to how orders may be sent. Specifically it is directed that remittances must not be made by Post Office Money Orders.

Mrs. Ballard travels less than formerly and spends a good deal of time in Chicago. Once when the writer asked one of the attendants in the reading room how access to the classes could be secured, she replied that one must enter a preparatory class first for a period of six weeks. She said that Mrs. Ballard was currently conducting the classes and that such power was being released that no uninitiated person could stand it.

Mrs. Ballard does call in leaders from various centers for group conferences and discussion, and these bring her letters and information which she could not receive through the mail. She maintains a remarkable degree of physical vigor. She is said to have accompanied the young people on long hikes in Rocky Mountain National Park during their two weeks' Youth Conference in the summer of 1944. She is sole head of the movement. She alone now receives the messages from the Ascended Masters, though less frequently from her now Ascended Master, former husband, than from others, less frequently even than from a former Roman Catholic prelate, Cardinal Bonzano, who made his Ascension shortly after the great Eucharistic Congress in Chicago. In contrast to Gerald B. Bryan's charge of her dictatorship of the movement, Mr. Potter asserted quite definitely that she was in no sense dictatorial in her control. "She will, when asked to, give her opinion as to whether or not one should or should not do a certain thing, saying, 'You must make your own call and follow the direction you get.'" He finds a reasonable degree of freedom in the movement, more, he thinks, than is present in the Christian Science Movement. Was Bryan mistaken, or have events had the effect of chastening somewhat the spirit of "Little Dynamite," as she was sometimes affectionately called?

Whether the movement had lost seriously after the trials, he could not say. He thought it likely, but since no statistics of general membership are kept it is impossible to know. He could not speak of other cities or the country generally, but in Chicago the number of One Hundred Percenters is as large as ever. They no longer have the great public meetings, but as many as fifteen hundred have been present in the central headquarters in Chicago in the various rooms. In 1948 they purchased a twelve-story downtown building, formerly a club, about two-thirds of which will be used for carrying on their many activities, including an expanding youth program, one of the more marked recent tendencies in the movement. More literature is being circulated in Chicago than ever. As to whether this is true of other centers, no information is available. Most of the larger cities have reading rooms similar to those maintained by Christian Science. Here one may read quietly, may borrow books, or purchase them.

Some measure of the extent of the Youth Movement may be gained from the fact that they hold a national conference each summer. The 1944 conference is fully reported in the Youth publication mentioned above. No statement is made as to the number in attendance, but from pictures in the periodical it was a group of considerable size. The program was something like that of other youth conferences with a definite recreational provision in the afternoons. Sessions every day were given to "decreeing" and almost every evening dictations from the Ascended Masters came through "Beloved Mama Ballard." In the evenings, frequently, some episodes taken from the *Unveiled Mysteries* or *Magic Presence* were dramatized, a different regional group being in charge each time.

Several times Mrs. Ballard conducted a question and answer period. Subjects discussed were various. Music was the center of attention in one period. Asked as to what instruments were undesirable, she listed the xylophone, accordion, cymbals, banjo, and saxophone as carrying "certain destructive vibratory action." [45] But the harp was the measure of a civilization. If many played the harp civi-

---

[45] *I Am Ascended Master Youth in Action,* November–December, 1944, p. 22.

lization was advancing. If only a few played it, that was a mark of its decline.[46] One evening the conversation turned on the "Beings of the Elements." Among these are Salamanders, Fairies, Undines, Elves, and Gnomes. Questions concerning them revealed that the Salamanders are involved in Fire activity, are about a foot in height and were created by Helios. Fairies have to do with flower formations and wear clothes of the color of the flower they are guarding. Undines have to do with water, and are about two-thirds the size of an average person. Elves learn their tricks from human beings. Gnomes, represented as distorted beings, were not originally so formed, but have become so by the impurity and discord among humans. Gnomes are builders, are larger in size than Fairies—two and a half to three feet tall. They also guard jewels.[47]

Concerning sports she answered that bowling was not so good because it was so often linked with gambling; skating was fine; swimming should be learned by everyone, but the going in and out of the water brings sudden temperature changes which open the door to sex. Movies are often enough degrading, though some films are good. Fashion shows lead to body consciousness. Going bare-legged is not acceptable except in a tennis game, or other sport where appropriate. Slacks should not be rolled up. Boys must not go around with shirt tails out. Anklets are appropriate for young girls, but from twelve to fifteen years on girls should wear stockings. Exposure and exploitation of the body lead inevitably to emphasis on sex! [48]

Still another Round Table discussed the various age groups. It appears that there is a "Youthlet" group, evidently of pre-adolescent age. The Youth group includes unmarried persons under thirty-three. The Young Married Peoples Group is from thirty-three to forty-five. Ordinarily these should be kept separate. The Radiation of each group is different. Only where there are too few to form separate groups should they be united in one.

The announced purpose of the Youth Magazine is that of bringing the Ascended Master Youth of America into closer touch one with another and to form an effective group whose sole aim is "to serve the Light so obediently that the 'Mighty I Am Presence,' the seven mighty Elohim, and all the Great Host of Ascended Masters

---

[46] *Id.,* p. 22.   [47] *Id.,* pp. 35–37.
[48] *I Am Ascended Master Youth in Action,* November–December, 1944, pp. 44–45.

can use them as a perfect channel to bring forth the New Golden Age." [49]

So the movement goes on—changed somewhat and changing. What of the future? To that we shall return later. Meanwhile, what are the cardinal beliefs of the movement, and the chief practices—and whence have they come?

III. *WHAT IT TEACHES*

A systematic presentation of the theological ideas of the I Am instruction is an impossible task, for as one reads their literature he becomes quickly lost in a maze of what are, to the uninitiated at least, meaningless terms. Words pile up on words, often enough used in other than their generally accepted meanings, as the Ascended Masters try to convey their teaching through the Messengers. Nor is there inner consistency. The system has undergone development. For example, the writer has found no single reference to the I Am in *Unveiled Mysteries,* the original text, the first revelation made by St. Germain to Guy Ballard. Only half a dozen individual Ascended Masters appear there, out of the score or more that have since been disclosed.

In the *Unveiled Mysteries,* near the close, in what was the climactic episode related in that book of unusual episodes, Lanto, one of the Ascended Masters, is made to say that nothing is Supreme but God; that only the Christ is eternal and real; that nothing is True but The Light, and that these Three are "The One." [50] This has almost a Trinitarian ring to it. But that does not represent the developed doctrine of the movement. The I Am is God, as now taught. It comes from the story of Moses who in the conversation with the voice out of the burning bush, asked, "Who shall I say sent me?" The answer was "I am that I am." (Exodus 3:13-14). The term has been used before. Charles Fillmore of Unity used it long before the Ballards appeared. Spalding in *The Masters of the Far East* used it, and indeed, among "metaphysical" students it has been quite commonly employed.

As at present used, it more often than not seems to be quite impersonal. It is usually spoken of as *It*. Yet to It are assigned such attributes as love, wisdom, will, and purpose which are ordinarily the attributes of personality. Students are exhorted to love, obey, adore, and give thanks to It. It is the source of all Power, Wisdom, Knowledge. It is Perfection. In a brief summary statement Mrs. Ballard declares that the I Am is the "individual God Presence" of all living persons, usually called the Mighty I Am Presence, and that it was to this individualized focus of the supreme source of all life that reference is made in the incident of Moses and the burning bush.[51] If the writer grasps her meaning rightly, there is a Supreme Source, an ultimate reality, of which the I Am, or as she usually calls it, the "Mighty I Am Presence," is an individualized expression. Yet this is not consistently maintained, for on another page in the same brochure she speaks of "the One Great Source" as the Mighty I Am Presence and asserts that the "Mighty I Am Presence" is Almighty, Limitless Intelligence.[52]

All this suggests to a student of comparative religion a conscious or unconscious paralleling of the neuter Hindu Reality, Brahman, and the personalized masculine Brahma, coming probably, through theosophic influence, to the Ballards.

If there is but one Real, one Source, one "Mighty I Am," there are hosts of cosmic beings to whom one may turn for help, and through whom the vast resources of cosmic power may be made available to mankind. A cursory glance through four or five issues of the *Voice of the I Am* revealed the following list. How many others there are, the writer does not know. He has seen no complete list, if one exists:—Mighty I Am Presence; St. Germain; Jesus; Great Divine Director; Seven Mighty Elohim; Queen of Light; Venus; Elohim of Peace; Lord Maitreya; Hercules; Archangel Michael; Goddess of Purity; Goddess of Justice; Arcturus; God of the Swiss Alps; Angel Deva of the Jade Temple; Cyclopei; Lanto; Mighty Aries; Chanera; Oromasis; Goddess of Light; Astrea; Ray-O-Light; Nada; Mary; Meta; Quan Yin; Helios; Diana; Seven Kumaras; Seven Mighty Chohans; Cassiopeia.

Some of these are known in Theosophy. Some of them are known to Spalding. Classic mythology provides some, astronomy or astrology others, and some appear to have come out of the Bible, directly or indirectly. Ray-O-Light could reflect the influence of modern advertising upon the "Messengers." Some of

---

[51] *Purpose of the Ascended Masters' I Am Activity*, p. 15.
[52] Id., p. 27.

these are Ascended Masters, of whom there are "Hosts" who do not appear by name. These Ascended Masters play a major role in the cult, for it was through one of them, St. Germain, that the revelation came to Mr. Ballard. Who are the Ascended Masters? Ballard himself says that they are truly God.[53] Yet they are tangible living beings of great wisdom, power and love who operate freely throughout the entire universe, performing naturally what is ordinarily considered to be supernatural acts.[54]

An Ascended Master is a human being who has by his own effort generated within himself enough power and love to break all the bonds of human limitation.[55] He is thus independent of time or space. He is able to manifest in any or many bodies or shapes as he wills. There is no limit to his power to dissolve or to assemble an atomic body.[56]

While there is a great brotherhood of Ascended Masters—the "Great White Brotherhood," two Masters stand out most prominently in the Movement—St. Germain and Jesus. It is their pictures that are most prominent in the sanctuaries, although now Guy Ballard also figures prominently along with them.

Who is St. Germain? According to an article in the *Voice of the I Am* he has appeared in many different periods. He was Samuel in the Old Testament. He appeared in the Middle Ages as St. Alban. He was last embodied as Lord Francis Bacon who, it is asserted, wrote the Shakespearean plays. Proof of this is found in the very name William Shakespeare. William is clearly only the will of the I Am, and Shakespeare could come from the fact that he shook the spear of wisdom at the ignorance and darkness of the age in which he chose to manifest himself.[57] Mrs. Ballard adds in her pamphlet that he was one who worked at the court of France before and during the French Revolution, and that the Revolution would not have occurred if they had heeded his advice.[58]

There was apparently a Comte de St. Germain who lived in Europe in the eighteenth century, a man who was interested in the occult, was known as a necromancer, but who did play a significant role in the political world of his day. He has been an object of interested study among occultists. Helen P. Blavatsky referred to him

[53] *Unveiled Mysteries*, p. 134.
[54] *Id.*, p. 135.   [55] *Id.*, p. 136.   [56] *Id.*, p. 137.
[57] *Voice of the I Am*, March 1936, pp. 5–6.
[58] *Op. cit.*, pp. 8–9.

as, "the greatest Oriental Adept Europe has seen during the last centuries" (Theosophical Glossary) and Henry Olcott, first president of the American Theosophical Society called him "a messenger and agent of the White Lodge." [59]

Whatever his actual historical character, he is the central figure in the I Am teaching—more often invoked, and more often heard from through the Accredited Messengers than any other.

He is especially important to Americans. It has been his ideal for centuries that somewhere shall emerge a nation of Ascended Masters, and he has chosen America to fulfill that ideal. A very important phase of his effort is directed to the purification and protection of the American people.[60]

Jesus is also an Ascended Master. He often speaks through the Accredited Masters, as indicated in the *Voice of the I Am*. For example, on December 25, 1944, he appropriately spoke. The message is reported in the April 1945 issue under the title "Beloved Master Jesus' Discourse, Chicago, Illinois, Christmas Day—Afternoon."

Various informants, one-time members of the movement, reported to the writer that this did not occur in the earlier days. Little place was given to Jesus, though reference to Jesus is found in the earliest publication, the *Unveiled Mysteries*.[61] There St. Germain declares that Jesus was the revealer to the outer world of the "Master Record" and that he is the living proof today that the individual may free himself from every limitation and manifest the divinity he was intended originally to express.

Bryan asserts that when they first came to Los Angeles in 1935 they "almost forgot to mention Jesus," but that "without the Christ even their most enthusiastic supporters balked at accepting their Saint (Germain)." [62]

They do seem to be somewhat on the defensive in their discussion of St. Germain referred to above, for in one paragraph of the above quoted article concerning St. Germain, effort is made to make students understand that they are in no way attempting to substitute St. Germain for Jesus. No one could do that, and besides there is

[59] For further information see Mrs. Cooper-Oakley *The Comte de St. Germain*, and the Encyclopedias. Also Bryan, *op. cit.*, Ch. 12.
[60] *Voice of the I Am*, March 1936, p. 9.
[61] *Unveiled Mysteries*, p. 138.
[62] Bryan, p. 195.

the utmost harmony among the Ascended Masters. However, each performs a distinctive service. Indeed, St. Germain's attitude toward Jesus is one of profound love, and together they are laboring to make a reality the dream of the I Am age on the earth.[63]

In a dictation, given February 15, 1939, at Oakland, California, and published in the April, 1939, *Voice of the I Am*, Jesus is reported to have said it was perfectly ridiculous for anyone to think of himself as the only authority on earth. Of course he was an authority under the love ray, as was St. Germain under the violet ray, but no one was ever to think of St. Germain as superseding himself or interfering in his work. On the contrary no greater blessing had ever come to earth than St. Germain.[64]

And in still another published discourse he is represented as saying that neither he himself, St. Germain, nor any other Ascended Master were giving out the I Am teachings in the west through any other channel than the Accredited Messengers, i.e., the Ballards, including Donald, and those whom they chose to use.[65] Thus Jesus seems to be in accord with the I Am teachings. Bryan asserts that he heard the announcer declare in the great Shrine classes, "Dear ones, these blessed Messengers (the Ballards) today are occupying the place that Jesus Christ occupied 2000 years ago."[66]

A distinction should be made here as so often, between Jesus and "the Christ," for the latter term is used by the Ballards, particularly in the earlier writings, very much as it is in Unity and other New Thought groups. Thus in *Unveiled Mysteries*,[67] St. Germain spoke at Mitla, in old Mexico, of the devotion of the Inca to the "Great Central Sun," today called the "Christ." In another connection St. Germain speaks of the Mighty God Presence as the Pure Christ.[68]

The function of the Ascended Masters is to help mankind. They are represented as having vast powers, and of being channels of Power. But they cannot, except in unusual circumstances, help man if he does not make "the call." Nothing is impossible to the power of the "Mighty I Am Presence" and the Ascended Masters, when the channels of power are opened. Everything is possible when they are.

[63] *Voice of the I Am*, March 1936, p. 6.
[64] *Voice of the I Am*, March 1936, p. 29.
[65] *Id.*, April 1936 issue, p. 26.
[66] Bryan, *op. cit.*, p. 194.
[67] *Unveiled Mysteries*, p. 127.
[68] *Id.*, p. 11.

Man's salvation individually and collectively depends upon opening the way for the Power to manifest itself. Salvation seems to mean Ascension, or becoming an Ascended Master. When men first came to birth on the earth they were "Perfect, Pure, God-Beings" and so remained until some two and a half million years ago. Then they almost forgot their creator and centered their thought upon things of the world. As a result they were reduced to "lower vibratory action." So they sank lower and lower; suffering and distress came upon them, and finally, so-called death. Thus began the round of rebirth which is the lot of man until he attains to the state of Ascended Master. In reality, of course, there is no such thing as death. Man cannot die even if he wishes to, for he is Life-Consciousness from the very heart of God and his Individualized Identity is Eternal.[69] The "Mighty I Am Presence," as represented in the chart, and of which much is made in the teaching, is above humanity. From it pours, through the top of the head, the Silver Cord of "Liquid White Light," [70] and anchors in the heart. Through this ray comes intelligence, energy, life, pure and perfect. But man has free will. This is insisted upon very strongly.[71] Discord and lack of harmony produce imperfection in physical form. When this discord becomes so marked that the God presence sees that nothing further constructive is possible, the sustaining Ray of Light is withdrawn, and what men call death ensues. But this is not the end. The life returns again embodied in a new physical form, and the process goes on until salvation is at last attained—which means, as indicated, until man makes his Ascension and becomes an Ascended Master.

Here in the reincarnation idea is the influence of Theosophy, or Hinduism. There are three conditions that affect the law of embodiment, according to Mrs. Ballard. Characteristics which an individual manifests draw him to a certain channel of embodiment, or he has criticized or condemned some race or group and so must incarnate as a member of it until he knows what it is to live under such conditions. Or, finally, one chooses a certain "channel" in order that he may help a given race or group toward perfection.

Thus the major good that can be sought is to make the Ascension, and it was the hope of achieving it that attracted many people to the

[69] *Purpose of the I Am Activity*, p. 17.
[70] *Unveiled Mysteries*, p. 255.
[71] *Purpose of the I Am Activity*, p. 33.

movement. It was the expressed hope of the Ballards and the purpose of St. Germain that America might become a nation of Ascended Masters, and that America might be the "carrier of the Cup of Light to all the Earth." [72] To die is to be born again. The Ascension is to be attained without death. It was the fact that Guy Ballard died, yet was said to have Ascended, that caused many to begin to doubt.

When does Ascension occur? How may it be attained—or in evangelical language, how is salvation achieved? That the Ascension may be long delayed and that reincarnation may take place over vast reaches of time is evident from the Ballard experiences. St. Germain tells him in their first meeting that mankind must be brought to understand that they have lived on earth in a physical body hundreds or thousands of times.[73] He took him back through numerous previous incarnations. Once he was son of a king, who was none other than St. Germain, ruling over a civilization in what later became the Sahara desert, but was then a gloriously productive land. This was some 70,000 years ago, and at the same time Lotus, or Edna Ballard, and Donald, were likewise of the royal offspring. He reappeared in other ages as a son of an Inca ruler—likewise Lotus and Donald; in more modern times as a famous concert singer in France—a woman—and, more importantly, from the standpoint of patriotic Americans he came to birth as George Washington, Edna Ballard as Joan of Arc, and Donald, Lafayette.

As in Indian thought man is on a cosmic wheel of existence which can only be escaped by a conscious effort at comprehension of the law of life. One must seek and constantly maintain contact with the God within, regardless of external conditions.[74]

In the various Ascensions reported in the Ballard experiences there was no death of the body. It simply disappeared "on a Radiant Pathway of Light" in one case.[75] In another, an aged white-haired man, David, lost all the marks of age, became youthful in appearance and disappeared in a "dazzling radiance of Light." [76] Would other persons, followers of the teaching, ascend thus? Numbers of them died, but of none was such an Ascension recorded. Mr. Ballard now and again reported ascensions as taking place from the "Royal Tetons" or "The Arabian Retreat," but always, it seemed, it was from

[72] *Purpose of the I Am Activity*, p. 9.
[73] *Unveiled Mysteries*, p. 17.
[74] *Id.*, pp. 26-27. [75] *Id.*, p. 242.
[76] *Magic Presence*, p. 84.

some secret or inaccessible place. It is reported that some followers went to Mt. Shasta and to the Tetons in search of the sacred retreats.

In November, 1938, as reported in the December, 1938, *Voice of the I Am*, St. Germain announced through the Messenger that under a New Dispensation it had been granted by Sanat Kumara, at the intercession of the Goddesses of Light and Liberty, that henceforth certain students would be permitted to make their Ascensions while their human forms, remained on earth.[77] That is, death of the physical body might not necessarily mean that the individual whom "so-called" death had taken, had failed of the Ascension, as before believed. There was no certainty, but one's friends or relatives could now hope at least that the desired end had been attained. As a matter of fact, in subsequent issues of the *Voice of the I Am* there appear statements by the Messengers that some have Ascended. The February issue asserts that in three different instances, those, who were thought to have died had really made the Ascension.[78]

It is apparently possible for one to win the right to Ascension, but to remain on in the physical body in order to perform some unfinished task. Mr. Ballard related in 1935 that in connection with the Ascension of Daniel Rayborn, he was given the opportunity to make the Ascension but the "Mighty I Am Presence" had commanded him to return to the world and serve. From that hour, he continued, his earthly pilgrimage was finished.[79] These facts, if recalled, should have made it easier for the followers to accept Mr. Ballard's Ascension after his death, but either they did not recall them, or expected more of the leaders themselves than of the students of I Am.

One of the principal means of attaining to the goal is, of course, the help of the Ascended Masters, and this is obtained through the "decree" or "call." This may be used for personal or for social or group ends. The decree is the I Am counterpart of prayer—but its spirit is not that of prayer in its Christian sense. It is not supplication; it is demand—or command.

If there are powerful constructive forces in the universe, there are also destructive, and there seems to be a perpetual war between them. Destructive forces are attempting to destroy America as well as to do evil to the individual. Much is made of "entities" by the

[77] *Voice of the I Am*, pp. 5 ff.
[78] *Voice of the I Am*, February, p. 19.
[79] Quoted by Byran, *op. cit.*, p. 73

movement, and it is only through the call of the faithful that these entities can be overcome and destroyed. What the origin of the evil is, is not wholly clear. In the case of the individual it is stated that he is responsible for every activity.[80] Because mankind centered its attention upon "the outer manifestations," it brought about the suffering and distress which humanity today experiences.[81]

At all events evil exists and is militant and must be destroyed. It is through the decrees of the faithful that this is to be accomplished. A typical decree against entities reads thus: (It is addressed to some one of the Ascended Masters or Gods or Goddesses)—

"Send legions of Thy Angel Devas of the Blue Lightning of Divine Love to seize, bind and remove from within and around me and my world all entities—carnate and discarnate—forever! If they be of human creation, annihilate them, their cause and effect this instant. If they be discarnate take them out of the atmosphere of earth." [82]

Reports were given from time to time of the number of entities destroyed in various cities—over 400,000 discarnate entities from Philadelphia, 332,000 discarnates from the New York City area, and a million from America in twenty-three hours' time one day.[83]

Also there seems to be a belief in black magic, for decrees were given for the destruction of black magicians, until everyone was said to have been removed from America and most of those from Europe.

But the most spectacular aspect of the I Am has been its Protection of America, which has been afforded by the constant decrees of the followers. The Ballards seem to have a passion for America. They have in their public meetings called it variously: God's country, the I Am Country, the "Land of the Light of God That Never Fails." A great many of the decrees are designed to afford this protection. How threatening are the dangers of destruction were often enough told in the public and closed classes. By the decrees, a wall of protection was thrown up about North and South America during the war, and it was this that kept them inviolate from invasion. More than once destructive forces were turned back. In the trial one of the witnesses told of the "disappearance of 346 foreign spies and the dissolution of three German submarines approaching the Panama

[80] *Purpose of the Ascended Masters' I Am Activity*, p. 33.
[81] *Id.*, p. 19.
[82] Quoted by Bryan, p. 59.
[83] Bryan, pp. 61–62, who cites the original published sources.

Canal," as a result of the timely decrees of the students.[84] A prominent member of the movement told the writer in conversation that he believed that it was the faithful decreeing of protection by the students that prevented the submarines that were near the East coast on V.E. Day, from injuring America, and that it was this same protection that made the incendiary balloons sent over by the Japanese so little destructive. He added, however, that he did not attribute this wholly to the I Am decrees, for he supposed that other people were also praying for the same end.

The Ascended Masters, through the Messengers, spoke frequently of evils averted from some city. St. Germain said in Washington, D. C., on December 8, 1938, that had it not been for the Messengers, mankind would already have been involved in a destructive war, and that the capital itself would not then be there.[85] Important cities were warned of "Gas Belts" beneath. Lord Maitreya told New York that their city would have been destroyed a year and a half before had there not been the call to the Light. San Francisco was in great danger and must be protected by decrees.

With this emphasis on patriotism it is not surprising that the announcer in one of their public meetings declared: "This is not a religion; it is a patriotic movement." [86] Nor is it surprising that it should appeal to many people of strong national pride and patriotism, the "one hundred percent Americans!" One of the auxiliaries of the movement is the "Minute Men of St. Germain" who, it is reported, wear uniforms, march to the music of bugle corps and drums, and engage in patriotic activities. There is a parallel organization—Daughters of Light.

Facts of this nature, plus the fact that the movement took over not a few of the ideas of the Silver Shirts, and the fact that at one time there was a pronounced political emphasis in the speeches of Guy Ballard, and that at one time during a meeting of Minute Men in Washington, D. C., Ballard was saluted as "Commander-in-Chief of the United States of America," led Bryan and others to look upon it, whether rightly or wrongly, as a dangerous incipient fascist movement.

That the movement is exceedingly conservative in its social and economic views is obvious on almost every page of its publications. It

[84] Los Angeles *Times*, December 19, 1941, Sec. 1, p. 19, cols. 2–3.
[85] *Voice of the I Am*, December 1938, p. 6.
[86] Bryan, p. 15.

is violently opposed to anything like strikes, or labor agitation or communism, or anything that threatens the status quo. The writer recalls hearing the great Civic Opera crowd, led by Mrs. Ballard, in a decree to blast all strike agitators, and in particular those who were leading a strike at that moment in a large industrial concern in Chicago.

They were uncompromisingly opposed to the New Deal and had a profound distrust of Mr. Roosevelt. Bryan declares that the inner circle, in secret, even went so far as to decree his destruction, using the form "Blast, blast, blast their (Mr. and Mrs. Roosevelt) carcasses from the face of the earth forever." He does not state his authority for this declaration, and obviously he was not himself one of the group. Such a charge could easily be made the occasion of a suit for libel. Dr. Bryan asserts that no legal cognizance of it has ever been taken. All of which doesn't, of course, prove its truth. He did, however, he declares, receive numerous anonymous telephone calls telling him to "lay off" the Ballards, which he assumes came from some of the "Minute Men." His early brochures attacking the movement were purchased and burned, he reports. The reader will draw his own conclusions. The charges form a part of the story which the historian may not ignore.

But there is more to it than just giving decrees. They also make a great deal of *affirmations*. Here the teaching runs very close to New Thought, from which it may very well have come. Mrs. Ballard asserts that whatever man puts his attention upon he compels to come into his world.[87] This is true of the good as well as the bad. St. Germain, in one of his discourses [88] advises that one never say, "I am sick," "I am broke." Rather when tempted to do so he should do just the reverse, and affirm silently but intensely that he lives and has his being in the I Am who is the source of all peace, power, and plenty.[89]

For there are many good things to be had aside from the ultimate goal of Ascension. Nothing is offered by New Thought or Christian Science or Psychiana in the way of health, prosperity, or happiness that may not be had through the I Am activity. Undoubtedly part of its appeal lies here, for there are many unhappy, troubled, poor, sick people who want these things desperately. It is probable that

[87] *Purpose of the I Am Activity*, p. 23.
[88] *I Am Discourses*, Vol. III.
[89] Quoted by Mrs. Ballard in *Purpose of the I Am Activity*, p. 25.

not a few persons were attracted from these other New Thought and kindred groups precisely because Mr. Ballard did what he told Dr. Robinson of Psychiana he was going to do—namely, dramatize the movement. Many people profess to have been healed of all sorts of diseases. Mrs. Ballard claimed that her husband had healed over 20,000 and that she herself had been instrumental in healing "thousands and thousands." There are many decrees for health in their publications. There are also affirmations of health.

One of the notable features of the I Am teaching is that of "precipitation." It occurred frequently in the Ballard experiences. He stretched out a cup—it was filled; St. Germain reached out his hand, a gold piece appeared in it. It was one of the charges made against the Ballards that they taught that wealth and things could be precipitated by decree. The book salesman, it will be recalled, said "If I need anything, I decree it."

In the court trial a letter was presented as evidence in which Mrs. Ballard, writing to one of the staff concerning another who was worried about finances, said: "Tell ——— not to worry about her channel of supply. It does not depend on R.T.'s insurance. I command ten times more than he has had or seen to be given ——— right now as her own individual channel, of which no one knows but her Presence! I command this to come forth instantly and become physically manifest as I write these words. Everybody keep harmonious and happy and it will come about sooner than you think. Everybody visualize a definite amount released into ———'s pocketbook this moment. . . .

(Written with pen, signed)

Mama and daddy." [90]

An informant reports that in a meeting in Los Angeles, members of the group waved stage money in large denominations as they decreed an abundance of substance. Many persons gave up their life insurance, preferring rather to depend upon the abundance of the resources of the Mighty I Am through decrees. Whether all these things were encouraged by the leaders is not certain. It is always possible for followers in their zeal to go beyond their leaders.

But that there is a non-material emphasis in the movement is clear. Especially in the early teachings there were personal disciplines imposed that were by no means devoid of spiritual possibilities.

[90] District Court Record, Los Angeles, No. 14496-B.H.

Thoughts and feelings must be brought under control. To accomplish this St. Germain suggested as a first step the stilling of all outer activity, both of body and mind, then the picturing and feeling the body enveloped in a "Dazzling White Light," and feeling intensely the unity of the self with the God within. . . . One should then acknowledge his joyous acceptance of the fulness of the Mighty God Presence. The period, which should occupy up to half an hour, should be brought to a close with a series of affirmations such as "I am a child of the Light—I love the Light—I serve the Light—I am protected, illumined, supplied, sustained by the Light, and I bless the Light." [91] Other directions follow throughout the book. "The continued use of affirmation is urged. By it the student raises his outer self into the full acceptance of its Truth and generates the feeling by which it becomes a thing manifested." [92]

Adoration of the Mighty I Am Presence is urged by Mrs. Ballard on rising in the morning, and repeatedly throughout the day whenever one has a free moment.

The Ballards make little use of the Bible and do not exhibit great familiarity with it. Now and then they quote it. They never suggest its reading; they do not distribute it, at least it is not in their catalogue of books, etc. Jesus, when he speaks through the Messengers, does not often quote from the gospels. We have already cited a reported message from Him that students "put aside everything else they have ever studied." Presumably this would include the Bible in many cases, for a great many of the followers have come from the churches in which the Bible is studied and used constantly.

Very little is said concerning the churches. The admonition to forget what they learned elsewhere would seem to cut students off from any divided loyalty, such as is freely allowed by others of the newer movements, such as Theosophy, Unity, Father Divine, etc. In the *Unveiled Mysteries*, Guy Ballard specifically asked St. Germain what the attitude of the Ascended Masters was toward the many channels through which partial Truth was being revealed. His reply reflected a generous attitude of tolerance. In effect he recognized that differences in understanding exist, but that after all, all men are God's children and serving according to their ability and understanding.

[91] *Unveiled Mysteries*, pp. 11–12.
[92] *Id.*, p. 68.
[93] *Unveiled Mysteries*, p. 233.

The general attitude toward other similar movements seems to be that in the I Am is the fulfillment of their partial understanding. Two of the Masters prominent in Theosophical teaching spoke through the Messengers to say that they were not yet Ascended when they gave their messages to Madame Blavatsky and "could only go so far." [94] Lady Master Leto declared that Mrs. Eddy had brought another phase of Knowledge to the world, but she declared that this teaching has revealed the final knowledge.[95] But when these groups opposed the I Am movement, St. Germain declared in one of his dictations that every group which condemned or criticized it, whether Unity, or Christian Science or any other, was bound to fail utterly and find their churches empty.[96]

We turn now to a consideration of the moral teaching of the movement. Mrs. Ballard once declared that their ideal for the student body was that it should be the finest, cleanest, most decent, refined, fearless and well-behaved group on earth, progressing constantly through their calls to the Mighty I Am Presence.[97] It is probable that this was never meant as a complete statement of the moral ideal, though with liberal interpretation of the terms it would stand up well. For example, what does "well behaved" mean? It could refer to one's personal individual relations or it could include a wide range of social implications. As a matter of fact, the movement largely stresses the individual rather than the social application. They are exceedingly strict in many requirements. For example, no I Am student should smoke, and he must not drink. They are extremely rigid in their control of sex relations. We have already cited Mrs. Ballard's answers to questions asked by young people at the Youth conference, in which she opposes anything in dress or sport that leads to "body consciousness," lest it lead to sex activity.

But they go even farther and condemn any sex activity, even within the marriage relationship, except for purposes of procreation. This naturally produced not a little trouble, particularly where only one member of the couple was of the faith. The result was, of course, the disruption of many families. The writer recalls a visit from a troubled mother whose daughter had become a follower of the movement. Her husband scoffed at it, and was unwilling to accept

---

[94] *Ascended Masters of Light*, p. 334.
[95] *Ascended Masters of Light* p. 226.
[96] *Voice of the I Am*, March 1937, p. 10.
[97] *Purpose of the I Am Activity*, p. 46.

the sex restrictions imposed by it. The marriage, otherwise apparently happy, was about to go on the rocks. What could be done about it?

Married couples who travelled with the Ballards in the hey-day of the movement's success occupied separate rooms in the hotels. When it became a question between loyalty to the movement and to marriage, it was the movement that came first, in the Ballard's teaching. For example, when the wife of an influential member of the party became disillusioned and critical of it, a letter from Guy Ballard informed him that he could not go on in his position of leadership "until such a time as you cut yourself free from such influence, if you should ever wish to do so." (See letter quoted above, page 277). An informant formerly well up in the movement said that only one marriage among a considerable group at one time gathered about the Ballards, remained intact.

Guy Ballard is quoted as saying in a Los Angeles class, August 19, 1935, "The sex urge was only to be used for procreation. When it is used for so-called pleasure, mankind loses the dominion of his physical form . . . When it is wasted, the body becomes decrepit and helpless . . . Your aura becomes charged with the most vicious entities you can imagine." [98]

To make the Ascension is to be preferred above family relationships and the rearing of children. The Goddess of Purity declared in a dictation reported in 1939 that sex or family relationship should not be considered by those who wished to make their Ascension and so escape human bondage. Having spent years in rearing children and in sex activity, ought they not forget it now? They need not fear for the race—enough of those who had no such high purpose could be counted on to perpetuate the species. One might not be free himself if he sought another from sex desire. [99]

Thus the I Am, like Father Divine and to a lesser degree Unity, inclines toward the celibate ideal. It is interesting, if not profitable, to speculate as to why this is. Is it, as some have suggested in the case of the Ballards, a result of unhappiness in their own experience growing out of the sex relation? One informant, very intimately acquainted with the Ballards, does not believe that they loved each other despite the almost touching devotion and loyalty within the

[98] Bryan, *op. cit.*, p. 181.
[99] Quoted by Bryan, *op. cit.*, p. 178, from *Voice of the I Am*, November 1939, v, pp. 25–26.

family, recorded in thir appearance together in some way or other in the various incarnations in the past, and as the three and only Accredited Messengers to this age. She cites the fact that they were separated for long periods prior to 1932 when he was in the west or, as represented in the *Magic Presence*, traveling in the Far East. This, of course, is not conclusive, for the fondest of couples are sometimes separated for long periods by the exigencies of modern existence. At all events the effects have been disastrous in many marriages and continue to be so. This is, of course, of moral concern.

The charges of fraud, sustained by a United States court, failed to convince many followers of any evil intent or moral fault. Despite the fact that the case was won by the government, many felt and still feel that intent to deceive or defraud was never effectively proven, and that the verdict really represents a religious intolerance and persecution. So present-day I Am followers have declared to the writer.

Charges have also been made that the attitude toward those who left the movement or who have criticized it has been one of vindictiveness and threat of dire consequences. One man avers that he was threatened with physical violence if he did not "lay off the Ballards." The Ballards may, of course, not have known of this zeal of their Minute Men, nor approved it.

Bryan quotes from a saying of the Ascended Master Sanat Kumara on July 3, 1939, in Los Angeles: "Do not again make the call for anyone to return to this Light. Rather call for their release from those bodies that they have chosen to desecrate by vicious falsehoods against the Messengers of Light (the Ballards)." [100] This he says means calling for their death. In the trial at Los Angeles a witness who had broken with the movement declared that I Am devotees were told to "Blast the Roosevelts, Secretary Morgenthau, and Cabinet Ministers, and annihilate them from the face of the earth." [101] This, to be sure, came from one of the former members of the inner circle who had become disillusioned. Bias is always a possibility in such a case—but it was given under oath to the court.

If these charges are true they have to be taken into account in estimating the moral emphases of the movement.

There is frequent mention by the Masters of God as Love, and

---

[100] Bryan, *op. cit.*, p. 189.
[101] Reported in Los Angeles *Examiner*, December 9, 1941, Sec. I, p. 19, cols. 2–3.

the admonition to act on the principle of love. There is a Law of Forgiveness upon which students are urged to call. Mrs. Ballard writes of a Law of Forgiveness upon which she urges each individual to call for forgiveness of the discord he has brought into the lives of others, past and present, and then for the forgiveness of the mistakes of all men, promising a truly remarkable relief from his own discord.[102] The writer has found no reference to repentance in any of the writings he has read.

The movement goes on. Mrs. Ballard continues to direct it. She, as "Accredited Messenger" receives and publishes regularly the Messages that continue to come from the Ascended Masters. She is vigorous and active, but in time her strength will fail and the dynamic leader will make her Ascension, as did her husband. What of the movement then? Will Donald, the remaining Messenger, take over? There is not much in the past to encourage that belief, though it is always a possibility. If not, where is the leadership that can hold it together? One prominent present leader thought it might break up into smaller groups, each going its own way under a regional leader.

Just how much vitality it has is not certain, whether enough to maintain itself no one certainly knows. But there is now an extensive literature direct from the Ascended Masters which they regard as authoritative in the same way the Bible is among the churches. Thus they have a body of scripture. It does not seem impossible that the Ascended Masters could find some channel of continuing communication with the group, though according to an important leader there is none at the present time. They have a ritual, an extensive cult paraphernalia, and in fact everything that is required as a basis for a continuing movement. That it will ever again attain the outward signs of success which attended it in the middle and late thirties, may well be doubted.

[102] *Purpose of the Ascended Masters I Am Activity*, p. 32.

Chapter Eight

The Liberal Catholic Church

The Liberal Catholic Church is one of the more recent of the newer religious movements in America. It had its origin in what was known in Great Britain as the "Old Catholic Church," which, in turn stemmed from an off-shoot of the Roman Catholic Church under the name of the Old Catholic Church in Holland. When in 1870 the Roman Catholic Church promulgated the doctrine of the infallibility of the Pope a number of eminent Catholic scholars on the continent refused to accept the doctrine and led by Dr. Von Döllinger, withdrew from the mother church. Resulting independent churches came into being which, because they felt they represented true Catholicism, in counter-distinction to the new Catholicism represented by an infallible Pope, they called the Old Catholic Church This church, while still holding to much that was Roman Catholic in belief and practice, but turning from the central authority of Rome, became much more liberal in its outlook than the mother church especially in Great Britain. It had, nevertheless, the genuine apostolic succession in its ministry, since its episcopal leaders had been properly ordained and consecrated by those legitimately within the succession, as held by the Roman Church. This proper succession is a much emphasized feature of the Liberal Catholic Church. It has prepared and published a highly detailed table of the succession through which the proper consecration of its present leaders is carefully legitimatized. Bishop Arnold Harris Matthew, first of the British Bishops of the Old Catholic Church, had his ordination at the hands of the archbishop of Utrecht, who, in 1892, had his ordination at the hands of the Bishop of Haarlem, who was in turn consecrated by Bishop Deventir, etc., on back to an earlier archbishop of Utrecht who was properly consecrated by Bishop Varlet, whose consecration is apparently unquestioned even by the Roman Catholic church. It is ultimately traced back through the famous Jacques Benigne Bossuet to Cardinal Barberini, nephew of Pope Urban VIII. Thus the succession seems to be validated. It is rather interesting, not to say amusing, and probably somewhat disconcerting to high Anglicans, that the Liberal Catholic Church "finds no adequate reason to deny the validity of Anglican orders," but in a footnote adds "at the same time the historical data bearing on the subject are confused and ambiguous and therefore difficult to estimate aright." The Liberal Catholic Church does not recognize the ordination of other churches as on the same plane as its own. Though it permits the exchange of pulpits with ministers of non-episcopal churches, it does not invite the latter to officiate at its altars. Anglican clergy wishing to enter the ministry of the Liberal Catholic Church must pass through a "form of conditional reordination to the priesthood, preceded by baptism, confirmation and the earlier grades of the ministry, namely cleric, door-keeper, reader, exorcist, acolyte, subdeacon and deacon, such rites being also administered *sub conditione*." [1]

The beginning of the Liberal Catholic Church is intimately bound up with Theosophy. Indeed, members of the theosophical group provided leadership for it in the early period of its existence.

Bishop Wedgewood under whose leadership the break with the Old Catholic group came and the formation of the Liberal Catholic Church, was a prominent figure in Theosophy, General Secretary of the Society at one time in Holland, and again in England and Wales, continuing as such at the same time that he carried on the work of promoting the newly founded body. He was instrumental in bringing Charles W. Leadbeater, one of the foremost leaders and exponents of Theosophy into the Church. Leadbeater had been ordained as an Anglican clergyman as long ago as 1878, but obviously could not continue his ministry in that body. He welcomed the opportunity to resume his clerical function in a church which carried over almost everything in the way of liturgy in the Anglican Church, but gave him complete freedom to pursue his occult interests. Leadbeater became regionary bishop of Australia of the Liberal Catholic Church and exercised this function at the same time that he served as head of the regional Theosophical Society. He was made Presiding

[1] *Liberal Catholic Church Statement of Principles,* Los Angeles, 1944, p. 9.

Bishop of the Liberal Catholic Church in 1923, succeeding Bishop Wedgewood in that position.

Bishop George S. Arundale was consecrated a bishop of the Liberal Catholic Church in 1925, and appointed as regionary bishop for India in 1926. This position he held until 1934 when he became president of the world organization of the Theosophical Society. Before the election, opposition by some members of the society to his ecclesiastical relationship led him to declare that if elected he would cease to wear clerical dress, as both he and Bishop Leadbeater were accustomed to do, and to be addressed only as Dr. or Mr. Arundale in order to "avoid all danger of confusion or identification between the Theosophical Society and the Liberal Catholic Church." [2] This the historian remarks "many members thought unnecessary." The fact that as late as 1933 this confusion was deemed possible, is a clear indication of the close relationship between the two organizations.

Bishop Irving Cooper, regionary bishop of the United States and the western hemisphere, while less conspicious as a Theosophist leader was a frequent lecturer to Theosophical gatherings. Bishop Mysseus a Belgian, regionary bishop of Western Europe, was listed as a delegate at an International Congress of Theosophists in 1906.

While not all Liberal Catholics are Theosophists, and by no means all Theosophists are Liberal Catholics, the Liberal Catholic Church does seem to have taken over a great deal of theosophical lore, and therefore provided Theosophists, who find little or no cult in the operation of the Theosophical Societies, that for which many of them doubtless feel strongly a need. It might be an overstatement of fact to suggest that the very occasion for founding the Liberal Catholic Church was the barrenness of Theosophy on its cult side, but as the Liberal Catholic Church has developed, it has provided precisely this opportunity for Theosophy-minded folk. Certain it is that there exists in the majority of men the feeling of necessity for worship which will not be easily denied.

On the side of its belief, the Liberal Catholic Church is precisely what its name indicates, liberal. Indeed there is nothing which the layman is obliged to hold. To quote its own statement, "The Liberal Catholic Church permits to its laymembers entire freedom

---

[2] Josephine Ransom, *A Short History of the Theosophical Society*, p. 515, Theosophical Publishing House, Adyar, India, 1938.

in interpretation of creeds, scriptures and tradition, and of its liturgy and summary of doctrine. It asks only that difference of interpretation shall be courteously expressed. . . . A truth is not a truth for a man, nor revelation a revelation until he sees it to be true for himself. . . ." [3]

This permits people of almost any faith to find a haven within the Liberal Catholic Church. That does not mean that the church does not have a doctrinal statement, for it does, but it seeks of its members "not profession of a common belief, but their willingness to worship corporately through a common ritual." It aims to help them to discover truth for themselves by providing them with opportunities for spiritual growth and explaining to them the ancient science of unfolding the divine potentialities which exist in every man. It asks of them sincerity, purity of motive, tolerance, breadth of mind, courteous expression, willingness to work and a constant pursuit of high ideals, confident, above all, that the power of the blessed sacrament of Christ's love may well be trusted to work God's own true purpose in their souls." [4]

While definitely Christian in its orientation, it is hospitable to truth wherever that may appear. Its affinity for the theosophical position may be seen in such a statement as this: "It holds that a theology can only justify itself and be of permanent value insofar as it partakes of the character of a theosophy. That is to say that while certain of its higher teachings remain within the category of revelation, because they are far beyond our grasp and attainment, others less remote are capable of reverification and even of development, by those who have unfolded within themselves the necessary spiritual faculties. Man being in essence divine can ultimately know the Deity whose life he shares, and by gradually unfolding the divine powers that are latent in him can grow into knowledge and mastery of the universe which is all the expression of that Divine Life. This method of approach to Divine Truth has often been called theosophy. . . . It is identical with the ancient Para-Brahmavidya of the Hindu Upanishads. It finds complete justification, of course, in scripture, and Theosophy has constantly appeared in the religious thought of both East and West, denoting not only mysticism, but also an eclectic philosophy underlying religion, which accepts as truth that

[3] *Liberal Catholic Church, Statement of Principles,* p. 6.
[4] *Liberal Catholic Church, Statement of Principles,* p. 7.

which commends itself universally to religious experience, where-
ever it is to be found and under whatever form." [5]

Holding such a view, the Liberal Catholic Church, while "moving
within the orbit of Christianity and regarding itself as a distinctly
Christian Church, nevertheless holds that other great religions of the
world are divinely inspired and that all proceed from a common
source, though different religions stress different aspects of this
teaching and some aspects may even temporarily drop out of recognition. These teachings as facts in Nature, rest in their own intrinsic
merit. They form that true Catholic Faith, which is Catholic, because it is the statement of universal principles in Nature." [6]
Naturally the Liberal Catholic Church makes no attempt to convert people from one religion to another.

The Church has, however, a definite theological statement. It
differs little in language from the accepted orthodox Christian teaching. God is infinite, eternal, transcendent but also immanent, the
"One Existence from which all other existences are derived." [7] God
is triune, Father, Son, and Holy Spirit. Since Charles W. Leadbeater, who was later presiding bishop of the church, was one of
the bishops at the time the statement was adopted, and himself
held the typical Theosophist view of divinity, it is clear that the
utmost freedom is allowed in the interpretation of the doctrine.
Leadbeater has written perhaps as much concerning Theosophic
thought as any other. [8]

A typical statement of belief held by Liberal Catholics is that of
Edward M. Matthews in a recent series of radio talks on religious
themes. In discussing the Trinity he asserts that triplicity is a constant
factor of existence. A basic manifestation of it is to be found in the
atom. In it is a nucleus or proton, an electron, and the cohesive
force which holds it together. God as the Father is "the central
nucleus of every atom, as the Son he binds together the electrons or
planets of the atom and keeps them in their orbit, or formation.
The electrons themselves are God, the Holy Spirit, in manifestation.
From this basic unit we can compound every material element or
substance. Thus we have *God in everything*." [9] According to the
Summary of Doctrine, the Father is the Source of All; the Son the
Word who was made flesh and dwelt among us; the Holy Spirit,
the Life-giver, the Inspirer and Sanctifier.

[5] *Id.*, p. 5.   [6] *Id.*, pp. 5–6.
[7] *Id.*, p. 13.   [8] See pp. 247 ff.
[9] *The Holy Trinity*, St. Alban's Press, Los Angeles, 1945, p. 17.

"Obviously, God is not and can not be a person," writes Mr. Matthews. "The Persons of the Holy Trinity are Representatives or Masks for the One God who is beyond individuality; is unlimited; immanent and transcendent." [10] In the case of Christ, or the Son, he manifests as one person, Jesus. So also "the Holy Spirit gives expression; but instead of one person, It expresses through many. . . . At Pentecost the Holy Spirit descended upon *all* the Apostles. . . . That is why it is sometimes called the Activity Aspect." [11]

The place of Christ is of course much more central than in Theosophy. In their summary of doctrine they say of him, "Christ ever lives as a mighty spiritual presence in the world, guiding and sustaining his People. The divinity that was manifest in Him is gradually being unfolded in man, until he shall come 'into a perfect man, unto the measure of the stature of the fullness of Christ.' [12] The language in which he is addressed in the liturgy differs little, if any, from that used in the orthodox liturgies, but there is a very real difference in belief concerning him. There is found in this group as in the New Thought and others a clear distinction between Jesus and the Christ. Christ, the "mighty spiritual Presence," is thought of as having come to the world again and again "founding one religion after another, at the time and according to the needs of the race. Thus it is thought that He was the Inspiration for each of the great religions of the world—all down through the ages of the history of mankind. . . . Jesus of Nazareth was the focal point of emphasis and teaching which we call Christianity." [13] This, the writer goes on to say, was, in a sense, an incarnation of God, but that so is each one of us also, the difference being only in degree, for in the end we, having passed through a series of lifetimes, "finally come to a full realization of our God-head and thus pass from the human world of existence to one of a greater degree of Divine Expression." This, it may be said, seems to be the meaning of salvation. The ultimate goal is a complete realization of our oneness with God and it is ultimately to be attained by everyone.[14] In an Act of Faith in the liturgy it is declared, "all God's sons shall one day reach His feet however far they stray." Jesus it appears was only one of those

---

[10] E. M. Matthews, *The One Existence*, St. Alban's Press, Los Angeles, 1945, p. 17.
[11] Matthews, *Holy Trinity*, p. 17.
[12] *Liberal Catholic Church, Statement of Principles*, p. 13.
[13] *The Holy Trinity*, pp. 11-12.
[14] *Id.*, p. 13.

who was "nearing His perfection" and so became "the Channel for the dissemination of Christ teachings." [15]

He is truly the Saviour of the World, not however "as a vicarious atonement to appease a vengeful God, but as the Way, the Truth and the Life. . . . He has travelled the road we travel, long ago. Now he stands ready to guide us on our way." [16] "He lifts us out of the darkness of earth into that glorious Light of eternal Love which comes from the Father of All." [17]

Christ is particularly present in the Sacraments of which there are seven recognized, as in the Roman Catholic Church although they are somewhat differently named and defined. Penance becomes absolution and extreme unction, holy unction. And it is the *living* Christ, not the dead Christ. They permit no image of the dead Christ in their sanctuaries. The living Christ is partaken of in the sacraments, which are not merely symbolical acts. "We speak from experience when we say that the sacraments are channels of Grace and spiritual blessing and in the case of Holy Communion, it is food indeed . . . not only for the body but for the Soul and Spirit of us. The spiritual value in the Sacraments is beyond evaluation, nor may it be measured, so vast is its potential." [18]

"Man is a spark of the Divine Fire," declares the Summary of Doctrine. This is the precise phrase Chas. W. Leadbeater uses in expounding the Theosophic belief regarding man.[19] Made in the image of God, and being himself divine in essence "he is eternal and his future is one whose glory and splendor have no limit." He has freedom of the will, and by his wrong choices produces evil. He is morally responsible for his choices and reaps what he sows in this life or the next. Sharing the nature of God, he is, of course, immortal. Being eternal he was therefore pre-existent, and his life does not end when his physical body is laid away. He is born again and again, just as in Theosophy, each successive birth providing him with opportunities for the development of qualities he must develop before he can realize the ultimate goal of achieving God-head.

---

[15] *Id.*, p. 13.
[16] *The Quarter Hour*, published by St. Alban's Press, Los Angeles, Vol. 5, p. 184, 1946.
[17] *Id.*, p. 172.
[18] *The Quarter Hour*, Vol. 5, p. 163.
[19] *Outline of Theosophy*, p. 38.

The Summary of Doctrine says, he "is a link in a vast chain of lives leading from the Highest to the lowest. As he helps those below him, so he is helped by those who stand above him on the ladder of lives, receiving thus a 'free gift of grace.' There is a 'communion of Saints' or Holy Ones, who help mankind, also a ministry of Angels." This last statement obviously makes a place for the Masters, or the Great White Brotherhood of Theosophy.

There is, of course, no place for everlasting punishment or hell, though Purgatory is provided for in the period between lives, as is also heaven, in so far as they follow Theosophy. They say, in describing their liturgy, that they have carefully eliminated all "fear of God and His wrath—the attitude of servile cringing and abject self-abasement, the oft-repeated appeals for mercy and naive attempts to bargain with God, and other crude survivals mainly of the Judaistic era, together with the haunting fear of everlasting hell—as derogatory alike to the idea of a Loving Father and to the men whom he has created in his own image." [20]

Concerning evil no specific statement is made, but it seems to be regarded very much as in Theosophy.[21] Evil is usually a misplaced or misinterpreted good. There is an inviolable law of cause and effect under which man's life is passed. An infraction of law brings its appropriate penalty in this or another existence. Yet, while the pain resulting from the infraction of the good law must run its course "acceptance of our just dues, accompanied by a corresponding determination to follow a righteous course will tend to balance out the former course of the law of retribution," according to E. M. Matthews.[22] While the familiar language is not used, he is here talking about "repentance and the remission of sins" as taught in orthodox theology. In the Confiteor, or Confession, in the ritual of the Holy Eucharist, there is confession of sin without using the word. "O Lord, Thou has created man to be immortal, and made him to be an image of Thine own eternity; yet often we forget the glory of our heritage and wander from the path that leads to righteousness. But Thou, O Lord has made us for thyself, and our hearts are restless till they find their rest in Thee. Look with the eyes of Thy love upon our manifold imperfections and pardon all our shortcomings,

[20] *The Liberal Catholic Church*, St. Alban's Press, Los Angeles, 1944, p. 9.
[21] See p. 251.
[22] *The Good Law*, St. Alban's Press, Los Angeles, 1945, p. 10.

that we may be filled with the brightness of the everlasting light, and become the unspotted mirror of Thy power and the image of Thy goodness. Through Christ our Lord. Amen."

Also the Absolution contains this phrase: "The Lord absolve you from all your sins."

The Bible, together with the creeds, is regarded as "the vehicle in which this teaching of the Christ has been handed down to his followers," but they do not consider them to be in any sense literally infallible, nor "in view of their contents and their historical career do they see how any other Church can logically do so." They make abundant use of scripture, particularly the New Testament in their liturgy. They think of the scriptures as inspired "in a general sense only" and follow Origen in an allegorical interpretation of some sections. The books of the Old Testament are of very unequal value. At the same time they assert that "there are evidences of the highest inspiration in other Scriptures of the world," and a knowledge of these "has thrown a great flood of light on the interpretation of doctrine." [23]

In the moral teaching of Liberal Catholicism there is nothing distinctive. It follows in general the pattern of Catholic Christian teaching. Brotherhood is stressed as basic to the religious life and "without mutual good will no system of social organization, whether democratic or not, can be other than chaotic." [24] They are too young a group to have developed an extensive program of social activity. If they maintain the usual hospitals, orphanages, clinics, settlements, etc., of the sort supported by the established churches, it has not come to the writer's attention. It is like so many other groups, strongly individualistic in its emphasis.

The worship practices are perhaps the most notable feature of the church. It has as "high" a service as any Anglo-Catholic or the Roman Catholic Church. It makes use of the complicated symbolism developed in historic Christianity, with here and there some modification or addition. Its liturgy is in the vernacular and follows rather closely the pattern of the Anglican Mass. Its vestments and general adornment of the altar are not unlike those in any high church. It has various grades of ministry who participate in the services in appropriate ways, priest, cleric, doorkeeper, reader, exorcist, acolyte, sub-deacon and deacons. But they do not require for ordination to

[23] *Id.*, pp. 9-10, *passim.*   [24] *Id.*, p. 7.

the priesthood, or even for consecration to the bishopric, that one devote himself wholly to the ministry. One of the ministers of a Chicago church personally known to the writer is a practicing physician. Another who was later consecrated as a bishop was a business executive, and as already observed in connection with Charles W. Leadbeater, he was at the same time presiding bishop of the entire world organization and head of the Australian section of the Theosophical Society. Yet we have already seen how jealously they regard themselves as standing within the Apostolic Succession.

Its ministry is not celibate, the church neither enjoining nor forbidding the marriage of its clergy. It does not require auricular confession, but provision is made for it if an individual desires it. Its frequent and systematic practice is not encouraged "as tending to defeat the true value of the Sacrament in the spiritual life of the individual." [25] But absolution is practiced either for individuals or in public services. The formula used in the liturgy for the absolution of the people is pronounced by the priest after all have repeated the confession quoted above, and while still kneeling.

"God the Father, God the Son, God the Holy Ghost, bless, preserve and sanctify you; the Lord in His loving-kindness look down upon you and be gracious unto you; the Lord absolve you from all your sins and grant you the grace and comfort of the Holy Spirit. Amen."

There is an emphasis on healing which the church believes to be in keeping with the practice of the early Christians. At the same time there is a "growing recognition that bodily ailments are in many instances the outcome of minor maladies of the soul and can best be remedied when the soul is at peace." [26] The means of healing are the "revivifying power of the Holy Spirit, the grace of Absolution, the Sacred Oil for the Sick and the Sacrament of Holy Unction." It is in no sense opposed to the use of medicine and resort to modern curative methods, but holds that each supplements the other. There is a detailed healing service arranged in their book of liturgy.

The Liberal Catholic Church is found chiefly where Anglican or Episcopal and Theosophical societies flourish most, England, Canada, Australia, New Zealand and the United States. There are some churches in the Dutch East Indies and elsewhere. The total number is not large, and the membership in the local churches is seldom

---

[25] *Id.*, p. 10. [26] *Id.*, p. 11.

large either. Statistics for the whole world are not available unfortunately. The 1936 U. S. Religious Census gives a total of 33 churches and 1,527 members, 96% of which are urban. World headquarters is in London, England, and there are regionary organizations, each in charge of a bishop named to that post. There is a General Episcopal Synod which is the official legislative body of the church.

What of the future of such an institution? Two features which it represents seem to respond very definitely to human needs, and they are not always found in combination. One is the deep-seated need for corporate worship, by means of a rather "high" type of ceremonial and ritual, in a great many people. Well, of course, there are several churches in which that need is abundantly met.

Then there is a demand on the part of many for the utmost freedom to think and believe. There are, needless to say, organizations a-plenty which offer abundant scope for independence in thought. But suppose these two demands meet in the same individual! Then it is not so easy to find a church in which the individual can feel at home. To be sure there is a great deal of liberalism in the left-wing Anglican group, but, even there, is hardly to be found a freedom to follow such ideas as Theosophy or what any of the other ethnic faiths offer.

In the Liberal Catholic Church there is room for any degree of syncretism in religious thought. There is a statement of doctrine, but one does not have to believe it, or can interpret it as he will. A personal letter from a prominent clergyman of the church declares, "I doubt if there can be any 'official' interpretation of the published Statement." Here then is a haven for some, though perhaps not a large number of people, in which they can combine complete liberty of thought with a highly ornate and stately form of worship.

The very breadth of the movement probably deprives it of any great driving power which seems to be a requisite for movements that are to win a world. But it will undoubtedly go on and probably increase, and may exercise some degree of influence on other churches, narrower in their belief and less stately in their ritual.

Chapter Nine

Spiritualism

There is a sense in which a discussion of Spiritualism does not belong in this book, which deals only with relatively modern religious movements, for Spiritualism is not new. At least what are generally regarded as spiritualistic phenomena are as old as man himself. One discovers them in very primitive religions, and in the most ancient faiths known to history. The Bible is full of them, Spiritualists claim, from beginning to end. "When an angel speaks, when a man is healed, when a prophet prophesies, when a man has a vision, when a spirit appears, then you are reading about Spiritualism in the greatest religious work of the age," enthusiastically writes Robert G. Chaney in his book *Biblical Spiritualism.*[1] Moses, Saul, Elijah, Isaiah, Daniel, Jesus, Paul, all of them had psychic experiences, we are told. Definitely, spiritualistic phenomena are not new.

But Spiritualism as an organized religion is new—newer than some of the other groups herein discussed, and it is possible to date its beginning very exactly.[2] It began, as most Spiritualists now agree, in 1848, at Hydesville, N. Y., with the Fox sisters, who were the first in the modern period, it is claimed, to establish communication with the dead.

It all began when these sisters heard strange knockings in the

---

[1] Psychic Books, Grand Rapids, Michigan, p. 22.

[2] For an extended study of Spiritualism as a religion in all its phases, see George S. Lawton, *The Drama of Life After Death,* Henry Holt and Co., New York, 1932. This is the definitive treatment of that movement down to the date of its publication. It is original, firsthand, thorough, objective, and exceedingly interesting. The present writer owes much to Mr. Lawton's study, even where no direct quotations are used; and gratefully acknowledges his debt. He has made many investigations similar to those of Lawton, and found his conclusions in every case to have been substantiated.

cottage, which were repeated over and over again, much to the disturbance of the Fox family. There was nothing essentially new in this either, for reports of haunted houses have appeared in every land and age. The unusual thing in this case was that in some way they were prompted to suggest a code by which whatever or whoever it was who was doing the rapping might convey meaning, if he had any to convey. So a code was evolved. A certain number of raps meant "yes," let us say, one, two meant "no," three, "I don't know," four "please repeat your question," etc. If questions were then asked, an answer could be given, and lo, a bridge connecting the world of the dead with that of the living had been built, making it possible for the dead to break through and talk with the living. It was this that furnished the impulse to modern Spiritualism.

The Fox cottage became a shrine for Spiritualists, and every year many pilgrims visited it. Finally the cottage was moved and set up, exactly as it had been, at Lily Dale, the summer capital of Spiritualism, in Western New York, and is open every day to visitors, of whom there are many during the season.

It is a simple five-room cottage, plain, ugly, like so many cheap wooden homes in American small towns, with nothing to distinguish it from any other of its kind. But it is a fascinating place to visit.

During a week end spent at Lily Dale I went twice to visit it. As I entered I noticed that there were perhaps a dozen persons seated in folding chairs, facing a pleasant-faced woman seated in a small rocking chair. She smiled a welcome at me. The place was completely quiet. No one said a word. Then I heard a very light tapping sound such as one might make by striking lightly with a wooden pencil on a desk. Tap, tap, tap, tap, tap! five times—then a pause, and again five times, the tapping was heard.

"That means greetings!" said the woman. "Our spirit friends want to greet you." So I responded with greetings. Each time a newcomer entered this was repeated.

Then someone in the group would ask a question, speaking in ordinary tones. Out of the stillness would come an answer, "yes," "no," "I don't know," etc. All sorts of questions were asked. The answer to one would lead to another. It was most interesting. The greater number of those present and asking questions were Spiritualists on pilgrimage, and they were entranced by it, certain that they were in communication with the spirit world.

The woman in charge, the one medium, seemingly, through which the rappings will occur, was open to any and all sorts of questions. She did not know how it was done. She had nothing to do with the rappings. She would move, on request, from one chair to another, and from one room to another. The rappings still continued to come and followed wherever she went. Some of us she permitted to go down into the cellar where, quite unknown to the Fox family, a murdered man had been buried years before the rappings were noted. This was of course a different cellar, for obviously one cannot move a hole in the ground, but it was a perfect copy of the original. While we were down there the rappings went on, but we were no more successful in localizing them than when in the rooms above.

All sorts of facile explanations have been given in the case of the Fox sisters, and of the medium whom I myself saw. Spiritualists simply accept it as a fact that the rappings are produced by those who have "passed over," and do not question how it is done. The important thing, they think, is to discover what they are trying to say and to give heed to it.

Wide publicity was given the phenomena at Hydesville and many came to investigate. Almost everyone has had, or knows someone who has had, an unusual experience, not easily explained in terms of ordinary known laws, a premonition of some sort, a meaningful dream, has seen a vision, or felt unaccountably moved to do or not do some particular thing. What could be the explanation of such experiences? Perhaps here was a clue to their understanding. Here might be an opening door to the exploration of the world of spirit.

This was not the first time that an interest in the spirit world had appeared. Emanuel Swedenborg's writings were known to many people of the day, and were of such a sort as to prepare the popular mind for an interest in the occurrence at Hydesville. Also it was the period in which mesmerism or hypnotism was beginning to be experimented with, opening thus a new world of investigation, and, by its very mysterious nature, serving as a preparation for the rise of an interest in Spiritualism. A year before the Hydesville rappings occurred, Andrew Jackson Davis had published his book *Nature's Divine Revelations*, which has, together with his later writings, been almost the Bible of Spiritualism. One Spiritualist group, the General Assembly of Spiritualists of New York State, passed a resolution at its 1930 convention accepting as the "fundamentals of Spiritualism the philosophy of Andrew Jackson Davis." At a "Thought Exchange" session at Lily Dale on Sunday evening I heard a leading figure affirm that "philosophically we date from Andrew Jackson Davis who copyrighted his book before the Fox sisters appeared in 1848." By some he is called the John the Baptist of the movement, by others the Founder. At all events it was he who wrote most convincingly concerning it, largely provided the terminology of Spiritualism, and much of its basic philosophy.

It was natural that others should attempt to duplicate the performance of the Fox sisters, and presently there were individual mediums who were purporting to be channels through which communication with the spirit world could be effected. Because of the intense desire of many to be able to talk with loved ones whom death had claimed, here was a lucrative field for any who might be able to act as mediums legitimately, or to pretend to act, using fraudulent means to exploit the credulity and affection of the bereaved.

Three rather well-defined interests in the phenomena developed. To thoughtful scientific minds here was a problem to be investigated. Were the phenomena real, or were they fraudulently produced, and if not fraudulent, how could they be explained? This led to the formation of Societies of Psychic Research, of which there are a number in America and elsewhere, dedicated to a study of the phenomena under test conditions. Many men of eminence in the world of science, the physical sciences, the biological sciences and from the psychological field, then almost unknown, have given much time and effort to its investigation. These men are usually not Spiritualists, although some of them have become such, convinced by their studies that the Spiritualist hypothesis was the only one adequate to explain what they have observed. An extensive literature has been published and still continues to appear. In more recent years elaborate studies have been carried on at one of the great American universities, Duke, in North Carolina, in what is now termed the field of parapsychology, dealing with the whole area of supersensory experience, of which the experience of the Spiritualistic medium is an extreme example. William James of Harvard University, James Hyslop, at one time of Columbia University, Morton Prince of Princeton University, were among the better-known American investigators of recognized standing as scholars. In England, Sir William Crooks, Alfred Russel Wallace, and Sir Oliver Lodge, among the scientists, and William T. Stead and Arthur Conan Doyle, among the prominent literary men, were active in studying it. Lodge became a convinced Spiritualist and wrote extensively concerning it. Arthur Conan Doyle likewise—indeed he became an active exponent of it, writing, traveling, lecturing constantly in its behalf. Most of the famous mediums have been investigated under rigid test conditions and the results published in journals and books.

Second, there was, as suggested, the commercial interest. Here was something that could be exploited to great personal advantage by those who were natively equipped or clever enough to do so; and it should be said that no excessive degree of cleverness is required in order to make a comfortable living as a medium, if one is not too scrupulous. Some have made much more than a living, they have become wealthy by its practice.

But third, it was seen that here was an answer to one of humanity's deepest needs, one with which religion was greatly concerned. Here was the assurance of immortality made doubly sure, for it was now possible actually to communicate with the dead. It was no longer a matter of faith. Faith in immortality had been much disturbed, and had become increasingly more difficult as the materialistic science of the nineteenth century developed. It was to become still more difficult as the nineteenth century gave way to the twentieth, but already there were many who had lost that confidence in the ongoing life which had been so much a part of the Christian heritage. Here was demonstration, actual proof; and if this cardinal tenet were established, might it not lend strength to other convictions associated with belief in a life after death?

So Spiritualism became a religion, and it is this phase of it with which this chapter deals. We are not here concerned with the truth or falsity of the phenomena. Maybe the dead come back, maybe they do not. What matters, so far as the present discussion is concerned, is that great numbers of people in America and elsewhere, believe that Spiritualism is true, they live by it, are comforted by it, strengthened, helped, healed by it. It is for them a living faith which they seek to perpetrate through an institution, the Spiritualist Church. As such, it falls definitely within the scope of this book to present a brief sketch of it.

All three of the divergent interests cross at times and interpenetrate. The avowed Spiritualist may use every scientific means in studying it, thus strengthening his faith, and he makes constant use of the results of scientific investigation in its propagation. The scientific researcher may, as in the case of not a few, become a confirmed Spiritualist, while the commercially interested individual may hide his real motive under the cloak of religion, in order to enjoy the constitutional guarantees of religious liberty, while personally profiting by the fraudulent production of spiritualistic phenomena.

The beginning of Spiritualism was in the rappings of the spirits. But many other kinds of phenomena have appeared since. In general these may be classified as mental or physical, and mediumship may be either on the mental or physical plane. In the former the communicating spirit operates through the mind of the medium. In the latter it operates through material things. Not to mention all the phenomena under each classification—one writer gives twenty varieties of each—the most common mental type is the ordinary platform message given in nearly every Spiritualist public meeting, where the medium simply gets, through some sort of mental impression, the messages as they come to her from the spirit world and passes them on to the individuals for whom they are meant. Here are listed telepathy, clairvoyance, clairaudience, clairsentience, trance, inspirational painting, speaking, writing, prophecy, and impression. Those classed as physical are, among others, rappings, the Ouija board, table-tipping, planchette, slate writing, spirit photography, levitation, direct voice (trumpet) note reading, materialization, and telekinesis. Some of these require a brief description.

Nearly everyone has had some experience with the Ouija board and table tipping. These do not require a high degree of "development" on the part of the experimenters. In the case of the latter four people sit around a table, usually in the dark, touching hands on the table top. After a time it may, for no apparent reason, begin to tip up at one side or another and drop back. If a code is suggested, answers may be gotten to questions asked of the spirit. Sometimes it may be lifted completely off the floor. In slate writing a double slate is used. Between the two seemingly clean inner surfaces of the slate, a slate pencil is placed. The slates are tied securely together. The client and the medium both grasp the slate across a table, and sit in complete silence, After a time the noise of a slate pencil is heard, and when, after a time the string is removed, a message is found written upon the slate.

In a trumpet séance, held in complete darkness, the medium goes into a trance and presently voices from the spirit world begin to speak from the trumpet, which, usually having about it a luminous band, may be seen floating about over the heads of those present.

In materialization, performed usually in a dim violet light, the medium goes into a trance in a cabinet made by curtaining off a corner of the room. After a time the voice of the medium's control or guide is heard, and in due time, helped by the singing of the sitters, encouraged to do so by the medium's assistant and the control, forms of a filmy, diaphanous character appear before the cabinet. These are often recognized by someone present as a long deceased friend or relative, and a conversation is carried on between them. The forms are generally visible to all in the room, though sometimes one is led to the curtains which part and he is shown the figure of one with whom he desires to speak. Such demonstrations are not common, much less so than in an earlier period, for it must be said, even in the world of spirit, that fashions seem to change.

One of the most baffling types of phenomena is telekinesis, the exertion of energy sufficient to move objects, sometimes quite large and heavy, at a distance from the medium, without any physically evident means of doing so. This is not usual at all in religious Spiritualism, but some remarkable telekinetic mediums have been studied by the Scientific Psychic Researchers. Nor is spirit photography much employed in Spiritualism as religion, though the use of spirit photographs as evidence is much stressed by religious spiritualists. I was shown many such by Spiritualist friends at Lily Dale. An ordinary landscape would be submitted. I would see nothing. But carefully they would point out, as peering from behind a rock, or hidden in the branches of a tree, what might be thought of as human faces, something like the Old Man of the Mountain, in *The Great Stone Face*. I was given what appears at first glance to be the picture of a snow-covered bush. But, turn it upside down, and the head of the Christ can be clearly seen in the light and shadows of the picture. The unbeliever is reminded of the puzzles which used to be quite popular, to find in a tree or a bush the head of a person or some other object which had been carefully drawn in it, and as carefully concealed.

But spirit photography goes far beyond this and many supposed spirit photographs have been published in the literature of the Psychic Research Societies.

In the earlier period a group would grow up about an individual medium forming a kind of independent church, if the medium were a religious person, or a minister of some one of the denominations who had been converted to Spiritualism. Rejected usually by his own church because of his Spiritualist leanings, it was but natural that he should seek to carry on his ministry, including the truth of Spiritualism, along with his traditional religious faith. Cities provided the most favorable soil for the development of such groups, so there grew up Spiritualist congregations in all the larger centers. But there was no organized body, no definite creed, no specific forms of worship. Side by side, there operated the sincere Spiritualist and the charlatan, and the world rather generally made no distinction between them—indeed, does not do so even now. Many mediums, in fact most, were persons of rather limited education, and little inclined to think or speculate about the implications of the phenomena, beyond proving that the dead still live. So a theology or a philosophy was slow in developing. But there were thoughtful people who were captured by it and did attempt to elaborate a philosophy of Spiritualism. Most of these were not themselves mediums. Andrew Jackson Davis, we have seen, was already thinking and writing concerning such matters when the Hydesville rappings occurred. These brought practical demonstration of what he was writing about, and immediately attracted him. He quickly became the outstanding figure in the field, though he always denied that he was a Spiritualist, that rather he was a "Harmonialist." [3] Nevertheless his works have almost the force of scripture even today among Spiritualists.

But the common interests of the independent groups gradually brought them together. One was the necessity of getting recognition from the civil authorities. Undeniably there was and is much fraud in the practice of mediumship. Mediums are still classed in some cities along with fortune-tellers and other operators of magic, which prey upon the public, and as such are subject to constant police observation. Legislation must be secured favorable to the legitimate practice of mediumship. But individuals could not achieve such ends alone. Concerted action was required. Thus there came into existence local Spiritualist federations, then regional, and at long last a national movement, or more exactly, several national groupings. It was not until 1893, just forty-five years after the Hydesville phenomena, that the largest and most representative group,

[3] Lawton, *The Drama of Life After Death*, p. 36.

the present National Spiritualist Association, hereafter designated as N.S.A., came into being, in Chicago. There are many others that claim to be national. At Lily Dale one speaker declared that there were twenty-six. Lawton said in 1930 that there were fourteen. *The Psychic Observer* carried paid advertisements of seven in February, 1945—though in an attempted check-up I was unable to make any contact with some in the list. Some represent only a small number of societies, some represent rather a paper plan or a hope than any substantial reality.

All of them are rather loosely organized. The movement as a whole is distinctly congregational in policy and allows only a limited amount of power to any central organization. The churches are in general rather small in membership. Often a local church represents nothing more than a personal following of a particular medium. There is little genuine cohesion in the group. Ordinarily there is a local board or council, to which the minister or medium is responsible, in theory. There is, in many states or sections, an association with its president and board, to which the local group is responsible, and at the head of all is the National Association with its president and board to which all auxiliary associations are responsible. This is the general scheme of organizations of the N.S.A. But where there is no state or regional association, responsibility of the local group is to the N.S.A. direct.

The N.S.A. has an official declaration of principles, to which all members are supposed to subscribe. It establishes the conditions of membership, and for the ministry; provides literature through books and periodicals; grants charters to newly organized societies; promotes the general work of the church through its officers and trained personnel; holds conventions at stated intervals; and, in general, watches over the work of the societies. Just as in the Congregational and Baptist churches, there is always a stubborn resistance to the assumption of powers of control over the local churches by the central body.

The local churches are often but loosely organized, and the turnover of membership is rapid. They are in general not very prosperous. Only a very few own their own property, or have a real church edifice. A great number of them meet in rooms in the homes of the mediums, or rent empty storerooms or public assembly rooms. The more aristocratic groups often meet in hotel parlors or small banquet rooms. Since they are frequently only the personal following of the medium, if he moves to another city the group disintegrates.

Most of the Spiritualist churches hold a regular religious service with singing, prayer, some special music, often a reading from the *Spiritualist Manual*, a sermon or address, and spirit messages in which the medium or mediums brings to most of those present some message from the spirit world. This is the most emphasized feature of the average Spiritualist church service, and is eagerly awaited—often rather impatiently so—for it is this for which most of those present come. It is the Spiritualist church's *raison d'être*. It has little if anything else that is distinctive. The messages are given sometimes by the minister himself or by other mediums, either attached to the local group, or visiting mediums. It is quite the custom for mediums to go "on tour," either hiring a hall and advertising their own meetings, as is done by some of the more widely known mediums, continuing for a few days or even weeks in a city, then moving on; or appearing as special attractions under the sponsorship of a local Spiritualist group, which thus gets added publicity and prestige.

Some well established Spiritualist churches are supported as other churches by systematic giving of the members, but probably much the greater number depend upon the "offering" which is usually fifty cents, or in some places a dollar. This is one reason, doubtless, why a number of public meetings are held. The number in attendance in the average Spiritualist church is not large. Lawton found it to be about twenty to twenty-five.[4] Hence the financial returns from this source are seldom very substantial. Mediums supplement this income from special "circles" or "development" classes where a regular fee is charged, often a dollar or more per person for each session, and in addition, private consultations or readings may prove quite lucrative. This was especially true during the recent war years. One Chicago medium told me she was in constant demand and could get no free time for rest. The charges for this vary greatly, depending upon the class of clientele which the medium serves.

One medium who is well enough known to hold an important national office told me that his regular salary from the church was forty dollars per week. He makes no stated charge for any private

---

[4] Lawton, *op. cit.*, p. 203. Of course, some churches have substantial congregations. The average membership as given in the U. S. Religious Census was 64 in 1936.

reading. The person served may give him nothing, or one dollar, or five. Besides this he has the ordinary perquisites of the minister from weddings, funerals, and public addresses or readings in other churches, or at conventions. Naturally only the better known mediums would be likely to be invited where a substantial honorarium would be paid. On a straight salary basis this compares very unfavorably with the salary of a person of equal reputation within his national body among the established churches, though probably the income of the Spiritualist minister from private consultations and other perquisites might be more than that of a comparably situated minister of one of the denominations. When on tour or at one of the summer assemblies, of which there are several, the income may, for a short time, be considerable. Probably only a comparatively few of the mediums in the service of the churches have a substantial income. Of those who make of mediumship a commercial tool, the same may not be said. Some of these have become wealthy.

While there is in the N.S.A., as well as some of the other national Spiritualist groups, an attempt to raise the educational standards of their mediums and ministers, the standard is at present not very high. In churches under some of the bodies, and in those which are run quite independently it is deplorably low. The N.S.A. maintains a seminary for the training of its ministers. Established at Whitewater, Wisconsin, and known as the Morris Pratt Institute, it is now planned to move it to Milwaukee, where much greater opportunities for practical experience are to be found. At the same time it is hoped that the entrance requirements can be raised to require high-school graduation, thus placing it on the college level. Most of the work is done by correspondence rather than in residence.

The present national director of education of N.S.A., Dr. Victoria Barnes, was for many years a practicing physician but retired from practice to give full time to the N.S.A. According to Dr. Barnes one must be a member of a church for a year before he is entitled to begin a course of training. The beginning course requires two years. At the end of that time one who has successfully done the work of the course becomes a licentiate, and may act as a lecturer in the churches. He must, however, have served at least one year as lecturer, and passed the two-year advanced course, and be examined by the National Board before he can receive ordination. The year of lectureship may run concurrently with the advanced course, just as a student may preach during his seminary course. Thus a minimum of five years must elapse after joining the movement before one can be ordained. This is in striking contrast to the older day when anyone who felt himself to be a psychic could set up his own church without any delay or necessary training. Of course he can still do this as a free lance, and the requirements of some of the other associations are less formidable, but it becomes increasingly difficult for a local church to operate without legal difficulties, unless it is associated with one of the recognized associations. There is the usual protest at raising the qualifications for mediums and ministers, some feeling that, in so doing, valuable workers are forced into the ranks of the less well established Spiritualist groups, precisely the complaint made in the orthodox churches. It does force some natively able preachers into the smaller and more extreme sects.

There is a distinction, of course, between ministers and mediums. While ministers are expected to have powers of mediumship, not all mediums aspire to ordination. In some of the associations they are called "missionaries." The question of licensing mediums is a perennial one. Some oppose it, but in the N.S.A. its necessity is recognized. There may be a number of mediums attached to a local group.

A medium is defined in the *Spiritualist Manual* as "one whose organism is sensitive to vibrations from the spirit world, and through whose instrumentality, intelligences in that world are able to convey messages and produce the phenomena of Spiritualism." [5] Mediumship is not regarded as a supernatural gift but is "subject to the operation of natural laws . . . which must be understood and complied with." [6] Nevertheless, not everyone can be a medium. Certain persons seem naturally to be potential "sensitives," even though they do not know it. Such persons can develop this power through proper exercises until they become effective mediums for spirit messages. Every Spiritualist church conducts "development classes" which are designed to enable such persons to develop their psychic powers.

By far the largest number of mediums are women. It is doubtless because of this that the great majority of pastors of Spiritualist churches are women, though the more conspicuous posts of leadership are usually held by men. In general, mediums are not highly educated persons, though Dr. Barnes sees no essential reason why

[5] P. 173.   [6] *Id.*, p. 178.

educating a sensitive would affect his powers of mediumship. The fact that the medium plays in no sense a creative role in communication, but serves largely as an instrument, may lead many mediums to feel that education is not essential. For those who exercise the full ministry in a church there is a more obvious need for education.

The N.S.A. holds an annual convention, which serves as the legislative body of the movement. Its officers, now elected triennially, were elected annually in the earlier years. Usually the president is re-elected again and again. There have been but four since the organization of the movement in 1893. The present incumbent, Mr. Charles R. Smith, is a business executive living in Milwaukee, who gives only part time to the movement. It has been a salaried, full-time position, but since he does not need the salary, he turns it back into the treasury of the association. He does accept a travel allowance when journeying on behalf of the movement. He is not himself a medium though he has had some unusual psychic experiences. He is a member of a local church in Milwaukee and sometimes assists in the service. He is a forward-looking individual, is keenly interested in raising the educational standards of the association and, interestingly enough, in his own local church, spirit messages are not given at the principal Sunday evening meeting. He favors eliminating them as part of the worship service and providing a special meeting when they can be given. This is nothing short of revolutionary in the Spiritualist churches generally. Whether such a reform can be effected is a question. Certainly it cannot be done overnight.

The N.S.A. represents what might well be called orthodox Spiritualism in the United States. But is by no means the only national body. New ones continue to appear. Lawton has described several in his book published in 1932. Here we can mention only a few of the newer ones.

The Spiritualist Episcopal Church was founded in Michigan in 1941, largely through the efforts of Rev. John W. Bunker, who is the present Presiding Clergyman. He was at one time a Methodist minister. Through the loss of a much loved daughter he became interested in spirit communication, and was converted to Spiritualism. He, together with Robert G. Chaney, was instrumental in creating the new movement, influenced, as he wrote, in a personal letter, by a desire for a more churchly type of worship in connection with Spiritualism.

It was inevitable that such a movement should appear sooner or later. The average worship service in Spiritualist churches leaves much to be desired. People are drawn to it from all sorts of churches. Those from Roman Catholicism, who are much numerous than would be suspected, and from the Episcopal and Lutheran churches, could be expected to want something more than the very very informal, often undignified, and barren worship service usually provided. Here is a fulfilment for that desire.

It is Spiritualist in that it teaches "true Spiritualism," it is Episcopal because "it is an Episcopacy, that is, it has an Episcopal form of church government and certain forms of ritual."

It is further described as "truly liberal, asking for the acceptance of no dogmatic creeds," and seeks friendly cooperation with "all spiritualists and psychic students." It has among its declared purposes "the establishment of churches, church homes, schools, sanatoriums, orphanages, homes for the aged, . . . and the dissemination of spiritual truths, as recorded in the Holy Bible, as revealed in the psychic teachings of Jesus the Christ, and as manifested in modern times through physical and mental mediumship." It seems to stress the distinctly Christian teaching more than some of the groups, emphasizing strongly the Spiritualistic teachings of the Bible. A liturgy for use in public worship has been prepared in which the people participate, very much as in an Episcopal service.

Although called Episcopal it does not use the term bishop. The two chief leaders are the Presiding Clergyman and the Appellate Clergyman—both elected by the annual conference, the former for a five- and the latter a three-year term. The annual conference is the legislative body, but the interim authority which administers the affairs of the church is the Board of Clergy consisting of the Presiding and Appellate Clergyman, a Missionary mental medium, a Missionary physical medium, three Divine Healers, an Associate Clergyman from each district, and the President and Secretary of the official board.

The headquarters of the movement is in Grand Rapids, Michigan. It has not yet become truly national, but is leaders are certain that it will become so. They are very active in the field of publication. There seems to be room for just such a branch within Spiritualism, as it at present exists.

In 1937, the Inter-National Constitutional Church was founded in Los Angeles, California, by Rev. Charles E. Kelso. It is really not concerned with churches since it deals only with ministers. Each minister has his own church which is independent. In 1946 the secretary wrote in a personal letter that there were 1200 ministers who were members of the organization, with an estimated 40,000 lay membership. He states that they believe in "Tolerance and the Divine gifts of God as set out in the 12th and 13th chapters of First Corinthians, and also Jesus' sermon on the mount."

Anyone who believes he has a call to preach the word of God has a right to be ordained, they think, but a very serious attempt is made to ordain only those who "will be a credit to the church." A college exists for the training of ministers, conducted by correspondence. Six subjects are taught in the course, and an advanced course in healing is offered which is open only to graduates of the seminary course.

The only requirement for members, that is of ministers, apparently, is that "they believe in God and agree to practice Tolerance." Local churches are entirely free to set their own standards for membership. Mediums are required to be endorsed by another member of the church and to take a course of study.[7]

Another recent organization destined to become national, if its founders' dreams are realized, is the Universal Psychic Science founded in 1942 by Rev. J. Bertram Gerling and his wife Rev. Helene Gerling at Rochester, New York. This is one which is definitely Spiritualist, but embraces as well a wide range of other metaphysical and occult interests. It uses on its letterhead just beneath the name of the movement the phrase, in quotation marks, "The Religion of Religions." It is definitely eclectic, or as the founders assert, *Universal*. They write: "Universal Science was born of all the Great Religions of the World. Its Inspiration springs from the Age Old Secrets of the Nile, from the Eternal Fire of Ancient Persia, from the Slopes of the Jordan and the Shores of Galilee, from the Mosques of Arabia, and the Temples of India, from the Sacred Shrines of China. . . . Here stands the bulwark of the essential Religious Truths and Spiritual Revelations of all times, expressed in the Enlightened Interpretation and Advanced Scientific Understanding of the New Day."

In its regular worship services it incorporates "a truly unre-

---

[7] All the foregoing is based on a personal letter of the Secretary of the Movement, January 11, 1945.

strained Breath of Universality . . . teaching, in 'Our Universal Bible Lessons,' the Scriptual Wisdom of all the Great World Religions of Man." A set of UPS scripture lessons is supplied to the churches for use in their services. A uniform plan is used in each lesson. It begins with the statement "In presenting Our Universal Bible Lesson we carry out the injunction revealed in the Christian Bible. 'God . . . hath made of one blood all the nations of men.' Our Scripture lesson is on the subject of ————." Then follow quotations from several of the scriptures of the various religions bearing on the topic, ending with, "In Universal Psychic Science we find this teaching on the subject" followed by a sentence of summary. "May this Universal Bible Lesson enlarge our vision of world Brotherhood. Let us pray." (Our Father-Congregational Expression.)

One finds echoes of Unity in a booklet on a "Personal Prosperity Plan;" of Hinduism in the encouragement of Hindu Rhythmic Breathing, as one of the steps in the healing process; and of New Thought in the injunction to *affirm* health and happiness. Verily this is a broad net, designed to gather in people of many interests.

It is too new to predict what success it may achieve, but the history of broadly and conscious syncretic faiths does not encourage too great optimism concerning its probable success.[8]

Still another quite recent movement is the "Federation of Spiritual Churches and Associations," which had its first organizational meeting at Bloomington, Illinois, in 1944. There had long been a feeling that some broadly conceived, united front for Spiritualists was needed. In the autumn of 1943, Rev. V. R. Cummins wrote an article suggesting such an organization, and, at the request of the editor of *Chimes*, prepared an outline of such an over-all organization. As a result of interest expressed in the suggestion, a meeting was called at Bloomington, for April, 1944, and progress made in drawing up an organization plan. Later in the year another meeting was held in Joplin, Missouri, with thirty members present. By 1945 when the convention was held in Tulsa, Oklahoma, there were ninety members, a 200% growth, and it continues to grow.

The purpose of the organization as stated in the publication *"The Whys and Wherefores of Federation"* is, primarily, to attain

---

[8] All quotations concerning UPS are taken from mimeographed materials sent to the writer by the founder.

strength through union. Religious freedom is at stake. Whenever one religious body can be denied its constitutional rights, no religious body is safe. The Federation would serve to "protect Spiritualists and unite them in Free and Unhampered Units so that the combined strength . . . will be unbreakable." Or as the president, Rev. V. H. Cummins, wrote in a personal letter: "Our Federation is an attempt to organize the minority groups that believe in intercommunion into a strong, united, and highly respectable body, on a par with the Council of Churches of Christ in America, or any other National Religious Council." [9]

Membership is open to "any duly organized church, legalized under its state provisions," but not to individual mediums who are not members of any legal church or organization; that is, it is a federation of organizations not individuals. One of its main purposes is the defense of mediums who are prosecuted by the law, but it will not attempt to defend mediums who are not members of legally organized churches and associations. The Federation intends "to make it plain to the nation that we stand as one body for *clean mediumship* which we will defend when attacked." There are no dues, the support of the Federation coming through voluntary contributions. No salaries are paid to officers. There is a Supreme Council made up of representatives from various sections of the country, elected at the periodical conventions for terms of 4, 3, 2 and 1 years to begin with, so as to assure rotation in membership. It serves as a clearing house of information and instruction, protests unwarranted attacks on the spiritual faith in the public press, and elsewhere, advises "of the existence of faults and corruption in our ranks wherever found, seeks to offer remedy and advice to correct the 'wrongdoing' in our own ranks and to take to task those responsible; fosters study and advancement of our cause and fights just as viciously every destructive force in and out of our fellowship." It works through appropriate committees, Educational, Legal, Public Relations, Membership, and Financial. The legal committee, for example, will codify all laws relating to Spiritualism in the various states. The Educational Committee will evaluate various courses of study, establish schools and eventually colleges for the teaching of the truths of Spiritualism. The late Rev. Carl Pierce, Bishop and head of the Spiritualist Science church and chairman of the Education

[9] December 1, 1945.

Committee, in a personal interview, told me that a substantial gift has already been made toward the founding of a Spiritualist college at Grand Rapids, Michigan.

With only a short period of existence behind it, one can hardly say what place it may play in Spiritualism, but it does seem that there is a distinct place for such a federation. That it will eventually include other minority groups is likely. Should this extension occur, it might develop into a very influential organization. In the aggregate the minority groups not included in the Federation's Council form a very substantial body.

We have so far dealt mainly with the development of the organizational side of the movement and their practices. What of their teaching? How do they think of the great central doctrines of Christianity?

Most of the Spiritualist churches accept, more or less fully, the Declaration of Principles formulated by the N.S.A. in 1899 and 1909. They are as follows:

1. We believe in Infinite Intelligence.
2. We believe that the phenomena of Nature, both physical and spiritual, are the expression of Infinite Intelligence.
3. We affirm that a correct understanding of such expression and living in accordance therewith constitute true religion.
4. We affirm that the existence and personal identity of the individual continue after the change called death.
5. We affirm that communication with the so-called dead is a fact scientifically proven by the phenomena of Spiritualism.
6. We believe that the highest morality is contained in the Golden Rule: "Whatsoever ye would that others should do unto you, de ye also unto them."
7. We affirm the moral responsibility of the individual, and that he makes his own happiness or unhappiness as he obeys or disobeys Nature's physical and spiritual laws.
8. We affirm that the doorway to reformation is never closed against any human soul, here or hereafter.

or in simplified form for use in Lyceums or Sunday School classes:

1. We believe in God.
2. We believe that God is in every living thing.
3. True religion is in obeying the laws of life.
4. We never die.

5. Spiritualism proves that we can talk with people in the spirit world.
6. We believe that we should treat others as we want them to treat us.
7. We are punished by our sins and we will be happy if we obey the laws of life.
8. Every day we can begin again.

This it will be clearly seen is a very general statement. With the exception of article 5, concerning communication with the dead and the last words of the 8th, "or hereafter," almost any member of any Christian church could accept it without difficulty. He would certainly believe in Infinite Intelligence; that man and nature are an expression of that Intelligence; that religion involves living in accordance therewith; that individual life goes on after death; that the Golden Rule is an expression of the highest insight; that man is a morally responsible creature; and that the door of reformation is always open while he is still alive in the body. Seemingly all he needs to add to become a Spiritualist is the belief in the possibility of communication with the spirit world. And that is precisely the fact. That is just what makes a Spiritualist.

But if the ordinary member of the Christian church could accept nearly all the Declaration asserts, it still would not express all his faith. There is so much left out, for example, there is nothing about God as Father, as well as Intelligence. There is not a word about Jesus as the Revelation of God, nor of any part which he plays in the scheme of human redemption. The Holy Spirit, God active on the present scene, except as Intelligence, is left out, though it might be implied in article 2. Nothing is said about the Bible or the word of God, or about the church.

Does this mean that Spiritualists do not believe these doctrines of traditional Christianity? Not necessarily. One may be a Spiritualist and believe them all, and that is exactly the case with great numbers of Christians who go over into Spiritualism from the churches, carrying all their old beliefs, only adding to them the distinctively Spiritualist ideas with reference to Spirit communication. But he does not have to hold orthodox views as true.

The Declaration is clearly a deliberately formulated minimum statement, in which both the orthodox and the unorthodox who accept communication with the spirit world can unite. Indeed, a member of almost any of the great ethnic religions could accept it as readily as a Christian. He too would add to it traditional elements from his own faith.

Historically, it will be recalled that Spiritualism was born in a period of not a little revolt against the current orthodoxy. Many were attracted to it who could no longer accept dogmatic Christianity. Furthermore the study of spiritualistic phenomena associated these, not alone with the Bible and Christianity, but with almost every religion. A Spiritualist faith need not, therefore, link itself with the beliefs of any particular religion. There might be Christian Spiritualists, Confucian Spiritualists, Hindu Spiritualists. Apparently it was thought there could not be atheistic Spiritualists.

When one turns to the official literature of the N.S.A. and reads the Invocations, prepared for use in worship services, he finds no specific reference to any personal deity. The terms of address are still of an impersonal nature, but the qualifying adjectives used with the impersonal terms clearly indicate that the essential nature of the Christian God is recognized officially. Thus "To the Infinite Spirit of the Universe, manifesting love and tenderness"; "Great Oversoul of All, that ever expresses through that still small voice within." [10] "O Spirit of Infinite Wisdom and Love." [11] "O Divine Spirit." [12] "O Spirit of Love and Tenderness." [13] "Infinite Love." [14] "O Great Guiding Force from out of the Lord of Spirit." [15] Here they are, Love, Wisdom, Guidance—not all the personal attributes, to be sure, but Love is certainly a central emphasis.

In a section of the *Manual* entitled "Philosophy of Spiritualism," it distinctly states that the Infinite Intelligence is "impersonal, omnipresent, and omnipotent." That is official, but go to an average Spiritualist service and you hear often enough "Our Father," God our Father," and other personal terms. It is routine with many mediums even in private séances to repeat the Lord's Prayer. The one point that matters to Spiritualism is a conviction concerning the possibility of communication with the spirit world.

Concerning Jesus no official statement is made. Some of the branches make a great deal of him. All Spiritualists, whatever they may think of Christ theologically, regard him as definitely a medium, and as manifesting psychic phenomena frequently in the course of his career. The annunciation was, of course, a message

[10] *Spiritualist Manual*, p. 36.
[11] *Id.*, p. 38.   [12] *Id.*, p. 48.   [13] *Id.*, p. 40.
[14] *Id.*, p. 46.   [15] *Id.*, p. 52.

from the spirit world. The transfiguration scene was a materialization of the spirits of Moses and Elias before the wondering eyes of his disciples. When he came walking on the water, when he appeared after his death on the road to Emmaus, in the upper room with the closed doors, by the seashore to his disciples—in all these he made use of spiritualistic phenomena, so also in the appearance to Paul on the road to Damascus. Conan Doyle wrote a brochure on *Jesus and Spiritualism*.

In the *Spiritualist Manual* there is a special reading for Easter day that reflects the Spiritualist attitude toward Jesus. Naturally it is his resurrection that is emphasized, because "it proves the personal identity of the individual continues after death. Jesus rising from the dead impinged [sic] upon the consciousness of man the fact that life includes a resurrection for all. His demonstration of this important cycle in mortals' external existence is proof of the continuity of life and the basis of man's conviction that Immortality is a fact. . . . Why was Jesus crucified and resurrected? To expiate our errors? No—so the great Christ Principle which he taught, and so ably exemplified might forever endure." [16]

The Easter story demonstrated several phases of mediumship," prophecy when Jesus said, "Today thou shalt be with me in Paradise"; *levitation* in the lifting of the stone; *apportism*, in the disappearance of his body, *materialization* when he appeared before his disciples, and *independent voice* when he spoke directly to them." [17] And, did he not say, "Greater things than these shall ye do," and "Go thou and do likewise?" Would he have said this "if demonstrations of Psychic Phenomena today are not produced through manipulations of the same law, the same Spirit Power?" [18]

Here, of course, is a quite different view from that held by the orthodox Christians, but there are some Spiritualist groups which much more nearly approximate the orthodox view, the Spiritualist Episcopal Church for example. And it cannot be too often stressed that any member who accepts the central Spiritualist view of the intercommunication between this world and the world of spirit may carry over as much of his orthodox traditional faith as he wishes. The golden rule which was given by Jesus is taken as the highest expression of moral insight, and his other teachings of a moral

---

[16] *Id.*, pp. 52–53, *passim*.
[17] *Id.*, p. 53.   [18] *Id.*, p. 53.

character are stressed in their preaching and teaching activities. The qualities of spirit which he exemplified, unselfish love, boundless sacrifice, endurance, courage, serenity and loyalty are "qualities that prepare the inner self for spiritual mediumship." [19]

Nowhere in the official declaration of principles is it stated that God is good, though the moral qualities attributed to Him in the passages quoted above, indicate that it is nevertheless believed that goodness is a part of His nature. It is affirmed in the section on Philosophy of Spiritualism that "the origin of the universe, for all practical purposes, may be said to be unknown and without special bearing on moral conduct." [20] There is no statement as to the nature of evil, though moral evil is of course recognized.

Man is defined as "a spiritual being, evolved from the lower forms of life, up through the period of consciousness, to the state of the higher moral and spiritual faculties which survive, unaffected, the decomposition of the physical body." [21] There is a minority left wing of Spiritualism which accepts the idea of rebirth, but to the majority of Spiritualists, man has not been here before when he comes to the moment of birth. Whether he was preexistent in some sense is not stated. However, once an individual, his identity is not lost at death, but passes into the spirit world to continue there its unfoldment. This is the heart of Spiritualism. It is its gospel. We shall therefore dwell at some length upon the nature of that world and man's development in it.[22] Man is threefold in his makeup. He is, in descending order, spirit, soul and body. As spirit, man is one with the eternal spirit, the impersonal intelligence of the universe. As such, man is of course eternal, has had no beginning and will have no end. In this sense all men are equal, because all are of the same divine essence. Therefore there is a bond between all men. They are brothers. Only in man does the formless spirit of the universe become actually organized and individualized. This took place not only once, when man as man first came to birth, to be handed on down through posterity to succeeding generations, but it occurs anew each time a human being is born. Indeed they purport to know just when the event occurs in the life cycle. A. J. Davis says that

---

[19] *Id.*, p. 53.   [20] *Id.*, p. 24.   [21] *Id.*, p. 24.

[22] Note: This is done in great detail in George Lawton's *Drama of Life After Death*, Chapters 1–3. The best concise statement of the matter by a Spiritualist writer is a chapter by a former leader in the N.S.A., Mark Barwise, in my *Varieties of American Religion*, pp. 201 ff.

about twelve weeks before the date of birth, "the spirit as a pre-existent entity descends into and becomes centered in the brain of the infant foetus." [23] The spirit never ceases to exist. It is immortal.

The soul is what is sometimes called the astral body. Davis says it is "that fine impalpable, almost immaterial body which clothes the spirit from the moment of death to all eternity. . . . The soul is the life of the outer body and the spirit is the life of the soul. After physical death the soul or life of the material body becomes the form or body of the eternal spirit." [24] It stands as a link between the spirit in man and the body. Animals have souls as do humans. But animals are lacking that which is distinctive of man, i.e., spirit. The soul seems to be made up of material elements taken in and refined by the body. It is not mind, as it is so often thought to be by non-spiritualists. Mind and thought belong to the realm of spirit. But soul includes the feelings, sensations, instincts, and whatever is animal.

The soul has a body of its own as substantial in its way as the physical body, though of a different order. It is exactly the same shape and form as the physical, possesses the same organs and parts, and is the body which the spirit will inhabit when, in physical death, the body we see and know has been laid aside. Then the soul becomes the body for the spirit, while the spirit becomes the life of the soul, apparently through all eternity.

The human body we know well enough. It serves as a covering for the soul. By reason of its lower vibratory rate it is impenetrable by the higher vibrations of the higher spiritual world. Technically it is "encased." Only a few, the psychics or mediums, are sensitive to these higher vibrations in ordinary life. So great is the gap between the spiritual and the material world, that direct contact between that higher world and the lower is possible only through the identification of the spirit and soul with the physical body. It is only through "a gradually descending scale of vibrations and substances" into the material body that the "spiritual body may concentrate itself and gain its individual form." [25]

At death the material body is discarded and the soul becomes the body of the spirit, which is but an individualized "portion of the external being or divinity. Without the soul, the spirit could not

[23] Lawton, p. 8.
[24] *Answers to Questions*, p. 20 (quoted by Lawton, p. 10).
[25] Lawton, p. 15.

maintain its individuality, but would reform to merge itself in the formless ocean of being. This union seems never to be broken and individuality lost, as in Hinduism or Buddhism, for example. Infinite progression through all eternity into ever higher and higher spheres seems to be the idea of salvation; "attaining higher and higher levels of perfection and beatitude," writes Lawton, "until finally it ascends into that vast region which ranges beyond the solar system—the cosmic immensities—and vanishes from earthly sight and knowledge." [26]

Death is thus but the liberating of the soul and spirit, allowing it to go on, untrammelled by the limitations of material existence, into what Spiritualists call the Summer Land. The process of death has been described often enough by those who, on this side, have been able clairvoyantly to observe it, and through spirit communication by those who have themselves passed through the experience. Death may of course come early or late, naturally or suddenly by accident or violence. In the normal process of growing old and dying naturally, death is simply the last stage of a gradual withdrawal of the soul and spirit from the fleshly body.

From about the age of thirty-five Spiritualists believe that a human begins to expend more energy than he receives and this is the beginning of a long process of decline, the deficit increasing with the years. However, not all the "vitality and magnetism" have disappeared. They have simply been turned inward. As Davis says, "The best parts of the bone, muscle, nerve, tissue—everything that makes up the physical organization—have progressively gravitated to the manufacture and development of spiritual deportment within, substantial and exquisitely appropriate to the atmosphere of a purer, better, and more beautiful sphere of existence." [27] Death, then, is really birth into a new and higher realm. When this is known and appreciated, then it loses its sting, they say. Of course Paul said precisely this also, "O Death where is thy sting? O Grave where is thy victory!"

As pictured by Spiritualists there is a cord of vital magnetic forces connecting the soul, or astral body, and the physical. It is usually pictured as passing from the head of the physical body to the foot of the astral or spirit body. So long as this cord is unbroken death has

[26] *Id.*, p. 16.
[27] *The Thinker*, pp. 402–404 (quoted by Lawton, p. 17).

not occurred. Now and then a soul has separated itself from the body temporarily, stretched the vital binding cord to a very tenuous one indeed, but later returned. Such is the case of those who appear to have died, but return to consciousness and tell of experiences "on the other side." This vital cord seems to serve precisely the function of the umbilical cord. Indeed, Davis calls it just that.

Death in old age is thus not a painful thing, and there is little shock. When death occurs in the case of the young, the strong, particularly when it has occurred suddenly, there is a terrific shock, and there ensues a period of confusion and painful maladjustment from which it requires some time to recover. It is rare that one in the spirit world is able to communicate soon with those on the earth plane. Sometimes months or even years must elapse before that becomes possible.

Well, after the transition, what of the life that goes on? In what conditions does it exist. What are its surroundings, its relationships, its activities? Concerning the details of the life beyond, no religious group has so much to say as the Spiritualists. Nor is it guesswork with them, for, they assert, those who have gone on into it have reported rather fully what they have found.

When one attends an average Spiritualist service and hears the messages from the other side, he is usually impressed by the banality of it all. Most communications have to do with only the most superficial things, "How are you? Are you well? I am happy, I am helping you all I can, etc." Why, it is often asked, do the spirits tell us nothing about the conditions of their life there, what they do, etc.?

In the first place it should be said that the spirits usually purport to answer the questions asked them and these are nearly all of the kind described. Indeed, that is about the level upon which the conversation of those who have been separated for some time usually opens. One does not at once plunge into the discussion of profound themes. But the real answer to the question is that spirits have told a great deal about the worlds beyond. Innumerable books deal with it in great detail, and every attempt has been made by Spiritualist leaders and investigators to discover the facts about the spirit world. There are two chief ways of doing so. One is through clairvoyant investigation, directly, by those who are clairvoyant. In this class may be named Emanuel Swendenborg, founder of the Church of the New Jerusalem, who antedated modern Spiritualism by almost a century; Andrew Jackson Davis, who had written in great detail about it before the Hydesville rappings first gave the clue as to how communications might be made with the dead; and others of less eminence. The other is through the reported experiences of those who have "passed over," speaking through accomplished mediums. Sir Oliver Lodge, in *Raymond*, records the most detailed probing concerning the nature of the realm beyond in conversation, through a medium, with his deceased son.

There is not complete agreement in every detail, among them, but reading several of these reports, some general features do seem to be held in common. Here only the barest outline can be given. For detail see Lawton, Chapters 2 and 3, and the extensive list of sources which are there noted.

Life goes on in the spirit world in a series of concentric "spheres," surrounding the earth. The number varies somewhat in the literature but usually it is seven. One is born into the sphere which his attainment in this life entitles him to enter, and therefore he progresses from sphere to sphere according to his development. When he has finished with the spheres belonging to earth, he apparently goes on into higher spheres involving ever higher and higher degrees of perfection in an infinite series. One hears of spheres of other planets, then of the entire solar system, then of galaxies. There seems to be no end. Continuous progress toward infinite perfection, which is eternally approached but apparently never achieved, seems to be the belief. Of what goes on in the planetary spheres adjacent to earth there is much apparent knowledge but of the spheres beyond, little is known certainly, it is said.

The Spiritualists completely repudiate the traditional concepts of heaven and hell, and of course all idea of "everlasting" punishment or reward. In the literature there is frequent report of the surprise of those who have recently passed over at not finding themselves in heaven or in hell. Yet there is something approximating the idea of both heaven and hell of a temporary nature. The lower spheres to which those of evil character and a low state of development go at death constitute a sort of purgatory, at least, where they must remain until they have developed to a higher degree. If not punitive it is at least purgative, and the soul remains at this level until it merits promotion to a higher sphere. In the upper reaches, indeed from the third on, existence approximates, in quality at least, what is meant by many of the orthodox when they use the term heaven.

These spheres lie at different distances from the earth from 300 miles in the case of the first, according to one estimate, to 18,500 miles for the seventh. They differ greatly in the degree and intensity of the light on each. The two lower are much darker than earth varying, it is estimated, from total darkness in its lowest portion to some 70% of that of earth in its highest. The third is about the same as earth while in the more distant spheres the luminosity increases steadily from sphere to sphere. Yet for those in each sphere above that of earth there is no discomfort in the augmented intensity of light since the sensitivity of the soul to external stimuli is modified as it ascends in the scale.

The sphere into which one is born is determined by the law of sowing and reaping. One determines for himself, by his own deliberate choices, where he will go at death. There is an exact correspondence between sowing and reaping. The vile, the sensual, the despicable, would be utterly out of place in the third sphere or Summer Land. They go, therefore, to the lower spheres and remain until they are fitted to proceed into the more elevated realms. Most ordinary, run-of-the-mine, good people go to the third sphere or Summer Land, skipping the lower levels. Theoretically it would seem to be possible to be born directly into the higher spheres from earth, in the case of the very exceptional, but once born into Summer Land the progression seems to be an orderly one with no skipping of spheres. Summer Land is the most densely populated. The first two spheres have no special name, the third, as indicated, is Summer Land, the fourth is the Philosophers Sphere; the fifth the Advanced Contemplative and Intellectual Sphere; the sixth the Love Sphere; and the seventh, the Christ Sphere.

Since it is in the third sphere or Summer Land that most of the people are found and about which most seems to be known and written, a few details of their belief concerning it are in point.

In general, life in Summer Land is a duplicate of life on earth, but without its handicaps and disabilities. All its imperfections are gone, all the evil and hatred, and all the discomforts from adverse physical or climatic conditions have been eliminated. People wear clothes— they do in every sphere—live in houses; have trees, and streams, and mountains; travel about; carry on work, though apparently they do not have to work for a living. The doctors in Summer Land were said to be enormously busy during the war years helping the great number of souls ushered into spirit land by the havoc of war. The violence of death of young men created a terrific problem for the inhabitants of the spirit world, for these came confused and maladjusted and had to be helped in their adjustment to the new life. There are animals there, according to some, though this is not universally believed, since the animal does not have a spirit. There are schools, and of course teachers and learners—this is also true of the lower spheres. While people ordinarily carry on the occupations which they followed on the earth plane, a chief preoccupation of the people of the third sphere is that of helping those they have left behind on earth.

There is social organization in Summer Land. There is marriage between the sexes, but the relationship is entirely a spiritual one. The fleshly element has disappeared. The marriage bond of earth is thought of as broken at death, so that one's spiritual mate may be an entirely different one than that on the earth plane, unless they had been real spirit mates. A view is widely held among Spiritualists that before human birth the Spirit is bi-sexual. However, before the moment of incarnation, the spirit is split into male and female, and each becomes an individual. Since they are really one, however, there is always a desire for reunion with the spiritual mate. This desire leads to marriage, but since the physical body with its animal inheritance sometimes dominates, the marriage may not be a union with the real mate. Released, however, from the physical body, in the spirit land, the spirit is free to seek its true affinity and eventually is sure to find it, although this may not occur for a long, long time. Some interesting psychic fiction has been written around this theme, e.g., *Alan's Alaine*, a novelette.[28]

Most of the communications that come from the spirit world are from Summer Land. Those who have gone on to higher spheres are less and less concerned with what goes on at the level of earth. At the fourth level dwell those whose interest is chiefly in intellectual or abstract matters. Here are the philosophers, artists, geniuses. They live in brotherhoods, apparently no longer concerned with such things as family. It is they who are held responsible for all the great discoveries and unusual advances which occur on earth. These are communicated to individuals on the earth plane usually through those still on the third plane, for direct contact with earth is not so easy.

[28] *Immortality*, New York City, serially March, 1928–March, 1930 (quoted at length in Lawton, *id.*, pp. 118–132).

Spiritualism believes that everyone ultimately will pass on into the higher spheres. No one is ever lost. Some tarry long on the way, for not all proceed at equal pace. It is thus universalist in its salvation ideal.

If the Spiritualist idea of God, officially at least, seems impersonal, in contrast to the warm personalism of much of orthodox Christian belief, it may be in part due to the fact that man practically depends for help and guidance, not so much upon God as upon the spirits of those in Summer Land, one of whose major preoccupations is in the care for those who are still on the earth plane. In the *Spiritualist Manual* one finds prayers directed to them like the following:

"Teach us, O Dwellers in the Land Supernal, to bear with patience and fortitude the burdens and vexations of fleeting time, and to accept all seeming disappointments as lessons in the development of our spiritual lives. May the work of bridging the chasm of death, of wiping the eyes of the mourner, be by us so faithfully done, so sweetly performed that pain may be transformed into joy, and sorrow into peace and happiness." [29]

"Help us, O Angel Loved Ones, to rise above the doubts, the fears, the pains and anguish of this life, that we may be fitting instruments to carry the word of assurance, of knowledge, of love to all who are in the shadows and have not found comfort for their souls and who are ignorant of the fact of spirit communion. The knowledge of this communion is the golden thread which glorifies and sanctifies and beautifies whatever of the sombre shade may work itself into the fabric of life. . . ." [30]

"May spirit loved ones help us in every effort to improve ourselves, and encourage us in our endeavors to uplift our fellow men and make their lives sweeter and brighter." [31]

In a reading designed for use in a Spiritualist service is found the following, which indicates the function the spirits perform in relation to life here: "How great the power of spirits! A host of invisible intelligences, exalted and wise, surround us everywhere. They cause men to purify their hearts and rectify their lives. They are everywhere, beside us, around us, above us. . . . All these with ceaseless praise, by day and by night behold the works of Infinite Intelligence, and adore them. Are they not all ministering spirits

---

[29] *Spiritualist Manual*, p. 32.
[30] *Id.*, p. 44.   [31] *Id.*, p. 48.

sent forth to minister to those who walk in the light and to save those who walk in darkness? . . . They come to lead the weary pilgrims from the rude scenes of this life to the mansions of the blessed. They come to guide the erring one and win his heart from evil. They breathe a holy calm into the wounded heart. The glory of their presence dissipates the darkness of this world.

"Who are these angel ministers? They are the wise and good of every age, of every land, who come laden with love, to bless, cheer and comfort sorrowing mankind. Under their loving tuition our spiritual senses may be unfolded so that they both appear and speak to us.

"O! Angels of Light and Wisdom, we solicit your presence with us this day, that you may illumine our minds, quicken our understandings, warm our hearts, and strengthen our adherence to truth. May your light drive away the mists of doubt and superstition from our minds, so that the light of Divine Truth may be ours forever." [32]

But how is the help of the spirits given? Unfortunately most humans are "encased," that is, because of their dullness of sensibility to the higher vibrations they are not able to commune directly with the other world. To be sure there do come to most people dreams, flashes of insight, warnings, premonitions, hunches, which, not ordinarily understood, are nevertheless the result of spirit influence. Some who are "sensitives" or "psychics" are able to get much more direct communication, and it is through the developed mediums that most persons must achieve whatever communication they may have with those who have passed over. It is thus one of the major services of Spiritualism to develop and provide mediums who can enable men and women to enter into communication with their dead.

A word of technical discussion of the way in which mediums work will be helpful. A spirit communication may be a direct two-way conversation, spirit with medium, but in most cases this is not the case. On the other side also not everyone apparently has the ability to communicate, even with a medium. Most mediums have in the spirit world what they call a guide or control, through whom they make contact with individual spirits on the other side. Thus four persons are involved in most communications, the spirit, the guide or control, the medium and the person to whom the message is given. Most mediums have one or more special guides through whom they work.

[32] *Id.*, pp. 32–33.

The guide may be a child or an adult, one of one's own race or from some totally different race. Thus some of the most famous guides of American mediums are American Indians. For some reason they are thought to have unusual psychic powers.

In the case of materialization séances the procedure is somewhat as follows. The medium goes into a trance—in a cabinet hidden from the view of the circle of those present. Presently the voice of the guide is heard, a voice utterly different from that of the medium. The writer recalls one such séance in which the medium, a woman weighing somewhere close to three hundred pounds had as her guide a little girl of seven or eight years of age who lisped as she talked in a childish voice. The guide was very informal, talked familiarly with us, told jokes, laughed, sang, in short acted (as a voice only, of course) just about as a child of that age would act. She told us what to do; had us sing songs, holding hands to form an unbroken circle, all this designed "to build 'em up." "Sing louder," she would command us, "I can't build 'em up if you won't help." We would sing louder. Presently at the foot of the curtains behind which the medium sat there appeared something filmy and white. It would push up, then fall back, then up again and back. "Sing louder," she would say and we sang, hymns, old familiar songs, college songs—it did not seem to make any difference what we sang. Finally the spirit form arose to its full height, and one of the women in the circle recognized her sister. She was almost beside herself with excitement, rushing to embrace the spirit form. She was restrained from this, but stood face to face with the spirit and the two carried on a lively conversation. Was it a real appearance of the dead, or only a clever fraud practiced by the supposedly entranced medium and some confederates? The critical unbelievers said fraud, though they did not know how it was done. The Spiritualist said it was a wonderful demonstration.

Curiously enough mediums themselves often get messages through other mediums. At an outdoor meeting place on the hill at Lily Dale, every evening a crowd, many of whom are mediums, gathers and several mediums are selected to bring messages to the people present. None seem more anxious to get messages than those who themselves practice mediumship. This would seem to be clear evidence that they are entirely sincere in their belief in spirit communication. That there is much conscious and deliberate fraud practiced by so-called mediums there can be no doubt whatsoever. This has been often and clearly exposed by Houdini and others. But that many, and one might venture to say, though proof would be difficult, the great majority of those who belong to the better Spiritualist churches, are deeply sincere people, is also true. Mediums may, of course, be self-deceived. Their sincerity does not at all establish the truth of their teachings, or that the phenomena which are produced through them are the result of activity in the spirit world. One distinguished leader in a national association said to me in conversation, "I don't know how these impressions come to me. But impressions do come. Maybe it isn't from the spirit world. Maybe it is the result of some perfectly natural but as yet little understood type of supersensory experience unrelated to the spirit world." He of course believed that the Spiritualistic explanation was the true one. Among the leaders a constant matter of concern is the fraudulent medium. How to deal with such persons is a problem. How to distinguish certainly what is fraudulent and what is true is not at all easy. Many of the recognized Spiritualist leaders are active themselves in exposing fraud and prosecuting those who practice it. It is a complaint of these folk that the public makes no discrimination between the legitimate and the fraudulent, but condemns all of them equally.

In a "thought exchange" session, a sort of free-for-all-discussion period at Lily Dale, I heard a lengthy discussion of the desirability even of dropping the name Spiritualist and adopting another which had no "bad" association in the minds of the public. It was hotly debated, the majority feeling that while the name was in some sense a handicap, it nevertheless had a history and a meaning which was honorable, and that a change would occasion a distinct loss with no compensating gain. For after all, they said, professed belief in and practice of spirit communication, under whatever name, would still be looked at askance by the unbelieving public.

Who are the Spiritualists? Whence do they come? Religiously they come from all the churches. Comparatively few are from the unchurched group. In a study made by a graduate student at Northwestern 81% had belonged to some church before becoming Spiritualists, 27% had belonged to more than one other church, 13.5% were from the Roman Catholic Church. This was a study of but one local Spiritualist church. On a national scale, while the majority are undoubtedly Protestant in background, there is a surprising proportion of Catholics. One very prominent leader in the N.S.A. estimated that about 50% of the membership was formerly Catholic. That would, of course, be out of relation to their numerical proportion of Catholic church members in America. Since Catholics form about 32% of the total church population in the country, any percentage higher than that would indicate a higher percentage of loss by Catholicism to Spiritualism than that of Protestantism. This will seem surprising to Protestants who generally think of Catholics as more loyal to their church than Protestants. But various prominent leaders pointed out to me that there is something in Catholic teaching that favors a Spiritualist view. One medium insisted that every priest in the course of his training had to commune with the dead. She was not too clear about it but seemed definitely to mean more than the mere prayers for the dead which, of course, all priests must offer. She knew a priest personally who told her that in almost every crisis experience he is conscious of his mother's presence. A Catholic writer has this to say about the dead: "Those then whose loss we deplore have not really left us; as immaterial beings they are unaffected by locality or distance; they are near us; clear sighted as they are, there are no opaque barriers, there is no dimness of vision. They know us, they follow our movements, and in the delicate consideration of a love that grows continually purer, and in the concentration of a gaze which becomes ever more intent, they hold us in their affectionate solicitude." [33] He adds, however, that "the church . . . has absolutely set her face against all attempts to hold intercourse with the souls of the dead by mediums or automatic writing, but she has no condemnations for such communion of thought and prayer as indicated in the passage cited."

Spiritualism is, of course, clearly Protestant in its freedom of inquiry, its rejection of ecclesiastical authority, and its loose congregational type of organization. The fact is that it deals with one of the most fundamental interests of humanity, the crisis of death and what happens thereafter. Since this is an experience common to all, it is not strange that men and women of all religious groups are attracted to it.

Three chief motives lead people to an interest in Spiritualism:
1. the desire for an assurance of immortality. Christian faith affirms it, but there have been many attacks upon that faith in recent times, and for many the scientific emphasis upon demonstra-

[33] Herbert Thurston, S.J., *Spectator*, October 19, 1937, vol. 139, pp. 8–74.

tion has left the doctrine of the future life in a weakened position. They want to believe in it. Most people have longed, through the centuries and still do, long for a life hereafter. Spiritualism has, it claims, utter proof of the doctrine, and many find in its phenomena just the evidence they need to uphold their faith as valid.

2. There is in many people a deep desire to keep unbroken the ties of love and affection which bind them to loved ones in their earthly life. They are unwilling to let their dead go. Who does not know one or more persons whose grief at the passing of a loved one has affected their whole subsequent life? They live a life that is embittered and empty and rebellious because of their loss. The hurt will not heal. Some such persons discover in Spiritualism the means of preserving these ties, continuing to commune with and even see their departed dead through the help of a medium. It is this that draws them into Spiritualism. Many persons keep a special room, or some special place sacred to the departed spirits and at periodical intervals enter into communion with them with the aid of a medium. Some seek to develop their own psychic powers so that the communion may be had without any intermediary. Spiritualism to such seems a great boon.

3. Many are appealed to by Spiritualism because through the mediums they are able to probe into the future, to find out what is around the corner. Spiritualism has from the first practiced prophecy. It is this fact which has brought them into ill repute and associated mediums in the popular mind with fortune-tellers, crystal gazers, numerologists, astrologers, and the like. This is a chief feature of the messages given in public meetings. Every person present is allowed to ask a question. The techniques for handling these varies. Sometimes the question is asked directly to the spirit when it appears, sometimes it is written on a piece of paper and placed in a sealed envelope which the medium reads and answers without opening the envelope. If one observes the nature of the questions he will find that almost all of them deal with the future. Some of them are full of heartache and anxiety. "Will John come home to me?" "Will my baby get well?" "Will I marry Henry?" Will I succeed in my new venture?"

How many this interest leads actually to join the Spiritualist Church, there is no way of knowing, but that this is a major contributing factor in the attendance upon public and private séances, there can be no doubt. Curiosity, of course, plays an important role, but this desire to discover what lies ahead is of very great importance in any study of motive.

A fourth appeal, though not as important as those mentioned, is that Spiritualism also purports to heal. This it has in common with nearly all the movements here studied. There are mediums who are especially helpful in this ministry, though most Spiritualist churches have a regular healing service of some kind. At Lily Dale there is a healing service almost every day. A description of such a service personally witnessed by the writer follows:

The session began with a short talk which I did not arrive in time to hear. As I entered the healer was standing behind a woman seated facing the audience of about twenty-five people. He stood with head bowed, hands extended at about a forty-five-degree angle. The room was in perfect silence. After two or three minutes the healer gasped, jerked his head, and said substantially, "Bless you, my sister. The forces are working, producing a condition in you favorable to your recovery of health. Your nerves are quieting, you are getting better. But tonight massage the inside of your feet just forward of the heel. You will find a tenderness there. Massage it for ten minutes every day and remain in silence, relaxed, and you will improve."

Then followed a man, then two other women. The man he told to massage just behind the base of the second toe, ten minutes a day.

Later I spoke with the man, poorly dressed, evidently a working man. "Did you feel helped?" "Yes." "What was the matter?" It was his eyes. "Did the healer know what was the matter with you?" "Yes, I had gone to him before." "Did he feel he was getting better?" "Yes."

One of the women I also asked several questions. The healer had never seen her, knew nothing about her condition or what her illness was. She felt some vibration, she said. She did not feel any sensitiveness in the foot as yet, but she would carry out instruction as to massage. She had had an operation for cancer, apparently successful. This had been predicted by a home town medium and it had come out precisely as indicated. She had been advised to seek this healer.

After individual healings the healer read a long list of names, then others added names audibly and the company went into silence to send out a prayer and vibrations for them.

Then the healer brought forward a special case, a woman afflicted for forty years with arthritis so that she was barely able to get to the assembly hall. As she came before him the forces were built up powerfully. As he stood by her she suddenly cried out that her limbs were paining her terribly. Was some healing process working? Then suddenly something happened and the *forces* ceased and she was unable to get up and walk. So they all concentrated upon her by name. After some moments of silence the healer said, "Now, Margaret, get up and walk. Come on, don't hesitate, get up walk, you can do it." Silence. "Come on, Margaret, try. Don't hesitate, come, Margaret." But she did not walk.

The service ended with a prayer and collection of funds to aid in carrying on Lily Dale activities.

A typical private healing will possibly be of interest. This also occurred at Lily Dale. I met a healer in the hotel lobby and she consented to answer questions. She had not known of healing powers until about ten years before. She was herself not interested in healing. She was a dressmaker. But once she attended a séance. The medium coming to her said, "You have power to heal, did you know it?" "No." "Well, you have. I feel powerful forces as I come to you. Would you heal if you could?" "Surely," she replied. Soon after came the opportunity and without any training at all she accomplished a difficult cure. Since then she has had remarkable cures, gradually giving up her dressmaking and devoting full time to healing.

Some cases she related seemed incredible. A man with gout, an athlete, desired to go to an important game. The doctor said it was impossible. The man came to her and within two days was healed. Some have been healed of cancer and of all sorts of diseases. She attributes her success to a doctor to whom she was once engaged, but who died. He is her guide and tells her what to do. I asked her about her method. First, she said, she talks to the patients, gets them in relaxed mood, mentally as well as physically. Sometimes this may take two or three hours. Then she prays with them, using a prayer appropriate to the condition. She lays her hands on them and—at this point she said, "I'll give you a treatment if you wish. It will cost you nothing and you will see." "But I've nothing to be healed of. I feel fine." "Oh," she said, "this will make you feel better. Come on."

She had me sit down sideways on a chair with my back to her, hands on my knees, legs not crossed (this would not do). She took hold of my head, one hand on forehead, one at the back of my head, and pressed firmly. Then she said a short prayer and recited a poem of several stanzas in a voice of great earnestness. As she came to the end of the poem I began to feel her hands trembling, vibrating almost as though an electric current were passing through. It was a strange feeling. After a little this ceased. Then she began to massage the back of my neck, higher up, then lower down. It was soothing. She rubbed by shoulders and back with a downward sweep of the hands (open), and quite vigorously, up and down the spine and out away from the spinal column, as though sweeping something out or away. It was invigorating and at same time soothing.

Then she turned me around and worked on the front side over my chest, abdomen, and down the thighs with the same downward sweeping movement of the open hands. A little before this, still from behind while hands were on my head, she said she could detect some agitation in my stomach, like butterflies moving about. She said it indicated a little sense of nervous hurry (as a matter of fact it was not long till my train time and I had several things yet to do).

Then she had me take off my shoes and, sitting facing me, she took my right foot up in her lap, rolled my trouser leg above my knee and began to work on my knee. She discovered a dark area there, she said. She had her eyes shut all the time. When she saw a dark place, that meant there was something the matter and she worked specially on that. When the dark spot became illuminated she moved on down the leg. (I had once had a pain in that knee and had had it treated by infra rays at a gymnasium. That was eight or ten years before). When she came to my ankle and bent it about, it cracked so she worked on that until it cleared. Then she took the left leg the same way.

At the conclusion of this she said, "Now take hold of my hands and something will happen you've never felt." I did so. "Tighter," she said, "Tighter." I did so, and there began again that intense vibration which grew and grew in intensity. It seems difficult to explain as simply her shaking my hands. It was a queer feeling. Then with a confident prayer of affirmation the treatment ended.

Spiritualism draws from all classes of society, though the majority are "from the lower and middle intellectual, social and economic classes," according to Lawton.[34] There is a small minority of professional men, lawyers, physicians, teachers, business men, who are usually interested in "research" in the psychic field, and who

[34] *Op. cit.*, p. 176.

disdain the average type of Spiritualist church service. They operate in small groups and under more or less "test conditions." Most of the members are adults. Only 8.2% are under thirteen years of age according to the U. S. Religious Census of 1926. In contrast the Roman Catholic Church reported 27.4%.

The number of Spiritualists according to the U. S. census is not large 27,352 in 1936. This does not tell the whole story, for it does not take account of many independent groups. Furthermore, many who are Spiritualists are not affiliated with any church. Lawton estimated that for every enrolled member there were at least ten or fifteen who were not enrolled. The U. S. census reports that the average attendance at every meeting of an active society is three times its membership. Of what other church body can this be said? Lawton ventured an estimate of from 500,000 to 700,000 Spiritualists in the United States and of 1,500,000 to 2,000,000 in the world.[35]

Spiritualism, aside from its beliefs and practices in connection with communication with the dead, has very little that is distinctive. There is little or no symbolism, no vestments, no sacred taboos. In the earlier day there was little stress upon the moral behavior either of mediums or of members. Indeed, many of the earlier Spiritualists were rebels against the mores of their day. The doctrine of free love was both preached and practiced by many of the early mediums. There seems to be little or no correlation between one's moral character and his psychic sensitiveness. It has often happened that mediums who have been under a long strain of trance, which, it is said, does "take it out of a person," have gone off into serious moral lapses. Similar results have sometimes occurred to ministers and evangelists after a prolonged revival effort.

Now, the Spiritualist churches do have moral requirements for their ministers and mediums, and in their lyceums or Sunday Schools and in their religious services do teach conventional Christian morals. However, there is little moral passion in the movement as a whole, even in respect to the individual virtues, much less is there any serious awareness of the demands of the so-called social gospel. The writer has never been in a Spiritualist gathering where there was sounded a clear ringing moral note. The impression is likely to be rather of an extremely "worldly," rather "hardboiled" attitude

---

[35] *Id.*, pp. 156–157. This estimate was published in 1932.

on moral and spiritual matters. When this judgment was expressed to Spiritualist leaders, they recognized and deplored it. There does seem to be a more wholesome moral outlook within the leadership of the movement today.

Spiritualism is as old as man, almost. It deals with a universal, inevitable, aspect of man's experience, death. It provides an answer to some of his most insistent questions. So deeply within him is the urge to a fulfillment of his present incomplete and little satisfying life that any group, with even a small degree of verisimilitude in its teachings concerning that life, is likely to get a hearing. Spiritualism is here to stay, organized or unorganized. Tendencies already observable within its more important branches lead one to believe that it will adapt itself to the passing scene, gradually purify itself of its earlier faults and come to serve an increasing number of people who do not find in the traditional churches an adequate ministry to man as he faces the great adventure, himself, or as he watches those whom he loves slip their moorings and move out into the unknown. A church which can offer a satisfactory faith and ministry in and around the crisis of death has little to fear from Spiritualism.

Chapter Ten

Jehovah's Witnesses

Jehovah's Witnesses deny indignantly that their movement is religious. This will sound strange to those who have heard them or read their literature which probably contains more scriptural quotations than any other current religious publication, and is replete with the familiar theological language of God, Christ, Kingdom of God, sin, salvation, etc. If this is not religion, then what is it?

The explanation of their denial rests upon their concept of religion which, it need hardly be said, is quite unique. "Religion is doing anything contrary to the will of Almighty God," they declare. "Religion is of the Devil." [1]

"The mask is down," declares an anonymous writer in a widely circulated pamphlet.[2] "The truth of God's word has ripped it off and organized religion stands exposed as being not of the Lord God and Christ but of their enemy, Satan—the Devil. It stands stripped of its Christian professions and stands naked as being demonism! Religion is revealed as the unchangeable foe of Christianity." [3]

Over against "religion" stand Jehovah's Witnesses, announcers of the gospel of the Kingdom, the coming of the Theocracy, or the rule of God, representatives of true Christianity, essentially as it was before it became corrupted and fell under the sway of Satan. Theirs is the authentic voice of warning, given by the prophets and apostles, of the coming day of judgment and the destruction of evil in the world.

[1] J. F. Rutherford, *Theocracy*, Watch Tower Bible and Tract Society, Brooklyn, 1944, p. 18.
[2] *Id.*, *Religion Reaps the Whirlwind*, Watch Tower Bible and Tract Society, Brooklyn, 1944, p. 58.
[3] *Id.*, pp. 58–59.

They have not always been called Jehovah's Witnesses. The name was officially adopted as late as 1931 at the suggestion of the then head of the movement, Judge J. F. Rutherford. Before that they were called "Russellites," "International Bible Students," "Millennial Dawnists" and other less complimentary names. But if the name came late in history, Jehovah's Witnesses are said really to have begun with Abel whom they recognized as the first of their line.[4] Once asked by a newspaperman concerning the beginnings of the movement, Judge Rutherford replied that Jehovah's Witnesses had been on earth as an organization for more than 5,000 years, citing as scriptural authority Isa. 43:10–12, Heb. 11 and Jno. 18:37. All true Christians, he said, were Jehovah's Witnesses.[5]

However, the movement now known as Jehovah's Witnesses was begun by Charles Taze Russell, better known as Pastor Russell, in 1872 in the city of Pittsburgh, Pennsylvania.

Russell was not a preacher but a layman, member of the Congregational Church and of the Y.M.C.A., though apparently in earlier childhood he had been brought up in the Presbyterian Church and learned its catechism. He "fell prey to the logic of infidelity," he says, when he began to think for himself. However, one night he attended a meeting of the Second Adventists "to see if the handful who met there had anything more sensible to offer than the creeds of the great churches." Though the scriptural exposition he heard there was not wholly clear or satisfactory, "it was sufficient, under God, to re-establish my wavering faith in divine inspiration and to show that the records of the apostles and prophets are indissolubly linked." [6]

This marked a turning point in the life of young Russell. He became an ardent student of the Bible and, although without college or theological training, he began to expound the scriptures with great assurance. And the people listened. Out of this grew the movement now known as "Jehovah's Witnesses," though Judge Rutherford was later to declare that "it would be blasphemy to claim that any man is the founder and organizer of Jehovah's Witnesses." [7] "Pastor Russell," he writes, "was the general organizer of the cor-

[4] *Theocracy,* p. 19.
[5] *Judge Rutherford Uncovers Fifth Column,* Watch Tower Bible and Tract Society, Brooklyn, 1940, p. 20.
[6] *Watch Tower,* July, 1906.
[7] *Theocracy,* pp. 22–23.

poration but he was not in any sense the founder or organizer of Jehovah's Witnesses. The claim that any man is the founder or organizer of Jehovah's Witnesses is blasphemy, for the obvious reason that it is the prerogative solely of Jehovah-God to select and organize his own witnesses, and no man has any authority whatever to select or organize them." [8] In the *Yearbook*, 1945, in the historical account of the movement, there appears no mention at all of Pastor Russell.

In 1879, Russell established a magazine, *Zion's Watch Tower and Herald of Christ's Presence*, and about 1880 published his first book, *Food for Thinking Christians*. In that same year he sent a representative to England to begin the work there. The first formal organization was in 1884 when Zion's Watch Tower Society was established. The movement spread rapidly. By 1888 it was reported that the "word" was being preached not only in the United States and England but also in China, Africa, India, Turkey and Haiti.[9]

The organization was simple, consisting of a Board of Directors made up of the President, Vice-president, Secretary-Treasurer and three others, all elected by those members who had contributed as much as ten dollars to the movement. For each added ten dollars an extra vote was allowed. Pastor Russell was, of course, president. It is said that no single vote was ever cast against him.

When in 1909 the headquarters of the movement was moved to Brooklyn, a new corporation was formed, chartered in New York State under the name "Peoples Pulpit Association," but changed in 1939 to the "Watch Tower Bible and Tract Society." In 1914 it was incorporated in England as "The International Bible Students Association."

Pastor Russell was tireless in the production and circulation of literature, a characteristic that has remained a constant throughout the whole life of the movement. No other group has used so extensively, or perhaps so successfully, the printed page as its means of propaganda. It was reported at the time of his death that more than 13,000,000 copies of his books had been distributed. One of them, *The Divine Plan of the Ages*, reached almost 5,000,000 circulation and *What the Scriptures Say about Hell*, 3,000,000. Evidently the matter of Hell was of no small concern to many people of his day.

---

[8] *Id.*, p. 18.
[9] Watch Tower, December, 1888.

The fact that he brought the comforting thought that there really is no Hell undoubtedly helped boost the circulation of that particular book.

But he also preached and travelled constantly, averaging some 30,000 miles a year. His most famous address was the *Photo Drama of Creation*, given innumerable times in person to overflow crowds, and to uncounted thousands more by use of a victrola record which carried the Pastor's voice to millions who saw the pictures shown, but to whom the Pastor himself never spoke personally.

It was while on one of his trips that the messenger of death came for him. One of his devoted followers called to the conductor and porter of the Pullman to come "see how a great man of God can die." This occurred in Texas in the year 1916. Judge J. F. Rutherford succeeded him as head of the movement, and gave it skillful and distinguished leadership for more than a quarter of a century.

Although democratically elected as leader, it was not unnatural that many within the movement should refuse to accept his leadership. To follow so colorful and so greatly beloved a figure as Pastor Russell could not be easy and Rutherford was almost completely different from the Pastor in many ways. Pastor Russell loved nothing so much as appearing before great crowds. There was about him a personal magnetism that drew people to him. Rutherford, on the other hand, seemed cold, distant, reserved. There was great respect for his ability to get things done, the cogency of his reasoning (from Scripture chiefly) and for his boldness of utterance. But the people did not love him as they did Pastor Russell. Rutherford avoided public appearances as much as possible. In later years he spoke usually by radio, and was little more than a voice. He appeared only very occasionally at great national or international conventions. He avoided meeting people. Few of the followers ever got close to him. He even disliked personal publicity, was seldom photographed, and the public knew but little concerning him. Although his position of leadership in the movement would certainly have entitled him to a place in *Who's Who in America*, his name is not included in this most inclusive reference work which describes its function as that of providing information about persons concerning whom information is most likely to be sought. Its omission, therefore, must have been because of his refusal to have it included.

Various groups have split off from the main body, believing that they were following the original teachings of Pastor Russell which they felt were being traduced in some degree under Judge Rutherford's leadership. Among them may be mentioned the Pastoral Bible Institute of Brooklyn.

It is true that Rutherford did not feel bound to adhere to everything Russell had taught. For example, the good Pastor, along with many another before and since, made much use of the Great Pyramid as a source of prophecy concerning the second coming of Jesus. On the basis of it he had worked out the date of that appearance which, like so many other such calculations, proved to be mistaken. Rutherford, who was completely Bible-centered in his belief, openly condemned resort to non-biblical sources in the attempt to discover the will and plan of God. He specifically mentioned the Great Pyramid as an example. This provoked violent criticism from older members of the movement who had grown up under Russell's teaching and many of them withdrew from it.

But Rutherford was an able administrator and gradually came to be recognized as its undisputed head and spokesman. With the passing years Russell and his writings fell more and more into the background. While they are still sold they are not advertised or pushed. Meanwhile, the Rutherford books, pamphlets, and voice records are being circulated literally by the million.

The Judge—he was not really a judge but a lawyer who did now and then serve as judge on a traveling circuit in Missouri—was a prolific writer. The current catalogue of the Watch Tower Bible and Tract Society lists fifteen titles of books, one of two volumes, another of three, making in the aggregate eighteen volumes averaging more than 350 pages per volume. The same catalogue advertises also thirty-two booklets of sixty-four pages each, containing lectures he delivered over the radio. Each one of the lectures, says the catalogue, was delivered "with the forcefullness, understandableness and conviction characteristic of Judge Rutherford: brevity, prompt getting at the subject, and plain setting forth of the pure Bible truth being sought for, with no fence straddling, pussyfooting or suppression of facts and truth for fear of man or devil." [10] In addition, the Judge's voice may still be heard, by the use of recordings, discussing in four and one-half minute speeches some eighty-three different topics, any one of which may be heard free of charge and without any obligation, in your own home if you desire it. All this sums up to nearly 10,000 printed pages.

[10] *Watch Tower Bible and Tract Society Catalogue*, p. 21.

Other items listed for sale by the Society are its *Yearbook*, a variety of Bibles, Bible translations, concordances and dictionaries, and all standard works. But no other publication by any writer other than Judge Rutherford is listed. The catalogue states that from 1921 through 1940, a total of 337,000,000 copies of his books and pamphlets were distributed, an average of almost 20,000,000 per year. In addition to this the Judge contributed regularly to the periodical publications of the movement. It is interesting to note that the books published since Rutherford's death have appeared anonymously. Thus Jehovah's Witnesses and their current teaching are far more intimately linked to Judge Rutherford than to Pastor Russell who launched the movement. We shall attempt to see later in what way, if any, the direction and teachings were modified by the Pastor's successors.

The Judge died January 8, 1942, at the age of seventy-two. He had lived during his last years at Beth-Sarim, California, the western headquarters. He left active direction of the movement to Mr. N. H. Knorr who succeeded him in the presidency. Little is known of Mr. Knorr personally. He refused the writer a personal interview, as he had consistently done to others who sought to make firsthand contact with him. Presumably it is he who does most of the writing that appears under the Watch Tower imprint today, but this is not certain. He is a man of middle age, apparently aggressive and capable. He had been vice-president for several years before the Judge's death. What direction the movement will take under his leadership, it is too early to say. So far there seems to have been no marked departure from the policies of his predecessor.

The organization of Jehovah's Witnesses is hierarchical and highly authoritarian. There is little democratic participation in the management or in the formation of policies of the movement as a whole. This is taken care of by a relatively small group of directors of the Society. There are, as already noted, three legal corporations through which the Society functions: (1) the Watch Tower Bible and Tract Society of Pennsylvania, the first incorporation of the movement, founded in 1884, as Zion's Watch Tower Society, (2) the Watch Tower Bible and Tract Society, incorporated in New York as the People's Pulpit Association, in 1909, but changed in 1939 to the present name, (3) the International Bible Student's Association, incorporated in 1914 in England, the name under which most of the work outside of the United States is carried on. In the Pennsylvania corporation all who contributed ten dollars or more to the movement were counted as members with an additional vote for each additional ten dollars contributed. At the annual meeting of the corporation in 1944, an amendment to the charter was proposed limiting membership to 500 and not less than 300. There was no mention of any money contribution in connection with membership. It was not stated how the members were to be chosen.[11] The New York corporation is really the controlling body. It is apparently self-perpetuating and made up of about forty members, most of whom are actively engaged in some phase of the movement's work. This group annually elects a Board of Directors who are the real power in the direction of the movement as a whole. According to the 1945 *Yearbook*, all three corporations are empowered to hold property, and other corporations have been formed for holding property in still other countries,[12] though Stroup declares that only the New York Corporation may hold property. What the basis of his statement is he does not say.[13]

The exact division of labor between the three corporations does not seem wholly clear, even after reading the official statement in the *Yearbook*, but it really doesn't matter for present purposes, for the 1945 *Yearbook* says, "The Corporations have the same president; thus the policies set for one organization are instituted in all."[14] The Boards are interlocking. The members of the Pennsylvania Board are elected by the general membership, as above defined, but in practice, only members of the New York Board are nominated for election. Tenure is generally, though not necessarily, for life, if the member desires to continue.

Mr. Stroup quotes a letter (written while Judge Rutherford was still alive) by an unnamed informant whom he simply designates as a "former higherup," as saying:

"Rutherford controls the organization completely. Directors' and members' meetings are a formality. The Judge sends a note stating whom he wants elected, or rejected, or what he wants done, and that is immediately done unanimously. Woe be unto that one who opposes. Anyone that opposes slightly gets a tongue lashing at the dinner table and if the opposition is serious or such one has too much

[11] *Yearbook*, p. 193.
[12] *Yearbook*, 1945, p. 33.
[13] H. H. Stroup, *Jehovah's Witnesses*, Columbia University Press, New York, 1945, p. 21.
[14] P. 33.

independence of mind he is liquidated from the organization." [15]

Whether his successor exercises as much power as Rutherford, is not known. It is very difficult to learn what goes on within the inner circles of the movement. Stroup says that "increasingly, in recent years, the organization has taken on the character of a secret society." [16] Criticism of the decisions or policies of the headquarters group are likely to be labeled as "Satan-inspired." A former head counsel of the movement was forced out because he ventured to write a letter to the Board of Directors criticising certain practices of Judge Rutherford and other officials and workers living at Bethel House. He asserts that his only interest was in bringing about some needed reforms, but he was dismissed without a hearing and "excommunicated from all meetings and activities of the organization. He sued Rutherford and the Board for libel and was awarded $25,000 damages by the court." [17]

In general, the membership of the movement seems not to be disturbed by this autocratic concentration of control at headquarters. They seem to accept whatever is handed down as from the Lord, though from time to time murmurings are heard, as at the convention at Cleveland, Ohio, during the summer of 1946.

Continuing from the top downward, the next step below the central controlling powers are what are called "regional servants." It will be noted that the term "servant" is used instead of minister, or preacher, or priest, though the functions are in many ways similar. In the United States there are six regional servants who superintend the work in their areas and report to the Board of Directors by whom they are appointed. These "servants" have little to do with local groups, but mainly with the next lower order of workers, the "zone servants" of whom there are 154 in the United States. If the regional servants were to be correlated with bishops in the Methodist Church, the "zone servants" would correspond to district superintendents, each being in charge of the work in a particular limited area. It is their responsibility to stimulate the workers in the local areas, see that they distribute their quota of literature, audit the local company's books, counsel with local groups and hold "zone assemblies," or district conferences, in short, stimulate, inspect, instruct and guide the local workers and their companies.

[15] H. H. Stroup, *Jehovah's Witnesses*, p. 22.
[16] *Id.*, p. 25.   [17] *Id.*, pp. 25–26.

The local group, corresponding to the local church, is called a "company," a term reminiscent of an early stage when military terms were employed, as in the case of the Salvation Army. At that time the "zone servant" was called captain. The local meeting place is called the "Kingdom Hall." This is usually a rented hall or storeroom, never a church building. It is simply furnished, with little or no attempt at adornment. The groups, which are rather more like study groups than congregations, are not large, seldom being more than two hundred in number. When this size is reached a new group is begun.

Appointed over the local company is "company servant" or "service director" who corresponds to the local pastor of a church. According to the *Yearbook*, "the company servant has general charge of and looks to all the interests of a congregation and, therefore, might be called the 'superintendent' or 'overseer.'" [18] In this whole organizational set-up they are, they think, following exactly the pattern of the New Testament. They quote, in support of this claim, the Goodspeed translation of Phil. 1:1–2, where "episcopos" is translated "overseer," and "diaconos" as "assistant." Where the work is more than the overseer can do, an "assistant company servant," or "assistant," is appointed. Indeed, there may be several assistants named, such as "accounts servant," "advertising servants," "literature servant," etc. Where the local company in a given center reaches two hundred, a new unit is opened, and in charge of it is placed a "unit servant," with his "unit assistant."

The main business of Jehovah's Witnesses is to witness. This all are supposed to do. "Being commanded to 'publish the glad tidings,' all servants of God naturally become publishers of the Kingdom, or Theocracy." [19] But there is a special group known as "publishers." They are part-time workers who are supposed to give a certain number of hours of work per month. Some give as little as fifteen hours, though the Society generally expects sixty. The work consists in calling upon people, playing the phonographic recordings of Judge Rutherford's talks for those who request it, distributing literature or other propaganda work. The 1948 *Yearbook* reported in the United States alone 67,680 publishers who devoted almost 18,000,000 hours to witnessing for the Kingdom during the year. Throughout the whole world 181,071 publishers gave 43,842,305 hours to their witnessing.

[18] P. 25.　　[19] *Yearbook*, 1945, p. 26.

Full-time workers are known as Pioneers, or Pioneer Publishers. Of these there are two classes, the Special Pioneers and the General Pioneers, or just Pioneers. The Special Pioneers are supposed to give a minimum of 175 hours service and make not less than 50 back calls in order to qualify for the regular financial allowance. They are sent to towns of 4,000 or more population where there is no local company, and to help the weaker companies in other communities. They may be sent anywhere. They get an allowance of $25 per month and get the regular Pioneer discount on all literature distributed. The Pioneers or General Pioneers are required to give 150 hours a month of service which may be in a place of his own choosing. Actually, the 1945 *Yearbook* reports an all-time high average of only 130.2 hours. It is supposed to be a full-time occupation, but the complaint is made that many try to hold down a regular job and do this beside. Also, some start bravely enough but give it up before they have worked a year. There is a small monthly allowance of $10.00 to the Pioneer. When the writer asked one, who had kindly brought him a number of books, how he managed to live, he replied that he lived around among the Witnesses, very much as the frontier circuit riders of an earlier day in America used to do. There were 3,834 Pioneer publishers in 1944 [20] who gave almost 6,000,000 hours service, distributed nearly 5,000,000 books and pamphlets, secured over 58,000 new subscriptions to publications and circulated 1,825,473 single copies of magazines. The Special Pioneers, 1,212 in number, the same year gave 2,413,084 hours of service, circulated 1,834,730 books and booklets, took 26,969 new subscriptions to periodicals and distributed 583,777 magazines. There were 3,056 organized companies in the United States, which, aside from what was done by the Pioneers, circulated over 8,000,000 books and booklets, gave over 10,000,000 hours of service, received 123,150 new subscriptions to periodicals and distributed over 5,000,000 copies of magazines. This was largely done, no doubt, by the "publishers." The Jehovah's Witnesses make great and effective use of their laymen.

The Pioneers are really the clergy of Jehovah's Witnesses. Formerly without specific training, there is now a training school located at South Lansing, upper New York, where professional training is given them. It is called the Watch Tower Bible College of Gilead, and was founded in February, 1943. The school can accommodate only 100 students with present facilities, so the number is

[20] Detailed statistics of work done by Pioneers not given in the 1948 *Yearbook*.

thus limited. The course runs for five months and is given chiefly to the study of the Bible and the techniques of witnessing. Thus far those attending the school have been workers with two or more years' experience in the field, rather than novices. The 1948 *Yearbook* reports 860 out of a total of 909 students enrolled as having graduated since the founding of the schools.

Concerning the question as to who are the real ministers of Jehovah's Witnesses, there has been great controversy. In normal times, strict definition may not be necessary, but when war comes and the question as to ministerial deferment from military service arises, some specific definition must be made. It was precisely the unwillingness of Jehovah's Witnesses to accept what they held to be an arbitrary definition of the ministry by the government which sent some 2,000 Jehovah's Witnesses to federal prison between 1940 and 1945. Some few accepted incarceration because of pacifistic belief, but the greater number were not pacifists at all, and resisted the State's order to enter military service as an infringement of their constitutional guarantee of religious liberty.

Some of Jehovah's Witnesses were recognized as ministers and given the 4D classification (ministerial deferment). This was generally accorded to those who carried a card from the central organization attesting to their full-time employment by the Society, or what corresponds ordinarily to ordination. Concerning the question of ordination, Judge Rutherford had this to say: "To be ordained means to be appointed by the proper authority to a position or office to perform the duties specifically assigned. Jehovah's Witnesses, being selected by Jehovah, it follows that Jehovah is the authority that ordains the servant." [21] Here the issue is squarely joined. It is no organization that ordains but God alone. To be sure, the organization sets its seal upon some as its full-time workers. "To each one who gives evidence that he is fully devoted to God and his kingdom and that he is wholly devoted to the service of God in obedience to his commandments, the Society issued a paper or card of identification showing that such person is recognized by the body of Christians composing the Society as an ordained minister and servant of the Lord. But," he continues, "this does not mean that no one else is an ordained minister who does not receive such a card of identification. The real ordination comes from

[21] *Theocracy*, p. 26.

God himself." [22] In practice, the Government accepted as ministers those who carried the card but refused deferment to those who had only their own individual witness of ordination by Jehovah to fall back upon, particularly when they did not give full time to the work but earned their living by some secular calling. This is not by any means the whole story of Jehovah's Witnesses' relation to the war which will be more fully discussed later.

Probably the most important phase of Jehovah's Witnesses' work is its publishing activity. It has its own great modern printing plant in Brooklyn, which annually turns out an amazing amount of printed matter for circulation all over the world. In 1944 [23] it printed 3,297,545 bound books and 20,885,719 booklets. It printed the weekly *Watch Tower* in eight different languages to the number of over 10,000,000 individual copies and in four languages issued more than 7,000,000 copies of *Consolation*, the monthly periodical. Besides this, it issued over 18,000,000 tracts of various kinds. Among the books, it produced 218,000 Bibles, including one Greek-English, diaglott edition. Even so, it is reported that they were unable to meet the demand for Bibles made upon them.

In the printing plant the workers are all Jehovah's Witnesses and all ordained, according to the *Yearbook*. They live in Bethel Home in Brooklyn and receive, besides maintenance, the sum of ten dollars per month. This is the sum generally given to workers from the president down to the lowliest. Judge Rutherford, like the rest, is said to have received only this amount. Of course, his maintenance allowances must have been much greater than that of others. But he is reported to have disposed of only some $200 in his will. He, too, lived at Bethel Home when in Brooklyn.

The society, however, owns a very palatial home called Beth Sarim at San Diego, California, where the Judge spent most of his time in his later years. The name means "House of Princes" and its purpose is, according to Rutherford, to serve as "some tangible proof that there are those on earth today who fully believe God and Christ Jesus and in his faithful kingdom, and who do believe that the faithful men of old will soon be resurrected by the Lord, be back on earth and take charge of the visible affairs of earth." [24] Beth Sarim stands ready for their occupancy when they return to

---

[22] *Theocracy*, p. 27.
[23] No detailed report of the publishing house is given in the 1948 *Yearbook*.
[24] *Salvation*, p. 311.

participate in the grand Theocracy soon to be established. It was purchased in 1929, and meanwhile serves as western headquarters of the movement.

The Witnesses also own several farms. The most notable perhaps is Kingdom-Farm at South Lansing, New York, which supplies much of the produce for Gilead Bible School and Bethel Home in Brooklyn. In addition, the Witnesses own various radio broadcasting stations. Their radio activity has been much more restricted in recent years since the strong anti-Catholic and anti-clerical pronouncement of Judge Rutherford caused many stations to refuse to carry his broadcasts.

In addition to their house-to-house canvassing, sale of literature, use of phonographs, and their public meetings, much use has been made in recent years of autos, or trucks, or trailers equipped with public-address systems by means of which large numbers of people can be reached, particularly in rural areas. As witnesses under divine constraint to make known the imminence of the end of the age and the coming of the Theocracy, they seek by every conceivable means to get their message to the people. One need never be surprised at any new method they may evolve.

Jehovah's Witnesses have literally covered the earth with their witnessing. The 1948 *Yearbook* contains annual reports of their work in eighty-six different countries. In the grand summary of the worldwide effort of the societies it is stated that altogether 181,071 publishers were active during the year; that they gave 43,842,305 hours of service, distributing more than 20,000,000 books and booklets. They made 11,710,832 back calls, that is second or additional calls on persons upon whom they had previously called. Over 12,000,000 individual magazines were distributed on the street corners of the world. It may be truly said that no single religious group in the world displayed more zeal and persistence in the attempt to spread the good news of the Kingdom than the Jehovah's Witnesses.

Just what is the gospel they teach?

The main teaching of the group may be stated rather simply. The Kingdom of Heaven is at hand. The end of the age is near. Armageddon is just around the corner, when the wicked will be destroyed and the Theocracy, or rule of God, will be set up upon the earth. Be warned! But behind this lie very definite theological concepts, some of them similar to, and some widely at variance with orthodox

Christian beliefs. Fundamental to everything else is the idea of God. Because God is the kind of a God he is, everything else follows quite logically.

What, then, do they hold with reference to God? First let it be noted that all their doctrines are based upon the Bible. The method of establishing the truth is to support it by an array of Bible quotations taken from any part of it—Old and New Testament alike. God appears, therefore, to possess all those attributes which are attached to him in the Bible. God is creator, Law Giver, Judge, Avenger, Father, Rewarder of Good, and Punisher of Evil. But the stress seems clearly to lie upon the side of His power and His inexorable justice rather than upon the side of His love and forgiveness. He is a jealous God, requiring submission. His name must be exalted and those who blaspheme it must be brought low. God is, to be sure, Father, or Life-Giver, the giver of every good and perfect gift. But this side of his nature is not the one that stands out. A casual check of the scripture passages dealing with the idea of God in Judge Rutherford's writings reveals that most of them come from the Old Testament and not the New.[25]

God is one, not three in one. Concerning the Trinity, Judge Rutherford writes, "The doctrine of the Trinity is a false doctrine and is promulgated by Satan for the purpose of defaming Jehovah's name."[26] There is no scripture which supports it, he declares. Indeed, there is much that proves God is but one, e.g., "I am Jehovah and there is none else; besides me there is no God," Is. 45:5, and many others, Ex. 20:2-4, Ps. 83:18. "The words 'holy ghost' do not refer to a person." Properly translated as "holy spirit," it means "the power of Jehovah, which power is invisible to human eyes and which power is entirely devoted to righteousness or holiness."[27] Though denying its place in a trinity, they make not a little of the Holy Spirit as, for example, inspiring the prophets and apostles at Pentecost.

But if God is one and the only one, there were nevertheless gods, spelled with a small letter. Lucifer, says Rutherford, was a mighty one among spirit creatures of old "and hence was a god."[28] To him was entrusted the duty of overseeing the creation of earth.

---

[25] For example, see *Children*, p. 50.
[26] *Uncovered*, Watch Tower Bible and Tract Society, Brooklyn, 1937, pp. 48-49.
[27] *Id.*, p. 52.   [28] *Children*, p. 55.

But when he heard the paeans of praise to God from his new creation he became covetous of that praise himself, rebelled against God and sought to trap man and bring about his destruction. Lucifer thus becomes Satan, or the Devil, and has carried on an incessant warfare with God since the creation. This seems to be their explanation of the origin of evil. Why God permits it to continue is not questioned so far as I have discovered. In one connection it was stated that God's power was sufficient to have crushed evil but that he desired the voluntary obedience of men so withheld his destructive power to give them every chance.[29] Yet in the end it is to be by that power that the end of evil will come and the day is not far distant. As in so many millennial groups Satan seems almost to have the upper hand. Rutherford says that "for many centuries Satan, the Devil, has operated as invisible ruler of the nations of the earth."[30] But his time is running out; the end of his rule is near.

"Jesus is the Son of the Almighty God," "the beloved and only begotten Son whom the Almighty, the Father, sent to earth to represent him and to declare his truth."[31] Yet in another place Rutherford speaks of Him as "that great prophet[32] who speaks with full authority conferred upon him by his Father." He was the Logos, "the beginning of God's creation," "the official representative of Jehovah—the one who carries into action Jehovah's purposes."[33] Three tasks were set for him (1) "the vindication of his Father's name, (2) the redemption and deliverance of those of mankind who believe on God and Christ and who are obedient to God's will, and (3) to set up the kingdom of Almighty God by and through which he accomplishes and completes his commission."[34]

The Devil had challenged Jehovah's power and caused multitudes to blaspheme His name. He had raised up many enemies against Jehovah-God. But to God "belongeth vengeance and recompense; their foot shall slide in due time—I will render vengeance to mine enemies and will reward them that hate me."[35] Those who have blasphemed and reproached Jehovah's name must be brought low. This is the will and purpose of Almighty God "which purpose," writes Judge Rutherford, "will be carried out in due time and executed by the Beloved Son."[36] Just how this is to be accomplished will appear a little later.

[29] *Id.*, p. 61.   [30] *Theocracy*, p. 3.   [31] *Id.*, p. 7.
[32] *Children*, p. 36.   [33] *Theocracy*, p. 8.   [34] *Id.*, p. 9.
[35] Dt. 32:35–43, *passim.*   [36] *Theocracy*, p. 11.

Man, by his disobedience in the Garden, fell under the condemnation of death. In Adam, all men sinned and, unless delivered, must perish. Only by the obedience of Christ Jesus in performing the will of his father is the way of redemption, deliverance and blessing opened to mankind.[37] This is simply the traditional Christian idea, held by Protestant and Catholic alike. In detail, however, it differs at some points. Adam had been created perfect. Because of his disobedience he had been pronounced imperfect and subject to death. But since is was the perfect man that sinned, "nothing less, nothing more than a perfect human life could purchase the descendants of Adam because his descendants had proceeded from one who was perfect at the time he was given authority to bring children into the earth." An angel could not do it, for an angel is greater than man. There were only imperfect men on earth, hence salvation could only come from Jehovah. "While the Logos, that is, Jesus, was purchasing the Kingdom, with all its rights and power, God provided that he should also purchase mankind."[38] In order to do this Jesus "laid aside his spirit life and became a man—born of woman, without spot or blemish."[39] He was a perfect man, perfect in his organism and with full and complete right to life as a perfect man."[40] He was thus fully qualified "as a perfect man to furnish the purchase price for mankind."[41] Crucified as though he were a sinner, "he died as a sinner, that sinners might live." Dying thus, however, "he did not forfeit his right to life as a man; hence when he was raised out of death, he possessed that right as a valuable thing, which constituted the purchase price or ransom price."[42]

Life is not the right of an imperfect man. Adam's sin forever lost to man that right. But God, the fountain of life, has provided "that Christ Jesus, who has bought mankind, may minister life as the free gift to those who obey him."[43] Salvation is therefore possible through Christ's work "to all those who believe on the Lord Jesus Christ and obey him."[44] It is a free gift forced upon no man, and no one who deliberately chooses to oppose God's kingdom can be expected to benefit by Christ's sacrifice.

Christ's third task is to set up the Theocracy or rule of God in the world. Here is the most distinctive teaching of Jehovah's Witnesses. It is their one constant point of emphasis. It is indeed the

---

[37] *Id.*, p. 11.   [38] *Children*, p. 111.   [39] *Id.*, p. 111.   [40] *Id.*, p. 114.
[41] *Id.*, p. 115.   [42] *Id.*, p. 115.   [43] *Id.*, p. 120.   [44] *Id.*, p. 120.

heart of their gospel. Jesus becomes God's *executive officer* in the setting up of Theocracy and rules as King over it. Participation in the life of the Theocracy is really salvation as they think of it. In discussing the Theocracy we are therefore discussing their concept of salvation. What then is it?

In the beginning the world was created perfect. It was under the rule of God. It was the Theocracy. "Under theocratic rule all was happiness, peace and blessedness on the earth. Sickness and disease and want and fear were unknown, the worship of God was pure and free and in spirit and in truth, and man was at peace with the lower animal creatures over which he had dominion." [45] Then came the rebellion of Lucifer, man's disobedience and consequent downfall with its fearful train of consequences for all humanity. Satan became the ruler of the nations. Evil flourished. Man was under the condemnation of death. Jesus came in fulfillment of prophecy, laid down his life, was resurrected and ascended to heaven, whence, in due time he will come "to rule in the midst of his enemies and bring Satan's uninterrupted rule to an end." Christ's rule did actually begin in 1914. In that year, they believe, "Christ Jesus the King, took unto himself his great power and began to reign. The King cleaned out the 'old heavens' and cast the Devil down to earth, as is recorded in Rev. 12:10–12." [46]

Why the year 1914? There seems to be no outward evidence of this having taken place. The answer seems to be that it comes from the prophecy Lev. 26:18–24 that Israel should suffer "seven times" for his sins. A "time" is taken by students of prophecy to be a period of 360 years. "Seven times," therefore, means 2,520 years. Since it is said that the overthrow of King Zedekiah, last of the kings of the Jews, occurred in 604 B.C., the fulfillment would take place in 1914. So Pastor Russell had calculated and taught. But nothing visible happened. It, therefore, must have occurred invisibly. At any rate it is a dogma among the Jehovah's Witnesses that in that year Christ began to reign. The outbreak of World War I in that year seemed to them evidence of something catastrophic having occurred. "The end of the world came in 1914," writes Rutherford. [47]

Then "in 1918 the Lord Jesus Christ came to the temple of

[45] *The New World*, Watch Tower Bible and Tract Society, Brooklyn, 1942, p. 23.
[46] *Yearbook*, 1945, p. 17.
[47] *Theocracy*, p. 32.

Jehovah," and began what is designated as the temple judgment.[48] In another place he writes that three and a half years after the time when Jesus was enthroned as King of the world, he appeared at the temple of Jehovah, gathered his faithful followers and sent them forth to preach. This marked the beginning of his judgment of the nations, foretold in Mt. 25:32–33.

The writer has sought diligently some explanation of this precise date for it is also a matter of dogma now. Of course, the war ended in 1918 but that would hardly seem to explain it. In 1917 Judge Rutherford and his associates, following Russell's example, refused to support the war. They were charged with obstructing the recruiting and enlistment service of the United States and causing insubordination in the military and naval forces of the United States. They were found guilty and in June 1918 were sentenced to the federal penitentiary where they were held for eight months. Then, on appeal of the case, they were admitted to bail. Later, the war having ended, the case was dropped. This was a serious blow to the movement and for a time the Brooklyn society was dissolved. Rutherford, however, even from prison, wrote letters to the followers. In 1922 a convention of 500, held in Cedar Point, Ohio, undertook a reorganization of the movement. This fits in exactly with a statement of the Judge that "although the temple judgment began in 1918, not until 1922 was it understood by the consecrated of the earth that the Lord was at the temple. From that time forward the Lord began to reveal to his followers the meaning of prophecy and all of the anointed now on earth can truly testify that since 1922 the Lord has continuously illuminated the prophecies, revealed the meaning and made them understandable by his people, greatly to the joy of all his servants." [49] It is frequently stated that there was "war in heaven" from 1914 to 1918.[50] Here it is noted that in 1919 the "Lord redeemed and delivered the faithful ones from Satan's organization, etc." [51] It was in 1919 that the Judge and his associates were released from the penitentiary.

But before the final establishment of the Theocracy there must first come the Battle of Armageddon and the destruction of the evil ones. This is thought to be imminent. One of the Judge's famous slogans was "millions now living will never die." That meant that

[48] *Id.*, pp. 32, 33.   [49] *Theocracy*, p. 33.
[50] *Salvation*, p. 206.   [51] *Id.*, p. 207.

Armageddon was expected within a generation. Signs abound that it is near—the signs customarily indicated by the millennialists, too familiar to need recounting here. What will it be like? Who will participate in it?

On one side in this greatest of all battles will be "Jehovah, the Almighty God, the Supreme Commander; Christ Jesus, the Field Marshal and Leader of the forces of war against unrighteousness; and all the holy angels of heaven who at all times obey Jehovah—God—and follow the lead of Christ Jesus." [52] On the other side will be "all who hold to religion or demonism, all the wicked angels and demons." Gog is Field Marshal of the wicked, serving under the Commander-in-chief of all evil, Satan.[53] The righteous of earth who are devoted to Jehovah and to Christ will witness the battle but take no active part in it. But let Judge Rutherford describe it in his own words. Jehovah gives the command to begin battle.

"Christ Jesus, the Vindicator of the Most High, hears and immediately obeys the command. He moves forward on his war mount to give battle to the enemy. The host of heaven, the holy angels, fully equipped, follow after the Lord Jesus Christ. It is the army of righteousness. The battle is on, and the forces of righteousness charge the enemy forces, hurl them back and literally cut them to pieces . . . the Lord Jesus Christ, fully supported by the Most High, strikes through the kings or ruling power, both visible and invisible . . . he wounds the head of every department of Satan's organization over the many countries; he fills the places with the dead." [54] "Complete annihilation of the army of Satan will be the result." [55] The battle will "forever put an end to religion and religious persecution . . . it is God's appointed time and place to settle all accounts with his enemies and this he will do by requiring the life blood of those who have deliberately violated his 'everlasting covenant.' " [56] "Those who die will not be a few million but all the wicked will God destroy—Ps. 145:20." [57]

"A small remnant, the righteous, will survive the destruction of Armageddon and shall remain on earth 'from generation to generation,' that is, forever. To them will be given the great and unspeakable privilege to 'be fruitful and fill the earth' with perfect creatures

[52] *Religion*, p. 339.   [53] *Id.*, p. 340.   [54] *Id.*, p. 345–346, *passim.*
[55] *Id.*, p. 341.   [56] *Id.*, p. 348.   [57] *Id.*, p. 347.

under the immediate direction and ministration of Christ, the King of the great Theocracy." [58]

To the Theocracy will be admitted also those who are resurrected from the dead, after Armageddon, but they will have no part in the divine mandate to repeople the world because "they must first be made righteous." [59] The order of resurrection will be, first, "the faithful apostles and others like them who have died in faith, waiting for the coming of the Lord"; [60] then, those of whom Paul wrote: 'they shall be changed, in a moment, in the twinkling of an eye'; then the faithful men of old who have a 'better resurrection.' Finally, will occur the general resurrection of those who have died without an opportunity to know the Lord, but the scriptures do not make clear just when this will take place." [61]

The wicked will not be resurrected. For them judgment has already occurred and there is no further hope for them. In other words, Jehovah's Witnesses teach the annihilation of the wicked. They are not condemned to hell or everlasting punishment but are destroyed. The willfully wicked who died before Armageddon are already destroyed. Those who resist the coming of the Theocracy, fighting on the side of Satan, will apparently be completely wiped out at Armageddon, thus leaving only those who had not had opportunity "to know the Lord" to be brought back to life. Apparently Pastor Russell had taught that the wicked would be raised, to be "turned into hell," but Rutherford says categorically that this interpretation was wrong. There will be no "nations" to be turned into hell because they will be destroyed at Armageddon.[62]

Those who have "had no opportunity to be justified by faith and obedience" will be brought back to life during the thousand-year reign of Christ and opportunity will be offered them to prove their integrity. Still others, "the rest of the dead" of Rev. 20:5, of whom it is said that they "lived not again until after the thousand years were finished," apparently are raised and stand judgment at the end of the thousand-year reign.[63] These have no part in the mandate to "fill the earth," for this must be done by the righteous. Paradise will already have been established in the earth before the general resurrection." [64]

[58] *Id.*, p. 354.   [59] *Salvation*, p. 355.   [60] *Id.*, p. 354.
[61] *Id.*, p. 342.   [62] *Id.*, p. 354.   [63] *Id.*, p. 356.
[64] *Id.*, pp. 355–356.

But there is yet one final act in the drama. After a thousand years, Satan, who was defeated and bound at Armageddon, is once again loosed to make test of the integrity of those who have been raised from the dead and some will be beguiled by the enemy and fall into destruction. But the end comes swiftly. Those who follow him, and the Devil himself shall be destroyed and the memory of such wicked shall cease forever.[65] The righteous live on eternally on the earth under the rule of Christ the King. Only the 144,000 participate with Christ Jesus in the first resurrection and "they are the only ones from among men to go to heaven." [66]

Thus salvation is not an otherworldly ideal of escape from earth to another life. It is to be experienced rather on earth but on an earth made over into a heaven-like place, a world in which there is no evil, pain, suffering, injustice, death. As a humble witness expressed it to the writer, "The righteous will live forever right here on earth, only it will be different than now."

"In what way?" I asked.

"Oh, there will be no more pain or suffering or poverty. There will be plenty for everybody and men will live together as one happy family and even wild animals will be at peace with one another and with men." She quoted the famous passage from Isaiah to support her belief—"And there will be no death."

"But there will be birth," I asked, "and children?"

At first she was not quite sure. Then she remembered. The Lord had said, "be fruitful and multiply, so there must be births."

In this she was right. The earth will be wellnigh depopulated at the battle of Armageddon. But the righteous shall fill the earth. Those who survive the destruction will have the great joy of repeopling the world. But those who have been raised from the dead are to have no part in it, since they are not righteous. After the final destruction of the evil one, paradise on earth will have been established. Since the world will have been "filled" and there is no death, there can be no more occasion for birth. Therefore, there will be no further marrying or giving in marriage.[67]

No one would grow old, thought my informant. Thirty-three seemed to be in her mind the upper limit men and women would reach. She and others are a bit hazy as to the details of that happy

[65] Rev. 20:10, 14.   [66] *New World*, p. 100.   [67] *Id.*, p. 359.

life. But what believers are not, even among the most orthodox? Life was to be good, ideal, really heaven on earth.

Details as to the nature of the Theocracy are not wholly lacking. Christ is to be king. He is to be aided by many of the ancient worthies of the Old Testament and New, brought again to life to rule with him.

Those faithful men of old may be expected back from the dead any day now. "The scriptures give good reason to believe that it shall be shortly before Armageddon breaks," writes the author of *The New World,* one of the books written since Judge Rutherford's death, and published anonymously.[68] It was to have a place in readiness for them that Beth-Sarim, or House of Princes, was built at San Diego in 1930, and is still maintained.

One brief glimpse may be given as to what is envisaged by the Witnesses as to the nature of the Theocratic government. "In the endless time to come there shall not be different governments on earth at the same time . . . there will be no self-determination of peoples . . . there will be only one government, indivisible, world wide, only one central authority and it will be heavenly, divine. It will be a paternal government because all that live will be children of the King, their Father, who gives everlasting life; and all mankind shall be one united, inseparable family relationship, doing justly, walking humbly with their God, worshiping him in spirit and in truth." [69]

The Jehovah's Witnesses' use of the Bible will already have appeared abundantly in what has thus far been written. They believe in its complete inspiration and divine authority. To quote a passage of scripture in support of anything is sufficient to establish its truth. No apparent difference is made between the parts of the Bible— Old Testament or New Testament. Typical of the use of scripture is their condemnation of Christmas trees based on Jeremiah 10:3 which they think definitely disposes of the matter. "The customs of the people are vanity; for one cutteth a tree out of the forest, the work of the hands of the workman with an ax. They deck it with silver and gold." Clearly this must be the familiar Christmas tree, and in an earlier verse it says, "Learn not the way of the nations." Therefore, it stands condemned. It is interesting to note, however, that

68 P. 104.   69 *New World.* p. 115.

while they circulate and use chiefly the King James version of scriptures, they also make use of other versions. Indeed, they publish what they call the emphatic Diaglott New Testament which gives in parallel columns the Greek text and the King James translation, the Greek column containing also a literal, interlinear translation, not unlike the familiar "pony" sometimes used by students. No modern Christians make a more constant use of scripture, or memorize it in greater quantities than the Witnesses. To argue successfully with them on scriptural grounds, one must know his scriptures better than most members of even the fundamentalist churches do today.

Toward the churches the Witnesses are quite hostile. They are religionists and teach religion. We have already quoted their definition of religion. They attack the Protestant and the Catholic churches alike, both as to their teaching, their organization and particularly their ministry. But it is for the Catholics that they reserve their bitterest attacks. Judge Rutherford repeatedly spoke and wrote exposing their doctrines and organization. His booklet *Uncovered* sums up best, perhaps, his indictment of that church and its doctrines. He openly charges them with inspiring most of the violent attacks made upon the Witnesses during recent years. Because of the violence of his attacks upon the church, as we have said, he was finally excluded from the air by many stations. This did nothing to soften his attitude, as may well be imagined. He challenged the hierarchy again and again to public debate on the issues raised but the challenge was ignored. Over two and a half million people petitioned the Federal Communications Commission to permit such a public debate over the air, in 1936, but nothing came of it. *Uncovered* was then published as Rutherford's statement of his case against the Roman Catholic Church.

Perhaps the most notable thing about the Witnesses is their insistence upon their primary allegiance to God, before any other power in the world. It was this that brought them into conflict with the State at two major points, first in the refusal of their children to salute the flag, and second in their refusal to participate in the war on the terms demanded by government.

The controversy over the salute to the flag was a long one. Children were excluded from schools and, in places, violent attacks were made upon them. The case was brought into the courts which at first decided against them. Appealed, the judgment was reversed in the lower courts. Appealed once more, it was carried to the United States Supreme Court which upheld the case against them. Thus it stood for a time, when later the Supreme Court reversed itself and decided the case in favor of the Witnesses. It is no longer necessary that their children salute the flag.

But why did they refuse to salute it? Not, certainly, because Jehovah's Witnesses are not loyal Americans but because as Judge Rutherford states it, "They are conscientious and sincerely believe that for them to indulge in the formalism or ceremony of saluting any flag is a violation of God's specific commandment as set forth in Exodus 20:3–5 and emphasized in many other scriptures. The reason that such flag saluting is a violation of that commandment is that the salute attributes salvation to the state which the flag represents, thus making the state a 'mighty one or a god, whereas' salvation belongeth alone to Jehovah, and violation of God's commandment would mean their certain destruction." [70]

The Judge suggested that they be allowed to make a pledge in somewhat different form, in part as follows: "I respect the flag of the United States and acknowledge it as a symbol of freedom and justice to all. I pledge allegiance and obedience to all the laws of the United States that are consistent with God's law as set forth in the Bible." [71]

The Jehovah's Witnesses are not pacifists.[72] They have no objection to the use of violence. The Battle of Armageddon which plays so important a role in their system is to be the greatest and most destructive of all battles. It was not, therefore, as pacifists that so many hundreds of Jehovah's Witnesses went to Federal Prison rather than accept induction into the armed forces during World War II. As we have seen, most of those were imprisoned because they insisted on their right to the 4D classification, which means deferment as ministers of religion. This the government refused to allow. But there is a deeper reason which sets the Witnesses apart from war. That is the principle of neutrality. Says Rutherford: "If the nations of Christendom or any other nations of earth desire to engage in war and do so, that is their affair, and it is the duty of God's

[70] Rutherford, *God and the State,* 1941, Watch Tower Bible and Tract Society, New York, pp. 18–19.

[71] *Id.,* p. 28.

[72] Rutherford, *Neutrality,* Watch Tower Bible and Tract Society, New York, 1939, p. 22 ff.

people to remain entirely neutral as to such wars. The war of one nation with another is not the fight of the followers of Christ Jesus. It is the privilege of each Christian to make his own position and relationship to the Lord to be clearly understood, that he is separate and apart from any of the nations of this world. Each one must determine for himself his relationship to God and his government. He must not, however, seek to induce others not to go to war." [73]

Such opposition to the generally accepted attitudes toward the State was not likely to go unnoticed and it has not been. In times of greatly heightened national feeling, when peoples' patriotic emotions are deeply stirred, it is almost inevitable that some persecution should be visited upon such persons. And it has been. The Witnesses have been persecuted as no other religious group in American history, save possibly the Mormons in an earlier day. They have been run out of town, beaten, stoned, shot, their houses destroyed, and have suffered every kind of indignity.[74] But they have not wavered. Rather they have thrived under persecution. They seem almost to welcome it. The woman quoted above, an ordinary lay witness, replied when I said, "but the witnesses are persecuted." "The Lord said we would be persecuted." Nothing more seemed to be necessary. "And think of the reward we are promised, 'for theirs is the Kingdom of Heaven.' " Clearly violence and opposition will not deter this people. They seem, some of them, to have almost a martyr's complex. They desire to suffer for their faith.

Against every sort of opposition they press ahead. They fight by every legal means for their civil rights, the right of public assembly —sometimes denied them—the right to distribute their literature, the right of conscience to put God above every other loyalty. They have performed a signal service to democracy by their fight to preserve their civil rights, for in their struggle they have done much to secure those rights for every minority group in America. When the civil rights of any one group are invaded, the rights of no other group are safe. They have therefore made a definite contribution to the preservation of some of the most precious things in our democracy.

The moral emphases of Jehovah's Witnesses are not greatly different from those of orthodox Christianity. They are largely individualistic. There is no apparent recognition of the social forces that

[73] Rutherford, *id.*, p. 9.
[74] *The Persecution of Jehovah's Witnesses,* published by the American Civil Liberties Union, New York, 1941.

make for evil and which must be met by the organization of the social forces of good. Their apocalypticism sees no human remedy for the vast evil of the world, but only the intervention of God with his great destructive power at Armageddon.

In some respects they are not as strict in their moral teachings and practices as the extremely conservative groups are. They have generally been against the use of tobacco and liquor, though in more recent years smoking and "chewing" has been more common in rural areas especially. Charges have been made of moral looseness among some of the higher-up leaders of the movement, especially in the use of liquor, but proof is lacking. Stroup finds that in sex matters the Witnesses follow in general the mores of their local communities.[75] Charges of sexual irregularities have been made against them but under bitter criticism, not to say actual persecution, by hostile neighbors, such charges might easily be only another form of persecution, without more foundation than might be found occasionally in almost any large religious group.

Marriage is not too warmly encouraged, owing to the imminence of the end of the world. Women are not held in too high esteem. They are definitely held, on scriptural grounds, to be weaker than men and a source of danger and temptation. Stroup expresses the judgment that there is more than the average amount of marital disorganization among them. Divorce is never approved "except on New Testament grounds," but separation is allowed. Stroup, in his studies, got the "impression that the number of separations among the witnesses is unusually high compared with that of other religious groups." [76]

What of their future? So far as this writer can see they will carry on and increase. They survived the passing of Pastor Russell. They survived the passing of Rutherford. If there is no such outstanding leadership at present as in the past, the leaders seem nevertheless to be capable. They know what they want and drive steadily toward their goals. There is much in the present scene to lend strength to their appeal. The confusion, the uncertainty, the fear—all are good soil for the growth of apocalypticism in our day, and Jehovah's Witnesses are well out in front among the apocalyptic movements.

They continue to attract, as in the past, the underprivileged, chiefly. The little people, who are especially confused, and troubled, and increasingly distrustful of any happy human outcome of the present world situation. In the Theocracy there lies the fulfillment of the hopes and dreams of which they see little chance of fulfillment in any present human set-up. And it has one appealing element in it that most other apocalyptic groups do not have. This New World is not in some far-off sphere—another world—but here on this good solid earth which, if only it could be rid of its evil and pain and suffering, would after all be the place of all places most desirable, really God's country. In it a man would feel at home as in no ethereal realm. This movement has in it the element of permanency. If Armageddon delays, it will nevertheless come—perhaps when least expected. It is well, therefore, to be prepared. And the certainty of a coming day not far distant, when the handicaps of the present life will disappear, when all that makes life presently hard and unlovely will give way to a blessed eternity of ideal living, may serve to make a little more tolerable the life that now is. This movement will very likely go on from strength to strength.

Chapter Eleven

Anglo-Israel

Having just passed through the bloodiest and costliest war in all history to save the world from a Master Race, it will be disheartening to many people to discover in their midst a movement which hinges, more than upon anything else, upon the belief that another race, the Anglo-Saxon, is uniquely the race chosen by God for the fulfillment of His purpose in the world. That that purpose is benign, namely the salvation of the nations, through this people, might seem to one who stands within the chosen group to rob it of any sinister significance, but scarcely to those who stand without it, and are to be the objects of its beneficent efforts. Suppose the chosen race were to become convinced of its superiority, but were to lose its moral controls. Suppose it were to confuse its own national aspirations with the purposes of God, and bring to bear upon this fulfillment the passion of religion. Suppose the race should get the notion that it was the executor of God's judgments upon other races and peoples.

One may be very sure that, however good the news may seem to Anglo-Saxon, British and Americans that they are heirs to all the promises made by God to Israel, there will be people of less fortunate lineage such as Indians, Africans, Germans, Italians, Greeks, Egyptians, Arabs, and Persians who will feel quite differently. Their plight is none too happy now in relation to the greater powers. What may it become if such a notion becomes universally held by Britons and Americans? Russia will certainly not be cheered by such knowledge. It will undoubtedly furnish one more motive to support her attack upon religion as dangerous to man, and upon the Judaeo-Christian religion in particular, as the purported source of such claims.

Properly speaking Anglo-Israelism is not a religion. It confesses

385

quite frankly that its chief tenet, that of the identification of the Anglo-Saxon people with the "true Israel," is in no sense necessary to salvation. "Of course not," writes one exponent of the belief. "How could belief in a purely historical identity in any way take the place of Spiritual belief in Our Saviour . . . who gave His sinless life to save the whole of mankind (regardless of race or color.)" [1]

"It cannot be too strongly urged," he continues, "that British-Israel Truth is NO NEW RELIGION. It is simply the master-key with which all religions can unlock the problems of the Bible . . . nevertheless, Christian truth and Israel truth are so interwoven, that neither is complete without the other, for *both are of God*. Both are taught in the Bible, and cannot be separated." [2]

Sensing that unbelievers might desire some more satisfying answer as to why, if not necessary for salvation, such a belief should be regarded as important, the same writer suggests a number of replies to the natural question, "Then what is the good of it?" Briefly they may be stated as follows:

1. It proves God right and vindicates his honor, for he promised Abraham, and later others, that so long as the sun and moon and stars endure, so long should Israel survive as a *Nation* before him, *forever*. ("When God says 'forever' surely we may take it that He means exactly what the words say.) If God is true, then Israel must be a nation somewhere today." [3] This is precisely the belief which Anglo-Israel followers hold, and claim to have proven beyond doubt. Thus is God proved right and his honor vindicated.

2. Again, he claims, it proves the truth of the Bible, which is

---

[1] M. H. Gayer, *The Heritage of the Anglo-Saxon Race*, Destiny Publishers, Haverhill, Massachusetts, 1941 (3rd ed.), p. 139.

[2] *Id.*, p. 139.

Note: Gayer's book, the one most frequently quoted in this chapter, was most highly recommended as the one which should be read for an understanding of the Anglo-Israel Movement. It is a sort of compendium of information, drawn from many sources rather than an original study, and thus represents something of a cross-section of belief as held today by the Anglo-Israelites. Accompanying the book, indeed the book is really only an explanation of it, is an elaborate chart showing graphically the descendants of the various tribes and presenting maps which give the supposed migration routes they followed to the British Isles. Another book mentioned as basic was J. H. Allen, *Judah's Scepter and Joseph's Birthright*, 13th ed., Destiny Publishers, Haverhill, Massachusetts, n.d.

[3] Gayer, *op. cit.*, p. 140.

held to be true in every word—"The inspired word of God." Just how is not explained, but presumably in the fulfillment of Biblical prophecy.

3. It is "the complete answer to infidelity . . . for it demonstrates the fulfillment of prophecy as no other subject does," "also in a day when the churches are losing so many of their young people, this subject arrests their attention, fires their enthusiasm, and wakes up some slumbering sense of awe and loyalty that no other does. The wonder of it touches them—British fair play urges that God has so faithfully carried out His part, He at least deserves the best *we* can offer in return." [4]

In addition, it is said to turn Communists into good citizens; provide the only solution of racial and international problems; to account, as nothing else can, for the growth, power, and influence of the British Empire; and finally to promote loyalty to God, King and Empire, and "bring all denominations together, making them realize as nothing else ever will how unimportant are the minor differences in our creeds, and how all important the Christ." [5] Just how this latter effect is to be wrought by this teaching is not stated.

If the question still arises, as to why God should have picked out the Anglo-Saxons as the favored race, the reply is that it was not we present-day members of that race that were chosen, but Abraham, "the friend of God." To him and his seed were the promises made. We Anglo-Saxons, the descendants of Israel, have simply inherited them. God, in the working out of his purposes, required a "Servant Race whom he could train to do His bidding."

If a king should desire to send a message to a group of people at the gate, he would send it by a servant. This would not mean that the servant was considered superior to the people to whom he bore the message, but wearing the uniform of the king he would be accepted by those people as His servant. "To Israel was entrusted the mighty responsibility of being God's 'Servants' and 'witnesses,' 'His Missionary Nation,' His 'Battle-axe and weapons of war,' His guardian of the seas, and the many other duties which were laid up for his people to fulfill in the world. *Is it not time that Great Britain Realized Her Inheritance?*" [6]

[4] *Id.*, p. 142.   [5] *Id.*, p. 142.   [6] *Id.*, pp. 135-139.
Note: The book though published in America was written by a citizen of Britain. A little later it will be seen how the United States is linked with Britain as joint heir of the promises.

But how does it come that the Anglo-Saxons are identified as Israel and are therefore, the carrier, in the modern age of the responsibility placed upon her, as well as being the special beneficiary of the promises made to her by God in ages long gone? Before answering that question which is of course the heart of the whole discussion, let it be pointed out that aside from this one teaching and certain implications that flow from it, there is nothing in the teaching of the movement to differentiate it from any fundamentalist religious group. Indeed, they insist that membership in their group does not separate people from their traditional churches. In some localities it is true they do have meeting places, with regular worship and preaching services, but not usually at the regular hours of service of most of the Protestant churches. In the Chicago centers they meet at 3:30 P.M. on Sundays, and some night during the week. They publish a great deal and are active in literature distribution. They are called, in Chicago, the Kingdom Gospel Institute, with the sub-title Anglo-Saxon Federation. It will not therefore be necessary to discuss in detail the theological beliefs of the movement. God, Christ, sin, salvation, atonement—all these great doctrines they hold just as they are held in the theologically conservative Protestant churches. If anything, they are more fundamentalist than most Christians. In their literal use of scripture they outdo even the most extreme Biblical literalists. The Bible is their chief reliance, as a source of doctrine, though they are obliged to make use of much secular history in their alleged proof that the true Israel in the modern age is Great Britain, or more broadly, the Anglo-Saxon people.

As long ago as 1694 a book was written by one John Sadler, linking Britain and ancient Israel very closely. The British Constitution was seen by him to have been derived from Israel. The author held that commerce existed between Britain and Phoenicia in the time of Solomon, Britain being a source of tin. The name Britain he derived from Phoenician as meaning field of tin. Israelites were supposed to have accompanied the Phoenicians in their journeyings and to have become acquainted with Britain, and might, he thought, have sought refuge there after the fall of Samaria.

But it was not until 1840 that John Wilson in his book *Our Israelitish Origin* clearly stated the theory as held by present Anglo-Israelites. The idea "caught on," and was supported by prominent Britons. One eminent Scotch astronomer found support for the theory in the Great Pyramid, and reliance upon the Pyramid as evidence has been an important feature of the movement ever since. A book by Edward Hines, published in 1871, *The Identification of the British Nation with the Lost Tribes of Israel,* had an enormous circulation, proving that the idea found a warm response among British people.

Gayer says that these men—Wilson and Hines (unknown to each other)—"gradually realized, to their amazement, that every mission foretold for Israel in 'the last days,' was now being undertaken by the British nation, and exactly at the time laid down." [7]

The idea was scorned at first, but says Gayer, "truth was bound to win. Many earnest thinkers, chief amongst them our wonderful Queen Victoria, took up this study, and came to believe in the identity of our race with Israel." [8]

The first Anglo-Saxon Association was founded in 1879 in England. A periodical, *Heirs of the World,* was published in America as early as 1880 (in New York), so the idea was evidently spreading. In 1919 a British-Israel-World-Federation was established with branches in Great Britain, Canada, Newfoundland, Australia, New Zealand, Tasmania, South Africa and the United States, that is, throughout the entire English-speaking world—which was natural enough, but, says Gayer, "it is owned as Truth by large numbers of thinking men and women of foreign nations." [9] One wonders how many and in what foreign nations. It was estimated as long ago as 1901 that there were over 2,000,000 people in the world who held the view. There is no way of discovering how many there are now. The circulation of *Destiny,* the official publication of the movement in the United States, was said by a leader, in personal conversation with the writer, to be about 16,000 in 1945, and increasing steadily. The sale of literature and the number of local meeting places in Chicago has increased notably in recent years. The leader, a layman, had begun with only a borrowed typewriter ten years before. In 1945 they had a property of their own half paid for, and twelve groups meeting in various sections of the city. Literature sales had run up to over five hundred dollars per month. There are no collections taken, no dues for membership, no funds solicited, yet seemingly they prosper.

National headquarters, formerly in Detroit are now at Haverhill,

[7] *Id.,* p. 137.   [8] *Id.,* p. 137.   [9] *Id.,* p. 137.

Massachusetts, where *Destiny*, a well edited and attractively printed monthly periodical is published, as are also tracts and books under the imprint "Destiny Publishers." [10]

The central teaching of the movement is that the Anglo-Saxon people are the descendants of Israel and heirs of all the promises made to Abraham and his successors in the Bible, including of course the utterances of the prophets. It is based upon an absolute belief that prophecy must be fulfilled. Its major premise is that every word of scripture is the literal word of God. Everything found in scripture must be true. Prophecies are a part of scripture, therefore prophecy must be true. Remove that premise and the whole edifice comes down like a house of cards. Therefore, the belief can only flourish among those who hold such a view of scripture—unless pride of race might lead one to accept as true certain parts of scripture that are favorable, while critically rejecting other parts, which do not support such a racial view.

With the promises to Abraham and others, most readers will already be familiar. Only a few need therefore to be repeated here. To Abraham, God said, "I will make of thee a great nation" Gen. 12:2. "Thy name shall be Abraham, for a father of many nations have I made thee" . . . "and Kings shall come out of thee." Gen. 17:6. To Jacob He said, "a nation and a company of nations shall be of thee" Gen. 35:1. "And thou shalt be called by a new name" Is. 62:2. "Wherefore glorify ye Jehovah in the east, even the name of Jehovah, the God of Israel, in the isles of the sea" Is. 24:15. All these they believe and many more are fulfilled in Britain or the Anglo-Saxon people. If they are not fulfilled in them they are not fulfilled, but prophecy must be fulfilled. So the argument goes.

But if Israel was the people chosen of God there were certain demands made upon her, and these she did not meet. She was to worship Jehovah only. She turned to the worship of idols. She was

---

[10] Among the books published or circulated by the movement may be listed the following titles: *Prophecy on Parade, Study in Revelation, God's Great Plan, One Man's Destiny, Great Pyramid Proof of God;* among the booklets and pamphlets: *Who and Where Are the Lost Ten Tribes?, The Challenge of the Great Pyramid, Anglo-Israelism, True or False?, The Marks of Israel.* This latter lists 72 marks, all of which are clearly to be found in Great Britain or the Anglo-Saxon people. A few of the tracts are *The Bible Answers the Race Question, Jesus Christ of Nazareth—Was He a Jew?, Suppose the Anglo-Saxons Are Not Israel.* Some of these are published locally in different centers rather than by the Destiny Publishers.

duly warned by the prophets but persisted in her iniquity. So judgment came upon her. She was to be punished "seven times" for her sins Lev. 26, 18–24. And so it happened. After having been made a great people under David and Solomon, she became divided and after a time Northern Israel fell before Assyria, and the ten tribes disappeared from history. Where did they go? Where are they now? This has been one of the perennially interesting questions raised by the Bible. Anglo-Israel has the answer. These tribes were not lost. They could not be, if prophecy was to be fulfilled, and God's promises made good. They were engaged in a long painful struggle, undergoing the "seven times" punishment of God. It was only after this had been completed that they began to benefit once more by the favor of God and experience the long-delayed fulfillment of prophecies spoken concerning them.

But all students of prophecy are agreed, says Gayer, "that a 'time' means 360 years. Scripture itself sets the scale—a day for a year." "Seven times" then would mean 7 x 360 = 2520 years. If Samaria fell in 720 B.C., then 2520 years after would fall in 1801, by adding one year which is said to be necessary to get the right astronomical date; and precisely in that year, on January 1st, occurred the union of Great Britain and Ireland to form the United Kingdom.[11] Then began the real expansion of the British Empire. Clearly, the British fulfill the specifications. But there is further evidence. Judah began her captivity in 604 B.C. (Modern scholars usually place it at 586 B.C.) Adding the 2520 years and making the necessary adjustment of one year this fell in 1917. Judah's captives shared the same judgment as Israel for they too were idolatrous. It was precisely in 1917 that General Allenby entered Jerusalem, delivering it from the Turks, indeed on the very anniversary of the recapture of the Temple by Judas Maccabeus in 168 B.C. This fulfilled exactly the words of Jesus in Lk. 21:24 "that Jerusalem shall be trodden of the Gentiles until the times of the Gentiles be fulfilled."

"If," writes another Anglo-Israelite, "Great Britain is not latter-day Israel, then Jerusalem is being trodden down still, and it remains for some other nation to expel us and lift the curse from it." [12] In 1948 there are many in Jerusalem who definitely believe that she is downtrodden still, even by Great Britain. And they also call themselves the sons of Abraham.

---

[11] *Id.*, pp. 115–116, *passim.*   [12] Quoted by Gayer, *id.*, p. 117.

But how did Israel ever get to the British Isles? That is a long story and takes us mainly outside of the Bible. It is generally held by Anglo-Israelites that there were two movements of Israel into England, Scotland and Ireland and that one of these occurred at an early date. They are called the western and the eastern migrations.

The western movement was composed of members of the tribes of Judah and of Dan. Judah had twin sons Zarah and Pharez. We can only sketch the story very briefly here without indicating in any detail the proofs offered for the claims that are made. Some general description of this method of proof will be given later. Enough here to say that Zarah, who, although the firstborn was not given the birthright, seems to have separated from the rest of Israel while it was still in Egypt and set out in search of adventure. Zarah had five sons of whom two played an important role in European history, for one of them Dara, called Dardanus by Josephus, is believed to have been the Dardanus who founded Troy, while the other Calcol or Cecrops founded Athens about 1556 B.C. The Zarah tribes moved westward across Southern Europe and sent colonies to Spain, or the Iberian (or Hebrew) Peninsula. Various geographical names such as Ebro, Ebrus, Eburo, are traced to the "Hebrew" root. This it may be said is a chief method of proof. Similarity of names is said to be evidence of the presence of the Hebrews in various European lands. It was from these Zarah descendants, recalled in the Saragossa of Spain today, which was said to have been their capital, that the Clan Milly, or Scots-Gaels, came into Britain somewhere about 1000 B.C. It was likewise from this group that the old Scottish kings of Ireland came. From these is traced the lineage of the royal house of England. Thus, through the Judah-Zarah line is the ruling family of Britain traced back to Israel, fulfilling the promise to Judah of "the sceptre till Shiloh come" (i.e., Christ) Gen. 49:10. But there are other lines which converge at the same point, as we shall presently see. Could there be any significance in the fact that the color of the official British military uniform is scarlet; that official British documents are tied with scarlet tape (hence red tape) or ribbon; and that it was a scarlet thread which the midwife tied about the wrist of Zarah to mark him as the firstborn? Gayer seems to think so for he cites not only these but other uses of "scarlet" in British custom.[13]

[13] *Id.*, pp. 51–52.

Dan, "the Pioneer," was the restless son of Israel. Turbulent, unruly, he too broke away from his brethren while they were still in Egypt and sailed away to Greece. He settled near Argos, became king and renamed the people "Danai." In the distribution of the land after the conquest the tribe of Dan was assigned a portion of the sea coast and became a maritime people. They established colonies in various parts. These migrating peoples seem to have followed the custom of giving places and rivers their own name, so it is easy to follow them through Europe, along the *Dan*ube, the *Dan*eiper (Dnieper), the *Don*, the Rho*dan*us (ancient name of the Rhone), the Rhine, ancient name Eri*dan*us, until they arrived in *Dan*mark (Denmark) and Scan*din*avia. These were the northern Danites.

The Southern branch became masters of the Mediterranean, eventually taking over the far-flung colonies of the Phoenicians, who had held most of the islands of the Mediterranean, and so also the British Isles. They were in these Isles sometime before 1000 B.C. Hibernia seems clearly to them to be from the same root as "Hebrew."

"Centuries before Greece had obtained her alphabet from Phoenicia and her mythology from Egypt," writes Gayer, "this intrepid people had inscribed their name Dan . . . from the Southern spars of the Lebanon, through Asia Minor and Central Europe to the Emerald Isle; from Denmark to the Straits of Gades." [14]

Thus two branches of Israel were in the British Isles by about 1000 B.C. at the time David was ruling his people, Israel, in Palestine. But this was only a beginning.

The third migration to the west was not large in numbers, but of supreme importance, for it brought to the Isles a Judean princess, descended from David, and she became the ancestress of the British royal family. It came about in this way, they say, though it should be noted that, chronologically, we are getting ahead of the eastern migration which had begun some two centuries earlier, but which came to the Isles much later in time.

At the time of the Babylonian captivity the Prophet Jeremiah was given his choice of going with the captives to Babylonia, or remaining in the homeland. He elected to remain, and he, Baruch, and others managed to hide away and keep with them the "king's daughters." Later, against the advice and stern warning of Jeremiah,

[14] *Id.*, p. 36.

they escaped to Egypt settling at Tahpanhes, according to Jer. 43:6–7. They were pursued by their Babylonian enemies and most of them were massacred, as had been foretold by Jeremiah. But he had also foretold that a remnant would escape (Jer. 44:28). Here the Bible story ends. It has been held generally that Jeremiah was among those who were killed. But the Anglo-Israelites believe otherwise, and from non-Biblical sources, which they regard as trustworthy, follow the remnant on to Britain.

It had apparently been foretold that the escaping remnant would revisit their homeland. While at Jerusalem the fugitives gathered together from the ruins of the temple certain sacred treasures, the stone upon which Jacob had rested his head at Bethel, a box which may possibly have contained the Ark of the Covenant, including possibly the tables of the Law, and such royal regalia or papers as might serve to accredit the princess as of the royal house of David.[15] Setting out with their precious cargo, Jeremiah and Baruch came by ship to Spain. This is said to be proven by ancient Spanish records which tell of the arrival at about this time of two eastern princesses accompanied by an ancient prophet and his scribe Brug (Baruch) bringing with them "a Sacred Stone, Box, and a golden banner inscribed with the Royal Lion of the Tribe of Judah." [16] From thence they must have sailed for "the Isles," for not long afterward news was brought to Eochaidh, described as a prince of Judah, descended from the Judah-Zarah migration, who had just been chosen as Heremon, or ruler of Ireland, and was awaiting his coronation, that a company including a princess, a prophet and his scribe had been shipwrecked on his shores. He had them brought to court, where he promptly fell in love with Princess Tamar Tephi and the two were wed. From this royal pair, both descendants of Israel, the one Eochaidh from the Judah-Zarah branch, the other from the Judah-Pharez line through Royal David, has descended the ruling house of Britain today. Thus was fulfilled the promise of God to Judah that "the Scepter shall not depart from Judah, nor a law-giver from between his feet until Shiloh come" (Gen. 49:10); and to David, "I will establish the throne of his kingdom forever . . . and thy house and thy kingdom shall be established forever before thee . . . thy throne shall

---

[15] *Id.*, p. 105.   [16] *Id.*, p. 106.

be established forever" (2 Sam. 7:16); "his seed shall endure forever and his throne as the sun before me." Ps. 89:36; "David shall never want a man to sit upon the throne of Israel" (Jer. 33:17).

The stone of Jacob which they brought with them has had an interesting history. Every king of Ulster was crowned upon it for a period of eight hundred years. It was then removed to Scotland where it remained until 1296 when it was seized by Edward I of England and brought thither where it has since remained in Westminster Abbey. It is a part of the coronation chair in which every English king since that time has been crowned, including the present monarch George VI.

Of the stone Gayer asserts, "There is the strongest reason for believing that this ancient Stone in the Abbey is the identical Stone, chosen by Jacob for his pillow, on the night of his wonderful vision in Luz or Bethel, and which he next morning set up and anointed with oil, vowing to Jehovah that this 'stone which I have set up for a pillar shall be God's house'" (Gen. 28:22).[17]

There has been much controversy about the Coronation stone or Stone of Destiny, as the Anglo-Israelites call it. It measures 26 x 16¾ x 10½ inches and is of a kind said by some to be found nowhere else except near Luz in Palestine. Others say it is a red sandstone commonly found in Scotland and bears no likeness to the stone found in the vicinity of ancient Bethel. Where lies the truth? Fortunately for present purposes it does not matter. We are only setting forth the belief of Anglo-Israel. They believe it to be Jacob's stone, and that it links the royal house to ancient Israel, and so fulfills prophecy.[18]

Thus far only two of the twelve tribes have reached "the isles," but the prophecies were made to all-Israel. What of the remaining tribes? Theirs is the story of the eastern migration.

The eastern movement began voluntarily at an early date. Already in the time of Solomon, "Under the protection of Israel's flag numbers of citizens were traveling and settling far beyond the geographical limits of Solomon's kingdom. Solomon's navy, sailing the seas to the Indian Ocean on the east and to the Atlantic on the west, doubtless carried many colonizing parties on their lengthy

---

[17] *Id.,* p. 108.
[18] For a discussion of the Coronation stone see *Encyclopaedia Britannica,* 14th ed., Vol. 12, p. 358.

voyages. Migration was continuous, especially towards the east and north." [19]

Chronicles 5:10–22 mentions a migration of 44,000 fighting men toward the Euphrates, accompanied by their families. Colonies known as Saccae, which Anglo-Israelites declare means sons of Isaac, were scattered from the Black Sea to the Persian Gulf, all voluntary migrants. Then came the fall of Samaria at the hands of the Assyrians, who carried away captive unknown numbers of Israelites. The ten tribes passed from history. Goard, a noted Anglo-Israelite authority, says that the remnant that remained in the Northern Kingdom were simply carried over "to join the greater number of Israelitish stock already in the country of their adoption." [20]

Those forcibly carried away were called the Kumri, from Omri, the name of the captured king. This is said to be the same as the later "Cymri." Afterwards the captive peoples and the whole of Migrant Israel came to be called the People of Guta, from the ancient name of Assyria, "Gutium." The long trek had begun which was to bring them ultimately to "the Isles," or present-day Britain.

The remaining two tribes, Judah and Benjamin, or Southern Israel, maintained their national life a little longer, but at last they fell before the Babylonians, and great numbers of them were carried into captivity. After Babylonia fell to the Persians, permission was given to the captives to return, but only 43,000 availed themselves of the opportunity. These rebuilt the temple and set up once again a kind of national existence, but always as vassals of a more powerful state, first the Persians, then the Greeks and finally the Romans. These were the Jews and are to be sharply distinguished from Israel as we shall see a little later. Most of the tribes of Judah and Benjamin remained in Babylonia, or were dispersed throughout the Persian Empire, "more as colonists than as captives." But Judah had already long since been established in Britain through the Zarah line, and the House of David was soon to be transplanted to "the Isles" to become the ancestors of those who were to rule all Israel, when once again they should reach the land toward which they were slowly and painfully moving from the East. As a matter of fact, shortly after the fall of Samaria, Sennecharib had carried away some 200,000 men of Judah, who had joined the other migrating sons

19 Quoted by Gayer, p. 58.
20 Quoted by Gayer, pp. 58–59.

of Israel, and were later to enter England possibly as the Jutes, at any rate Jutes sounds not unlike Judah.[21]

Meanwhile, Israel is said to have escaped from the Assyrian Babylonian Empire, through the Caucasus, into what are known as the Scythian Steppes. Remains are said to be found in the Crimea, which may itself be a variant of Cymri. The Ephraem-Manasseh tribes went to the Danube, known as the Getae; Dan was known as Thyssa—Getae, and the other seven tribes the Massagetae. The latter aided the Persians in their attack on Babylonia and were besought by Daniel to return to the worship of Jehovah, but they refused. Later they were driven west by the Persians into the region of the Don and Dneiper, in the regions of Asgard.

Here is an interesting joining of the Hebrew prophecy and ancient Norse mythology. Asgard is, in Norse mythology, the home of the Gods, similar to the Greek Mount Olympus. These Massagetae became Norsemen or Northmen. Odin, the chief of the Norse gods becomes their king. They are now called Asar. As in the word Israel one finds the name of their god El, so also is it found in Asar, "As" meaning "God," just as "An" in Getic means Divinity, and appears in the word Angles, the name of a people who together with the Saccae or Saxons invaded England later.

Odin is said to have introduced a new religion, "which," says Gayer, "included the Fatherhood of God, the immortality of the Soul, future rewards and punishments, etc. . . . not the barbarous religion depicted by the Romans and our histories . . . it weaned the Massagetae from their gross idolatries and drew them away from heathenism to a higher, nobler civilization." [22]

With his people Odin migrated to Scandinavia. From him descended the kings of Denmark, and through them Queen Alexandra. The Israel tribes thus entered Britain as Anglo-Saxons, Celts, Jutes, Danes, etc. The Welsh were the Cymri.

The Getae, i.e., Ephraem-Manasseh, became the Goths. They were converted to Christianity by Ulfilas, the Arian, and became "the most tolerant of all religionists." They played an important role in the history of Europe, participating in the invasion of the Roman Empire but, eventually defeated, they fled into Scandinavia, and the name Goths disappears. But they reappear at a later time as the Northmen or the Normans. They came out of Norway once

---

[21] *Id.*, pp. 60-61.   [22] *Id.*, p. 92.

more, are said to have captured Constantinople in 911 A.D. and 941, and to have found a firm footing in France, whence in 1066 they entered England under William the Conqueror, helped undoubtedly, "by the kinship of Normans, Danes and English." [23] Thus was fulfilled the prophecy of the coming of the tribes of Israel to the "Appointed Place" 2 Sam. 7:10. The number was complete. All the tribes were there, and the throne of David was still established.

This is the belief of Anglo-Israelites. There is an extensive literature which attempts to prove all their claims. Many people have been convinced by these writings. The one major evidence of these complicated movements of peoples seems to be the similarity of sound or root of names, places, rivers, and persons to Hebrew names. Is this a dependable method? Though utterly unconvinced, personally, the author nevertheless leaves any attempt to confirm or refute their theories to abler linguistic and historical specialists. He is concerned, rather, only with the fact that very large numbers of people do so believe, and that this belief is tied up intimately with their religious faith. What practical consequences might such a faith have for human relations?

What, for example, of the tying in of America with British-Israel as the Manasseh tribe? Just how America comes to be Manasseh does not seem clear. That, of course, the English or Anglo-Saxon element in America has been and is dominant can hardly be disputed, and if the Anglo-Saxon people are Israel then a large part of the American people and perhaps the American nation may share whatever responsibilities and benefits grow out of their identification with Israel. But why Manasseh? A sample of the evidence is this.[24] Manasseh was the thirteenth tribe. Now note how often the number thirteen appears in our national flag and seal: there were thirteen original colonies; thirteen stars and strips on the flag; there are thirteen stars in the glory cloud of the official seal; thirteen bars in the escutcheon on the breast of the eagle; thirteen letters in "E pluribus unum." The eagle holds an olive branch in one talon, a symbol of Ephraem—but why not Manasseh? In the other talon he holds thirteen arrows.

In the earlier days there was no mention of America. It was British-Israel, not Anglo-Saxon Israel. The words "Britain" and

[23] *Id.*, p. 103.
[24] See chart accompanying Gayer, *The Heritage of the Anglo-Saxon Race*, Destiny Publishers, Haverhill, Massachusetts, 3rd ed., 1941.

"British" are said to be Hebrew derivatives. British comes from, "Berith"-covenant and "ish"-man and means, therefore Covenant-man. "Ain"-country. Britain, therefore, is country of the Covenant. It was natural, however, that persons of British descent should want to be counted in on the benefits. So the concept had to be broadened. As to the practical effects, it would certainly mean that America would be tied in more closely to the British Empire, for in Britain is found not alone the people, Israel, but the royal house of David, which is to endure forever. The practical effect would be to cement with religion, and all the emotional drive which it affords, the solidarity of Britain and America. Certainly fellow Israelites in America will feel impelled to keep alive the British Empire, for it is clearly of God. It must endure forever. Writes one British Israelite, "In due time Manasseh and Ephraem will be joined, because Manasseh must return to Israel." [25]

An interesting complication arises in respect to Manasseh, according to the writer just quoted, for he distinguishes an East and a West Manasseh who were divided by the Jordan. The Eastern group, according to the studies of Odlum, went eastward as far as Japan, where it is alleged, there are found many names that are Hebrew in sound and meaning. The "ruling families of the White Japanese—the Samurai are our own people of Joseph's seed who took their names from Samaria" the capital of Northern Israel. He points out many similarities between the two island empires, among them the fact that Shinto is monotheistic and very similar to the religion of the Jews (one wonders where he got his knowledge of Shinto). Thus America shares with Japan her identification with Manasseh. All this was of course written before Pearl Harbor.

But a much more important question is, what are the implications for the Jews, the people ordinarily supposed to be of the seed of Israel? Are Britons Jews? By no means! The Anglo-Saxons are Israel not Judah, and therefore not Jews. No distinction is more sharply drawn than that between Israel and the Jews. Some Jews are, to be sure, Israelites, but not all Israelites are Jews. At great length it is explained that the Jews are descended from Judah alone— as the similiarity of sound of their names makes clear. Abraham, Isaac, and Jacob cannot rightly be referred to as Jews. Fully five-sixths of the Bible was written to Israel—not Judah, and that portion

[25] E. Odlum, *God's Covenant Man*, p. 21.

directed to Judah was addressed "to literal men and women of Judah." Out of Judah came David and the throne that was to endure forever, upon which today sits the British sovereign. Many of the tribe of Judah refused to return from the captivity and ultimately reached "the isles" as part of all Israel, but those who lived on in Palestine became the Jews. "That they would always be a marked race was foretold in the Bible. That the prophecies regarding Judah have been amply verified, no one can deny." [26]

Are the Anglo-Israelites therefore anti-Semitic? I asked that question of certain present day American leaders of the movement. "Of course not," they replied, "for are we not Semites, all of us of the Anglo-Saxon world?"

"Well, then, are you anti-Jewish?" I countered.

"No," they answered, "we are not against any race or people. We are against those who defy the Constitution of the United States, of whatever race."

Interesting light is thrown on the question by a pamphlet, *"The Bible Answers the Race Question."* It begins by establishing the fact that there is a great difference between races, and refutes the argument that races appear to be inferior only because being in the minority they are therefore denied equal opportunity of development. Africans, Haitians, and others are cited as examples. Since all races are equal in origin, and therefore have an equal start, their differences must be due either to some special gift of God or else He has established and confirmed differences in races, or the difference lies in race itself. The fact that the Nazis overdid race differences does not invalidate the fact of difference. The author of the pamphlet goes on to assert that intermarriage of disparate races has evil results and weakens the race. He quotes various authors to show definite mental differences between races.

If races are different can we treat all alike? He asks. The reply is that all must of course have equal justice, but, is the same treatment just for all races. He defends the poll tax in the South, "it simply rules out those who have not sufficient foresight to plan two or three months ahead. They should be ruled out . . . it would be a crime to repeal or otherwise destroy the poll-tax law." [27]

Concerning education the pamphlet acknowledges that in the

[26] Gayer, *op. cit.*, p. 15.
[27] *The Bible Answers the Race Question*, published by the Kingdom Gospel Institute, Chicago, Illinois, 1945, p. 14.

South not all are given equal facilities, but declares that economic conditions in the South are such that they cannot give equal opportunity to all. It is logical, therefore, that this greater opportunity be given to those capable of profiting by it, the white people, of course. The Biblical curse upon Ham is defended, and the care of Abraham, Isaac and Jacob to maintain the purity of the race is applauded.

"The equality of men and races is in Christ. When one is a Christian all racial lines cease to exist (Are not Negroes in the South supposed to be Christians?), but "it does not mean that in the physical realm we should run over the boundaries God has fixed." [28]

Specifically concerning anti-Semitism, it aserts that all Anglo-Saxons are Semites and that there is no anti-Semitism in their teaching. The Jews, it is asserted, are not all seeking to establish dictatorships, but many subversives hide behind the smoke screen of anti-Semitism. According to Mt. 27:25 the Jews pronounced a curse upon themselves ("his blood be upon us and our children") and until they repudiate that action and acknowledge the Son of God as their Messiah and Savior there is nothing that any man can do materially to better their condition. "It is in God's hands." [29]

Let the reader make up his own mind whether on the basis of this summary, they are, or are not, anti-Semitic.

That they are so regarded by others is abundantly clear.

Dr. Harold W. Ruopp in a paper on *Organizations That Build Prejudice*, presented at the Chicago Conference on Home Front Unity,[30] says of the Anglo-Saxon Federation in part, "This group is the American counterpart of the British Israelites, well known for their Nazi ideologies. It hides behind the respectability of the word 'religion' and is pseudo-religious in character. It has printed and exploited Hitler-loving George Mosely's vicious articles on the Jews and has printed and distributed many other anti-Semitic pieces. . . .

"This organization, through its magazine, uses religion to cover up its spread of the poison of disruption. It preaches under various cloaks the right to rule of a 'master race,' disunity, chaos, intolerance, and bigotry."

[28] The extreme rarity of any outstanding success among those with no white blood is noted, *id.*, pp. 20–21.
[29] *Id.*, p. 22.
[30] May–June, 1945. Published by Mayor's Committee on Race Relations, 134 N. LaSalle Street, Chicago, pp. 18–21.

In their literature the obligation of Israel as the Servant of Jehovah is insisted upon. The fact that 90 per cent of Protestants are of the Anglo-Saxon peoples is held as proof of the theory that they are Israel. "That thou mayest be my salvation unto the ends of the earth" (Is. 49:6). If one could always be sure that Israel would operate thus! But also it is said, "Thou Israel art My battle-axe and weapons of war; for with thee shall I break in pieces the nations and with thee shall I destroy Kingdoms" (Jer. 51:20). Which shall it be? Recent history is likely to convince most people that the whole idea of a uniquely chosen race is a danger to the rest of the world!

Chapter Twelve

The Oxford Group Movement

Religion at a house party! That is news. Indeed, it was news that was spread far and wide through the national press when word of Frank Buchman's earliest house parties first got about. Somehow religion and house parties did not quite seem to belong together, yet here was a man who was choosing the house party as his method of reaching and changing men's lives.

Buchmanism, otherwise known as the Oxford Group Movement, or sometimes in this country as the First Christian Century Fellowship, is no different theologically or in its ethical teaching from what is ordinarily found in the Evangelical Christian churches. Indeed, Sam Shoemaker, an Episcopalian rector who was for many years identified with the movement, says specifically, there is nothing new "in the Oxford Group Movement—it only believes what the Church believes, is only re-emphasizing the inwardness of the Church's message, and only does what the Church does at its best. It is simply the Church at work in the lives of individuals. I emphatically say the Group is the Church on the march, and that every church should be a Group." [1]

What distinguishes it is its method of work and the degree of emphasis upon certain points of belief and practice. One does not have to leave his own church to become a member of the Oxford Group Movement. Rather it was an attempt to intensify religious devotion and to make it function within the church. Perhaps the most insistent emphasis of the movement has been its emphasis upon what used to be called "personal work," that is, the winning of individual souls.

[1] Samuel M. Shoemaker, *Conversion of the Church*, Fleming H. Revell, New York, 1932, p. 7.

About this there is, of course, nothing new. In every evangelistic campaign conducted within the Christian church this has been emphasized. But it was almost always associated with a special evangelistic effort and generally made part of a completely planned campaign, with much publicity and an appeal to the masses by an evangelist from the platform. In the Oxford Group Movement it is a constant. It goes on all year, every day, sometimes in connection with church, more often without any special relation to public services.

The Oxford Groupers, as they are called, are men and women who have themselves been "changed." The old word was conversion. A first evidence of the change that has been wrought in their own lives is the eager desire themselves to change the lives of others. They are supposed to become what they have often been called, *life-changers*.

It all began when Frank Buchman, a graduate of a Lutheran Theological Seminary, went one day into a small church in an English village and heard a simple sermon which deeply moved him. He had entered the little church, he later related, "with a divided will, nursing pride, selfishness, ill will, which prevented me from functioning as a Christian minister should. The woman's simple truth personalized the Cross for me that day and suddenly I had a poignant vision of the Crucified. There was infinite suffering on the face of the Master and I realized for the first time the great abyss separating myself from Him. That was all, but it produced in me a vibrant feeling as though a strong current of life had suddenly been poured into me and afterwards a dazed sense of a great spiritual shaking up. There was no longer the feeling of a divided will, no sense of calculation or argument, of oppression and helplessness; a wave of strong emotion following the will to surrender rose up within me from the depths of an estranged spiritual life and seemed to lift my soul from its anchorage of selfishness, bearing it across that great sundering abyss to the foot of the Cross." [2] This experience marks an epoch in Buchman's life.

After graduating from the seminary he had taken a small church in Philadelphia and made a success of it. Out of his work there had grown a settlement house in which he ministered particularly to the young men of the community. A disagreement with his board of trustees led him to sever his relations with the settlement, and he

[2] A. J. Russell, *For Sinners Only*, Harper and Brothers, New York, 1932, p. 43.

had gone to England for a period. There he had the spiritual experience already related. He had felt resentful of the committee's action and had been uneasy about it. He now saw that he must rid himself of this feeling of resentment, so sat down and wrote to each of the board individually, saying that he had nursed ill will against them, was sorry, and asked their forgiveness. As a result he at once experienced a sense of spiritual release. The note of restitution, in so far as humanly possible, was to be a matter of great emphasis in his teachings ever afterward. He at once felt a keen desire to share with others the joy that his experience had brought him, and that has ever since been the earmark of a member of the Oxford Group Movement. Sharing is a central principle for them. From that time until this, Frank Buchman has never ceased to seek out individual persons and share with them his Christian experience. With him it became a passion to win men to Christ, to change their lives, and make of them in their turn life-changers.

Buchman served for some years as a YMCA secretary on a college campus where he was noted for his individual approach to men. Later he went to the Orient with Sherwood Eddy on one of his evangelistic campaigns. It was in China, to which he had returned at a later date, in 1918, that the first house party was held. This was to be his method all through the years to the present day.

The house-party technique, while it seems strange at first, has a definite underlying philosophy. In the first place it separates men for a time from their regular pursuits so that they have time to consider religion and their own particular religious experience. Second, it provides an informal setting, over against the formality of church and public services. Third, it provides an opportunity for more intimate and prolonged fellowship between individuals and small groups than is possible in the formal setting of a church. Fourth, and perhaps more important than all the rest, it somehow brings religion into contact with the common life, brings it down to the level at which men live from day to day. There seems ordinarily to be a certain restraint among men in talking about religion. In the setting of a house party it seems perfectly natural, since religion is a central theme of the gathering, to talk about it freely and frankly without the usual inhibitions.

The method has proved most effective. Because house parties are ordinarily associated with people of leisure or privileged position, it is generally regarded as a technique designed to reach that class rather than humbler folk, and such has actually been the case; although it is strongly stressed among Groupers themselves that in a house party there are no distinctions of class or race or creed. A recent study made of a considerable number of members of the group at an earlier date, revealed that the median family income had been between five and ten thousand dollars, with 28 per cent of the group having an income of more than ten thousand dollars a year. That income twenty years ago was quite substantial. It is still probably true that a larger percentage of those attracted to the movement are from the more comfortable income groups, but not so large as in an earlier day.

What goes on at a house party? Well, there are meetings, to be sure, held usually in the living room of the home or ballroom of the hotel in which the group happens to be staying. In these meetings talks are made upon life-changing, and the principles that underlie the movement generally; but, most of all, opportunity is provided for public testimony as to what Christ has done for the individual who testifies. Testimony, or witnessing, is a highly important feature of their faith. Besides the public meetings there are intimate talks between persons attending. Some have already experienced the change and are glad to share with those who are interested the experience that they themselves have had. Or, burdened by a sense of guilt, an individual wants to talk to somebody and make a confession. Many of the confessions are made not to the whole group but to other individuals of the group. This is one of the main contributions which the house party makes. Often men find their lives changed as a result of these personal confessions.

It would be a mistake to suppose that house parties are solemn and entirely austere gatherings. On the other hand, every effort is made to make them joyous and full of fun. There is always recreation. There are always games. There are books to be read. There are things to be done together in which the various persons participate. The common meal is often a time of hilarity and genuine fun. Through this it becomes apparent, very much to the surprise of some who have met it for the first time, that religion is a thing of joy and good fellowship. That this is so makes a great appeal to many who have felt that religion was a wet blanket, merely a matter of inhibitions and negatives. But another constant feature of the house party is the quiet time, or the quiet hour. Opportunity is provided for each individual to be alone, and he is encouraged to keep, preferably early in the morning, a period of private study, meditation and prayer. In this period comes, as they think, direct guidance from the Holy Spirit. The practice is to sit quietly after Bible reading and prayer and to note down on a piece of paper the impressions that come. They call it guidance, and what one is guided to do through this experience often determines what he is to do during the day.

At the Kuling houseparty were two Anglican bishops. One of them, Bishop Roots, was to become a leading member of the group and to die, finally, during a house party at the precise moment that a wedding was being performed in a room below. Both bishops had sons at Cambridge University, in England, about whom they were greatly concerned religiously. Frank Buchman visited these young men on his return to England and, learning of the religious conditions among university undergraduates, determined to do something about it. In the summer of 1921 he held a house party for Oxford and Cambridge men. Here students from both schools were changed. Three of these went with him to Oxford which became the center of the slowly growing movement, and eventually gave it its name.

Undergraduates, who in the aftermath of the war had grown cynical and disillusioned, and had given up all religious convictions and associations, were drawn into the movement. Lives were changed, largely as a result of the testimonies of men who had experienced the change and had found a new joy and purpose in life. They talked of religion naturally and easily in the little informal groups that met together, not of religion in general or as a problem or as a phenomenon, but in terms intensely personal. Each man who found the new life was expected to share it, and he did so. Buchman always emphasized this. One found his own experience of God deepened as he shared it with another. Some of the leading ministers in Oxford churches were caught up in the movement and made effective use of group methods in their own churches as well as with students. University deans and professors were gradually won, and were quick to speak in favor of the movement when it was attacked, as it certainly was. It was a great moment for the Group when the great scholar B. H. Streeter, who was Provost of Queen's College, stood up one evening in the Group meeting to declare: "I have been watching this Movement more particularly during the last two years and a half. Hitherto my attitude towards it has been what diplomatists call 'a benevolent neutrality.' . . . It is my duty to associate myself with a Movement which seems to have got on to the secret of giving well-meaning people new hope, and new courage, and also of increasing their number and power. You cannot reform the world merely by improved social machinery; you must first reform the men who will work the machine." [3] Much earlier Dr. Grensted, Professor of Philosophy of Religion, had lent it his wholehearted support and travelled with teams who were carrying their witness to distant places.

From Oxford the movement spread in many directions. Students who had been changed went out to carry the Group message into every part of England and even into foreign lands. In 1927 fifteen Oxford students were on a team that carried the movement to Holland. A year later, invited by a Rhodes scholar from South Africa, a team of seven spent several months in various South African centers. Everywhere lives were changed and groups formed to carry on the witness.

Frank Buchman believed in teamwork. The work was largely for individuals by individuals, but a team made an impact on a community that an individual could not easily make. Public witnessing of the Group aroused interest, set people thinking. The variety of witnesses made the appeal wider. Left completely unmoved by the witness of a dozen other persons an individual might be deeply challenged by the testimony of the thirteenth witness and yield his life to Christ—be "changed."

A strange and valuable feature of these witnessing teams was that they were for the most part made up of non-professionals, laymen with a passion for Christ, who volunteered their services, received no compensation for it and often enough paid their own expenses.

No salaries are paid in this movement. Buchman has never had a salary nor have his workers. They have operated on a "faith" basis. Money has usually come, sometimes in very substantial amounts, but also there have been times when the margin was too low for comfort. But they have gone on, and somehow the needs are met. That its appeal has been, to a considerable degree, to people of more than average income whose gratitude has been stirred by what the movement has done for them, is perhaps the secret of its generous support. Its house parties have often been held in homes of wealth

[3] Quoted by R. H. Murray, *Group Movement Throughout the Ages,* Hodder & Stoughton, London, 1936, pp. 337–339, *passim.*

amid rich surroundings, or in country clubs, or big expensive hotels. People have been impressed by the seeming prosperity of the movement. It is nevertheless a "faith"-supported movement. It has sometimes been called a movement to the "up and outers" instead of "down and outers." In a sense this is true. Compare the message of Buchman with that one hears in the mission halls on the Bowery or South State street and it is not very different. Man has sinned. He needs salvation. Christ is man's savior. In surrender to him lies the way out of the old life into a new one of peace, joy, satisfaction.

Nor is the method so different. At a house party there are talks to the group, but the most effective part of both is the personal testimony of men who have been changed. Opportunity is given for decision—the methods differ of course—and the first requirement upon both is that they share with others what they have found. Both stress "personal work," not only as a duty, but as a means of deepening one's own experience.

Naturally to appeal to the "up and outer" one must go where he is likely to be found and adapt the precise method to the situation. This Buchman and his followers have learned to do.

All during the late twenties and early thirties the movement continued to grow. In 1931 seven hundred attended the Oxford house party. In 1935 ten thousand attended. Teams visited the United States, Canada, India, China, South America, pretty much the whole world. Many men in public life came under its influence, members of Parliament, ministers of state, public officials, great industrialists, journalists, educators. Its influence was steadily growing. Individual men of great influence were being won and their experience of a new birth was beginning to affect the way in which they carried out their public duties.

A criticism often voiced in the earlier days of the movement was that it was lacking in social vision; that it was merely a carry over, in a new setting, of the old emphasis on individual salvation. It had remained essentially true to a principle enunciated by F.B., or Frank, as his followers like to call him, in his earlier days, before there was anything like a movement in existence. He wrote: "This principle of personal evangelism is the essential of Christianity and the absolute essential of all progress. The depersonalization of all activity is one of the great problems of our day. In business, education, and in every mission activity we must return to the fundamental principle of Christ as a constant and get into touch with men individually." [4]

To get proper social relations, proper government, proper use of economic goods, it is necessary to get good men. If only men in strategic positions of influence and power could be brought to surrender their lives to Christ the consequences would be incalculable. The shadows in Europe in the middle thirties were deepening. Mussolini, Hitler, Franco were rising to power, and threatening the peace of the world. At one time Buchman is reported to have said if he could but "change" the lives of four men, political leaders of great states, there would be no fear of war in Europe. He undoubtedly believed just that. To many that represents a definite over-simplification of a very complex problem. Not a few felt that there was a lack of sensitivity in Buchman to the enormity of the crimes that Facism in Germany was committing. A reported saying of Buchman concerning Hitler was later to react rather disastrously upon the movement. Whether he ever said just what he is quoted as saying may be open to doubt. There can be no doubt that the belief that he did say it had the practical effect of bringing both Buchman himself and the movement into bad repute. Reported as having been uttered in 1937, it was in the years of mounting fear of war and war hysteria that it bore its greatest fruit and caused a decided recession in the public acceptance of the group. Here is his statement:

"I thank heaven for a man like Adolf Hitler who built a first line of defense against the Anti-Christ of Communism. . . . Think what it would mean to the world if Hitler surrendered to God. . . . Through such a man God could control a nation overnight and solve every last bewildering problem." [5] As late as 1943 this was still being quoted as indicating possible Fascist sympathies of the movement. The circumstance that gave rise to the article from which the quotation is taken was the unsuccessful attempt to secure deferment from military service for Group members who were engaged in morale-building efforts during war-time.

One distinguished statesman, president of the Norwegian Parliament, came under Buchman's influence at a meeting in Geneva at which a number of delegates to the League of Nations were present,

[4] Quoted by John McCook Roots, *Atlantic Monthly* article *An Apostle to Youth*, December 1928, republished in pamphlet form, p. 10.

[5] *Time*, Vol. 41, January 18, 1943, p. 65.

and was changed. He served more than once as member of a Group team, speaking once to more than a hundred members of Parliament in a committee room of the House of Commons in London. It was he who invited the Group to come to Norway where it scored perhaps its most notable success. All Norway was aware of it. Thirteen hundred attended the great house party just outside of Bergen where one hundred and twenty-five had been expected. One of those who was won was Freddie Ramm, who was later to die in a concentration camp in Germany because of his loyalty to conviction. He is one of the Group's heroes, universally loved and honored. Hambro said of it: "What is happening all over Norway is truly a miracle." Groupers believe that it was, in part, the result of their impact on Norwegian life that produced the courage and morale manifested later by Ramm, Bishop Bergraev and hosts of other ordinary citizens of Norway.

Teams covered also Denmark, Finland, Latvia, France, Switzerland and countries of Asia. It had become truly world-wide in its influence.

Sometime in 1937 or 1938 the movement began to use the term *Moral Re-Armament*. A speech delivered by Frank Buchman in London in 1938 launched a new world program of Moral Re-Armament, or M.R.A. He said in part: "The world's condition cannot but cause disquiet and anxiety. Hostility piles up between nation and nation, labor and capital, class and class. The cost of bitterness and fear mounts daily. . . . Is there a remedy that will cure the individual and the nation and give the hope of a speedy and satisfactory recovery? . . . The crisis is fundamentally a moral one. The nations must re-arm morally. Moral recovery is the forerunner of economic recovery. . . . We need a power strong enough to change human nature and build bridges between man and man, faction and faction. . . . God alone can change human nature." [6]

Since that time the name of the movement itself has become Moral Re-Armament. Not that there has been a legal change of name. After much legal trouble the name Oxford Group Movement had been legitimatized. It is not likely to be given up. But in the press, everywhere M.R.A. seems now to be the designation most used.

Whether consciously or not the movement has become more

---

[6] *Remaking the World*, abridged ed. Moral Re-Armament, Washington, D. C., 1945, p. 18.

socially oriented. It still talks of changing individual lives, and still employs all the old Group techniques, but the individual is thought of less as an end in himself. There is a definite attack upon economic and social problems, but it is through changing individuals. Individuals are made much more conscious, in recent years, of the obligations which a changed life has for the total social body. At least it seems so to the writer on the basis of comparative reading in the earlier and later literature of the movement.

At the Oxford house party as early as 1934 F.B. described the Oxford Group as a Christian revolution. "It's aim is a new social order under the dictatorship of the Spirit of God making for better human relationships, for unselfish cooperation, for cleaner business, cleaner politics, for the elimination of political, industrial and racial antagonism." [7]

In London the old Clive house on Berkeley Square, home for generations of Lord Clive of India and his descendants, was put up for sale. It was purchased by M.R.A. and became headquarters of the movement. All during the war it performed a varied ministry. Meeting place of statesmen from various countries, representatives of labor and management, of rich and poor, it has been a center for the building of mutual understanding between men who represent opposite points of view on vital questions. M.R.A. writers tell of problems of national and even international importance solved because men on both sides have been "changed."

But under war-time conditions troubles occurred. Some of Buchman's earlier statements about Hitler and other dictators arose to embarrass the movement. The attempt to get deferment for M.R.A. workers from military service aroused popular reaction against it and failed. In both Europe and America there was a recession of interest in it. It drops almost entirely out of the magazines from 1939 on. In 1941 *Time* and *Newsweek* carried stories of the "recent disastrous decline" in both America and Britain. The headquarters in America had been for some years in the parish house of Samuel Shoemaker's Calvary Episcopal Church but, for reasons never fully stated, Shoemaker broke with the movement in 1941 and it sought sanctuary elsewhere. It was in Washington, D. C., until recently when it was transferred to Los Angeles, California. Since 1945 it has published a small monthly magazine *New World*

[7] Quoted by R. H. Murray, *op. cit.*, p. 336.

News in which appears news of what the movement is doing around the world. It was suggested by *Newsweek* that Shoemaker's break was because "he resented a Buchman tendency to assume authority instead of letting converts run their lives by the old Oxford Group method of listening for direct orders from God." [8]

Shoemaker's own statement in a letter dated November 1, 1941 and directed to his parishioners seems to indicate that it was a change in respect to the Group's relationship to the church. "When the Oxford Group was by its own definition," he writes, "a movement of vital personal religious working force today, we fully identified ourselves with it. Certain policies and points of view, however, have arisen in the development of Moral Re-Armament about which we have had increasing misgivings."

The life-changing principles of the movement he still uses and will continue to use, for they are, he considers, as quoted above, essential elements in the propagation of the Christian faith.

In England bitter attacks upon the movement were made in open Parliament sessions, one going so far as to impugn the "absolute honesty" of the founder, Frank Buchman, and to ridicule the claims of the movement to having settled important labor troubles by the methods of the Group. Rather, said a member of Parliament, they had been solved by "sordid means like better pay and better hours." This will seem an unfair statement to many who know that often enough the better wages and better hours came precisely because the men who were doing the bargaining had been sensitized to the needs of labor by the moral and spiritual change they had undergone under Group influence.

As a matter of fact in recent years great attention has been given to the solution of industrial conflicts, through the method of changing the lives of men in the labor and management group who have to make decisions in the conflict. There are not a few well-known labor leaders now who have become members of M.R.A. Likewise a considerable number of influential industrialists have experienced the change under the influence of the movement. These leaders are brought into close personal fellowship through the medium of the house party. Here they learn to know each other as men, and come to have a respect and affection for each other. When they come into conference, therefore, over points in dispute

[8] Vol. 18, November 24, 1941, p. 65.

between the bodies they represent, they do not come as sworn enemies but friends who have learned to know and to trust each other.

Quite recently M.R.A. was given Island House, a large hotel at Mackinac Island, and there during the summers have held continuous house parties from the beginning until well after the close of the normal vacation season. When the hotel came to the movement it was old and dilapidated, and had fallen into bad disrepair. Members of the Group undertook by volunteer labor to rehabilitate the place. They painted it, repaired broken windows, gave it a thorough overhauling, then moved in. All the work of maintenance, care of rooms, cooking, setting tables, in fact all the work is shared without remuneration by members of the Group. It is a salutary experience when it becomes the turn of a powerful industrialist and a union head to dry the dishes together after a common meal.

People come from all over the world but chiefly from the United States to this great house party. Over 2,000 were in attendance during the past season. There is no fixed charge for accommodation. One may pay much or little as he is guided and, of course, everyone shares in the work.

During the war years the movement went all out in support of the war effort. Pacifist Christians may wonder if they got divine guidance to do this, but evidently they thought they had. Their means of helping the effort was made in two directions, one, in stimulating the growth of productivity in industry, and two, that of building general morale among the people. The method devised for doing it was chiefly through the use of the drama. At the house party dramas were planned, written, and staged, then later, after continual criticism and overhauling, were put on the road, going from city to city wherever invited, carrying their religion and influence. This would seem to be somewhat of a letdown from the more distinctive religious emphasis of an earlier day, but in conversation with participants in some of the efforts, the writer was assured that there is still the same emphasis upon the necessity of changing lives and that the whole project is carried out very much in the spirit of the earlier specifically religious effort. No one is paid for his services. The Group relies for support on whatever funds may be forthcoming from the city where their plays are put on. No admission charge is ever made. Often the play may be given in public schools or municipal auditoriums or churches, indeed wherever opportunity is afforded.

There can be little doubt of the benefit that may be derived by those who participate in the planning, building and staging of these dramas, especially when it is carried out in an atmosphere created by the central Group emphasis of changed lives, joint sharing, and upon the four absolutes which are central to the Group teaching.

One of the most remarkable features of house parties in recent years has been the presence of a number of juveniles in attendance. They too have worked out dramas and staged them and put them on all across the country. Remarkable testimonials are forthcoming as to the effectiveness of the plays put on by these young people in creating a better spirit among the youth in the cities where they have appeared.

These activities seem likely to go on. What new directions the movement may take now that the war period is past it is to early to say. Frank Buchman grows old. He travels less than formerly and spends more time at the London headquarters, but his faith in the principles with which he began the movement is apparently unshaken. He persistently calls upon the men of the movement to carry out with increasing faithfulness the tried and proven principles upon which he has so successfully operated.

What in detail are these principles? First of all let it be noted again that the movement holds no specific theological positions that differ from those found in the churches. People of all denominations, even Catholics, have been caught up into the movement. Some are of liberal theological outlook, some conservative. It would probably be true to say that more are conservative than otherwise. But theology has not been the primary concern of the group. If some very fundamentalist people have found themselves at home within it so also did Bernard H. Streeter, great, liberal Biblical scholar of Oxford.

Four absolutes are insisted upon by the movement as an ideal: absolute honesty, absolute purity, absolute unselfishness, and absolute love. With these theology has little to do. Each Grouper who surrenders his life to Christ seeks constantly the realization of these absolutes, and is always checking his performance against the ideal. There are likewise four requisites for the attainment of these absolutes. These are sharing, surrender, restitution and guidance.

The principle of sharing has some very farreaching applications. They distinguish two specific bases of sharing, one, sharing for confession, the other, sharing for witness. A basic presupposition underlying the whole thought and method is man's sinfulness and his need of redemption, or of "change," as they like to call it. A primary requirement upon one who is guilty of sin is confession, and in the Oxford Groups this confession is neither to a priest, as in the Catholic church, that is, to one who can pronounce absolution, nor is it alone confession in secret to God, but confession before man. This need not be public confession in a meeting. It may be only confession to a friend, or to some other individual. So long as sin goes unconfessed it festers and works havoc within the spiritual life of the individual. He cannot experience the joy and release that come through the sharing in confession of sin.

It was the nature of some of the public confessions made in the early student group meetings which brought heavy criticism upon Buchman and his movement. Some of the men felt impelled to confess their sex sins. The frank uninhibited confessions that were sometimes forthcoming in the informal student groups were shocking to outsiders, and led them to believe that there was an unhealthy sex emphasis in the movement. As to just what one should confess, and to whom one should confess, whether to an individual or at a public gathering, one must depend upon guidance. If one feels guided to confess publicly then there is nothing else to be done.

These public confessions of sin, which have sometimes been highly entertaining to the idle listener, have also sometimes had the moral effect of bringing a sense of guilt to other listeners, and, as a result of this guilt, a pronounced change in their whole lives. At all events, confession is an important feature of the Group's teaching.

The sharing for witness we have already said enough about. The testimony of what has been wrought in one's own life must be given, and such testimonials have been the chief means of interesting and ultimately changing the lives of innumerable persons who have listened to the testimonies. Again, besides the testimony in public, which, on occasion, may be called for, there is the other testimony not simply of good works which, of course, is a most effective testimony, but that of actively sharing with individuals whom one meets on the train, in hotels, and during recreation hours, or wherever he may be. That is a mark of a good Grouper. Naturally such witnessing has repelled some, but, as followed under "guidance," they think it is the most highly productive of all means of changing lives. It must not be sanctimoniously done, but when such sharing is the obvious outflow of a life that has been deeply and vitally affected by religious faith, it is undoubtedly one of the most effective ways in the world of reaching other people for Christ.

Surrender means the complete surrender of the will to Christ. They make no claim that this is easy. It may mean an entire change of one's whole life plan. It has meant just that for many of the Groupers. But it is necessary. So long as there are reserved areas in a man's life, they assert, he cannot expect to enter into a wholly satisfying experience of God. He will not achieve the four absolutes, surely, so long as his will is a divided one.

Restitution is an absolute requisite for spiritual growth. It is the practical test of one's sincerity. Frank Buchman felt it necessary to do his part in restoring the broken relationship with his former trustees by confessing his sense of resentment and seeking their forgiveness. A first step on the way to a changed life is the attempt to make restitution for the evil that has been committed. If one has stolen, he must restore to its owner what he took, or if this is impossible, say because of the death of the victim of his theft, he must dispossess himself of his ill-gotten gain in some way, giving it to charity or for some constructive purpose. If he has lied, he must undo the damage his lie has caused. One prominent student who had cheated his way through school felt he must confess it and refuse to take the degree thus falsely won. Sometimes this reaches far into one's past. F.B., himself, tells how, at his first house party, there came to him in his quiet time the memory of something he had done which by most people would have been considered quite harmless. But he felt that it must be confessed and restitution made. But he was leader of the house party. What would people think if he the leader should confess such a wrong? Nevertheless he felt it must be done, and that publicly. So at the first opportunity he did confess and declared his purpose to make necessary restitution. The effect of his confession was electric. In so far from bringing upon himself the adverse feeling of the Group, it started a chain of confessions and restitution that had farreaching consequences in the lives of many of those present and upon the future of the movement itself.[9]

---

[9] See A. J. Russell, *For Sinners Only*, pp. 99 ff.

After the visit of a Group team to any city there is usually a wave of gifts to some "conscience fund" through which persons are able to make deferred restitution, as a step toward a changed life.

Guidance is a basic feature of Group practice. It rests upon a confident belief that God has a plan for every life, and that God will speak to man and lend him guidance if man will but seek it. How is this done? Mainly through the "quiet time." If a man desires divine guidance he must take time and fulfill the conditions necessary for its reception. A primary requirement is that he have a special time for it, and that he listen as well as pray during that period. This is nothing new. The mystics have all taught and practiced it. Long before Buchman came along the "morning watch" had been taught and practiced by the leaders of the Student Christian Movements. But Buchman added one element which was not commonly advocated by them. One should go into a "quiet time" with a notebook and pencil and write down the guidance received. "The advantage of this," writes one Grouper, "is two-fold; it is an aid to concentration, and acts as a reminder of duties to be performed, and is of value in checking at the close of the day the thoughts received each morning and through the day." One should be alone. He should get into the position which for him "gives greatest relaxation of body and mind," and "cultivate stillness of the mind by an act of the will, thinking peaceful and restful thoughts. Have unhurried quiet and sense of leisure, avoiding all tenseness." Bible study is helpful, the reading of some great devotional passage, confession of sin, seeking of forgiveness, dedication of body and mind to God for the day, prayer, of course, and then *listening*. This is an important part of the procedure and the point at which failure is said most frequently to come. Men do not listen to God.

But guidance comes not only in the formal morning quiet times. It comes through "circumstances, through reason, through Church, Group or Fellowship." "Luminous thoughts," flashes of insight, may come unexpectedly at any moment. Often in the course of the day's work a Grouper will say when there is some problem to be solved, some decision to be made, "let us observe a 'quiet time' together and seek guidance." Then ensues a period of silence, prayer and listening and often guidance comes.

But how shall one know that it is God's guidance and not merely one's own judgment? The little pamphlet from which the above quotations came [10] suggests four tests.

1. Does it go counter to the highest standard or belief which we already possess?
2. Does it contradict the revelations which Christ has already made in or through the Bible?
3. Is it absolutely honest, pure, unselfish and loving?
4. Does it conflict with our duties and responsibilites to others?

The Group has practiced "guidance" from the first. Remarkable stories of special guidance are found in their literature. Frank Buchman has moved across the world, entered this country and that, sought out this individual or that, attempted this task or that, as he has felt guided. What happens when two persons get guidance that seems to be in conflict? There is more than a suggestion that some who have separated themselves from the movement have done so because their own guidance did not coincide with that of F.B., and who felt that there was a growing tendency on Buchman's part to assume authority rather than to allow others to be guided by the Group method of listening to God. If this is an actual fact, it is by no means the first time such a thing has occurred in history. Perhaps it may be said to be one of the dangers inherent in the belief that one is under direct guidance from God.

In the main, however, the method has been the chief one in the unfolding life of the movement. There are many within the great churches who are now stressing the necessity of *listening* as well as talking to God. Prayer is a two-way conversation, at its best, and he prays best who gives opportunity for God to speak to him. Probably the Group emphasis upon this has been one of its major contributions to the religious life of our time.

Absolute honesty, absolute purity, absolute unselfishness, absolute love! Who can attain to them? The Groupers would be the first to admit that they have not yet attained their goal, but they remined the world that Jesus long ago lifted up the standard of perfection, "Be ye perfect," or "ye shall be perfect as your Father in heaven is perfect."

We have not here indicated as in most of the chapters what are the beliefs of the Oxford Group Movement about God, salvation,

[10] *The Quiet Time*, n.d., no author, but published in England.

Jesus, the Bible, etc., because, as we have said before, they have no distinctive beliefs. They are a cross-section of Christianity, chiefly Protestant, to be sure, and believe as the rest of Christians do. It is their emphasis and primarily their method that sets them off as peculiar. Will they continue and grow? Or is it a passing phase of Christian history? Will the movement end, as has so often happened, as another sect? Some fear this. So far there has not developed much in the way of an institution. It has mainly been a fellowship. They have sought not to conflict with the church. They have met at hours other than those of regular public worship. They own little property—some indeed, but not much. There has developed as yet no set of paid workers who have vested rights they feel bound to perpetuate.

One cannot, of course, say with certainty what will happen when Frank Buchman passes from the scene. Already he is past the usual age of retirement. He suffered a heart attack in 1943. There are able men who have enlisted in the movement. There is obvious need for continued emphasis within the church upon a vital life-changing religious experience. If it does pass after a while, it is far more than probable that another such movement will arise to take its place in time. For religion is vital. It is life-changing and it is revolutionary in the best sense. When now and again it becomes too deeply encrusted over with externals, life will break out anew. Of that one may be sure. Meanwhile, the Oxford Group marches on. It is worth while watching it as it goes!

Chapter Thirteen

Mormonism

It was just a little more than one hundred years ago, July 1847, that Brigham Young, leader of an indomitable company which had made an epic journey across the plains to escape religious persecution, let his eye range over the broad valley of Salt Lake and announced, "This is the place." Salt Lake City, built by the Mormons as their capital, remains today as the great Mormon center, but members of the faith, now more than three-quarters of a million in number, are found in many lands. Some 4,000 men and women, most of them young, are laboring through 34 missions in North and South America, Europe, Australia, New Zealand, and in the islands of the Pacific. This they do largely at their own expense, but aided by families and friends. Two years' missionary service from each member is the normal expectation, though this may not necessarily take them to distant fields. Many give a much longer period of service.

Differing from the better-known churches in their conception of the priesthood, as will later appear, more than 191,000, about a fourth of the total membership, have been ordained to act in some official capacity in the church. Three hundred thirty-six thousand are enrolled in their Sunday schools, taught or directed by some 30,000 volunteer teachers. Over 25,000 boys are in Boy Scout organizations under the church, and nearly 150,000 young men and women are being trained in various fields through the Young Men's and Young Women's Mutual Improvement Organization. The Primary Association which concerns itself with the spiritual training and recreation of children enrolls over 100,000 boys and girls. The Relief Society, an organization for the women of the church, has over 70,000 members. Quick to build schools and colleges, the Mormons now, like others, are educated chiefly in state schools, though they do have their own universities and several colleges; but they maintain institutes in connection with 11 universities and 85 high schools, where theological training as well as recreation is provided.

While the great temple at Salt Lake City is the best known and loved of their temples, there exist six other impressive temples in such widely scattered cities as Logan, St. George, and Manti, Utah; Mesa, Arizona; Cardston, Alberta, Canada; and Laie, Hawaii.

While the largest concentration of members is in Utah, there are substantial groups in all the adjacent states, particularly Idaho. There are small groups in most of the states. England has furnished a considerable following from the very early period until now.

All this is a far cry from those early days in up-state New York, where young Joseph Smith, Junior, son of a not too prosperous farmer, announced the finding, under divine direction, of certain golden plates in Hill Cumorah, plates inscribed and left there centuries before by a prophet about to die. Written in an ancient hieroglyphic, they were deciphered by Smith with the aid of the Urim and Thummim, providentially found with the plates. Through these Joseph Smith, a very meagerly educated youth, was able to translate the meaning of the obscure characters into English. He is said to have sat on one side of a curtain and dictated to an amanuensis on the other side, who wrote it all down. Published finally, it was called the Book of Mormon, from which Mormonism gets its popular name, though the official church title is The Church of Jesus Christ of Latter Day Saints.

Naturally, even in as credulous a period as the early nineteenth century, such a claim was questioned, and there has been a long and bitter controversy over the origin of the book. Did it all happen as reported, or was Joseph Smith made the tool of more designing persons, who were able, through him, to launch a movement that alone they were unable to bring to birth? Mormons and Mormon writers in their latest publications warmly defend the truth of Smith's claims. An official publication, issued by the Church Radio Publicity and Mission Literature Committee in 1938, declares: ". . . if it is not true, then the entire structure of Mormonism is built on a false foundation." [1] They adduce as evidence of its genuineness the signed statement of eight witnesses who solemnly affirm

[1] *A Short History of the Church of Jesus Christ of Latter-Day Saints*, Salt Lake City, 1938, p. 20.

". . . that Joseph Smith, Junior . . . has shown us the plates . . . which have the appearance of gold; and as many leaves as the said Smith has translated we did handle with our hands; and we also saw the engravings thereon, all of which has the appearance of ancient work and of curious workmanship." Every published edition of the Book of Mormon carries this signed statement.

Opponents assert that, assuming the sincerity of the eight—there were eleven, all told, who are supposed to have seen the plates—three on another occasion—it would have been easy to deceive them. Doubt is cast upon the sincerity of most of them by one writer or another. One sums up his opinion thus: "The only one whose life might warrant a judgment of sincerity is Whitmer, and he expressed faith in the Book of Mormon until his death. Nevertheless, even he was guilty of the most serious imposture, attempting to succeed Smith by means of revelation." [2] Mormon writers, on the other hand, cite the fact that although six of the eleven left the church—two of these later returned—". . . not one of them . . . ever hinted a denial of his testimony of the divine origin of the Book of Mormon. On the contrary, every one of them affirmed his testimony to the last." [3]

But the Mormon claim is also upheld, they affirm, by the discoveries of archaeologists and anthropologists which confirm "the record (in the Book of Mormon) in many respects with proof of once populous cities, of highly organized social systems, and of destructive wars that destroyed great numbers of people." [4]

Furthermore, "the doctrinal unity of the book, its consistency of language, its general harmony, and Joseph Smith's inability to compose such a work without divine help," are convincing evidences to the Mormon mind that the divine origin of the book must be accepted. [5] Mormons assert that a Professor Anthon of Columbia College, shown a reputed copy of the text of the plates, said the characters were Egyptian, Chaldaic, Assyriac and Arabic and that the translation given by Smith was essentially correct. [6] Arbaugh says that Professor Anthon "told Harris what the figures were and that he was being swindled." [7]

[2] G. B. Arbaugh, *Revelation in Mormonism*, University of Chicago Press, 1932, p. 43.
[3] *Short History of the Church*, p. 26.
[4] *Id.*, p. 27.   [5] *Id.*, p. 27.
[6] Talmadge, *Articles of Faith*, p. 267.
[7] *Op. cit.*, p. 37.

Anthon is said to have repudiated the Mormon claim of his corroboration of their text, but Mormons deny that he did so. Talmadge asserts that another linguist, a Doctor Mitchell of New York, not otherwise indentified, "having examined the characters, gave concerning them a testimony in all important respects corresponding to that of Professor Anthon." [8]

The most commonly accepted explanation of the book's origin by non-Mormons is that it was based upon a historic novel written by a Presbyterian clergyman named Spaulding which he intended calling *The Manuscript Found in the Wilds of Mormon; or Unearthed Records of the Nephites*. He offered it for publication to a printer in Pittsburgh, as yet without title. The printer agreed to publish it if the author would provide a title page and preface. Financial difficulties at this time caused Spaulding to move to Amity, Pennsylvania, leaving the manuscript in the hands of the printer. When he returned later with title and preface, the manuscript was missing. A young man, Sidney Rigdon, an employee of the establishment, was suspected of taking it. Sidney Rigdon was a primary figure in the beginnings of Mormonism. Arbaugh asserts boldly that Rigdon was the real founder of Mormonism,[9] and that he used Joseph Smith as a ready tool in carrying out his purpose to found a new religion. The Spaulding story, it is asserted, reworked by Rigdon, and given to the world through the medium of Joseph Smith, became the Book of Mormon, and the basis of the new faith.

The argument in support of this thesis is too long and involved to repeat here, but probably most non-Mormon writers believe that Spaulding's work was basic to the Book of Mormon. On the other hand, Talmadge declares: "The fanciful theories of its origin, advanced by prejudiced opponents are in general too inconsistent and in most cases too thoroughly puerile to merit serious consideration. Assumptions that the Book of Mormon is the production of a single author or of men working in collusion, a work of fiction, or in any manner a modern composition are their own refutation." [10]

Obviously, the controversy cannot be resolved here. It is no part of the author's purpose to prove or disprove the truth of the origin of the book and its teachings. Here, however, is a great modern reli-

---

[8] *Op. cit.*, p. 268.
[9] *Revelation in Mormonism*, p. 9.
[10] *Op. cit.*, p. 269.

gious movement of marked vigor and aggressiveness. This book is the basis of its faith. *The Short History of the Church*, p. 23, declares: "Practically all the main ideas which we find in the Bible are to be found in the Book of Mormon; only in simpler and clearer form. The spirit of the book is equally intense, fervent, and spiritual as that of the Hebrew scriptures." To them, it is unquestionably of miraculous origin. But the same might be said of the Bible as a whole, as viewed by conservative Christians. To the Mormons the miraculous in their modern revelation is no more of an obstacle to belief than the miraculous in the ancient Biblical revelation is to traditional Christian believers. The age of revelation has not passed. God continues to reveal himself. That he chooses still to do so in unusual or miraculous fashion need cause the reverent believer no concern, Mormons hold.

As Joseph Smith himself tells the story, as a boy of about fifteen he experienced something of a religious awakening. It was a time of revival in that section. He was troubled about the divisions in the church. Drawn to Methodism, he went one day into the woods to inquire of the Lord which church he should choose. Here he had a vision. A pillar of light appeared about him. He saw two figures. One of them, pointing to the other, said: "This is my beloved son; hear Him." When he asked which church he should join, he was told he must join none, since all of them were wrong and their creeds an abomination. He related the vision to a Methodist preacher who said it was of the devil, for there were no longer any revelations. He did not join a church, rather for a period of some three years fell into foolish ways "offensive in the sight of God"—not, he hastens to add, any great or malignant sins, for "a disposition to commit such was never in my nature"—but conduct "not consistent with that character which ought to be maintained by one who was called of God as I had been.[11] Then, in 1823 came another vision, thrice repeated, in which an apocalyptic figure revealed to him that he was to find the golden plates and the Urim and Thummim. Under divine direction he went to the spot indicated near the top of Hill Cumorah, near Manchester Village. He removed the stone covering of the box in which the plates were hidden and saw them, but was forbidden to remove them until the time for bringing

[11] *Short History*, p. 8.

them out had arrived. Every year for four years he returned to the site only to be told to wait. But in September 1827 they were delivered to him.

The countryside had been aroused by the story of Joseph's visions and when it was known that he had the golden plates "the most strenuous exertions were used to get them from him." He sought relief from this public pressure by moving to Harmony, Pennsylvania, the home of Emma Hale whom he had married that year. And here he set about translating the plates with the help of a former schoolteacher, Oliver Cowdery. In this he was occupied much of the time, through 1829, having moved once more to Fayette, New York. Martin Harris, a well-to-do farmer, financed the printing of the first edition of 5,000 copies by mortgaging his farm.

Thus, almost ten years passed between the first vision of Joseph Smith and the completion of the Book of Mormon. It was a time of training and preparation. But, says the *Short History of the Church,* "this did not give him a right to set up a church." [12] This came one day while Joseph and Oliver were in prayer when "a messenger laid his hands upon us and ordained us, saying: 'Upon you, my fellow-servants, in the name of Messiah, I confer the priesthood of Aaron, which holds the keys of the ministering of angels, and of the gospel of repentance, and of baptism by immersion for the remission of sins,' " whereupon each baptized the other and were mutually ordained to the Aaronic priesthood. Some time later, they were ordained to the higher priesthood and given authority "to establish the church on earth, with all that belongs to it by way of gifts, ordinances and divine blessings." [13]

On April 6, 1830, the first organization of the church was effected with six members, the oldest of them but thirty-one years of age. Smith and Cowdery were recognized as the spiritual head of the church. During the first service, Joseph received a revelation designating him as "a seer, a prophet, an apostle of Christ." [14] Known at first simply as The Church of Christ, the name was changed four years later to The Church of Jesus Christ of Latter-Day Saints. [15]

The newly formed church became at once an active aggressive group and quickly added to its numbers. It met serious opposition and persecution. Joseph Smith was twice arrested and imprisoned

[12] P. 29.   [13] *Short History,* p. 30.   [14] *Id.,* p. 31.
[15] G. B. Arbaugh, *Revelation in Mormonism,* pp. 13–14.

within the first year. Meanwhile, revelations continued to come to Joseph elaborating the simple organization of the church to meet the practical needs of the people until it assumed its present form, soon to be described. Once the principle of a living, continuing revelation was established, it was inevitable that revelations would be forthcoming as necessity arose. So grew the church in numbers and in complexity of form.

Since the Book of Mormon was the story of the ancestry of the American Indians and was preserved "that the Lamanites might . . . believe the gospel . . . and be saved," it was natural that the early Mormons should feel a sense of mission to the Indians. Accordingly, four men set out to go to the Lamanites. They worked their way westward into Ohio. At Kirtland they met with unusual success, baptizing over a hundred new converts, but they pressed on as far as Independence, Missouri, where they made contact with the Delaware Indians. They were well received by the Indians' chief, but the U. S. Commissioner forbade them to preach to the Indians, so they returned to report to the head of the church. Coming once again to Kirtland, they found that the headquarters of the church had been moved thither. The prophet arrived there in 1831.

This was the beginning of a period of intense activity. Missionaries were sent out to many parts—some to Canada, some to England, some to the South. The Mormon population grew steadily. Converts, won by the efforts of these missionaries, came to settle either in or near Kirtland, Ohio, or in Jackson County, Missouri, where another large Mormon center was developing. A temple—the first—was erected at Kirtland and an ideal city projected by the prophet at Independence, Missouri. For the prophet, it was a time of great literary effort. Revelations came on many subjects. The Book of Commandments was issued. He translated the Book of Abraham from an ancient manuscript which had been discovered; the Doctrines and Covenants were compiled and published; and the prophet worked at length on a revision of the Hebrew scriptures. His closest associate and collaborator was now Sidney Rigdon, former "Disciple" minister, who is said to have influenced greatly the theological beliefs of Mormonism.

At a conference of the church in 1831, it was decided that a group originally from New York, who had migrated to Thompson, Ohio, near Kirtland, should migrate further west to Zion as they had come to call Independence, in Jackson County, Missouri.

At first, the inhabitants of Jackson County welcomed the newcomers. They streamed in from the East until by 1833 there were 1,200 in the region. It was their Promised Land. A temple was projected and an ideal community planned. A man would own his own home, take whatever was necessary out of his earnings for the maintenance of his family, but the rest he must turn over to the church. There were to be no rich and no poor. All this disturbed the native inhabitants. Their own way of life was threatened. In addition, the newcomers were anti-slavery while the local residents were pro-slavery. A clash was inevitable and it came. Appeal was made to the governor and protection promised, but it availed nothing in the form given. In the end, the Mormons were forced out and much of their property destroyed. They fled into Clay County, and later settled in Davies and Caldwell Counties. Far West, the principal center, was declared by revelation to be a "holy and consecrated land." As many as fifteen thousand Mormons settled in this section, and hither came Joseph Smith and Sidney Rigdon when a series of events—the failure of the Kirtland Safety Society Bank among them—led the Saints to abandon Kirtland. There were many who, disillusioned by these experiences, renounced their faith, but the majority moved westward to Missouri in 1837 or 1838.

They had barely gotten settled when trouble again developed. They had just begun the erection of a temple in Far West when violent opposition once more broke out. Pitched battles were fought between the settlers and the Mormons. The state militia intervened at the order of the governor. Forced to surrender, their leaders, Joseph Smith and several others, were court-martialed and sentenced to be shot at sunrise. The sentence was not carried out but the entire Mormon community was expelled from the state. This entailed the greatest loss and hardship, and the Saints had no redress.

Joseph Smith and his fellow prisoners were not executed because the officer designated to carry out the order refused to do so. They were kept in prison for several months but eventually all escaped and joined the Saints in Illinois, whither they had fled. While imprisoned, Joseph Smith continued to receive revelations. He is said to have told one of his companions that he would not live to see his fortieth birthday.

In 1839, Joseph chose a site on the Mississippi River about fifty miles above Quincy, Illinois, as their new home. He called it Nauvoo, the beautiful. Incorporated as a sort of city-state by a most liberal charter which allowed it to maintain a militia and an independent judiciary, it grew rapidly until in a short time it was the largest city in the state. A temple was built, reputedly at the cost of a million dollars, an unheard-of sum in that period. Religious liberty was extended to all, with penalties for disturbing the worship of any church.

Intense missionary activity was carried on. Converts were made in many distant places: Canada, England, and in the Pacific Islands. Representation of Mormon interests was made to the national government in Washington. Talk of Joseph Smith for president of the United States was heard. He issued a pamphlet setting forth his platform which included purchase of all slaves by the U. S. Government for the purpose of freeing them, thus compensating their owners. An active propaganda in his behalf was carried on by friends all over the country.

But all was not peaceful. Several attempts were made to have Joseph and Hyrum Smith, his brother, returned to Missouri, where they had escaped from prison. Then internal enemies published certain statements regarded as libelous by the Mormon leaders. The city council acting, as they declared, under the city charter declared the paper a nuisance and ordered the mayor, Joseph Smith "to abate it." Smith issued an order to destroy the press and the libelous handbills. This was done by the city marshal. A little later, the mayor and council were charged with rioting and hailed before a justice of the peace in Carthage, Illinois. Fearing mob violence, they refused to go. Smith, it is asserted, wrote the governor inviting him to investigate the case in person in Nauvoo and offering to abide by his decision. The governor ordered them, however, to appear, adding, "I will guarantee the safety of all such persons as may be brought to this place either for trial or as witnesses for the accused." [16]

The prophet, knowing that his life was in danger if he went, resolved to go west and make a home for his people. He even crossed the Mississippi into Iowa, but, besought by his wife to return and stand trial, he acquiesced and in company with his brother and others, went to Carthage for trial. Bound over by the judge to the next term of court on the charge of rioting, they were later charged with treason. An appeal to the governor having failed, they were thrown into the jail where on the 27th of June a mob shot

[16] *Short History*, p. 9.

Joseph Smith, his brother, and John Taylor to death. The prophet was martyred at the age of thirty-nine years. The Saints were without a leader. What would they do?

There was naturally great confusion at this unexpected turn of events. None had contemplated the necessity of determining a successor to the prophet. He was young—under forty—and active. The natural expectation that he would long continue to lead them left them with no plan for the future direction of the church. Sidney Rigdon presented himself as divinely appointed "guardian," and sought acceptance by the group before some of the more outstanding leaders who were away on various missions could return. They did return, however, before a meeting could be called and though Rigdon was given a chance to present his claim, the people did not respond favorably. On the other hand, when, at a later meeting the same day, Brigham Young spoke before them, they were quickly convinced that the movement needed no "guardian," but that control belonged properly to the "apostles" of whom Brigham was the president. Indeed, Mormon sources declare that when President Young rose to speak, "the people were astonished, for he stood transfigured before them and they beheld the Prophet Joseph Smith and heard his voice as naturally as ever they did when he was living. It was a manifestation to the Saints that they might recognize the correct authority." [17] Thus, Brigham Young became the head of the church and to his organizing and administrative ability the church owes more than to any other man since the death of the prophet.

It was at once apparent that Nauvoo offered no security for the development of the movement. They must seek a home elsewhere. Already before his death Joseph Smith had foreseen this necessity and was contemplating such a move. Now it must be quickly made, for active persecution of the Saints began. The charter of the city was revoked by the legislature. A mass meeting of citizens at Quincy demanded their withdrawal from the state. Preparations began in 1845 and they worked feverishly to provide the necessities for the long journey. In early February 1846 the first of the Saints crossed the river into Iowa and began the epic journey to the west. This migration is too well known through books, articles, stories and moving pictures to need recounting here. Certain it is that there is

[17] Joseph Fielding Smith, *Essentials in Church History*, Deseret Book Company, Salt Lake City, 11th ed., 1946, p. 388.

no more thrilling story in the annals of the American frontier than this. For daring, patient acceptance of incredible hardships, and for dogged persistence on the part of a people seeking freedom to worship God according to the dictates of their own faith, it ranks among the great stories of all time. The necessity for the migration reflects little credit upon the American people of that day who were the descendants of an earlier generation which had fled their European homes in search of religious freedom, and had written into the fundamental law of the land a guarantee of religious liberty.

Thus, in 1847, they came to the valley of Salt Lake and began the building of their new home. But they had not yet come to the end of their hardships nor indeed of religious opposition. It was no easy task to convert a desert into a fabulously rich agricultural area. But wise planning, vigorous activity and an indomitable will to live, wrought the wellnigh impossible. A person today who motors through Utah, or goes by train, who visits Salt Lake City and other prosperous Utah cities, cannot fail to be impressed by the results of their labors. The two most familiar landmarks of Salt Lake City are the tabernacle, a building marvel for its time, and the great temple, the center of worldwide Mormonism. From here have gone forth literature and human representatives that have carried Mormonism around the world. There have been difficulties. At one time the United States sent armed forces against the Mormons. It was with difficulty that statehood was achieved. This came only after an agreement to abandon the practice of polygamy which was a primary source of opposition to the Mormons. Finally, in 1896, Utah became a sovereign state, and for more than half a century has taken its own part in the national life. Utah is no longer exclusively a Mormon state. The division of the population was in 1936, 61% Mormon and 39% Gentile. Mormonism has been accepted, or more accurately, it has passed the stage of overt persecution, but its missionaries are still looked at askance by the communities they visit, and members of the small Mormon churches are likely to be regarded as queer. A vigorous missionary program to reclaim Mormons still is carried on in the Mormon country and a bitterly controversial literature attacking Mormon beliefs is still circulated, chiefly by the more conservative branches of Protestantism. It is proper that some inquiry as to the organization and beliefs of these people be made. First, how are they organized as a church?

II. *THE CHURCH—HOW IT IS ORGANIZED AND HOW IT FUNCTIONS*

In a lesson book designed for the use of intermediates in the Sunday School is stated, in perhaps oversimplified form but with crystal clarity, the Mormon doctrine of the church.

"When Jesus lived among men he organized the Church. It was called the Church of Jesus Christ because he was head of it. After many years people became careless; they changed His Church; they also changed many things He had taught. It was no longer His Church.

"So Jesus told a young man, Joseph Smith, to organize the Church of Jesus Christ again. Jesus told Joseph Smith to name the new church the Church of Jesus Christ of Latter-Day Saints. Members of the church are sometimes called Latter-Day Saints." [18]

The organization of the church and the Mormon community is not as it was in the beginning. Like every other movement, it has evolved slowly, adapting itself to meet the needs as they developed. At first it will be recalled (p. 426) Joseph Smith and Oliver Cowdery were divinely directed to baptize and ordain each other as priests of the Aaronic order. Later, they were ordained to the higher or Melchizidek order. At the organization of the church in April 1830 they were formally accepted by the six members as spiritual leaders of the group. By revelation, Joseph Smith was declared to be a prophet and seer at the first meeting. Others were ordained to the lower order of priesthood. Those of the higher order were called "elders." By this time the principle of a continuing revelation, chiefly through Joseph Smith, though others also purported to receive revelations, had been well established. Subsequent organizational changes were usually in obedience to divine revelation.

Shortly after the founding of the church with its six members, the first conference was held in Fayette, New York. There were now twenty-seven members. At this and subsequent conferences, new machinery was announced. A revelation in the summer of 1830 [19] was the basis of a most important feature of Mormon life,

[18] A. Hamer Reiser and Marion G. Merkley, *What It Means to Be a Latter-Day Saint*, Deseret Sunday School Union Board, Salt Lake City, 1946, p. 1.
[19] *Doctrines and Covenants*, Sec. 29.

the "doctrine of the gathering of the Saints." The Saints having been chosen out of the world were to gather together in one place "upon the face of this land to prepare their hearts and be prepared in all things against the day when tribulation and desolation are sent forth upon the wicked." It was this belief that led converts from many widely separated places to migrate to the different Mormon centers, and made of the group something more than just a church, for where people came together thus they formed not only a religious community, but also a socio-economic group which, in isolation from majority political control, became of necessity a political group—a kind of theocracy. In this respect, Mormonism has frequently been likened to Islam. Even when in a minority they tended to form a solid economic and political bloc and to vote as a group. This was a major cause of the feeling of antagonism felt toward them wherever they settled. Their religious beliefs seemed to their neighbors to be queer and to many blasphemous; their social practices, such as polygamy, bolstered by religious belief were offensive, but when they threatened to become controlling political and economic forces, there was violent opposition on the part, first of individuals, and later of organized groups, who conspired to drive them out of the country. The coming of a few scattered individual families in a given area is easily accepted even if they be queer, but when an area becomes a center for the "gathering of the Saints," and they continue to come in great numbers, local resistance is sure to be aroused. Only in the empty spaces of the semi-desert western mountain country, where no other white settlers lived, could they hope to find peace and the full opportunity to develop their doctrine to its logical conclusion, the formation of a theocratic commonwealth which controlled the whole of man's life. That is what developed in Utah, and ultimately led to sharp conflict with national policies as the United States spread westward over the mountains. The Mormon empire ultimately had to bow to the advancing tide of national life. It was all part consequence of the doctrine of the gathering of the Saints.

Without attempting to follow chronologically the evolution of church government, it gradually assumed the present form which may be briefly sketched as follows:

The church as a whole is divided into *stakes of Zion* which in turn are subdivided into *wards*. These each hold quarterly conferences and elect the officials who preside over them. One hundred and fifty-one stakes, still in existence, are listed in a recent publication.[20]

At the head of the church stands the First Presidency, consisting of the President and two other High Priests elected by the Quorum of Twelve Apostles or Council of Twelve. There have been but eight presidents of the church during its one hundred seventeen years existence, Joseph Smith and Brigham Young being the first two. The Council of Twelve, when its decision is unanimous, is equal in power and authority with the First Presidency. In the event of the death or disability of the President, authority reverts to the Council. Next in authority is the Presiding Quorum of Seventy whose unanimous decision on matters properly brought before it for official action is equal in authority with the Council of Twelve. There are many Quorums of Seventy, but the seven presidents of the Presiding Quorum preside over all other quorums and their presidents.

The remaining general authority is the Presiding Bishopric, consisting of a presiding bishop and two counselors. It has jurisdiction over other bishops and over all the activities and organizations of the lower or Aaronic priesthood. Ordinarily, the Presiding Bishop is the oldest bishop of the church if he is qualified, or he may be chosen by the First Presidency, assisted by two high priest counselors. All members of these governing bodies must be ordained members of either the lower Aaronic or the higher Melchizidek priesthood. As indicated earlier,[21] roughly one fourth of the total membership are ordained to one order or the other. Obviously, this means that the ministry of the church is conceived quite differently than is the case in the general Protestant and Catholic churches. There is nothing inconsistent in being at the same time a business or professional man and a priest. Probably the greater part of the propagation of the Mormon gospel has been done by what the churches would call laymen but who are ordained Mormon priests.

The lower order comprises deacons who deal largely with temporal matters and teachers who are local officers. They exhort the members, may lead meetings or preach, but neither may baptize

---

[20] *Essentials in Church History*, pp. 685–689.
[21] See page 421.

nor administer the sacrament. Priests of this order, however, may baptize, administer the sacrament and, under proper direction, ordain deacons and teachers, and may assist the elders in their duties. Deacons are organized into bodies or Quorums of Twelve, teachers of twenty-four, and priests of forty-eight. The two former quorums elect their presiding officers, but the priests' quorums are presided over by bishops who belong to the higher order.

The higher order of Melchizidek consists of bishops, elders, seventies, high-priests, patriarchs or evangelists and apostles. These are all qualified to perform any functions of the lower order, and others in addition. The elders may ordain elders, confirm, confer the Holy Spirit, bless children and, in the absence of a high-priest, perform his functions. Seventies are traveling elders—usually among the Gentiles, or non-Mormons. High-priests may perform all the ordinances of the church. A bishop is a high-priest ordained and set apart to preside over a ward. Patriarchs likewise may perform all the ordinances of the church and have the duty of blessing the members of the church. Joseph Smith's father was first Patriarch and the office of Presiding Patriarch is regarded as hereditary. Apostles travel among the Saints, regulate the affairs of the church, ordain Patriarchs and others to the priesthood and act generally under the direction of the first Presidency.

It is clear from the nomenclature used that an attempt was made to follow the pattern of the early Christian church in their organization and ministry. Talmadge declares: "The Latter-Day Saints declare their high claims to the true Church organization, similar in all essentials to the organization effected by Christ among the Jews." [22]

So long as the Mormons constituted the entire community, the president, Brigham Young, was civil as well as religious head. He himself or with the other higher officers laid down the rules under which the community lived and was responsible for its social and economic arrangements, subject to the ratification of the conference held each half year. Thus, they planned Salt Lake City on its generous lines, determined the conditions of occupancy by the settlers, laid down rules concerning Sabbath observance, superintended the colonization of the valley and more distant parts, built irrigation systems, created cooperative enterprises both for produc-

[22] *Articles of Faith*, p. 204.

tion and distribution of goods, loaned money, in short, pretty largely controlled the social, economic, and later the political life of the growing community.

III. *WHAT IT TEACHES*

Though in part a socio-economic group, Mormonism was and is, first of all, a religion. It has a specific set of beliefs, many of them differing in no serious respect from traditional Christianity. But it has some very distinctive beliefs not held by the church at large. These must be given in some detail, though little need be said of that which is commonly accepted. What are these distinctive Mormon beliefs? It will be well to begin with their conception of religious authority. This may be stated simply as divine revelation. How has God revealed his will to men? In the past, preeminently through holy men as recorded in the Bible. At this point they are in agreement with traditional Christianity. They accept the Bible, the Old and New Testaments as basic to their faith. In the Articles of Faith as stated by Joseph Smith, it is affirmed simply: "We believe the Bible to be the word of God, as far as it is translated correctly." To be sure, he did not think that the King James version current in his day was a correct translation, and he dedicated a great deal of time in Kirtland to a revision of the scriptures. In any Mormon book of theology frequent appeal is made to the Bible as proof of the correctness of all their beliefs. Talmadge calls the Bible "the foremost of her (the Mormon) standard works, first among the books which have been proclaimed as her written guides in faith and doctrine." [23] In his chapter on the organization of the church there is approximately the same number of footnote references to the Bible as to other Mormon sources. That they have their own interpretation of the Bible which does not always agree with that of the church in general, is true, but so, of course, have many other Christian groups.

They differ from traditional Christianity, at least Protestants, in holding that revelation is continuous and that there are other revelations of God later than the Bible—specifically the Book of Mormon and other Mormon scriptures, as given through the prophet Joseph Smith. These have the value of Holy Scripture,

[23] *Articles of Faith*, p. 236.

but they go farther, as does the Catholic Church, in the belief in a continuing revelation through the head of the church. The head, or President, of the church is still "called to be a seer, a revelator, a translator and a prophet." [24] Concerning revelation the Articles of Faith declare: "We believe all that God has revealed, all that he does now reveal, and we believe that He will yet reveal many great and important things pertaining to the Kingdom of God." [25]

The scriptures which Mormons accept, along with the Bible, include the *Book of Mormon, The Book of Doctrines and Covenants,* and *The Pearl of Great Price.* There is room here for only a very brief description of the Book of Mormon. We have already told how it was delivered to Joseph Smith and by him translated and given to the world. It is believed by Mormons to be a divinely inspired record "made by the prophets of the ancient peoples who inhabited the American continent before and after the time of Christ." [26]

The main division of the book recounts the history of the migration of a group from Jerusalem about 600 B.C., in the time of Jeremiah, led by a prophet not mentioned in the Bible, Lehi. They reached the shores of the Arabian Sea, constructed a ship, provisioned it and set sail eastward across the Indian and Pacific oceans, coming at last to the American continent, just where it is not stated certainly. Here they prospered and became a numerous people but divided eventually, one group following Nephi, the other Laman, both sons of the prophet Lehi, and thus they became two separate nations, the Nephites and the Lamanites. The former advanced in enlightenment and culture, became the builders of great cities, the ruins of which have since been found in South and Central America and Mexico. The Lamanites on the other hand degenerated, fell under the Lord's displeasure, went naked, became dark skinned and forgot the faith of their fathers, becoming savages. The American Indians are their descendants. The two peoples warred one with another and ultimately the Nephites were destroyed as a nation about 400 A.D., the final struggle taking place in northern New York near the hill where the golden plates were found by Joseph Smith.

Shortly after his ascension, Jesus appeared among the Nephites and taught them, much as he had done the Jews in Palestine. Here

---

[24] *Doctrines and Covenants, 107:91, 92*; Talmadge, *op. cit.,* p. 210.
[25] Article 9. [26] Talmadge, p. 255.

among them a church was founded according to directions given by Jesus very much as in the Holy Land. The section of III Nephi which records Jesus' appearance and teachings reads indeed like the gospels. The Nephites were responsive and there followed a period of idyllic existence—the golden age of the Nephites.

Record of their history, culminating in Jesus' appearance among them, had been faithfully kept on plates of gold. These, the prophet Mormon abridged on other golden plates and gave to his son Moroni to make any additions he saw fit and to hide away in the ground. He added only a few chapters to complete the Nephite story, but added another entire book, Ether, which relates the story of the Jaredites, followers and descendants of one Jared, who with his brother at the building of the Tower of Babel escaped the confusion of tongues and at the command of the Lord migrated across the great waters, in boats built by divine direction, for a period of 344 days and landed at last upon the shores of America. Here they lived prosperously, developed a culture of their own, had a church, and, through prophets and seers, experienced the direction of divine revelation. But in a series of conflicts the Jaredites were all destroyed save one. The record of this people was written by the last one of their prophets, Ether, who hid it away, to be found several hundred years later by a Nephite ruler. Abridged by Moroni, it was attached to the Book of Mormon, and so becomes a part of the sacred book of the Latter-Day Saints.

While much of the book is narrative in form, telling of the history of these various peoples, much doctrinal teaching is likewise included, most of it taken from the Bible directly, sometimes verbatim. The Book of Mormon "in no sense supplants the Bible, but supports it," writes a member of the Council of the Twelve Apostles of the Reorganized Church of Latter-Day Saints.[27] "Its spiritual depth and inherent Christian merit are readily perceived. It is an important witness—a second witness—speaking from the Western Hemisphere, providing additional proof of the divinity of Christ." [28]

But while basic to Mormon faith, it is doubtful if it is as important a source concerning the beliefs, organization and practice of the Mormons as two other collections of the prophecies, translations and

[27] Paul Hanson, *Jesus Christ Among Ancient Americans*, Independence, Missouri, 1945, p. 143.

[28] *Id.*, p. 143.

other writings of Joseph Smith, the *Doctrines and Covenants,* and *The Pearl of Great Price.* The Book of Mormon stands at the beginning and is a revelation of the past. The other two are the record of continuing revelation during the early years when doctrine and organization were being formulated. They are what Smith referred to in the statement quoted above as "all that he does now reveal." [89] The *Doctrines and Covenants* contains a series of seven lectures on faith delivered in Kirtland to a class of elders. There is no specific indication that these were by Joseph Smith. The remaining portion of the book consists chiefly of revelations given through Joseph Smith. Each is dated, and usually also located, in an introductory sentence which also states to whom it was directed, e.g., Section 28 is a "Revelation given through Joseph the Seer, to Oliver Cowdery in Fayette, N. Y., September, 1830." Many are directed to individuals, some are general, thus Section 48: "Revelation given through Joseph the Seer, at Kirtland, Ohio, March 1831." One section, #134, "Of Governments and Laws in General," seems to be a declaration of Mormon belief made not by Joseph Smith but probably later. It reads simply, "We believe, etc." This section and one entitled "The word and will of the Lord given through President Brigham Young, etc.," and one other under the title "Revelation, called the Appendix, given through Joseph the Seer, etc." make up the Appendix to the *Doctrines and Covenants.*

The Pearl of Great Price is a small volume containing the "Book of Moses," the visions of Moses as revealed to Joseph the Seer in 1830; the "Book of Abraham" which is described as a "translation of some ancient records that have fallen into our hands from the catacombs of Egypt; the writings of Abraham while he was in Egypt," and a section called "Writings of Joseph Smith," comprising (1) an "extract from a translation of the Bible," a part of Matt. 24; (2) Joseph Smith's story of his first visions, the finding of the plates, their translation, his baptism and ordination; and (3) The Articles of Faith of the Church.

These two supplementary scriptures are of the utmost importance to present-day Mormonism, more so probably than either the Bible or the Book of Mormon, though Mormons would unhesitatingly affirm that they are supported by the earlier works. In all of them critical non-Mormon scholars see the hand of Sidney Rigdon, as

[29] See page 437.

the really formative theological influence of the Mormon Church.

But revelation still continues and by its means the church is guided, the President being the mouthpiece through which it is given. In this respect, Mormonism closely resembles Roman Catholicism.

The Idea of God

If one takes the simple statement of the articles of faith, there is little to indicate that Mormons differ from traditional Trinitarian Christianity in respect to their belief about God. "We believe in God, the Eternal father, and in His Son, Jesus Christ, and in the Holy Ghost." Whence then the popular idea that Mormonism is polytheistic, believing in many gods? There are at least two possible sources, one that men in the end become gods—a doctrine to be considered at some length later; another, some utterances of Brigham Young. On one occasion he declared: "How many Gods there are, I do not know, but there was never a time when there were not Gods and worlds," etc.[30] In a sermon preached in the tabernacle April 9, 1852, he said concerning Adam: "When our father Adam came into the Garden of Eden he came into it with a celestial body. He helped to make and organize the world. . . . He is our Father and God, and the only God with whom we have to do. . . . Jesus, our Elder Brother, was begotten in the flesh by the same character that was in the Garden of Eden, and who is our Father in Heaven." Some Mormons undoubtedly believed this and preached it. The Reorganized Church of Latter-Day Saints repudiated any such doctrine, and a Utah Mormon paper in 1900 declared that "the doctrine is not preached either to the Latter-Day Saints or to the world as a part of the creed of the Church." [31] It is possible, too, that the charge may have arisen from the conception of the relationship between the persons of the Godhead. Here they differ sharply from traditional Christian interpretation.

"The one-ness of the Godhead, to which the scriptures so abundantly testify, implies no mystical union of substance, nor any unnatural and therefore blending of personality. Father, Son, and Holy Ghost are as distinct in their persons and individualities as are

[30] *Journal of Discourses,* Vol. 7, p. 333.
[31] *Deseret Evening News,* March 21, 1900.

any three personages in mortality," writes Talmadge.[32] Their unity, he says, is one of purpose and operation, not substance. Against the traditional view that God is "without body parts or passion" he affirms that "to deny the materiality of God's person is to deny God, for a thing without parts has no whole and an immaterial body cannot exist." [33]

Brigham Young voiced the common belief when he declared "Our God and Father in heaven has a body, with parts, the same as you and I have." [34] Nevertheless, the same attributes are assigned to Him as in traditional Christian theology. He is Father Eternal, Creator Omniscient, Omnipotent, Omnipresent, Merciful, Gracious, a God of Truth and Love. The Son, like the Father, is a being of body and parts. He lived as Jesus in the flesh, a man, was resurrected "in the same form and so ascended into heaven." We have seen that he appeared in human form to the Nephites and to modern Prophets. Talmadge says: "We know that both the Father and the Son are in form and stature perfect men; each of them possesses a tangible body, infinitely pure and perfect and attended by transcendent glory, nevertheless, a body of flesh and bones." [35]

In 1916 the First Presidency and the Council of the Twelve Apostles issued an exposition of the doctrine of the Father and the Son which is official and has the weight of revelation. They assert, first of all, that God is really not Creator but Organizer. "He certainly did not create in the sense of bringing into primal existence the ultimate elements of the materials of which the earth consists for 'the elements are eternal' according to Doctrines and Covenants, 93:33." [36] Life also is eternal, they declare, not created, but "may be infused with organized matter." [37]

Christ is Savior and Redeemer, as we shall see in more detail as we discuss salvation.

A clear distinction is made between Elohim and Jehovah, the relationship being that of father and son. Jehovah is Jesus in his pre-natal state. In the Book of Mormon, Ether 3:14, Jesus Christ asserts "I am the Father and the Son." How could this be? Being Jehovah, "the executive of the Father, Elohim," he was the Creator, and "being Creator, he is called the Father of heaven and earth." [38]

[32] *Articles of Faith*, p. 41. [33] Talmadge, *op. cit.*, p. 48.
[34] *Journal of Discourses*, 1:50. [35] *Articles of Faith*, p. 42.
[36] Talmadge, *op. cit.*, p. 466. [37] *Id.*, p. 466.
[38] Talmadge, *op. cit.*, pp. 465-473, *passim*.

The Holy Ghost, unlike Father and Son, has no body or parts, but is "a personage of spirits," though the Spirit has manifested himself in human form. Indeed, the Father and Son may operate through the Spirit in the dealings with men. Through the Spirit revelations are made and the purposes of the Father and Son effected.[39] So much does the Holy Ghost differ from Father and Son that in a set of questions on one of the Lectures on Faith when it is asked, "How many personages are there in the Godhead?" the answer is "Two; the Father and Son."[40] But later in the same series when it is asked, "Do the Father, Son and Holy Spirit constitute the God-head?" the answer given is, "They do."

Man and His Salvation

Mormons believe in the pre-existence of spirits. In his mental state man "is the union of a pre-existent spirit with a body composed of earthly elements."[41] The number of them is fixed and when all those have been born who were appointed to take fleshly form, "then and not until then, shall the end come."[42] Placed upon earth, man was given free will but made accountable for his acts. Our first parents fell, and thereby forefeited their deathless state, becoming subject to mortality, which made necessary a plan of salvation. As children of Adam, we inherit their ills and imperfections, but we are not adjudged sinners simply because of the sin of our common parents. Original sin as commonly held is repudiated by the Mormons. "We believe," says Article 2 of their creed, "that men will be punished for their own sins and not Adam's transgression."

The plan of salvation does not, in its main outlines, differ essentially from the traditional orthodox view, as stated in Article 3. "We believe that through the atonement of Christ, all mankind may be saved, by obedience to the laws and ordinances of the gospel," which are "Faith in the Lord Jesus Christ, Repentance, Baptism by immersion and laying on of hands for the gift of the Holy Ghost," as shown in Article 4. It is in the details of the scheme that the novel element enters. By his vicarious sacrifice, "in a manner to us incomprehensible and inexplicable, He bore the weight of the sins of the whole world," writes President Taylor.[43] And Talmadge adds,

[39] Talmadge, *op. cit.*, p. 42.   [40] Lecture V, 1.
[41] Talmadge, *op. cit.*, p. 475.   [42] *Id.*, p. 194.
[43] Quoted by Talmadge, *op. cit.*, p. 76.

"The means may be to our finite minds a mystery, yet the result is our salvation." [44] There is no official philosophy of the atonement that I have been able to discover.

Though man may fail to fulfill the conditions of salvation in this life, he is not thereby completely lost. Mormonism believes that salvation is universal and that there is still a chance beyond the grave. Punishment both here and in a future life there will be, but it is not everlasting. But how can man be saved after this life? The conditions of salvation as stated in the Articles of Faith are faith, repentance, baptism by immersion, the remission of sins and laying on of hands for the gift of the Holy Spirit. A modern Mormon source already quoted adds to this confirmation, and marriage for eternity and time.[45] But these can be performed only in the flesh, and how can this be done for those who have died? The answer is, says this source, "The baptism, confirmation, the ordination and the sealing of some one else for them." Here are accounted for two of the most distinctive Mormon practices: baptism for the dead and sealing in marriage for eternity.

To the many who have died, having deliberately refused to accept the gospel, must be added innumerable others who died never having heard the gospel. What provision is there for them? The former are not to be punished "beyond the time requisite to work the needed reformation and to vindicate justice, for which ends alone punishment is imposed." [46] And it would be blasphemous, Talmadge asserts, to believe that God would condemn a soul under any law not known to him.[47] It becomes plain, then, that the gospel must be preached in the spirit world where these dead dwell. Authorization for this is found in the Bible, Peter declaring (I Peter 4:6): "For this cause the gospel was preached also to them that are dead that they might be judged according to men in the flesh, but live according to God in the Spirit." I Peter also declares that Christ went and preached to the spirits in prison (I Peter 3:18–20) while his body lay in the tomb. Since baptism is "essential to the salvation of the living, it is likewise indispensable for the dead." A word of Paul is taken as authorization for performing such baptism, I Cor. 15:29: "Else what shall they do which are baptized for the dead, if the dead rise not at all? Why are they then baptized for the dead?"

[44] *Id.*, p. 78. [45] *Short History of Church*, p. 81.
[46] Talmadge, *op. cit.*, p. 147. [47] *Id.*, p. 146.

The practice arose during the Ohio period, though there seems to have been no revelation to account for it. Smith, in an article written in 1842 (*Times and Seasons*, April 15), claims to have originated it. It was first performed as any other baptism in a convenient stream or body of water. But in a revelation given in Nauvoo in 1841, Joseph Smith declared that the time had come to build a temple and that, after a reasonable time, if the temple were not built, baptism for the dead which must thenceforth be in a suitably appointed place would not be acceptable.[48] After the erection of the temple such baptisms were restricted to it. "It is necessary for some reason," declares the *Short History of the Church*, "that the ordinances for the dead shall be performed in houses specially built for that purpose." [49] This has led to the multiplication of temples until there are now seven. Other ordinances as well, such as marriage for eternity, can be performed only in temples, and the baptisms could only be performed upon persons who had paid their tithe. In a conference in Nauvoo in 1841, Joseph Smith declared that those who neglected the baptism of the dead "did it at the peril of their own salvation." [50]

That the dead are saved by the baptism is not claimed, any more, declared an article in the *Times and Seasons*, than baptism will necessarily save the living.[51] Faith and repentance are essential conditions and baptism for either the living or dead without these will not effect one's salvation. It is performed precisely as is the rite for the living, the living simply standing proxy for the dead.

But while salvation is universal and no one is entirely lost (save the sons of Perdition) not everyone will be exalted. That is, there are degrees or levels of salvation, three according to a revelation of the prophet given in 1832.[52] They are the celestial, terrestrial, and telestial, in order from higher to lower. In the higher, those who attain it are made priests of the Most High, and kings. They shall have celestial bodies. Indeed, declares the prophet, "they are Gods," [53] or in another place "they shall be Gods, because they have no end; therefore, they shall be from everlasting to everlasting,

---

[48] *Doctrines and Covenants*, Sec. 124:30–31.
[49] P. 4.
[50] *Times and Seasons*, Vol. 2, p. 578.
[51] May 1, 1841.
[52] *Doctrines and Covenants*, Sec. 76:50 ff.
[53] *Id.*, 76:58.

because they continue. . . . They shall be Gods, because they have all power, and the angels are subject to them." [54]

"Those who attain to this are those who overcome by faith and are sealed by the Holy Spirit of Promise." [55] But the more elaborate statement of becoming gods is found in connection with a revelation on celestial marriage, another doctrine peculiar to the Mormons.

There are two kinds of marriage, marriage for time and marriage for eternity or celestial marriage. A marriage for time has no validity in the life hereafter. Those who are so married "when they are out of the world neither marry nor are given in marriage . . . for these did not abide by my law; therefore, they cannot be enlarged but remain singly and without exaltation in their saved condition, to all eternity; and from henceforth are not Gods, but are angels of God forever and ever." [56] The church provides for the lower form of marriage for those it deems not fitted for the higher, or those who prefer it. The celestial form can only be performed in the temples—and is performed with mystic and secret rites never disclosed to the outsider. Only those who have been so married apparently attain to the celestial or highest grade of exaltation. This belief has had some very important implications for Mormon life. What if one were already married to someone "for time," and he were not willing or eligible according to the church to marry for eternity? Must one thus lose the chance of exaltation? Or, what if one were not married at all?

This difficulty is met by the idea of spiritual marriage. It became possible for more than one woman to be sealed to one man. Since, at least after 1852, when the revelation concerning polygamy was first promulgated publicly, though it had been practiced since the days in Ohio by some, and since Nauvoo by the prophet and the principal leaders, plural marriage for time and eternity was generally accepted. This arrangement gave the answer. In the course of the revelation given in 1843 permitting polygamy, the prophet speaks of women "given unto him to multiply and replenish the earth . . . and for their exaltation in the eternal worlds, that they may bear the souls of men," i.e., says a note, "the souls or spirits of men to be born in heaven." [57]

About no teaching of Mormonism has there been more contro-

---

[54] *Id.*, 132:20.   [55] *Id.*, 76:53.
[56] *Doctrines and Covenants*, 132:17.
[57] *Doctrines and Covenants*, 132:63.

versy than that concerning polygamy. That the practice was born of unholy lust and concupiscence on the part of the prophet and the leaders of the movement, and given a supposed divine sanction through a revelation of the prophet, is the charge of most non-Mormon writers. That it was a doctrine at first resisted, and accepted finally by Joseph and his associates only with the greatest reluctance lest they be cut off by the Lord, is claimed by Mormon apologists. Certain it is that nothing in Mormon practice offended more deeply the sensibilities of the citizenry of that day, and it was only after a pledge given by the then president of the church to renounce the practice, that Utah was finally admitted to statehood. Some of the divisions of the church repudiated the doctrine completely. However, the revelations permitting its practice still stand in the *Doctrines and Covenants.* A few Mormon fundamentalists have been tried within recent years for contracting plural marriages. A modern Mormon source declares that "at best less than three percent of the men in the church practiced plural marriage." [58]

There seems no doubt that many women were convinced that apart from being sealed to a man there was no salvation for them. This led many women "to be sealed" to men with whom they never cohabited or had any physical relationship.

With the abandonment of the practice of polygamy as announced by the President of the Church, the sealing of women to already married men ceased, since it might lead to charges of polygamous marriage and this had become a criminal offense. A vestige of it remains even yet, however, in that a woman may be "sealed" to a man who has passed from this life even though he was once married and his widow is still alive, provided that the consent of the widow is secured and the President of the Church gives permission. It is asserted, however, that the deceased man in the spirit world is not obliged to accept the "sealing," and if he refuse the "seal" is not effective.

Just as the relationship between husband and wife who are married only for time does not carry over into the spirit world so also is the bond of parents and children broken by death, unless they be sealed by the proper temple rite. It is a part of the celestial marriage rite to seal the children to the parents for eternity. But for a son whose parents were not so sealed for eternity a way is provided whereby

[58] *Short History,* p. 167.

the family connection in the future world may be continued. He can by proxy marry his parents for eternity and be sealed unto them through these proxies. This is frequently done today by new converts to the faith. But here, too, the "sealing" is not effective unless it is freely accepted and all the conditions met by those who are so sealed.

But the final word has not been spoken concerning salvation until their ideas concerning the millennium and the final judgment have been set forth.

Man existed as spirit before his mortal birth. "Physical death is but a temporary separation of spirit from the body," declares a modern Mormon tract. The righteous are ushered at once into a state of happiness, Paradise, to await the resurrection. The evil go away into a state of awful "darkness, fearful, looking for the fiery indignation of the wrath of God upon them; thus, they remain in this state as well as the righteous in paradise until the time of their resurrection." [59]

In the fullness of time Christ will come again to usher in the millennium. The tribes of Judah will be gathered at Jerusalem, but the tribes of Israel—here generalized to mean the rest of mankind who are heirs of the promise—will be gathered in Zion whose center is to be the New Jerusalem. This Joseph Smith located by revelation at what is now Independence, Missouri, the site of the original Garden of Eden. Here Christ will set up his Kingdom. The just men of all the ages will be resurrected and dwell in Zion for a thousand years. "During the millennium there shall be both mortals and immortals living upon the earth together." [60] "Satan shall have no power to tempt any man. And there shall be no sorrow because there is no death." [61] During the millennium the gospel will be preached to all those who live or who have died not knowing the law of the gospel—so that the salvation of all may be made possible. But at the end of the thousand years men will again fall away from God, Satan will be loosed and rule for a time. Then will come the battle of Armageddon, the resurrection of all the dead and the final judgment. Then shall the heavens and the earth pass away and there shall be a new heaven and a new earth.

---

[59] *Book of Mormon*, Alma, 40:11–14.
[60] Milton R. Hunter, *The Gospel Through the Ages*, Salt Lake City, 1946, p. 284.
[61] *Doctrines and Covenants*, 101:24.

Stated in strictly Mormon terms the earth at the fall of Adam became "telestialized," at the second coming of Christ it becomes "terrestrialized," and now once again it becomes celestialized, and forms the abode of those who have merited the highest or celestial glory. Those of lesser glory, the terrestrial or telestial glory, take up their abode on other planets (from a personal interview with a prominent Mormon leader). The fate of the sons of Perdition no man knows or can know. It is too terrible, but an informant told me that Joseph Fielding Smith, one of the greatest Mormon leaders, had asserted that these were so few that they could be counted on the fingers of one hand. Thus it becomes a practical universalism in respect to its salvation doctrine.

There is a mixture of both this-worldliness and other-worldliness in the Mormon concept. While undoubtedly, in the end, the concept is other-worldly, in that it does not find its fulfillment in this life, or even on this earth, save as it is celestialized, there has been a strong this-worldly element in it from the first. A whole chapter is given in a recent Mormon book to the discussion of what it calls "temporal salvation." Latter-Day Saints, the author writes, "believe not only in the gospel of spiritual salvation, but also in the gospel of temporal salvation," and this means, he says, social security. The fear of want and poverty must be banished, for it is "the thing that has caused more unhappiness and social unrest throughout the world." [62] The church must concern itself with the total welfare of men.

To this end there was adopted in the midst of the depression in 1936 the Mormon Church Welfare Program. Not that before this time the church had been indifferent to the temporal needs of men, but conditions now obliged them to a more concerted effort than ever before. The Program announces three main objectives: (1) the distribution of the necessities of life among the needy, (2) the provision of employment for members out of work, (3) the gradual improvement of conditions among the dependent or the low-income groups "by furnishing opportunities for better use of individual talents and resources, and through a solution of local community problems. Funds for the aid of the needy are raised by a fast, two meals on one Sunday a month, and the giving of the amount so

---

[62] George Stewart, *et al.*, *Priesthood and Church Welfare*, Deseret Book Co., Salt Lake City, 1939, pp. 262–263, *passim.*

saved to the church for distribution. But the principle of self-help is strongly emphasized, even here. "One gives what one has and gets what one needs." The person out of a job has time. This he may give to some project; for this he is issued a "work receipt" and this entitles him to draw from one of the many storehouses that have been set up for the needs of his family—though not necessarily on a strict basis of the value of services rendered. These storehouses are filled by use of vacant lands, unsalable surplus materials, by tithing in kind, etc., and there is an exchange of products among the store houses so that each has a variety of commodities to dispense. There is a central clearing house for all this in Salt Lake City where there is a warehouse, administration building, milk evaporating unit, modern creamery, sewing center—shoemaking shop, and along with other features, an elevator with a storage capacity of over 300,000 bushels of wheat, all built by welfare labor.

The aim is to get unemployed persons into jobs under private enterprise, but this is not always possible. The unemployables, for example—so jobs have to be created for them. Projects are set up, productive in so far as possible. Sometimes these may be in building operations for the church. Much ingenuity has been exercised in discovering and developing worthwhile projects.

The long-time objective, designed, not for an emergency, but to better the economic and social status of the people, involves education in better and more profitable ways of farming or marketing, development of cooperatives, credit unions and like devices, so that life may be lived more richly and securely. It is all a part of the sense of obligation to bring men temporal as well as spiritual salvation.[63]

While the appeal of Mormonism is no narrow one, it is not altogether unlikely that one of the strong appeals to people of moderate or straitened circumstances is this concern for practical human welfare and security. "They never let you down," it is said. "They look after their own." It is reported that during the great depression no Mormons had to be taken care of by public relief funds.

Nothing has been said concerning the divisions of Mormonism. But they have not escaped this common evil of sectarianism. Given the principle of a continuing revelation, it was inevitable that others

[63] Facts here taken from a pamphlet, *Helping Others to Help Themselves— The Story of the Mormon Church Welfare Program.*

than the prophet should claim to receive revelations. This was a constant source of difficulty in the early days. The most important branch is known as the Reorganized Church of Jesus Christ of the Latter-Day Saints with headquarters at Independence, Missouri. They hold that the direction of the church should be hereditary, and are sometimes called the Josephites. They have repudiated the teaching regarding polygamy as well as some other ideas held in the Utah church. There was an Iowa branch and the Strang group in Wisconsin, as well as others, but there is no space for a consideration of these.

It is a fact that the Mormon church has grown and continues to grow steadily. The following table gives the membership of each of the two main branches and the total of all the branches as given in the United States Religious Census reports for the decades 1906–1936.

TABLE IX

Total Membership

Year	Utah Church	Reorganized Church	Total *
1906	215,796	40,851	256,639
1916	403,378	58,941	462,329
1926	542,194	64,367	606,561
1936	678,217	93,470	783,969
1945 **	870,346	113,064	987,086

* Includes other small groups
** From *Year Book of the Churches*, 1946

Naturally, the greatest concentration of membership is found in Utah. At first the only people in Utah, Gentiles soon began to come, so that by 1900, only forty percent of the population were Latter-Day Saints. But comparing Mormon membership with the total state population, there was a steady gain in the proportion of Mormons to total Utah residents until the last decade. In 1906 the rate was 40%; in 1916, 57%; in 1926, 66%. In 1936 the percentage dropped to 61%.[64]

[64] Since the religious census was taken in 1906, 1916, etc., and population figures were for 1900, 1910, etc., comparison was here made between the 1910 state census and the 1906 religious census figures.

The second most numerous Mormon group is found in neighboring Idaho where, in 1936, there were almost a third as many as in Utah. Then follow in order California with 34,623; Arizona—22,062; Wyoming—16,497; Nevada—7,744; Colorado—6,945; Oregon—5,400; Montana—3,368; and Washington—2,566 (1936 religious census figures). California shows the most marked percentage of increase among all the states. The New England states, as a whole, seem to have been least responsive to Mormonism according to the religious census figures, the number reported in 1936 being less than that in either 1916 or 1926. The South Atlantic states, the East South Central and West South Central States also reported a decline in membership in 1936 over the previous decade, but in every other section of the country the membership has increased steadily decade by decade. In 1906 only two states, New Hampshire and Rhode Island, reported none. Thus the Mormon faith has become truly nation-wide in its coverage of the United States.

Though the Mormon church is growing, it has its troubles, doubtless. One, not unknown to the other churches, is that of holding its young people to its rather strict prohibition of smoking, drinking of liquor and even of tea and coffee, the requirements known among them as the Word of Wisdom. But even greater difficulty meets the church in the maintenance of so fundamentalist a faith in an age of modern science, especially when young Mormons go to "Gentile," i.e., non-Mormon schools.

Other internal conflicts have arisen over the social and economic practices of the church. In a day of growing democratic participation in the control of the social and economic life of the people, the highly centralized power of the church in the hands of a few, and the definitely capitalistic point of view of those in positions of power (in strong contrast to the earlier day) have caused a degree of restlessness among many of the members of the church.[65] But it is a vigorous faith. There is enthusiasm and zeal and commitment to the program of the church enough to lead some four thousand members, most of them young, to give one or more years at their own expense and without compensation to spreading their gospel. It is essentially a great lay movement. Less than thirty-five persons in the active leadership of the church receive a salary. It is teachers,

[65] For a discussion of the inner strains in Mormon life, see E. E. Ericksen, *The Psychological and Ethical Aspects of Mormon Life,* University of Chicago Press, Chicago, 1922, especially part III.

lawyers, doctors and merchants who carry on the ministry of the church. A dentist earning $20,000 a year gives up his practice for three years to head a regional mission. A great lawyer refuses a salary of $100,000 a year to accept an official position of leadership at a salary of one-twentieth that amount.

So long as this kind of conviction and self-giving continue one need not question the future. That changes will come in time, no one will doubt. One of the great leaders of the church contributed a chapter to a book edited by the writer.[66] Many readers did not recognize anything distinctive about it. It might have been written by a religious liberal of almost any one of the denominations save for one reference to Joseph Smith. One finds in examining the literature published for the various ages in the Sunday schools a skill in writing, and an understanding of the educational process, which betoken thorough preparation for the task of religious educational leadership.

Already serious problems have been raised as Mormon scholars have begun to study critically the Book of Mormon and the other revelations. If they should become convinced of an element of fraud in the character of the prophet, could they still go on accepting the revelation? As a matter of fact, the Reorganized Church recognizes weakness in some of the prophet's revelations and yet it has not caused them to repudiate the rest of his revelations. Already it has been asserted that the truth of the revelation does not depend upon the character of the medium through which it is given. Thus, some at least have come to the position held by many theosophists in respect to their seer Helena P. Blavatsky.[67]

Mormonism seems clearly to be capable of coming to terms with the world about it. It survived the struggle over polygamy, repudiated its practice and still thrives. It will meet other situations as they arise.

[66] *Varieties of American Religion*, 1936.
[67] See p. 222.

Appendix A

A Selected Bibliography on
Modern American Cults and Minority Religious Movements

I

General

Ferguson, Charles W., *The Confusion of Tongues*, Doubleday Doran and Co., New York, 1928. Also published under the title *The New Book of Revelations*, 1929. An excellent though not wholly objective treatment. Unfortunately out of print, and somewhat out of date.

Van Baalen, Jan Karel, *The Chaos of Cults*, Wm. B. Eerdmans Publishing Co., Grand Rapids, Michigan, 1942. 3rd edition. Presents not a little material from the cults themselves, expressing their point of view. The general purpose of the book is not, however, an objective one, but to help refute them and to reveal their pagan character.

Wyrick, Herbert M., *Seven Religious Isms*, Zondervan Publishing House, Grand Rapids, Michigan, 1940. A definite attack by a conservative minister.

Lieb, Frederick, *Sight Unseen*, Harper and Brothers, New York, 1939. A not unsympathetic treatment of several movements by a journalist who was much interested in some of them from a personal standpoint as well as journalistically.

Clark, Elmer T., *Small Sects of America*, Abingdon-Cokesbury Press, Nashville, 1937. While the greater part of the book deals with the smaller sects within the orthodox Christian tradition, it does treat some of the cults which are farther from the normal Christian point of view.

Bach, Marcus, *They Found a Faith*, Bobbs Merrill Co., Indianapolis, 1946. A most fascinating book dealing with eight movements, written from firsthand study, not so much of the literature, but of the actual functioning of the faiths in the lives of leaders and people. Warmly sympathetic and understanding of the people who seek satisfaction of their religious needs in these non-"regular" groups. A more recent volume, *Report to Protes-*

453

tants, Bobbs Merrill Co., Indianapolis, 1948, deals with still other groups not covered in the earlier book.

Braden, Charles S., *Why Are the Cults Growing?* A series of four articles in *The Christian Century*, Vol. 61, pp. 45–47; 78–80; 108–110; 137–140; Jan.–Feb., 1944. Here the writer attempted to analyze the appeals made by the various movements, including most of those discussed in this book, but others also, particularly, what he calls the "emotional cults."

Braden, Charles S., *Varieties of American Religion*, Willett Clark and Co., Chicago, 1936. Here several of the movements discussed are treated by distinguished representatives of the groups themselves. Unfortunately it is out of print.

Braden, Charles S., "What Can We Learn from the Cults?" *Religion in Life*, Vol. 14, pp. 52–64, winter 1944–45.

Braden, Charles S., *Protestantism—A Symposium*, edited by Wm. K. Anderson, Abingdon-Cokesbury Press, New York, 1945. The chapter on "Sectarianism Run Wild," pp. 110–125.

Atkins, Gaius Glenn, *Modern Cults and Religious Movements*, Fleming H. Revell, New York, 1923. A very thoughtful analysis of the teachings of a number of the major movements, sympathetic, but also critical in tone.

II

On the Particular Movements

Here no pretense to completeness is made. There is a wealth of material published by each one concerning its own teachings of which only a very few are named.

On Father Divine

Hoshor, John, *God in a Rolls-Royce*, Hillman-Curl, New York, 1936.

Parker, R. W., *The Incredible Messiah*, Little, Brown and Co., Boston, 1937. These two books exploit the more spectacular and bizarre elements of Father Divine's movement, and can in no sense be regarded as objective treatments of it. They do, however, contain valuable materials, and are very interestingly written.

Cantril, Hadley, *Psychology of Social Movements*, chapter on Father Divine. A serious attempt to analyze the motivation that leads so many people to follow Father Divine.

The New Day, published weekly by the New Day Publishing Co., 126 Howard St., Newark, New Jersey, is the official publication in which everything Father Divine says in public appears. Indispensable for an understanding of Father Divine and his people.

On Psychiana

There has been no extended objective study published as yet. Marcus Bach has an excellent chapter in *They Found a Faith* (see above) and a volume on it by him is said to be forthcoming.

Your God Power, 1943, *The Strange Autobiography of Frank B. Robinson,* 1941, and a set of the *Psychiana Lessons,* 1932, all published by Psychiana at Moscow, Idaho, are the best sources for a study of the founder and his teachings.

On New Thought

Mind Re-makes Your World, edited by Ernest Holmes, Dodd Mead and Co., New York, 1944. A symposium in which leaders of the New Thought Movement all over America participate.

Dresser, Horatio W., *A History of the New Thought Movement,* Thomas Y. Crowell, New York, 1919. The official history of the movement from within.

Holmes, Ernest, *New Thought Terms and Their Meanings,* Dodd Mead and Co., New York, 1942. A real help to an understanding of what New Thought writers are trying to say.

On Unity

There is no extended published objective study in print. An unpublished doctoral thesis at the University of Chicago, 1942, by Dr. James W. Teener is the most thoroughgoing attempt yet made to study it. The thesis should be published. The major books of the movement have been mentioned in the footnotes of the chapter on Unity. The titles are *Metaphysical Dictionary,* 1944, *Talks on Truth,* 1943, *Prosperity,* 1940, *Jesus Christ Heals,* 1944, *Christian Healing,* 1909, *Mysteries of Genesis,* 1944, and *The Twelve Powers of Man,* 1943, all by Charles Fillmore, and published by Unity, Kansas City, Mo.

On Christian Science

Wilbur, Sibyl, *The Life of Mary Baker Eddy*, Christian Science Publishing Co., Boston, 1938. The official life.

Powell, Lyman P., *Mary Baker Eddy*, Lyman P. Powell, New York, 1930. Considered as second only to the Wilbur "Life." In striking contrast to an earlier book by the same author. Supposedly had complete access to official files, but fails to take account of other important sources.

Dakin, Edward F., *Mrs. Eddy, the Biography of a Virginal Mind*, Charles Scribner's Sons, New York, 1930. First published in an expensive edition, later in the cheaper Blue Ribbon Book series. Considered highly offensive by Christian Science leaders. Very well documented throughout, and presents an amazing amount of material. Unfortunate disposition to ridicule his heroine, lends plausibility to charges of unfair partisanship.

Bates, Ernest F., and Dittemore, John W., *Mary Baker Eddy, The Truth and the Tradition*, George Routledge and Sons, London, 1933. Written largely by Mr. Bates on the basis of materials made available by Mr. Dittemore who was one of the leaders of the movement in the earlier years, but later became alienated from Mrs. Eddy and her movement. Excellent documentation. It is asserted that Dittemore by reason of his disaffection becomes a biased source. This does not seem to be the case. Much of the material he supplied was in the nature of letters, diaries, etc., to which he had access. See footnote, p. 185.

Mrs. Eddy's own writings, all published by the Christian Science Publishing Society are, of course, basic sources. The more important are *Science and Health with Key to Scriptures*, and *Miscellaneous Writings*. The *Church Manual* while not assigned to her authorship was chiefly the product of her mind. All her writings have undergone numerous editions and have long since been standardized. The *Christian Science Journal* and *Christian Science Sentinel* are the chief current publications. The *Christian Science Monitor* carries comparatively little distinctively Christian Science matter.

Swihart, Altman K., *Since Mrs. Eddy*, Henry Holt and Co., New York, 1931, tells the story of two dissident movements arising out of Christian Science, that of Augusta E. Stetson of New York and of Mrs. Annie C. Bill in England.

On Theosophy

Kuhn, Alvin B., *Theosophy, A Modern Revival of Ancient Wisdom*, Henry Holt and Co., New York, 1930. A relatively objective study.

Farquhar, J. M., *Modern Religious Movements in India*, Macmillan Co., New York, 1918. The author, a distinguished missionary to India, discusses the Indian phase of the movement. Theosophists regard missionaries as biased against them.

Ransome, Josephine, *A Short History of the Theosophical Society*, Theosophical Publishing House, Adyar, India, 1938. An official history of the movement.

Jinarajadasa, C., *The Golden Book of the Theosophical Society*, Theosophical Publishing House, Adyar, 1925. Written in celebration of the Fiftieth Anniversary of the founding of the society.

Chief original sources are the writings of

1. the founder Helena P. Blavatsky, perhaps most important *Isis Unveiled* and *The Secret Doctrine*
2. Annie Besant, numerous titles and
3. Charles W. Leadbeater. The latter's *Outline to Theosophy*, 3rd edition Theosophical Book Concern, Los Angeles, 1916, and *Textbook of Theosophy*, 3rd edition, Theosophical Publishing House, Los Angeles, 1918, are as clear and understandable statements of theosophical belief as any that have appeared.

On I Am

Bryan, Gerald B., *Psychic Dictatorship in America*, Truth Research Publications, Los Angeles, 1940. See footnote p. 265 for discussion of this book and list of other writings by Mr. Bryan, concerning which the same observations may be made.

Chief original sources are the writings of the founders, Mr. and Mrs. Guy Ballard and the periodicals, all published by the St. Germain Press, Chicago, Ill. The principal titles are: *Unveiled Mysteries*, 1934; *The Magic Presence*, 1935; *The I Am Discourses* by St. Germain, 1935; *Ascended Masters Discourses*, by the Ascended Masters, 1937; *The "I Am" Adorations and Affirmations*, 1936. *The Voice of the I Am* is the official monthly periodical.

On the Liberal Catholic Church

There has been no extensive objective study published.
Original Sources are pamphlet material issued by St. Albans Press,
Los Angeles, Cal., especially the *Statement of Principles*, 1944.
Also a monthly periodical issued by the Press, *The Quarter
Hour*.

On Spiritualism

Lawton, George S., *The Drama of Life After Death*, Henry Holt
and Co., New York, 1932. An excellent detailed, objective and
scholarly study of every aspect of the movement.
The Spiritualist Manual, seventh edition, 1944, published by the
National Spiritualist Association, Washington, D. C. The best
statement of Spiritualism as a religion.
There is an enormous literature, books and pamphlets, dealing with
the subject, published by various branches of Spiritualism and
by individuals; also various periodicals. Among these *The
National Spiritualist*, official monthly organ of the National
Spiritualist Association, published at Chicago, Ill.; and *The
Psychic Observer*, published at Lily Dale, New York, circulate
widely.

On Jehovah's Witnesses

Stroup, H. H., *Jehovah's Witnesses*, Columbia University Press,
New York, 1945. An objective, scholarly study of the movement, the only one yet to appear in America.
Chief original sources are the writings of Charles Taze Russell, the
founder, and of Joseph F. Rutherford, all published or circulated
by the Watch Tower Bible and Tract Society, Brooklyn,
New York. Judge Rutherford's publications include 15 books
and innumerable pamphlets. The book titles are: *Religion, Salvation, Enemies, Riches, Light, Government, Prophecy, Creation,
Reconciliation, Preservation, Deliverance, The Harp of God*,
and *Preparation*. Among his pamphlets perhaps *Theocracy,
Armageddon*, and *God and the State* are of chief importance.
The Yearbook, published annually since 1933 contains the annual
reports of the society's activity throughout the world.
The Watchtower, issued twice monthly, and *Consolation*, issued
every other Wednesday, are the official periodicals of the
movement.

On the Anglo-Israel Movement

No extended objective treatment is available.

Gayer, M. H., *The Heritage of the Anglo-Saxon Race*, Destiny Publishers, Haverhill, Mass., 1941. A widely used and highly recommended summary of the claims of the Anglo-Israelites and their Biblical and other bases. It is accompanied by a large and complicated chart revealing the relation of Britain and the Anglo-Saxon peoples to Israel. Probably the best modern compendium of information concerning the movement.

Allen, J. H., *Judah's Scepter and Joseph's Birthright*, Destiny Publishers, Haverhill, Mass., thirteenth edition, 1917. Particularly emphasizes the scriptural basis of Anglo-Israelism.

The national official monthly periodical, *Destiny*, is published at Haverhill, Mass. Numerous tracts and pamphlets published at the national headquarters, Haverhill, Mass., and by individuals and local groups are widely circulated.

On the Oxford Group

No really extensive objective study has been published.

Russell, A. J., *For Sinners Only*, Harper and Brothers, New York, 1932. An interesting inside study of Frank Buchman and his movement.

Howard, Peter, *Ideas Have Legs*, Frederick Muller, Ltd., London, 1945. A more recent inside account, particularly of the Moral Re-Armament phase of the movement.

There is an extensive booklet and pamphlet literature of the movement, much of it highly pictorial, e.g., *Democracy's Inspired Ideology*, and *The Rising Tide*.

New World News is the monthly publication in America, issuing from the headquarters, Los Angeles, Cal.

On Mormonism

Chief original sources are:

The Book of Mormon, The Doctrines and Covenants, The Pearl of Great Price and *Brigham Young's Discourses*, edited by John A. Widtsoe, Deseret Book Co., Salt Lake City, 1925.

Valuable Mormon sources:

Smith, Joseph Fielding, *Essentials in Church History*, Deseret Book Co., Salt Lake City, 11th ed. 1946.

Short History of the Church of Jesus Christ of Latter Day Saints, published by the Church Radio Publicity and Mission Literature Co., Salt Lake City, 1938.

Talmage, James E., *Articles of Faith*, 12th ed., Salt Lake City, 1924.

Hunter, Milton R., *The Gospel Through the Ages*, Melchizidek Priesthood Course of Study—1946, Stevens and Wallis, Salt Lake City, 1945.

Reiser, A. H. and Merkley, Marion G., *What It Means to Be a Latter-Day Saint*, Course of Study for the First Intermediate Department, Deseret Sunday School Union Board, Salt Lake City, 1946.

Berrett, Wm. E., *The Gospel Message*, Course of Study for Sunday Schools, Deseret Sunday School Board, Salt Lake City, 1945.

Stewart, George, et al., *Priesthood and Church Welfare*, A Study Course for the Quorums of the Melchizidek Priesthood for the year 1939, Deseret Book Co., Salt Lake City, 1939.

A few non-Mormon sources:

Linn, W. A., *The Story of the Mormons*, Macmillan Co., N. Y., 1902. Although old now it is rather generally regarded as the best and most objective study of the Mormons.

Arbaugh, G. B., *Revelation in Mormonism*, University of Chicago Press, 1932.

Erickson, Ephraim E., *The Psychological and Ethical Aspects of Mormonism*, University of Chicago Press, 1922.

APPENDIX B

A brief account of a number of the modern cults and minority groups not included in the study. No claim is made that this is a complete list. As a matter of fact there may be scores that are known locally, and some perhaps more widely, which we have omitted. Those here included are the ones that in the experience of the writer have been the most frequently asked about. Numerous sects, some of them with strange names, might have been included, but they represent little or nothing strikingly different from the major religious groups so far as belief is concerned. For a brief account of most of these see Elmer T. Clark, *Small Sects in America*, Abingdon-Cokesbury Press, New York. A new edition is scheduled for early appearance. Also see the *United States Religious Bodies*, 1936, the last religious census to be published.

THE AHMADIYYAT MOVEMENT IN ISLAM

A modern sect of the Moslem faith. Originating in India in the latter half of the nineteenth century, it has become quite aggressively missionary and has sent missionaries to many parts of the world, including England and America. It differs from Orthodox Islam chiefly in its belief that the founder, a promised Messiah, appeared in India as the fulfillment, not alone of the expectation of one to come held by the Moslems, but also of that held by Hindus, Buddhists and Christians. Indian headquarters were until lately in Qadian, in the Punjab, but recent rioting in India, as a result of the division of India into a Hindu and a Moslem state, caused its removal to Lahore. The American headquarters are in Chicago where the head of the American mission resides and where the *Moslem Sunrise*, a quarterly magazine, and other materials are published.

Until 1945 there was but one missionary in America, Sufi M. R. Bengalee, who had small groups of members in various cities in the United States, but there are now three, and it is planned to increase this number considerably. They adhere to the basic teachings of Islam in most respects, but stress strongly the belief not only in the Prophet Mohammed but in all the prophets. Jesus, they hold, did not die on the cross, but swooned, was released from the tomb by his friends and went away to India where he spent some forty years, teaching and preaching. His tomb is a center of pilgrimage in Srinagar, in Kashmir, today.

See Sufi M. R. Bengalee, *The Life of Muhammed*, Moslem Sunrise Press, Chicago, 1940 and *The Tomb of Jesus*, Moslem Sunrise Press, Chicago, 1944. Also *Ahmadiyyat, or The True Islam*, Qadian, India, 1924.

THE AMANA CHURCH SOCIETY

An outgrowth of a German movement in the early eighteenth century, which held that inspiration and revelation had not ceased, but that living persons were quite as capable of receiving inspiration as the ancients. A revival of this movement in the nineteenth century led to a conflict with the state church and forced migration to America, where a group led by Christian Metz and Barbara Heinman, established a community at Buffalo, New York, in 1842. Later, in 1852, they migrated to Iowa and established seven villages. They were incorporated in 1859 under a charter which provided that all property be held in common, that all surplus earned through farming, industry or business should be applied to community improvement, education or benevolent purposes. The community is not celibate as so many of the communistic societies have been. Anyone entering the community must surrender all his property and claim to wages. In return he gets a guarantee of security, the provision for his needs. If a person withdraws he is given back what he originally contributed to the society.

The last four religious census reports show a steady decline in membership. The number of churches remained the same, seven, through the four decades, but the membership in 1906, 1916, 1926, and 1936 was 1,756, 1,534, 1,385, and 847.

See W. A. Hinds, *American Communities*, Chicago, 1908; also *A Brief History of the Amana Society*, published by the society in 1900.

AMERICAN ETHICAL UNION

The Society of Ethical Culture in the City of New York was founded on May 15, 1876, by Felix Adler, at that time a professor in Cornell University, but later for more than a quarter of a century professor of Social and Political Ethics in Columbia University. Societies were subsequently founded in Chicago, 1882; Philadelphia, 1885; St. Louis, 1886; Brooklyn, 1905; and Boston, 1920, each as a separate, completely autonomous group holding like views and seeking common ends. In 1889 the existing groups were formed into the American Ethical Union "for the purpose of establishing new Societies, supporting foreign secretaries for the furtherance of the Ethical movement abroad and to publish literature interpreting the movement's principles and aims." It publishes a monthly periodical *The Standard*.

The membership has never been large, but a number of people of great influence have been a part of it, thus extending its influence out of all proportion to its size and numbers.

Its central emphasis has, from the beginning, been upon ethics rather than creed or ceremony. Some of its leaders as well as members have been theists, some non-theists. There is no requirement in this respect. But "the ethical end is the sovereign, supreme end of life to which all other ends must be subordinated," as Felix Adler declared. However much religious belief might help to reinforce the moral law it was his contention that "the authority of the moral law is not borrowed; it is aboriginal and also sovereign." [1] It was his conviction that it was harmful to teach that one's moral obligation was derivative from certain religious beliefs, since when those beliefs ceased to be convincing morality itself might be cast off. "If morality rests on extraneous props, it will fall to the ground when the props crumble, as they were sure to do, and as more and more they have done," he declared.[2]

The Ethical Societies hold regular public meetings, closely resembling church services, with music, periods of quiet meditation, the reading of scripture or some inspired bit of prose or poetry, and an address by the leader upon some pertinent theme, social, political, philosophic, ethical or religious. But they are also active in practical social efforts designed to lift the level of community life, through clubs, settlements, playgrounds, forums, etc., etc.

The headquarters of the Union is in New York City.

THE AMISH MENNONITES

Often spoken of simply as the Amish, this group is really only one of the several Mennonites sects, differing but little in doctrine from the rest; but they are more strict in their interpretation of that doctrine. There are two Amish bodies, what is now called the Conservative Amish Mennonite Church, but is really the more liberal wing of the Amish group, and the Old Order Amish Men-

---

[1] Felix Adler address, in *Fiftieth Anniversary of the Ethical Movement*, p. 13.
[2] *Id.*, pp. 11-12.

monite Church, which adheres strictly to earlier beliefs and practices. These Mennonites worship chiefly in private homes rather than churches, maintain no full-time paid ministry, use the German language generally, and enforce the ban upon those who are expelled for non-conformity to church doctrine and practice. They dress very plainly, and use hooks and eyes rather than buttons on coats and vests. Ninety-five percent of the churches are rural. They are found mainly in Pennsylvania, Ohio and Indiana.

See *The New Schaff-Herzog Encyclopedia of Religious Knowledge,* Art. Mennonites.

THE BAHAI FAITH

The Bahai Faith originated in Persia near the middle of the last century, an offshoot of Shiah Islam, built about the coming of one, who, like the Jewish Messiah, had been long expected. Preceded by a forerunner, the Bab, very much as John the Baptist preceded Jesus, Bahá 'u' lláh, the Splendor of God, after the liquidation of the Bab by the rulers, became the head of the movement. Though himself of a wealthy and influential family, he too was bitterly persecuted, and spent many years either in prison or in a prison colony. Here he thought deeply and wrote much which is now regarded by his followers as scripture. At his death he passed the direction of the movement on to his son, Abdul Baha, who, when finally liberated by the Young Turks, travelled to Europe and America where he wrote and lectured widely and established the Bahai Faith.

Arising within Islam, it is in no sense a purely Moslem faith, but a syncretic movement which asserts the essential unity of all religions. Its great temple at Wilmette Illinois, a suburb of Chicago, overlooking Lake Michigan, is one of the remarkable buildings of America, a symbol, with its nine sides and nine doors, of the oneness of the great religions of the world. Entering by any door and walking straight forward, one meets at the center, beneath the magnificent dome, all those who enter by any other door.

The present head of the faith is Shoghi Effendi, eldest grandson of Abdul Baha. The movement stresses among other things the oneness of mankind, world peace, a world language. There is no professional ministry.

Chief original sources for a study of Bahia are the writings of Baha Ullah and Abdul Baha. See also J. E. Esslemont, *Bahá 'u' lláh and the New Era,* rev. 2nd ed. G. Allen and Unwin, London, 1940.

The Black Jews *or* Black Hebrews

A name commonly given to the Church of God, founded by the Prophet, F. S. Cherry, a wholly self-educated Negro, who claims to have been called by the Lord in a vision to be his prophet. He knows and uses both Hebrew and Yiddish, and employs the Talmud along with the Bible. He teaches that his followers are the real Jews, and that the so-called Jews today are not real Jews at all. Jesus is believed to have been a Negro. They observe Saturday as their Sabbath; look forward to the end of the world at the end of the twentieth century. They substitute the Passover for Holy Communion, but practice baptism. Secular dancing is forbidden, also drunkenness, but moderate drinking is encouraged. Pork is taboo, and marriage with outsiders is forbidden unless the other person agrees to join the movement. Divorce is not permitted.

The prophet Cherry is the head of the church and the final religious authority. Membership is open to any Negro who wishes to join. Apparently white persons are excluded.

See Arthur H. Fauset, *Black Gods of the Metropolis*, Univ. of Penn. Press, Philadelphia, 1944, chapter IV.

Divine Science

One of a number of New Thought groups of varied names, associated together in the International New Thought Alliance. It was founded by Mrs. Malinda E. Cramer in 1885, after experiencing a notable healing from a serious illness through the realization of God's presence. The same method, applied to others, worked equally well. Systematizing her teachings, she went from city to city, lecturing, healing and establishing centers. The present headquarters of the movement are in Denver, Colorado, where it publishes and circulates periodicals and other printed material.

Unlike Christian Science it "does not deny the existence of visible matter, but interprets both form and force as manifestations of God." Healing is more than restoring harmony to the bodily organism, "it is cleansing the inner man from all that is unlike God." It differs in no essential respect from the general New Thought Movement as discussed in chapter III.

See Horatio W. Dresser, *The History of the New Thought Movement*, Thomas Y. Crowell Company, New York, 1919.

DOWIEISM, *properly* THE CHRISTIAN CATHOLIC APOSTOLIC CHURCH IN ZION

A movement founded by John Alexander Dowie (1847–1907) in Chicago, Illinois, in 1896. In 1901 he established Zion City, on the shore of Lake Michigan some forty miles north of Chicago, as its center, and it has so remained until the present. For many years it was an exclusive religious community, the whole of its population members of the church; its industries as well as its schools and churches being run on the principles taught by its prophet and founder. It has never spread widely, as it had been hoped, although there are members in other sections of the country and foreign missions are carried on.

Zion City itself is no longer exclusively a religious community. Gentiles are found in considerable numbers, even other churches are there now. The former communal industries retain the name of Zion but they are no longer under community control. There appear to be certain tendencies among the younger leaders to modify to some extent the original teachings of the group. Zion City is now becoming famous for its annual presentation of the Passion Play, very much like the one given in the village of Oberammergau. It draws capacity crowds from far and near each spring. Two periodicals are published, *The Theocrat* and *Leaves of Healing*.

See *The New Schaff-Herzog Encyclopedia of Religious Knowledge*, Articles, John Alexander Dowie, and Christian Catholic Apostolic Church in Zion.

THE DUKHOBORS

Sect originating at an uncertain date in Russia, which, about the beginning of the twentieth century, migrated to Saskatchewan, Canada, in order to escape persecution because of their peculiar beliefs and practices. They were welcomed to Canada, which was at that time seeking colonists and gladly conceded to them the right not to bear arms, and excused them from the performance of certain other obligations ordinarily accepted by Canadian citizens, because of their religious beliefs.

They are strictly vegetarian, and extremely considerate of animals, the more conservative wing refusing to use them for ploughing and other heavy farm work, preferring rather to do this heavy work themselves. They are strictly communistic and make no use of money within the group. They worship in homes, not churches, have no paid ministry. They do not drink and are very strict in most respects. The more extreme sect has offended public taste by appearing in procession wholly naked, a common method of protest employed by the group. They have a long history of successive Messiahs who have appeared in the person of their leaders.

Later the group spread into British Columbia where large land holdings were acquired by their leader, Peter Verigin. His son, who succeeded him, is said to have lost most of the communal wealth that had been built up, and the community is said to be disintegrating. There are three sects, the Orthodox, the Named Dukhobors, and the Sons of Freedom, the latter the most extreme of the three. As late as January, 1946, *Newsweek* reported a conference of Dukhobors which urged upon the entire community a new code of conduct that would outlaw the employment of nudity and the burning of schools and other buildings as methods of protest against the enforcement of Canadian law.

See *Slava Bohu, The Story of the Dukhobors*, by J. C. F. Wright, Farrar and Rinehart, New York, 1940; Chas. W. Ferguson, *Confusion of Tongues*, Doubleday, Doran, New York, 1928, Ch. 6; Mrs. W. G. Foster; *Canadian Communists, Amer. Journal of Sociology*, Vol. 41, pp. 327-340.

House of David

Founded in 1903 by Benjamin Purnell, who regarded himself as the seventh of the messengers prophesied in Revelation, the famous Johanna Southcott of England being the first, in 1792. The community, located at Benton Harbor, Michigan, was organized by him "as a commonwealth, according to apostolic plan." As stated in their own literature, "All persons making application for membership must first make all necessary settlements of their worldly affairs, then as a point of faith, give all they possess into the Commonwealth of the Association for which they voluntarily of their own free will, labor and receive all necessary benefits therefrom." Though suffering gravely from the charges of immorality brought against the founder in the courts, the movement survived that crisis and the subsequent death of Benjamin, and still operates in Benton Harbor, where they do a thriving business selling fruit and other products of their farms, and catering to the vacationists who throng that lakeside region.

They are strict vegetarians. Men wear their hair long; their travelling baseball team and band are widely known. They continue to publish and circulate the writings and teachings of Benjamin, but they do not grow. There is one outpost of the movement in Sydney Australia. They publish a periodical *Shiloh's Messenger of Wisdom.*

See Charles W. Ferguson, *Confusion of Tongues,* Doubleday Doran, New York, 1928, chapter III.

HUMANISM

Religious humanism, in contradistinction to literary humanism, is a relatively recent movement in America. It is more than just an organization, although there is an American Humanist Association with headquarters at present at 569 South 13th Street, Salt Lake City, Utah, which publishes a substantial quarterly magazine, *The Humanist,* and distributes other literature. Rather it is a point of view shared by a large number of people who are related in no way to the formal movement. Considerable numbers of left-wing, liberal Protestants, found principally, but not alone, in the Unitarian churches are essentially humanists in outlook. The late Dr. John H. Dietrich, Unitarian pastor in Minneapolis for many years, is often called the father of the movement. Others who have written as Humanists have been J. A. C. F. Auer of Harvard Divinity School, Curtis Reese of Chicago, A. E. Haydon of the University of Chicago, Max Otto of the University of Wisconsin, and Charles F. Potter of New York.

The best statement of the position is that of the Humanist Manifesto, issued in 1933 and signed by a number of prominent religious leaders, most of them Unitarians. (See *The Christian Century,* Vol. 50, pp. 743-745, June 7, 1933). The essence of the position is that there is nothing outside or beyond man upon which he can depend for his salvation. It must be self-won, here and now—for there is no life beyond this—by his control and manipulation of the physical and social forces of the world which determine his destiny. Science, an increasing knowledge of his world, is the clue to his full realization of all his capacities, the really good life, which is for him the meaning of salvation.

See A. E. Haydon, *The Quest of the Ages,* Harper Brothers, New York, 1929; Curtis W. Reese, *Humanist Sermons,* Open Court, Chicago, 1927; Charles F. Potter, *Humanism a New Religion,* Simon and Schuster, N. Y., 1930; J. A. C. F. Auer, *Humanism States Its Case,* American Unitarian Ass'n, Boston, 1933.

INSTITUTE OF RELIGIOUS SCIENCE AND PHILOSOPHY

A New Thought movement, founded by Dr. Ernest Holmes in Los Angeles, California, in 1927. It now has branches in many parts of the United States, and has spread to Canada, North Africa and Australia. Headquarters are at Los Angeles, where a very active center is maintained, including a school, public lectures, healing, and counselling, as well as the preparation and circulation of the literature of the movement. For years Dr. Holmes has lectured to a great crowd every Sunday afternoon. He has been president of the International New Thought Alliance, and is author of some of the most widely circulated New Thought books. See the chapter on New Thought for an elaboration of the teaching of the Institute of his founding and other New Thought centers. The movement continues to expand. A new regional college is being opened in San Francisco. The magazine, *Science of Mind*, has a nationwide circulation, far beyond the membership of the movement.

See Bibliography on The New Thought Movement, p. 688 for some of Dr. Holmes' own books which clearly set forth the teachings of the Institute as well as that of the general New Thought Movement.

MOORISH SCIENCE TEMPLE OF AMERICA

A movement limited strictly to Asiatics (Negroes really) founded by a Negro, Timothy Drew, about 1913. He had reacted violently to Christianity in his youth and found happiness finally only in Islam, moved powerfully by the fact of racial discrimination as practiced by Christians. He became convinced the Negro people's salvation lay in the discovery of their true origin as Asiatics. They must refuse to be called Negroes, Colored People, Black Folk, Ethiopians, and henceforth call themselves Moors or Moorish Americans. He wrote a *Holy Koran* which has become the scripture of the movement, and came himself to be called the Prophet Noble Drew Ali. Centers were established in a number of American cities. Dissension developed within the group in Chicago and a slaying occurred. Although absent at the time, Noble Drew Ali was arrested and held for trial. But before the trial he died under circumstances not yet clear. The movement split into several sects. Some of the sect leaders are regarded as reincarnations of Noble Drew Ali.

The organization is secret in character. There was a period during World War II when no outsiders were permitted to attend their meetings. Members must be Asiatic, no white person may join. Christianity is for them, the Moslem faith for the Asiatics. Men must wear the fez at all times. They are vegetarian; they pray three times a day facing the East. Shaving, use of cosmetics, straightening the hair, smoking, and drinking intoxicants are forbidden. They observe Friday as their Sabbath.

See Arthur H. Fauset, *Black Gods of the Metropolis,* University of Pennsylvania Press, Philadelphia, 1944, chapter V.

THE ORDER OF THE CROSS

The Order of the Cross is a relatively new movement, quite unknown in America until the late thirties, when it was introduced by the Rev. and Mrs. H. Kemmis from England, where it first appeared. It was founded by J. Todd Ferrier, (1858–1942), a former Congregational minister who, as a result of certain experiences, came to believe that he was a channel through which a new revelation had come to man. This revelation came, it is claimed, as a "recovery" of wisdom that he had accumulated in past incarnations, for reincarnation is a central belief of the movement. Much that Jesus said has been lost, they claim, but through Mr. Ferrier has been brought to light. Some of the sayings of Paul and the other New Testament writers were really sayings of Jesus, it is alleged. The chief book of the founder is *The Logia,* or sayings of Jesus, thus restored and accompanied by a commentary of highly esoteric character.

Three teachings of Jesus conspicuously absent from the writings of the Apostles are, they hold: (1) reincarnation; (2) the unjust taking of any life, animal or human; and (3) complete refusal of the righteous to engage in war or violence. Members of the Order of the Cross, therefore, must believe in reincarnation, must be vegetarians and anti-vivisectionists, and absolute pacifists.

The movement is not in the least aggressive, but has made some progress in America, particularly on the west coast where there are a few local groups, all meeting in someone's home. In 1947, Mr. and Mrs. Kemmis journeyed to Australia and New Zealand to introduce the movement there.

Here is a rather unusual movement which appears to be a grafting on to Christianity of certain ideas usually associated with the religions of India. Members need not withdraw from the churches to which they belong when they join the order. Mr. Kemmis still retains his standing as an Anglican clergyman, and is frequently invited to speak before church groups. A periodical *Herald of the*

Cross is published in England and a dozen or more books by the founder and others of the movement are circulated. American head-quarters are at 229½ N. Western Avenue, Los Angeles, 4, California.

ROSICRUCIANISM

A movement which insists that it is not a religion at all, but a fraternal order. Indeed, the head of the leading branch of the movement in America—there are several branches—Amorc, with headquarters at San Jose, California, felt so strongly about the matter that he refused to allow the writer to quote from their copyrighted sources in an attempt to describe it. He compares it with the Masonic Order with which it does indeed have much in common, but in the mind of large numbers of people, including many who follow it, it is regarded as a religion, and functions as such in their lives.

Usually held to have been founded by one Christian Rosenkreuz, in the seventeenth century—Max Heindel, founder of the Rosicru-cian Fellowship, Oceanside, California, says in the thirteenth century —H. Spencer Lewis, historian of Amorc, traces it back to Egyptian sources and makes Thutmose III the organizer of the secret brother-hood in 1489 B.C. It was Amenhotep IV or Akhnaton, he thinks, who contributed most to the early formulation of its philosophy.

Amorc has an impressive headquarters, a number of striking buildings, advertises widely in the periodical press, and claims to mail out over 6,000,000 pieces of mail per year. The teaching of Amorc, it is claimed, is never published, but is to be obtained only as one becomes a student under the guidance of those who have been initiated into it. The Rosicrucian Fellowship is much more definitely religious in its orientation. It also makes a great deal of use of astrology.

See *Encyclopedia of Religion and Ethics,* Art., Rosicrucian. H. Spencer Lewis, *Rosicrucian Questions and Answers with Complete History of the Rosicrucian Order,* Amorc, San Jose, California.

THE SHAKERS *or* UNITED SOCIETY OF BELIEVERS

A movement which has all but disappeared in America—the 1936 religious census reported but 3 congregations with a total of only 92 members. In 1906 it had reported 15 societies with 516 members; 1916, 12 with 367; in 1926 only 6 societies with but 192 members. It was founded in England about the middle of the eighteenth century by one Jane Wardley, among the Quakers. Because of the violence of their physical expression under intense religious emotion, the little group were called the Shaking Quakers.

Ann Lee became their leader. In a vision it was revealed to her that the Christ Spirit had come through her as it had long ago through Jesus. She is said to have regarded sex as the root of all evil. A group of the Shakers migrated to America. After the death of Ann Lee, Joseph Meachem and Lucy Wright organized them into communistic societies. At one time the membership was in excess of 5,000, but it has declined steadily since 1860. There were 56 communities in 1874 which owned a hundred thousand acres of land. The communities were generally rural. They were entirely celibate. All property was held in common. Great stress was laid upon open confession of sin.

See *Encyclopedia of Religion and Ethics,* Article, Communistic Societies of America.

SWEDENBORGIANISM *or* THE CHURCH OF THE NEW JERUSALEM

A movement which grew out of the experiences and writings of a distinguished Swedish scientist, Emanuel Swedenborg (1688–1772) who, after fifty years of age, and an active career as scientist, engineer, and inventor, began to receive revelations from the other world which he carefully recorded in more than twenty volumes. Actual organization began with the formation of a class to study his writings by Robert Hindmarsh in London in 1782. The first American branch of the organization which came to be called the General Church of the New Jerusalem, was founded in Baltimore in 1792. There are two Swedenborgian bodies in the United States, both quite active in propagating their faith by means of the circulation of the writings of Emanuel Swedenborg and other literature, and by the radio. The entire works of Swedenborg have been translated into English and at least some of them are to be found in most libraries. The movement has often been described in Encyclopedias, and other reference works. A graduate theological seminary of the New Church is located near Harvard University in Cambridge, Massachusetts.

See The New Schaff-Herzog, *Encyclopedia of Religious Knowledge, Encyclopaedia Britannica.*

THE VEDANTA SOCIETY

A movement founded in America by Swami Vivekananda, following the World Parliament of Religions at Chicago in 1893. Disciple of the Hindu seer, Sri Ramakrishna, he was the real founder of the Ramakrishna Movement in India, one of the most vigorous modern reform movements in Hinduism. Unlike traditional Hinduism, which has not been missionary minded, this movement has established Vedanta Societies in many parts of the world, particularly in the larger cities of America, each one directed by a monk of the Ramakrishna Order.

The movement stresses the oneness of all religions, basing its teaching upon the Upanishads and the Bhagavad Gita. Regular public lectures are given by the Swamis, and special classes in the study of Hindu philosophy and the Bhagavad Gita are conducted. Their leaders profess no interest in the conversion of anyone to Hinduism. Some of them have been very able interpreters of the East to the American people. The writings of Swami Vivekananda, and the published sayings of Sri Ramakrishna are the best sources for an understanding of the movement.

Index